The Cambridge Handbook of Instructional Feedback

This book brings together leading scholars from around the world to provide their most influential thinking on instructional feedback. The chapters range from academic, in-depth reviews of the research on instructional feedback to a case study on how feedback altered the life-course of one author. Furthermore, it features critical subject areas – including mathematics, science, music, and even animal training – and focuses on working at various developmental levels of learners.

The affective, noncognitive aspects of feedback are also targeted, such as how learners react emotionally to receiving feedback. The exploration of the theoretical underpinnings of how feedback changes the course of instruction leads to practical advice on how to give such feedback effectively in a variety of diverse contexts. Anyone interested in researching instructional feedback, or providing it in their class or course, will discover why, when, and where instructional feedback is effective and how best to provide it.

ANASTASIYA A. LIPNEVICH is an associate professor of educational psychology and a director of faculty research development at Queens College and the Graduate Center, the City University of New York.

JEFFREY K. SMITH is a professor in the College of Education at the University of Otago, New Zealand.

The Cambridge Handbook of Instructional Feedback

Edited by

Anastasiya A. Lipnevich
Queens College and the Graduate Center, City University of New York

Jeffrey K. Smith
University of Otago, New Zealand

CAMBRIDGE
UNIVERSITY PRESS

CAMBRIDGE
UNIVERSITY PRESS

University Printing House, Cambridge CB2 8BS, United Kingdom

One Liberty Plaza, 20th Floor, New York, NY 10006, USA

477 Williamstown Road, Port Melbourne, VIC 3207, Australia

314–321, 3rd Floor, Plot 3, Splendor Forum, Jasola District Centre, New Delhi – 110025, India

79 Anson Road, #06–04/06, Singapore 079906

Cambridge University Press is part of the University of Cambridge.

It furthers the University's mission by disseminating knowledge in the pursuit of education, learning, and research at the highest international levels of excellence.

www.cambridge.org
Information on this title: www.cambridge.org/9781107179394
DOI: 10.1017/9781316832134

First published 2018

Printed and bound in Great Britain by Clays Ltd, Elcograf S.p.A.

A catalogue record for this publication is available from the British Library.

Library of Congress Cataloging-in-Publication Data
Names: Lipnevich, Anastasiya A., editor. | Smith, Jeffrey K., editor.
Title: The Cambridge handbook of instructional feedback / edited
   by Anastasiya A. Lipnevich, Jeffrey K. Smith.
Description: Cambridge ; New York, NY : Cambridge University Press, 2018. |
   Includes bibliographical references and index.
Identifiers: LCCN 2018021298 | ISBN 9781107179394 (hardback : alk. paper) |
   ISBN 9781316631317 (paperback : alk. paper)
Subjects: LCSH: Feedback (Psychology) | Communication in education.
Classification: LCC BF319.5.F4 C36 2018 | DDC 302.2–dc23
LC record available at https://lccn.loc.gov/2018021298

ISBN 978-1-107-17939-4 Hardback
ISBN 978-1-316-63131-7 Paperback

Contents

Figures

Tables

Contributors

MARYAM ALQASSAB, Ludwig-Maximilans-Universität, Munich, Germany

HEIDI L. ANDRADE, University at Albany–SUNY, Albany, NY, USA

MASAHIRO ARIMOTO, Tohoku University, Japan

VIDYA S. ATHOTA, School of Business, University of Notre Dame, Australia

SUSAN M. BROOKHART, School of Education, Duquesne University, USA

GAVIN T. L. BROWN, University of Auckland, New Zealand

JEREMY BURRUS, ACT, Inc., Center for the Assessment of Social, Emotional, and Academic Learning, USA

IAN CLARK, Tohoku University, Japan

PHILLIP DAWSON, Centre for Research in Assessment and Digital Learning (CRADLE), Deakin University, Australia

CHRISTOPHER C. DENEEN, RMIT University, Australia

N. RUTH GASSON, University of Otago, New Zealand

THOMAS GOETZ, University of Konstanz, Germany, and Thurgau University of Teacher Education, Switzerland

KATARZYNA GOGOL, University of Konstanz, Germany, and Thurgau University of Teacher Education, Switzerland

STEVE GRAHAM, Mary Lou Fulton Teachers College, Arizona State University, USA

THOMAS R. GUSKEY, University of Kentucky, USA

LOIS R. HARRIS, Central Queensland University, Australia

MOLLY HOLINGER, Neag School of Education, University of Connecticut, USA

BRUCE D. HOMER, The Graduate Center, CUNY, USA

ANDERS JONSSON, Faculty of Education, Kristianstad University, Sweden

ANIL KANJEE, Tshwane University of Technology, South Africa

ALLISON B. KAUFMAN, Department of Ecology and Evolutionary Biology, and Department of Psychology, University of Connecticut, USA

JAMES C. KAUFMAN, Neag School of Education, University of Connecticut, USA

MAIKE KRANNICH, University of Konstanz, Germany, and Thurgau University of Teacher Education, Switzerland

HEIDI KROOG, Brock University, St. Catharines, Ontario, Canada

AMY LIN, Brock University, St. Catharines, Ontario, Canada

ANASTASIYA A. LIPNEVICH, Queens College and the Graduate Center, City University of New York, USA

ASHISH MALIK, University of Newcastle, Australia

JONATHAN E. MARTIN, ACT, Inc., Program Director of K12 Consulting Services, USA

CASSIM MUNSHI, National Institute of Education, Singapore

DANA MURANO, The Graduate Center, City University of New York, and ACT, Inc., Center for Assessment of Social, Emotional, and Academic Learning, USA

JACQUI MURRAY, Whitireia, New Zealand

TERESA M. OBER, The Graduate Center, CUNY, USA

MICHELE M. PAGEL, Adventure Aquarium, USA

ERNESTO PANADERO, Department of Evolutive Psychology and Education, Faculty of Psychology, Autonomous University of Madrid, Spain

KELLY A. PARKES, Department of Arts and Humanities, Teachers College, Columbia University, USA

JAN L. PLASS, CREATE Lab, New York University, USA

RICHARD D. ROBERTS, RAD Science, USA

MARIA ARACELI RUIZ-PRIMO, Stanford University, USA

JOAN SARGEANT, Faculty of Medicine, Dalhousie University, Halifax, Nova Scotia, Canada

VALERIE SHUTE, Florida State University, USA

MARIAN SMALL, University of New Brunswick, Canada

JEFFREY K. SMITH, University of Otago, New Zealand

RICK STIGGINS, Founder and retired President, Assessment Training Institute, USA

GORDON STOBART, Oxford University Centre for Educational Assessment (OUCEA) and Institute of Education, University College London, UK

KELVIN H. K. TAN, Curriculum, Teaching and Learning Academic Group, National Institute of Education (NIE), Singapore

JACQUES VAN DER MEER, University of Otago, New Zealand

CHRISTOPHER WATLING, Schulich School of Medicine and Dentistry, Western University, London, Ontario, Canada

DYLAN WILIAM, University College London, Institute of Education, London, UK

HWEI MING WONG, Centre for Research in Pedagogy and Practice, National Institute of Education (NIE), Singapore

Foreword

"Feedback, like rain, should be gentle enough to nourish a person's growth without destroying the roots." This quote (modified from the original by Frank A. Clark) is a simple reminder that feedback can be helpful or not, assume a variety of forms, be provided at different times, and have diverse effects on different people. But what if there were a drought (no rain, no feedback)? Consider the following two questions: If a tree falls in the woods and nobody's around to hear it – does it make a noise? If a teacher instructs some content or skill and doesn't assess and support learning – can students deeply learn? In both cases, the answer is no.

So feedback is really important – not just for learning new things, but pretty much across all of life. There are countless examples of feedback in nature – with both positive and negative functions. For example, our hypothalamus reacts to changes in temperature and responds appropriately. If the temperature drops, we shiver to bring up the temperature, and if it's too hot, we sweat to cool down via evaporation. Predator–prey relations in nature are also well-known examples of feedback loops, as is climate change. The key difference between positive and negative feedback is their response to change – positive feedback accelerates change while negative feedback delays change.

What does all this have to do with the book that you're about to dive into? We're all giving and getting feedback throughout our lives – in the classroom, on the job, as part of family life, and so on. How can we ensure that the feedback we give and get is effective and constructive? That's covered in the book. For example, as a teacher, I want my students to excel and grow so I provide lots of feedback (and they similarly return the favor, with the goal to improve my teaching skills). As an employee, I need valid feedback to perform my best, and as an employer, I need to give constructive feedback to those who work for me. Finally, as a parent, I want my kids to grow into awesome adults, and I'm fairly certain they want me to be a good parent. Can one book possibly cover the wide range of feedback contexts and types? This one comes close.

I suspect that I was asked to write this foreword because of the literature review I published a decade ago in the *Review of Educational Research* titled "Focus on Formative Feedback." That particular project was something I'd been longing to do for years – to wrap my head around the slippery, often conflicting feedback findings in the literature, then provide a things-to-do (and things-to-avoid) set of tables at the end for practitioners. Since then, there has been considerably more work in the feedback arena. This book – *The Cambridge Handbook of Instructional Feedback*, edited by Anastasiya A. Lipnevich and Jeffrey K. Smith – is an excellent convergence of the most current feedback work in a wonderful one-stop book. The chapters comprise a delicious smorgasbord of feedback-related topics ranging from theoretical to empirical research, qualitative to quantitative work, in the contexts of K-12 classrooms to higher education and the workplace, and spanning different countries for cross-cultural perspectives (e.g., Singapore, the United States, South Africa, Japan, Spain, Sweden). Feedback is examined relative to who is giving it (e.g., a computer or game vs. teachers vs. self vs. peer), who is receiving it, and the content areas in which the feedback is employed (e.g., math, science, writing, medicine, and music). Cognitive as well as affective states can benefit from feedback too – which is also covered. The twenty-seven chapters are not only diverse, but they're written by luminaries in the field. I close as I started, with a quote: "Feedback may be a gift, but constructive feedback is an investment" (Brad Boyson).

Valerie Shute
Florida State University

Preface

The focus of *The Cambridge Handbook on Instructional Feedback* is on feedback as it manifests itself across various instructional settings and contexts. Learners at all levels receive a wealth of feedback messages on a daily – or even hourly – basis. Teachers, coaches, parents, peers – all have suggestions and advice on how to improve or sustain a certain level of performance. In a classroom context, sharing learning intentions, clarifying criteria for success, providing information that moves learners forward, and activating students as the owners of their learning are essential functions of feedback (Black & Wiliam, 2009). Inarguably, feedback is a key element of successful instructional practices – those that lead to best improvement (see, e.g., Hattie and Timperley, 2007). Researchers agree that feedback is essential for improved performance, but we also know that learners often dread feedback and dismiss it and that the effectiveness of feedback varies depending on specific characteristics of feedback messages that learners receive (see, e.g., Lipnevich & Smith, 2008). This volume brings together extant literature on feedback across multiple academic domains, contexts, and levels of schooling, and attempts to clarify a range of questions that relate to various aspects of feedback, including its type, level of specificity, frequency, context, and timing. The book paints an expansive picture of the current state of research on instructional feedback, discussing both the theory and areas of application. The volume focuses specifically on the most important constituents and components of feedback:

1. Those who provide feedback
2. Those who receive feedback
3. Characteristics of feedback
4. The context of feedback.

The volume comprises five parts. Part I focuses on existing theory, presenting definitions, characteristics, methodological issues, and a general conceptual framework of instructional feedback, and describing existing taxonomies of instructional feedback (see Table 0.1 for a brief description of chapters included in this volume). The contributors situate feedback within the framework of formative assessment. Wiliam (Chapter 1) opens this part with a discussion of feedback in the larger historical context. Wiliam discusses whether feedback works, the magnitude of the impact on learning, and what kinds of feedback work best. One of the key points of this chapter is that feedback interventions need to take greater account of the crucial difference between learning and performance that has been a fundamental concept in memory research for decades. In Chapter 2, Stobart argues that feedback has to be carefully related to the proficiency of the learner and cannot be treated as a generic template to be applied mechanically. He discusses different types of feedback and how they should be matched to different levels of student performance. In Chapter 3, Brookhart juxtaposes feedback in summative and formative contexts and emphasizes the importance of student agency, whereas in Chapter 4, Murray, Gasson, and Smith propose a taxonomy of written feedback messages, allowing for a more systematic look at how feedback influences achievement. Brown and Harris (Chapter 5) conclude this part with a survey of the different methods currently being used to investigate feedback in empirical studies.

Part II covers research on feedback at different levels and areas of schooling, discussing specifics of cognitive, emotional, and psychosocial development of learners as well as best approaches to feedback delivery at different developmental levels. The contributors explain the specifics of feedback delivery across subject domains and other instructional settings. Tan and Wong (Chapter 6) attempt to answer the question of whether feedback in primary schools can enhance students' "independent" learning and at the same time aid students in achieving necessary learning outcomes for high-stakes examinations. The discussion is situated in the context of schooling in Singapore. Chapters 7 through 10 describe specifics of presenting feedback in the domains of writing, math, science, and music. Graham (Chapter 7) summarizes research on feedback effectiveness in the domain of writing and discusses challenges of providing good quality feedback on students' written assignments. Small and Lin (Chapter 8) explore various aspects of offering feedback to students who are learning mathematics. This chapter includes examples at a variety of grade levels of how to connect feedback to learning objectives, including attention to assumptions students do or do not make. In Chapter 9, Ruiz-Primo and Kroog present results of a study in which they closely examined assessment artifacts, focusing on feedback presented to students in math and science classrooms. Music represents yet another academic domain with unique characteristics of teacher–student relationships and consequently the characteristics of assessment and feedback. Parkes (Chapter 10) explores three broad areas of feedback in music instruction that include teacher behaviors, peer and student feedback, and sensory feedback in the performance of music.

The importance of noncognitive (or psychosocial) skills in education is no longer disputed; researchers and practitioners are pondering these issues as they relate to feedback that may help students to enhance such skills. What kind of information should be provided to students that will help them to become more conscientious, motivated, or resilient? In Chapter 11, Murano, Martin, Burrus, and Roberts try to formulate answers to these questions and discuss the role of feedback in the development of noncognitive skills. The researchers present various approaches to feedback for cognitive skills and argue that feedback recommendations for cognitive skills transfer to noncognitive skills as well.

Chapter 12, by van der Meer and Dawson, and Chapter 13, by Sargeant and Watling, discuss challenges and specific characteristics in the context of higher education and medical education, respectively. The authors argue that effective feedback should go beyond its corrective purpose and should contribute to students' developing dispositions, perspectives, and skills for life beyond academia. Chapter 14, by Athota and Malik, concludes this section and discusses 360-degree feedback in a workplace. The authors describe a multi-rater approach and possible issues that might arise when providing feedback in a workplace context.

In Part III the researchers discuss various modes of feedback delivery and the diversity of contexts for feedback presentation. Munshi and Deneen (Chapter 15) explore issues and make suggestions on technology-enhanced feedback in a systematic review of literature. Key points include the implications of who is driving the dialog around technology-enhanced feedback, what works well in technology-enhanced feedback, and where there seem to be persistent and significant gaps in research and practice. In Chapter 16, Homer, Ober, and Plass examine the ways in which digital games can be used to authentically evaluate learners' knowledge and skills. Challenges are examined, including lack of general acceptance of games as assessment tools, potential for extraneous cognitive load caused by the gaming environment, and a culture of exploration and "cheats/hacks" in games. The researchers conclude with some examples of current "best practices" in game-based assessment and recommendations for next steps in the field. In Chapter 17, Andrade focuses on self-assessment, defined as the act of monitoring one's processes and products in order to make adjustments that deepen learning and enhance performance. Andrade suggests that self-assessment is most beneficial, in terms of both achievement and self-regulated learning, when it is used formatively. Panadero, Jonsson, and Alqassab (Chapter 18) examine the concept of peer feedback, discussing the key empirical themes that have been investigated. Issues related to trust, relationships between peers, and the nature of the task are discussed, along with recommendations and specific conditions that influence the effectiveness of peer feedback. In Chapter 19, Guskey discusses feedback in the context of Bloom's mastery learning theory, exploring the concept of "pre-assessment" and how it plays into instructional practice. Kanjee (Chapter 20) and Arimoto and Clark (Chapter 21) explicate feedback in international contexts of South Africa and Japan, respectively. Kanjee explores primary school teachers' written feedback practices in South Africa, and how they expect their learners to respond to this feedback. Arimoto and Clark extend the cross-cultural exploration and contrast the Western perspective of the child as a "student" or "pupil" with the Japanese practice of "zenjin education," translating most closely to "whole-child education." This part concludes with Kaufman and Pagel's (Chapter 22) discussion of feedback presented in the context of animal training. The authors draw parallels with situations in which one person's language or understanding thereof is not the same as another's.

In Part IV the contributors focus on characteristics of learners and discuss variables that relate to students' receptivity and active use of feedback. Stiggins (Chapter 23) examines the effectiveness of feedback from the student's (information recipient's) perspective. In Chapter 24, Jonsson and Panadero discuss ways that help to facilitate students' engagement with their feedback, whereas Goetz, Lipnevich, Krannich, and Gogol (Chapter 25) focus on students' emotional reactions to feedback. Holinger and Kaufman in Chapter 26 explicate the relationship between creativity and feedback (and the related construct of evaluation) from several different research perspectives: the motivational approach, the cognitive approach, and the individual differences/personality approach.

In Part V, the editors (Smith and Lipnevich, Chapter 27) join forces in an attempt to integrate these various elements into a coherent whole. In the process, we make a series of recommendations for future research, policy, and practice.

All in all, this book provides a comprehensive summary and evaluation of current research and can serve as a resource for scholars and practitioners to make informed decisions about the inner workings of instructional feedback in their respective educational programs. Humbly, we hope that researchers, students, policymakers, and practitioners alike will find this volume to be of value.

Table 0.1 *Summary of chapters that appear in this volume*

Title	Authors	Country	Feedback Context	Brief Summary
1. Feedback: At the Heart of – But Definitely Not All of – Formative Assessment	Dylan Wiliam	UK	General academic context	Discusses whether feedback works, the magnitude of the impact on learning, and what kinds of feedback work best
2. Becoming Proficient: An Alternative Perspective on the Role of Feedback	Gordon Stobart	UK	General academic context	Argues that feedback has to be carefully related to the proficiency of the learner and cannot be treated as a generic template to be applied mechanically
3. Summative and Formative Feedback	Susan M. Brookhart	US	General academic context	Juxtaposes feedback in summative and formative contexts and emphasizes the importance of student agency
4. Toward a Taxonomy of Written Feedback Messages	Jacqui Murray, N. Ruth Gasson, and Jeffrey K. Smith	New Zealand	University	Discusses an approach to categorizing feedback
5. Methods in Feedback Research	Gavin T. L. Brown and Lois R. Harris	New Zealand	General academic context	Surveys the different methods currently being used to investigate feedback in empirical studies that examine real-world processes in the design, delivery, and impact of feedback
6. Assessment Feedback in Primary Schools in Singapore and Beyond	Kelvin H. K. Tan and Hwei Ming Wong	Singapore	Elementary schools in Singapore	Attempts to answer the question: Can feedback in primary schools enhance students'

Table 0.1 (*cont.*)

Title	Authors	Country	Feedback Context	Brief Summary
				"independent" learning, and at the same time assist students to achieve requisite learning outcomes for high-stakes examinations?
7. Instructional Feedback in Writing	Steve Graham	US	Writing assignments	Summarizes research on feedback effectiveness in the domain of writing and discusses challenges of providing good quality feedback on students' written assignments
8. Instructional Feedback in Mathematics	Marian Small and Amy Lin	Canada	Math	Explores various aspects of offering feedback to students who are learning mathematics
9. Looking Closely at Mathematics and Science Classroom Feedback Practices: Examining Artifacts, Students' Products, and Teachers' Communications	Maria Araceli Ruiz-Primo and Heidi Kroog	US	Math and Science	Presents results of a study in which researchers examined feedback presented to students in math and science classrooms
10. Instructional Feedback in Music	Kelly A. Parkes	US	Music	Explores three areas of feedback in music instruction: (1) teacher behaviors, (2) peer and student feedback (assessment), and (3) sensory feedback in the

Table 0.1 (*cont.*)

Title	Authors	Country	Feedback Context	Brief Summary
				performance of music
11. Feedback and Noncognitive Skills: From Working Hypotheses to Theory-Driven Recommendations for Practice	Dana Murano, Jonathan E. Martin, Jeremy Burrus, and Richard D. Roberts	US	General academic context, non-cognitive skills	Discusses the role of feedback in the development of noncognitive skills
12. Feedback in Tertiary Education: Challenges and Opportunities for Enhancing Current Practices	Jacques van der Meer and Phillip Dawson	New Zealand and Australia	University	Focuses on the questions of what the particular purposes and the specific challenges and opportunities of feedback processes are in higher education
13. Instructional Feedback in Medical Education	Joan Sargeant and Christopher Watling	Canada	Medical schools	Discusses challenges and specific characteristics in the context of medical education
14. 360-Degree Feedback at the Workplace: A Transformative Learning Perspective	Vidya S. Athota and Ashish Malik	Australia	Work settings	Describes a multi-rater approach and possible issues that might arise when providing feedback in a workplace context
15. Technology-Enhanced Feedback	Cassim Munshi and Christopher C. Deneen	Singapore and Australia	General academic context, technology	Explores issues and makes suggestions on technology-enhanced feedback
16. Digital Games as Tools for Embedded Assessment	Bruce D. Homer, Teresa M. Ober, and Jan L. Plass	US	Technology	Examines the ways in which digital games can be used to authentically evaluate learners' knowledge and skills

Table 0.1 (*cont.*)

Title	Authors	Country	Feedback Context	Brief Summary
17. Feedback in the Context of Self-Assessment	Heidi L. Andrade	US	Self-assessment across academic contexts	Explores the process of self-assessment and suggests that self-assessment is most beneficial, in terms of both achievement and self-regulated learning, when it is used formatively
18. Providing Formative Peer Feedback: What Do We Know?	Ernesto Panadero, Anders Jonsson, and Maryam Alqassab	Spain, Sweden, Germany	Peer-assessment in general academic context	Explores the complexity of peer feedback and discusses issues related to trust and relationships between peers
19. Feedback, Correctives, and the Use of Pre-Assessments	Thomas R. Guskey	US	General academic context	Discusses feedback in the context of Bloom's "mastery learning"
20. Teacher Expectations and Feedback Practices in South African Schools	Anil Kanjee	South Africa	Elementary/primary schools	Explores primary school teachers' written feedback practices in South Africa, and how they expected their learners to respond to this feedback
21. Interactive Assessment: Cultural Perspectives and Practices in the Nexus of "Heart or Mind"	Masahiro Arimoto and Ian Clark	Japan	General academic context in Japan and Western Countries	Contrasts the Western perspective of the child as a "student" or "pupil" with the Japanese practice of "zenjin-education," translating most closely to "whole-child education"
22. Instructional Feedback in Animals	Allison B. Kaufman and	US	Animal training	Discusses feedback in situations in which a person's language (or one's

Table 0.1 (*cont.*)

Title	Authors	Country	Feedback Context	Brief Summary
	Michele M. Pagel			personal understanding of it) is not the same as another's, using animal training as a context but drawing parallels with humans
23. The Emotional Dynamics of Feedback from the Student's Point of View	Rick Stiggins	UK	General academic context	Examines the effectiveness of feedback from the student's (information recipient's) perspective
24. Facilitating Students' Active Engagement with Feedback	Anders Jonsson and Ernesto Panadero	Sweden and Spain	General academic context	Discusses ways that help to facilitate students' engagement with their feedback
25. Performance Feedback and Emotions	Thomas Goetz, Anastasiya A. Lipnevich, Maike Krannich, and Katarzyna Gogol	Germany and US	General academic context	Presents an overview of student emotional responses to feedback
26. The Relationship between Creativity and Feedback	Molly Holinger and James C. Kaufman	US	General academic context	Discusses the relationship between creativity and feedback (and the related construct of evaluation) from several different research perspectives
27. Instructional Feedback: Analysis, Synthesis, and Extrapolation	Jeffrey K. Smith and Anastasiya A. Lipnevich	New Zealand and US	General academic context	Brings the discussion together

Acknowledgments

The idea to write a book that presents a comprehensive overview of research into instructional feedback, and offers a mixture of theory and practical recommendations, has been evolving for several years. We would like to thank our editor, David Repetto, for seeing the value in such a volume and for inviting us to join the effort and prepare the Handbook. We would like to also thank Professor Valerie Shute, a recognized authority in the field of assessment and feedback (and far beyond), who graciously agreed to write the Foreword to this edited volume, and did it in record time.

Edited volumes can be very difficult to produce, as anyone who has set out on this onerous task will testify. We are indebted to Fiona Stuart for her work pulling together the important pre-production pieces, including formatting all the chapters, tracking references, and editing the volume. Fiona was the first person to read through the entire Handbook and to provide her ever-positive feedback. Thank you for that!

Anastasiya would also like to thank her incredible husband Sergey Lipnevich for all of his love, support, and constant encouragement throughout this endeavor. I get so touched when you casually discuss new research on feedback with our houseguests (despite being immersed in a field that is far removed from psychology and education). You do listen to my exhilarating accounts of current research findings! Anastasiya also thanks her children, Emilian and Evan Lipnevich, for being the amazing people that they are. I marvel at you each and every day and I look forward to watching your superhuman powers further unfold. And to the three of you – I value your feedback, realizing that it may be positively biased. Despite all that we know about optimal feedback practices, "You are the best" does mean a lot when it comes from the three of you. Words cannot describe how much I love you and hope that my work on this Handbook will help you in various domains of your lives. Many thanks to my parents, Larisa and Andrey Tsobkalo; grandparents, Elena and Stepan Khinevich; my sister Viktoria; my uncle Vladimir; and all extended family. Your unending support helped me to take this project to fruition. And to the Krivtsova-Ricchiuti family – this book will always be associated with the marvelous time that we spent with you, in beautiful Abruzzo, Italy. To all of my friends and family – many thanks for your advice, for listening to me as I vented my frustrations, and for just plain being there.

Jeff would like to thank his wonderful wife and partner in crime, Lisa Smith, who was gracious enough not to remind him how many times he said, "This is the last book I'll ever edit," through the past three edited volumes he has worked on. And he thanks his children, Benjamin and Leah Smith, and his stepdaughter, Kaitlin Bishop, for their willingness to provide him with unflinchingly honest feedback on his tastes in clothing, music, jokes, and many other aspects of life. I hope your wonderful partners Andrea Livi Smith and Ben Bishop always do the same for you. To Jeff's beautiful and brilliant granddaughters, Daria Smith, Olenna Smith, and Gwendolyn Bishop, may you one day read this paragraph and say, "Hey, I'm in a book!" And may the feedback you receive always be honest, kind, timely, and help you grow.

Ana would also like to thank her PhD students with whom we spent the entire semester discussing the mechanics of feedback. Dana, Elise, Francesca, Kalina, Maggie, Maria, Tai, and Zebing – it was a great privilege to have a group of enthusiastic and interested students by whom I could run my feedback-related ideas. Your feedback is incorporated throughout this volume – and I thank you for it. And both Ana and Jeff thank David Berg for being David Berg throughout the whole process.

Finally, an edited book would be nothing without contributions from the acclaimed scholars whom we asked to give of their time, expertise, and knowledge to prepare chapters on topics that we felt needed special attention. We are indebted to each and every one of you for the various chapters appearing in this volume. We appreciate your critical contributions and willingness to cope with a challenging task and time constraints and to respond to our suggestions with grace and efficiency. We learned a lot from you and are very grateful for your work. Because of your joint efforts, we believe the volume is coherent and informative. It has been a tremendous privilege to work with you, and we look forward to future projects and opportunities to collaborate.

Our work on this volume coincided with quite a bit of traveling. Between the two of us, this volume developed and evolved as we traveled through seventeen countries. The time that we spent working side by side in Dunedin, New Zealand, was the most memorable, but our calls at odd hours from various corners of the world were no less enjoyable. We hope this book will give readers a deeper understanding and appreciation of the current state-of-the-art in the field of instructional feedback and give a flavor of different cultures and countries from which our multinational crew comes. Please enjoy this volume and do not hesitate to drop us a line should the book raise any questions. As you may have guessed, we love feedback!

PART I

Theoretical Foundations

Methods and Concepts

1 Feedback

At the Heart of – But Definitely Not All of – Formative Assessment

Dylan Wiliam

Introduction

In 1996, Avraham Kluger and Angelo DeNisi, two psychologists at Rutgers, the State University of New Jersey, published a rather remarkable review of the research conducted from 1905 to 1995 on the effects of feedback. In their conclusion, they suggested that most of the research that had been conducted into feedback had shed little light on how to make feedback more effective because more attention had been given to whether, rather than how, feedback worked, and most of the studies had focused on the short-term effects of feedback, taking little account of whether the effects would be sustained over time. In this chapter, I review the history of feedback research and suggest that feedback research will be more effective if this research is located within a wider theoretical framework, taking more account of both micro and macro features of learning. Specifically, feedback research is likely to be more effective if it places greater attention on the cognitive processes that are involved in learning (the micro level) and on the social situations within which feedback is given and received (the macro level).

The Origins of the Concept of Feedback

In 1948, Norbert Wiener, then professor of mathematics at the Massachusetts Institute of Technology, published a book titled *Cybernetics, or control and communication in the animal and the machine* (Wiener, 1948). In it, he pointed out that in many physical systems (whether mechanical or organic), effective action required not only a mechanism for producing the action required but, in addition, some means for monitoring whether the mechanisms had produced the required effect. In railway signaling, when a lever is moved to change signals or points (switches in US English), a light or other confirmatory device shows that the intended change has indeed taken place. In the Navy, on receipt of an order, subordinates repeat the order to show that it has been heard correctly.

Such systems are needed only when the effect of the action taken is uncertain. If the desired effect always occurs, there is no need to check whether the action has been effective. For example, at typical atmospheric temperatures, it takes around 1,200 joules of energy to raise the temperature of 1 cubic meter of air by

1 degree Celsius. So if we know the volume and the temperature of the air in a building, and we know the temperature we would like the air to be, then it appears to be a straightforward task to calculate the heating requirements of the building. Unfortunately, things are not quite that simple. The building loses heat, and the rate at which the building loses heat depends on the quality of the insulation, the exterior temperature, the speed of the wind, and a whole host of other factors. That is why thermostats are used to measure the temperature of the air in rooms, to compare it with the desired temperature, and when the measured temperature goes too far below the desired temperature, some action, such as increasing fuel to a boiler or opening up a damper, is taken to change the temperature of the air. In discussing this "chain of the transmission and return of information" Wiener suggested that it should be called "the chain of feedback" (Wiener, 1948, p. 114).

In the middle part of the nineteenth century, the term "feed back" had been used in the United States to describe the reversion of a system back to some previous state. For example, a patent application in 1865 described what an operator of a machine for making spindles for wagon axles should do when "the carriage is about to feed back" (Jay, 1865). However, the first use of the term in its current sense seems to have been by Karl Ferdinand Braun, winner (jointly with Guglielmo Marconi) of the 1909 Nobel Memorial Prize in physics. In his acceptance address he pointed out that it was possible to separate out two electrical oscillations with a special circuit "*so long as care is taken* that as far as possible the circuit has no feed-back into the system being investigated" (Braun, 1909, p. 233, emphasis in original).

Of course, the idea of self-correcting systems had been around for thousands of years. Some versions of the ancient Greek clepsydra (water clock) incorporated a conical float to regulate the flow of water into the reservoir, and this is probably the earliest known example of a self-regulating device that needed no control from an external agent. James Watt's steam engine employed a "governor" to control the speed of the engine. Two solid metal balls swung on pendulum rods on opposite sides of a rotating shaft, and when the speed of the shaft's rotation increased, the balls swung outward. The pendulum rods were in turn connected to the intake valves of the steam engine, so that when the shaft speeded up, the valves closed down, slowing the speed of the engine, and when the speed of the engine dropped too much, the valves opened up, speeding up the engine. In this way, the system regulated or "governed" the speed of the engine.

Wiener described Watt's governor as an example of *negative* feedback because, in a governor, "the feed-back tends to oppose what the system is doing" (Wiener, 1948, p. 115). The alternative, where the feedback tends to reinforce what the system is already doing, is termed positive feedback. Although positive feedback loops can be useful – for example in amplifying a faint sound or a weak electrical signal – they are unstable. Most people are aware of the problem encountered in sound amplification in which sound from a loudspeaker is picked up by a microphone, which is then further amplified, which in turn increases the sound received by the microphone, increasing the sound coming out of the loudspeaker further still, leading to a howling sound that is often just called "feedback." Another example of a positive feedback loop is the growth of a population of animals with plentiful food and no predators; the population just keeps on growing exponentially.

A less obvious example of a positive feedback loop is an economic recession, in which people lose their jobs, or have their hours cut back, so they have less money, and so rein in spending, leading to further job losses, leading to further losses of confidence, and so on. This is a positive feedback loop because the information being fed back (there's a recession) has the effect of pushing the system further in the direction it was already going (less economic activity). In engineering, therefore, "positive" feedback is generally not good, since it leads either to explosive increase (as in the case of the amplification system) or collapse (as in the case of a recession). In contrast, negative feedback loops are useful, since they tend to produce stability.

For example, where the supply of food is limited, a population of animals will grow quickly at first, but as competition for food intensifies, the rate of increase will slow. The population will then tend toward a steady state, known as the "carrying capacity" of the environment (Levins, 1966, p. 427). In a similar way, the effect of the room thermostat is an example of negative feedback since the effect of the system is to heat the room when it is too cold, or to cool the room when it is too hot.

Feedback in Psychology and Education

As the term "feedback" was used more and more in engineering, it was picked up in psychology. Early uses of the term focused on motor control or the electrical circuits involved in nerve stimulation (see, for example, Washburne, 1935), but in research on the effects of reinforcement, rewards or other sensory information given to subjects in experiments were sometimes described as "feedback" (W. O. Jenkins & Stanley, 1950; Skinner, 1950). More interestingly, researchers on human performance in organizational psychology were also using the term "feedback" to describe information given to individuals or groups about their own performance (D. H. Jenkins, 1948; Roseborough, 1953; Wilson, High, & Beem, 1954). By 1954, the use of the term was sufficiently established for Robert Gagné – one of America's leading psychologists of education – to suggest that issues about the quality, grain size, and frequency of feedback, and how they impacted performance, were key areas for research on learning (Gagné, 1954).

An important focus for early research in this area examined whether corrective or reinforcement feedback was the most useful. In other words, was feedback more effective when it provided reassurance to learners that they were "on the right track" or was it better if feedback was given only when the actions of the learner deviated from what was desired in some important respect?

Intuitively, there are plausible arguments for each of these ideas. If someone is following a set of driving directions, it can be helpful to be told, "You will pass a BP petrol station on your right" but it is also helpful to know that, "If you pass under the motorway, you've gone too far."

It is tempting to regard the relationship between corrective and reinforcement feedback as being equivalent to the relationship between negative and positive feedback in engineering, but there are important differences. In engineering, whether feedback is positive or negative depends on its effect; if the effect is to push the system further in the direction in which it is already moving, it is positive, while if the feedback serves to oppose the existing trend, it is negative. In psychology, the terms "corrective" and "reinforcement" describe the intent of the feedback, and, as researchers commonly found, the actual effects of the feedback were different from what was intended.

As Kulhavy noted in his review of research on feedback in 1977, much of the early research into the effects of feedback was rooted in the behaviorist paradigm and strongly tied to the "programmed learning" movement (Skinner, 1968). The idea was that telling students that their answers were correct "reinforced" the cognitive processes through which the student had gone in order to arrive at the correct response, and thus would increase the likelihood that the correct response would be given to a similar prompt in the future. B. F. Skinner summed it up as follows:

> the machine, like the private tutor, reinforces the student for every correct response, using this immediate feedback not only to shape his behavior most efficiently but to maintain it in strength in a manner which the layman would describe as "holding the student's interest." (Skinner, 1968, p. 39)

Kulhavy defined feedback as "any of the numerous procedures that are used to tell a learner if an instructional response is right or wrong" (Kulhavy, 1977, p. 211). At its simplest, this would involve simply indicating whether a learner's response to an instructional prompt was correct or not (often called "knowledge of response" or "knowledge of results" or simply "KR"). Other examples included feedback that, for incorrect responses, provided a correct response ("knowledge of correct response" or "KCR") or gave the learner multiple further attempts to produce a correct response, possibly with additional support, such as an explanation provided by the teacher ("repeat until correct"). More complex forms of feedback included feedback that provided the learner with information on what needed improvement ("correctional review"). Ultimately, as it became more and more complex, feedback became indistinguishable from instruction:

> If we are willing to treat feedback as a unitary variable, we can then speak of its form or composition as ranging along a continuum from the simplest "Yes-No" format to the presentation of substantial corrective or remedial information that may extend the response content, or even add new material to it. Hence, as one advances along the continuum, feedback complexity increases until the process itself takes on the form of new instruction, rather than informing the student solely about correctness. (Kulhavy, 1977, p. 212)

However, it is clear that the evidence about the superiority of reinforcement, rather than correction, was not that clear cut:

> [Referring to the statement made by Skinner quoted above] With such confident statements available, it is no surprise that scholars have worked overtime to fit the round peg of feedback into the square hole of reinforcement. Unfortunately, this stoic faith in feedback-as-reinforcement has all too often led researchers to overlook or disregard alternate explanations for their data. One does not have to look far for articles that devote themselves to explaining why their data failed to meet operant expectations rather than to trying to make sense out of what they found. (Kulhavy, 1977, p. 213)

Kulhavy pointed out that many studies (e.g., Anderson, Kulhavy, & Andre, 1971) had found that telling learners that they were on the wrong track (negative reinforcement) was more effective than telling them they were on the right track (positive reinforcement) – something that should not occur if the primary benefit of feedback was as reinforcement. More serious for the "feedback-as-reinforcement" hypothesis was the finding that delaying feedback for a day or more often had no impact on its effectiveness – what is sometimes called the "delay-retention effect" (Kulhavy, 1977). In fact, as a later review by Bangert-Drowns, Kulik, and Kulik (1987) found, delaying feedback until after the learner had been required to attempt a task – called "reducing presearch availability" – consistently enhanced the effects of feedback.

During the 1980s, a number of attempts were made to make sense of the often apparently conflicting research findings. Some used what Robert Slavin (1986) termed a "best evidence" approach (the approach used by Kulhavy), while others, such as Schimmel (1983) and Kulik and Kulik (1988), used meta-analysis. Most of the reviews found that, on average, providing feedback was better than providing no feedback, but beyond that, clear results about how to maximize the benefits of feedback were hard to find.

For example, Kulik and Kulik found that delayed feedback appeared to be more effective than immediate feedback in what they called "applied" studies, where students were tested on material related to, but different from, what they had been taught. In the twenty-eight studies they found where the material to be learned took the form of lists of words or terms, the results were less clear cut. In ten of the studies, immediate feedback was significantly better, while in four of the studies, delayed feedback was significantly better. In the remaining thirteen, the differences were nonsignificant (with six favoring immediate feedback and seven favoring delayed feedback).

A clue as to the mechanisms involved was provided by a review of studies of feedback in "test-like events typical of classroom education and of text-based and technology-based instruction" (Bangert-Drowns, Kulik, Kulik, & Morgan, 1991). Their review focused on feedback that was intentional (i.e., intended to improve learning) and mediated (i.e., given by answers in a text or through computer-based instruction, rather than by direct human interaction), and generated four main findings.

Feedback Type: "Correct/incorrect" feedback (what Kulhavy had termed "knowledge of results") produced no benefit; providing correct answers ("knowledge of correct results") provided some effect (Cohen's $d = 0.22$), while "repeating until correct" or providing an explanation provided larger effects ($d = 0.53$ in each case).

Presearch Availability: Where learners were able to find answers before they had attempted the task, feedback did not improve learning, but where this was not possible (where there was, in the jargon, "control for presearch availability"), feedback had a substantial positive impact on learning ($d = 0.46$).

Study Design: Feedback had no effect in studies where students were given a pre-test, but in the studies that relied only on post-tests, there was a significant impact on learning ($d = 0.40$).

Type of Instruction: Feedback in programmed instruction and in computer-assisted instruction had no impact on learning, but in text comprehension exercises, and test performance, feedback had a significant positive effect ($d = 0.48$ and 0.60, respectively).

Bangert-Drowns et al. concluded that the crucial determinant of the effects of feedback was the extent to which the feedback was received in a "mindful" way, and similar conclusions were reached in other reviews of research into feedback conducted at the same time (see, for example, Dempster, 1991, 1992), and a review of research studies published in Dutch also underscored these main findings (Elshout-Mohr, 1994).

In 1996, Kluger and DeNisi published what is perhaps still to this day the most important study on the effects of feedback on performance. They defined a feedback intervention as "actions taken by (an) external agent(s) to provide information regarding some aspect(s) of one's task performance" (Kluger & DeNisi, 1996, p. 255). They searched a number of bibliographic databases, including the Social Science Citation Index, PsycInfo, and National Technical Information Services, for any studies – going back as far as 1905 – that included either "knowledge of results" or "feedback" as one key word and "perform-ance" as another, a process that yielded approximately 2,500 papers and 500 technical reports.

To ensure that only high-quality feedback studies were included in their review, Kluger and DeNisi (1996) rejected:

- Studies where feedback was combined with some other intervention, such as target-setting. Even if the intervention was effective, it would be impossible to know whether the increased performance was due to the feedback or the target-setting component of the intervention.
- Studies that lacked a control group. Where performance was measured before and after a feedback intervention, it would be impossible to attribute any increase in performance to the feedback since it could have been achieved simply by maturation.

- Studies where performance was estimated qualitatively rather than measured quantitatively, since the lack of measurement obviously introduces a substantial element of subjectivity into the results.
- Studies where the experimenter participated as a subject (!) or those that involved fewer than ten participants, due to the large errors of sampling involved.
- Studies where the reports of the results did not allow an effect size to be estimated (e.g., studies where the standard deviation of the performance measure was not provided and could not be estimated from the information provided in the report).

Of the original 3,000 studies identified as potentially relevant, only 131 (fewer than 5%!) of the studies met all five of these criteria, and the reports of the selected studies allowed Kluger and DeNisi (1996) to calculate 607 effect sizes based on 12,652 participants (with a total of 23,663 observations). They found reasonably strong evidence that feedback that directed recipients' attention to themselves (e.g., general praise, comparison with others, other general threats to self-esteem) tended to be less effective than feedback that focused attention on the tasks in which they were engaged. They also found that where initial feedback showed a large gap between actual and desired performance, what was crucial was whether subsequent feedback showed a rapid improvement. Where learners saw such improvement, feedback had a substantial positive effect on achievement, but where they did not, the benefits of feedback were much smaller.

However, their most important conclusion was that little could be drawn from a review of the literature on feedback because the quality of the existing studies was relatively poor. A large number of studies were not included in their review due to the lack of a control group, presumably because researchers assumed that the effects of feedback would be positive. Also, in most of the studies included in the review, the impact of feedback was evaluated just once, with the impact being measured very shortly after the feedback intervention. Studies that included measurement of performance on several occasions, with feedback interventions between each, often yielded different results from the "one-off" studies. Moreover, in many of the studies, feedback was evaluated in terms of effects on shallow learning, which Kluger and DeNisi (1996) pointed out might interfere with deeper learning, and thus restrict the ability of individuals to transfer their learning to similar, but different, tasks. Perhaps even more importantly, they pointed out that even if a feedback intervention produced large increase in achievement, it might not be a good idea to implement it widely if the feedback made the recipient more dependent on the feedback for continued progress, especially if that feedback was expensive to provide.

Since Kluger and DeNisi's (1996) review, two further major reviews of the effects of feedback have been published. Shute (2008) sought to provide advice on the best ways to provide feedback to learners in intelligent tutoring systems. Echoing the conclusions of Kluger and DeNisi, she found that there was no simple answer to the question, "What feedback works?" The effectiveness of feedback varied according to the instructional context, the kinds of tasks, and the characteristics of the students themselves. However, again echoing Kluger and DeNisi, she found that feedback was less effective when it focused on the learner, when it provided information only on the correctness of responses, or when it was so prescriptive that learners did not have to think for themselves. Feedback was more effective when it provided guidance – but not instructions – on how to improve performance – in other words, feedback should encourage mindfulness. She also found that for procedural learning and for tasks well beyond the learner's current capability, immediate feedback tended to be more effective, while delayed feedback was more effective for tasks within the learner's capability, or where the outcome measure involved transfer to other contexts.

Around the same time, Hattie and Timperley (2007) summarized the results of seventy-four meta-analyses of factors affecting student academic achievement that specifically included feedback. Building on the work of Ramaprasad (1983), they defined feedback as "specifically relating to the task or process of learning that fills a gap between what is understood and what is aimed to be understood" (p. 82). They confirmed the earlier findings of Kluger and DeNisi (1996) that feedback about the self as a person tended to be less effective, while feedback about the processing of the task and about self-regulation of learning tended to be more effective. Feedback about the task itself showed positive benefits when the feedback focused on strategy processing, or to enhance self-regulation of learning. Hattie and Timperley also noted that the conditions necessary for feedback to be optimally effective were not commonly found in practice.

Quantifying the Effects of Feedback

In the discussion of the review of research by Bangert-Drowns et al. (1991) above, a number of standardized effect sizes (Cohen, 1988) were quoted, with the most beneficial forms of feedback generating effect sizes of the order of 0.4–0.6. In Kluger and DeNisi's (1996) review, weighting the 231 effect sizes in proportion to the size of the sample generated a mean effect of 0.41 standard deviations, and Shute (2008) suggested that the effect of feedback on student achievement was in the range of 0.4–0.8 standard deviations. An unpublished review of the effects of feedback in college students by Nyquist (2003) found an average effect size, over 185 studies, of 0.4, but the effect varied substantially across different kinds of studies. In the thirty-one studies where feedback took the form of simply indicating the correctness of the results, the average effect size was 0.14, but in the forty-one studies where feedback provided information about guidance for improving performance, the effect size was 0.39, and where the feedback provided the learner with a specific task (ten studies), the average effect size was 0.56. For a detailed description of this study, and details of how feedback was classified, see Wiliam (2013).

In interpreting their results, Kluger and DeNisi (1996) concluded that feedback interventions "had a moderate positive impact on performance" (p. 258). In deciding that an effect size of 0.41 was "moderate," it seems likely that Kluger and DeNisi were influenced by the work of Jacob Cohen, who is often, but incorrectly, quoted as saying that effect sizes in the range 0.2–0.3 should be regarded as small, those around 0.5 should be regarded as moderate, and those in the range of 0.8–1.0 should be regarded as large. In fact, what Cohen was proposing was the opposite of this.

Cohen's suggestions appear in a book on conducting power calculations for experiments in the behavioral sciences (Cohen, 1988). The statistical power of an experiment is the likelihood that an experiment will yield a statistically significant finding given that the effect being investigated actually does exist. The power of an experiment depends on the number of cases (larger experiments have greater power), the significance level chosen for regarding results as significant (lower significance levels mean less power), and the magnitude of the effect being investigated (the larger the effect, the more powerful the experiment). Estimating the power of an experiment is an important step in experimental design, because it can provide the researcher with an indication of whether the experiment is likely to detect the effect being investigated. If an experiment has a power of 0.40 – the typical value in education and psychology according to Sedlmeier and Gigerenzer (1989) – then even if everything goes according to plan, and the effect being researched is real, the results will fail to reach statistical significance 60% of the time.

In order to perform a power calculation, the experimenter needs to make an estimate of the magnitude of the effect being investigated, and it is on this matter that Cohen was providing advice:

> Thus, if the investigator thinks that the effect of his treatment method on learning ability in phenylpyruvia is small, he might posit a **d** value such as 0.2 or 0.3. If he anticipates it to be large, he might posit **d** as 0.8 or 1.0. If he expects it to be medium (or simply seeks to straddle the fence on the issue), he might select some such value as **d** = 0.5.   (Cohen, 1988, p. 25, emphasis in original)

He went on to say:

> The terms "small," "medium," and "large" are relative, not only to each other, but to the area of behavioral science or even more particularly to the specific content and research method being employed in any given investigation ... In the face of this relativity, there is a certain risk inherent in offering conventional operational definitions for these terms for use in power analysis in as diverse a field of inquiry as behavioral science. This risk is nevertheless accepted in the belief that more is to be gained than lost by supplying a common conventional frame of reference *which is recommended for use only when no better basis for estimating the ES index is available.*   (p. 25, emphasis added)

This is particularly important in looking at the effects of feedback on educational achievement, since, for students over the age of nine, an effect size of

0.41, where achievement was measured with standardized tests, would be equivalent to more than doubling the rate of student learning (Bloom, Hill, Black, & Lipsey, 2008). This would be a very large effect indeed.

Another feature of their findings that may have led Kluger and DeNisi (1996) to regard an effect size of 0.41 as "moderate" was the extraordinary dispersion of their results, with twelve effect sizes in excess of four standard deviations (and one, implausibly, over twelve standard deviations). In fact, the standard deviation of the effect sizes, weighted to take account of the size of the experiments, was around 1 and, in what has to be one of the most counterintuitive results in all of psychology, they found that 231 of the 607 effect sizes they calculated were *negative*. In other words, in almost two of every five scientific studies, the effect of feedback was actually to lower performance; participants would have performed better if the feedback had simply been withheld. To complicate matters even further, Hattie and Timperley found that, across 74 meta-analyses involving 4,157 studies, feedback increased student achievement on average by 0.94 standard deviations.

Why different studies of the effects of feedback produce such different estimates of impact on student achievement is not clear, but there is increasing evidence that, in education at least, the results of meta-analyses are generally difficult – and often impossible – to interpret, for at least five reasons (for a fuller discussion of these issues, see Wiliam, 2016b):

1. The outcome measures used in education seem to vary more in their sensitivity to the effects of instruction than is typically the case in other areas where meta-analysis is used (e.g., medicine, psychology). For example, Ruiz-Primo, Shavelson, Hamilton, and Klein (2002) found that the effects of feedback were *five times* greater when student achievement was evaluated with measures of achievement that directly related to the content of instruction rather than those that measured the same concepts in different settings.

2. As noted above, many educational experiments have relatively low power, and, as it is generally easier to get studies published if their results are statistically significant, published effect sizes tend to dramatically overstate the actual effects. While there are some straightforward techniques for identifying and correcting this kind of publication bias, such as through the use of funnel plots (see, for example, Borenstein, Hedges, Higgins, & Rothstein, 2011) the use of such techniques is not yet standard in education.

3. The most commonly used effect size (Cohen's d) involves dividing the difference in control and experimental group means by the population standard deviation (or some estimate of it). Experiments conducted on populations with restricted range (gifted students, student with special educational needs) will yield larger effect sizes. More importantly, since the dispersion of achievement tends to increase with age (Wiliam, 1992), studies conducted with younger children will tend to yield much larger effect sizes than those conducted with older children.

4. There is little agreement about key words in education, so it is difficult to ensure that automated searches are identifying all relevant research studies. Moreover, when the vast majority of studies are carried out in a particular kind of setting (e.g., laboratories) generalizing to other studies (e.g., schools) is problematic, especially as the setting of the experimental work is rarely included in moderator analyses.

5. Many experimental reports do not contain sufficient details of the experimental manipulation for these to be used as moderators of effect in moderator analyses. For example, the typology of feedback developed by Ruiz-Primo and Li (2013) proposed analyzing feedback studies in terms of nine factors that would appear to be important as variables to consider:

   (i) Who provided the feedback (teacher, peer, self, or technology-based)?

   (ii) How was the feedback delivered (individual, small group, or whole class)?

   (iii) What was the role of the student in the feedback (provider or receiver)?

   (iv) What was the focus of the feedback (e.g., product, process, self-regulation for cognitive feedback, or goal orientation, self-efficacy for affective feedback)?

   (v) On what was the feedback based (student product or process)?

   (vi) What type of feedback was provided (evaluative, descriptive, or holistic)?

   (vii) How was feedback provided or presented (written, video, oral, or video)?

   (viii) What was the referent of feedback (self, others, or mastery criteria)?

   (ix) How and how often was feedback given in the study (one time or multiple times; with or without pedagogical use)?

However, many reports of feedback studies do not provide details of many of these questions, so that even if the meta-analysis used these as moderators of effect, too much data would be missing to place much confidence in the results.

Therefore, while it is clear that feedback does seem, on average, to produce relatively large effect sizes compared with other educational interventions, what these effect sizes actually mean is far from clear. It may be possible, for specific examples, to develop metrics that allow easily interpreted comparisons of different feedback interventions. For example, where students are learning multiplication facts, or predetermined vocabulary lists, then a simple percentage increase in the number of facts or words learned would be readily interpretable. However, when measures such as standardized effect size are used, then age norms need to be taken into account. Given that for students over the age of nine, one year's schooling increases student achievement by no more than 0.4 standard deviations, it is clearly nonsense to suggest that feedback could increase this by 0.79 standard deviations (i.e., in effect students would be making three years' average progress per year).

However, the far more serious problem with research on feedback is that, given the large number of negative effects, unless we have a better understanding of how feedback works, any advice that we should be giving students more feedback is profoundly misguided, because we may end up giving students more of the feedback that actually lowers achievement. Teachers may spend huge amounts of time on something that is actually lowering student achievement.

In the conclusion of their meta-analysis on the effects of feedback, Kluger and DeNisi (1996) pointed out that the most important thing about feedback was not the characteristics of the feedback itself – whether it was written or verbal, whether it was immediate of delayed, whether it was specific or generic – but what the recipient did with it.

In their "preliminary feedback intervention theory" they suggested that recipients could do one of four things with the feedback they were given: change behavior, change the goal, abandon the goal, or reject the feedback. However, for the first two of these, whether the response was productive or not would depend on the situation. Where performance fell short of the goal, changing behavior, in order to try to reach the goal, would be an adaptive response. However, where the feedback indicated that a learner had already reached the desired goal, changing behavior – to exert less effort, for example – would generally be maladaptive. Where the feedback indicated that a learner had reached a goal, the desirable outcome is that the learner would change the goal, to set a higher one, but where the feedback indicated the learner was still falling short of the goal, changing the goal to one that could be more easily achieved would not be conducive to learning.[1] One way of illustrating these responses is shown in Table 1.1.

The final sentences of Kluger and DeNisi's (1996) review are worth quoting at length:

> These considerations of utility and alternative interventions suggest that even an FI [feedback intervention] with demonstrated positive effects on performance should not be administered whenever possible. Rather, additional development of FIT [feedback intervention theory] is needed to establish the circumstance under which positive FI effects on performance are also lasting and efficient and when these effects are transient and have questionable utility. This research must focus on the processes induced by FIs and not on the general question of whether FIs improve performance – look at how little progress 90 years of attempts to answer the latter question have yielded.   (p. 278)

To sum up, after (now) over one hundred years of research we know very little about feedback. While methodological differences could account for some difference in the effect sizes found, the fact that several reviews suggest that the

---

1 Hattie and Timperley made similar points by suggesting that learners could reduce the discrepancy between current and desired performance *either* by changing efforts to reach the goal (by increasing effort or using more effective learning strategies) *or* by lowering the goal, making it less specific, or abandoning it entirely. Teachers could also "close the gap" by reducing the difficulty or the specificity of the goals or by providing more support (for example, by giving direct help or providing more structure).

Table 1.1 *Possible responses to feedback (adapted from Wiliam, 2011a)*

	Feedback indicates performance...	
	falls short of goal	exceeds goal
Change behavior	Increase effort	Reduce effort
Change goal	Reduce aspiration	Increase aspiration
Abandon goal	Decide goal is too hard	Decide goal is too easy
Reject feedback	Ignore feedback	Ignore feedback

feedback increases student achievement by 0.4 standard deviations and others suggest that the effect is almost two and a half times as large (Hattie & Timperley, 2007) suggests we have no clear idea of the benefits of feedback. Some might argue that the actual magnitude of the effect is less important than the sign – if feedback increases student achievement, we should do more of it anyway – but this ignores two things. The first is the large – and largely unexplained – number of feedback studies that show negative effects on learning. Without a clear understanding of why so many feedback studies have found that feedback lowers achievement, mandating more feedback may, as noted above, result in more of the feedback that lowers achievement. The second is the issue of opportunity cost. Even if we could be sure that feedback would raise achievement, teachers and students have only so much time, and if teachers spend time on giving their students feedback, and students take time to act on that feedback, we need to know the likely impact on achievement so that we can compare it with other uses of the same time.

Moreover, we know little about what kinds of feedback are likely to be helpful in a given situation. It seems plausible that either telling learners that they are on the right track, to encourage them to maintain their efforts, or informing them when they need to change what they are doing in order to improve could be beneficial. While we know, as Jeffrey Nyquist showed, some forms of feedback *tend* to be more effective than others, the range of effects is huge, and for any kind of feedback, the answer to the question, "Does it work?" seems to be "Sometimes." Now, in a way, this is not at all surprising. As Kluger and DeNisi (1996) pointed out, the effect of feedback depends on the reaction of the recipient, and that will depend on many factors. Feedback given to one student may prompt that student to increase effort, while the same feedback, to a very similar student, may result in the student giving up, and an important determinant of the response of the student is the relationship between the donor and the recipient. Teachers give students feedback assuming that students know that the purpose of the feedback is to help students improve, but many students seem to believe that critical feedback is just given by teachers in order to be hurtful. David Yeager and his colleagues have shown that just explaining to high school students why they are being given feedback (what they call "wise feedback") – and in particular that critical feedback indicates a belief by the teacher that the student can reach high academic standards – improves student achievement and college enrollment (Yeager, Purdie-Vaughns, Hooper, & Cohen, 2017).

Given all this, and, in particular, given the difficulty of describing, categorizing, or measuring the relationships between donors and recipients of feedback, it seems that developing Kluger and DeNisi's (1996) "feedback intervention theory" to a point where it is likely to be useful is a significant undertaking that is likely to take decades, rather than years, even if it is possible. For that reason, in the remainder of this chapter, I want to explore how existing feedback research can be applied more effectively in the service of learning. This will inevitably involve going somewhat beyond the evidence base, drawing some speculative inferences about what is likely to be most effective, but given the potential that feedback seems to have to improve learning, such an approach seems justified. Researchers always conclude that "more research is needed" and this is not only – or even primarily – a self-serving claim to provide more work for researchers; research tends to make things more complicated rather than simpler. But practitioners need to make decisions right now about where to focus their efforts, and the remainder of this chapter proposes that placing feedback within a more general framework of formative assessment, while also taking into account recent advances in our understanding of learning and memory, can contribute to that aim.

Learning, Memory, and Feedback

One of the most surprising things about the field of feedback research is how many studies of feedback pay relatively little attention to the nature of learning and the cognitive processes involved. In most feedback studies, it is generally assumed that information about current performance will, if acted on by the learner, produce improvements in performance, and, as noted above, researchers have focused more on the way that feedback is given than the nature of the feedback provided. Studies have examined whether feedback is more effective if it is immediate or if it is delayed; if it specific, or if it is generic; if it is spoken rather than being given in writing; and so on. Of course, these can be important questions, especially where the purpose of the feedback is to improve an individual's performance in the short term, but where the focus – as it most often tends to be – is on improving the capabilities of individuals over the longer term, then feedback interventions that improve performance are likely to be ineffective and may even be counterproductive.

As Kirschner, Sweller, and Clark (2006) point out, "The aim of all instruction is to alter long-term memory. If nothing has changed in long-term memory, nothing has been learned" (p. 77). The purpose of feedback, therefore, is almost always to improve long-term memory of the things on which feedback is being provided. There will be times when the purpose of the feedback is to improve an artifact – such as when an English language arts teacher notices a typographical error on the front page of a student newspaper that a class has prepared and points out the error to the students so that the error can be corrected. However, most of the time, the purpose of the feedback is to improve the learner, and not the work, the work being merely the source of evidence for the teacher about what kinds of feedback interventions are likely to be most effective. This observation is particularly important in view of the clear differences between *learning* and *performance* that have been noted in the psychological literature for well over eighty years.

In 1929, Hugh Carlton Blodgett showed that rats that were rewarded with food for reaching a goal box within a maze reached the box more quickly than rats that were simply removed from the maze when they reached the box. The error-rate of those given rewards dropped by 87% over the first seven days of the experiment, while those not given rewards improved much less quickly, with a 20% reduction of errors over the same time period. A third group of rats was given no reward for the first two days, and, as might be expected, their improvement was indistinguishable from the second group. However, rats in this third group received rewards on the third day, and their performance *the next day* was as good as those who had received rewards since the first day. They had been learning, even though the evidence of that learning was not apparent in their performance on the maze task (Blodgett, 1929). Since then a huge number of studies have shown that, for humans and other animals, learning can occur even though there is no discernible change in performance, and this seems to hold for both motor learning and verbal learning (for a review of this research, see Soderstrom & Bjork, 2015). More recently, the converse has also been demonstrated: increases in performance can occur with no increase in long-term learning, and increases in performance on a learning task can actually be accompanied by a *reduction* in long-term learning. This is an important observation because it is clear that learners base their judgments of their own learning on the quality of performance rather than learning. They show a clear preference for study strategies that improve short-term performance rather than long-term learning, although this tendency does seem reasonably easy to counteract (McCabe, 2011).

These insights go some way to explaining many of the contradictory and ambiguous findings on feedback interventions. Feedback can appear to be effective in the short term (by improving performance) but have no impact – or even a negative impact – on learning. Conversely, feedback might appear to be completely ineffective, in that it has no impact on performance immediately after the feedback, but, over time, might generate learning that leads to higher levels of performance in the longer term. A crucial focus for future feedback research is therefore to understand the circumstances under which feedback improves learning (rather than just performance). While many factors will clearly be important to disentangle, one particularly important aspect of this research will be to build on new theories about the nature of human memory, and particularly the work of Robert Bjork.

The New Theory of Disuse

Perhaps the most common view of memory is as a kind of recording device, where things that are learned are recorded in some way. Over time, unless they are constantly refreshed, these memories decay – what Edward Thorndike called the "law of disuse" (Thorndike, 1913, p. 4). If facts or events cannot be recalled, the general assumption is that the memories of those facts have decayed so much that they have disappeared. However, it seems that when things have been well learned in the past, the problem is rather one of retrieval. For example, as Yan (2016) points out, many people remember being taught their home telephone number as a child and can remember knowing it very well, but often cannot recall the number in adulthood. However, even if they cannot recall the number, adults can usually identify the number from a list of telephone numbers. If the memory really had disappeared, this would not be possible. The number is still stored in memory. What is hard is retrieving it. The same insight provides an explanation of the "tip of the tongue" phenomenon – the fact that someone cannot recall something at a particular time, but know that they know it, and are often able to recall it a short time later, especially if they stop trying to recall it. Other things can, at a given point in time, be easily recalled but are never effectively learned. For example, when staying at a hotel, most people can remember the number of their room during the stay but weeks later cannot recall it and, more importantly, would not be able to pick out the number from a list of numbers. While the number is easily recalled during the stay, it is not effectively learned (in the sense of changing long-term memory).

Bjork and Bjork (1992) point out that human memory works very differently from physical or digital storage mechanisms. With physical or digital storage, retrieval does not change the stored information, nor any other information. In contrast, when humans retrieve things from memory, the material that is retrieved becomes more memorable, and – more surprisingly – things that are not retrieved become less easy to retrieve in the future. Bjork and Bjork's "new theory of disuse," which appears to account for existing observations about memory better than any other theory, makes five assumptions:

1. The contents of memory can be characterized by two parameters: storage strength and retrieval strength. Storage strength is a measure of how well something has been learned, while retrieval strength measures the ease of access to something in memory. These two parameters are independent of one another, since something can have high storage strength and low retrieval strength (a childhood telephone number) or can have low storage strength and high retrieval strength (the number of a flight just before boarding).
2. Storage strength can increase but cannot decrease, so that, to all intents and purposes, once something has been learned, it is never lost (except through physical changes to the brain).

3. Retrieval strength is limited, so that retrieving some items makes retrieving other items more difficult.
4. Storage strength is increased both by successfully retrieving an item from memory and by restudying the item, but retrieval produces a larger increase in storage strength than restudy.
5. The reduction in an item's retrieval strength caused by learning or retrieving other items is greater when the item's retrieval strength is higher, and when the item's storage strength is lower.

A full examination of the consequence of Bjork and Bjork's new theory of disuse is beyond the scope of this chapter, but it is clearly an important priority for future research on feedback interventions. For the time being, it seems appropriate to draw attention to two consequences of the assumptions of the "new theory of disuse" that seem to be particularly important in terms of understanding the existing research on feedback and for guiding future research. The first is that it is now clear, from extensive empirical work, that learning activities increase storage strength to a greater extent when retrieval strength is *low*. The greater the difficulties encountered during the retrieval process, the greater the increase in storage strength will be if the retrieval process is successful. In other words, learning is enhanced when learners encounter "desirable difficulties" (Bjork, 1994, p. 193) in their learning. Feedback that reduces the extent to which learners struggle to retrieve things from long-term memory is likely to be less successful than feedback that supports learners in a productive struggle for retrieval. This is a particularly important observation in view of the fact noted above that learners and teachers seem to prefer feedback that makes learning easy.

The second consequence of the assumptions of the new theory of disuse is that, because retrieval has a greater impact on storage strength than restudy, for a given level of retrieval strength, activities that support learners in retrieving items from memory, rather than providing correct answers (which are a form of restudy) are likely to be more successful. This insight goes at least some way to explaining the results described in the historical review of feedback research earlier in this chapter, such as the fact that "presearch availability" reduces the effects of feedback (Bangert-Drowns et al., 1991) and the relatively small effects of "knowledge of results" compared with other forms of feedback reviewed by Nyquist (2003).

The more general point is that if learning is, indeed, as Kirschner et al. suggest, "a change in long-term memory," then feedback research needs to pay greater attention to what we know about the counterintuitive aspects of the nature of human memory. In particular, feedback research needs to pay greater attention to the fact that learning is not the same as performance and that both learners and teachers seem to prefer instructional activities and feedback interventions that focus on performance rather than learning – activities that therefore fail to enhance and, in some cases, impede learning. This particular distinction does not seem to have been used as a moderator of feedback effects in meta-analyses and may prove a useful first step in explaining the considerable variation in feedback effects that have been observed.

Feedback in a Wider Context: The Formative Assessment Frame

As noted above, as well as connecting feedback to research on learning and memory, an adequate response to Kluger and DeNisi's (1996) suggestions about the development of feedback intervention theory would also require embedding the process of feedback in a wider theoretical frame. In 1998, Paul Black and I published a review of the effects of classroom evaluation processes that was intended to update the reviews produced by Gary Natriello and Terry Crooks a decade earlier (Natriello, 1987; Crooks, 1988). Our review (P. Black & Wiliam, 1998) convinced us that feedback had considerable potential to improve student learning in classrooms:

> Thus, whilst we cannot argue that development of formative assessment is the only way, or even the best way, to open up a broader range of desirable changes in classroom learning, we can see that it may be peculiarly effective, in part because the quality of interactive feedback is a critical feature in determining the quality of learning activity, and is therefore a central feature of pedagogy. (P. Black & Wiliam, 2005, p. 100)

Shortly after we published our review, we began working with groups of teachers to explore the potential for improved use of feedback in classrooms. The charity from which we sought funding had a particular interest in the teaching of mathematics and science, and so we focused our initial work with teachers of these subjects.

We recruited a group of twelve mathematics teachers and twelve science teachers from six secondary schools in two local education authorities (Medway and Oxfordshire) and we began by surveying the kinds of feedback that these teachers provided to their students. We found that most of the feedback took the form of "knowledge of results" (i.e., an indication of whether the work students submitted was correct or not) with some feedback also providing information about "knowledge of correct results." We suggested to teachers that feedback would be more effective if, as well as indicating whether results were correct, the feedback also identified what students should do to move their learning on. To our surprise, they found this very difficult. By looking at their students' responses to the tasks they had been assigned, the teachers were able to evaluate the extent to which students had learned the intended material. However, where students had not reached the required level, the students' responses provided no guidance for the teacher about what kind of instructional response the teacher should make, except to teach the material again but, presumably, to do so more effectively.

A few months into the project, the teachers asked us for some formal information about the psychology of learning. At first, this too surprised us, but perhaps we should not have been so surprised. We had asked them to provide feedback that their students could use, and to do that, they needed models of their students' thinking. Despite the fact that most of the teachers had substantial teaching experience (well over ten years in most cases), they had managed – and indeed in many cases been regarded as highly effective teachers – without any clear idea of what was happening in their students' heads.

The teachers also began to think much more carefully about the tasks they set their students. They had realized that to provide effective feedback to their students, they needed to find out more about their students' thinking, and that the tasks they routinely used varied considerably in the extent to which they provided useful, instructionally tractable, information about student achievement. That, in turn, led teachers to an awareness that they needed much greater clarity about the aims of their instruction, in order to be clear about what kinds of questions or tasks would be most appropriate. While the project had focused originally on feedback, real implementation of these ideas required attention to the ways in which evidence of learning was elicited, which in turn necessitated clarity about the learning goals.

At the same time, the kinds of practices that the teachers were adopting in their classrooms placed much greater responsibility for learning on the learners. Put bluntly, changing what teachers were doing in classrooms also required changing what students were doing. In particular, harnessing the power of assessment and feedback to improve learning involved greater use of students assessing their own work and that of their peers.

This, of course, was exactly the point being made by Kluger and DeNisi (1996) in the closing paragraphs of their review: the importance of considering the reactions of learners in examining feedback interventions. A similar point was made by Phillippe Perrenoud in his response to our 1998 review:

> This [feedback] no longer seems to me, however, to be the central issue.
> It would seem more important to concentrate on the theoretical models of
> learning and its regulation and their implementation. These constitute the
> real systems of thought and action, in which feedback is only one
> element.   (Perrenoud, 1998, p. 86)

At around this time, many writers had begun to use the phrase "assessment for learning" to describe the use of assessment to improve learning (for an extended discussion of the term "assessment for learning," see Wiliam, 2011b). The phrase appears to have been first used by Peter Mittler in the title of an edited collection of chapters on teaching children with special educational needs (Mittler, 1973), and a few years later, it was used by Harry Black as the title of a chapter in the book *Assessing educational achievement* (H. Black, 1986). In 1992, the term was used as the title of a paper given by Mary James at the annual meeting of the American Educational Research Association (James, 1992) and three years later as the title of a book by Ruth Sutton (Sutton, 1995). While many authors have suggested using the term "assessment for learning" rather than "formative assessment," as Bennett (2011) points out, this merely moves the definitional burden. Moreover, the distinction between assessment for learning and assessment of learning is of a different kind from the difference between formative and summative assessment. The former distinction relates to the purpose for which the assessment is carried out, while the second relates to the function it actually serves:

> Assessment for learning is any assessment for which the first priority in its design and practice is to serve the purpose of promoting students' learning. It thus differs from assessment designed primarily to serve the purposes of accountability, or of ranking, or of certifying competence. An assessment activity can help learning if it provides information that teachers and their students can use as feedback in assessing themselves and one another and in modifying the teaching and learning activities in which they are engaged. Such assessment becomes "formative assessment" when the evidence is actually used to adapt the teaching work to meet learning needs.
> (Black, Harrison, Lee, Marshall, and Wiliam, 2003, p. 10)

To complicate matters even further, many authors used the term "formative assessment" to describe processes of monitoring student achievement with little student involvement (see, for example, the discussion of this in Shepard, 2008), and more recently, some authors have used "assessment for learning" to describe the teacher's role, while referring to the role of learners as "assessment as learning" (Earl & Katz, 2006).

In an attempt to draw together the different definitions in a coherent way, Paul Black and I proposed the following definition:

> Practice in a classroom is formative to the extent that evidence about student achievement is elicited, interpreted, and used by teachers, learners, or their peers, to make decisions about the next steps in instruction that are likely to be better, or better founded, than the decisions they would have taken in the absence of the evidence that was elicited.   (P. J. Black & Wiliam, 2009, p. 9)

While this definition was relatively straightforward to apply to determining whether an assessment was functioning formatively, it was less useful for teachers in deciding how to develop their use of formative assessment.

In our early work with teachers (see, for example, P. Black, Harrison, Lee, Marshall, & Wiliam, 2003), we had introduced teachers to formative assessment through five kinds of classroom activity:

- Sharing success criteria with learners
- Classroom questioning
- Comment-only marking
- Peer- and self-assessment
- Formative use of summative tests.

While all these activities seemed to be connected, their precise relationship to each other, to feedback, and to formative assessment was not clearly articulated. More importantly, the lack of a theoretical rationale raised the possibility that these five activities did not collectively exhaust the possibilities for formative assessment. After several false starts, we realized that the definition of

	Where the learner is	Where the learner is going	How to get there
Teacher	Clarifying, sharing, and understanding learning intentions	Engineering effective discussions, activities, and tasks that elicit evidence of learning	Providing feedback that moves learning forward
Peer		Activating students as learning resources for one another	
Learner		Activating students as owners of their own learning	

Figure 1.1 *Five key strategies of formative assessment.*

feedback proposed by Arkalgud Ramaprasad (1983) provided a useful starting point. Ramaprasad had defined feedback as "information about the gap between the actual level and the reference level of a system parameter which is used to alter the gap in some way" (p. 4). Applying this to educational settings, the key aspects of formative assessment could be conceptualized as the result of crossing three processes in learning (establishing where the learner is, establishing where the learner is going, and establishing how to get there) with three kinds of individuals in the classroom (teacher, peer, and learner). The resulting framework is shown in Figure 1.1 (Wiliam & Thompson, 2008).

Extensive discussions of the application of this framework for formative assessment can be found in Wiliam (2011a, 2016b) and Wiliam and Leahy (2015), but for the purpose of the present discussion, the important point is that this framework seems to provide teachers with a useful framework for thinking about their practice. Of course, this framework itself needs to be embedded in a wider theory of pedagogy, but the framework seems to represent a reasonable compromise between bland generalizations about, on the one hand, practice that teachers find unhelpful and, on the other hand, overly prescriptive approaches to teacher education that, in Lawrence Stenhouse's memorable phrase, treats the teacher "as a kind of intellectual navvy" who is told where to dig but not why (Stenhouse, 1980).

While this framework developed from a "bottom-up" perspective, starting with the concept of feedback, it can also be derived from a "top-down" perspective such as that provided by the Educational Endowment Foundation's Teaching and Learning Toolkit (Education Endowment Foundation, 2015). The Toolkit was originally developed as a resource to assist schools in England to use more wisely the additional funds they had been given to address the needs of socioeconomically disadvantaged students. However, many schools found the format of the Toolkit, which provides information on the costs and benefits of various interventions and policy proposals, together with an indication of the quality of the available evidence, useful for examining other aspects of the work. Using a best-evidence synthesis (Slavin, 1986) rather than meta-analysis, the Toolkit provides estimates of the impact of thirty different policy interventions, in additional months of learning per year, together with a rough indication of the cost of the intervention (on a five-point scale) and a judgment about the quality of the available evidence (on a four-point scale).

According to the Toolkit, the three most cost-effective interventions are feedback, promoting metacognition and self-regulated learning, and peer-tutoring. The last two are clearly central aspects of "activating students as owners of their own learning" and "activating students as learning resources for one another." In other words, the three most cost-effective interventions, according to the EEF's Toolkit, are closely linked to three of the five strategies of formative assessment as defined in Figure 1.1. Moreover, as the teachers working on formative assessment discussed earlier realized, the starting point for effective feedback is to have relevant information about students' current levels of achievement, which requires evidence to be elicited, and this in turn requires clarity about the learning intentions.

The five strategies of formative assessment described in Figure 1.1 therefore represent a "minimum set" of the highest impact strategies and provide a framework within which teachers can think about feedback in a more integrated way. It also establishes reasonably clear boundaries for what is, and what is not, formative assessment, and thus helps focus attention on the aspects of teacher practice that are likely to be most effective priorities for development. More-over, the model appears to be quite general. It has recently been used with social workers, community support workers, those involved with adult education, and instrumental music teachers, and all these groups have found it relevant and applicable to their work. It can also be used as a framework for teacher professional development (Wiliam, 2016a).

Conclusion

In this chapter, I have tried to present some initial suggestions about how the challenge laid down by Kluger and DeNisi in the closing sections of their 1996 review of the effects of feedback might be met. As they pointed out, attempts to discover whether feedback works, the magnitude of the impact on learning, and what kinds of feedback work best have yielded little progress because they failed to take into account the longer-term effects, the costs of providing the feedback, and the reactions of the recipients of feedback. In addressing this challenge, I have suggested that feedback interventions need to take greater account of the crucial difference between learning and perform-ance that has been a key concept in memory research for decades. Specifically, feedback interventions should be designed so as to maximize the impact on storage strength, rather than focusing on retrieval strength, which means delaying feedback until retrieval strength is low, creating "desirable difficul-ties" for learners in taking on board the feedback, and, wherever possible, by providing feedback that requires learners to retrieve rather than restudy previously learned material. I have also suggested that, for work with teachers, it is helpful to locate feedback within a wider theoretical frame that takes into account the different roles of teachers, learners, and their peers. In particular, I have suggested that by defining formative assessment inclusively, focusing on the extent to which assessment-elicited evidence is used to improve educational decisions, we can place feedback at the heart of effective formative assessment in a way that supports teachers in harnessing the power of feedback to improve learning.

References

Anderson, R. C., Kulhavy, R. W., & Andre, T. (1971). Feedback procedures in programmed instruction. *Journal of Educational Psychology, 62*, 148–156.

Bangert-Drowns, R. L., Kulik, C.-L. C., Kulik, J. A., & Morgan, M. (1991). The instructional effect of feedback in test-like events. *Review of Educational Research, 61*, 213–238.

Bangert-Drowns, R. L., Kulik, J. A., & Kulik, C.-L. C. (1987, April). The impact of peekability on feedback effects. Paper presented at the annual meeting of the American Educational Research Association, Washington, DC.

Bennett, R. E. (2011). Formative assessment: A critical review. *Assessment in Education: Principles, Policy and Practice, 18*, 5–25.

Bjork, R. A. (1994). Memory and metamemory considerations in the training of human beings. In J. Metcalfe & A. P. Shimamura (Eds.), *Metacognition: Knowing about knowing* (pp. 188–205). Cambridge, MA: MIT Press.

Bjork, R. A., & Bjork, E. L. (1992). A new theory of disuse and an old theory of stimulus fluctuation. In A. F. Healy, S. M. Kosslyn, & R. M. Shiffrin (Eds.), *From learning processes to cognitive processes: Essays in honor of William K. Estes* (vol. 2, pp. 35–67). Hillsdale, NJ: Lawrence Erlbaum Associates.

Black, H. (1986). Assessment for learning. In D. L. Nuttall (Ed.), *Assessing educational achievement* (pp. 7–18). London: Falmer Press.

Black, P., Harrison, C., Lee, C., Marshall, B., & Wiliam, D. (2003). *Assessment for learning: Putting it into practice*. Buckingham, UK: Open University Press.

Black, P., & Wiliam, D. (1998). Assessment and classroom learning. *Assessment in Education: Principles, Policy and Practice, 5*, 7–74.

Black, P., & Wiliam, D. (2005). Developing a theory of formative assessment. In J. Gardner (Ed.), *Assessment and learning* (pp. 81–100). London: Sage.

Black, P. J., & Wiliam, D. (2009). Developing the theory of formative assessment. *Educational Assessment, Evaluation and Accountability, 21*, 5–31.

Blodgett, H. C. (1929). The effect of the introduction of reward upon the maze performance of rats. *University of California Publications in Psychology, 4*(8), 113–134.

Bloom, H. S., Hill, C. J., Black, A. R., & Lipsey, M. W. (2008). Performance trajectories and performance gaps as achievement effect-size benchmarks for educational interventions. *Journal of Research on Educational Effectiveness, 1*, 289–328.

Borenstein, M., Hedges, L. V., Higgins, J. P. T., & Rothstein, H. R. (2011). *Introduction to meta-analysis*. Chichester: Wiley.

Braun, K. F. (1909). Electrical oscillations and wireless telegraphy. In Alfred Nobel Memorial Foundation (Ed.), *Nobel prize lectures* (pp. 226–245). Stockholm: Alfred Nobel Memorial Foundation.

Cohen, J. (1988). *Statistical power analysis for the behavioral sciences* (2nd edn.). Hillsdale, NJ: Lawrence Erlbaum Associates.

Crooks, T. J. (1988). The impact of classroom evaluation practices on students. *Review of Educational Research, 58*, 438–481.

Dempster, F. N. (1991). Synthesis of research on reviews and tests. *Educational Leadership, 48*, 71–76.

Dempster, F. N. (1992). Using tests to promote learning: A neglected classroom resource. *Journal of Research and Development in Education, 25*, 213–217.

Earl, L. M., & Katz, S. (2006). *Rethinking classroom assessment with purpose in mind: Assessment for learning, assessment as learning, assessment of learning.* Winnipeg, MB: Manitoba Education, Citizenship and Youth.

Education Endowment Foundation. (2015). Teaching and learning toolkit. Retrieved from https://educationendowmentfoundation.org.uk/toolkit/toolkit-a-z/.

Elshout-Mohr, M. (1994). Feedback in self-instruction. *European Education, 26*(2), 58–73.

Gagné, R. M. (1954). Training devices and simulators: Some research issues. *American Psychologist, 9*(3), 95–107.

Hattie, J., & Timperley, H. (2007). The power of feedback. *Review of Educational Research, 77*, 81–112.

James, M. (1992, April). Assessment for learning. Paper presented at the annual meeting of the American Educational Research Association, New Orleans, LA.

Jay, J. M. (1865, May 16). Improvement in machines for making the spindles of wagon-axles. US Patent No. US47769 A. US Patent and Trademark Office, Washington, DC.

Jenkins, D. H. (1948). Feedback and group self-evaluation. *Journal of Social Issues, 4*(2), 50–60.

Jenkins, W. O., & Stanley, Julian C. Jr. (1950). Partial reinforcement: A review and critique. *Psychological Bulletin, 47*, 193–234.

Kirschner, P. A., Sweller, J., & Clark, R. E. (2006). Why minimal guidance during instruction does not work: An analysis of the failure of constructivist, problem-based, experiential, and inquiry-based teaching. *Educational Psychologist, 41*, 75–86.

Kluger, A. N., & DeNisi, A. (1996). The effects of feedback interventions on performance: A historical review, a meta-analysis, and a preliminary feedback intervention theory. *Psychological Bulletin, 119*, 254–284.

Kulhavy, R. W. (1977). Feedback in written instruction. *Review of Educational Research, 47*, 211–232.

Kulik, J. A., & Kulik, C.-L. C. (1988). Timing of feedback and verbal learning. *Review of Educational Research, 58*, 79–97.

Levins, R. (1966). The strategy of model building in population biology. *American Scientist, 54*, 421–431.

McCabe, J. (2011). Metacognitive awareness of learning strategies in undergraduates. *Memory & Cognition, 39*, 462–476.

Mittler, P. (1973). Purposes and principles of assessment. In P. Mittler (Ed.), *Assessment for learning in the mentally handicapped* (pp. 1–16). Edinburgh: Churchill Livingstone.

Natriello, G. (1987). The impact of evaluation processes on students. *Educational Psychologist, 22*, 155–175.

Nyquist, J. B. (2003). The benefits of reconstruing feedback as a larger system of formative assessment: A meta-analysis. Master's thesis, Vanderbilt University.

Perrenoud, P. (1998). From formative evaluation to a controlled regulation of learning. Towards a wider conceptual field. *Assessment in Education: Principles, Policy and Practice, 5*, 85–102.

Ramaprasad, A. (1983). On the definition of feedback. *Behavioral Science, 28*, 4–13.

Roseborough, M. E. (1953). Experimental studies of small groups. *Psychological Bulletin, 50*, 275–303.

Ruiz-Primo, M. A., & Li, M. (2013). Examining formative feedback in the classroom context: New research perspectives. In J. H. McMillan (Ed.), *Sage handbook of research on classroom assessment* (2nd edn., pp. 215–232). Thousand Oaks, CA: Sage.

Ruiz-Primo, M. A., Shavelson, R. J., Hamilton, L., & Klein, S. (2002). On the evaluation of systemic science education reform: Searching for instructional sensitivity. *Journal of Research in Science Teaching, 39*, 369–393.

Schimmel, B. J. (1983, April). A meta-analysis of feedback to learners in computerized and programmed instruction. Paper presented at the annual meeting of the American Educational Association, Montreal, Canada.

Sedlmeier, P., & Gigerenzer, G. (1989). Do studies of statistical power have an effect on the power of studies? *Psychological Bulletin, 105*, 309–316.

Shepard, L. A. (2008). Formative assessment: Caveat emptor. In C. A. Dwyer (Ed.), *The future of assessment: Shaping teaching and learning* (pp. 279–303). Mahwah, NJ: Lawrence Erlbaum Associates.

Shute, V. J. (2008). Focus on formative feedback. *Review of Educational Research, 78*, 153–189.

Skinner, B. F. (1950). Are theories of learning necessary? *Psychological Review, 57*, 193–216.

Skinner, B. F. (1968). *The technology of teaching*. New York: Appleton-Century-Crofts.

Slavin, R. E. (1986). Best-evidence synthesis: An alternative to meta-analytic and traditional reviews. *Educational Researcher, 15*(9), 5–11.

Soderstrom, N. C., & Bjork, R. A. (2015). Learning versus performance: An integrative review. *Perspectives on Psychological Science, 10*, 176–199.

Stenhouse, L. (1980). Product or process? A reply to Brian Crittenden. *New Education, 2*, 137–140.

Sutton, R. (1995). *Assessment for learning*. Salford, UK: RS Publications.

Thorndike, E. L. (1913). *The psychology of learning*. New York: Teachers College, Columbia University.

Washburne, J. N. (1935). An electro-chemical theory of learning. *Journal of Educational Psychology, 26*, 99–122.

Wiener, N. (1948). *Cybernetics, or control and communication in the animal and the machine*. New York: John Wiley & Sons.

Wiliam, D. (1992). Special needs and the distribution of attainment in the national curriculum. *British Journal of Educational Psychology, 62*, 397–403.

Wiliam, D. (2011a). *Embedded formative assessment*. Bloomington, IN: Solution Tree.

Wiliam, D. (2011b). What is assessment for learning? *Studies in Educational Evaluation, 37*, 2–14.

Wiliam, D. (2013). Feedback and instructional correctives. In J. H. McMillan (Ed.), *Sage handbook of research on classroom assessment* (2nd edn., pp. 197–214). Thousand Oaks, CA: Sage.

Wiliam, D. (2016a). La evaluación formative del desempeño de la enseñanza. In G. G. Niebla, M. T. M. Irigoyen, F. E. R. Castaño, H. S. Pérez, & F. T. Segura (Eds.),

La evaluación docente en el mundo (pp. 166–199). Mexico City: Instituto Nacional para la Evaluación de la Educación.

Wiliam, D. (2016b). *Leadership for teacher learning: Creating a culture where all teachers improve so that all learners succeed.* West Palm Beach, FL: Learning Sciences International.

Wiliam, D., & Leahy, S. (2015). *Embedding formative assessment: Practical techniques for K-12 classrooms.* West Palm Beach, FL: Learning Sciences International.

Wiliam, D., & Thompson, M. (2008). Integrating assessment with instruction: What will it take to make it work? In C. A. Dwyer (Ed.), *The future of assessment: Shaping teaching and learning* (pp. 53–82). Mahwah, NJ: Lawrence Erlbaum Associates.

Wilson, R. C., High, W. S., & Beem, H. P. (1954). A factor-analytic study of supervisory and group behavior. *Journal of Applied Psychology, 38,* 89–92.

Yan, V. (2016). Retrieval strength vs. storage strength. Learning Scientists. Retrieved from www.learningscientists.org/blog/2016/5/10-1.

Yeager, D. S., Purdie-Vaughns, V., Hooper, S. Y., & Cohen, G. L. (2017). Loss of institutional trust among racial and ethnic minority adolescents: A consequence of procedural injustice and a cause of life-span outcomes. *Child Development, 88,* 658–676.

2 Becoming Proficient

An Alternative Perspective on the Role of Feedback

Gordon Stobart

Introduction

Two learners are given feedback – they are both told, "You're wrong." The first is a novice, for whom this feedback is unhelpful ("How is it wrong?") and demotivating ("I'm no good at this"). The second is an expert who takes the feedback as a challenge and draws on self-regulation skills to energetically review the processes involved to see if this is the case.

This is a stark illustration of the main claim of this chapter, that feedback has to be carefully related to the proficiency of the learner and cannot be treated as a generic template to be applied mechanically. This argument is made throughout this handbook in relation to different domains and phases of education. The distinct focus here is how it varies in relation to the *proficiency* of learners, as they move from novice to expert. An individual's proficiency may vary by domain (I may be competent at mathematics but a novice at art). It is also not necessarily phase related; a ten-year old may be a proficient chess player while a university student is a novice. It is the learner's proficiency that determines the feedback in a domain or phase. Failure to recognize this may lead to what Ericsson (2006) has called "arrested development" (p. 685) in which we settle for an unchanging level of proficiency.

This chapter considers understandings of feedback based on expertise studies of how we move from novice to expert. This occupational context provides three main challenges to the widely established educational theory and practice of feedback. The first is that feedback is defined more broadly and incorporates activities and practices that in education are generally not treated as part of the feedback process. The second is on a heightened recognition of the emotional impact of feedback, even when it is task based. The third is that the quality of feedback is judged by what learners do, rather than teacher-related criteria such as its timing or clarity. This links to the concept of "deliberate practice": what practice and improvement has the feedback encouraged in the work of those who receive it?

The chapter offers a synthesis of proficiency models and illustrations of how we move from novice to expert. This leads to considerations of the kind of feedback needed at different stages of proficiency. The synthesis draws on the work of the Dreyfus brothers (1980, 2005), Chi (2006), Ericsson (2006, 2009), and Eraut (2007), all of whom use variations of a progression model that moves from *novice* to *competent* to *proficient* to *expert and master*.

One of the key features of these proficiency models is that they see ability as something that is developed through deliberate practice, instruction, feedback, and the development of effective mental frameworks and working memory. I have argued elsewhere (Stobart, 2014) that this expertise tradition, which has been widely researched since the chess studies of the 1950s onward (De Groot, 1946/1965; Chase & Simon, 1973) and the music studies of the 1990s (see Lehmann & Gruber, 2006), has had limited impact on education and has received little input from educational research.[1]

Feedback Models

This section offers a very brief review of current understandings of classroom feedback, formulations that are elaborated throughout this handbook. It then seeks to complement them with theory and practice from expertise research into skill progression – in which feedback plays a major role. The intention is to flesh out feedback practices in relation to proficiency progression, particularly how feedback varies in relation to proficiency.

The "Educational" Model of Feedback

This is set within the widely adopted framework provided by those such as Sadler (1989), Kluger and DeNisi (1996), Hattie and Timperley (2007), Shute (2008), and Wiliam (2013). Others in this handbook are also significant contributors to developments within this model. It draws on cybernetic thinking, which sees feedback as "closing the gap" between current and desired performance in a way that learns and adapts from the information provided (Roos & Hamilton, 2005). Kluger and DeNisi's classic 1996 meta-analysis led to a framing of feedback in terms of the level ("locus of attention") at which it is addressed. Hattie and Timperley (2007) developed, and made more accessible, this approach using task, self, process, and self-regulation as the levels. Shute (2008) added considerations of timing and of scaffolding feedback. Wiliam (2013) has reviewed this development of current theorizing and his conclusion sits well with the expertise model: "it is clear that a useful theory of feedback would need to be very broad, including instructional design and a much fuller understanding of learners' affective reactions in instructional settings" (p. 21).

Kluger and DeNisi (1996) concluded that while feedback had a significant effect on average, this masked the fact that more than a third of feedback

---

1 In the 900-plus pages of *The Cambridge Handbook of Expertise and Expert Performance* (Ericsson et al., 2006), there is not a single chapter from mainstream educational researchers. This may be because expertise studies have often focused on occupational and professional development and draw on the historic "apprenticeship" model. I argue (Stobart, 2014) that this neglect by education of expertise studies is in part the result of a different historical approach to ability, in which it has been seen as inborn and fixed, a proxy for intelligence.

interventions had the negative effect of decreasing performance. Synthesizing these educational feedback models, classroom practices that are more likely to "close the gap" focus on the following:

- The feedback is effectively timed.
- It is specific and clear.
- It is clearly linked to the learning intention.
- The learner understands the success criterion/standard.
- It focuses on the task rather than the learner (self/ego).
- It gives cues at the right levels on how to bridge the gap.
- It offers strategies rather than solutions.
- It challenges, requires action, and is achievable.

This general approach, derived from the major reviews above, has been widely utilized in feedback practices within education, with an emphasis on giving informative feedback, preferably at a process rather than merely corrective level and focusing on the task rather than the person.

While the expertise tradition has much in common with this, it brings at least three challenges to this conventional approach. These involve the definition of feedback, the role emotion plays in attending to feedback, and a greater emphasis on "deliberate practice" as part of feedback.

Challenges from Expertise Research

Defining Feedback

One challenge from the expertise tradition is to see the closing-the-gap model as a narrow, and essentially cognitive, view of feedback in which teacher-generated information "closes the gap" between where learners are and where they need to get to. Molloy, Borrell-Carrio, and Epstein (2013) challenged some of the assumptions of this approach: "Best-practice principles are often founded on the idea that feedback occurs in a contextual vacuum, in which learners will respond reliably and consistently to a given stimulus provided by the teacher" (p. 52). Within the expertise tradition, Eraut (2007) adopted a much broader definition of feedback than the narrow cybernetic closing-the-gap approach by emphasizing that feedback often comes from sources other than direct instruction. His definition of feedback is: "Any communication that gives some access to other people's opinions, feelings, thoughts or judgements about one's own performance" (p. 6). This is a much broader concept, which focuses on how the learners' antennae respond to the way their work is being received, with the implication that this could be either positive or negative.

This is a very different emphasis from the educational model's somewhat circular and narrow cybernetic use of the term in which something qualifies as feedback only if it helps close the gap between where learners are and where they need to get to (Sadler, 1989; Assessment Reform Group, 2002; Hattie & Timperley 2007). It also aligns with everyday understandings of feedback, though these often consider only the giver's viewpoint ("I've given them feedback but they just don't use it") as if it is a gift to be gratefully received without evaluating how it might be received (Askew & Lodge, 2000). The importance of *some access* in the definition is that it leaves open how the learner construes the feedback. Eraut's (2007) point is that there may be considerable gaps between the intention of the giver and how it is received by the learner, particularly as it will be mediated by the emotions that accompany any feedback. This has been recognized in educational feedback research by those such as Boerkaerts (2006) and Gamlem and Smith (2013).

The implication of Eraut's (2007) approach is that much that we do that is not generally considered feedback sends messages about how the learner is being evaluated. For example, the tasks apprentices are given to do may be taken as feedback on what the supervisor thinks of their capabilities. So, in relation to school, if students are put in ability sets for mathematics, this sends a signal about what the teacher, or school, thinks of this group. To be put in the bottom class may send a clear feedback message about perceived capability that will affect both learners' and teachers' expectations. Boaler (2009), who researched differences between "streamed" (selected by ability) and non-streamed classes, has shown the power of this kind of message on expectations and progress. She found that in England, 88% of the children in the bottom group at age five (the policy in England has encouraged early streaming) were still in the bottom group at age sixteen.

This broader approach also means that curricular choices will feed back to students how their institution sees them. The range of options in the curriculum and how a student is steered toward certain courses, for example toward vocational rather than academic, will be viewed as feedback under this broader definition. The effects of selective examinations on a learner's identity provide a powerful example – to pass affirms potential as a successful student, to fail means the candidate "was not up to it." Life-changing assessments, such as selection for selective schools at age eleven, send a powerful feedback message. This is captured by Broadfoot's (1979) haunting judgment on the English 11+ intelligence test, which 75% failed, which decided whether a student went to grammar school (academic) or not: "Intelligence testing, as a mechanism for social control, was unsurpassed in teaching the doomed majority that failure was the result of their own inbuilt inadequacy" (p. 44).

Recognizing the Emotional Impact of Feedback

Eraut (2007) has emphasized the emotional component in feedback, arguing that even when it is task focused it is still personal and therefore emotional. The educational model often gives the impression that by focusing on the task rather than the self (two of Kluger & DeNisi's levels of feedback), it is possible to minimize the often negative emotional impact of feedback. However, from the perspective of occupational learning, any judgment about my product (the task) is a judgment about me, since my identity is bound up with my performance:

> This strong emotional dimension ... may lead to feedback intended to be narrow being interpreted as broad. Moreover, even when the provider of feedback stresses that it is the action or performance that is the subject of the feedback, many recipients interpret it as being a comment on their person. Thus messages intended for guidance may be interpreted as judgemental. (Eraut, 2007, p. 1)

This emotional filter is developed by Molloy, Borrell-Carrió, and Epstein (2013):

> Although the judgement is made about students' work, students themselves can see work as a presentation, or a manifestation of their own amateur knowledge, ideas or behaviours ... Even if they tell themselves that feedback is about the task or performance, they can interpret the constructive criticism as an affront to their self or person. (p. 52)

Deliberate Practice

This makes even more important the need to provide specific information about how performance might be improved. A key concept in the expertise literature is that of "deliberate practice" (Ericsson, Krampe, & Tesche-Romer, 1993; Ericksson & Pool, 2016) in which a more expert mentor identifies the next step in the development of a complex skill. It is through repeated practice of this activity that performance becomes increasingly fluent. The emphasis here is on *using* feedback through practicing it, rather than just receiving it. Foer (2011) pointed out that people often reach "OK plateau," a point at which they stop improving at a skill despite performing it regularly. To improve requires retaining some degree of conscious control while practicing in order to stay out of autopilot.

The assumption in this is that a key element of feedback is choosing the most effective "next step" that will again take learners out of their comfort zones. Sports coaches use the idea of "the sweet spot" in which the chances of success in an activity are around 50/50. This is a perfect feedback situation; skilled, and usually immediate, feedback will improve the odds of success. Further practice will see the skills becoming increasingly automatic so that the learner can take on more difficult challenges. Feedback then leads to immediate practice of the specific behavior that has been targeted as the next step, and practice continues until it is mastered. So feedback is largely evaluated in terms of generating successful action rather than the analysis of the features of the message.

John Wooden, the legendary college basketball coach, exemplifies this approach. His teaching methods, so effective that they were studied by educators Nater and Gallimore (2010), involved rapid correction in which the correct performance is quickly modeled by the coach, and the learner immediately goes back and does it again until there is improvement. So rather than offering critique, involving telling the learner what is wrong and how to do it better, he used correction – going back and doing it correctly. Over 80% of the 2,000-plus feedback comments studied were about how to perform the task, with only 7% involving praise and 7% critical.

Lemov, Woolway, and Yezzi (2012) used a similar classroom approach in which they encouraged teachers to "shorten the feedback loop" so that any correction comes as quickly as possible and the learner repeats the activity as soon as possible. They remind us of those sports lessons in which we queued for our turn at a particular practice drill and, if we got it wrong, we went to the back of the line to try again sometime later – by which time we had forgotten the feedback so were likely to make the same mistake again. "Shorten the loop" means getting an immediate chance to incorporate the feedback. Lemov et al. also echoes Wooden when they emphasize that the teacher should focus on the solution rather than the problem.

This might be seen as adding another element to the already muddled picture around the timing of feedback. The suggestion in Shute (2008) that sometimes on simple tasks it may be best to delay feedback (p. 18) is clearly not the advice here – with Wooden arguing that any delay is a wasted opportunity as the sooner an error can be rectified the better.

Proficiency Models and Feedback

How does somebody become an expert – and what does being an expert involve? These questions have been systematically researched since the 1950s (see Ericsson et al., 2006 for an overview). A common experimental topic has been chess: how does chess skill develop and what do grand masters do differently from other players, especially novices? The same questions have been asked of experts in music, medicine, science, sports, and other skilled professions (see Ericsson et al., 2006).

The model used here draws on two main traditions, one that studies relative expertise (what makes an expert better than a novice?) and one that has focused on how problem-solving develops in the progression to expertise. The relative expertise model can be represented by Ericsson et al. (1993), Chi (2006), and Ericsson (2006), while the Dreyfus brothers (1980, 2005) provided an influential and contested model of skill development that focuses on the progression toward expert intuition. The Dreyfus model is regularly used in medical and health training.

A Synthesis of Proficiency Models. This also incorporates progression models such as Eraut's (2005) synthesis of expertise. The actual labels for each stage vary across authors (and over time by the same authors) but the progression is similar (see Figure 2.1). I have used "proficiency" because "mastery," which is also used, may be confusing given its other uses in education, for example, "mastery learning." I have also minimized the use of "stages" and "levels" as these often lead to over-rigid progression models, given that skill development may be much patchier and better seen as a continuum with many overlaps.

Naive	*One who is totally ignorant of a domain* (Chi)
1. Novice	Someone who is new to the domain and has minimal knowledge/exposure. Sticks to taught rules or plans and responsible only for following the rules to complete task.
2. Advanced beginner	Still rule following but able to apply across similar contexts. Rules become *guidelines*. Will try new things but has difficulty troubleshooting. Focus still on completing tasks.
3. Competent	Excessive rules sorted into *perspectives* ("coping with crowdedness") which generate conceptual models. Uses deliberate planning and past experience in problem-solving. Makes decisions and accepts responsibility for outcomes so is more emotionally involved. Chi's *journeyman,* who can be trusted to do a day's work unsupervised.
4. Proficient	Conceptual models develop into a conceptual framework covering a whole skill, which leads to a holistic view of a situation. Develops *maxims* for guidance and prioritizing, which are then adapted to the situation. Problems identified more intuitively while decision-making is still largely deliberate and conscious.
5. Expert	Extensive practice leads to "intuitive grasp of situations based on deep, tacit understanding" (Eraut), which transcends reliance on rules, guidelines, and maxims. Identifies and solves problems intuitively. More analytical approaches in unfamiliar problem situations (Gobet & Chassy 2009)
6. Master	(often merged with Expert – Dreyfus & Dreyfus, 2005). Is "capable of experiencing moments of intense absorption" and "does not need to pay conscious attention to his performance" (Dreyfus & Dreyfus, 1980). For Chi (2006), it is elite performance that set the standards or ideals. Also recognized as "the" expert in a domain.

Figure 2.1 *A proficiency progression model (adapted from Dreyfus & Dreyfus, 1980, 2005).*

What Leads to Skill Progression?

There is general agreement around some of the key dynamics in skill progression (see Feltovich, Prietula, & Ericsson, 2006). These can be summarized in terms of the following:

- Opportunities, expectations, clear goals
- Motivation, resilience, and risk-taking
- Extensive deliberate practice and widening experience
- Effective mental frameworks/conceptual models
- Skilled diagnostics and feedback.

Each of these comes into play and interacts as skills develop. They may also take a progressively different form. In the Dreyfus model, progress is based on being increasingly exposed to situational complexities, to more holistic approaches, to more intuitive problem recognition, and to taking more responsibility for decisions.

Glaser (2009) treats the progression as a *change in agency*, which he describes in three interactive phases:

(a) *External support*, involving early environmental structuring influenced by parental dedication and interests and the support of teachers and coaches
(b) *Transition*, characterized by decreasing scaffolding of environmental support and increasing of apprenticeship arrangements that offer guided practice and foster self-monitoring, the learning of self-regulatory skills, and the identification and discrimination of standards and criteria for high levels of performance
(c) *Self-regulation*, a later stage of competence in which much of the design of the learning environment is under the control of the learner as a developing expert. In this phase, the conditions of deliberate practice are arranged so that performers can obtain feedback on their own performance. There is very selective use of external support. (p. 305)

Two Examples of Progression from Novice to Expert

Dreyfus and Dreyfus (2005) thread two examples through their account of the movement from novice to expert. Like many other expert performance researchers (De Groot, 1965; Gobet & Simon, 2009) they draw heavily on studies of chess. They also use driving as a more familiar activity.

Chess. When learning chess the *novice* has to learn the moves and other rules, for example, "always exchange if the total value of pieces captured exceeds the value of pieces lost." These are to be mechanically applied, and the novice's role is to apply them accurately. As an *advanced beginner* she will be exposed to more complex situations for which *instructional maxims* will be needed:

> With experience, the chess beginner learns to recognize overextended positions and how to avoid them. Similarly, she begins to recognize such situational aspects of positions as a weakened king's side or a strong pawn structure, despite the lack of precise and situation-free definitions. The player can then follow maxims such as: attack a weakened king's side. Unlike a rule, a maxim requires that one already has some understanding of the domain to which the maxim applies. (Dreyfus & Dreyfus, 2005, p. 783)

The *competent* learner operates with more experience at which point:

> the number of potentially relevant elements and procedures that the learner is able to recognize and follow becomes overwhelming. At this point, since a sense of what is important in any particular situation is missing, performance becomes nerve-racking and exhausting, and the student might well wonder how anybody ever masters the skill. (p. 784)

So the competent chess player may decide after studying a position that her opponent has weakened his king's defenses so that an attack against the king is a viable goal. If she chooses to attack, she ignores weaknesses in her own position created by the attack, and the timing of the attack is critical. "Successful attacks induce euphoria, while mistakes are felt in the pit of the stomach." What is important here is the emotional involvement involved in taking responsibility for the tactic. This brings with it risk taking and the need for resilience – mistakes will be made. "In general, resistance to involvement and risk leads to stagnation and ultimately to boredom and regression" (p. 785).

The *proficient* chess player "can recognize almost immediately a large repertoire of types of positions. She then deliberates to determine which move will best achieve her goal. She may know, for example, that she should attack, but she must calculate how best to do so" (p. 787). The key shift here is that the proficient learner can immediately see what needs to be done, though in deciding what to do will fall back on rules and maxims. Failure at this point does not just lead to analyzing mistakes, it is about "letting them sink in," again the importance of emotional commitment.

At the *expert/master* level the player sees not only what needs to be done but also immediately how to do it. This is the Dreyfus brothers' contested concept of intuition (see Gobet and Chassy, 2009). The support for this is that the chess grandmaster can select moves in five to ten seconds without serious degradation of performance. This involves drawing on recognition of a vast range of types of position and making an immediate situational response. Where there is deliberation, as in normal chess, this is a "deliberative rationality" that allows observation of the intuitive decision with an eye to improving it.

Car Driving. A more familiar example is the way we progress as drivers. The novice driver is rule bound: check your seat belt and rear mirror before starting, always come to a complete stop at a stop at a stop sign, change into second gear when you reach 10 mph.

The advanced beginner uses (situational) engine sounds as well as (nonsituational) speed in deciding when to change gear. He learns the maxim: "Shift up when the motor sounds like it's racing, and down when it sounds like it's straining." Engine sounds cannot be adequately captured by a list of features, so features cannot take the place of a few choice examples in learning the relevant distinctions.

A competent driver exiting the motorway on an off-ramp curve learns to pay attention to the speed of the car, not whether to change gear. After taking into account speed, surface conditions, criticality of time, etc., the driver may decide he is going too fast. He then has to decide whether to let up on the accelerator, remove his foot altogether, or step on the brake, and precisely when to perform any of these actions. He is relieved if he gets through the curve without mishap, and shaken if he begins to go into a skid.

The proficient driver, approaching a curve on a rainy day, "may feel in the seat of his pants that he is going dangerously fast" (Dreyfus & Dreyfus, 2005, p. 787). He must then decide whether to apply the brakes or merely to reduce pressure by some specific amount on the accelerator. Valuable time may be lost while making a decision, but the proficient driver is certainly more likely to negotiate the curve safely than the competent driver who spends additional time considering the speed, angle of bank, and felt gravitational forces, in order to decide whether the car's speed is excessive.

The expert driver not only feels in the seat of his pants when speed is the issue; he knows how to perform the appropriate action without calculating and comparing alternatives. On the off-ramp, his foot simply lifts off the accelerator and applies the appropriate pressure to the brake. What must be done, simply is done.

Implications for Feedback in the Classroom

The temptation is to equate levels of feedback (corrective, process, and self-regulation) with stages along the proficiency continuum. However, ambiguities around self-regulation make any equating more complex. While it is treated as a separate level of feedback by Kluger and DeNisi (1996) and Hattie and Timperley (2007), I would argue that it is also found *within* each level. So, for novices receiving task-based corrective feedback, there is an element of being aware of why they need to improve, something that is easier to grasp in performance skills such as learning tennis or producing an artifact. The range of studies in the Kluger and DeNisi (1996) meta-analysis meant that many outside education were included, some of them occupational. The assumption with these was that "the individual knows how to do the task; hence the purpose of feedback concerns whether performance is up to expectation" (Lipnevich, Berg, & Smith 2016, p. 171). This form of self-regulation may be less apparent to students when introduced to basic algebra or classic literature. Framed in terms of motivation, there may be a stronger intrinsic drive to develop skills in occupational or sporting areas than in school subjects where motivation may often have to be largely extrinsic; it is society's and the teacher's job to encourage participation in mastering the rules (Hidi & Harackiewicz, 2000).

Novice Learners. This model of progression raises provocative questions for the classroom, for example, the assertion that for *novices* what is being learned should be decontextualized, as basic knowledge is about "nonsituational" rules. This involves unambiguous instructions that, for success, need to be correctly followed. The novice is not asked to take responsibility for anything other than following the rules, and the focus is on completing the task. In classrooms this could be the learning of vocabulary in a second language or learning multiplication tables in mathematics.

This is a live issue in education, reflected in the controversies around E. D. Hirsh's Core Knowledge curriculum, which seeks to identify the knowledge every American child needs. Hirsch argues that this is a matter of social justice and it is the assumed cultural, and often traditional, knowledge that is the basis for effective communication, even if one is arguing for change (Hirsch, 1987).

The notion of learning basic facts, which then become automatic and free up working memory as the basis of more skilled performance, has been taken up by Christodoulou (2014) in the UK context. Young (2008) also makes the argument for "powerful knowledge" in education. It is most apparent in sports coaching where complex skills are broken into basic drills, some of which may bear little direct relationship to the target skill, for example, boxers doing skipping exercises. This challenges approaches such as "learning to learn" or critical thinking when they are applied independent of a knowledge base. Willingham (2009) claims that we should not expect novices to know how experts think because

> cognition in early training is fundamentally different from cognition late in training. It's not just that students know less than experts; it's also what they know is organized differently in their memory. Expert scientists did not think like experts-in-training when they started out. They thought like novices.   (p. 128)

Advanced Beginners

These will be familiar to most classroom teachers. More complex material is introduced and the teacher helps the students "pick out and recognize the relevant aspects that organize and make sense of the material" (Dreyfus & Dreyfus, 2005, p. 783). The teacher will provide guidelines (maxims) – "What is the main point of the passage?" Feedback is a means of guiding choice. Learning at this stage is still largely about following instructions with a focus on completing tasks. They point out, as do top sports coaches, that this is not the time for lengthy theorizing or interesting the learner in the big picture. The focus is on completing increasingly complex tasks. The barista-in-training does not need to know the history of coffee; the task is to put together the elements that make the cup of coffee that has been ordered.

This may see the start of a "mixed-level" model of feedback in which corrective task feedback is still present, but process level feedback is beginning to be introduced. This is because exposure to more varied situations means that a range of differing strategies may need to be considered, so feedback maxims ("What kind of mathematics problem is this?") may be used to alert the learner to choices that have to be made.

Who is best placed to give the feedback at this early stage of proficiency? From different occupational studies, Eraut (2004) concludes that sometimes feedback may be most effective when it is given on the spot from those who are just ahead in their skills, especially when they are all working as part of a team. He cites accountancy audit teams as a context for effective feedback. This comes from more experienced trainees "who were themselves novices only a few months earlier; so they feel able to ask them silly questions in the safe knowledge that they had faced the same problems themselves in the very recent past" (Eraut, 2007, p. 10). Despite trainee nurses having a great need of on-the-spot feedback, nursing was a more mixed picture. This was because of the cultures of different wards: "constructive feedback in areas where their performance was adequate but capable of being improved was most likely to occur when membership of a ward community provided access to significant social and emotional support" (p. 10). However, in many wards trainees were more likely to get negative feedback on one mistake than positive feedback on the things they did well.

Ericsson (2009) summarizes progression at the beginner stage in terms of individuals often reaching "an acceptable level of proficiency during a brief period of instruction followed by a limited period of effortful adaptation ... individuals typically gain immediate feedback about errors and inferior performances" (p. 35). The risk is that performance soon plateaus and we settle for a "stable adaptation to the demands of a domain" (think social tennis or guitar playing). This often means we can perform with limited errors – so only by setting more demanding goals, with more failures, are we likely to progress significantly.

The Competent Learner

This learner is operating with more complex tasks and situations that require the many rules and guidelines to be organized into a *conceptual model*. Effective exposure to a variety of "whole" situations will help the learner grasp the connections between the different contexts. A key change here is that the competent learner has to devise plans and choose the perspective to adopt. The willingness to select a plan is critical to further development at this point as individuals have to take on responsibility for the consequences of their actions. Choosing the course of action requires emotional involvement. Action is no longer about the detached application of rules; it is a risk-taking process that involves personal success or failure. When things work out well, the competent student may experience a kind of elation unknown to the beginner. This is Chi's (2006) "journeyman" stage, when it is decided that the learner is competent to be sent off alone to handle new tasks.[2] We can no doubt remember the feelings aroused by the first day in a new job or our first solo drive after passing our driving test.

In nurse education Benner (1984) studied trainees at each stage of skill acquisition. She found that unless trainees stay emotionally involved and accept the joy of a job well done, as well as the remorse of mistakes, they will not develop further and will eventually burn out trying to keep track of all the features and aspects, rules and maxims that modern medicine requires. The paradox here is that progression to expert sees *more* emotional engagement, rather than increasing analytical detachment.

---

2 The origins of the terms "sacked" and "fired" seem to come from this process. If your work was unsatisfactory, your tools were bundled up in a sack and you were sent away. If your work was catastrophic, your tools would be burned to prevent any recurrence. You had been fired.

Since students tend to follow the teacher as a model,

> teachers can play a crucial role in whether students will withdraw into being
> disembodied minds or become more and more emotionally involved in the
> learning situation. If the teacher is detached and computer-like, the students
> will be too. Conversely, if the teacher shows involvement in the way he or she
> pursues the truth, considers daring hypotheses and interpretations, is open to
> students' suggestions and objections, and is ready to be shown wrong, the
> students will be more likely to let their own successes and failures matter to
> them, and rerun the choices that lead to successful or unsuccessful
> outcomes.   (Dreyfus & Dreyfus, 2005, p. 785)

Feedback and Emotion. As we develop competence, our successes and
failures become more emotionally charged since they are increasingly the
result of personal choices and decisions. Responses to feedback in this context
are also emotionally loaded, since any feedback may be perceived as a personal judgment, even if task related. This immediately brings self-regulated
learning into play, as the learner has to decide how to handle the feedback.
A helpful model here is the dual pathway theory proposed by Boekaerts (1993,
2006), which deals with both metacognition and emotions. In essence, the
model assumes that students make choices as they appraise the cognitive and
emotional demands of a task and respond along one of two pathways, the
growth or the *well-being* pathway. The growth pathway involves learners
seeking to increase their competence, while the well-being pathway is used
to protect the learners from negative feelings of incompetence or anxiety by
using avoidance and denial.

The emotional pressures felt by competent learners who want to improve,
and yet are alert to the costs of any negative feedback even when diagnostic,
have been explored as a self-control issue by Trope, Ferguson, and Raghunathan (2001). They found a similar cost–benefit analysis to that of Boekaerts.
Learners may want to know:

> what skills they need to improve, what kinds of tasks to choose or avoid, and
> how much effort and preparation to invest in those tasks they choose. At the
> same time, individuals may be deterred by the emotional costs of negative
> feedback. These costs involve negative esteem-related feelings such as shame,
> dejection and disappointment.   (p. 257)

Feedback in this context tries to steer the learner down the growth pathway.
But feelings of competence are precarious, for example feeling overwhelmed by
the complex demands of new tasks, and so there may be a motivational need to
also address the well-being element. The intention may be to minimize the costs
of failure or reduce anxiety so that the growth pathway can be attended to. This
challenges the conventional mantra that feedback should always be task
related; there are performances for which we may need a good deal of encouragement to attempt or continue. "I know you can do it" may count as effective
feedback under these circumstances.

Normative Feedback. As competence develops, the conventional belief that
feedback should not compare performance of learners needs scrutinizing. The

research is clear on the negative effects of giving grades or marks alongside written feedback (Butler, 1987; Lipnevich & Smith, 2009), and these are partly explained by grades being used for comparison ("what grade did you get?") and therefore being self-related to the neglect of any task-related feedback that may move learning forward.

However, we need to consider the longer-term appraisal of where a learner is relative to a program or other learners. Eraut (2007) found that all the respondents in every project his team conducted wanted "longer-term normative feedback, how they are doing relative to their cohort and relative to training expectations" (p. 14). So, in addition to on-the-spot feedback that enhances ongoing learning, there is still a need to discuss "their own and their employer's view of their progress" (p. 14).

The implication is that we may need to consider, along with immediate feedback on a task, the longer-term feedback that offers a more general appraisal of progress relative to program expectations and relative achievement – an intention of school reports?

The Proficient Learner

Through exposure to multiple examples and situations, proficient learners develop a conceptual framework around their whole skill set. We are now historians or scientists rather than students of history or science. In approaching a task, what needs to be done can be intuitively recognized, though deciding what to do will involve largely deliberate and conscious planning based on maxims and rules. We may see what the question is that needs answering but then have to work out how to answer it. The proficient teacher or coach immediately sees what is happening but then has to think through what needs to be done. The proficient learner designs practice to further develop skills, though Lemov et al. (2012) argued that teachers do not practice in the way other performance professionals do, for example, musicians. Teachers "go live" many times a day and they listen, discuss, and reflect during professional development sessions, yet they do rehearse how to ask questions or how to start a class. The risk here is that they reach the "OK plateau" and stay there.

In this progression to proficiency, much of the feedback will be self-initiated, a monitoring of performance that seeks to adapt to the specific situation. Where feedback is given by others, it will be contextual. General maxims or advice are of little value – the proficient learner knows the big picture; it is the specifics of the situation that need a response. The expert golf coach does not need to explain to the proficient golfer general strategies for improvement. What is wanted is nuanced feedback on a specific performance, for example, how to modify the follow-through on the swing.

A Norwegian study of trainee teachers (Kristiansen, 2016) illustrated this shift. Trainees who were in their fourth and final year of training were interviewed about the feedback they were receiving from their trainers. Kristiansen found they were no longer satisfied with the kind of codified feedback they had received earlier in their training. One of the practices then was to write down in advance what they wanted their trainer to give feedback on. Not surprisingly, in the early stages classroom management was a topic that dominated; however, by the final year "it became a word we just wrote to have something on the paper" (p. 9). They no longer wanted transparent objectives and criteria; "they did not want to be locked into such criteria, but wanted instead to receive assessment and feedback on what occurred spontaneously along the way" (p. 10) – "feedback on what pops up" as one student put it. These same students also wanted less feedback – "by now we're pretty confident in ourselves" – and felt capable of far more self-assessment – "in practice I think about what went well and what went poorly" (p. 9).

This element of self-feedback is a common feature in the expertise literature. For example, Charness, Krampe, and Mayr (2009) found that proficient chess players' performance is more directly related to the amount of individual study of published chess masters' moves than the amount of time playing chess with others. Glaser (2009) sees the role of teachers and coaches as providing scaffolding for assisted practice in monitoring, in the design of situations for self-analysis, and in feedback. "The coach who does this and then fades out of the picture in order to enable learners to provide these environmental situations for themselves is teaching a most important skill of deliberate practice and self enhancement of performance" (p. 307).

The Expert

We would be pleased when, as trainers or teachers, any students reached a proficient level of performance in terms of developing expertise in the class-room. What is of more interest is the teacher's progression from proficiency, which I assume sufficient training and experience will have brought about, to expert. In the Dreyfus model, this is when extensive practice and reflection means that the expert can recognize what is happening and what is needed without conscious recourse to guidelines or rules. Like chess grand masters or expert firefighters, the expert teacher intuitively knows what to do. The source of this intuition is a wide repertoire of refined situational discriminations that can be instantly drawn on and that distinguish the expert from the proficient performer (Dreyfus & Dreyfus, 2005)

I find the Dreyfus position on intuition a problematic concept, not least because intuition can be wrong – "usually they guide us in the right direction but sometimes they are mistaken" (Klein, 2004, p. 3; Kahneman, 2011).[3] Intuition also suggests no need for thought – an issue nicely captured in Eriksen's (2010) paper, "Should Soldiers Think before They Shoot?" My own

---

3 There has been a long-running controversy between the Dreyfus brothers and researchers who use information processing and artificial intelligence to explain intuition and insight in terms of the rapid "chunking" of information (Simon, 1989; Klein, 2003). Gobet and Chassy (2009) have offered a template theory to reconcile some of the differences.

preference is to move to the way expert performance is framed as a more deliberate approach in the "relative expertise" tradition.

Chi (2006) defined experts as excelling in the following:

1. Choosing the appropriate strategy to use
2. Generating the best solution, often faster and more accurately than others
3. Using superior detection and recognition, for example, seeing patterns and deep structures of problems
4. Applying extensive qualitative analyses to a problem
5. Accurately monitoring their own performance
6. Retrieving relevant information more effectively.

The assumption here is that knowledge has been acquired in such a way that "it is highly connected and articulated, so that inference and reasoning are enabled as is process to procedural actions. The resulting organization of knowledge provides a schema for thinking and cognitive activity" (Glaser, 2009, pp. 305–306). This structured knowledge reflects exposure to a learning environment in which there are opportunities for problem-solving, reasoning, and transfer to unfamiliar environments.

This approach sits comfortably with educational theorizing such as Schon's (1983) *knowing-in-action* and his emphasis on *reflection-in-action* while one is engaged in an activity and with Biggs and Collis (1982) and Biggs and Tang's (2011) SOLO taxonomy. The progression in SOLO is from simple and unrelated ideas ("unistructural") through multiple but unrelated facts ("multistructural") to a more coherent understanding of the whole ("relational") and finally to a more questioning and hypothetical stance ("extended abstract").

Expert Teachers

Hattie's (2003) work, building on that of Berliner (2001), on expert teachers relates more directly. Hattie's research contrasts novice, experienced, and expert teachers. He found that while the profile of experts and others differed on sixteen dimensions, the three most important were the degree of challenge in the classroom work, the extent that this required "deep representation" of the domain, and the quality of monitoring and feedback. He found that expert teachers:

1. Can identify essential representations of their subject(s) – and spontaneously relate what is happening to these deeper sets of principles and are better decision makers in the classroom.
2. Have a greater appreciation of the classroom context.
3. Are more adept at assessing students' levels of understanding and provide more useful feedback.
4. Are passionate about teaching and learning and have a high respect for their students.
5. Provide more challenging tasks and goals that positively influence student performance.

Experts and Feedback

Much of the feedback experts receive will come from their own self-monitoring of their performance. The expert pilot will constantly be monitoring feedback from the environment and using it as part of "what if . . ." anticipatory behavior (the same is true of expert drivers). Sometimes the initial reaction may be at the level of "something isn't quite right here," a response found in expert clinical work, well fictionalized in the TV series *House* in which the irascible Dr. House regularly follows hunches while his young interns scour the textbooks to find a diagnosis. Klein (1999) provided a powerful case study of a firefighter who leads his team into what they believed was a kitchen fire. They pull back after a first unsuccessful attempt to douse the flames and then go back in again. The firefighter then commands his team to immediately leave the building, shortly after which the floor they were standing on collapses – it was a basement, not a kitchen fire. Klein was interested in what led the chief to suddenly call his men out, the fire team having put it down to extrasensory perception in their leader. What slowly emerged was the tacit sense that something was awry; his intuition, which could not be put into words until much later, was that the fire was too hot and too quiet for it to be a routine kitchen blaze.

The feedback in these cases comes from a sensitivity, often tacit, to the environment. For the expert teacher, entering a deathly quiet classroom does not lead to the "oh good, they're going to be quiet today" response we might see from a novice; rather, it rings alarm bells – what's gone on or is about to go on here?

This does not mean that experts do not need feedback from others. In sport, top players constantly receive corrective feedback from their coaches. Elite tennis players travel with their coaches. While they are not allowed to coach during the game, they will be constantly analyzing the game in order to build it into the deliberate practice of the next training session. Expert scientists will often seek feedback from their peers for their ideas. The development of quantum mechanics provides a fascinating study of how the pioneers would get together to challenge each other's ideas often in a very robust fashion.[4] Perhaps more surprisingly, leading artists have also conducted lengthy correspondences and visits among themselves discussing and critiquing each other's views of art. For example, Matisse and Picasso were in regular contact through letters and visits and the development of their art was often in reaction to the other's work and feedback (Spurling, 2005).

A potential hazard of being an expert is that feedback may not always be welcome. Having to battle to get an idea accepted requires a certain

---

4 See, for example, Kumar's (2009) account of the Fifth Solvay Conference of 1927 at which the giants of quantum physics and quantum mechanics all came together to discuss and argue over the nature of reality – "more philosophy than physics." Einstein was there but did not present a paper because he felt he "was not competent enough" to present a report for the reason that "I have not been able to participate as intensively in the modern development of quantum theory as would be necessary for that purpose" (pp. 255–256).

stubbornness. This may develop into entrenched views that resist feedback because it is taken as criticism. Expertise is often so domain-specific that feedback from outside the specialty is ignored or diminished. Chi (2006) gives the example of medical experts who are drawn to offer diagnoses in terms of their own field, so a blood specialist will look for a "blood" explanation.

Feedback for experts is therefore complex as they draw on a variety of sources. The primary one is self-feedback based on information from their environment, which uses their experience of multiple similar situations. It will also come from colleagues and other experts who may challenge findings. Yet even at the expert level the role of corrective feedback has not disappeared, especially in sport and other performance activities. Here activities are continuously honed through deliberate practice, often based on minor adjustments to technique. The top golfer will regularly call on a swing coach or a putting coach when accuracy falters, which is part of maintaining expertise, as is continuously monitoring performance.

Conclusion

Drawing on the findings of the expertise literature, with its focus on the more occupational and professional development, this chapter has highlighted the need to address feedback in relation to the level of proficiency of the learner. Failure to do this can lead to "arrested development" (Ericsson, 2006) because inappropriate feedback may hold the learner at an earlier stage of proficiency. This has much in common with the need for feedback varying by domain or phase of education discussed elsewhere in this volume.

This chapter departs in three main respects from the conventional educational model of feedback, which is seen as an essentially cognitive and cybernetic model involving "closing the gap" between current and intended performance. These departures are:

1. A much broader definition of feedback that involves information and responses that the learner gathers from the environment, including teachers and others. So apprentices evaluate the task they are given as feedback on what the tutor or institution thinks of their competence. This would also be true of whether they are directed toward vocational or more general academic studies; it is feedback about perceived capabilities.
2. A fuller recognition of the role played by emotion in mediating any feedback messages. Because apprenticeship and the progression to proficiency largely focus on products, self-esteem and personal identity will often be bound up with how these products are viewed by others. The exhortation to focus on the task rather than the learner (self) in the educational literature is a misleading oversimplification; the product is a highly personal piece of work. Any criticism of the product is likely to be interpreted as criticism of the person. Paradoxically, this may need some feedback to be addressed at the

self level in order to reduce anxiety and the risk of going down Boekaerts's "well-being" avoidance route.

3. A greater focus on feedback leading to immediate action and being judged by the difference it makes to practice. The key concept here is that of *deliberate practice* in which a weakness in performance is identified and immediately practiced. One reason that feedback often has a limited impact is because of the lack of action and practice that accompanies it. This call for on-the-spot feedback further compounds the findings in the educational literature about the timing of task-based corrective feedback (see Shute, 2008). This also places far more emphasis on action in response to feedback – it is not just about thinking but also doing.

At the same time proficiency feedback does not avoid longer-term normative feedback – how the trainee is doing in terms of expected progress and in relation to others. This is separate from immediate feedback and is best viewed as informal or, in some cases, formal appraisal.

Feedback and Proficiency

As proficiency improves the nature of feedback changes, though at every stage feedback is more complex than identifying a single level of Hattie and Timperley's taxonomy of task, process, self-regulation, and person. Progression involves dealing with ever more varied and complex situations in which the learner has to make more choices. Even at the novice level, where much of the feedback is task-based corrective feedback, there is still an element of self-regulation in the sense of knowing what the end goal is.

Feedback at the advanced beginner stage means scaffolding a limited range of choices. By the time they are competent learners they will be making more of their own choices about what action to take. This involves more self-regulation and emotional commitment as learners take on more responsibility for choices and outcomes. At this point the emotional element in the response to feedback becomes much stronger and becomes an important factor in how feedback is dealt with. For some it may provoke sufficient anxiety or distress that the avoidance path of preserving a sense of well-being is considered, in Kluger and DeNisi's (1996) terms, modifying the goal or devaluing the messenger. At this point motivational "self" feedback may be in order to continue with the challenge of becoming competent.

At the proficient level there is a shift to self-feedback that the proficient performer uses to monitor and improve performance. Feedback from others is still needed, but this is much reduced and likely to focus on the specific rather than the general. For experts, feedback comes from a range of sources but primarily from monitoring the environment for feedback, for example, noticing that something "is not quite right." Along with this comes feedback from colleagues and other experts, some of which may be robust as ideas are challenged. Even as an expert, particularly in sporting and other performances, there is still a need for corrective feedback on aspects of the tasks – hence the coaching entourage that accompanies top tennis players and golfers.

The main message about feedback from the expertise literature is that we need to see feedback in broader terms than the current restrictive cybernetic model. We should recognize that learners are receiving far more feedback than the well-timed and informative feedback of the educational model. The environment and those in it are continuously sending feedback messages and learners are seeing these through their own emotional lenses.

This is well captured by Boud and Molloy (2013):

> Expectations of feedback change throughout a program, especially across major transitions: from school to higher education, from higher education to the workplace and from workplace to workplace. Feedback practices need to be staged and designed to anticipate and accommodate such transitions. As learners become more experienced, their reliance on "external feedback from the teacher" should be reduced as they increasingly seek feedback from other useful sources including peers and consumers. Their self-monitoring and self-regulatory practices should be more finely tuned (and utilised) compared to their entry point into a program or discipline of study. Discrepancies in judgements between learners and others almost always have emotional import and commonly touches on the emerging professional. (p. 204)

References

Askew, S., & Lodge, C. (2000). Gifts, ping-pong and loops: Linking feedback and learning. In S. Askew (Ed.), *Feedback for learning* (pp. 1–18). London: Routledge Falmer.

Assessment Reform Group (2002). *Assessment for learning: 10 Principles*. Assessment Reform Group.

Benner, P. (1984). *From novice to expert: Excellence and power in clinical nursing practice*. Reading, MA: Addison Wesley.

Berliner, D. C. (1988). The development of expertise in pedagogy. Charles W. Hunt Memorial Lecture presented at the annual meeting of the American Association of Colleges for Teacher Education, New Orleans.

Berliner, D. C. (2001). Learning about and learning from expert teachers. *International Journal of Educational Research, 35*(5), 463–482.

Biggs, J. B., & Collis, K. F. (1982). *Evaluating the quality of learning: The SOLO Taxonomy*. New York: Academic Press.

Biggs, J., & Tang, C. (2011). *Teaching for quality learning at university: What the student does* (4th edn.). Maidenhead, UK: McGraw-Hill.

Boaler, J. (2009). *The elephant in the classroom: Helping children to learn to love maths*. London: Souvenir Press.

Boekaerts, M. (1993). Being concerned with well-being and with learning. *Educational Psychologist, 28*, 149–167.

Boekaerts, M. (2006). Self-regulation and effort investment. In K. A. Renninger & I. E. Sigel (Eds.), *Handbook of child psychology*, vol. 4: *Child psychology in practice* (6th edn.). Hoboken, NJ: Wiley.

Boud, D., & Molloy, E. (Eds). (2013). *Feedback in higher and professional education, understanding it and doing it well*. Abingdon, UK: Routledge.

Broadfoot, P. (1979). *Assessment, schools and society*. London: Methuen.

Butler, R. (1987). Task-involving and ego-involving properties of evaluation: The effects of different feedback conditions on motivational perceptions, interest and performance, *Journal of Educational Psychology, 79*, 474–482.

Charness, N., Krampe, R., & Mayr, U. (2009). The role of practice and coaching in entrepreneurial skill domains: An international comparison of life-span chess skill acquisition. In K. A. Ericsson (Ed.), *The road to excellence: The acquisition of expert performance in the arts and sciences, sports, and games* (pp. 51–80). Hove, UK: Psychology Press.

Chase, W. G., & Simon, H. A. (1973). Perception in chess. *Cognitive Psychology, 4*, 55–81.

Chi, M. T. H. (2006). Two approaches to the study of experts' characteristics. In K. A. Ericsson, N. Charness, P. J. Feltovich, & R. R. Hoffman (Eds.), *The Cambridge handbook of expertise and expert performance* (pp. 21–30). Cambridge: Cambridge University Press.

Christodoulou, D. (2014). *Seven myths about education*. Abingdon: Routledge.

De Groot, A. D. (1946, trans. 1965). *Thought and choice in chess*. The Hague: Mouton.

Dreyfus, H. L., & Dreyfus, S. E. (1980). *A five-stage model of the mental activities involved in directed skill acquisition*, Berkeley: University of California Operations Research Center.

Dreyfus, H. L., & Dreyfus, S. E. (2005). Expertise in real world contexts. *Organization Studies, 26*, 779–792.

Eraut, M. (2004). Informal learning in the workplace. *Studies in Continuing Education, 26*, 247–274.

Eraut, M. (2005). Expert and expertise: Meanings and perspectives. *Learning in Health and Social Care, 4*, 173–179.

Eraut, M. (2007). Feedback and formative assessment in the workplace, 3rd Seminar, Assessment of significant learning outcomes project. Retrieved from www.researchgate.net/publication/237739544_ASSESSMENT_OF_SIGNIFI CANT_LEARNING_OUTCOMES_3RD_SEMINAR_Feedback_and_For mative_Assessment_in_the_Workplace1.

Eriksen, J. W. (2010). Should soldiers think before they shoot? *Journal of Military Ethics, 9*, 195–210.

Ericsson, K. A. (2006). The influence of experience and deliberate practice on the development of superior expert performance. In K. A. Ericsson, N. Charness, P. J. Feltovich, & R. R. Hoffman (Eds.), *The Cambridge handbook of expertise and expert performance* (pp. 683–783). Cambridge: Cambridge University Press.

Ericsson, K. A. (2009). The acquisition of expert performance. In K. A. Ericsson (Ed.), *The road to excellence: The acquisition of expert performance in the arts and sciences, sports, and games* (pp. 1–50). Hove, UK: Psychology Press.

Ericsson, K. A., Charness, N., Feltovich, P. J., & Hoffman, R. R. (Eds.) (2006). *The Cambridge handbook of expertise and expert performance*. Cambridge: Cambridge University Press.

Ericsson, K. A., Krampe, R. T., & Tesche-Romer, C. (1993). The role of deliberate practice in the acquisition of expert performance. *Psychological Review, 100*, 363–406.

Ericsson, K. A., & Pool, R. (2016). *Peak: Secrets from the new science of expertise.* London: Bodley Head.

Feltovich, P. J., Prietula, M. J., & Ericsson, K. A. (2006). Studies of expertise from psychological perspectives. In K. A. Ericsson, N. Charness, P. J. Feltovich, & R. R. Hoffman (Eds.), *The Cambridge handbook of expertise and expert performance* (pp. 41–67). Cambridge: Cambridge University Press.

Foer, J. (2011). *Moonwalking with Einstein.* London: Allen Lane.

Gamlem, S. M., & Smith, K. (2013). Student perceptions of classroom feedback. *Assessment in Education: Principles, Policy and Practice, 20,* 150–169.

Glaser, R. (2009). Changing the agency for learning: Acquiring expert performance. In K. A. Ericsson (Ed.), *The road to excellence: The acquisition of expert performance in the arts and sciences, sports, and games* (pp. 41–67). Hove, UK: Psychology Press.

Gobet, F., & Chassy, P. (2009). Expertise and intuition: A tale of three theories. *Minds and Machines, 19,* 151–180.

Hattie, J. (2003, October). Teachers make a difference: What is the research evidence? Paper presented at the Australian Council for Educational Research Conference on Building Teacher Quality, University of Auckland, New Zealand.

Hattie, J., & Timperley, H. (2007). The power of feedback. *Review of Educational Research, 77,* 81–112.

Hidi, S., & Harackiewicz, J. M. (2000). Motivating the academically unmotivated: A critical issue for the 21st century. *Review of Educational Research, 70,* 151–179.

Hirsch, E. D. (1987), *Cultural literacy: What every American needs to know.* Boston: Houghton Mifflin.

Kahneman, D. (2011). *Thinking fast and slow.* London: Allen Lane.

Klein, G. (1999). *Sources of power.* Cambridge, MA: MIT Press.

Klein, G. A. (2003). *Intuition at work.* New York: Currency and Doubleday.

Klein, G. (2004). *The power of intuition: How to use your gut feelings to make better decisions at work.* New York: Doubleday.

Kluger, A. N., & DeNisi, A. (1996). The effects of feedback interventions on performance: A historical review, a meta-analysis, and a preliminary feedback intervention theory. *Psychological Bulletin, 119,* 254–284.

Kristiansen, C. W. (2016). Assessment practices in teacher education: Presenting preliminary data analysis. Unpublished paper, Agder University.

Kumar, M. (2009). *Quantum, Einstein, Bohr and the great debate about the nature of reality.* London: Icon Books.

Lehmann, A. C., & Gruber, H. (2006). Music. In K. A. Ericsson, N. Charness, P. J. Feltovich, & R. R. Hoffman (Eds.), *The Cambridge handbook of expertise and expert performance* (pp. 457– 470). Cambridge: Cambridge University Press.

Lemov, D., Woolway, E., & Yezzi, K. (2012). *Practice perfect.* San Francisco, CA: Jossey-Bass.

Lipnevich, A. A., Berg, D. A. G., & Smith J. K. (2016). Toward a model of student response to feedback. In G. T. L. Brown & L. R. Harris (Eds.), *Handbook of human social conditions in assessment* (pp. 169–185). Abingdon, UK: Routledge.

Lipnevich, A. A., & Smith, J. K. (2009). "I really need feedback to learn": Students' perspectives on the effectiveness of the differential feedback messages. *Educational Assessment, Evaluation and Accountability, 21,* 347–367.

Molloy, E. K., Borrell-Carrio, F., & Epstein, R. (2013). The impact of emotions in feedback. In D. Boud & E. Molloy (Eds.), *Feedback in higher and professional education: Understanding it and doing it well* (pp. 50–71). Abingdon, UK: Routledge.

Nater, S., & Gallimore, R. (2010). *You haven't taught until they have learned.* Morgantown, WV: FIT.

Roos, B., & Hamilton, D. (2005). Formative assessment: A cybernetic viewpoint. *Assessment in Education: Principles, Policy and Practice, 12,* 7–20.

Sadler, D. R. (1989). Formative assessment and the design of instructional systems. *Instructional Science, 18,* 119–144.

Schön, D. A. (1983). *The reflective practitioner: How professionals think in action.* New York: Basic Books.

Shute, V. J. (2008). Focus on formative feedback. *Review of Educational Research, 78,* 153–189.

Simon, H. A. (1989). *Models of thought* (vol. 2). New Haven, CT: Yale University Press.

Spurling, H. (2005). *Matisse the master.* London: Penguin.

Stobart, G. (2014). *The expert learner: Challenging the myth of ability.* Maidenhead, UK: Oxford University Press/McGraw-Hill.

Trope, Y., Ferguson, M., & Raghunathan, R. (2001). Mood as a resource in processing self-relevant information. In J. P. Forgas (Ed.), *Handbook of affect and social cognition* (pp. 256–274). Mahwah, NJ: Lawrence Erlbaum.

Wiliam, D. (2013). Feedback and instructional correctives. In J. H. McMillan (Ed.), *SAGE handbook of research on classroom assessment* (pp. 196–214). Los Angeles, CA: SAGE.

Willingham, D. T. (2009). *Why don't students like school?* San Francisco, CA: Jossey-Bass.

Young, M. F. D. (2008). *Bringing knowledge back in.* Abingdon, UK: Routledge.

3 Summative and Formative Feedback

Susan M. Brookhart

Interest in the effects of feedback long pre-dates current discussions of formative assessment. Early investigations of feedback conceived of it as comments on summative assessment. Historically, behaviorist and associationist approaches to both the topic of teacher feedback on classroom work and to designing research to investigate it focused on classroom summative tests, often objective tests. Learning was understood as acquiring a command of facts and concepts, teaching as transmitting that material, and feedback as knowledge about the correctness of responses on summative assessment, generally tests. Results of research on feedback in this summative context gave only weak support to the effectiveness of teacher feedback on student work. From the perspective of today's understanding of what students do when they learn, we can say that those studies investigated only a narrow and, we can say now, understandably unhelpful aspect of feedback.

With the rise of interest in cognitive learning theory, student self-regulation of learning, and formative assessment, conceptions of learning and feedback – and the research designed to investigate it – changed. Learning was understood as students reaching intended learning goals, some to do with command of facts and concepts and some to do with applying those to solve problems or extend thinking. Feedback was understood as information to the student about a learning goal he or she was pursuing. Importantly, the usefulness of that information was referenced to the learning goal itself – not just to help students score better but to help them increase work quality relative to criteria, on which that learning goal could be evaluated. This moved feedback from the summative arena into the formative. With the change in learning theories behind conceptions and investigations of feedback came a concomitant change in the results of feedback research. Results of studies of formative feedback indicate that teacher feedback on student work is one of the most powerful supports for classroom learning.

In this chapter, I review these two eras in feedback research. I conclude that the power of feedback lies in its formative use, although I try to salvage some small nuggets from the studies of feedback in summative assessment that might be helpful even in an era of cognitive learning theory. In this effort, I draw on studies of student perceptions of assessment and feedback. Finally, I point out that in order to give their students effective feedback, educators will need to make what I have called the "sea change" (Brookhart, 2017) to a view of learning that takes seriously the importance of student agency in their own learning.

The Argument in a Nutshell

- Early twentieth-century studies of feedback were based in behaviorist and associationist views of learning.
- These early studies conceived of feedback as a reward or punishment for performance on summative assessment.
- Studies done under these behaviorist/summative approaches found feedback had very small effects on learning.
- By the late twentieth century, cognitive and constructivist views of learning eclipsed behaviorist views.
- Studies in this period conceived of feedback as information for students during the course of their learning, an aspect of formative assessment.
- Studies done under these constructivist/formative approaches found feedback had large effects on learning.
- Studies of student perceptions of feedback, even those done in the context of summative assessment, find that students prefer feedback that gives them information for improvement (formative feedback).
- The most appropriate role for feedback is as part of a formative approach to learning.
- Feedback on summative assessment may be used strategically for specific, limited purposes.

Feedback in the Context of Summative Assessment

In the early twentieth century, before cognitive learning theory and the rise of interest in formative assessment, feedback was studied mostly in the context of summative assessment. The prevailing theories of learning were behaviorist. Kluger and DeNisi (1996) claimed, "The single most influential theory in this area [feedback] is Thorndike's (1913) law of effect" (p. 258). The law of effect states that reinforcement increases the likelihood of a behavior and punishment decreases it. Positive feedback was likened to reinforcement and negative feedback was likened to punishment in early feedback research. The problem was that results of many early feedback studies were not consistent with this theory.

Skinner (1958), a noted behaviorist, credited Pressey and the teaching machines he devised in the 1920s with the first exploration of the effectiveness of feedback. Pressey devised teaching machines in which students responded to multiple choice questions. If correct, the machine moved to the next item for the student's consideration. If incorrect, the student had to keep choosing responses until he was correct and was able to move on. Skinner (1958) wrote: "Pressey seems to have been the first to emphasize the importance of immediate feedback in education and to propose a system in which each student could move at his own pace" (pp. 969–970). When teaching machines did not catch on, Skinner reported, Pressey was disappointed.

Skinner (1958) proposed that part of the reason that Pressey's teaching machines, and with them his views of effective feedback, did not catch on was that the prevailing learning theories at the time had to do with memory. He went on to describe the more current (in 1958) understanding of how learning occurs: "By arranging appropriate 'contingencies of reinforcement,' specific forms of behavior can be set up and brought under the control of specific classes of stimuli" (p. 970). Therefore, the teaching machines on which Skinner worked with his colleagues at Harvard required the students to "*compose* his response rather than select it from a set of alternatives ... we want him to recall rather than recognize – to make a response as well as see that it is right" (p. 970). However, in the examples Skinner gave, the student's "composition" amounted to putting letters or numbers in response boxes or supplying a word in a blank. The feedback given by the machine was still about the correctness of the response, and if a student's response was incorrect he was not allowed to move to the next frame of programmed instruction.

So while the theory of learning had changed somewhat from Pressey's to Skinner's time, the conception of feedback had not. Feedback was still conceived of as information about the correctness of one's response given after one had a chance to make that response. Reading the article "Teaching Machines," I was struck with the inescapable inference underlying all of the discussion of learning and examples of teaching machines: that learning meant having a command of facts and concepts that a student could use to supply right answers to the teacher's (or the machine's) questions. At the end of the article, Skinner did briefly deal with the question of thinking, but from a clearly behaviorist approach: "A more [than then-conventional approaches to teaching] sensible program is to analyze the behavior called 'thinking' and produce it according to specifications" (p. 975). Presumably, that would have led to feedback about the correctness of thinking, as well.

At the same time as Skinner and colleagues were working on teaching machines, Page (1958) conducted an original study investigating the effects of providing comments on graded work. The context, therefore, was summative assessment. This study had a large impact on the field, for several reasons. First, this may have been the first such study investigating whether teacher comments caused significant improvement in student performance. Second, it became somewhat famous as a model study. Sample size was large for classroom research (74 teachers and 2,139 students). Because Page adhered to principles of experimental design, including random selection and random assignment to treatment groups, and yet conducted the study in the context of the normal conduct of schooling (avoiding reactive arrangements and testing-by-treatment interactions), Campbell and Stanley (1963, p. 21) praised its "excellent utilization" of these principles. Garnering praise from such an influential publication as Campbell and Stanley's book drew both fame and replications.

What Page (1958) did was to randomly select secondary (seventh to twelfth grade) teachers in various subject areas. Each teacher gave the next objective test in the course of study and graded it as she normally would, using the letters

A to F. Then, the teacher ranked the papers from the highest to lowest grade. Papers were then organized by rank into groups of three, and the teacher rolled a die to put the papers into one of three treatment groups: no comment (just the grade), a free comment (whatever the teacher wanted to write) along with the grade, or a specified prewritten comment. Each group of three papers was thus randomly assigned to treatment groups, until the teacher reached the bottom of the pile. The specified comments were evaluative and general (for example, "A: Excellent! Keep it up" (p. 174)). The criterion used to investigate improvement was simply the next objective test given in the class, whether or not it was on the same topic as the first test and its feedback. Page's (1958, p. 180) major finding was that students who received free comments scored better on their next test than students who received specified comments, who in turn scored better on their next test than students who received no comments. Keep in mind that all students received a grade – which in today's language might be termed "knowledge of results." Because the measures were two tests in sequence, Page interpreted the comments as motivational: he termed his study a "classroom experiment in school motivation" (p. 173). Comments about the substance of students' learning intended to stimulate future thinking were not really possible with feedback defined in this way, as comments on summative work.

Unfortunately, support from replications was not proportional to the fame Page's study produced. Stewart and White (1976) found that by 1976, twelve different researchers had replicated Page's study; however, only two reported replicating the treatment effects. The remaining ten studies found no significant differences in learning between treatment groups. Stewart and White (1976) extended Page's study by using five treatment groups, in grades five and seven only, and by having an immediate criterion (the next test in the class) and a long-term criterion (the last test given in the study's six-week period). First, they did a pre-survey to find out what kinds of comments students would judge to be consistent with which letter grade (for example, the comment chosen for A was "Excellent" for both fifth and seventh grades, and for D was "You must do better next time" for fifth grade and "Careless work" for seventh grade). Then, using the same method as Page (1958) except for the number of groups, students were randomly assigned to receive: (1) letter grades only, (2) letter grades and evaluative comments, (3) evaluative comments only (the same evaluative comments, presented without the grade), (4) positive comments only (chosen from a menu of positive comments like "Good work"), and (5) whatever the teacher normally did in her current practice. Notice that all the feedback was evaluative (not descriptive or suggestive of next steps) and the context was still summative assessment. Stewart and White (1976) found no significant treatment effects on either the immediate or long-term tests.

Kulhavy (1977) published a review of studies of feedback on what he called "written lessons" (p. 211). Most of the studies he reviewed were studies of teacher feedback on objective tests; "written" meant that the work was done on paper, not that it was about writing composition. He argued that a behaviorist interpretation of feedback as a type of reinforcement was misplaced and was perhaps the reason that feedback research had not been able to establish strong effects on learning. First, he argued using the behaviorists' own terms "only that which reinforces is a reinforcer" (p. 213), and, given the results of early feedback studies, clearly feedback was not a reinforcer. Classroom feedback does not fit the requirements of operant contingency and does not necessarily result in learning, so clearly feedback cannot be a reinforcer in the behaviorist sense. Then, he pointed out that studies of the delay-retention effect (DRE) showed that delaying feedback for a day or more led to increases in retention as measured by a subsequent test. If feedback were a reinforcer in the behaviorist sense, it would not improve by increasing the interval between students' responses and feedback.

Notice, however, that while Kulhavy argued against a behaviorist approach to studying the effects of feedback on learning, he retained an associationist view of what learning is (learning is associating correct answers with test questions) and a summative context for feedback. Regarding a definition of feedback, Kulhavy wrote, "Throughout this paper the term 'feedback' is used in a generic sense to describe any of the numerous procedures that are used to tell a learner if an instructional response is right or wrong" (p. 211). The studies he reviewed mostly investigated teacher feedback on tests. Of course there is a sense in which studying feedback to see whether it has an effect on future learning can be thought of as "formative" because we are investigating the improvement and enhancement of learning. However, classroom tests that contribute to final grades are by definition summative. In addition, the kind of tests described in the review focused on recall and comprehension, did not necessarily assess the same learning goals, and mostly used multiple choice tests, implying learning meant mastery of a set of facts and concepts to be gauged by test performance. This approach to learning is summative in flavor ("I'll know how well I've learned when my teacher tells me how I did on the test").

Kulhavy (1977) then showed that studies of feedback that did not produce increases in learning used designs that "either allow learners to see the feedback before responding or are so heavily cued and prompted that students are able to answer correctly with only a cursory reading of the content" (p. 216). In other words, students could copy the answer without digesting the material. He used the term "pre-search availability" for this condition, where students could copy without learning, and demonstrated that this condition was responsible for the weak support for feedback in the literature. He concluded that pre-search availability should be low in order to design meaningful studies of feedback. He also concluded that instructional materials should be designed to minimize the possibility of pre-search availability, to facilitate learning, not copying (p. 219).

He concluded his review by describing studies designed in his laboratory that showed learners' confidence in their ability interacts with students' attention to and use of feedback and that this approach led to more meaningful conclusions about feedback. In this laboratory context, high-confidence students spent more time studying feedback that pointed out errors (incorrect answers) than correct responses and benefited more from feedback. While Kulhavy's team's studies were more successful than many of the studies in his review, they still operationalized learning as correct recall or comprehension as measured by objective tests. Kulhavy's review, then, began to move the study of feedback from the behaviorist paradigm, paying some attention to students' use of feedback, but still viewed learning as an associationist activity.

Changes in the Understanding of Feedback with the Advent of Cognitive and Constructivist Learning Theories

Why did studies of feedback in the context of summative assessment produce such mixed and disappointing results? The passing of six decades and major developments in learning and motivation theories give us some answers to this question that researchers did not have at the time. Two developments in particular are of interest here: the advent of cognitive and constructivist theories of learning and motivation and the appearance of formative assessment or assessment for learning.

Cognitive and Constructivist Theories of Learning and Motivation

The term "cognitive and constructivist approach to learning and assessment" may be applied broadly to approaches based on cognitive learning theory, constructivism, social cognitive theory, social constructivism, and sociocultural theory. All these theories of learning posit that the learner constructs meaning, whether individually or in dialogue with others, as opposed to receiving and memorizing information (Ormrod, 2014). The latter approach derives from behaviorist or associationist theories of learning. As we saw in the previous section, behaviorist and associationist theories of learning align well with a view of feedback as knowledge of results from summative assessment. In contrast, cognitive and constructivist approaches to learning align well with a view of feedback as information given during the process of learning based on formative assessment.

As cognitive and constructivist perspectives on learning developed, motivation theory developed a more cognitive orientation, as well. Several separate lines of research began, including attribution theory (Weiner, 1979), cognitive evaluation theory (Ryan, Connell, & Deci, 1985), expectancy value theory (Eccles, 1983), goal theory (Ames & Archer, 1988), self-efficacy theory (Pintrich & Schrauben, 1992), and amount of invested mental effort (Salomon, 1983, 1984). Advances in motivation theory have brought together these motivational constructs that were at one time studied separately. Self-efficacy, for example, has taken its place as one of the important components of self-regulated learning (Zimmerman & Schunk, 2011). Intrinsic and extrinsic sources of motivation and control have become important components of self-determination theory (Deci & Ryan, 2002). Thus motivation theory and learning theory are converging on the notion that students' taking up feedback, understanding it, being disposed to use it, and applying it in their work are at least as large a determinant of the effects of feedback on learning as are characteristics of the feedback message from teachers and others.

Formative Assessment

The definition of formative assessment, or assessment for learning, is still somewhat in flux (Wiliam, 2010). Sadler (1989) described the term "formative assessment" in the sense we will use it in this chapter: "Formative assessment is concerned with how judgments about the quality of student responses (performances, pieces, or works) can be used to shape and improve the student's competence by short-circuiting the randomness and inefficiency of trial-and-error learning" (p. 120). He stressed the involvement of the learner in this process and the fact that the learner must have a concept of the goal he is aiming for, compare current performance to that goal, and take some action to close the gap (p. 121). This idea of comparing current performance to desired performance was influenced by Ramaprasad's (1983) definition of feedback in organizational systems: "Feedback is information about the gap between the actual level and the reference level of a system parameter which is used to alter the gap in some way" (p. 4).

The formative assessment script that must be running inside a learner's head is now often characterized as three questions (Hattie & Timperley, 2007): "Where am I going? How am I going? and Where to next?" (p. 86). These questions derive from Sadler's (1989) description of students' participation in the formative learning process. While many authors and groups have crafted their own definitions of formative assessment, they all share the basic concept that assessment information comes as information to a student who is aiming toward a learning goal of some sort. The information can come from teacher feedback, from student self-assessment, from peers, or from various materials, but the idea that feedback is informational to a student is central in formative assessment. This idea aligns with cognitive and constructivist theories of learning and self-regulation and self-determination theories of motivation. If learning means that students make their own meaning, then feedback means information to facilitate that process.

Some define "assessment for learning" as assessment undertaken with the intention of enhancing learning and, in a more restricted use, term such assessment "formative" if the assessment information is actually used for students' regulation of learning (James & Pedder, 2006). In this chapter, I will consider formative assessment and assessment for learning to be synonyms. The Assessment Reform Group (2002) defined assessment for learning as "the process of seeking and interpreting evidence for use by learners and their teachers to decide where the learners are in their learning, where they need to go and how best to get there" (p. 2). Sadler's three learner processes, popularized as Hattie and Timperley's three questions, are clearly apparent in this definition as well.

Moving from Associationist to Cognitive Views of Learning and Feedback

The transition from associationist to cognitive views of learning and feedback, and the concomitant transition from viewing feedback in the context of summative assessment to the context of formative assessment, happened over time and in different scholarly circles. Remember that the theme of this chapter is that the notion of *feedback for learning* has been around for a long time, at least from the beginning of behaviorism; however, feedback fits better with a cognitive and constructivist model of learning and has assumed an important place as an aspect of *assessment for learning*, or formative assessment. Reviews of the feedback research have borne out this generalization, as studies done during the reign of behaviorism have found lesser effects on learning than those done under more contemporary views of learning. But there was a transition period, as formative assessment gradually emerged and feedback came to be seen as part of formative assessment (or, sometimes, synonymous with it: Crooks, 1988).

In the United States, Scriven (1967) used the terms *formative evaluation* and *summative evaluation* to refer to evaluation functions in education (pp. 40–43). Evaluation was formative if it was used to develop or improve educational programs or processes, and summative if it was used to make final decisions about them. Bloom, Hastings, and Madaus (1971) "borrowed the term 'formative evaluation' from Scriven (1967)" (p. 54) to refer to their use of brief assessments in the context of mastery learning. Thus they applied the term *formative evaluation* to the learning process of individual students (not programs), so that teachers could apply "feedback and corrections." This is still not formative assessment as described above, because teachers are the only ones using the information. As more constructivist views of learning gained prominence, however, it was a short leap from seeing formative evaluation as information about the learning process that teachers could use to Sadler's (1989) view of seeing formative assessment as information about the learning process that teachers could use and that students could use for improving their own performance (Brookhart, 2007).

In the United Kingdom, Elton (1982) titled his chapter in a book about improving higher education "Assessment for Learning" (the earliest use of the term I am aware of). The bulk of the chapter is about how to conduct summative assessment effectively. His goal, however, was not better memorization and recall, but rather helping students leave higher education with more interest in their subject matter, a deeper understanding of their subject area, and more ability to "stand on their own feet intellectually, emotionally, and morally" (p. 107). Thus the chapter is not about what we would now call assessment for learning – because the context is summative assessment – but it moves beyond an associationist view of learning and begins to focus on the students as learners and not just as those who take teachers' tests. I do not know whether the title of this chapter was known to subsequent authors who use the term "assessment for learning" in its current, formative, and student learning–focused meaning or not, but it does give evidence that the idea was in circulation and was changing.

In my view, the clearest milestone in the transition from considering feedback as something that teachers do to maximize the likelihood of students giving correct answers to considering feedback as information supplied to students to help clarify a learning goal, their current status regarding that goal, and their next steps in learning was Kluger and DeNisi's (1996) review of the feedback literature.

Kluger and DeNisi's Review of the Feedback Literature: Enter Cognitive Learning Theory

Kluger and DeNisi (1996) are widely cited for their meta-analysis of feedback literature, showing that feedback improved performance with an average effect size of 0.41; however, more than a third of the 607 effect sizes in their study were negative. Kluger and DeNisi wrote that they did their meta-analysis to demonstrate that feedback effects are very variable and that the widespread assumption that feedback helped improve learning was not true, or at least not always true. Kluger and DeNisi (1996) defined feedback – or, more specifically, feedback interventions (FIs) – as "actions taken by (an) external agent(s) to provide information regarding some aspect(s) of one's task performance" (p. 255). They interpreted FIs to encompass both historical studies of knowledge of results and more recent studies including elaborated feedback. In this way they were poised on the fence, considering feedback according to both the old and new paradigms.

In their milestone study, Kluger and DeNisi (1996) also did two other things, less often cited but relevant to my argument in this chapter that feedback studies and their findings were hampered by historically inadequate views of learning and assessment. First, they conducted a historical review of feedback studies. They showed that early feedback studies usually operationalized feedback as knowledge of results, as I have already noted. These studies were often flawed methodologically and did not pay attention when results were inconsistent, typically proclaiming feedback useful anyway. They described how this tendency was exacerbated when a widely cited review by Ammons (1956) promulgated the same view that feedback was useful despite reviewing evidence to the contrary.

In addition, Kluger and DeNisi (1996) identified the need for an updated theoretical framework to ground feedback research. Similar to Kulhavy (1977), they showed that viewing feedback as reward and punishment did not account for the results in early feedback studies, which meant that a new theory was needed. To fill this need, they posited feedback information theory (FIT), which they based on several current theories, including Bandura's social cognitive theory and others compatible with it. They presented a theoretical argument to support the propositions of FIT:

(a) Behavior is regulated by comparisons of feedback to goals or standards, (b) goals or standards are organized hierarchically, (c) attention is limited and therefore only feedback-standard gaps that receive attention actively participate in behavior regulation, (d) attention is normally directed to a moderate level of the hierarchy, and (e) FIs change the locus of attention and therefore affect behavior.   (Kluger and DeNisi, 1996, p. 259)

Kluger and DeNisi conceptualized the hierarchy to which they referred as a self-level (in which they considered both personal concerns and meta-cognition) at the top, a task level in the center, and a detail level at the bottom of the hierarchy. FIT called for feedback to direct learners' attention to the task, not to the self and not to the small details involved in completing the task. They also predicted goal-setting, affect, and some other variables (e.g., the familiarity of the task) would affect how people would take up the feedback they were given, thus acknowledging the role of the learner in the feedback process. Then, they tested their model by adding moderators into their meta-analysis. They cautioned that they still found variability in results, but concluded that in general, feedback could potentially have large, positive effects on performance:

> Specifically, an FI provided for a familiar task, containing cues that support learning, attracting attention to feedback-standard discrepancies at the task level (velocity FI [self-referenced feedback] and goal setting), and is void of cues to the meta-task level (e.g., cues that direct attention to the self) is likely to yield impressive gains in performance, possibly exceeding 1 SD.   (p. 278)

Hattie and Timperley's Review of the Feedback Literature

Fast-forward a decade and we find another much-cited review of the feedback literature and another model of feedback clearly consistent with cognitive learning theory and formative assessment. Hattie and Timperley (2007) defined feedback as "information provided by an agent (e.g., teacher, peer, book, parent, self, experience) regarding aspects of one's performance or understanding" (p. 81). This definition is very similar to Kluger and DeNisi's (1996) and, like theirs, encompasses a broad range of feedback studies including both knowledge of results and elaborated feedback. Summarizing the results of twelve meta-analyses (including Kluger and DeNisi's), Hattie and Timperley (2007) reported the average effect size for feedback as 0.79, twice the effect of a year of typical schooling and twice the overall effect reported by Kluger and DeNisi (1996). However, Hattie and Timperley also noted that the effects of feedback were quite variable and that the task at hand was still to describe what made feedback effective or not.

As I noted in the introduction, Hattie and Timperley (2007) are much cited for the model of feedback they offered to show how feedback could enhance learning. To explain part of the theoretical background for their model, Hattie and Timperley stated (2007):

> Effective feedback must answer three major questions asked by a teacher and/
> or by a student: Where am I going? (What are the goals?), How am I going?
> (What progress is being made toward the goal?), and Where to next? (What
> activities need to be undertaken to make better progress?) These questions
> correspond to notions of feed up, feed back, and feed forward.   (p. 86)

Hattie and Timperley's (2007) model clearly rests on cognitive learning theories, because the student is conceptualized as asking where she is going, having goals, and striving to meet them by incorporating information about current progress and next steps. It also clearly invokes formative assessment principles, echoing Sadler's (1989) three questions. Hattie and Timperley's model posits that feedback works at four levels: task, process, self-regulation, and self. The bulk of their review is spent looking at evidence of how feedback answers the three questions and the effectiveness of feedback at each of the four levels. They conclude that feedback about the task is effective, especially if it is about misconceptions (less so if the problem is learners' lack of information). Feedback about the process the student used to do the task is also effective and may lead to deeper learning. Feedback about self-regulation, for example, helping students to attribute their success in learning to their own effort, is effective if students have sufficient self-efficacy and willingness to do the learning. Feedback about the self, for example, general praise of a student, is usually ineffective.

These descriptions show that Hattie and Timperley's (2007) model of feedback is more solidly grounded in cognitive learning theory and formative assessment than Kluger and DeNisi's (1996) FIT. In particular, Hattie and Timperley separate self-regulation and the personal self into two levels, whereas Kluger and DeNisi considered both self-feedback and meta-task feedback as part of the same level of hierarchy of feedback. Hattie and Timperley have also added a level about the process students use to do the task, reflecting the importance of self-regulation. The point for this chapter is that as learning and motivation theory continues to develop over time, we see increases in the roles that student agency, student's learning intentions, and formative assessment play in feedback.

Other Influential Developments in Feedback Research

I have highlighted the contributions of Kluger and DeNisi's (1996) and Hattie and Timperley's (2007) meta-analyses because they illustrate the move toward more cognitive understandings of the role of feedback – a theme of this chapter – so clearly, and because they are large, much-cited meta-analyses. Because of both the size of their research base and their widespread citations, these two reviews have had, and will continue to have, a great influence on the evolving understanding of feedback. However, many other authors have provided theory and research in this evolving understanding, and there is not enough space in this chapter to detail them all. In this section, I briefly highlight some studies that I believe have also been influential in our understanding of feedback. They certainly have influenced my thinking and they, too, are much cited in the field.

In the 1970s and 1980s, educational psychologists began to study the effects of intrinsic and extrinsic motivation on learning. They began to realize that students' understanding of their competence and success were important for mastery and self-determination, which has direct implications for the functioning of feedback. Butler and Nisan (1986) designed a classic study to test the effects of different feedback conditions on learning and motivation with a sample of sixth graders in Israel. They hypothesized that learners receiving individualized, task-related feedback comments on their performance on interesting tasks would express more interest in the tasks and that they would perform better on both a "quantitative" task (finding as many words as they could in a longer word) and a "qualitative" task (a divergent thinking task). They also hypothesized that learners receiving numerical grades (on the 100-point scale) would perform better than learners who received no feedback on the quantitative task, but not the qualitative one. All their hypotheses were supported and were interpretable in terms of intrinsic motivation. Those in the feedback/no grades group received both positive and negative comments, and yet were more interested in the tasks and attributed their success to effort and other internal factors. Those in the no-feedback group attributed their success to the examiner's mood, the neatness of their work, and other external factors. All groups, even the group that received numerical grades, reported a preference for receiving comments.

Fast-forward a quarter-century. Lipnevich and Smith (2009a) expanded this design to test the effects of feedback on essay performance with university students in the United States. Their design included three factors: feedback (three groups – no feedback, detailed feedback perceived to be from the instructor, and detailed feedback perceived to be from a computer), grade versus no grade, and praise (two groups – statement of praise versus not). Detailed feedback, specific to a student's work, was strongly predictive of improvement in essay performance. Receiving a grade as well reduced performance somewhat, although not as much if accompanied by praise. Overall, detailed, specific feedback without grades or praise was most effective, with little difference according to whether the feedback was perceived to come from the instructor or a computer.

Both of these studies, at very different grade levels and at either end of a range of progress in the field of motivation theory, reached similar conclusions. It seems clear that detailed, descriptive feedback and grades occupy different places in students' motivational space. Both remind us that we need to take into account motivation theory, and not just learning theory, to understand the effects of feedback. Both support the theme of this chapter that feedback is best understood as formative.

The shift to formative feedback is evident in Tunstall and Gipps's (1996) typology of feedback, which they created based on observations of feedback in primary classrooms and categorized based on formative assessment ideas from Crooks (1988) and Sadler (1989), among others. They found that evaluative feedback can be classified as positive or negative, but descriptive feedback is in a sense all positive. Feedback in the form of description of students' strengths included (Tunstall & Gipps, 1996, p. 394) "specifying attainment" and "constructing achievement" (teachers and students mutually constructing concepts of what learning looks like). Description of weaknesses, however, were not considered negative but rather "specifying improvement" and (my personal favorite phrase) "constructing the way forward." In other words, when children are engaged with information that will help them reach their own learning goals, motivation is engaged even – and sometimes especially – when there is more work to be done. What matters is that the student understands what work is to be done, believes she can do it, and has a concept of what learning will result.

Current Conceptions of Feedback in the Context of Formative Assessment

In the historical review in the previous sections, I advanced the argument that early feedback research characterized feedback as something that occurred after summative assessment, mainly because conceptions of assessment were grounded in behaviorist and associationist theories of learning. These theories viewed learning as training and assessment as evaluating the status of that training. Only when our understanding of learning shifted to cognitive and constructivist theories did the notion of formative assessment arise, as the emphasis shifted from what training the teacher would provide to what apprehending and comprehending the student would be actively seeking to do. In that context, feedback shifts in two ways: from summative to formative, and from something "nice to have" to something that is an integral part of most learning episodes.

In the first section below, I describe the role of feedback in the formative learning cycle described by Sadler (1989), Hattie and Timperley (2007), and others. In the next section, I cite research to support expanding our understanding of a feedback episode beyond the words provided to students. Both of these expand our understanding of feedback in the context of formative assessment. Finally, I turn to research on students' perceptions and opinions about feedback. Studies of students' perceptions serve to "triangulate" the argument that the main function of feedback is formative, to support further learning. Students are unanimous in their support of, and preference for, feedback that provides constructive advice for next steps accompanied by opportunities to take those next steps. Thus the voices of researchers, practicing educators, and students converge on the notion that feedback's main role is formative.

The Role of Feedback in a Formative Learning Cycle

In this chapter, I will use the term "formative learning cycle" for the formative learning process described by Sadler (1989) and others and summarized in Hattie and Timperley's (2007) three questions. Formative assessment can occur only when students have a concept of the learning goal they are aiming for

(Sadler, 1989). In a formative learning cycle, students are mentally pursuing the script: Where am I going? Where am I now? How can I close the gap?

Learning goals come in different grain sizes, from broad learning standards that are found in state or national curriculum documents to unit-sized goals for instruction to daily learning targets that form the basis for individual lessons. When teachers help students understand their learning targets and goals and give examples of what competency or mastery looks like (Bransford, Brown, & Cocking, 2000; Ryan & Deci, 2000), they support students in their quest for mastery (Sadler, 1989; Hattie & Timperley, 2007). Daily learning targets should be arranged in a learning trajectory (Sztajn, Confrey, Wilson, & Edgington, 2012) and include criteria for success so that students know what to look for in their work as they proceed (Sadler, 1989):

> The indispensable conditions for improvement are that the *student* comes to hold a concept of quality roughly similar to that held by the teacher, is able to monitor continuously the quality of what is being produced *during the act of production itself*, and has a repertoire of alternative moves or strategies from which to draw at any given point. In other words, students have to be able to judge the quality of what they are producing and be able to regulate what they are doing during the doing of it.   (p. 121)

The most powerful formative learning cycles occur within lessons in pursuit of what Wiliam (2010) terms short- and medium-cycle learning goals. Students' active learning is fed with minute-by-minute formative feedback such as comments on students' class work. Feedback on short-cycle, in-class learning targets is usually informal and often oral. Students and teachers both take part in this feedback, which may be in dialogue, and either may initiate. Feedback on medium-cycle learning goals, for example, unit goals or objectives that span several lessons, often takes the form of feedback on more formal formative assessment evidence, for example, written feedback on quizzes or drafts of assignments (Wiliam, 2010).

Thus feedback plays a huge part in formative assessment, second only to clarifying learning targets and success criteria for students (Sadler, 1989; Hattie & Timperley, 2007; Ruiz-Primo & Brookhart, 2018). This is the most important, most effective, and most profound role feedback plays in learning. Butler and Winne (1995) analyzed the cognitive processes involved in self-regulated learning (SRL), concluding that feedback is "a prime determiner of processes that constitute SRL" (p. 245). They distinguish between two general types of feedback, outcome feedback and cognitive feedback. Outcome feedback, or knowledge of results, simply informs students about their achievement status. Current students and teachers are well aware of this kind of feedback, as evidenced by the common phrases "How did I do?" and "Here's how you did." In terms of the theme of this chapter, this is summative feedback. Butler and Winne's (1995) review concludes that this kind of feedback is not particularly helpful for supporting the self-regulation of learning.

In contrast to outcome feedback, cognitive feedback draws students' attention to qualities of their work in relation to criteria for the task or suggests ways students might attend to aspects of the task. In terms of the theme of this chapter, this is formative feedback. This kind of feedback *is* conducive to learning in general and the self-regulation of learning in particular. Students' beliefs about learning, about the task, and about themselves as learners affect how, and how well, students will be able to process and benefit from this feedback. Butler and Winne (1995) show how students use feedback, mediated by their own beliefs and understandings, during all aspects of the self-regulation of learning: selecting goals, selecting tactics and strategies to reach the goals, and monitoring their progress. They review and reinterpret feedback research and find support for their model of feedback and self-regulated learning, in the process demonstrating that feedback is indeed a "prime determiner" of student self-regulation and learning.

A recent meta-analysis of studies of formative assessment and writing (Graham, Hebert, & Harris, 2015) underscores the fact that feedback not only is formative but is the primary formative mechanism, at least in learning writing. Their meta-analysis examined the effects of students' receiving and using feedback on their writing on the quality of their subsequent writing. The authors concluded: "We found that feedback to students about writing from adults, peers, self, and computers statistically enhanced writing quality, yielding average effect sizes of 0.87, 0.58, 0.62, and 0.38, respectively" (p. 523).

Hattie and Timperley's (2007, p. 83) estimate of the overall effects of feedback across twelve meta-analyses was in a similar range, 0.79. In fact, prior to publishing his major work, *Visible Learning*, Hattie (2009) described how he had synthesized many reviews of feedback and famously prescribed that students should receive "dollops" (p. 173) of feedback. Other contemporary reviews of feedback literature reach similar conclusions about the importance of cognitive feedback – which your childhood teachers, if they were like mine, may have called "constructive criticism" – or elaborated feedback (Mason & Bruning, 2001) and about its crucial and primary role in student learning from cognitive, constructivist, and formative perspectives (Shute 2008; Evans 2013; Van der Kleij, Feskens, & Eggen, 2015).

A Formative Feedback Episode Is More than a Message

As the reviews explicated above suggest, feedback research stops short of supporting a simple generalization like "Summative feedback doesn't work, and formative feedback does." On balance, summative feedback doesn't work very well, in the sense of enhancing future learning, and formative feedback does, but there is much variability in both types of feedback research. The persistent findings in the feedback literature that not all feedback is helpful signals that something more is needed than simply well-crafted, descriptive, and informational comments. This section will use a broader literature base to support the claim that an appropriate feedback message itself is necessary but not sufficient to enhance future learning.

To affect future learning, or at least to maximize it, a feedback episode needs three characteristics (Ruiz-Primo & Brookhart, 2018). First, of course, the feedback message must be appropriately worded and delivered – descriptive, constructive, and so on. The literature I have reviewed so far is clear on that. Second, a feedback episode must be an episode of learning for both student *and teacher*. Third, the student must have a timely opportunity to use the feedback, usually in intentionally designed follow-up lessons.

Both Parties Must Learn from Feedback

In effective feedback episodes, both the teacher and the student learn something. The student learns the current status of her learning and what next steps she should take. The teacher learns about how the student is thinking about the concept she is learning. To support this claim, I need to draw on studies of teacher participation in formative assessment and studies of student self-regulation of learning.

Studies of teachers who are experts in formative assessment show that they collect and interpret evidence about student thinking: about how students are understanding concepts, processes, problem-solving approaches, or principles and where they have misconceptions (Minstrell, Anderson, & Li, 2009; Kroog, Ruiz-Primo, & Sands, 2014). This allows them to consider what comments or immediate next instructional moves will take the student from that point to the next logical step in learning. In contrast, teachers who are *not* effective with formative assessment simply assess the correctness of student work (e.g., this student got 80% of the problems right). Then, they make corrections or give assignments to review areas where students had low scores, without effectively addressing specific misconceptions or learning needs.

If the role of teacher feedback to students in formative assessment is to help students move to the next step toward a learning goal, then teachers *must* learn what students are thinking. Sadler (1989) suggested that the role of formative assessment information is to short-circuit for students the ineffective strategy of trial-and-error learning. In effect, formative assessment research suggests the same holds true for teachers. Teachers who merely look for the quantity of correctness in students' work miss the key opportunity to focus their feedback on specific learning needs. This is an instructionally weak position for the teacher to be in; the only response is to assign more of the same work that the student did not do very well in the first place.

I have already mentioned Hattie's (2009) enthusiasm for the power and potential of feedback to enhance student learning. Supporting the view that teachers should learn about student thinking during feedback episodes, Hattie (2009) reports that his views about feedback changed as he reviewed additional research evidence, and he realized that feedback was more than the responses teachers provide to students about their work. He wrote:

> It was only when I discovered that feedback was most powerful when it is
> from the *student to the teacher* that I started to understand it better. When
> teachers seek, or at least are open to, feedback from students as to what
> students know, what they understand, where they make errors, when they
> have misconceptions, when they are not engaged – then teaching and learning
> can be synchronized and powerful.   (p. 173, emphasis in original)

In other words, a feedback episode should result in learning for both the
student, who learns about where he is in his learning and what to do next, and
the teacher, who learns about how the student is thinking and understanding, in
order to focus both feedback comments and next instructional moves.

Studies of student self-regulation of learning suggest that students actively set
learning goals and pursue them and that assessment information from both self
and others is critical in this process (Butler & Winne, 1995; Allal, 2011;
Zimmerman & Schunk, 2011; Andrade & Brookhart, 2016). Thus for feedback
to enhance future learning, students must be able to hear feedback as information that they can use to improve, they must understand what they should do
next, and they must believe they have the capacity to use the feedback to
improve. Only then can students effectively revise work, focus studying, or
consider a concept differently to correct a misconception. To effectively use
feedback, students must apprehend the information contained in the comments
and make sense of it the same way they do any other learning – by relating it to
other concepts and understandings they already possess. If students do not learn
from feedback, they cannot use it. The converse is also true. If students do not
use feedback, they are not likely to learn from it.

All told, then, crafting feedback messages that are descriptive, well focused,
and timely goes only so far toward making feedback effective. Feedback
episodes must contribute to teachers' learning about students' thinking and
students' learning more about their learning goal and their own next steps. As
we have seen in the first part of this chapter, most of the feedback literature to
date has centered on students' learning from feedback. The claim of this chapter
is that two more pieces must be in place for feedback to be effective, teachers'
learning from feedback and then providing students with opportunities to use
the feedback while learning is still ongoing. These pieces are consistent with the
chapter's prior claim, that the most effective use of feedback is formative.

Students Must Have Opportunities to Use Feedback

Simply providing comments on an assignment does not guarantee, or even
necessarily encourage, students to use the feedback to improve their work or to
further their learning. Even if feedback is provided without a grade, which is
known to interfere with students' attention to comments (Butler & Nisan, 1986;
Lipnevich & Smith, 2009a), many students will still simply ignore feedback. Some
will not understand it. Others will become angry or frustrated, and absent
guidance in using the feedback will throw their work with teacher's comments
away. The common teacher notion that students will use their feedback "next

time" is a misconception, as well. Most students will not memorize feedback comments and pull them from memory the next time they are relevant. The teacher needs to provide students an opportunity to use the feedback immediately or at least while the feedback is still relevant to what the students are learning.

Actually, providing students with an opportunity to use feedback will not only ensure that the feedback is used; it can also work to equalize opportunity. High-achieving students will use any piece of information they can get to improve their work and their learning (Brookhart, 2001). Providing lesson time and scaffolding as needed for students to use feedback can extend some of these benefits to all students (Covington, 1992). Unfortunately, there is some evidence that teachers find providing immediate follow-up difficult (Heritage, Kim, Vendlinski, & Herman, 2009; Schneider & Gowan, 2013; Wylie & Lyon, 2015). On the other hand, skillful teachers can structure immediate opportunities for students to use feedback, for example, blending feedback comments into pedagogic questioning (Heritage & Heritage, 2013).

For final support of this chapter's argument, I turn to studies of students' perceptions of feedback. Results of these studies support the claim that the most effective feedback is formative but that the notion of "formative feedback" extends beyond comments made during formative assessment, to include teachers' learning about student thinking and helping students actually use their feedback.

Students' Views of Feedback

Dann (2016) pointed out that feedback by definition cannot be a one-way process, because by its very nature it is intended to help students improve. Students' interpretation of the feedback they receive is as critical as teachers' feedback messages and intentions. Consistent with most formative approaches to feedback, Dann (2016) grounds her remarks in the concept of formative assessment, a social constructivist approach to learning, and Habermas's theory of communicative action, which holds that communication between two parties, by speech and/or action, requires mutual negotiation and interpretation. Evans (2013) called for more research on students' perceptions of feedback, finding that research base thin. However, the research base does seem to be growing.

Students' views of feedback underscore the value of formative feedback and the lack of value – and sometimes negative value – of summative feedback. That is, current studies of students' perceptions of feedback are congruent with the observations we have made about older studies of summative feedback, based on outdated learning theories, showing limited effectiveness, and more recent studies of formative feedback, based on more current understandings of learning and motivation, showing larger positive effects.

Studies of students' perceptions of feedback have been done at the middle and secondary level (Pajares & Graham, 1998; Peterson & Irving, 2008; Gamlem & Smith, 2013; Harris, Brown, & Harnett, 2014; Murtagh, 2014; Zumbrunn,

Marrs, & Mewborn, 2016) and at the university level (Weaver, 2006; Lipnevich & Smith, 2009b; Pokorny & Pickford, 2010; Ferguson, 2011; Douglas, Salter, Iglesias, Dowlman, & Eri, 2016; Zhan, 2016). Some of the studies asked about feedback in contexts where feedback was given only on summative assessments (e.g., Ferguson, 2011), some of the studies asked about feedback in a formative context (e.g., Pajares & Graham, 1998), and some of the studies asked students about their perceptions of feedback in general (e.g., Harris et al., 2014).

Despite this variation in the formative/summative context of studies, differences in country and curriculum, and differences in grade level and subject matter, the one thing that all the studies of student perceptions had in common was students' preference for specific suggestions they could use for improvement and learning, coupled with opportunities to use the feedback. Ferguson (2011), for example, surveyed graduate and undergraduate university students in Australia. Even though the topic of his study was feedback on summative assessments, students still preferred comments that could make the work better, like comments on key ideas in their writing or the approach they took in a paper. That is, they were looking for formative feedback even in what was supposed to be summative feedback.

In perhaps the most generalized of the student perception studies, Peterson and Irving (2008) asked New Zealand secondary students what they thought the definition and purpose of assessment was. Although they were aiming to study students' perceptions of assessment in general, what students in their focus groups told them was that the whole purpose of assessment was to get feedback, primarily to help them improve and secondarily to show progress to parents and others. Students did not separate the purposes of feedback and assessment in general. In terms of the argument being made in this chapter, these students are telling us that formative feedback is not only the most effective kind (thus corroborating the research findings reported above) but that formative feedback is the essence of assessment.

Studies of students' perceptions of feedback in basic education have identified what students think is "positive feedback" and what they think is "negative feedback." Gamlem and Smith (2013) found that students perceived as positive both feedback that registered approval of their work and feedback that identified areas for improvement coupled with suggestions for how to proceed with that improvement and time to do so. Students perceive disapproval as negative feedback. They also perceive feedback as negative when constructive comments are given but teachers do not give students time to work with feedback they receive. They experience this situation as disapproval and report that it makes them feel "useless" (p. 160).

Harris et al. (2014) surveyed students in years five through ten in New Zealand, a context with a strong commitment to formative assessment. They also asked students to draw pictures of feedback. Students' responses were overwhelmingly positive, and although they often drew pictures of feedback in summative contexts (on graded work), they registered a strong preference for feedback that gave suggestions for improvement. Similarly, Murtagh (2014) studied two literacy classes in the United Kingdom, where students also registered a strong preference for descriptive feedback that helped them understand their own strengths and weaknesses, as opposed to ticks (check marks) or general comments ("good"). Basic education students in the United States (Pajares & Graham, 1998; Zumbrunn et al., 2016) also wanted teachers to engage with the content of their work and give them honest and clear information about what they were doing well and what they could do to improve.

Studies of students' perceptions of feedback in higher education have also described the type of formative information students seek and prefer. Similar to the findings in basic education, Douglas and colleagues (2016) found that Australian university students in blended (online and face-to-face combined) courses preferred detailed feedback on their work and did not value general comments. Lipnevich and Smith (2009b) found US university students also preferred detailed comments. In a design that investigated the interaction of grades with feedback, they found that students felt grades were unnecessary if learning was the goal, and high grades decreased students' motivation to revise work. Praise and other general comments were not valued.

Pokorny and Pickford (2010) found that UK university students saw summative feedback as coming too late to be useful and stressed the importance of receiving formative feedback on their work before assignments were due. Similar to findings in basic education, these university students also said feedback was not helpful if students did not have an opportunity to use it. Pokorny and Pickford's (2010) findings extend our understanding of the kind of detailed feedback students want. They want their feedback to give cues to teachers' criteria and expectations, in time to use it, and they want the feedback to be from a tutor with whom they have a positive relationship. Weaver's (2006) survey of UK university students also found that constructive criticism should be detailed enough to support improvement and, importantly, understandable to the recipient. Some of Weaver's students reported they did not always understand the feedback they were given. They also reported wanting feedback that described strengths and did not focus only on weaknesses or needs for improvement.

Thus a pretty clear picture emerges. Students consider that feedback is effective when it is formative, comes from a teacher with whom they have a positive learning relationship, helps them understand teachers' expectations, identifies strengths and weaknesses based on those expectations, makes detailed constructive suggestions for improvement, and provides students time to act on those suggestions. A study by Zhan (2016) suggests that future feedback research done in subject-area contexts might illuminate even more specific details, which will differ by subject and learning goal. In the context of Chinese university students learning to write in English, Zhan (2016) found that students wanted feedback that focused on organization, content, and language use and gave less emphasis to formatting and mechanics. Presumably, future studies of students learning different content and skills could identify specific kinds of feedback that students seek in other learning contexts. I would expect – although it is an empirical question – that if this future research were framed in terms of cognitive and constructivist learning theories, researchers would find that the specific kind of feedback students want in content areas is related to what they perceive as areas of greatest need for learning or areas of central importance to the content, or both.

Where Does That Leave Feedback in the Context of Summative Assessment?

I hope I have succeeded in mounting a persuasive argument that the most appropriate role for feedback is as part of the formative learning cycle. For all of the reasons in this chapter, when I work with teachers, I usually advise them to give feedback during formative learning time and just grade summative assessments. I tell them it is a waste of time and energy to give detailed feedback on summative assessment, which comes too late to be useful and may not even be read.

However, I would argue that feedback on summative assessment may be used strategically for specific, limited purposes. Part of this argument rests on the fact that, except in a few cases of final evaluations of grant-funded projects or self-contained, one-shot programs, no assessment is ever only summative. In the case of classroom learning, there is always more to learn. The research I reviewed in this chapter, plus my own study of how successful students process and use information from their assessments (Brookhart, 2001), suggests that feedback on summative assessment is useful to the extent that the "sum" – the certification of what has been learned, typically for grading and reporting – is not an ultimate summation of learning but does in fact feed into ongoing learning in a class or course.

This suggests two possible cases in which feedback on summative assessment may be helpful. The first is when your grading policy allows for revision of summative assessment (e.g., revising a final project) or retaking tests, as long as the redoing is carefully planned. In general, revision yields the best evidence of new learning after feedback for complex performances (e.g., a final project, a term paper). Retaking a new form of a test (same blueprint, different test questions) yields the best evidence of new learning after feedback for tests with right-answer questions. In both cases, though, if students use feedback to learn more, additional summative assessment and a revised grade is a better indicator of final student status on a standard or unit learning goal.

The second case in which feedback on summative assessment may be helpful is when the summative assessment follows a unit of instruction that will lead to another unit that builds on the skills students learned in the first unit. This happens more regularly in some subjects (e.g., mathematics) than others. Consider, for example, a student who finds out from feedback on her unit test about factoring quadratic equations that she is making a consistent mistake with the addition and subtraction signs in the factors. If the next unit is about graphing quadratic equations, and the factored equations are a source of information needed for the graphs, feedback on the first unit test, coupled with practice using the feedback as the next unit begins, could be helpful to her.

A limited amount of research on using summative feedback to further learning already exists. The formative use of summative tests (FUST) was a strategy described in the Kings, Medway, Oxfordshire Formative Assessment Project (Black, Harrison, Lee, Marshall, & Wiliam, 2003). This strategy can include using formative practices to support revision; having students write review questions, answer, and mark them as a means of studying; and using test results as a springboard for continued formative work. Carless (2011) found that FUST was one formative assessment strategy more easily accepted in Confucian-heritage settings where historically summative assessment has dominated.

Notice that in both of these specific cases, feedback on a summative assessment is actually used formatively. The "summative" nature of the assessment was temporary, for the purpose of ending a unit or reporting a grade; however, learning was still in progress.

The Conclusions in a Nutshell

- The most appropriate role for feedback is as part of a formative approach to learning.
- Therefore, formative learning cycles where students have opportunities to receive and use feedback should be the building blocks of instructional planning.
- Basing instructional planning on formative learning cycles represents a sea change in beliefs about teaching and learning for many instructors, whose instructional planning is built on cycles of transmission of material followed by summative assessment.
- Feedback on summative assessment may be used strategically for specific, limited purposes.
  - Feedback on summative assessment may be useful if students are given an opportunity to revise their work or retake a test.
  - Feedback on summative assessment may be useful if the next instructional unit after a summative assessment builds on the concepts and skills that are the subject of the feedback.

Before I conclude the chapter, it is important to note that just because learning and motivation theorists have moved past a behaviorist or association-ist view to cognitive and constructivist views of how students learn, it does not follow that all instructional practices have moved, as well. There are many closet behaviorists out there (Shepard, 2001). Many educators even give lip service to cognitive and constructivist views of learning, but plan instruction and assessment as a series of instructional activities followed by a summative assessment. This happens in both basic education (Ruiz-Primo & Brookhart, 2018) and higher education (Boud & Molloy, 2013), revealing an underlying "transmission" view of learning.

Because of their own understanding of learning, assessment, and feedback, such educators have difficulty taking the student's perspective and producing feedback that suggests next steps in the student's personal learning trajectory, keeping in mind where the student is and where he or she needs to go next. Educators who really want to become expert at formative assessment must jettison outdated learning theories and vocabulary (e.g., stop saying they did something to "reinforce" a student's learning) and begin to understand what constructing one's own learning means for instruction and assessment. Elsewhere, I have called this the "sea change" (Brookhart, 2017) that needs to happen if formative assessment is to realize its potential. Because, as I have argued in this chapter, feedback provides the information and motivates the student energy that fuels the formative learning cycle, it follows that this sea change needs to happen in order for feedback to realize its full potential. Formative assessment and feedback are intimately related, and you cannot have one without the other. Until all those who teach experience the sea change, feedback will remain what the teacher needs to say and not what the student needs to hear.

References

Allal, L. (2011). Pedagogy, didactics and the co-regulation of learning: A perspective from the French-language world of educational research. *Research Papers in Education, 26*, 329–336.

Ames, C., & Archer, J. (1988). Achievement goals in the classroom: Students' learning strategies and motivation processes. *Journal of Educational Psychology, 80*, 260–267.

Ammons, R. B. (1956). Effects of knowledge of performance: A survey and tentative theoretical formulation. *Journal of General Psychology, 73*, 87–95.

Andrade, H., & Brookhart, S. (2016). Classroom assessment as the co-regulation of learning. In press. *Assessment in Education: Princples, Policy and Practice.*

Assessment Reform Group. (2002). Assessment is for learning: 10 principles. Retrieved from www.aaia.org.uk/content/uploads/2010/06/Assessment-for-Learning-10-principles.pdf.

Black, P., Harrison, C., Lee, C., Marshall, B., & Wiliam, D. (2003). *Assessment for learning: Putting it into practice.* Berkshire, UK: Open University Press.

Bloom, B. S., Hastings, J. T., & Madaus, G. F. (1971). *Handbook on formative and summative evaluation of pupil learning.* New York: McGraw-Hill.

Boud, D., & Molloy, E. (2013). Rethinking models of feedback for learning: The challenge of design. *Assessment and Evaluation in Higher Education, 38*, 698–712.

Bransford, John D., Brown, Ann L., and Cocking, Rodney R. (Eds). 2000. *How people learn: Brain, mind, experience and school.* Washington, DC: National Academy Press.

Brookhart, S. M. (2001). Successful students' formative and summative use of assessment information. *Assessment in Education, 8*, 153–169.

Brookhart, S. M. (2007). Expanding views about formative assessment: A review of the literature. In J. H. McMillan (Ed.), *Formative classroom assessment: Theory into practice.* New York: Teachers College Press.

Brookhart, S. M. (2017). Formative assessment in teacher education. In D. J. Clandinin & J. Husu (Eds.), *International handbook of research on teacher education*. London: Sage.

Butler, R., & Nisan, M. (1986). Effects of no feedback, task-related comments, and grades on intrinsic motivation and performance. *Journal of Educational Psychology, 78*, 210–216.

Butler, D. L., & Winne, P. H. (1995). Feedback and self-regulated learning: A theoretical synthesis. *Review of Educational Research, 65*, 245–281.

Campbell, D. T., & Stanley, J. C. (1963). *Experimental and quasi-experimental designs for research*. Chicago: Rand McNally.

Carless, D. (2011). *From testing to productive student learning.* New York: Routledge.

Covington, M. V. (1992). *Making the grade: A self-worth perspective on motivation and school reform*. Cambridge: Cambridge University Press.

Crooks, T. J. (1988). The impact of classroom evaluation practices on pupils. *Review of Educational Research, 58*, 438–481.

Dann, R. (2016). Developing understanding of pupil feedback using Habermas' notion of communicative action. *Assessment in Education, 23*, 396–414.

Deci, E. L., & Ryan, R. M. (Eds.). (2002). *Handbook of self-determination research*. Rochester, NY: University of Rochester Press.

Douglas, T., Salter, S., Iglesias, M., Dowlman, M., & Eri, R. (2016). The feedback process: Perceptions of first and second year undergraduate students in the disciplines of education, health science and nursing. *Journal of University Teaching and Learning Practice, 13*(1), article 3.

Eccles, J. (1983). Expectancies, values, and academic behaviors. In J. T. Spence (Ed.), *Achievement and achievement motives* (pp. 75–146). San Francisco, CA: Freeman.

Elton, L. (1982). Assessment for learning. In D. Bligh (Ed.), *Professionalism and flexibility in learning* (pp. 106–135). Guildford, UK: Society for Research into Higher Education.

Evans, C. (2013). Making sense of assessment feedback in higher education. *Review of Educational Research, 83*, 70–120.

Ferguson, P. (2011). Student perceptions of quality feedback in teacher education. *Assessment and Evaluation in Higher Education, 36*, 51–62.

Gamlem, S. M., & Smith, K. (2013). Student perceptions of classroom feedback. *Assessment in Education: Principles, Policy and Practice, 20*, 150–169.

Graham, S., Hebert, M., & Harris, K. R. (2015). Formative assessment and writing: A meta-analysis. *Elementary School Journal, 115*, 523–547.

Harris, L. R., Brown, G. T. L., & Harnett, J. A. (2014). Understanding classroom feedback practices: A study of New Zealand student experiences, perceptions, and emotional responses. *Educational Assessment, Evaluation and Accountability, 26*, 107–133.

Hattie, J. A. C. (2009). *Visible learning: A synthesis of over 800 meta-analyses relating to achievement*. London: Routledge.

Hattie, J., & Timperley, H. (2007). The power of feedback. *Review of Educational Research, 77*, 81–112.

Heritage, M., & Heritage, J. (2013). Teacher questioning: The epicenter of instruction and assessment. *Applied Measurement in Education, 26*, 176–190.

Heritage, M., Kim, J., Vendlinski, T., & Herman, J. (2009). From evidence to action: A seamless process in formative assessment? *Educational Measurement: Issues and Practice*, *28*(3), 24–31.

James, M., & Pedder, D. (2006). Beyond method: Assessment and learning practices and values. *The Curriculum Journal*, *17*(2), 109–138.

Kluger, A. N., & DeNisi, A. (1996). The effects of feedback interventions on performance: A historical review, a meta-analysis, and a preliminary feedback intervention theory. *Psychological Bulletin*, *119*, 254–284.

Kroog, H. I., Ruiz-Primo, M. A., & Sands, D. (2014). Understanding the interplay between the cultural context of classrooms and formative assessment. Paper presented at the annual meeting of the American Educational Research Association, Philadelphia.

Kulhavy, R. W. (1977). Feedback in written instruction. *Review of Educational Research*, *47*, 211–232.

Lipnevich, A. A., & Smith, J. K. (2009a). Effects of differential feedback on students' examination performance. *Journal of Experimental Psychology: Applied*, *15*, 319–333.

Lipnevich, A. A., & Smith, J. K. (2009b). "I really need feedback to learn": Students' perspectives on the effectiveness of the differential feedback messages. *Educational Assessment, Evaluation and Accountability*, *21*, 347–367.

Mason, B. J., & Bruning, R. (2001). Providing feedback in computer-based instruction: What the research tells us. University of Nebraska-Lincoln. Retrieved from http://dwb.unl.edu/Edit/MB/MasonBruning.html.

Minstrell, J., Anderson, R., & Li, M. (2009). Assessing teacher competency in formative assessment. Annual Report to the National Science Foundation.

Murtagh, L. (2014). The motivational paradox of feedback: Teacher and student perceptions. *Curriculum Journal*, *25*, 516–541.

Ormrod, J. E. (2014). *Educational psychology: Developing learners* (8th edn.). Boston: Pearson.

Pajares, F., & Graham, L. (1998). Formalist thinking and language arts instruction: Teachers' and students' beliefs about truth and caring in the teaching conversation. *Teaching and Teacher Education*, *14*, 855–870.

Page, E. B. (1958). Teacher comments and student performance: A seventy-four classroom experiment in school motivation. *Journal of Educational Psychology*, *49*, 173–181.

Peterson, E. R., & Irving, S. E. (2008). Secondary school students' conceptions of assessment and feedback. *Learning and Instruction*, *18*, 238–250.

Pintrich, P. R., & Schrauben, B. (1992). Students' motivational beliefs and their cognitive engagement in classroom academic tasks. In D. H. Schunk & J. L. Meece (Eds.), *Student perceptions in the classroom* (pp. 149–183). Hillsdale, NJ: Lawrence Erlbaum.

Pokorny, H., & Pickford, P. (2010). Complexity, cues, and relationships: Student perceptions of feedback. *Active Learning in Higher Education*, *11*, 21–30.

Ramaprasad, A. (1983). On the definition of feedback. *Behavioral Science*, *28*, 4–13.

Ruiz-Primo, M. A., & Brookhart, S. M. (2018). *Using feedback to improve learning*. London: Routledge.

Ryan, R. M., & Deci, E. L. (2000). Self-determination theory and the facilitation of intrinsic motivation, social development, and well-being. *American Psychologist*, *55*(1), 68–78.

Ryan, R. M., Connell, J. P., & Deci, E. L. (1985). A motivational analysis of self-determination and self-regulation in the classroom. In C. Ames and R. Ames (Eds.), *Research on motivation in education*, vol. 2: *The classroom milieu*. New York: Academic Press.

Sadler, D. R. (1989). Formative assessment and the design of instructional systems. *Instructional Science*, *18*, 119–144.

Salomon, G. (1983). The differential investment of mental effort in learning from different sources. *Educational Psychologist*, *18*, 42–50.

Salomon, G. (1984). Television is "easy" and print is "tough": The differential investment of mental effort as a function of perceptions and attributions. *Journal of Educational Psychology*, *76*, 647–658.

Schneider, M. C., & Gowan, P. (2013). Investigating teachers' skills in interpreting evidence of student learning. *Applied Measurement in Education*, *26*, 191–204.

Scriven, M. (1967). The methodology of evaluation. In R. W. Tyler, R. M. Gagne, & M. Scriven (Eds.), *Perspectives of curriculum evaluation* (pp. 39–83). Chicago: Rand McNally.

Shepard, L. A. (2001). The role of classroom assessment in teaching and learning. In V. Richardson (Ed.), *Handbook of research on teaching* (pp. 1066–1101). Washington, DC: American Educational Research Association.

Shute, V. J. (2008). Focus on formative feedback. *Review of Educational Research*, *78*, 153–189.

Skinner, B. F. (1958). Teaching machines. *Science,* 128, 969–977.

Stewart, L. G., & White, M. A. (1976). Teacher comments, letter grades, and student performance: What do we really know? *Journal of Educational Psychology*, *68*, 488–500.

Sztajn, P., Confrey, J., Wilson, P. H., & Edgington, C.(2012). Learning trajectory based instruction: Toward a theory of teaching. *Educational Researcher*, *41*, 147–156.

Thorndike, E. L. (1913). *Educational Psychology*, vol. 1: *The original nature of man*. New York: Columbia University Teachers College.

Tunstall, P., & Gipps, C. (1996). Teacher feedback to young children in formative assessment: A typology. *British Educational Research Journal*, *22*, 389–404.

Van der Kleij, F. M., Feskens, R. C. W., & Eggen, T. J. H. M. (2015). Effects of feedback in a computer-based learning environment on students' learning outcomes: A meta-analysis. *Review of Educational Research*, *85*, 475–511.

Weaver, M. R. (2006). Do students value feedback? Student perceptions of tutors' written responses. *Assessment and Evaluation in Higher Education*, *31*, 379–394.

Weiner, B. (1979). A theory of motivation for some classroom experiences. *Journal of Educational Psychology*, *71*, 3–25.

Wiliam, D. (2010). An integrative summary of the research literature and implications for a new theory of formative assessment. In H. L. Andrade & G. J. Cizek (Eds.), *Handbook of formative assessment* (pp. 18–40). New York: Routledge.

Wylie, E. C., & Lyon, C. J. (2015). The fidelity of formative assessment implementation: Issues of breadth and quality. *Assessment in Education: Principles, Policy and Practice*, *22*, 140–160.

Zhan, L. (2016). Written teacher feedback: Student perceptions, teacher perceptions, and actual teacher performance. *English Language Teaching, 9*(8), 73–84.

Zimmerman, B., & Schunk, D. (Eds.). (2011). *Handbook of self-regulation of learning and performances.* New York: Routledge.

Zumbrunn, S., Marrs, S., & Mewborn, C. (2016). Towards a better understanding of student perceptions of writing feedback: A mixed methods study. *Reading and Writing, 29,* 349–370.

4 Toward a Taxonomy of Written Feedback Messages

Jacqui Murray, N. Ruth Gasson, and Jeffrey K. Smith

Consider the sentence in high school student William's essay, and the possible feedback messages it might have generated (Figure 4.1). If you were William, which of these alternative approaches would engender the most positive or most negative reaction in you as a writer? What would provide the most help? How much variation in feedback messages might there be among different teachers marking the same written work? In this chapter, we explore the nature of written feedback message options available to teachers engaged in marking with a goal of developing a type of "taxonomy" of feedback messages. Such a taxonomy would be helpful in understanding how we communicate to students and in providing a framework for conducting research on the reliability, validity, and effectiveness of communication in feedback settings. We wanted to develop a system that would be understandable and usable by teachers and would provide a structure that would allow for research to be conducted on feedback, such as by looking at intermarker reliability. We also wanted it to be complete in being able to categorize almost all types of feedback encountered. This chapter is based on the doctoral thesis work of the first author; we refer the reader to that thesis for more detail on various aspects presented here (Murray, 2018).

Approaches to Feedback Coding Systems

There have been a number of attempts to develop feedback-coding systems over the years, and we began by examining several of those to see if they would fit our purposes. Perhaps the most widely known system is the model developed by Hattie and Timperley (2007). Their model has four levels of feedback: task, process, self-regulation, and person. The power of the Hattie and Timperley model is that it focuses attention on the cognitive processes that underlie the content of the feedback, much as Bloom's taxonomy did over half a century ago (Bloom, Engelhart, Furst, Hill, & Krathwohl, 1956). Hattie and Timperley's (2007) approach concerned the focus of the feedback message but leaves many of the aspects of particular feedback messages open. If one looks at the five feedback messages in Figure 4.1, it can be seen that three exist at the task level, and two at the processes level. And yet these five comments are different in many other ways. For example, as Hattie and Timperley pointed

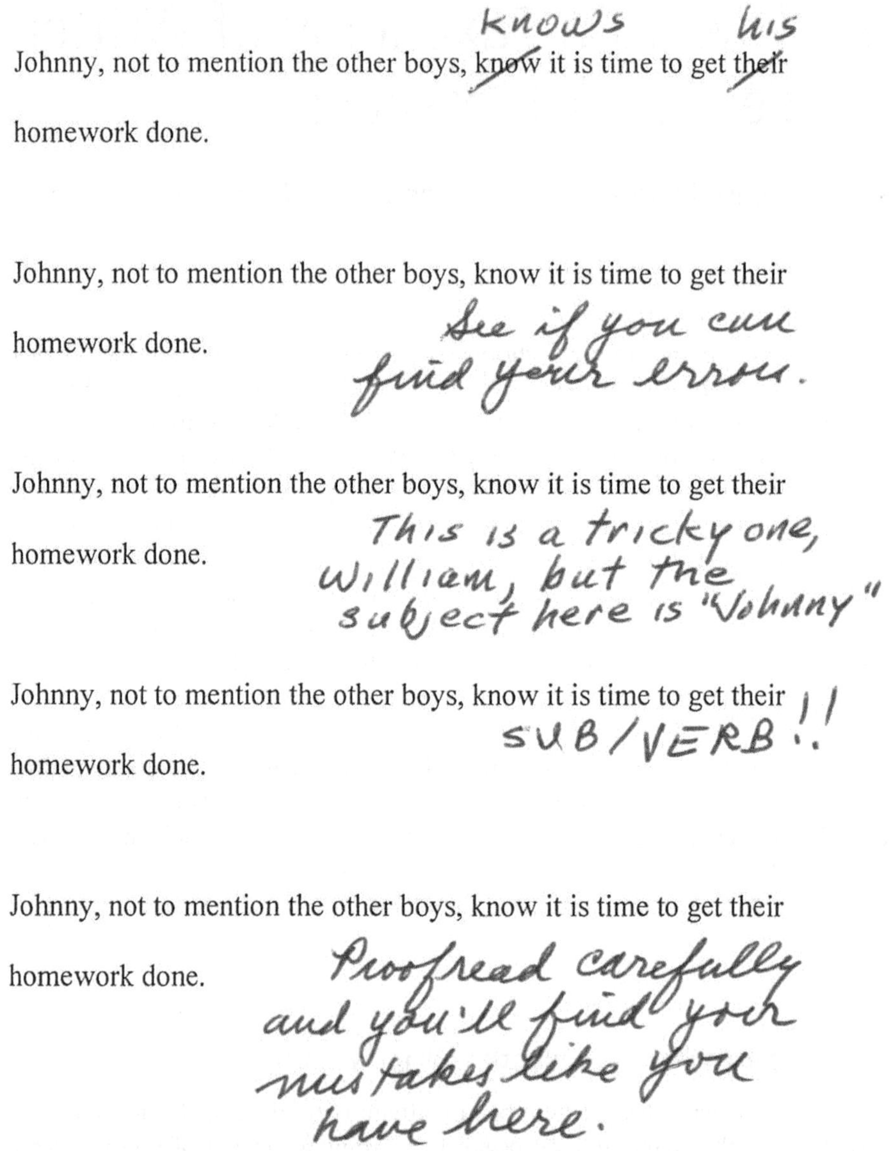

Johnny, not to mention the other boys, ~~know~~ knows it is time to get their his

homework done.

Johnny, not to mention the other boys, know it is time to get their

homework done. *See if you can find your error.*

Johnny, not to mention the other boys, know it is time to get their

homework done. *This is a tricky one, William, but the subject here is "Johnny"*

Johnny, not to mention the other boys, know it is time to get their //

homework done. SUB/VERB !.

Johnny, not to mention the other boys, know it is time to get their

homework done. *Proofread carefully and you'll find your mistakes like you have here.*

Figure 4.1 *Different feedback messages to William's sentence.*

out, there are also differences in terms of whether the tone of the feedback is positive or negative. Also, there are many varieties of feedback within their four major categories. Thus, there are a number of approaches to the issue of categorizing feedback in addition to Hattie and Timperley's exemplary work. We examine them below.

Spinks (1998) developed a feedback coding system with six categories: non-verbal notations, grammar and expression, subject matter, structure, referencing, and professional induction. Nonverbal notations concerned the various graphic devices that markers use as shortcuts in their marking (e.g., crossing out incorrect material). Grammar and expression concerned comments about diction, spelling, and punctuation along with comments about syntax. Subject matter concerned comments relating to the student's handling of content. Structure concerned the overall outline of the assignment such as the introduction, conclusion, and organization of paragraphs. Referencing concerned comments relating to compliance with guidelines (such as APA style). Professional induction concerned the kinds of comments that were designed to induct the student into the discipline in which they were studying. All five of the marker comments in Figure 4.1 would be categorized as concerning grammar and expression. (Note: To describe the individuals who provide feedback to students, we are using the term "markers." Although this may seem a bit prosaic, the term makes it clear that we are talking about the educators who read the student papers and respond by sending written messages.)

Ivanic, Clark, and Rimmershaw (2000) had a very different take on feedback messages. They collected a selection of responses by tutors on students' writing from five subject tutors at a UK university and four "English for academic purposes" tutors, some working in the UK university, others in an African university. They coded feedback responses into six categories: explained the grade in terms of strengths and weaknesses, evaluated the match between the student's essay and an ideal answer, corrected or edited the student's work, engaged in a dialogue with the student, gave advice that would be useful in writing the next essay, and gave advice on rewriting this essay. What is particularly interesting here is how different this approach is from the Spinks (1998) approach, *and* from the Hattie and Timperley (2007) approach. They took a very broad view of feedback messages; all of the messages in Figure 4.1, for example, would fit into the "corrected or edited the student's work" or possibly the "engaged in a dialogue" categories.

Using the sentence as the unit of analysis in providing feedback, Mutch (2003) investigated the content of comments on a set of feedback sheets given to students. He conducted the research following anecdotal evidence from a variety of stakeholders that feedback was uninformative or too brief. His system looked at feedback in relation to whether it was about understanding the question, structuring and argument, concepts, knowledge, communication, or presentation. He also coded feedback according to whether it was positive or negative, and then further coded comments by category into factual, developmental, implied developmental, conversational, or neutral comments. In this system, feedback messages can be categorized in multiple fashions. Although all five of the comments in Figure 4.1 would be categorized as concerning communication or presentation, they would differ as to whether they were positive or negative and to whether they were factual, implied developmental, or developmental.

Stern and Solomon (2006) developed an elaborate categorization scheme that included twenty-three different categories. They looked at feedback at the global level, the middle level, and the micro level, as well as an "other comments" category developed to capture personal comments and tracking marks.

At the global level, comments were coded according to whether they were about overall quality, paper structure and organization, creativity, or voice. At the middle level, comments were coded according to whether they were about quality of specific thoughts and claims, procedure and technique, support/evidence for claims, request for content clarification, or paragraph and sentence structure/style. At the micro level, comments were coded according to word choice/phrasing, missing words and pieces, grammar and punctuation, spelling/typos, technical style, and references or citations. The other comments category included invitations to discuss the paper, personal expressions and advice, scholarly advice, "roadmaps," tracking marks, rubric/grading sheet, unidentifiable, and other. The Stern and Solomon scheme has a number of attractive features, including its hierarchical structure. What it does not address, however, are issues such as tone and whether feedback is forward looking. The five comments in Figure 4.1 would all be categorized the same, as being at the micro level and concerning sentence structure.

Although there are other approaches that might be examined, this sampling provides enough information and variety to allow for a critical analysis of the work in the field to date. Perhaps the issue that stands out most clearly is that feedback messages have multiple characteristics. They can be about structure, grammar, content, etc.; they can have a tone to them (positive, neutral, negative); they can concern just the piece of work at hand or be forward looking; and they can speak to the student in a kind of dialogue, or not. Additionally, implicit in these models is an underlying purpose or focus to the scheme. They raise the questions of: What does one want to accomplish in a given categorization scheme? For whom will this scheme be useful?

Considerations in a New Taxonomy of Feedback Messaging

In thinking about whether a new approach to categorizing feedback messages might be developed, three overarching purposes came to mind in its development: the approach should be useful to the people who give and receive feedback messages; it should encompass almost all possible feedback messages; and it should be a vehicle that will facilitate research in this area. But before getting too far down that road, a definition of feedback is necessary. Ramaprasad (1983) offered what might be considered the classic definition of feedback: "information about the gap between the actual level and the reference level of a system parameter which is used to alter the gap in some way" (p. 4). This definition is endorsed by Wiliam (Chapter 1, this volume). There are many variations on the themes that Ramaprasad presented, but the heart of the definition is that feedback tells the learner about current status, desired status, and how to close the gap between the two.

Although we accept this definition for our purposes here, we have to admit that it is a bit disquieting. Does feedback have to tell a student his/her current status? Does feedback have to include an ultimate desired state? Does feedback have to inform about *how* to close the gap? If, for example, a teacher looks at a student working on a math problem and says, "Check your calculations," the teacher has not told the student where the student is ultimately headed, nor where the student currently is (except, perhaps, indirectly), nor how to find and correct calculation errors. We note that Ramaprasad (1983) said that the reference level could be implicit. And still, clearly the teacher has provided feedback about a current weakness. Furthermore, there does not need to be a gap between a current and desired state in order to provide feedback that is useful. Imagine some kind of performance (playing a flute piece, throwing a discus, doing a math problem) that generates the response: "That was perfect!" In this case, there is no gap, and yet, providing the information that there is no gap is probably very helpful feedback. Finally, there may be no ultimate desired state; there might just be progress. If a teacher is working with a third-grade pupil on reading comprehension, does the teacher have some notion of the student's final level of comprehension, or rather just a strong idea of what the trajectory of growth looks like in the early elementary years? Does feedback require a clear objective? These are issues perhaps best discussed in a different venue, but they are issues on our minds, and we thought it best to at least put them in play for consideration.

In looking at the research literature on feedback and in considering more than a hundred years of teaching experience among the three authors, we started our journey toward a taxonomy of feedback by generating a set of seven broad categories of feedback for consideration: developmental, topic-specific/ content, generic, corrective/editorial, discourse, dialogical, and feed-forward. We describe each briefly.

Developmental Feedback

Developmental feedback was defined by Hyatt (2005) as comments written "with the intention of aiding the student with subsequent work in relation to the current assignment" (p. 344). Hyatt stated that developmental feedback offers alternatives for the learner, tells learners what they need to address next, poses a question, or is informational, offering comments or information on related and complementary topics. Hyatt suggested that this type of feedback provides learners, in most instances, with information on how to progress with their work.

Topic-Specific/Content Feedback

The second feedback type identified from literature was topic-specific or content feedback. This feedback type was defined as providing information about "student knowledge and understanding of the topic being assessed" (Brown & Glover, 2005, p. 2). Spinks (1998) stated that this feedback relates to comments about concepts, issues, and theories that lie within and behind each topic. She suggested that these comments either provide positive reinforcement for good points made or, more often, question the writer about something lacking in relation to the topic. Topic-specific feedback generally provides very little information that would help with future assignments or writing skills (Brown & Glover, 2005).

Generic Feedback

Generic feedback was the third feedback type identified in the literature. This feedback type was defined as providing information about the structure or mechanics of writing; it was considered transferable because it suggests new approaches to future assignments (Lea & Street, 2008; Orsmond & Merry, 2011). Lea and Street referred to it as being information about syntax, punctuation, layout, or structure. Orsmond and Merry pointed out that it also allows learners to improve aspects of future work. Generic feedback relates to the structure and mechanics rather than the content of written work. Feedback about structure concerns learners' handling of an assignment at the macro level. This includes comments such as whether introductions and conclusions are correct and whether the assignment is well organized (Spinks, 1998). It also looks at the transition of ideas within and between paragraphs.

Corrective/Editorial Feedback

Corrective or editorial feedback was the fourth feedback type identified in the literature. This feedback type focuses on correcting errors (Bitchener, 2008; Price, Handley, Millar, & Donovan, 2010). It is concerned with surface-level corrections of written work. Discussion in the literature alluded to corrective feedback being either direct or indirect (Bitchener, 2008). Direct corrective feedback provides the correct linguistic form above or near the error, while indirect corrective feedback indicates in some way that an error has occurred but no explicit correction is given (Bitchener, 2008; Ellis, 2009). Examples of direct corrective feedback include crossing out of unnecessary words or phrases and insertion of words and phrases that may be missing (Bitchener, 2008). Examples of indirect corrective feedback include underlining or circling of errors with no indication of how the error could have been correctly written or, alternately, the recording of the number of errors in the margin. It is important to note that corrective feedback can also be classified as generic, depending on the nature of the feedback.

Discourse Feedback

Discourse feedback, the fifth feedback type identified in the literature, was defined as feedback that contains terminology that the teacher, rightly or wrongly, assumes the student understands, but which the student may not have understood (Hyatt, 2005). This terminology is often commonly referred to as "jargon" in an academic context. Terms considered to be discourse feedback could include "argument," "structure," "plagiarism," "explicitness," and "clarity" (Lillis & Turner, as cited in Hyatt, 2005). These are understandings and terminology that appear straightforward and clear to markers but can be confusing for students (Hyatt, 2005).

Dialogical Feedback

Dialogical feedback, the sixth feedback type identified in literature, involves sharing or reciprocity between learners and markers (Sutton, 2009; Nicol, 2010; Carless, Salter, Yang, & Lam, 2011; Tuck, 2012). It is feedback that invites further discussion. This feedback type has been defined in a variety of ways. Carless et al. (2011) described it as being an interactive exchange between the marker and the student. They stated that during this interactive exchange, "interpretations are shared, meanings negotiated, and expectations clarified" (p. 397). They suggested that this is a type of feedback that supports and informs learners while also helping them to develop self-regulation skills. Bakhtin (as cited in Sutton, 2009) referred to dialogical feedback as being a "shared enquiry which uses endless posing and answering of questions" (p. 3). He stated that open communication is used where there is no first or last word. Nicol (2010) stated that in dialogical feedback, feedback activities are shared across markers and learners.

Feed-Forward Feedback

Feed-forward feedback is the last and arguably most important type of feedback identified in the literature. This was defined as feedback that provides comments for improvement in future work (Bevan, Badge, Cann, Wilmott, & Scott, 2008; Nicol, 2010). According to Brown and Glover (2005), feed-forward feedback enhances future understanding and achievement. It provides learners with opportunities to close the gap between their current performance and their desired level. Feed-forward feedback is forward looking rather than being concerned with the work that has just been completed (Price et al., 2010). It is about "longitudinal development not only including feedback directed at supporting improvements, but also providing advice and guidance that supports slowly learnt literacies" (Knight & York, as cited in Price et al., 2010, p. 279). With feed-forward feedback, the aim is to shift away from informing learners about what is right or wrong to having them see and understand underlying reasons (Sadler, 2010). This aids learners in making judgments about their own work, while working and after (Sadler, 2010). We note that developmental feedback and feed-forward feedback are highly similar.

A Taxonomy of Written Feedback

The taxonomy presented here was developed by starting with the literature, and then taking the perspective of wanting to produce a system that would assist educators in understanding their feedback efforts to students. Such a taxonomy should allow for the ability to categorize all types of feedback and should be usable in looking at issues such as the reliability of the feedback messages that are delivered to students from one marker to another. We began with the categories from the literature, and then looked extensively at feedback messages on student papers to see how they aligned with developing categories. A more thorough description of our approach than can be provided here is found in Murray (2018).

We first developed a set of categories that were somewhat narrower than the seven described above, but broad enough that subcategories were required for several of them. The broad feedback types that were generated for the taxonomy are presented here along with brief mention of subcategories.

1. Topic-specific feedback: Information about the content of the current piece of written work. This is information that is typically irrelevant to future written work.
2. Corrective feedback: Information that corrects written work at the sentence level. This is mainly about mechanics, correcting grammar, spelling, and formatting issues.
3. Generic feedback: Information about the structure or mechanics of written work. This is information that is transferable to future written work.
4. Simple feedback about something correct: Information that simply tells writers what they have done right. There is no mention of why it is right.
5. Simple feedback about something not correct: Information that simply tells the writer what has been done wrong. There is no mention of why it is wrong.
6. Complex feedback about something correct: Information that tells the writer what has been done right and why it is right.
7. Complex feedback about something not correct: Information that tells the writer what has been done wrong and why it is wrong. There is no mention of how it could be improved.
8. Feed-forward feedback: Information that tells the writer "where to next." It tells the writer *what is right or wrong and why*. It also tells or shows the writer *how to make improvements.*
9. Connective feedback: Information that connects the writer back to a previous feedback comment made in either the current essay or a past essay.
10. Dialogical feedback: Information where the marker tries to connect with the writer through posing a question. The marker asks the writer to think more deeply about something to do with content or another part of written work.
11. Personal feedback (three types): Information that is personalized to the writer by using the student's name, by using "you" or "your," or personalized to the marker by using "I" or "My."
12. Positive feedback (feedback that offers praise): Information that is positive, using a friendly tone that is encouraging.

13. Negative feedback (feedback that is critical or discouraging): Information that is negative in tone and often discouraging to the student.
14. Neutral feedback: Information that is considered neither positive nor negative or that is considered to be both positive and negative.
15. Nondescript feedback: Information that uses symbols only with no explanation in words for the symbols used. Symbols are used to simplify the feedback.
16. Discourse feedback: Information that uses academic words that students may not understand.

Consistency in Provision of Feedback across Different Markers

Having developed a system for coding written feedback, we next pursued the question of whether the formative feedback that markers provide is consistent from one marker to the next. That is, does the help that is provided to students to improve their work depend mostly on what their demonstrated needs are, or rather on who is providing the feedback? Do different feedback providers give different feedback? Naturally, this will vary widely across contexts, but we decided to use a setting available to us to see how this might work, and how it might be examined. This study involved looking at the feedback provided by five different markers who all taught sections of a nursing course at the tertiary level that involved developing student writing skills. Full details can be found in Murray (2018). Ethics approval for the study was obtained; all participation was voluntary and no remuneration or reward was given for participation. There were three basic components to the study. The first component involved looking at whether different evaluators could reliably code feedback comments according to the taxonomy described above. The second component consisted of looking at the interrater reliability of five different markers who all taught in the same first-year course marking a random sample of five papers from the course. The third component consisted of looking at an additional eight papers from each of the five markers to see if their marking of the interrater sample was consistent with their typical course marking. These three approaches are explained in more detail as they are presented.

Coding Reliability

The first question concerned whether the coding system could be used consistently to code feedback. To assess this, the lead author in this chapter and a research assistant each coded two research papers using the coding scheme. Using Cohen's kappa, initial interrater reliability (Bryman, 2008) results showed that the measure of agreement between the two coders was very good for all but two of the sixteen categories. After adjustments to the codes, a second set of ratings showed that all the categories had a Cohen's kappa of 0.80 or above except for one. This category had a Cohen's kappa of 0.73. It was decided at this stage that no further adaptions to the feedback definitions needed to be made. The final evaluation of interrater reliability was completed through the co-coding of another eighteen assignments. The results of this final evaluation were very good across all categories in the coding schedule. The Cohen's kappa for all categories was 0.78 and above with most categories at 0.90 and above. The reliability level was considered to be of a high enough standard to allow for the taxonomy to be used in the research.

The Uses of Different Feedback Messages and Interrater Reliability

The course used in the study was an undergraduate nursing course at a tertiary institution. (It should be noted that the study used markers from both the first and second year of the program. The results were mostly consistent across the two years of the course. For space purposes, we omit the discussion of the study conducted with the second-year markers.) The first-year course focused on developing the writing skills of the students. Five of the course lecturers agreed to participate in the study (referred to here as "markers"). Each of the markers assessed their own assigned paper and four additional papers, one from each of the other four markers in the course. Names were removed from all papers in the class so the markers were blind to whose papers they were marking. They did, however, know that they were marking four extra papers for the research. The five papers that had been marked by each of the five markers became the data corpus for this component of the research. The researcher (the first author of this chapter) then coded all twenty-five papers (five original papers times five markings) using the taxonomy. All feedback comments on all papers were coded.

The goal of this analysis was to look at the distribution of various feedback categories in terms of frequency of usage and to examine how consistent markers are in providing formative feedback intended to help students develop their skills in a given area. The reliability aspect of this analysis has a degree of parallelism to classical reliability (Feldt & Brennan, 1989) and to reliability considered from a classroom assessment perspective (Smith, 2005), but differs in some important respects from each. It should be kept in mind that there really is not a notion of the "correct" feedback that should be given to a student on an assignment, as one might argue there is for a score on a summative assessment. Different markers may reasonably differ on what they feel is important. At the same time, one would think that a given assignment within the context of a given class should generate feedback consistent with the quality of the work presented and consistent with norms and expectations for performance and growth within the class. And since all markers were experienced lecturers in the course, a degree of intermarker consistency would be expected. With that caveat, we examine the feedback presented for some of the aspects of the

Table 4.1 *Means, standard deviations, and raw values for total number of comments*

Marker	n	Mean	Standard Deviation	Raw Values for Students				
				S1	S2	S3	S4	S5
1	5	24.20	7.39	19	19	27	36	20
2	5	40.60	10.57	46	43	38	52	24
3	5	50.60	9.12	43	45	48	66	51
4	5	48.60	14.87	63	29	42	64	45
5	5	40.80	12.25	43	35	39	60	27

taxonomy presented above. Space limitations prohibit presenting details for all sixteen categories within the taxonomy, so we will select what we feel are the most salient findings here. What kinds of messages do we send to students, and do we do so consistently from one marker to the next?

We begin by looking at the total number of comments that appeared on the five papers that were in the study. Table 4.1 presents the means, standard deviations, and raw counts for each marker for each paper. We include the raw counts on each variable to give an idea of variability that might not be well captured by the standard deviation in such a small sample.

We see that there is wide variability in the number of comments provided, with Marker 3 providing more than twice the number of comments as Marker 1. We also see that the number of comments on a given paper might vary by a factor of three (see column S1). Using a repeated measures analysis of variance, the differences among markers and among student papers were strongly statistically significantly different (for details, see Murray, 2018).

Turning to the feedback categories, we see that four of the feedback categories have to do with aspects of work that are either correct or incorrect, and where the feedback is either simple or complex. Hence, there can be correct/simple, correct/complex, incorrect/simple, and incorrect/complex. What we find here is that there is substantially more feedback that is simple than complex, and more feedback concerning work that is incorrect as opposed to correct. Across all markers and student assignments, there were 3.8 *simple* comments about something that was correct versus 33.6 *simple* comments about something incorrect. There were 0.68 *complex* comments about something correct versus 3.04 *complex* comments about something incorrect. Overall, there were four times as many simple comments about something incorrect than the other three categories combined, and roughly nine times as many comments about something incorrect than correct. With regard to reliability, three of the four categories (all but complex feedback about something not correct) showed significant differences among markers. Table 4.2 presents the means and standard deviations of feedback in this category. It is interesting to compare this table with Table 4.1; we see that the bulk of comments that are made by all five of the markers fall into this category. This raises the question of what message are we

Table 4.2 *Means, standard deviations, and raw values for simple feedback about something not correct*

Marker	n	Mean	Standard Deviation	Raw Values for Students				
				S1	S2	S3	S4	S5
1	5	18.00	3.87	14	17	21	23	15
2	5	34.40	10.35	32	34	35	50	21
3	5	39.40	10.06	33	36	38	57	33
4	5	41.20	12.55	53	24	36	54	39
5	5	35.00	13.65	35	29	34	57	20

sending overall to students when the bulk of what they see are short messages about errors – for some students, more than fifty times on a short essay.

Next we look at the tone of the messages sent, whether they are positive, negative, or neutral. On average, 2.68 of the comments on the papers were positive in tone; 0.88 were negative in tone; and 34.29 were neutral in tone. There were no significant differences among markers on the use of negative tone. The markers varied significantly in their use of a positive tone, with one marker using it only on average 0.60 times across the five papers, while another used it an average of 5.40 times. Markers were also significantly different on the use of neutral tone, although the differences mostly reflected the overall number of comments made by markers. Combining this information with the simple/complex, correct/incorrect data, we see that most of what students see on their papers are simple comments about something incorrect presented in a neutral tone.

Depicting Feedback Patterns via Star Graphs

To show more clearly the variability across several measures within individual assignments, star graphs were developed. A star graph is a visual representation of multiple data points for a single observation. In this case, they represent eight feedback dimensions presented at once. Each variable is placed on a scale from 0 in the center of a circle to the maximum possible value on the circumference of that circle. Thus, each variable represented is standardized against all the other variables (by making the distance from 0 to the maximum possible the same as the distance from the center of the circle to its circumference). For example, if a particular score is 7 and the maximum score is 10, then the line will go 70% of the way from the center toward the circumference. It would have the same length as if the score were 21 out of a maximum score of 30.

Star graphs are a very useful way of depicting multivariate data for a relatively small sample of observations, particularly when the observations can be characterized in some useful way, such as looking at students on one axis and markers on the second axis, as is done here. The graphs tend to be effective with between four and twelve variables to examine. It should be noted

Table 4.3 *Codes for variables in the star graphs*

Code	Variable Name
A	Total score
B	Total number of comments
C	Total number of words
D	Simple feedback about something not correct
E	Complex feedback about something not correct
F	Generic feedback
G	Feed-forward feedback
H	Neutral feedback

that the appearance and comparability of the graphs depend very much on the variables selected to depict as well as how they are ordered.

To produce the star graphs for this analysis, eight variables were chosen. The variables included total score, total number of comments, total number of words in the comments, simple feedback about something not correct, complex feedback about something not correct, generic feedback, feed-forward feedback, and neutral feedback. Simple, complex, generic, and feed-forward feedback types were chosen because they were feedback types that offered information with varying levels of depth. Neutral feedback was chosen as this was the tone of the feedback most often provided by markers. Total score, total number of comments, and total number of words were chosen even though they are not part of the taxonomy because they provided essential background information in relation to the marking. The letter codes for the variables in the star graphs can be seen in Table 4.3.

The star graphs are presented in Figure 4.2. Each graph represents a set of scores given to one student (vertical axis) by one marker (horizontal axis). Looking at the figure horizontally allows one to see how the same marker marked different papers. Looking vertically allows one to see how the same paper was marked differently by different markers.

Note: As presented in Table 4.3, the variables used here (starting at 12 o'clock and going clockwise) were: (A) grade assigned, (B) total comments made, (C) total words, (D) simple feedback on incorrect material, (E) complex feedback on incorrect material, (F) generic feedback, (G) feed-forward feedback, and (H) neutral feedback.

If we begin by looking at Student 1 (first column), we see that the five markers have rather different profiles of feedback provision. Although the total score (A) is fairly similar across markers, Marker 3 provides a lot of comments, especially compared with Markers 1 and 5. Also note that this student gets no feed-forward feedback from any of the markers. Compare this with Student 5, who gets a similar pattern from Markers 1, 2, and 5, and a second pattern from Markers 3 and 4. Markers 1, 2, and 5 gave a high total score, few comments overall, and a modicum of feed-forward feedback. Markers 3 and 4 also gave a good total score, but wrote more to Student 5 and were more likely to use neutral feedback.

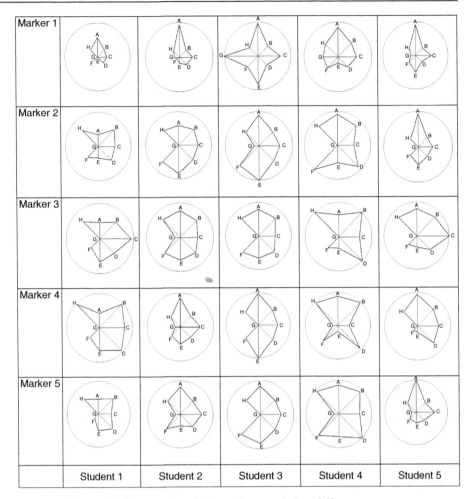

Figure 4.2 *Star graphs of the marks awarded to different papers.*

Taking the marker perspective, several issues stand out. Markers 1–3 tend to have similar profiles across papers, whereas Markers 4 and 5 show different patterns for different students. Also note that Marker 1 is the only marker that uses any level of feed-forward feedback on a consistent basis.

Marker Consistency in Other Markings

To check if the markers consistently used the same approach to marking work that they knew was not part of the main study, each marker agreed to have an additional eight papers coded from a previous assignment in the course. Thus, these papers were marked without the markers having any sense that their work was being evaluated by someone else. The feedback from these assignments was coded using the taxonomy. The means and standard deviations for each marker for each feedback type were then compared with the means and standard deviations in the original study. Also, for each feedback type the percentage per total number of comments was calculated.

The feedback was fairly consistent across all categories, with only one marker showing any variation from the marking patterns seen in the main study. Thus, we are confident that the main study did not suffer in any real degree from the Hawthorne effect, where simply being observed can change a person's behavior (Roethlisberger & Dickson, 1939).

Examples of Consistency and Differences in Messages

Before concluding, we take a brief look at feedback messages from a more qualitative perspective. Tables 4.4 and 4.5 present verbatim quotes from the five markers on identical sections of an assignment. In Table 4.4 we see that there is consistency as well as difference in the messages that have been sent. Marker 1 makes a specific criticism as well as a feed-forward message about how the material can be improved in future work. Marker 2 makes a vague comparative statement about the quality of the paragraph. Marker 3 indicates, somewhat quaintly, that the material is "muddly." Marker 4 appears to communicate the same sentiment as Marker 3, but does so in a more direct fashion. And Marker 5 seems to indicate that because the material is brief it demonstrates limited

Table 4.4 *Comments made by markers on same material, example 1*

Marker Number	Paragraph Comment
1	"you are tending to list ideas here – next time try to write a sentence of your own which explains in your own words what the direct quote means"
2	"This is a better paragraph"
3	"Muddly"
4	"This could be explained more clearly – it is a bit confusing"
5	"This is brief and therefore demonstrates limited understanding"

Table 4.5 *Comments made by markers on same material, example 2*

Marker Number	Paragraph Comment
1	"Good paragraph 1) main idea is introduced 2) good use of relevant references, 3) a concluding sentence of your own to show that you understood the topic"
2	"Good understanding shown. Well written but you need to refer to APA guidelines re citations"
3	"Muddled. I don't follow what you mean. Sentence structure not quite right. Incorrect"
4	"Good ideas in this paragraph. You explained them well"
5	"Overall a good demonstration of understanding"

understanding. So much for "To be or not to be." Although Markers 3–5 are similar in their message, Marker 2 takes an opposite view, and Marker 1 addresses form rather than content.

In looking at Table 4.5, we see a somewhat similar pattern. Marker 1 provides detailed information on why the material is good and could be used in future work. Markers 2, 4, and 5 communicate that the writer has understood the material and that this understanding has been communicated effectively. Marker 3, on the other hand, is apparently still stuck in the muddle. What we see in these two tables is a degree of consistency in the overall assessment of the material, although there are some clear disagreements as well. But we also see stylistic differences in how the markers communicate to the writer. Marker 1 is distinguishable from the other markers in that the communication is clear, specific, and oriented toward the future work of the student. In those regards, it seems to us that this is simply superior to the messages sent by the other markers in these instances.

Summary and Reflection

The development of the taxonomy allows us to talk about feedback in ways that we feel are informative and useful to those who provide feedback. For example, we find that the majority of feedback that we encountered here was simple corrective feedback provided in a neutral fashion. We also note that next to no feedback was provided that might be classified as feed-forward messages, even though the research makes clear how effective such feedback might be (Hattie & Timperley, 2007). We saw that markers varied substantially in the types of feedback they provided and the amount of feedback provided.

In looking at the lack of a personal tone or dialogic feedback in the messages sent, it occurred to us that these papers were marked without the markers knowing who the students were (as names were removed). To a degree, this creates a bit of artificiality in the study. Without knowing who the student is, what kind of progress this work represents, or what the student has been focused on learning, it is difficult to personalize the feedback messages. But this raises an interesting point. Typically, it is recommended that markers mark papers without knowing who the student is in order to ensure fairness in the marking. But – and this is a critical point – if the purpose of the assessment is formative in nature rather than summative, then the notion of not knowing who the student is becomes not only *not* a positive factor but actually detrimental to providing good feedback. Hence the formative/summative split in assessment becomes more pronounced. And we must acknowledge that the study presented here suffers to a degree because of this artificiality.

Another point of concern for us has to do with seeing the large number of neutral, simple, corrective feedback messages and the very small number of feed-forward messages. Our initial reaction was one of disappointment, but it is necessary to be somewhat tempered in that concern. We do not really know what type of feedback message is the most helpful to students, nor whether a certain approach is always best, or best for all students. Although there has been a fair amount of good work looking at the efficacy of feedback (see Hattie & Timperley, 2007; or Carless et al., 2011), there is still much work to be done. Our hope is that this taxonomy will be helpful to researchers in crafting more targeted research into the efficacy of different feedback messages.

The feedback message does not sit by itself on an assignment but is inextricably linked to the work of the student that engendered the message, the goal of the marker who constructed the message, as well as how that message is received by the student on the return of the assignment (Lipnevich, Berg, & Smith, 2016). The generation and reception of feedback involves a complex set of interactions that are inherently difficult to investigate. There are many variables to be controlled and others to be explored in any given study. But the challenges presented by studying feedback should not prevent us from making our best efforts to understand how feedback leads to learning and where it might impede learning. We owe that to those whom we endeavor to teach.

References

Bevan, R., Badge, J., Cann, A., Wilmott, C., & Scott, J. (2008). Seeing eye-to-eye? Staff and student views on feedback. *Bioscience Education*, 12, 1–15.

Bitchener, J. (2008). Evidence in support of writing corrective feedback. *Journal of Second Language Learning*, *17*, 102–118.

Bloom, B. S., Engelhart, M. D., Furst, E. J., Hill, W. H., & Krathwohl, D. R. (1956). *Taxonomy of educational objectives: The classification of educational goals. Handbook I: Cognitive domain.* New York: David McKay Company.

Brown, E., & Glover, C. (2005, September). Refocusing written feedback. Paper presented at the 13th Improving Student Learning Symposium, Sheffield Hallam University.

Bryman, A. (2008). *Social research methods.* Oxford: Oxford University Press.

Carless, D., Salter, D., Yang, M., & Lam, T. (2011). Developing sustainable feedback practices. *Studies in Higher Education*, *36*, 395–407.

Ellis, R. (2009). A typology of written corrective feedback types. *ELT Journal*, *63*, 97–107.

Feldt, L. S., & Brennan, R. L. (1989). Reliability. In R. L. Linn (Ed.), *Educational measurement* (pp. 105–146). New York: Macmillan.

Hattie, J., & Timperley, H. (2007). The power of feedback. *Review of Educational Research*, *77*, 81–112.

Hyatt, D. F. (2005). "Yes, a very good point!": A critical genre analysis of a corpus of feedback commentaries on Master of Education assignments. *Teaching in Higher Education*, *10*, 339–353.

Ivanic, R., Clark, R., & Rimmershaw, R. (2000). What am I supposed to make of this? The messages conveyed to students by tutors' written comments. In M. Lea & B. Stierer (Eds.), *Student writing in higher education: New contexts* (pp. 47–65). Buckingham, UK: Open University Press.

Lea, M., & Street, B. (2008). Student writing and staff feedback in higher education: An academic literacies approach. In M. Lea & B. Stierer (Eds.), *Student writing in higher education: New contexts* (pp. 32–46). Manchester, UK: Manchester University Press.

Lipnevich, A. A., Berg, D. A. G., & Smith, J. K. (2016). Toward a model of student response to feedback. In G. T. L. Brown & L. R. Harris (Eds.), *Handbook of human and social conditions in assessment* (pp. 169–185). Abingdon, UK: Routledge.

Murray, J. (2018). The consistency and effectiveness of written feedback provided by markers in tertiary education. Doctor of Education thesis, University of Otago.

Mutch, A. (2003). Exploring the practice of feedback to students. *Active Learning in Higher Education, 4*, 24–38.

Nicol, D. (2010). From monologue to dialogue: Improving written feedback processes in mass higher education. *Assessment & Evaluation in Higher Education, 35*, 501–517.

Orsmond, P., & Merry, S. (2011). Feedback alignment: Effective and ineffective links between tutors' and students' understanding of coursework feedback. *Assessment & Evaluation in Higher Education, 36*, 125–136.

Price, M., Handley, K., Millar, J., & O'Donovan, B. (2010). Feedback: All that effort, but what is the effect? *Assessment & Evaluation in Higher Education, 35*, 277–289.

Ramaprasad, A. (1983). On the definition of feedback. *Behavioral Science, 28*, 4–13.

Roethlisberger, F. J., & Dickson, W. (1939). *Management and the worker.* Cambridge, MA: Harvard University Press.

Sadler, R. D. (2010). Beyond feedback: Developing student capability in complex appraisal. *Assessment & Evaluation in Higher Education, 35*, 535–550.

Smith, J. K. (2005). Reconsidering reliability in classroom assessment and grading. *Educational Measurement, 22*(4), 26–33.

Spinks, S. (1998). Relating marker feedback to teaching and learning in psychology. In C. Candlin & G. Plum (Eds.), *Researching academic literacies* (pp. 148–203). Sydney, Australia: Macquarie University.

Stern, L. A., & Solomon, A. (2006). Effective faculty feedback: The road less travelled. *Assessing Writing, 11*, 22–41.

Sutton, P. (2009). Towards dialogic feedback. *Critical and Reflective Practice in Education, 1*, 1–10.

Tuck, J. (2012). Feedback-giving as social practice: Teachers' perspectives on feedback as institutional requirement, work and dialogue. *Teaching in Higher Education, 17*, 209–221.

5   Methods in Feedback Research

Gavin T. L. Brown and Lois R. Harris

Feedback is meant to inform and guide improvement (Hattie & Timperley, 2007). Researchers have been striving to understand how feedback can be optimized so it is of maximum value to learners, leading them to adaptive and growth-oriented action (Lipnevich, Berg, & Smith, 2016). Understandably, multiple methods of research have been utilized and this diversity of approaches is encouraged since each method has its own strengths and limitations. However, as Guénette (2007) notes, part of the problem in answering questions about feedback efficacy is that studies suffer from design inconsistencies. This has significant impact on review studies and meta-analyses that seek to make sense of the field because the variability in results in those reviews may arise from the variability of methods used in contributing studies. Because feedback studies use differing methods of data collection and analysis, these design differences lead to divergent results and conclusions. Thus, some of what we claim to know about feedback may be a consequence of researchers' methodological decisions, making it essential that not only are studies carefully designed but that comparability is increased.

This chapter surveys the different methods currently being used to investigate feedback in empirical studies that examine real-world processes in the design, delivery, and impact of feedback. While grounded in our own almost decade of work on the topic, this chapter is not an encyclopedic review of all studies having to do with feedback. Rather, we have surveyed the literature to identify common methods being used and for each have reported a few studies that make use of it to illustrate how it is being applied. Readers will no doubt know of others that we have not included; the goal within this chapter is simply to identify methods being used and describe some strengths and limitations for each, allowing readers to make informed methodological decisions in their own research endeavors and adopt a more critical stance toward the research that they read.

As the focus is on empirical work, we have excluded many excellent sources that are conceptual or theoretical analyses of feedback, along with the many literature reviews, so as to concentrate on the methodological choices made in individual studies. Additionally, given the chapter's focus on feedback designed to directly enhance student learning, we have also excluded studies of student feedback on or evaluations of courses, teaching, or teachers since such studies do not examine how feedback is related to student learning; instead, such studies are more properly considered institutional evaluation (e.g., Kember, Leung, & Kwan, 2002; Richardson, 2005). This exclusion includes reviews of departments or programs within institutions used as feedback for self-improvement (e.g. Maier, 2010; Schildkamp & Visscher, 2010).

We have structured this chapter first around methods used for collecting data within feedback studies and second around methods used for analysis of these data. Especially under data collection, we have taken an approach that links quantitative and qualitative methods such that the mixing of methods to overcome method effects is prioritized. This means that we are not methodological purists and in this chapter are trying to prioritize a pragmatic approach.

Data Collection

We have grouped data collection methods in descending order of researcher control. Experimental studies achieve control through random assignment of participants into treatment or control conditions, and all materials and activities administered in the treatment group are controlled by the researcher. Slightly less control occurs in quasi-experimental studies where naturally occurring groups or units are assigned to experimental treatments or not. Researchers still have control over data collection when they stimulate participants with highly structured processes such as closed-response questionnaires or stimulated recall of previous events. Free-response techniques (e.g., focus groups, semi-structured interviews, or draw-a-picture evaluations) give the researcher control over the general content of the data, while participants are able to freely respond as they see fit. Observation of naturally occurring data (e.g., video-recordings of classroom activities or traces in course books) may reflect the pinnacle of ecological validity because researchers do not prompt or solicit such data, but much data may not be relevant to the empirical goals of the study.

Experiments

Experimental studies exercise the greatest control over conditions and participants by randomly assigning members of a sample, derived from a population, to one or more conditions that experience different processes (Campbell & Stanley, 1963). It is presumed in the random assignment process that differences between individuals are canceled out in the group membership; that is, the average ability, attitude, or background variables are equivalent between treatment and control conditions. Feedback experiments generally control either the content of feedback or the processes of how feedback is implemented. A few studies have actually developed interventions and experimentally tested whether learners can be taught to provide better feedback.

As an example of the kind of control exhibited in experimental studies, consider the design of Ashwell's (2000) experiment where he manipulated the content of feedback foreign-language students received on drafts one and two of a composition. Students were randomly assigned into four conditions. The conditions were: (1) content feedback (draft 1) followed by form feedback (draft 2); (2) form (draft 1) before content (draft 2); (3) mixed form and content feedback (drafts 1 and 2); and (4) no feedback. Statistical analysis of data indicated that there were no significant differences between the four conditions in relation to changes in content. Students receiving feedback did improve their accuracy significantly more than those in the control group; however, the particular pattern of feedback they received did not appear to matter.

Other examples of studies that have manipulated different kinds of feedback include Chase and Houmanfar (2009); Butler, Godbole, and Marsh (2013); Harks, Rakoczy, Hattie, Besser, and Klieme (2014); Narciss et al. (2014); and Pekrun, Cusack, Murayama, Elliot, and Thomas (2014). Experimental studies that have examined the process of feedback delivery include Corbalan, Kester, and van Merriënboer (2009); Lipnevich and Smith (2009b); Cho and MacArthur (2010); Harber, Gorman, Gengaro, Butisingh, Tsang, and Ouellete (2012); Bayerlein (2014); and Hamer, Purchase, Luxton-Reilly, and Denny (2015). Some studies have mixed process and content factors of feedback, including Strijbos, Narciss, and Dünnebier (2010) and Vollmeyer and Rheinberg (2005). Perhaps on the edge of future research is the experimental study that examined, using fMRI, the brain activity of participants when given bogus performance information within the neuroscanner (Kim, Lee, Chung, & Bong, 2010). This study found that brain regions associated with negative affect were activated when norm-referenced feedback was given to low-competence participants, while the same region was activated when criterion-referenced feedback was given to high-competence participants. Further, they found that performance-approach goal scores correlated positively with activation in the negative emotion brain areas during norm-referenced feedback. Although negative emotions can be activating (Pekrun, Goetz, Titz, & Perry, 2002), the authors use these results to caution against the use of norm-referenced feedback. Clearly, further research into this matter is required.

These studies allow reasonably strong claims to be made as to which factors have the greatest impact through the power of the random assignment of reasonably large to large samples of participants to a variety of controlled conditions. Replication studies and use of multiple dependent measures also contribute to the strength of such claims. Such highly controlled designs are often accompanied by sophisticated analytic processes to establish the impact of demographic variables as moderating or mediating variables (path or structural equation modeling) and evaluation of mean differences (multiple analysis of variance or multiple regression).

A critique of such research is that results in a controlled study do not necessarily generalize to natural environments (e.g., classrooms) where multiple factors simultaneously impinge on the planned treatment, which itself may not necessarily be implemented with fidelity. This contrast between 'in vitro' experimental studies and 'in vivo' natural environments can mean that results do not translate into the real world (Autoimmunity Research Foundation, 2012; Zumbo, 2015). Even when experimental studies do take place in natural classroom environments, it is virtually impossible to control for all differences as there are so many potential points of variation, even between hypothetically comparable class groups (e.g., enthusiasm of the teacher, quality of classroom relationships between teachers and students). A further complication arises in the ethics of some students not receiving a treatment that is believed to benefit all; variations such as delayed or counterbalanced treatments need to be considered.

A second important issue with these studies is that, from an inspection of the listed studies, few are true replication studies in which the same methods and variables are used. This means that an important aspect of modern science is missing – replication of experiments demonstrates the robustness of results (National Research Council, 2002; Simons, 2014). Although the frequency of replications is rising (Makel, Plucker, & Hegarty, 2012), there is still little academic incentive to conduct or publish replication studies (Neuliep, 1990; Earp & Trafimow, 2015), and arguably too few occur to achieve accurate measurement of effect (Hunter, 2001). These concerns are raised in the discipline of psychology, while levels of concern about the same issue in the field of education are somewhat less prominent. Hence, there is a need to substantiate that findings reported as statistically significant are in fact significant and not artifacts of chance (i.e., all statistically significant results could be the 'chance' event) and that they may legitimately be generalizable to other similar environments. Successful replications seem to occur most often when the original researcher is kept in the research team (Makel, Plucker, & Hegarty, 2012). Obviously, for any kind of replication to be possible, a highly detailed explanation of procedures must be included in reports. Standards as to how experimental studies need to be conducted should be considered by all seeking to use this method (Lindsay, 2015). Nonetheless, the existence of meta-analytic summaries around psychological processes, including feedback (Kluger & DeNisi, 1996; Hattie & Timperley, 2007), does support the idea that sufficient information about how a phenomenon has been studied exists to allow replicable study, even if the findings differ; otherwise, there would not be sufficient comparable studies of a phenomenon to reach any conclusions about the robustness of effect (Smith, Smith, & Smith, 2017).

Quasi-Experiments

Similar to the experiment is the quasi-experiment in which naturally occurring samples are randomly assigned to controlled conditions (Shadish & Luellen, 2006). These studies exercise control over the intervention but not over who is within each group, meaning that differences between groups may preexist that can impact results. Normally, techniques like analysis with covariates can help to account for such preexisting differences.

A strength of quasi-experimental feedback studies is that they are more likely to take place within classrooms, meaning they may more accurately emulate real-world feedback conditions than laboratory experiments. For example, in Gielen, Peeters, Dochy, Onghena, and Struyven's (2010) quasi-experimental study, they adopted a repeated measure design to examine if peer feedback was more effective if the student had to reflect on and write a response to the peer feedback or not. The study drew on forty-three year 7 (sixth-grade) students all taught by the same teacher, but belonging to two different class groupings, and found no difference in the quality of the final student products based on the two conditions. Another example is Gan and Hattie's (2014) quasi-experimental intervention study where one naturally occurring group of students was taught how to give feedback with a parallel group acting as control. The study found that prompted peer feedback had a significant effect on the number of comments students made related to knowledge of errors, suggestions for improvement, and process-level feedback. Clearly, as such studies have great potential for better identifying what may be effective within in vivo classroom situations, it is hoped that more studies adopt such a design in the future as it is currently one of the least represented methods.

Nonexperimental Methods

A wide variety of nonexperimental data collection techniques has been used in the study of feedback. These include interviews (including stimulated recall), focus groups, surveys, free response, observations, collection of traces, and case studies. Under this label, we include studies that have a treatment but no control group. For example, similar to an experimental study of not reporting grades (Lipnevich & Smith, 2009b), Sendziuk (2010) reported, without a control group, feedback without grades being given to students who then self-assessed their own writing, with subsequent statistical comparison of peer and tutor marking.

Although nonexperimental studies lack random assignment and control groups, they can vary in the degree of control researchers exert. Clearly, surveys require considerable control over the design of data collection tools (i.e., the survey questions and response formats) and the selection of the participating sample. In contrast, semi-structured interviews and focus groups give the researcher control over what task or questions will be posed but much less control over how participants respond or what they substantively contribute. Free-response mechanisms are deliberately low-control data collection techniques as the researcher explicitly directs the participants to respond in an individual way (e.g., consider the variety of student responses to a poem in the film *Dead Poets Society*). Observations of naturally occurring data or inspection of traces left behind by teachers or students give control to the researcher only in terms of which behaviors or objects will be selected for analysis.

Survey Studies. A large number of survey studies about feedback have been conducted, particularly around participant understandings of and attitudes toward feedback and/or their feedback experiences. Effective surveying generally depends on large samples drawn from a clearly defined population. There is greater power to generalize when the sample is fully representative of all key aspects of the population and when the researcher selects participants rather than relying on a convenience sample. The issue of how many participants comprise an appropriate sample size is complex and outside the scope of this chapter. Interested readers will find some general guidance from NIST/SEMA-TECH (2003) and Raosoft (2017).

Survey methods are frequently used within the feedback literature. For example, our own work has surveyed students (Harris, Brown, & Harnett, 2014b, N=193; Brown, Peterson, & Yao, 2016, N=278) and teachers (Brown, Harris, & Harnett, 2012, N=518) concerning their understandings of feedback. Indeed, the development of a standardized self-report questionnaire about the function and nature of feedback has been the subject of a series of studies among New Zealand students (Irving, Petersen, & Brown, 2007, 2008; Brown, Irving, & Peterson, 2009; N=705, 536, 499, respectively). Other large to reasonably large feedback surveys include a study of feedback perceptions among Cantonese-speaking students and teachers (N=1740, 460, respectively, Carless, 2006), a survey of Portuguese university students (Flores, Veiga Simão, Barros, & Pereira, 2015, N=502, in two sites), and a two-study survey of Australian university students (Lizzio & Wilson, 2008, Study 1, N=57; Study 2, N=277). In contrast, smaller-scale surveys include Robinson, Hope, and Holyoak (2013) with 166 university students; Jodaie, Farrokhi, and Zoghi (2011) with 100 high school students and 30 teachers; Bayerlein (2014) with 103 undergraduate and 30 postgraduate students; and Bevan, Badge, Cann, Willmott, and Scott (2008) with just 45 students. Clearly, inconsistency in results can arise from the differences in the design of survey questions, response scales, and samples. A constant threat to the validity of claims is the large errors in reported survey results attributable to smaller sample sizes; simply put, more is better in survey work (Marsh, Hau, Balla, & Grayson, 1998).

Interviews. An obviously direct way of collecting information concerning people's perspectives, experiences, opinions, attitudes, and beliefs about feedback is to ask them. The interview allows participants to state directly for themselves their own thoughts, ideas, and emotions. Even quite young interviewees are able to answer questions about intentions, attitudes, thoughts, and experiences. Obviously, interviews that follow a more rigid schedule of questions or topics administered in the same way (de Leeuw, 2008) will generate more comparable information across informants. However, relaxing the structure and sequence of the interview will generate more natural and potentially more insightful responses (Brenner, 2006) and allow interviewers to ask probing questions and follow up on statements of interest. Regardless, institutional review boards or ethics committees will probably require at least a schedule of 'semi-structured' questions to establish that the study will do no harm.

The majority of interview studies about feedback include relatively small numbers of participants. The number of interviewees needed to create a sense of saturation concerning the range of responses is difficult to estimate and the answer seems to depend on many factors, including pragmatic issues of time needed to collect and analyze data (Baker & Edwards, 2012). Nonetheless, recommendations seem to gravitate to at least twenty or thirty interviewees. Given that small sample sizes are common, how participants are chosen is particularly important. While some sampling strategies (e.g., selecting prospective interviewees from a larger pool based on particular criteria; Harris & Brown, 2016) may help increase the generalizability of findings, caution must be taken when drawing conclusions based on any kind of convenience sample.

There is concern about the potential influence of the interviewer, whose presence and manner may inadvertently influence the informant to say what the person believes is expected by the interviewer, sometimes referred to as socially desirable responding. As interviewer influence can range from mild and inadvertent to oppressive and controlling, researchers must attend carefully to the way knowledge is constructed within an interview context and minimize the potential of interviewer distortion in the interview. The type and nature of the interviewer impact should be acknowledged and considered when interpreting results (Kvale, 2002). The challenge is how to elicit appropriate information without distorting data.

Interview studies commonly focus on the perspectives of teachers (e.g., Bailey & Garner, 2010; Price, Handley, Millar, & O'Donovan, 2010), students (e.g., Tunstall & Gipps, 1996a; Higgins, Hartley, & Skelton, 2002; Bruno & Santos, 2010; Gamlem & Smith, 2013), or both (e.g., Tjeerdsma, 1997). For example, one study of forty-eight UK university lecturers showed that the idiosyncratic perceptions and practices of the lecturers did not reflect the intentions of institutional policies (Bailey & Garner, 2010). Because this study was situated in one institution, it is difficult to know if the results generalize beyond this context, though such an expectation seems probable.

An interesting method that potentially reduces interviewer effects is the use of stimulated recall as a trigger for the interview. Recall can be stimulated with samples of previously given or received written feedback or audio or audiovisual recordings of a feedback situation; these real-life prompts then become the basis of discussion focused on aspects that seem relevant to the theme of the interview (Dempsey, 2010). Examples of studies that use stimulated recall around feedback experiences are Hargreaves (2013) and Van der Kleij, Adie, and Cumming (2016).

Another useful interview style to consider is the think-aloud. Think-aloud protocols require that individuals conduct a task while verbalizing their thoughts, reasons, and reactions while doing a task (Kuusela & Paul, 2000). This information provides insights into the underlying reasons for why participants do what they do (e.g., Why might teachers provide particular feedback? Why might students respond to feedback in particular ways?). No doubt the challenge with 'talking about thinking while doing' is that it depends on the ability of participants to be aware of their thinking and their skill at putting those thoughts into spoken words. Clearly, this requires significant skills and substantial training and prompting to ensure participants do not 'go quiet' while they concentrate on a novel task or alternately begin to make inferences about their thinking instead of reporting their actual thoughts (Ericsson & Simon, 1980). At least one think-aloud study has investigated what students do with the feedback they are given (Handley, Price, & Millar, 2011).

Focus Groups. Increasing the number of participants by creating a focus group can also potentially decrease the influence of the moderator. The focus group method aims to elicit open and rich responses by allowing participants to interact and discuss the topic; because of this group interaction, the discussion is potentially less interviewer centered (Kitzinger, 1994; Morgan 1997; Rabiee, 2004). Such free-flowing conversations generate data based on group interactions that are different from the sum of individual contributions in an interview setting. Focus group discussions about feedback have included teachers (Irving, Harris, & Peterson, 2011), as well as primary (Burnett & Mandel, 2010), secondary (Peterson & Irving, 2008), and university students (Poulos & Mahony, 2008; Lipnevich & Smith, 2009a). Obviously, the makeup of focus groups matters; preexisting relationships among group members may make some participants hesitant to share particular opinions, while others may be more open due to friendship. An important element to a well-constructed focus group is having a starter task that ensures all members have something to contribute, reducing the impact of negative social practices, such as 'loafing' or 'free-riding,' collusion, friendship bias, or decibel control of discussion (Pond & Ul-Haq, 1997). For example, an interesting free-response technique that has been used as a focus group task is to ask students to draw a picture of their own personal perception of the phenomenon of interest (Harris, Harnett, & Brown, 2009). The fact that the picture is personal and usually not artfully drawn (unless by art students) means it requires explanation and discussion, the very grist of focus groups.

Observation. Gaining access to learning spaces and processes in real-world classroom settings is the antithesis to the laboratory environment of the experiment. Actual behaviors being observed are generally naturalistic once those being observed are accustomed to the presence of the observer or camera. However, researchers have to exercise control of observation by developing sampling systems (i.e., How often should particular behaviors or events be recorded? Whose actions (e.g., the teacher, particular students) are the focus of observation?). Mechanisms for recording data (e.g., checklists; see an example in Voerman, Meijer, Korthagen, & Simons, 2012) have to be developed and checked for validity and reliability. The downside, unsurprisingly, is that the phenomenon of interest may not occur in front of the observer or may not occur very often when it is not elicited by the researcher. This means that observation depends on the visibility and sufficient presence of the behavior of interest to make the observation of value. Length of observation varies: Voerman et al. (2012) observed only one lesson per teacher to examine feedback practices, while Björklund Boistrup (2010) attended all mathematics lessons for the entire week.

However, even if many observations take place, there is still the potential of researcher impact on results (e.g., the potential that Margaret Mead was deceived by her informants; Kawulich, 2005). Observation studies of classroom feedback processes often are augmented by complementary methods (e.g., interviews or focus groups) to ensure that the observed behaviors are interpreted from subject rather than researcher perspectives (e.g., Harris & Brown, 2013). Observed data are often a powerful starting point for stimulated recall interviews, such as the ones discussed in the previous section.

Traces. A related data collection technique to observation is the study of the traces or artifacts teachers and students create as a result of their normal classroom practice (e.g., comments left on essays or course books). The collection and analysis of traces left behind in natural processes is an old and well-established tradition in social science research (Webb, Campbell, Schwartz, Sechrest, & Grove, 1981). These traces are created naturally without any input from the researcher and so have great validity, although sampling bias can occur (e.g., when participants select only what they consider to be their 'best' examples to share). Manual trace data dominate research into feedback currently, with much arising from written teacher feedback comments (Hyland & Hyland, 2001; Matsumura, Patthey-Chavez, Valdes, & Garnier, 2002; Lee, 2007; Ruiz-Primo & Li, 2013). Similar data can come from student written comments to their peers or themselves as part of peer or self-assessment practices (Harris, Brown, & Harnett, 2014a).

Research that analyzes examples of feedback online has also gained popularity, made possible by increased computer and social media usage alongside the development of digital tools that allow researchers to have access to significant information about the person's online behaviors (e.g., time spent, places visited, and so on). Two examples of digital log files as a way of exploring how students use feedback can be seen in Narciss et al.'s (2014) use of log files recorded in a web-based intelligent learning environment to trace student actions on a task following varying types of feedback and Harper and Brown's (2017) use of log files of students' voluntary use of hints in an online teaching and testing resource. These digital traces are the core material of 'big data' research (Hofferth et al., 2017) and may be a potential source for further research.

Case Studies. While studying a large sample of individuals or sites has potential to create robust estimates of parameters, it is sometimes useful to examine in great detail how things take place in a much narrower sample of situations. Researchers often choose to study smaller samples much more intensively with multiple methods and modes of data collection. Such rich but small-scale investigations, often called case studies, may be particularly valuable to feedback research because the complexities of how feedback works are still being clarified. Case studies involve purposefully selecting a small sample of individuals or sites that are studied intensively, often making use of multiple methods so as to create a deep understanding of the complexity of factors acting on a phenomenon (Yin, 2006).

For example, Harris and Brown (2013) selected three teachers out of a pool of twenty-six interviewees and intensively studied their classroom assessment and feedback practices. Data collection involved video-recorded observations, teacher interviews, and student focus groups. Other examples of case study include Bruno and Santos (2010), who studied three middle school students' experiences of written feedback via interviews with the students, observation of them in their classroom environment, and analyses of their assignments; Hyland (2003), who studied six students via interviews and analysis of teacher feedback on their written work; and Li and Barnard (2011), who studied the feedback beliefs and practices of a group of tutors via survey, individual interviews, 'think aloud' and stimulated recall sessions, and focus group interviews. This approach, especially when combined with multiple observations or data types, can create powerful and insightful descriptions of how processes in a domain take place.

Mixing Methods

Throughout this grand tour of data collection methods, many studies use more than one method. This is popularly known as mixed methods (Johnson & Onwuegbuzie, 2004), because methods that have different assumptions about knowledge are brought together to investigate a phenomenon. However, it may be better to think of this approach as 'mixing' methods (Brannen, 1992) since each method is integral in itself and, as yet, there do not appear to be methods that somehow inherently cross paradigmatic boundaries. The case studies described above mix methods; likewise, several studies have used two or more methods sequentially to understand feedback. For example, Lizzio and Wilson (2008) used content analysis of student comments to create a construct frame for a subsequent survey study.

Mixing methods has a long provenance in multimethod research (Brewer & Hunter, 1989), where multiple methods, usually drawn from a pool of philosophically aligned methods (e.g., surveys with multiple batteries), are used to investigate a phenomenon. More recently, mixing of methods has focused on crossing paradigmatic boundaries so as to increase the probability of fully understanding a phenomenon by approaching it from multiple perspectives, multiple informants, and multiple data sources. The logic of triangulation is invoked as a rationale for mixing methods, though considerable caution needs to be exercised in believing that contrasting methods will deliver corroboration (Smith, 2006; Harris & Brown, 2010). Nonetheless, increasingly, feedback studies are using multiple or mixed methods to overcome method artifacts.

Data Analysis

Having collected the data, the researcher must turn that raw information into interpretation using systematic, rigorous methods of analysis. Generally, the goal is to document procedures such that readers can verify the credibility of subsequent interpretation. Data analytic techniques can be grouped into two major classes: content classification and statistical analysis.

While statistical techniques of analysis may be governed by conventions and rules, there is still a subjective element in deciding which technique to apply and which standards to adopt (Brown, 2016). Hence, a sufficient warrant for findings depends on credible techniques of analysis.

Content Classification Methods

A variety of classification methods exist. All these methods require analysts to assign a categorical attribution to elements of the raw data (Bartholomew, Henderson, & Marcia, 2000). Rules or rubrics for assigning data objects to classifications can be derived from a priori theoretical categories (i.e., deductive analysis) or from a close inspection of the data (i.e., inductive analysis).

Deductive analysis of data involves mapping aspects of the raw data to preexisting categories derived from a theory or model of how the phenomenon should work (Elo & Kyngäs, 2008). A large body of inductive methods exist (e.g., grounded theory, phenomenography, content analysis, thematic analysis, etc.), but there are many similar features to such methods (Thomas, 2006). General principles involve discovering thematic categories that efficiently and effectively group common phenomena within the data and which allow for a simplification of the data (Braun & Clarke, 2006). Validation of classification can be determined through having two or more analysts conduct coding of a sufficient sample to establish a measure of consensus between analysts (e.g., percentage agreement) or consistency of classification (e.g., kappa or Krippendorf coefficients) (Stemler, 2004).

Deductive Analysis. A number of studies have adopted preexisting feedback frameworks and used them to guide analysis of feedback data. For example, Hattie and Timperley's (2007) four levels of feedback framework (i.e., task, process, self-regulation, and person) has been used to classify the types of feedback students give each other (Harris, Brown, & Harnett, 2014a) and teachers give students (Harris, Harnett, & Brown, 2013). Other studies that used the Hattie and Timperley framework to guide analysis include Björklund Boistrup (2010), Gan and Hattie (2014), and Ajjawi and Boud (2017). Another framework for coding feedback was developed by Tunstall and Gipps (1996b), and this has also been used by many other authors (e.g., Parr and Timperley, 2010). These are just two of the frameworks available for other researchers to draw on, with a further example being Chi's (1996) four types of feedback: corrective, reinforcing, didactic, and suggestive (Tseng & Tsai, 2007).

Inductive Analysis. As mentioned earlier, a large number of inductive techniques have been used to investigate feedback. The rationale for this choice of technique is not always obvious, and, unsurprisingly, results are extremely variable since quite different techniques are used. An example of a reasonably replicable technique arising from the research goals is seen in the work of Van der Kleij et al. (2016), who, among other things, measured the length of each feedback conversation and counted the number of words spoken by teacher and student, along with the number of times each person stopped the replayed video recording to comment on what was happening in the prerecorded student–teacher feedback conversation. More difficult to replicate are such techniques as content analysis (e.g., Mayring, 2000; Weaver, 2006), as used by Lizzio and Wilson (2008); phenomenology (e.g., Groenewald, 2004), as used by Orsmond and Merry (2011); or phenomenography (e.g., Marton, 1981; Harris, 2011), as used by McLean, Bond, and Nicholson (2015). The adoption of these techniques can allow novel and important discoveries about not just categories of interest but also the relationship of such phenomena to each other. The challenge facing inductive analysis is to establish credibility in the process of classification and the potential replicability of the classification systems. Some inductive analytic studies in feedback report the development of robust coding schema and the testing of the schema through the ability of independent judges to reasonably replicate each other's classification (e.g., Lizzio & Wilson, 2008; Nelson & Schunn, 2009; Parr & Timperley, 2010), but many could be improved via more rigorous reporting of the coding process.

Statistical Analytic Methods

Survey and experimental studies about feedback tend to depend heavily on statistics to make sense of results. A major goal in statistical analysis is to identify whether the observed results are unlikely to be due to chance (null hypothesis significance testing) and how large and substantive the results are (i.e., effect size) (Field, 2016). A common early step in many statistical studies is the evaluation and determination of measurement quality, which is a substantial challenge when attempting to grapple with psychological phenomena (Crocker, 2006). The evaluation of scale attributes assumes that multiple indicators are needed to reduce error in measuring complex phenomena and is often summarized, albeit inappropriately (Sijtsma, 2009; Teo & Fan, 2013), through Cronbach's alpha estimate of internal reliability, and more robustly through model to data fit indices generated by confirmatory factor analysis (Bandalos & Finney, 2010). Once robust measurement properties are established (e.g., scale reliability, fit to the data, validation evidence for the constructs being measured), many studies go further into determining whether paths between constructs are both statistically and practically significant. While conventional regression analysis can achieve this, structural equation modeling is a more powerful causal-correlational analysis approach since it retains latent structures and errors and allows for correlated predictors and outcomes (Hoyle, 1995). The causal paths introduced in such analysis, of course, are not proven in nonexperimental studies. Alternately, rather than establish regressions among constructs, analysis may examine whether there are differences in responses (e.g., mean scores or parameter estimates) between participant groups (i.e., analysis of variance and invariance testing, respectively). The use of such techniques can test empirically the credibility of theoretical claims about feedback and generate hypotheses about the relationship of feedback factors to outcomes.

Large-scale survey studies that have used a combination of factor analytic techniques (to establish measurement properties) and structural equation modeling (to establish potentially causal relationships among constructs) include Burnett (2002); Brown, Harris, & Harnett (2012); Rakoczy et al. (2013); Harks et al. (2014); Harris, Brown, and Harnett (2014b); and Brown, Peterson, and Yao (2016). A simpler approach than structural equation modeling is to correlate factor scores once these are determined (e.g., Lizzio & Wilson, 2008). This approach reduces the latent score to a single scale score and does not establish directionality in paths. Correlations, which are nondirectional linear relationships, can be used to identify relationships, without suggesting causal direction (Nelson & Schunn, 2009; Parr & Timperley, 2010).

An even simpler approach is to determine a set of factors or scales and generate mean scale scores for participants to examine differences between time, group, or condition. Reporting the means and standard deviations can permit eyeball inspection as to whether the means differ (Tang & Harrison, 2011), but a more sophisticated approach is to use an inferential technique such as analysis of variance (Nesbit & Burton, 2006) and multivariate analysis of variance (Kim, Lee, Chung, & Bong, 2010; Kerssen-Griep & Witt, 2012) not only to determine whether the observed differences are unlikely to occur by chance but also to establish the size of difference after taking into account the variability of scores within each group. When noncontinuous variables are used (e.g., proportion of feedback falling into certain categories), statistical methods exist (e.g., McNemar's test) to determine whether there are differences in the distribution of these categorizations between times or groups (e.g., Parr & Timperley, 2010).

Conclusion

This examination of methods used in feedback studies may read somewhat like a research methods textbook, but the concerns readers should have about research results often have to do with researchers ignoring well-established threats to the validity of their claims due to the methodological choices made. What this means is that editors and reviewers of studies need to insist that authors provide enough detail about methodological choices to permit critical evaluation and potential replication. While statistical analytic studies are potentially easy to critique (e.g., if a parametric test is applied to nonparametric data), it is somewhat more challenging to critique subjective coding if authors simply report that "themes emerged from the data." The importance of clarity and completeness in reporting of methods decisions cannot be overemphasized. It also seems clear from this review that the method issues raised in the general literature apply equally to research into feedback.

An important aspect of research into feedback that we have not seen extensively in the field is attention to the importance and influence of cultural context on results. It is highly likely that there are differences in how various groups respond to methods that impact results (e.g., starting values for Asian groups may be more modest than Western groups on items having to do with self-evaluations of behaviors), yet very few studies include participants from different countries (an exception is Furneaux, Paran, & Fairfax, 2007). Hence, the comparability of data collection methods across contexts may be much more problematic than expected. Translation and adaptation of instruments across languages and contexts is not guaranteed by 'translation, back-translation' procedures since the meaning of a phenomenon in a different context is not necessarily captured by literal rather than functional equivalence logic (Werner & Campbell, 1973). Our own study with a self-report survey inventory of teacher conceptions of feedback generated completely different analytic structures and incompatible models between New Zealand and Louisiana, in the United States, which was attributed to the very different policy frameworks around assessment and feedback (Brown, Harris, O'Quin, & Lane, 2017). This means that identical replication is probably an extremely laudable but potentially impossible goal when attempting to cross large cultural, social, or policy boundaries. This suggests that there will always be discrepancy and inconsistency in results; it will always probably 'depend.' This issue means that research users must be careful about how research findings are applied in a different context.

Nevertheless, researchers have to make decisions about the 'best' or most appropriate method. Going back to the big questions of what we need to know about feedback in this context is perhaps the most defensible way to approach feedback research. It is outside the scope of this chapter to decide what those questions are, but we encourage researchers to consider: What are the big questions we need to answer about feedback? What kinds of methodologies or designs might be appropriate to investigate these questions? What new or innovative approaches might be worth adopting? Considering questions around 'what we know we don't know' would be a good start. For example, we suggest that the field needs a deeper understanding of what students actually do or do not do with feedback and why those choices are made. The teaching and curriculum world is creating new modes of feedback delivery (e.g., computerized feedback, feedback from peers/self), and how these can be structured to ensure positive impact on learning is still uncertain. The one fMRI study suggests that potential insights into the effect of feedback can be found using this high technology approach, though the validity of such studies is still in question (Vul, Harris, Winkielman, & Pashler, 2009).

It is clear in reading the literature that feedback elicits highly personal responses, partly because feedback is so complex (Lipnevich, Berg, & Smith, 2016). Having a clear understanding of the participants in a study is important if we hope to make any claims about what is or is not effective. Participants (i.e., students, teachers, etc.) are not homogenous groups; hence, methods need to be able to identify and account for within-group variation.

Our conclusion is that the world of feedback research has a long way to go to establish robust and consistent findings due, in part, to the lack of clarity in reporting how research was conducted and the lack of consistency in methods, samples, and tools across studies. The field is being enriched by many small and exploratory studies, but many claims about feedback are not well and consistently supported by data. It is necessary that educational decisions about feedback are informed by approaches that are empirically supported rather than ideologically driven. It is hoped this review will contribute to the development of a more robustly described and conducted body of research into feedback. We encourage increased scrutiny from research users, which will lead to more evidence-based feedback strategies being implemented in schools for the benefit of learners.

References

Ajjawi, R., & Boud, D. (2017). Researching feedback dialogue: An interactional analysis approach. *Assessment & Evaluation in Higher Education, 42*(2), 252–265.

Ashwell, T. (2000). Patterns of teacher response to student writing in a multiple-draft composition classroom: Is content feedback followed by form feedback the best method? *Journal of Second Language Writing, 9*(3), 227–257.

Autoimmunity Research Foundation. (2012). Differences between in vitro, in vivo, and in silico studies. Retrieved from http://mpkb.org/home/patients/assessing_litera ture/in_vitro_studies.

Bailey, R., & Garner, M. (2010). Is the feedback in higher education assessment worth the paper it is written on? Teachers' reflections on their practices. *Teaching in Higher Education, 15*(2), 187–198.

Baker, S. E., & Edwards, R. (2012). *How many qualitative interviews is enough? Expert voices and early career reflections on sampling and cases in qualitative research.* Southampton, UK: National Centre for Research Methods. Retrieved from http://eprints.ncrm.ac.uk/2273/4/how_many_interviews.pdf.

Bandalos, D. L., & Finney, S. J. (2010). Factor analysis: Exploratory and confirmatory. In G. R. Hancock & R. O. Mueller (Eds.), *The reviewer's guide to quantitative methods in the social sciences* (pp. 93–114). New York: Routledge.

Bartholomew, K., Henderson, A. J. Z., & Marcia, J. E. (2000). Coded semistructured interviews in social psychological research. In H. T. Reis & C. M. Judd (Eds.), *Handbook of research methods in social and personality psychology* (pp. 286–312). Cambridge: Cambridge University Press.

Bayerlein, L. (2014). Students' feedback preferences: How do students react to timely and automatically generated assessment feedback? *Assessment & Evaluation in Higher Education, 39*(8), 916–931.

Bevan, R., Badge, J., Cann, A., Willmott, C., & Scott, J. (2008). Seeing eye-to-eye? Staff and student views on feedback. *Bioscience Education, 12*(1), 1–15.

Björklund Boistrup, L. (2010). Assessment discourse in mathematics classrooms: A multimodal social semiotic study. PhD dissertation, Stockholm University.

Brannen, J. (Ed.). (1992). *Mixing methods: Qualitative and quantitative research.* Aldershot, UK: Avebury Ashgate Publishing.

Braun, V., & Clarke, V. (2006). Using thematic analysis in psychology. *Qualitative Research in Psychology, 3*(2), 77–101.

Brenner, M. E. (2006). Interviewing in educational research. In J. L. Green, G. Camilli, & P. B. Elmore (Eds.), *Handbook of complementary methods in education research* (pp. 357–370). Mahwah, NJ: Lawrence Erlbaum Associates.

Brewer, J., & Hunter, A. (1989). *Multimethod research: A synthesis of styles*. Newbury Park, CA: SAGE.

Brown, G. T. L. (2016). The qualitative secret within quantitative research: It's not just about numbers. In C. J. McDermott & Kožuh, B. (Eds.), *Modern approaches in social and educational research* (pp. 33–42). Los Angeles, CA: Antioch University.

Brown, G. T. L., Harris, L. R., & Harnett, J. (2012). Teacher beliefs about feedback within an assessment for learning environment: Endorsement of improved learning over student well-being. *Teaching and Teacher Education*, *28*(7), 968–978.

Brown, G. T. L., Harris, L. R., O'Quin, C., & Lane, K. E. (2017). Using multi-group confirmatory factor analysis to evaluate cross-cultural research: Identifying and understanding non-invariance. *International Journal of Research & Method in Education*, *40*(1), 66–90.

Brown, G. T. L., Irving, S. E., & Peterson, E. R. (2009, August). The more I enjoy it the less I achieve: The negative impact of socio-emotional purposes of assessment and feedback on academic performance. Paper presented at biennial conference of the European Association for Research in Learning and Instruction, Amsterdam.

Brown, G. T. L., Peterson, E. R., & Yao, E. (2016). Student conceptions of feedback: Impact on self-regulation, self-efficacy, and academic achievement. *British Journal of Educational Psychology*, *86*(4), 606–629.

Bruno, I., & Santos, L. (2010). Written comments as a form of feedback. *Studies in Educational Evaluation*, *36*(3), 111–120.

Burnett, P. C. (2002). Teacher praise and feedback and students' perceptions of the classroom environment. *Educational Psychology*, *22*(1), 5–16.

Burnett, P. C., & Mandel, V. (2010). Praise and feedback in the primary classroom: Teachers' and students' perspectives. *Australian Journal of Educational & Developmental Psychology*, *10*, 145–154.

Butler, A. C., Godbole, N., & Marsh, E. J. (2013). Explanation feedback is better than correct answer feedback for promoting transfer of learning. *Journal of Educational Psychology*, *105*(2), 290–298.

Campbell, D. T., & Stanley, J. C. (1963). *Experimental and quasi-experimental designs for research*. Chicago, IL: Rand McNally.

Carless, D. (2006). Differing perceptions in the feedback process. *Studies in Higher Education*, *31*(2), 219–233.

Chase, J. A., & Houmanfar, R. (2009). The differential effects of elaborate feedback and basic feedback on student performance in a modified, personalized system of instruction course. *Journal of Behavioral Education*, *18*(3), 245–265.

Chi, M. T. H. (1996). Constructing self-explanations and scaffolded explanations in tutoring. *Applied Cognitive Psychology*, *10*, 33–49.

Cho, K., & MacArthur, C. (2010). Student revision with peer and expert reviewing. *Learning and Instruction*, *20*(4), 328–338.

Corbalan, G., Kester, L., & van Merriënboer, J. G. (2009). Dynamic task selection: Effects of feedback and learner control on efficiency and motivation. *Learning and Instruction*, *19*(6), 455–465.

Crocker, L. (2006). Introduction to measurement theory. In J. L. Green, G. Camilli, & P. B. Elmore (Eds.), *Handbook of complementary methods in education research* (pp. 371–384). Mahwah, NJ: Lawrence Erlbaum Associates.

de Leeuw, E. (2008). Self-administered questionnaires and standardized interviews. In P. Alasuutari, L. Bickman, & J. Brannen (Eds.), *The SAGE handbook of social research methods* (pp. 313–327). London: SAGE.

Dempsey, N. P. (2010). Stimulated recall interviews in ethnography. *Qualitative Sociology, 33*(3), 349–367.

Earp, B. D., & Trafimow, D. (2015). Replication, falsification, and the crisis of confidence in social psychology. *Frontiers in Psychology, 6*(621).

Elo, S., & Kyngäs, H. (2008). The qualitative content analysis process. *Journal of Advanced Nursing, 62*(1), 107–115.

Ericsson, K. A., & Simon, H. A. (1980). Verbal reports as data. *Psychological Review, 87*(3), 215–251.

Field, A. (2016). *An adventure in statistics: The reality enigma.* London: Sage.

Flores, M. A., Veiga Simão, A. M., Barros, A., & Pereira, D. (2015). Perceptions of effectiveness, fairness and feedback of assessment methods: A study in higher education. *Studies in Higher Education, 40*(9), 1523–1534.

Furneaux, C., Paran, A., & Fairfax, B. (2007). Teacher stance as reflected in feedback on student writing: An empirical study of secondary school teachers in five countries. *IRAL – International Review of Applied Linguistics in Language Teaching, 45*(1), 69–94.

Gamlem, S. M., & Smith, K. (2013). Student perceptions of classroom feedback. *Assessment in Education: Principles, Policy and Practice, 20*(2), 150–169.

Gan, M. J. S., & Hattie, J. (2014). Prompting secondary students' use of criteria, feedback specificity and feedback levels during an investigative task. *Instructional Science, 42*(6), 861–878.

Gielen, S., Peeters, E., Dochy, F., Onghena, P., & Struyven, K. (2010). Improving the effectiveness of peer feedback for learning. *Learning and Instruction, 20*(4), 304–315.

Groenewald, T. (2004). A phenomenological research design illustrated. *International Journal of Qualitative Methods, 3*(1), 1–26.

Guénette, D. (2007). Is feedback pedagogically correct? Research design issues in studies of feedback on writing. *Journal of Second Language Writing, 16*, 40–53.

Hamer, J., Purchase, H., Luxton-Reilly, A., & Denny, P. (2015). A comparison of peer and tutor feedback. *Assessment & Evaluation in Higher Education, 40*(1), 151–164.

Handley, K., Price, M., & Millar, J. (2011). Beyond "doing time": Investigating the concept of student engagement with feedback. *Oxford Review of Education, 37*(4), 543–560.

Harber, K. D., Gorman, J. L., Gengaro, F. P., Butisingh, S., Tsang, W., & Ouellete, R. (2012). Students' race and teachers' social support affect the positive feedback bias in public schools. *Journal of Educational Psychology, 104*(4), 1149–1161.

Hargreaves, E. (2013). Inquiring into children's experiences of teacher feedback: Reconceptualising assessment for learning. *Oxford Review of Education, 39*(2), 229–246.

Harks, B., Rakoczy, K., Hattie, J., Besser, M., & Klieme, E. (2014). The effects of feedback on achievement, interest and self-evaluation: The role of feedback's perceived usefulness. *Educational Psychology, 34*(3), 269–290.

Harper, A., & Brown, G. T. L. (2017). Students' use of online feedback in a first year tertiary biology course. *Assessment Matters*, 11, 99–121.

Harris, L. R. (2011). Phenomenographic perspectives on the structure of conceptions: The origins, purposes, strengths, and limitations of the what/how and referential/structural frameworks. *Educational Research Review*, 6(2), 109–124.

Harris, L. R., & Brown, G. T. L. (2010). Mixing interview and questionnaire methods: Practical problems in aligning data. *Practical Assessment, Research & Evaluation*, 15(1). Retrieved from http://pareonline.net/pdf/v15n11.pdf.

Harris, L. R., & Brown, G. T. L. (2013). Opportunities and obstacles to consider when using peer- and self-assessment to improve student learning: Case studies into teachers' implementation. *Teaching and Teacher Education*, 36, 101–111.

Harris, L. R., & Brown, G. T. L. (2016, April). "Everything you do is giving them feedback": A phenomenographic study of teacher conceptions of feedback. Paper presented at the American Educational Research Association annual meeting, Washington, DC.

Harris, L. R., Harnett, J. A., & Brown, G. T. L. (2009). "Drawing" out student conceptions: Using pupils' pictures to examine their conceptions of assessment. In D. M. McInerney, G. T. L. Brown, & G. A. D. Liem (Eds.), *Student perspectives on assessment: What students can tell us about assessment for learning* (pp. 321–330). Charlotte, NC: Information Age Publishing.

Harris, L. R., Brown, G. T. L., & Harnett, J. (2014a). Analysis of New Zealand primary and secondary student peer- and self-assessment comments: Applying Hattie & Timperley's feedback model. *Assessment in Education: Principles, Policy and Practice*, 22(2), 265–281.

Harris, L. R., Brown, G. T. L., & Harnett, J. (2014b). Understanding classroom feedback practices: A study of New Zealand student experiences, perceptions, and emotional responses. *Educational Assessment, Evaluation and Accountability*, 26(2), 107–133.

Harris, L. R., Harnett, J., & Brown, G. T. L. (2013, April). Exploring the content of teachers' feedback: What are teachers actually providing to students? Paper presented at the annual conference of the American Educational Research Association, San Francisco, CA.

Hattie, J., & Timperley, H. (2007). The power of feedback. *Review of Educational Research*, 77(1), 81–112.

Higgins, R., Hartley, P., & Skelton, A. (2002). The conscientious consumer: Reconsidering the role of assessment feedback in student learning. *Studies in Higher Education*, 27(1), 53–64.

Hofferth, S. L., Moran, E. F., Entwistle, B., Aber, J. L., Brady, H. E., Conley, D., . . . & Hubacek, K. (2017). Introduction: History and motivation. *Annals of the American Academy of Political and Social Science*, 669(1), 6–17.

Hoyle, R. H. (1995). The structural equation modeling approach: Basic concepts and fundamental issues. In R. H. Hoyle (Ed.), *Structural equation modeling: Concepts, issues, and applications* (pp. 1–15). Thousand Oaks, CA: Sage.

Hunter, J. E. (2001). The desperate need for replications. *Journal of Consumer Research*, 28(1), 149–158.

Hyland, F. (2003). Focusing on form: Student engagement with teacher feedback. *System*, 31(2), 217–230.

Hyland, F., & Hyland, K. (2001). Sugaring the pill: Praise and criticism in written feedback. *Journal of Second Language Writing*, 10(3), 185–212.

Irving, S. E., Harris, L. R., & Peterson, E. R. (2011). "One assessment doesn't serve all the purposes" or does it?: New Zealand teachers describe assessment and feedback. *Asia-Pacific Education Review, 12*(3), 413–426.

Irving, S. E., Petersen, E. R., & Brown, G. T. L. (2007, August). Student conceptions of feedback: A study of New Zealand secondary students. Paper presented at the biannual conference of the European Association for Research in Learning and Instruction (EARLI), Budapest, Hungary.

Irving, S. E., Peterson, E. R., & Brown, G. T. L. (2008, July). Feedback and academic achievement: The relationship between students' conceptions of feedback and achievement. Paper presented at the sixth biennial conference of the International Test Commission, Liverpool, UK.

Jodaie, M., Farrokhi, F., & Zoghi, M. (2011). A comparative study of EFL teachers' and intermediate high school students' perceptions of written corrective feedback on grammatical errors. *English Language Teaching, 4*(4), 36–48.

Johnson, R. B., & Onwuegbuzie, A. J. (2004). Mixed methods research: A research paradigm whose time has come. *Educational Researcher, 33*(7), 14–26.

Kawulich, B. B. (2005). Participant observation as a data collection method. *Forum Qualitative Sozialforschung/Forum: Qualitative Social Research, 6*(2). Retrieved from www.qualitative-research.net/index.php/fqs/article/view/466/996.

Kember, D., Leung, D. Y. P., & Kwan, K. P. (2002). Does the use of student feedback questionnaires improve the overall quality of teaching? *Assessment & Evaluation in Higher Education, 27*(5), 411–425.

Kerssen-Griep, J., & Witt, P. L. (2012). Instructional feedback II: How do instructor immediacy cues and facework tactics interact to predict student motivation and fairness perceptions? *Communication Studies, 63*(4), 498–517.

Kluger, A. N., & DeNisi, A. (1996). The effects of feedback interventions on performance: A historical review, a meta-analysis, and a preliminary feedback intervention theory. *Psychological Bulletin, 119*(2), 254–284.

Kim, S.-I., Lee, M.-J., Chung, Y., & Bong, M. (2010). Comparison of brain activation during norm-referenced versus criterion-referenced feedback: The role of perceived competence and performance-approach goals. *Contemporary Educational Psychology, 35*(2), 141–152.

Kitzinger, J. (1994). The methodology of focus groups: The importance of interaction between research participants. *Sociology of Health & Illness, 16*(1), 103–121.

Kuusela, H., & Paul, P. (2000). A comparison of concurrent and retrospective verbal protocol analysis. *American Journal of Psychology, 113*(3), 387–404.

Kvale, S. (2002, March 7–9). Dialogue as oppression and interview research. Paper presented at the Nordic Educational Research Association Conference Tallinn, Estonia. Retrieved from http://bit.ly/2mROjhH.

Lee, I. (2007). Feedback in Hong Kong secondary writing classrooms: Assessment for learning or assessment of learning? *Assessing Writing, 12*(3), 180–198.

Li, J., & Barnard, R. (2011). Academic tutors' beliefs about and practices of giving feedback on students' written assignments: A New Zealand case study. *Assessing Writing, 16*(2), 137–148.

Lindsay, D. S. (2015). Replication in psychological science. *Psychological Science, 26*(12), 1827–1832.

Lipnevich, A. A., & Smith, J. (2009a). "I really need feedback to learn": Students' perspectives on the effectiveness of the differential feedback messages. *Educational Assessment, Evaluation and Accountability, 21*(4), 347–367.

Lipnevich, A. A., & Smith, J. K. (2009b). Effects of differential feedback on students' examination performance. *Journal of Experimental Psychology: Applied*, *15*(4), 319–333.

Lipnevich, A. A., Berg, D. A. G., & Smith, J. K. (2016). Toward a model of student response to feedback. In G. T. L. Brown & L. R. Harris (Eds.), *The handbook of human and social conditions in assessment* (pp. 169–185). New York: Routledge.

Lizzio, A., & Wilson, K. (2008). Feedback on assessment: Students' perceptions of quality and effectiveness. *Assessment & Evaluation in Higher Education*, *33*(3), 263–275.

Maier, U. (2010). Accountability policies and teachers' acceptance and usage of school performance feedback: A comparative study. *School Effectiveness & School Improvement*, *21*(2), 145–165.

Makel, M. C., Plucker, J. A., & Hegarty, B. (2012). Replications in psychology research. *Perspectives on Psychological Science*, *7*(6), 537–542.

Marsh, H. W., Hau, K.-T., Balla, J. R., & Grayson, D. (1998). Is more ever too much? The number of indicators per factor in confirmatory factor analysis. *Multivariate Behavioral Research*, *33*(2), 181–220.

Marton, F. (1981). Phenomenography: Describing conceptions of the world around us. *Instructional Science*, *10*, 177–220.

Matsumura, L. C., Patthey-Chavez, G. G., Valdes, R., & Garnier, H. (2002). Teacher feedback, writing assignment quality, and third-grade students' revision in lower- and higher-achieving urban schools. *Elementary School Journal*, *103*(1), 3–25.

Mayring, P. (2000). Qualitative content analysis. *Forum Qualitative Sozialforschung/ Forum: Qualitative Social Research*, *1*(2). Retrieved from www.qualitative-research.net/index.php/fqs/article/view/1089/2385.

McLean, A. J., Bond, C. H., & Nicholson, H. D. (2015). An anatomy of feedback: A phenomenographic investigation of undergraduate students' conceptions of feedback. *Studies in Higher Education*, *40*(5), 921–932.

Morgan, D. L. (1997). *Focus groups as qualitative research* (2nd edn.). Thousand Oaks, CA: SAGE.

Narciss, S., Sosnovsky, S., Schnaubert, L., Andrès, E., Eichelmann, A., Goguadze, G., & Melis, E. (2014). Exploring feedback and student characteristics relevant for personalizing feedback strategies. *Computers & Education*, *71*, 56–76.

National Research Council. (2002). *Scientific research in education*. Washington, DC: National Academy Press.

Nelson, M. M., & Schunn, C. D. (2009). The nature of feedback: How different types of peer feedback affect writing performance. *Instructional Science*, *37*(4), 375–401.

Nesbit, P. L., & Burton, S. (2006). Student justice perceptions following assignment feedback. *Assessment & Evaluation in Higher Education*, *31*(6), 655–670.

Neuliep, J. W. (1990). Editorial bias against replication research. *Journal of Social Behavior and Personality*, *5*(4), 85.

NIST/SEMATECH. (2003). *e-Handbook of statistical methods*. Retrieved from www.itl.nist.gov/div898/handbook.

Orsmond, P., & Merry, S. (2011). Feedback alignment: Effective and ineffective links between tutors' and students' understanding of coursework feedback. *Assessment & Evaluation in Higher Education*, *36*(2), 125–136.

Parr, J. M., & Timperley, H. S. (2010). Feedback to writing, assessment for teaching and learning and student progress. *Assessing Writing, 15,* 68–85.

Pekrun, R., Cusack, A., Murayama, K., Elliot, A. J., & Thomas, K. (2014). The power of anticipated feedback: Effects on students' achievement goals and achievement emotions. *Learning and Instruction, 29,* 115–124.

Pekrun, R., Goetz, T., Titz, W., & Perry, R. P. (2002). Academic emotions in students' self-regulated learning and achievement: A program of qualitative and quantitative research. *Educational Psychologist, 37*(2), 91–105.

Peterson, E. R., & Irving, S. E. (2008). Secondary school students' conceptions of assessment and feedback. *Learning and Instruction, 18*(3), 238–250.

Pond, K., & Ul-Haq, R. (1997). Learning to assess students using peer review. *Studies in Educational Evaluation, 23*(4), 331–348.

Poulos, A., & Mahony, M. J. (2008). Effectiveness of feedback: The students' perspective. *Assessment & Evaluation in Higher Education, 33*(2), 143–154.

Price, M., Handley, K., Millar, J., & O'Donovan, B. (2010). Feedback: All that effort, but what is the effect? *Assessment & Evaluation in Higher Education, 35*(3), 277–289.

Rabiee, F. (2004). Focus group interview and data analysis. *Proceedings of the Nutrition Society, 63*(4), 655–660.

Rakoczy, K., Harks, B., Klieme, E., Blum, W., & Hochweber, J. (2013). Written feedback in mathematics: Mediated by students' perception, moderated by goal orientation. *Learning and Instruction, 27,* 63–73.

Raosoft. (2017). Sample size calculator. Retrieved from www.raosoft.com/samplesize.html.

Richardson, J. T. E. (2005). Instruments for obtaining student feedback: A review of the literature. *Assessment & Evaluation in Higher Education, 30*(4), 387–415.

Robinson, S., Pope, D., & Holyoak, L. (2013). Can we meet their expectations? Experiences and perceptions of feedback in first year undergraduate students. *Assessment & Evaluation in Higher Education, 38*(3), 260–272.

Ruiz-Primo, M. A., & Li, M. (2013). Analyzing teachers' feedback practices in response to students' work in science classrooms. *Applied Measurement in Education, 26*(3), 163–175.

Schildkamp, K., & Visscher, A. (2010). The use of performance feedback in school improvement in Louisiana. *Teaching and Teacher Education, 26,* 1389–1403.

Sendziuk, P. (2010). Sink or swim? Improving student learning through feedback and self-assessment. *International Journal of Teaching and Learning in Higher Education, 22*(3), 320–330.

Shadish, W. R., & Luellen, J. K. (2006). Quasi-experimental design. In J. L. Green, G. Camilli, & P. B. Elmore (Eds.), *Handbook of complementary methods in education research* (pp. 539–550). Mahwah, NJ: LEA.

Sijtsma, K. (2009). On the use, the misuse, and the very limited usefulness of Cronbach's alpha. *Psychometrika, 74*(1), 107–120.

Simons, D. J. (2014). The value of direct replication. *Perspectives on Psychological Science, 9*(1), 76–80.

Smith, J. K., Smith, L. F., & Smith, B. K. (2017). The reproducibility crisis in psychology: Attack of the clones or phantom menace? In M. C. Makel & J. A. Plucker (Eds.), *Toward a more perfect psychology: Improving trust, accuracy, and transparency in research* (pp. 273–287). Washington, DC: American Psychological Association.

Smith, M. L. (2006). Multiple methodology in education research. In J. L. Green, G. Camilli, & P. B. Elmore (Eds.), *Handbook of complementary methods in education research* (pp. 457–475). Mahwah, NJ: LEA.

Stemler, S. E. (2004). A comparison of consensus, consistency, and measurement approaches to estimating interrater reliability. *Practical Assessment, Research & Evaluation, 9*(4). Retrieved from http://tinyurl.com/m7grwph.

Strijbos, J.-W., Narciss, S., & Dünnebier, K. (2010). Peer feedback content and sender's competence level in academic writing revision tasks: Are they critical for feedback perceptions and efficiency? *Learning and Instruction, 20*(4), 291–303.

Tang, J., & Harrison, C. (2011). Investigating university tutor perceptions of assessment feedback: Three types of tutor beliefs. *Assessment & Evaluation in Higher Education, 36*(5), 583–604.

Teo, T., & Fan, X. (2013). Coefficient alpha and beyond: Issues and alternatives for educational research. *Asia-Pacific Education Researcher, 22*(2), 209–213.

Thomas, D. R. (2006). A general inductive approach for analyzing qualitative evaluation data. *American Journal of Evaluation, 27*(2), 237–246.

Tjeerdsma, B. L. (1997). Comparison of teacher and student perspectives of tasks and feedback. *Journal of Teaching in Physical Education, 16*(4), 388–400.

Tseng, S.-C., & Tsai, C.-C. (2007). On-line peer assessment and the role of the peer feedback: A study of high school computer course. *Computers & Education, 49*(4), 1161–1174.

Tunstall, P., & Gipps, C. (1996a). "How does your teacher help you to make your work better?" Children's understanding of formative assessment. *Curriculum Journal, 7*(2), 185–203.

Tunstall, P., & Gipps, C. (1996b). Teacher feedback to young children in formative assessment: A typology. *British Educational Research Journal, 22*(4), 389–404.

Van der Kleij, F., Adie, L., & Cumming, J. (2016). Using video technology to enable student voice in assessment feedback. *British Journal of Educational Technology*. Advanced online publication. doi:10.1111/bjet.12536.

Voerman, L., Meijer, P. C., Korthagen, F. A. J., & Simons, R. J. (2012). Types and frequencies of feedback interventions in classroom interaction in secondary education. *Teaching and Teacher Education, 28*(8), 1107–1115.

Vollmeyer, R., & Rheinberg, F. (2005). A surprising effect of feedback on learning. *Learning and Instruction, 15*(6), 589–602.

Vul, E., Harris, C., Winkielman, P., & Pashler, H. (2009). Puzzlingly high correlations in fMRI studies of emotion, personality, and social cognition. *Perspectives on Psychological Science, 4*(3), 274–290.

Weaver, M. R. (2006). Do students value feedback? Student perceptions of tutors' written responses. *Assessment & Evaluation in Higher Education, 31*(3), 379–394.

Webb, E. J., Campbell, D. T., Schwartz, R. D., Sechrest, L., & Grove, J. B. (1981). *Nonreactive Measures in the Social Sciences* (2nd edn.). Boston: Houghton Mifflin.

Werner, O., & Campbell, D. T. (1973). Translating, working through interpreters, and the problem of decentering. In R. Naroll & R. Cohen (Eds.), *A handbook of method in cultural anthropology* (pp. 398–420). New York: Columbia University Press.

Yin, R. K. (2006). Case study methods. In J. Green, G. Camilli, & P. Elmore (Eds.), *Handbook of complementary methods in education research* (pp. 111–122). Mahwah, NJ: Lawrence Erlbaum Associates.

Zumbo, B. D. (2015). Consequences, side effects and the ecology of testing: Keys to considering assessment in vivo. Paper presented at the plenary address to the 2015 annual conference of the Association for Educational Assessment – Europe, Glasgow, Scotland.

PART II

Domain-Specific Feedback

6 Assessment Feedback in Primary Schools in Singapore and Beyond

Kelvin H. K. Tan and Hwei Ming Wong

Introduction: Assessment Feedback in Primary Schools Has Diverse Purposes

Primary school students, ages six through twelve, are in a developmental period for academic learning characterized by the ability to use logical and coherent actions in thinking and solving problems or at the "concrete operations" stage of Piaget's cognitive development theory (Wadsworth, 2003). During this period, primary school students have learned to master the more formal skills of life such as following rules and mastering literacy and numeracy. They are more aware of their own feelings and those of others and are better able to link their thoughts and feelings. However, when compared with adolescents, ages thirteen through twenty, primary school students' thinking is less advanced, less efficient, and generally more simplistic. They are less developed in their executive control in the management of emotions in self and interpersonal systems (Larson & Brown, 2007). As such, primary school students are perceived as cognitively less able and developmentally too immature to reflect on their own learning and to assess themselves productively. This prevents them from performing self-assessment accurately (Fontana & Fernandes, 1994; Ross, 2006) compared with older students.

It is tempting to view primary school students as being more amenable to, and in need of, teachers' careful guidance and "scaffolding" in the form of assessment feedback. Such a view depicts young students as being deficient or lacking in literacy and numeracy skills, and assessment feedback is part of a pedagogical package to ensure students understand and demonstrate curriculum knowledge to the teacher's satisfaction. Yet it is equally plausible to argue the opposite – that young minds not yet exposed to the full socialization and normalization effects of formal education should be left to develop their own ways of thinking and understanding the world. In this more constructivist view of education, assessment feedback is a complex and contested endeavor – feedback may represent the expertise of others, such as teachers, in guiding students to independent learning (Tan, 2013a, 2013b). But, at the same time, by unduly imposing curricular and ideological strictures on students, feedback may simply be a corrective device to normalize students' behavior and knowledge. How, then, can feedback in primary schools be approached to balance the provision of teachers' expertise into students' assessment experiences to enhance their independent learning, and at the same time assist students to achieve requisite learning outcomes for high-stakes examinations?

Perhaps a good example of such tension(s) in assessment feedback purpose and practice would be found in a context that concurrently emphasizes assessment feedback for the preparation to achieve high-stakes examination performance and develops students' confidence in and enjoyment of their own learning. This is certainly the case in the city-state of Singapore, which revamped its public primary school education in 2010 with the ambitious remit of "Holistic Assessment," for which one of its key changes was that

> the school-based assessment system should be balanced to place greater emphasis on skills development and to provide constructive feedback which enables more meaningful learning in support of both academic and non-academic aspects of a pupil's development ... and [this] shifts the focus away from an end-outcome where students and parents concentrate too much on assessment of learning in the form of examinations.
> (Ministry of Education, 2009, p. 35)

This statement encapsulates the tensions of assessment feedback purposes in primary schools: assessment feedback should be constructed to support meaningful learning, yet prepare students for tests and examinations. It should support student development in both academic and nonacademic areas, yet be understood and practiced mostly to enhance academic achievement. It should recognize that pupils in primary schools are in their early formative years and in need of careful nurturing of their interests in learning, yet assessment feedback is depended on to assist students to perform well in high-stakes national examinations.

In this chapter, we use the examination-oriented context of Singapore primary schools as a backdrop to explore how assessment feedback may be practiced more effectively for its various, and at times conflicting, purposes. We examine recent research studies on assessment feedback in Singapore primary schools to identify areas of improvement for assessment feedback.

We propose a simple framework for effective feedback practice in terms of assessment standards, assessment design, and feedback dialogue. In this framework, assessment design provides and structures the instances where feedback is generated and (imminently) applied, thus ensuring that learners are always provided with opportunities to apply feedback into action. And feedback should also be directed toward a purposeful goal – closing gaps in students' learning, which in turn necessitates clarity in identifying what students' gaps in learning are in the first instance. This highlights the importance of clarity in achievement standards against which students' gaps in learning may be gauged.

We argue that feedback that is effective in supporting and enhancing students' learning is best understood as a dialogue between teachers and students, rather than a unilateral provision of feedback from teachers to students (Nicol, 2010; Carless, 2016). It is not enough merely to provide useful feedback to students on their assessment tasks. In order to enhance students' subsequent learning, feedback needs to be understood and then used by students to close the gap between their previous demonstrated level of learning and their desired next level of learning or performance to be attained within a specific period of time.

Finally, we recommend various factors that enhance students' ownership of learning – this helps in developing students to become self-regulated agents and beneficiaries of assessment feedback practices in primary schools.

Assessment in Singapore Primary Schools

The education system in Singapore is characterized as examination oriented (Cheah, 1998; Gopinathan, 2001; Heng, 2001; Tan, 2011b; Lim-Ratnam, 2013). Clear lines of progression to tertiary education and vocational institutes are drawn based on how students perform in the high-stakes national examinations. In the anxiety for their children to survive in an examination-based system, parents often exert pressure on teachers to focus more on promoting academic outcomes with the objective of preempting the work of the next level of schooling, rather than the holistic development of the child (Lim-Ratnam, 2013).

In 2008, the Primary Education Review and Implementation (PERI) Committee was appointed to study and recommend wide-ranging changes to primary education in Singapore. The Committee recognized that some parents "felt the need to shift towards a less exam-oriented culture where academic results are not the only measure of a child's success" (p. 35) and pointed out that "While assessment remains important, a preoccupation with examinations can hinder the overall development of the student and make learning dreary and less engaging" (p. 34).

The PERI Committee explained that "Assessment is an important aspect of teaching and learning which should be effectively used to support the holistic development of our pupils" (p. 34) by providing "stakeholders such as teachers, parents and pupils with meaningful information about how well pupils have progressed by highlighting their strengths and areas for improvement" (p. 34). The Committee also noted that some parents "felt that students needed to be prepared from young to sit for examinations" (p. 35). These two recommendations reflect the tension of purposes for assessment feedback in Singapore primary schools – that assessment feedback should be informative to identify strengths and areas for improvement and also should be a form of examination preparation. Consequently, the Committee recommended that "schools should provide more qualitative feedback to students on their learning and development of skills in both academic and non-academic areas, and to suggest how they can make improvements" (p. 35). This new assessment discourse has subsequently been labeled as "Holistic Assessment" by the Ministry of Education (MOE), and several concrete measures were recommended to effect these changes.

In summary, the desired purposes of assessment feedback identified by the PERI committee may be summarised as:

1. Providing more qualitative feedback on their learning and development of skills
2. Providing more meaningful information on students' strengths and areas for improvement
3. Preparing the young to sit for their examinations
4. Supporting the holistic development of students.

It is instructive to observe the language used to suggest the intent of assessment feedback in these recommendations – assessment feedback is framed as the *provision* of *information* to *support* educational outcomes. Such a discourse paints a passive and provisional view of assessment feedback practice. Assessment feedback is understood here as the generation of information that may or may not be acted on by learners and stakeholders. It is understood as a useful resource that may or may not be used, rather than a set of essential actions that form a coherent approach to assisting learners to make sense of and improvements in their learning.

In this chapter, we argue that the diverse needs of assessment feedback in primary schools – to assist learners in whole-child development and yet adequately prepare them for high-stakes national examinations – requires a more comprehensive and integrated practice of assessment feedback. It is not sufficient for assessment feedback to be merely and passively limited to information provided for discretionary use by teachers and students for general purposes. Assessment feedback should be understood and used as a series of practices that generates information on students' learning and structures imminent opportunities for such information to be put to use by learners. Recent research on assessment practices in Singapore primary schools suggests several areas of improvement for assessment feedback practice that are pertinent for primary schools (Ratnam-Lim & Tan, 2015; Wong, 2016, 2017; Rahmat & Wong, 2017; Safii & Wong, 2017). We will discuss this research in greater detail in subsequent sections in this chapter.

Assessment Feedback in Singapore Primary Schools

Since July 2009, the MOE has been working with a small number of primary schools to "prototype" the concept of Holistic Assessment (MOE Press Release, 2010). Since then, the MOE has been systematically implementing Holistic Assessment in all primary schools in phases.

When PERI Holistic Assessment was first implemented in 2010 in 16 partner prototype schools, and subsequently in 171 primary schools between 2011 and 2013, capacity building was an important aspect of the implementation. Teachers attended ongoing job-embedded professional development to improve their classroom assessment practices to better engage their students and improve their students' learning. Key components of PERI Holistic Assessment capacity-building framework for teachers included seminars and exhibitions, assessment literacy and subject-specific workshops, networking and learning journeys, teacher learning communities, and PERI Holistic Assessment professional learning lectures and workshops conducted by assessment experts looking into the five keys/principles of sound assessment practice discussed later. The PERI Holistic Assessment capacity-building framework aims at building teachers' assessment literacy and assessment competencies.

One of the five keys/principles of sound assessment practice is developing the teachers' capacities in effective communication (why, what, when, and how) in providing feedback to students. Various assessment experts have highlighted the importance of feedback in their respective PERI Holistic Assessment professional learning lectures and workshops. At the 2012 professional learning lecture, Wiliam (2012) summarized feedback as the information provided to students to better understand problems and solutions that helps to move learning forward. In a separate lecture in 2013, Fisher (2013) discussed the use of assessment information to feed-forward as a significant factor in the learning process. In feed-forward settings, students make meaningful gains when they are provided with feed-forward ideas and related instruction that supports their continuing growth. The importance of the feedback loop was highlighted by Chappius (2015) in her 2015 lecture where teachers can check for understanding and continue teaching guided by information about students' mastery or nonmastery of knowledge or skills.

In addition to building up teachers' fundamental understanding of assessment principles, teachers also reviewed and refined existing assessment practices that could both effectively support and report learning. Holistic reporting systems, guided by principles of sound grading and reporting (O'Conner, 2009; Guskey & Bailey, 2010), were planned and designed to gather information on and report on students' progress in achieving the key learning outcomes and development of skills, dispositions, and values. Other practices that support feedback are activating students as learning resources for one another (peer feedback) and activating students as owners of their own learning (self-feedback) (Wiliam, 2011).

However, two recent research studies suggest that teachers view and utilize assessment feedback in ways that may not directly support or contribute to learning effectively. For example, Ratnam-Lim and Tan (2015) reported on a study of forty-three teachers on their assessment practices in primary schools from a random sample of thirty schools. Several of the respondents noted that "for feedback to be meaningful to pupils, they have to be able to understand how the feedback can help them improve" (p. 69). As the pupils in Primary 1 and 2 are young (ages six to eight), "they may not be able to fully appreciate and understand the feedback, much less to know what to do with the feedback" (p. 69). One of the teachers explained that if the feedback is couched in "child language," it "may not be practical enough to guide them" (p. 69). Some teachers explained that the feedback was "mainly for the parents to read and support their children's learning at home" (p. 69). The teacher respondents also felt that "teachers don't know exactly what to ask and how to guide so that students could benefit from the feedback on their learning and make improvement in their area of weaknesses" because they are "used to the summative assessments that focus more on what students have achieved since summative assessments were of greater importance in the past" (Ratnam-Lim & Tan, 2015, p. 69).

To provide rich feedback, "teachers need a good understanding of the child's skills and competencies. The only way teachers can get this insight is when they interact with the child and take the time to review their daily work" (Ratnam-Lim & Tan, 2015, p. 70). This is time consuming, as the teacher needs to "really look at each child and assess the child individually" (p. 70). As there are thirty to forty children in a class, the teacher may not know each and every child intimately enough to give customized comments that are useful enough to help each child improve. A teacher in the study concluded that "it is practically impossible to provide constructive feedback for every answer in every question, for every student and for every piece of assignment" (p. 70).

Teachers could become overworked or overloaded when they attempt to provide feedback for every question and every task to every single student. The assumption that there is a need to provide feedback to every student for every question brought to the surface the teachers' perceptions/misconceptions of how feedback is used. In order to challenge this assumption, we therefore need to examine how feedback is defined.

Feedback can be defined as "information provided by an agent (e.g., teacher, peer, book, parent, self, experience) regarding aspects of one's performance and understanding" (Hattie and Timperley, 2007, p. 81), and its main purpose is "to reduce discrepancies between current understandings and performance and a goal" (p. 86). There are three kinds of feedback questions: "feed-up," "feed-back," and "feed-forward." Feed-up ("where am I going?") aims at providing information about "the attainment of learning goals related to the task or performance" (Hattie and Timperley, 2007, p. 88). Feed-back ("how am I going?") aims at providing information "relative to a task/performance goal, often in relation to some expected standard, to prior performance, and/or to success or failure on a specific part of the task" (p. 88). The third notion, feed-forward ("where to next?"), aims to provide information on the strategies a student can adopt or processes he or she could go through that can facilitate in achievement of the learning goals. Feeding forward is effective when the information provided "leads to greater possibilities in learning" (p. 90).

In 2010, a large-scale, representative, nation-wide project on classroom practices (Hogan et al. 2013) was conducted where 114 primary and secondary school teachers were interviewed in a semi-structured format about their assessment practices. Responses were coded for feedback use and were analyzed using Hattie and Timperley's framework, particularly their notions of feed-up, feed-back, and feed-forward. These were subsequently examined in relation to teachers' beliefs about the high-stakes testing environment in Singapore schools, about student abilities, about instructional practices, and innovative pedagogies.

The findings indicated that teachers largely used feedback in highly limited ways: to correct or highlight mistakes and students' weaknesses, reteaching, giving students suggestions on improvements, using good performance tasks for students to model, and giving students praise (Rahmat & Wong, 2017). The responses relating to goals (feed-up) were predominantly absent, and feed-forward was very limited. Teachers seemed more concerned with providing student feedback on current levels of performance and believed that feedback was necessary only when students performed below expectations. The teachers did not seem to monitor whether students had understood or had benefited from the feedback given to them by improving their performance beyond the current levels. This suggests that the feedback given by Singaporean teachers might not be actively used by students to improve their progress or learning or that the feedback seemed low level, aimed only at correcting the current level of performance rather than stretching students' capability. Furthermore, teachers' perceptions of their students' abilities shaped how they use feedback. They construed student abilities in negative ways, which has consequences for instructional practices including the kinds of feedback teachers deemed suitable for students. In conclusion, we feel that teachers need to be consistently aware of and keep their negative views of their students, especially in terms of their abilities, in check. Their negative views about their students' abilities can influence what and how feedback is given to their students. Teachers could therefore be limiting their own students' progress unknowingly.

It is possible that the teachers in Singapore classrooms who used feedback largely in a corrective, evaluative manner may have a narrow understanding of what feedback is or may not know how to give feedback effectively. Also, given the high-stakes examination culture in Singapore schools, teachers may perceive their role as merely delivering the curriculum and teaching to the test. Such corrective feedback tendencies were also observed in other studies on Singapore assessment feedback practices.

Effective feedback consists of information about progress and how to proceed to the next level or stage of learning for the students. Based on the findings from Ratnam-Lim and Tan (2015) and Rahmat and Wong (2017), it seemed to be an issue for teachers to give effective feedback to students as they tended to focus only on corrective feedback aimed at the task level of what is correct or incorrect. They provided little information to students on how to proceed to the next step. There is also a perception on some teachers' part that students were not capable of taking in and using feedback. Teachers seemed to see the role of students as that of only passively receiving feedback, and low-level corrective feedback at best. This also seemed to be related to teachers being uncomfortable and not confident in giving effective feedback, especially that of feed-forward.

Perhaps teachers had assumed that primary school students were too young to play an active role in their own assessment and learning. As such, teachers compensated by correcting students rather than teaching them to understand

and use feedback. Additionally, teachers might also be afraid to relinquish partial control to students; thus students' learning was still very much teacher controlled and the responsibility of teachers, instead of the students' responsibility where they would do their own learning. Based on our work and personal observations, teachers from the two studies were not able to realize and maximize the full potential of feedback in their classrooms. There were various reasons for this, ranging from teachers' beliefs and perceptions that students were too young to understand the feedback to teachers' own perceived lack of competencies in giving effective feedback to students and to constraints such as the lack of time to give customized feedback to each student.

It is important to consider the students' role in assessment and assessment feedback as they are the ones using the feedback to improve their learning. Students can be ready for feedback and can be capable of using feedback for their learning if they are properly trained and are given the opportunities to use it. At the same time, we cannot assume that only teachers can give feedback. Students are capable of giving feedback too, for their own learning and also for the teachers' learning and teaching. We next look at two recent studies that examined students' role in assessment and assessment feedback.

Student Involvement in Feedback Practices

Wong (2012a, 2012b, 2016, 2017) examined primary school students' and teachers' perceptions of self-assessment in Singapore. She found that the Primary 4 students (aged ten) believed that there was information that only they could provide as feedback to their teachers that would help the teachers to support them in their learning. Therefore, the students wanted their teachers to know about their self-assessment. The following interview excerpts from individual students illustrate their beliefs:

> "We know some information that teachers don't know, and we can understand ourselves better than teachers." (2012a, p. 326)

> "Yes, because sometimes students know some things that teachers do not know [about students]." (2012b)

> "They [students] know some things about themselves better." (2012b)

> "We can get more information about ourselves that teacher don't know." (2012b)

> "Yes. I know myself better and can help me to learn more." (2016, p. 12)

Wong (2012a) also reported that teachers were not averse to their students using self-assessment and that they were interested to know how their students assessed themselves because it would be feedback about their students' learning as well as their own teaching. The following are the teachers' interview excerpts:

> "Yes. Let me know. Yes, it would be information. Can use in my teaching, like their weak areas." (p. 235)

"Oh, definitely. Definitely, because this one will help me to plan my lessons as well as for me to assess how well have they understood the lessons. And this will actually help me to plan my lessons … So from the [students'] self-assessment results, I know more or less how should I cater [to] the needs [of different children] and from there, I will base on needs and then I will teach."   (p. 235)

The current formative assessment feedback practices in Singapore seem to focus only on teachers giving feedback to students in the day-to-day classrooms rather than the other way around. The teachers seemed to focus only on their role as teachers and focused on giving feedback to students, telling them how or what to do for their work, and rarely going beyond correction of work. It was not within the teachers' usual practices to refer to information provided by students via their work and self-assessment (Wong, 2012a). The teachers only realized the potential of using the information from students as feedback to improve or change their own teaching practice when it was brought to their attention. Therefore, one recommendation is that assessment feedback should be a two-way feedback loop with both teachers and students giving feedback to one another to improve teaching and learning.

Although there is a perception that primary school students may not be cognitively and emotionally mature enough to self-assess, findings from Wong (2016) indicated otherwise. Students as young as ten years of age have the ability to assess themselves. This finding is in line with other studies conducted with primary school students (e.g., Munns & Woodward, 2006; Andrade, Du, & Wang, 2008; Brown, 2008; Wong, 2017) that illustrated that students as young as seven and eight years old could do self-assessment. When provided with the opportunity to use self-assessment and with training in self-assessment (see Andrade & Valtcheva, 2009; Andrade, 2010), students were able to take ownership for their learning and were open to using self-assessment. The need to practice using self-assessment was emphasized by the students. This indicated that they were not confident in assessing themselves accurately and needed more practice to self-assess. The students' perceived need for more self-assessment practices was reflected by the results that compared the teachers' scoring of the student work and the students' own self-assessment. The students tended to be more modest than necessary and depressed their own scores when assessing themselves as compared with the teachers' scoring (Wong, 2016). A possible reason for the students not feeling confident enough to self-assess accurately is that teachers traditionally have been the ones to assess the students, be it conventional or alternative assessment. It would therefore take students time to become accustomed to and get into the habit of assessing themselves. The students' self-awareness of a need for more practice also implied their openness to using self-assessment, which could potentially contribute toward a regular use of self-assessment in the classrooms.

In general, the primary school students felt that they should assess themselves and that they have assessed themselves fairly. They believed that they had information about themselves that they could use that the teachers did not have. At the same time, the students also indicated that they needed more practice to be confident in assessing their own work. The teachers also commented that their students were capable of assessing themselves but that they needed guidance and training to do so. The students believed that they could play a bigger role in their own assessment and giving feedback about their own work. However, it remains to be seen how teachers can give effective feedback to students, and especially how teachers will use feedback from students to improve teaching and learning.

Safii and Wong (2017) observed five primary mathematics classrooms, as they studied how feedback was given in the class in terms of the four levels described in Hattie and Timperley (2007): task, process, self-regulation, and person. The study also observed how teachers used the students' self-assessment rubrics. Based on the preliminary findings, teachers gave mostly evaluative and corrective feedback to students about their work. A majority of the Primary 3 students (nine years old), who were randomly selected to participate in focus group discussions, stated that they received feedback on their careless mistakes. A number of students mentioned that they were advised to be neater in their writing. These comments on their schoolwork often included strategies to improve the quality of their work, for example, taking time to complete schoolwork instead of rushing through it. Another student shared that her teacher showed the class the mistakes she had made to show an example of bad quality work. Even though she did not like it, she understood the teacher's intention of helping the class.

Feedback is often merely an acknowledgment of an exchange of information ("tick and flick") (described as phatic feedback by Murtagh, 2014). Students received feedback such as "you have to improve" and "well done" on their work, with no additional information that could support in-depth learning. This type of feedback was mostly at the task level and at the person level (Safii & Wong, 2017).

Even though most students used the feedback given by their teachers to do better in their work, with a few mentioning that the feedback was helpful, some students did not use their teachers' feedback often. One student said that she seldom worked on the feedback she received as the feedback was not helpful. Another student shared that she only used the feedback for her work sometimes as she "doesn't feel like caring about it." This could be indicative of a consequence of the lack of follow-up by the teachers on the students' use of feedback. As there was no consequence/punishment for the student, she was not obliged to use feedback except when she wanted to.

The responses gathered during these students' focus group discussions were reflective of the responses collected from a self-assessment questionnaire that was done by a Primary 3 cohort in the same school. Seventy percent of the cohort responded positively (i.e., choosing agree or strongly agree on a five-point Likert scale) to the statement "I can use the feedback that my math teacher gives me to improve my work."

Based on the focus group discussion data, some students reported that they wanted more helpful comments, suggestions, and advice from their teachers on how to do their work. The excerpts that follow are the kind of feedback that students wanted to hear from their teachers. It was interesting that the students wanted more feedback that could move them forward in their work, but, at the same time, they wanted feedback that was praise from their teachers:

> "I want to receive both advice and comments."
>
> "Helpful comments."
>
> "Give us encouragement, so that we'll try to do better and give us motivation to learn math more."
>
> "Sometimes good, sometimes bad. Like good job, well done. Like, you must improve handwriting, be more careful and don't be distracted."
> (Safii & Wong, 2017)

It seemed that younger students still looked up to their teachers and needed the affirmation from them even though person-level feedback was not helpful in improving their work. But it is the positive affirmation, the praise of "well done," "good job," that enhanced the students' self-esteem and motivated them to make an effort in their work. As indicated by the findings in Safii and Wong (2017), students actually looked forward to receiving praise as feedback from their teachers. To the students, receiving praise was equally as important as feedback on how to improve their work as it evoked a sense of achievement and success in them.

Teachers' responses collected in a questionnaire conducted at the start of the study revealed similar results to the classroom observations of the teachers on the nature of feedback in classrooms. When asked to rate how frequent they gave feedback that focused on task (i.e., choosing from 1, not at all; 2, seldom; 3, sometimes; 4, often; 5, a lot), the teachers' aggregated mean was 4.00 for verbal feedback and 4.40 for written feedback. On the same scale, the teachers' mean rating of feedback that focuses on self-regulation was 2.20 for verbal feedback and 3.00 for written feedback. These results showed that feedback in the classroom was centered on teachers' directives, aimed at improving the quality of schoolwork, but did not actively engage the students to reflect on their learning.

The findings showed that students are capable and, more often than not, willing to work on comments they receive from their teachers about their schoolwork. However, it seemed that monitoring of how the feedback is actually used by the students does not occur in typical classrooms (see Crisp, 2007). It also seemed that sometimes teachers did try to seek feedback from students about their teaching, but more could be done.

There appears to be a gap between teachers' knowledge of assessment literacy and principles and the teachers' actual practice in giving effective and quality feedback. Based on the research, teachers have professed that they did not know when and how to give feedback. They seemed to be focused on giving feedback at the task level and at the person level. They seldom moved to the process and self-regulation levels, which are more powerful in guiding students toward deep processing and mastery of tasks. There is also deficit thinking on some teachers' part that students are not capable of taking in and using feedback, and they continue to see students as passive learners and passive recipients of feedback. Teachers seemed to presume that students would use the feedback given to improve their learning without checking if students had actually used it (see Crisp, 2007; Sadler, 2010a).

Even with student self-assessment, the challenge for teachers is to move out of merely giving evaluative and corrective feedback and toward providing meta-cognitive feedback for students to contemplate their work. Teachers need to consciously think about the kind of feedback they can give to their students that will be helpful for them to improve their work. The challenge is also for teachers to maintain a two-way feedback loop with their students: giving feedback to and getting feedback from their students.

Recommended Assessment Feedback Practices for Primary Schools

We recommend four distinct and yet related practices to enhance assessment feedback practice and outcomes in primary schools:

- Establish clear standards to identify gaps for feedback to address.
- Design assessment tasks to generate useful feedback and then apply that feedback.
- Engage in feedback as a dialogue with students instead of providing feedback as information.
- Develop in students the ability and disposition to be active generators and beneficiaries of their own feedback.

The first three are presented as a "trifecta" of practices to frame how feedback may be understood and used for students' immediate benefit. It is a trifecta because all three elements are required to be successful. Tan (2013a) argued that assessment standards, design, and feedback broadly constituted the minimal requirements for assessment for learning to succeed in enhancing student's learning and achievement in concrete ways. Feedback information is not useful in itself unless it is directed toward a specific need. A gap in what students had and can (imminently) achieve is a direct need that assessment feedback information can help to address. Hence, identifying precise gaps for assessment feedback to bridge is an important precondition for ensuring that feedback information is directed toward a specific target for students to achieve.

Likewise, the source material as well as the opportunity to generate and apply assessment feedback information cannot be left to chance or random occurrence. There should be an intentional design for assessment tasks to ensure students are provided with feedback as well as timely opportunity to use it. Teachers can only confirm that learning has resulted from feedback if students have been required to act on feedback, to complete the feedback loop (Sadler 1989). Similarly, Boud (2000) stated that "unless feedback is applied and used to demonstrate improvement, there is no way to tell if it has been effective"

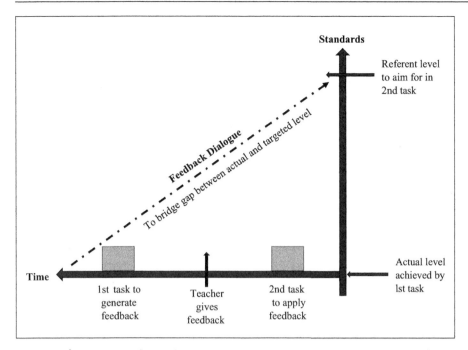

Figure 6.1 *Trifecta of practices: assessment standards, design, and feedback.*

(p. 10). Effective assessment design to generate and apply feedback would therefore constitute the second prerequisite for effective feedback practice.

Clear standards and purposeful assessment design ensure that primary school learners can be provided with timely feedback information to address appropriate gaps in their learning. The third practice that completes the trifecta of assessment feedback practice is to reframe feedback as a dialogic practice between teachers and students that focuses on their learning, rather than limiting assessment feedback to information that is unilaterally provided to, or imposed on, students as an end in itself. In fact, the prior existence of assessment standards' clarity and assessment design of feedback opportunity frames the targets and the timings for teachers and students to focus on in their feedback dialogue.

Figure 6.1 provides a visual representation of how the three elements of assessment standards, design, and feedback can be seen as working together as a trifecta. These three elements need to be considered in relation to each other. For example, the nature and timing of the assessment task(s) (horizontal axis) is influenced by the extent of the gap (vertical axis) that the assessment feedback is meant to bridge. Likewise, the amount of time between the assessed past learning and the anticipated enhanced learning (horizontal axis) would also affect how ambitious the assessment feedback should be (vertical axis). The triangulation of these three elements represents distinct contexts in which assessment can be understood and used for enhancing students' learning. Hence, there should be clarity of assessment standards, and clear focus and timing to design and use assessment tasks, before assessment feedback may be given, interpreted, and applied by teachers and learners.

Clarity of Standards as a Precondition for Assessment Feedback

A popular assertion of formative assessment advocates is that an assessment is considered to be formative only to the extent to which its use improves student outcomes (Wiliam, 2010). This implies that formative assessment should not merely generate useful information for teachers and students, but should also be used by students in ways that enhance their learning outcomes. This presumes (1) that the enhanced learning outcome, or improvement in performance/scores, is important enough to be recognized and (2) that there is clarity and certainty of standards to ascertain whether there has been any improvement in learning.

A common and popular version of feedback theory is Ramaprasad's (1983) definition that "Feedback is information about the gap between the actual level and the reference level of a system parameter which is used to alter the gap in some way" (p. 4). In the same vein, Sadler (1989) lists three essential conditions for student feedback to be effective:

- Students must understand what good performance is (i.e., the student must possess a concept of standard being aimed for).
- Students must understand how current performance relates to good performance (for this, the students are able to compare current and good performance).
- Students should understand how to act to close the gap between current and good performance.

What Ramaprasad's (1983) definition and Sadler's (1989) conditions for feedback have in common is the need for clear standards of learning to be articulated in order to identify a student's gap in learning that feedback may address. In common discourse, standards are whether a program of study or examination result shows a level of satisfaction/achievement. But in terms of functioning as a yardstick for gauging whether learning or enhancement of learning has actually taken place, standards need to be more unambiguously defined *before* tests and examinations are created and utilized.

Gauging the Proper Amount of Feedback to Provide on a Given Assessment

The potential of formative assessment feedback to enhance learning is thus limited by two main factors: first, the realistic gap in students' learning that may be bridged within that time (vertical axis of the formative assessment triangle) and, second, the amount of time in which formative assessment is practiced (horizontal axis of the formative assessment triangle).

While it is important to define clear standards in order to identify a suitable gap for feedback to address, it is also critical to analyze the different levels of ambition within a gap and to be realistic about how much feedback would be optimally useful for students to understand and act on. Shute (2008) warned that "if feedback is too lengthy or too complicated, many learners will not pay attention to it, rendering it useless" (p. 159). Likewise, Nicol (2010) identifies one of the key recommended good feedback practices from the literature in higher education contexts as being *"Selective* by commenting in reasonable detail on two or three things that the student can do something about" (p. 512). The challenge, however, is in deciding which "two or three" things feedback should direct students to address. In this regard, the argument is made that sparse feedback should also focus students on what they must do, and not only on what they should do, as it would not be logical to focus only on what is encouraged ("should") and neglect what should be mandatory ("must").

A gap in students' learning to be addressed by assessment feedback may be analyzed as comprising two different levels – what they must do with feedback (the accountability level) and what they should do with the feedback (the responsibility level) (Tan, 2011a), and that assessment feedback should strive to help students improve their learning at both levels. This requires teachers and assessors to be clear about the distinction between students' accountability and responsibility for their enhanced learning. An accountability level of feedback is pitched at what a student is in all likelihood able to achieve. A responsibility level of feedback targets what a student should reasonably achieve with sufficient effort and guidance. The characteristic of a responsibility level of feedback is that it targets a student's plausible scope of improvement, as distinct from an accountability level of feedback, which is pitched at the student's definite improvement.

Assessments Should Be Designed to Generate and Apply Feedback

The only way to tell if learning results from feedback is for students to make some kind of response to complete the feedback loop (Sadler, 1989). Boud (2000) strongly argues that "unless feedback is applied and used to demonstrate improvement, there is no way to tell if it has been effective"(p. 10). Hence, it is important that (1) students are given a task from which useful feedback could be given, (2) there is a subsequent task for which students may apply the feedback, and (3) the feedback is suitable for assisting students to improve their learning toward an identified level of improvement.

These conditions have implications for how to design assessment as well as post-assessment tasks for students to benefit from by using the feedback. The enhancement of student learning in formative assessment depends on the opportunities for students to receive and act on feedback. This is premised on the availability of assessment tasks that engage the students in displaying the initial learning and subsequent tasks or other opportunities that permit the students to apply feedback to their learning. As Sadler (1989) argued, students need more than information on how to close the gap between their current and desired performance levels – they require opportunities to use teachers' feedback.

The emphasis on students being able to use, and not just understand, teachers' feedback in subsequent assessment tasks has received considerable recent attention. Orsmond, Maw, Park, Gomez, and Crook (2013) observed a new trend of research into feedback and learning to "consider students' perceptions of feedback and their *use* of feedback" (p. 5, emphasis added). Likewise, Hounsell, McCune, Hounsell, and Litjens (2008) and Scoles, Huxham, and McArthur (2012) emphasized the value of feedback to students as focusing on what the students might do (or aim to do) with the feedback in their next or future assignments. Such an emphasis is known and labeled by some as "feedforward," the notion of effective learning from feedback whereby teacher feedback is utilized by the students to inform their efforts in future assessments.

Recommended Feedback Practice: Feedback as Dialogue, Not Commodity

Young students in primary schools are often perceived as being more receptive to (adult) teachers' instructions compared with older adolescent students. Such reception may tempt teachers to unilaterally transmit assessment feedback to primary students without taking care to ensure that the feedback is understood and acted on. It is therefore of vital importance that teachers in primary schools are able to converse or dialogue with students to enable young learners to understand and respond to feedback.

Crisp (2007) highlighted a tendency for "unilateral pronouncements by assessors" as one reason why students do not respond to feedback (p. 578). Likewise, Sadler's (2010b) argument for developing student capability in making complex appraisals appeals for feedback to be used as dialogue *with* students (as opposed to providing feedback unilaterally *to* students).

Nicol (2010) took the argument for a dialogic model of feedback even further, by suggesting that enhancing the quality of feedback by letting students experience and benefit from feedback as dialogue is possible, even with large groups of students and without necessarily unduly increasing teachers' workloads in the long term. Drawing from Laurillard's (2002) conversational framework for learning, Nicol (2010) suggested four important characteristics of feedback as dialogue:

1. Adaptive: It is continually adapted to individual students' needs.
2. Discursive: Feedback is a discussion or exchange of knowledge that constructs and enhances students' learning.
3. Interactive: Feedback is linked to the targets or goals for learning.
4. Reflective: Feedback enables learners to think back, and think through, on his or her own learning and what should be improved.

Beaumont, O'Doherty, and Shannon (2011) argued for feedback practice as "a system of guidance that provides not only a summative judgment of performance, but support through opportunities for a discussion which identifies areas of improvement and scaffolds the student to help achieve higher grades"

(p. 4). To achieve this, Beaumont and associates suggested three stages in their dialogic feedback model:

Stage 1: The *preparatory guidance stage* where students are prepared to understand the context of the assessment and the standards and criteria against which teachers' feedback is given. In this stage, teachers are encouraged to make explicit marking schemes and assessment criteria available to students for discussion *before* students attempt the assessment task.

Stage 2: The *in-task guidance stage*, which is important for creating opportunities for teachers and students to discuss ongoing work and construction of tasks against standards and criteria. They recommended that assessment assignments are broken down into smaller tasks for discussion and detailed specific feedback and that students could submit multiple drafts to the teacher for verbal and/or written feedback.

Stage 3: The *performance feedback stage* where feedback on students' final performance of their task is given in verbal or written form in summative fashion. Such feedback should be related to formal standards and criteria of the assessment task, which also permit students to understand how they should learn from their assessment experience and consequently prepare differently (or better) for future assessment challenges.

This systematic approach ensures feedback dialogue is paced prior to and throughout students' applying themselves to assessment tasks, and enhances students' focus on realizing learning outcomes in the course of dialoguing about assessment, rather than confining their attention to only completing the tasks. Extending assessment feedback dialogue before, during, and beyond tasks is therefore a direct approach to dissuading students from adopting a task-level orientation to feedback practice.

The trifecta of practices described in the earlier sections frames how feedback is understood and used by students to enhance their learning. Knowing how to use feedback to improve learning is a lifelong skill that goes beyond schooling. Hence, it is never too early to start training students at the primary school level to be active assessors of their own learning. Another recommended feedback practice is therefore to develop students to become self-regulated agents and beneficiaries of assessment feedback practices.

Developing Students to Become Self-Regulated Beneficiaries of Assessment Feedback Practices

Related to the trifecta for assessment is developing students' ability to self- and peer assess. For assessment feedback to be provided by teachers and successfully used by the students in classrooms, several factors need to be in place for the implementation of self- and peer assessment. In terms of students, first, self- and peer assessment should be an important part of the learning culture in the classrooms where time and space is provided for the students to use them (see Munns & Woodward, 2006; Nichols & Berliner, 2008). Second, students need to understand that the purpose of self- and peer assessment is to improve their learning. Third, the students need to be taught how to use self- and peer assessment. This includes explaining the criteria and standards used and making sure the students understand them clearly, as well as the modeling of the use of the self- and peer assessment (see Andrade, 2008; McMillan & Hearn, 2008). Fourth, the role of the students needs to change from passive learners to active learners and from being only passively assessed by teachers to actively assessing their own learning in terms of self-assessment (see Andrade et al., 2008). The students will begin to take on more decision-making as they take more responsibility for their own learning. They need to be encouraged to do so. Fifth, the students need to believe that they have the ability to learn to self-assess and to use such assessment (Wong, 2016).

Teachers need to change beliefs and expectations about their teaching and about their students. Teachers need to believe that their students have the ability to learn for themselves and to assess themselves (Wong, 2012a, 2016, 2017). Teachers need to change their expectations of their students and to see them as active learners, because, ultimately, students are the ones who have to do the learning. Teachers need to rethink students' roles in learning and assessment as well as rethink and develop relationships with students, seeing them as partners in making decisions about their own learning. Teachers who believe in their students are more receptive to creating opportunities for those students to learn. In addition, teachers must be willing to rethink their assessment practices, pedagogical practices, and students' learning needs when necessary in order to incorporate more formative assessments, in particular, self-assessment and peer assessment, into the students' day-to-day learning.

Traditionally, teachers are the instructors – the source of knowledge – as well as the assessors. However, with self- and peer assessment, students can be the teachers for themselves and for others, for example, deciding what learning strategies to use themselves and giving suggestions to their peers. Students know their own strengths and weaknesses and can be activated as a source of knowledge for their peers. In other words, with self- and peer assessment, the students take responsibility for and control of their own learning rather than just relying on the teachers to tell them what is not working or what to learn next. Teachers need to create a learning culture in their classrooms (see Nichols & Berliner, 2008). It is in this learning culture where self-assessment, peer assessment, and other formative assessments that inform learning and teaching should be placed. They should be an integral part of instruction where finding and using suggestions for improvement are valued, and opportunities for students to use the assessment feedback to plan and execute steps for improvement are present. It is imperative that there is trust between the teachers and the students (Popham, 2008). Students need to believe and trust that their teachers are devoted to having all students do well. As indicated by the findings in Wong (2012a, 2016, 2017) and Safii and Wong (2017), primary school students can self-assess, but teachers need to provide the training and opportunities so that the students can self-assess more effectively and confidently. Although we hope for teachers to give more feedback at the process and self-regulation levels, there is utility at this level in praise. In Safii and Wong (2017), the younger students actually looked forward to praise as it evoked feelings of success and motivated students to try to persevere in their work.

Conclusion

This chapter examined assessment feedback practices in primary schools against the backdrop of an instructional context of preparing young learners for high-stakes examinations. Faced with such pressures, there is a temptation for teachers to focus on imposing corrective feedback on students to address deficiencies, rather than to enable improvement. Such imposition also leaves little room for students to clarify the intent and meaning of feedback, rendering the feedback information as an extra burden or correction to be dealt with in addition to assessment tasks.

A trifecta of methods is recommended for assessment feedback to be practiced, rather than merely provided, in a more constructive fashion for primary students to enhance learning. These methods create a framework of clear and appropriate standards, assessment tasks designed to generate and apply feedback, and a practice of using feedback to engage in dialogue with students on understanding and using feedback information for their learning. In addition, we argue that it is vitally important for students to be supported to become active agents and beneficiaries of assessment feedback. A combination of enlightened teachers and empowered students engaged in dialogue on student learning can then ensue.

References

Andrade, H. (2008). Self-assessment through rubrics. *Educational Leadership*, *65*(4), 60–63.

Andrade, H. (2010). Students as the definitive source of formative assessment: Academic self-assessment and the self-regulation of learning. In H. L. Andrade & G. J. Cizek (Eds.), *Handbook of formative assessment* (pp. 90–105). New York: Routledge.

Andrade, H., Du, Y., & Wang, X. L. (2008). Putting rubrics to the test: The effect of a model, criteria generation, and rubric-referenced self-assessment on elementary school students' writing. *Educational Measurement: Issues and Practice*, *27*(2), 3–13.

Andrade, H., & Valtcheva, A. (2009). Promoting learning and achievement through self-assessment. *Theory into Practice*, *48*, 12–19.

Beaumont, C., O'Doherty, M., & Shannon, L. (2011). Reconceptualising assessment feedback: A key to improving student learning? *Studies in Higher Education*, *36*, 671–687.

Brown, W. (2008). Young children assess their learning: The power of the quick check strategy. *Young Children*, *63*(6), 14–20.

Boud, D. (2000). Sustainable assessment: Rethinking assessment for the learning society. *Studies in Continuing Education, 22*, 151–167.

Carless, D. (2016). Feedback as dialogue. In M. A. Peters (Ed.), *Encyclopedia of educational philosophy and theory* (pp. 1–6). Singapore: Springer Singapore.

Chappuis, J. (2015). *Seven strategies of assessment for learning* (2nd edn.). Upper Saddle River, NJ: Pearson Education.

Cheah, Y. M. (1998). The examination culture and its impact on literacy innovations: The case of Singapore. *Language and Education, 12*, 192–209.

Crisp, B. (2007). Is it worth the effort? How feedback influences students' subsequent submission of assessable work. *Assessment and Evaluation in Higher Education, 32*, 571–581.

Fisher, D. (2013). The purposeful classroom. Keynote address at the Primary School Education Seminar and Exhibition 2013, Ministry of Education, Singapore.

Fontana, D., & Fernandes, M. (1994). Improvements in mathematics performance as a consequence of self-assessment in Portuguese primary school pupils. *British Journal of Educational Psychology, 64*, 407–417.

Gopinathan, S. (2001). Globalisation, the state and education policy in Singapore. In J. Tan, S. Gopinathan, & W. K. Ho (Eds.), *Challenges facing the Singapore education system today* (pp. 213–251). Singapore: Prentice Hall.

Guskey, T. R., & Bailey, J. M. (2010). *Developing standards-based report cards*. Thousand Oaks, CA: Corwin.

Hattie, J., & Timperley, H. (2007). The power of feedback. *Review of Educational Research, 77*, 81–112.

Heng, M. A. (2001). Rethinking the meaning of school beyond the academic "A." In J. Tan, S. Gopinathan, & W. K. Ho (Eds.), *Challenges facing the Singapore education system today* (pp. 108–118). Singapore: Prentice Hall.

Hogan, D., Chan, M., Rahim, R., Kwek, D., Khin, M. A., Loo, S. C., ... & Luo, W. S. (2013). Assessment and the logic of instructional practice in Secondary 3 English and mathematics classrooms in Singapore. *Review of Education, 1*, 57–106.

Hounsell, D., McCune, V., Hounsell, J., & Litjens, J. (2008). The quality of guidance and feedback to students. *Higher Education Research & Development, 27*, 55–67.

Larson, R. W., & Brown, J. R. (2007). Emotional development in adolescence: What can be learned from school theatre program? *Child Development, 78*, 1083–1099.

Laurillard, D. (2002). *Rethinking university teaching: A conversational framework for the effective use of learning technologies* (2nd edn.). London: Routledge Falmer.

Lim-Ratnam, C. (2013). Tensions in defining quality pre-school education: The Singapore context. *Educational Review, 65*, 416–431.

McMillan, J. H., & Hearn, J. (2008). Student self-assessment: The key to stronger student motivation and higher achievement. *Educational Horizons, 87*, 40–49.

Ministry of Education. (2009). *Report of the primary education review and implementation committee*. Retrieved from www.moe.gov.sg/initiatives/peri/files/peri-report.pdf.

Ministry of Education (2010). Press release. PERI Holistic Assessment seminar 2010: 16 schools share Holistic Assessment practices and resources. Retrieved from http://archive-sg.com/sg/m/moe.gov.sg/2015–12 25_7252662_131/Ministry_of_Education_Singapore_Press_Releases_PERI_Holistic_Assessment_Seminar_2010_8212_16_Schools_Share_Holistic_Assessment_Practices_and_Resources/.

Munns, G., & Woodward, H. (2006). Student engagement and student self-assessment: The REAL framework. *Assessment in Education*, *13*, 193–213.

Murtagh, L. (2014). The motivational paradox of feedback: Teacher and student perceptions. *The Curriculum Journal*, *25*, 516–541.

Nichols, S. L., & Berliner, D. C. (2008). Testing the joy out of learning. *Educational Leadership*, *65*(6), 14–18.

Nicol, D. (2010). From monologue to dialogue: Improving written feedback processes in mass higher education. *Assessment & Evaluation in Higher Education*, *35*, 501–517.

O'Connor, K. (2009). *How to grade for learning: Linking grades to standards* (3rd edn.). Thousand Oaks, CA: Corwin.

Orsmond, P., Maw, S. J., Park, J. R., Gomez, S., & Crook, A. C. (2013). Moving feedback forward: Theory to practice. *Assessment & Evaluation in Higher Education*, *38*, 240–252.

Popham, W. J. (2008). *Transformative assessment*. Alexandria, VA: Association for Supervision and Curriculum Development.

Rahmat, F. A., & Wong, H. M. (2017, June). Analysing the nature of feedback in classrooms in Singapore. Paper presented at the Seventh Redesigning Pedagogy International Conference, Singapore.

Ramaprasad, A. (1983). On the definition of feedback. *Behavioural Science*, *28*, 4–13.

Ratnam-Lim, C. T. L., & Tan, K. H. K. (2015) Large-scale implementation of formative assessment practices in an examination-oriented culture. *Assessment in Education: Principles, Policy & Practice*, *22*, 61–78.

Ross, J. A. (2006). The reliability, validity, and utility of self-assessment. *Practical Assessment, Research & Evaluation*, *11*(10). Retrieved from http://pareonline.net/pdf/v11n10.pdf.

Sadler, D. R. (1989). Formative assessment and the design of instructional systems. *Instructional Science*, *18*, 119–144.

Sadler, D. R. (2010a). Beyond feedback: Developing student capability in complex appraisal. *Assessment & Evaluation in Higher Education*, *35*, 535–550.

Sadler, D. R. (2010b). Fidelity as a precondition for integrity in grading academic achievement. *Assessment & Evaluation in Higher Education*, *35*, 727–743.

Safii, L., & Wong, H. M. (2017, June). Seeing self-assessment and teacher feedback through students' lenses. Paper presented at the Seventh Redesigning Pedagogy International Conference, Singapore.

Scoles, J., Huxham, M., & McArthur, J. (2012). No longer exempt from good practice: Using exemplars to close the feedback gap for exams. *Assessment and Evaluation in Higher Education*, *8*, 631–645.

Shute, V. (2008). Focus on formative feedback. *Review of Educational Research*, *78*, 153–189.

Tan, K. H. K. (2011a). Assessment for learning in Singapore: Unpacking its meanings and identifying some areas for improvement. *Educational Research for Policy and Practice*, *10*, 91–103.

Tan, K. H. K. (2011b). Assessment reform in Singapore: Enduring, sustainable or threshold? In R. Berry & B. Adamson (Eds.), *Assessment reform in education: Policy and practice* (pp. 75–88). London: Springer.

Tan, K. H. K. (2013a). A framework for assessment for learning: Implications for feedback practices within and beyond the gap. *International Scholarly Research Notices.*

Tan, K. H. K. (2013b). Variation in teachers' conceptions of alternative assessment in Singapore primary schools. *Educational Research for Policy and Practice, 12,* 21–41.

Wadsworth, B. J. (2003). *Piaget's theory of cognitive and affective development: Foundations of constructivism* (5th edn.). Upper Saddle River, NJ: Allyn & Bacon.

Wiliam, D. (2010). An integrative summary of the research literature and implications for a new theory of formative assessment. In H. Andrade & G. Cizek (Eds.), *Handbook of formative assessment* (pp. 18–40). New York: Routledge.

Wiliam, D. (2011). *Embedded formative assessment.* Bloomington, IN: Solution Tree Press.

Wiliam, D. (2012, April). Sustaining formative assessment with teacher learning communities. PERI HA Professional Learning Series Workshop, Ministry of Education, Singapore.

Wong, H. M. (2012a). The perceptions of Singaporean teachers and students toward academic self-assessments. Doctoral dissertation, National Institute of Education, Nanyang Technological University.

Wong, H. M. (2012b). Students' interview transcripts. In The perceptions of Singaporean teachers and students toward academic self-assessments. Doctoral dissertation, National Institute of Education, Nanyang Technological University.

Wong, H. M. (2016). I can assess myself: Singaporean primary students' and teachers' perceptions of students' self-assessment ability. *Education 3–13: International Journal of Primary, Elementary and Early Years Education, 44,* 442–457.

Wong, H. M. (2017). Implementing self-assessment in Singapore primary schools: Effects on students' perceptions of self-assessment. *Pedagogies: An International Journal, 12,* 391–409.

7 Instructional Feedback in Writing

Steve Graham

Feedback is essential to good writing. This becomes especially obvious when feedback is not successful. Take, for example, the spacecraft *Mariner 1* bound for Venus at a cost of $18.5 million (Hendrickson, 1994). It had to be destroyed five minutes after takeoff due to an editing error involving a comma. Not as costly, but embarrassing nonetheless is this retraction: "IMPORTANT NOTICE. If you are one of the hundreds of parachuting enthusiasts who bought our Easy Sky Diving book, please make the following correction: on page 8, line 7, the words 'state zip code' should have read 'pull rip cord'" (Lederer, 2000, p. 116).

While feedback is not always successful in writing, it is necessary because authors sometimes write things that either are incorrect or do not make sense. This is illustrated in the following two comments written by different students: (1) "With all of the uses to be made of rubber it was necessary to find a substitute. After all rubber does not grow on trees" (Linkletter, 1962, p. 219) and (2) "The French flag is one half white, one half red, and one half blue" (Abington, 1952, p. 39). Even the inadvertent omission of a single letter can change a student's intended meaning, as in: "Pavlov studied the salvation of dogs" (Lederer, 1993, p. 13).

While these examples demonstrate why students and even professional writers need feedback, instructional feedback in writing involves more than just response to what is written. It also involves feedback designed to enhance students' learning of writing skills, strategies, knowledge, and motivations. Further, teachers can use instructional feedback to gauge their effectiveness as well as modify and enhance their instruction.

In this chapter, I define instructional feedback in writing, and then examine its purposes and functions as well as its effectiveness, providing recommendations for future research. I close by offering several additional observations on instructional feedback in writing based on my interactions with those who teach it – teachers.

What Is Instructional Feedback in Writing?

Drawing on multiple definitions of feedback (Balzer, Doherty, & O'Connor, 1989; Kluger & DeNisi, 1996; Hattie & Timperely, 2007), I define instructional feedback in writing as information provided by another person, group of people, agency, machine, self, or experience that allows a writer, one learning to write, or a writing teacher/mentor to compare some aspect of performance to an expected, desired, or idealized performance. To illustrate, accomplished or developing writers can receive feedback from a teacher or mentor on something written or in the process of being written. They can also receive feedback on their writing from peers, parents, computer programs, and even agencies or companies that score writing. Writers can further self-assess their own writing or derive information through their experiences writing and sharing their writing with others. As they are learning new writing skills, they can receive feedback on their progress from teachers, mentors, or other learners or by assessing their own progress. Feedback on learners' writing or their development as writers can provide teachers and mentors with information on their teaching effectiveness.

Each of these examples of instructional feedback is a consequence of the actions or performance of the writer. These outcomes may be solicited as part of a formal assessment, as when students are tested or a written assignment is graded, or they may occur in a less formal manner, as when a student asks a friend for feedback on his paper or a teacher monitors how well students apply a writing skill after its use is modeled. In all of these cases, the perceptions and evaluations of the actions and performance of the writer are compared with one or more standards. For example, when rereading what was written earlier, a writer may recognize that what was written was not exactly what she intended to write (a mismatch between realized and expected standards). A computer may underline words that were not spelled correctly (a mismatch between the realized and idealized standards). A teacher may inform a student that he or she did not combine two smaller sentences as directed during an instructional exercise (a mismatch between observed and desired actions).

Providing instructional feedback in writing is not a one-way street. Those receiving feedback can accept, modify, or reject it (Beach & Freidrich, 2006; Hattie & Timperely, 2007).

For instance, Zumbrunn, Marrs, and Mewborn (2016) found that middle and high school students differed in their openness to receiving feedback about their writing. Some students appreciated receiving feedback because it provided a means to improve their current and future writing, helped them understand the perspectives of others, made it clear which aspects of their writing were well done, or evoked positive emotions and feelings. Other students did not view writing feedback favorably because they viewed their writing as their own, did not care about the opinions of others, were uninterested in writing, or found that feedback evoked negative emotions.

Further, as Hattie and Timperely (2007) suggested, an ideal learning environment occurs when both teachers and learners are active agents in the instructional feedback process. Instead of just waiting on others to provide them with feedback, students and teachers can actively and directly seek feedback from others on their own.

What Are the Purposes and Functions of Instructional Feedback in Writing?

Formative and Summative Feedback

Instructional feedback in writing can be formative, summative, or both. Formative feedback is derived from assessments that involve collecting information or evidence about student learning, interpreting it in terms of learners' needs, and using it to alter what happens (Wiliam, 2006). Such assessments are often viewed as a process applied by teachers, mentors, students, peers, self, and even computers to provide feedback for making adjustments in everyday teaching and learning (e.g., Stiggins, 2005; Heritage, 2010). For instance, this might involve a peer providing a fellow student with feedback on his initial plan for a paper, a parent writing questions on a child's paper to indicate areas in need of clarification, a teacher telling a student during a conference what he liked most about a paper, a computer highlighting a phrase or sentence in text that may be poorly constructed, or a student using a scoring rubric to assess specific aspects of her writing such as word use, organization, and sentence structure. It might also involve feedback during learning where a peer tells a fellow student where a comma goes and why during a lesson on punctuation; a teacher provides a student with feedback on how to more effectively apply the planning strategy being taught; a mentor praises a student's persistence when learning a new writing strategy; or a computer informs a student when a mistake is made when matching specific words with similar spelling patterns.

A popular example of a formative assessment and feedback system within the context of writing is the 6 + 1 trait writing program (Culham, 2003). This program teaches students and teachers how to analyze writing using a specific set of traits that include ideation, organization, voice, word choice, sentence fluency, conventions, and presentation. Students use this evaluation system to provide feedback on their own and others' writing. This program involves more than assessment and feedback, however, as students acquire a vocabulary and criteria for planning and discussing writing as well (Coe, Hanita, Nishioka, & Smiley, 2011).

Formative assessment in writing and the resulting feedback can also be used by teachers to shape the writing curriculum in at least three ways. This includes using the information provided by formative assessments to decide what to teach (e.g., students typically use the same sentences patterns over and over in their writing and the teacher designs a series of lessons to address this), to modify a particular lesson as it is occurring (e.g., the teacher notices that students are misapplying strategy for giving each other feedback that is being taught and provides verbal guidance on how to correct this), or to modify instruction more broadly. This last approach is exemplified by the curriculum-based measurement (CBM) approach. With CBM, teachers monitor students' writing progress in order to make changes in their teaching with the goal of making it more effective (Deno, 1985; Saddler, 1989). This typically involves regularly monitoring students' writing progress using test stimuli drawn from the annual writing curriculum. Feedback from these assessments is used to monitor the progress of the class as well as individual students to determine if the instructional procedures are working and to modify them to produce better instructional programs if needed.

Summative feedback is drawn from assessments designed "to determine a student's current performance or attainment of material that was the focus of instruction" (Hosp, 2012, p. 97). Summative assessments are often cumulative evaluations given at particular time points to determine students' growth, mastery of learning standards, or what they do or do not know. Such assessments often follow the end of an instructional unit, and unlike formative assessments, which may occur quite frequently, summative assessments may occur only a few times over the course of an academic year or semester. Examples of writing summative assessments in the classroom that provide feedback to teachers and students are midterm or end-of-term exams assessing students' mastery of specific writing skills, assigned writing projects evaluating students' capabilities to use writing in a particular way (e.g., write a convincing argument that addresses multiple viewpoints), or a particular recurring assessment involving students' sentence construction skills to evaluate growth over time.

Summative assessments and the feedback they provide can also be used for accountability purposes. According to Elliott, Kurz, and Neegaard (2012), the basic theory underlying this approach is that "by setting standards and measuring achievement annually relative to these standards, both teachers and students will work harder and more learning will occur" (p. 111). In the United States, for example, accountability tests in writing are quite common with writing assessed at the national level (i.e., National Assessment of Educational Progress; https://nces.ed.gov/nationsreportcard/), by most states, and in many school districts (Beck & Jeffrey, 2007; Graham, Hebert, & Harris, 2011). Such tests are often administered once a year to students in specific grades or even all grades.

The results or specific feedback from these national, state, or district summative writing assessments can have high-stakes consequences for students, teachers, and school districts (Jeffrey, 2009). Scores from summative assessments may determine if a student receives a high school diploma, indicate readiness for college, or establish eligibility for a merit-based scholarship (Beck & Jeffrey, 2007). The summative findings may be used by policymakers, educators, and the public to make judgments about the effectiveness of writing instruction in specific district or schools. They may further be used to evaluate the effectiveness of teachers, and such data may provide evidence when teachers are reviewed each year.

While high-stakes summative assessments provide feedback that can be used to measure writing achievement, evaluate students' mastery of important skills, determine the effectiveness of instructional practices in writing, and monitor writing educational systems for accountability, they can also provide formative feedback that can be used to guide instructional decision-making. This can occur at multiple levels. For instance, a school district whose writing scores have been consistently low for several years may make a decision to invest greater attention to writing instruction, changing how writing is taught and increasing professional development for teachers.

Feedback from high-stakes summative tests can also be aimed at making more immediate changes in classrooms. The assessments envisioned by Smarter Balanced (www.smarterbalanced.org/higher-education) to assess students' mastery of Common Core State Standards (CCSS) in writing (www.corestandards .org/ELA-Literacy/) provide an example of this. The goal of Smarter Balanced was to develop a summative test to assess students' performance at the end of the school year as well as interim assessments that teachers could administer throughout the school year. In addition to providing feedback on students' mastery of CCSS objectives (allowing one to compare student performance across classes, schools, districts, and states), it was anticipated that the feedback from the summative and interim tests would provide teachers with timely feedback about their students' writing, allowing them to tailor instruction to students' needs. While one could argue about whether the feedback from the summative and interim tests occurs frequently enough or whether it is adequately tied to classroom practices, the basic idea envisioned by Smarter Balanced is consistent with the view that formative assessments collect information or evidence about students' learning, interpret it in terms of learners' needs, and use it to alter instruction (Wiliam, 2006).

Focus of Instructional Feedback in Writing

The examples in the sections above demonstrate that instructional feedback in writing can take many different forms and serve a variety of purposes. The purposes of instructional feedback dictate the focus or form that feedback takes. Instructional feedback to students can be aimed at virtually all aspects of writing including, but not limited to, supporting the learning maintenance and generalizations of new writing skills and strategies, establishing current levels of performance, improving what is written and extending or challenging thinking about a particular piece of writing, demonstrating how readers react to writing or use the information written, shaping how writing unfolds and takes place, enhancing motivation and writing persistence, facilitating self-evaluation and promoting personal responsibility, managing the writing environment or one's writing behavior, working with writing collaborators, applying new tools for writing, praising accomplishments or efforts, clarifying or establishing goals for writing or learning, emphasizing standards or criteria for good writing, controlling negative emotions about writing, making the process of writing more manageable, and reinforcing or establishing new identities for writers (Peterson, 2003; Beach & Freidrich, 2006; Rijlaarsdam et al., 2012; MacArthur, 2016; Graham, in press).

Hattie and Timperely (2007) indicated that instructional feedback generally focuses on the task or product; the processes used to create a product or complete a task; the personal processes of regulating the task so that it can be done better, more effortlessly, and more confidently; and the self in terms of personal feedback that expresses positive or negative evaluations about the student. Examples of feedback on the writing task or product include comments about the content of a paper, the grammatical correctness of a sentence, or whether a newly learned writing strategy is executed correctly. Feedback on process in writing mainly involves information, cues, or guidance designed to help writers apply processes involved in producing text such as goal setting, planning, drafting, revising, and editing. Self-regulation feedback in writing focuses on supporting commitment (e.g., investment of effort), control (e.g., generating internal feedback to monitor, evaluate, and modify task or product execution), and confidence (e.g., self-efficacy). The aim of self-regulatory feedback is to foster autonomous, self-directed, and self-disciplined writing. Examples of personal feedback focused on the self in writing include praise such as "You are a great writer," "You worked really hard," and "That is a really intelligent thing you said here." Such praise carries little information about the processes, effort, confidence, or control related to the task and the writer's performance. As Hattie and Timperely noted, however, praise can provide such information, as when a writer is informed: "You are really an ace editor because you corrected every error in this piece of writing."

Hattie and Timperely's (2007) taxonomy captures most of the examples of feedback in writing presented in the chapter so far. Even so, I want to direct attention to feedback aimed at writers' emotions, personality traits, audience, and the social context in which writing takes place. Discussions of how instructional feedback can be directed at influencing these aspects of writing are relatively uncommon. However, feedback may serve a purposeful and facilitative role in each. I provide an example for each below.

First, a writer may be uncertain about who will ultimately read her text, influencing her evaluation of what she writes and the feedback she gives to herself. As a result, she may create an imaginary audience and keep this audience in mind as she self-evaluates the text produced so far and the possible text to be produced.

Second, students who experience anxiety about writing may benefit from self-directed feedback reminding themselves to reduce negative self-talk and increase positive coping thoughts (see, for example, Salovey & Haar, 1990). To illustrate, a teacher might encourage a student to identify positive self-statements they say to themselves while writing, as is done in the self-regulated strategy development model (Harris, Graham, Mason, & Freidlander, 2008), and ask students to self-evaluate periodically to determine if they are using them and if they are accomplishing the desired purpose.

Third, in social contexts where students are expected to work together on some aspects of their compositions, teachers can establish a routine for carrying out these tasks, and then provide students with feedback that helps them do this effectively and smoothly. For instance, MacArthur, Graham, Schwartz, and Shafer (1995) taught students a framework for providing feedback to each other, and then provided them with feedback on how well they were implementing once they started to apply it routinely in the classroom.

Fourth, for students who are less concerned with presenting themselves in an agreeable way (a personality trait; see Costa & McCrae, 1992), some feedback from the teacher might focus on the importance of planning, as these students are less likely to do this before writing than students who control their expressive behavior to present themselves in a pleasing way (see Galbraith, 1999). Unfortunately, I was not able to locate any studies that tested how feedback should be matched to personality traits.

Instructional feedback also differs on whether it is designed to address feed-up, feed-back, feed-forward, and side-shadowing. Hattie and Timperely (2007) indicated that feed-up provides information to writers and their teachers/ mentors on their attainment of learning goals based on task performance. Such feedback addresses the question, "Where am I going?" The goals for such feedback can range widely from performance on a written composition (e.g., provide at least three forms of support for your argument), learning a new writing skill (e.g., summarize in a written paragraph the gist and three most important details), and teaching writing (e.g., students can correctly combine two simple sentences into a complex one using a subordinating conjunction). The feedback provided may be direct ("You exceeded the requirement for this assignment by providing four forms of support for your argument"), comparative ("This summary is better than the last one you did because you accurately identified the main idea"), social ("Alphonso, I like the way you listen to Mark's ideas for how these two sentences can be combined"), motivational ("We are now really good at creating complex sentences"), or more general ("You need to take on more challenging topics when you write").

Feed-back information addresses the question, "How am I going?" (Hattie & Timperely, 2007). This aspect of instructional feedback focuses on progress on a task or some part of it and/or how to proceed with the task. Such information is often provided in relation to a specific instructional goal (e.g., "You met the goal of doubling the number of substantive revisions made"), past performance (e.g., "I did so much better than the last time I taught my students this skill, as all of them now apply it in their writing"), or success in carrying out the task ("You did the first step or the strategy, but forgot to do the second one").

The focus of feed-forward information is aimed at answering the question, "Where to next?" (Hattie & Timperely, 2007). This often involves informing students about what they will be working on next, but it can lead to feedback that opens the door for greater possibilities for learning. For example, Graham, Harris, and Mason (2005) asked pairs of third-grade students to identify contexts in which they could use one or more of the skills or strategies they were learning. Students then set a goal to apply this in one or more new contexts, considering how they would need to modify the skill or strategy. In the next instructional meeting, each student assessed and discussed his or her application of the new skill or strategy in the new context, identified what worked and did not work, and considered any needed modifications. The information students gathered about their own performance and shared with others provided opportunities for them to extend their thinking about how what they learned could be applied more broadly.

Side-shadowing feedback focuses on considering alternative perspectives and dialogic intentions (Welch, 1997). In contrast to providing comments aimed at giving information on how to further develop a piece of writing, side-shadowing comments and questions are designed to challenge writers' certainty by encouraging them to consider their writing from a different angle such as how another character might interpret the same events.

Modes for Delivering Instructional Feedback in Writing

Instructional feedback in writing can be delivered through a variety of different modes. It can involve oral feedback, as when teachers conduct conferences with students asking them questions like: "How is the writing going?," "I like how you open your piece by . . .," "I am having trouble visualizing what you wrote – what other information can you tell me?," or "How can we say this using different words?" Oral feedback can be delivered face to face or via a tape recorder, phone, or other device. It can also involve students' listening to their compositions being read back to them via text-to-speech voice synthesis (e.g., Jones, 1998).

Feedback can be delivered through written cues, comments, and directions, as when a teacher or peer provides marginal notes, edits, or questions directly in the composition, or summative statements at the beginning or the end of the paper. Such feedback can be handwritten or provided digitally.

Students and teachers can deliver feedback about writing or writing instruction to themselves through an internal or external self-directed dialogue where they self-assess performance, process, commitment, control, confidence, emotions, audience reaction, and so forth. For example, while teaching a writing lesson, a teacher may covertly tell herself, "I need to slow down and go back over this; I don't think everyone understood what I showed them."

Instructional feedback can be quantitative, as when teachers grade students' writing or use a rubric to provide numerical grades on specific features of writing. Students can also grade their writing, as when they sort the writing in their portfolio so they can highlight their best work. Teachers can collect quantitative feedback using clickers, as when they pose a question to check students' understanding of a concept they are presenting. Some computer-automated essay-scoring programs give students a score after evaluating their writing (see Crossley & McNamara, 2017, for examples).

Feedback can be visual. For example, students may use emojis to express how they feel about a story written by a peer; word-processing programs may use color to highlight problematic areas in text; and writers may watch other people try to deal with their text (see Rijlaarsdam et al., 2008, for examples). Of course, instructional feedback can involve multiple combinations of these modes, as when a student puts together a portfolio, including rubric scores for each composition selected, written commentary on why each piece was selected, and a prominent gold star on her favorite paper.

It is important to note that methods for delivering instructional feedback have expanded considerably in recent years, as a result of new computer programs and the Internet. To illustrate, students can use Google Docs to write and exchange feedback (Zheng, Lawrence, Warschauer, & Lin, 2015). They can develop, showcase, and process electronic portfolios for their writing online or on a computer (Nicolaidou, 2013). A weblog can be created where students write cooperatively, providing each other with feedback (Karask, Fer, & Orhan, 2014). An automated essay evaluation program can be used to provide students with feedback for revising their papers (Wilson & Czik, 2015; Moore & MacArthur, 2016). Students can send each other feedback anonymously through a digital computer program (Cho & MacArthur, 2011).

The potential advantage of computer programs and digital systems like the ones above include immediacy of feedback and potential access to more reviewers. While there is a general perception that immediate feedback is better than delayed feedback, a review by Kulik and Kulik (1988) found that some delay is beneficial when feedback is focused on the task, whereas more immediate feedback may be better when the focus is on process. A good example of the former is when an author puts aside a draft of a paper for a couple of days so it can be viewed with fresh eyes. In terms of multiple reviewers, expanding the number of collaborators who provide feedback to an author is likely to be seen as advantageous by many, but the effects of increasing the number of reviewers is uncertain.

What Are the Effects of Instructional Feedback for Writing?

Reviews that examine the effectiveness of feedback across academic domains indicate that it generally improves performance (Balzer et al., 1989; Kluger & DeNisi, 1996; Hattie & Timperely, 2007; Sanchez, Atkinson, Koenka, Moshontz, & Harris, in press), but there is considerable variability in outcomes, and feedback is not always effective. Even though feedback is one of the oldest tools used to teach writing, research examining its effectiveness is quite limited, especially in terms of studies designed to draw a causal inference about its effects (i.e., true and quasi-experiments). As a consequence of this limitation, I cannot examine the effectiveness of all of the different types of instructional feedback presented so far. There is enough evidence to draw some tentative conclusions about formative and summative instructional feedback in writing though.

In examining the impact of formative assessment, I draw on meta-analyses that summarize the effects of feedback intervention studies in writing. These meta-analyses mostly involve school-aged students, although a review by Hillock includes studies conducted with college students. There is overlap (at times considerable) between studies included in these reviews, but each of these meta-analyses is presented. I did this for two reasons. First, the reviews provide a historical examination on the shifting focus of formative feedback intervention studies in writing, and, second, some aspect of each review provided new evidence or a new focus on an aspect of formative feedback not covered in the other reviews. The studies included in these meta-analyses almost always involved typically developing writers, and little to no attention was directed at examining cultural differences. Thus, it is not possible to draw with any certainty the impact of formative feedback on struggling writers, students with disabilities, or specific cultural groups.

When examining the impact of summative feedback, I was unable to draw on meta-analyses, as such a review does not exist in the area of writing, and intervention studies are extremely rare. As a result, I draw on other forms of evidence, such as descriptive and qualitative studies, investigations examining the reliability and validity of summative assessments, and correlational research.

Formative Feedback

Formative feedback can come from teachers, peers, self, or computers. Hillocks (1986) was the first scholar to apply meta-analysis to determine the effectiveness of peer and self-feedback on the writing of students in grade three to college. He limited the studies reviewed to true and quasi-experiments writing intervention studies. He located six studies that tested students' use of criteria embodied in a scale or set of questions to evaluate and generate feedback about writing (these are often referred to as rubrics today; Andrade, Wang, Du, & Akawi, 2009). Across studies, students applied these criteria to assess their own writing, the writing of their peers, writing supplied by teachers, or some combination of these methods. All participants in these six investigations were either freshmen in college or typical students in grades ten to twelve. Two-thirds of the studies produced a positive effect size. The average effect for all studies was 0.36, providing evidence that engaging in formative assessments where specific criteria are used to evaluate and generate feedback about writing is effective.

In a more recent meta-analysis, my colleagues and I (Graham, Hebert, & Harris, 2015) examined the impact of multiple forms of formative feedback on the quality of students' writing. All investigations included in our meta-analysis involved true or quasi-experiments conducted with elementary and middle school students.

One basic finding from this review was that formative feedback from adults improved the quality of students' writing. The seven studies examining adult feedback tested specific forms of adult feedback including teacher or parent feedback on writing as well as teacher feedback on students' progress while learning specific writing skills. Examples of adult feedback on writing includes providing students with verbal feedback about unclear or missing information in text, scores and comments on specific features of writing based on the criteria from a writing rubric, and information about number of words written and accuracy of spelling in text. An example of feedback on progress while learning a writing skill includes providing students with information on their success in applying a strategy for organizing text as it is being taught to them. Taken together, the seven studies testing adult feedback to students statistically improved the quality of students' writing (average weighted effect size = 0.87), with all studies producing a positive effect.

A second finding from our 2015 meta-analysis (Graham, Hebert, & Harris, 2015) was that peer feedback (giving it or giving and receiving it) statistically enhanced the quality of text produced by elementary and middle school students. All eight studies examining peer feedback produced a positive effect, resulting in a collective effect size of 0.58. Examples of peer-feedback procedures tested in these studies ranged from directions to meet with a classmate and provide feedback on their paper to teaching students to use a rubric or scale for providing feedback.

We further found that teaching elementary and middle school students to provide self-feedback was a successful strategy to improve the quality of their writing. All ten studies testing the effectiveness of this form of formative feedback produced a positive effect, resulting in an average effect of 0.62. The form of self-feedback most commonly tested in the studies reviewed involved teaching students to use a rubric to score their writing, but also included instruction designed to evaluate their text and carry out specific revising processes such as substituting, adding, deleting, and moving text.

Our 2015 analysis (Graham, Hebert, and Harris) also found that feedback from computer programs improved students' writing. All four studies conducted with middle school students enhanced the quality of what students wrote, yielding a collective effect of 0.38. Three of these investigations tested Summary Street, a computer program that provides students with feedback when writing a summary. The other study was a web-based feedback system.

Not all of the approaches to formative feedback that my colleagues and I examined in 2015 (Graham, Hebert, & Harris) were found to be effective. First, even though all five studies testing the impact of curriculum-based measurement in writing with elementary and middle school students produced a positive effect, the average effect of 0.18 for these studies was not statistically significant. In these studies, curriculum-based measurement procedures involved teachers monitoring their students' progress on one or more writing variables over time. Writing assessments were typically administered weekly.

We also found that the popular 6 +1 Trait program described earlier in this chapter was not effective in improving the quality of students' writing. While all four studies conducted with elementary grade children resulted in a positive effect, the collective effect size of these investigations was 0.05. This effect was not statistically significant.

Last, in our 2015 meta-analysis (Graham, Harris, & Hebert) we did not specifically test if there were differential effects depending on who delivered the feedback (adults, peers, or self). This was examined by Graham, Kiuhara,

McKeown, and Harris in 2012 with a meta-analysis that focused solely on elementary grade students. In this review, my colleagues and I conducted a moderator analysis to examine if source of feedback was related to the magnitude of effects obtained for formative feedback in writing. This was the case, as the effect for adult feedback was statistically greater than the average weighted effects for peer and self-feedback. Unfortunately, a similar analysis involving older students and adults has not been conducted.

It should also be noted that my colleagues and I (Graham, Harris, & Hebert, 2011) conducted an earlier meta-analysis that was more expansive than either of the 2015 analyses described above, as it included elementary, middle, and high school students. While the accumulated evidence in all three reviews supports the effectiveness of formative feedback in writing, this earlier 2011 meta-analysis provided some additional and useful information. We found that (1) when students received feedback from adults or peers their writing improved (average effect in eight studies was 1.01), and (2) giving and receiving feedback enhanced writing quality (the average effect for six studies was 0.71).

Finally, in another meta-analysis, my colleagues and I (Graham, Harris, & Santangelo, 2015) found that praise had a positive impact on students' writing. The studies that tested the effectiveness of praise involved single subject design investigations. Like true and quasi-experiments, single-subject designs are experimental and provide controls for threats to internal validity (see Horner et al., 2005). Contingent praise had a large and positive effect on specific features of elementary students' writing in four studies (nonoverlapping data = 96%). For example, when a teacher praised a positive feature of a student's writing, such as good word choice, students were more likely to make such choices in future papers. The effects of praise requires further study, though, as Lipnevich and Smith (2009a) reported that older university students indicated that praise did not facilitate learning even though it had a positive influence on their emotions.

The findings from these various reviews support the commonly held view that formative writing assessments where students receive feedback about their writing or writing progress during the course of everyday teaching and learning improves students' writing. This conclusion comes with a number of caveats, though. First, the findings from the meta-analyses described above are based on a relatively small number of experimental studies. Collectively, there were fifty-three such investigations in the five meta-analyses above. Second, many of these studies involved weaker designs. For instance, 57% of the studies in Graham, Hebert, and Harris (2015) were quasi-experiments. Whereas overall study quality was not related to variability in effect sizes in this review, there was great variability in the overall quality of studies, with issues ranging from attrition to failure to control for teacher effects.

It is also clear that students' writing does not always improve as a result of formative evaluation and feedback. This was evident in Graham, Hebert, and Harris (2015). This review found that two approaches did not enhance students' writing: (1) the 6+1 Writing Trait program and (2) the curriculum-based measurement approach. On a more positive note, all of the thirty-nine studies that my colleagues and I reviewed in this meta-analysis produced a positive effect, with 82% yielding an effect size greater than 0.22. In a moderator analyses, we also found that variability in the effects of feedback was not statistically related to grade (elementary versus secondary schools) or type of formative feedback (structured versus unstructured). Nevertheless, many forms of writing feedback have not been adequately tested. For example, I was able to locate only two studies testing the effectiveness of writing feedback focusing on process (Schunk & Schwartz, 1993a, 1993b). Experimental research examining the impact of feedback in writing that focuses on self-regulation, emotions, personality traits, audience, self, and social context is notably absent and needed.

Summative Feedback

Effectiveness

Most of the research on summative assessment and feedback in writing involves writing assessments that are used for accountability purposes, which mainly includes writing assessments administered by states and school districts in the United States (Graham, Hebert, & Harris, 2011). Very little research has been directed at determining the effects of other summative writing assessments such as grades, mid-term and end-of-term exams, or graded writing projects. As a result, I examine the impact of high-stakes accountability tests on students' writing as well as on classroom practices.

Supporters of high-stakes state and district tests argue that the findings or feedback from such evaluations are beneficial because they raise expectations for students' writing and make these expectations more explicit. This in turn leads to better writing instruction and encourages students to become better writers. This view is also shared by the general public (Afflerbach, 2005).

In contrast to formative instructional feedback in writing, where the impact of such information has been tested via true and quasi-experiments, the value of feedback from high-stakes writing assessments rests primarily on correlational data and qualitative analyses (Graham et al., 2011). Available studies provide some limited support for the positive effects of these assessments, including student writing gains (based on correlational data), making writing instruction more central to the mission of schools, and changing teachers' writing practices in positive ways (e.g., Callahan, 1999; Parke, Lane, & Stone, 2006; Dappen, Iserhagen, & Anderson, 2008).

Despite these positive findings, high-stakes writing assessments produce negative and unintended consequences (Graham, Hebert, & Harris, 2011). For example, high-stakes writing assessments can narrow what is taught, as teachers place greater emphasis on teaching the types of writing tested, minimizing or even excluding the teaching of other types of writing not included in these assessments (Hillocks, 2002). Another unwanted consequence is that these tests can encourage teachers to teach and students to use a formulaic approach to writing, reducing students' voice and originality when writing. To illustrate, Albertson (2007) found that 78% of grade eight and 66% of grade ten students used the same basic formula (five-paragraph theme) or a variation of it on the state's direct writing assessment. A third negative consequence of these tests is they send the unintended message that writing is the job of the language arts teachers. This happened in a study where English teachers were expected to implement the state's writing assessment framework (Callahan, 1999). Consequently, many content teachers came to view writing as something done by the English department.

Even more important, the assessments from which high-stakes feedback are derived are of questionable validity. A basic assumption underlying the validity of a high-stakes writing assessment is that it produces reliable findings. A review by Graham, Hebert, and Harris (2011) of fifteen studies found that such tests are not reliable enough to provide valid information about students' writing or teachers' writing practices.

It is further assumed that the findings from high-stakes writing assessments allow educators to determine students' general writing performance. Most assessments collect a single sample of writing in a specific genre (Jeffrey, 2009). Basing an assessment on a single piece of writing is like administering a one-item test. In the area of writing, such tests do not provide a valid measure of students' overall achievement. To illustrate, Coffman (1966) found that five writing tasks were needed to reliably assess high school students' writing. Similarly, Huang (2008) reported that three writing tasks were needed to obtain a reliable estimate of writing achievement for English-language learners, whereas Graham, Hebert, Sandbank, and Harris (2016) indicated this would require eleven compositions when students were young, struggling writers. While it is unlikely that any writing assessment can reasonably require five to eleven writing samples, it is clear that a single sample is not adequate.

Concerns about the technical adequacy of high-stakes writing assessments raise issues about the consequential validity of feedback from such tests for relevant stakeholders: students, teachers, and schools. Is it fair to use these tests as currently conceptualized and constructed to provide feedback that is used to make high-stakes decisions about students, teachers, or schools? I would argue that it is not. However, if these tests are eliminated at the state and district level, an unintended consequence may be that writing instruction becomes even more minimized in schools than it currently is (Graham, 2014).

Future Research

Formative Assessment

While there are many issues that researchers can address in the future, I would like to highlight several that I think are particularly important. One, we know little about the reliability and validity of the different types of formative writing assessments teachers apply. Some initial work in this area has been done (e.g., see appendix B, tables 10–13 in Graham et al., 2011), but the psychometric principles of many assessments used to provide formative feedback in the classroom are unknown. As part of this work, I hope researchers will examine if teachers view specific assessment and formative feedback procedures as useful and acceptable (see, for example, Graham, Harris, Bartlett, Popadopoulou, & Santoro, 2016). We also need to know what level of accuracy by the user is needed for an assessment and its resulting feedback to be effective. For instance, how accurate does peer or self-assessment need to be in order to improve performance?

Surprisingly little empirical research has been devoted to determining the attributes that make formative writing feedback effective (see Lipnevich & Smith, 2009b; Smith & Lipnevich, 2009, for exceptions to this statement). This has not stopped experts from rendering their opinions, such as "Effective teacher feedback is specific, descriptive, nonjudgemental, and varied according to students' phases of development, ZPD [zone of proximal development], language skills, perceived persona, and self-assessment abilities" (Beach & Freidrich, 2006, p. 231). I suspect that much of this is true for writing and formative feedback in general, but such a definition is not complete, as it does not address factors such as focus, mode, timing, source, or context. Further, feedback involves judgments comparing some aspect of performance to expected, desired, or idealized standards (see the definition at the start of this chapter). A writer's knowledge of the standard, with which performance is compared, may be especially important in determining the effectiveness of formative feedback. Consider, for instance, a student self-assessing his own writing; judgments may be particularly difficult to make if the writer is unclear of his own goals or intentions when writing a text (Fitzgerald, 1987). Unless there is some other standard against which to compare performance, evaluation and the resulting self-feedback may be unclear, imprecise, or ineffective. This is also likely to happen when the reasons for teaching writing skills or strategies are uncertain, or when teachers do not have a clear idea of how writing instruction should proceed.

The study of what makes formative writing feedback effective (or ineffective) likely depends on the interaction between the context in which writing occurs and the internal resources that writers and collaborators bring to the act of composing. Most theoretical models of writing, and by extension evaluation and feedback, focus on one or the other (see Bazerman, 2016; MacArthur & Graham, 2016). One model of writing that emphasizes the interaction between context and individual writers and collaborators is the Writers in Community Model (Graham, 2018). The basic tenet of this model is that the community in which writing takes place and the cognitive capabilities and resources of those who create it simultaneously shape and constrain writing.

A writing community in this model involves a group of people who use writing to accomplish specific goals,[1] such as a science classroom using writing to facilitate learning or an English classroom where both writing and literature are taught. As these examples illustrate, writing does not have to be the main or only goal of a community, and one can be a member of multiple writing communities. Writing communities range in size, purpose, and the distribution of power among members, and members vary in terms of their affiliations and identities. Writing in a community is accomplished through the use of specific tools and recurring actions. Tools include writing machinery (e.g., pencil and paper, word processors, Internet-based programs), artifacts created by writers (e.g., author notes, drawings, past drafts of text), and sources of information writers draw on (e.g., texts, pictures, film, interviews, exemplars). Recurring actions, on the other hand, are the typical practices that a writing community employs to achieve its objectives, and include the activities that members of the community engage in to define the writing task, structure the writing environment, distribute responsibility, execute the process of composing, and manage the social, motivational, emotional, and physical aspects of writing. How a writing community comes to carry out its purposes does not occur by happenstance but is shaped by its physical and social context as well as the collective history of the community and macro forces outside it (e.g., rules and policies set by an organization under which the community operates). The Writers in Community Model proposes that these factors shape the nature and form of writing within a community and by extension the process of formative evaluation and feedback. Even in seemingly similar communities like two fourth-grade writing classrooms, formative assessment and feedback will differ in multiple ways.

The act of writing in a community is undertaken and shaped by its members. In other words, what writers and their collaborators bring to the task of composing is also important. Within a specific community, writers and possible collaborators must decide to engage in the act of writing and determine how much effort to commit, what cognitive resources to apply, what tools to use, how to carry out the task, and who to work with in some instances. These decisions are driven by each individual's views on the value, utility, and interest in the writing task, expectations for success, attributions for success or failure, and beliefs about the community in which this writing takes place and their role and identity in it. Writing is further influenced by the relevant knowledge an individual can bring to bear. These resources are initiated and coordinated through control mechanisms (i.e., attention, working memory, and executive functioning) that writers and collaborators use to regulate the writing environment, tools for writing, and the production processes involved in planning, producing, and polishing text. These control mechanisms further regulate motivational beliefs, emotional states, personality traits, and physiological

---

1 In some instances a writing community can involve a single person as when a writer composes a diary only he or she reads.

factors that impact the writer. The Writers in Community Model proposes that these individual factors shape the nature and form of writing within a community and, by extension, the operation of formative evaluation and feedback.

The Writers in Community Model (Graham, 2018) envisions writing as an extremely complex process operating in complex and diverse environments. Future research studying formative instructional feedback in writing and its effects should concentrate on context, individual differences, and their interactions. Take, for instance, writing in school. We know very little about how formative assessment is enacted in different writing communities. In a national survey by Kiuhara, Graham, and Hawken (2009), a majority of high school teachers reported they used praise for writing weekly or more often, but there was considerable variation among teachers and differences in academic areas (e.g., English teachers reported praising writing more often than social studies and science teachers). There was also considerable variation in teachers' use of scales and personal judgment to assess writing, including differences across academic areas (e.g., scales were used more often by English teachers). Contextual effects were also identified by Matsumura et al. (2002), who found that teachers in low-achieving urban schools were more likely to provide their students with feedback on the content of their paper than teachers in higher-achieving urban schools. While neither of these studies drilled deeply into the multiple and interacting attributes of a writing community as described above, they demonstrate the value of studying varying communities to gain a better understanding of how instructional feedback in writing operates within and across settings.

Consistent with the Writers in Community Model, there is evidence that individual differences in writing influence the effectiveness of formative feedback. For instance, my colleagues and I (Graham, 1997; De La Paz, Swanson, & Graham, 1998) provided struggling writers with supports designed to enhance their revising behavior. This included procedures that prompted students to identify parts of text that might be problematic, diagnose the problem if possible, decide how to address the problem, and execute the decision. While these procedures did result in more substantive and higher-quality revisions for the participating students collectively, we observed instances where the effectiveness of the self-derived feedback was influenced by what the student brought to the task. Students differed in their ability to identify and diagnose problems in text, as when one student deleted three sentences central to the plot because readers would not understand that part or when another student changed "love" to "like" in the sentence "He loved farm work" because readers would not understand why he loved farm work. They also differed in their ability to execute planned changes, as when one student correctly identified that "We got to ride horses go to rodeo" did not sound quite right, but was unable to address this problem successfully when he changed this to: "We got to ride horses go and a rodeo." Similar issues in the use of feedback have been identified in a review on revising by Fitzgerald (1987).

I suspect we would have found greater variation in the effects of self-feedback on revising behavior in our studies if we had taken into account other individual factors such as attention, working memory, beliefs, emotions, and personality factors. A study of how these individual differences played out in different writing communities would be even better. Thus, I encourage researchers not only to conduct more research on formative assessment and instructional feedback in writing but to consider the complex interplay between individual differences and context when doing so.

Summative Feedback

Given the importance of summative assessments and feedback in standards-based reform today (Elliott et al., 2012), additional research is needed to improve such measures. This includes improving the reliability of such assessments and determining what combination of writing samples, raters, and or other facets of assessment is needed to obtain a valid measure of writing achievement. This is not to say that such research is not already under way (see, for example, appendix B, table 14, in Graham et al., 2011). Rather, additional research is needed in order to make summative writing feedback from high-stakes tests more trustworthy.

An especially important issue in high-stakes assessments is the cost of scoring writing samples. New methods for scoring need to be explored and tested, with an eye to providing affordable assessment and feedback. One new approach for scoring students' writing that has garnered considerable attention of late is the development of computer programs for assessing writing (e.g., Burdick et al., 2013). An example of this is the research and subsequent computer programs the Educational Testing Service has developed for scoring writing on the Graduate Research Exam (see www.ets.org/erater/publications/). While there is currently considerable consternation in some parties about the use of these assessments for both summative and formative purposes (e.g., "How can a computer match the feedback given by a teacher?"), innovators and researchers have made incredible strides in the last several decades in developing and testing ever more sophisticated computer marking systems. These programs ease the scoring burden and are just as reliable as human scorers (Coniam, 2009). While these programs are not ready to replace human scoring, they can clearly be used in conjunction with it (Graham, 2014).

Research on summative assessment and feedback needs to be expanded to examine the effects of grades, exams, projects, and so forth on writing. As with research on formative assessment, high-quality experimental designs should be employed to test if summative feedback causes changes in students' writing and the teaching of writing. Likewise, the role of context, individual differences, and the interaction between the two need to be part of this research.

Finally, more attention needs to be directed at how summative feedback is used by teachers and students. For instance, high-stakes tests often occur at the end of the school year, and teachers do not receive feedback on their students' performance in time to make changes in classroom instruction for these students.

Concluding Comments

I recently conducted a workshop on formative feedback in writing with several hundred elementary grade teachers in Texas. I asked them to work in small groups to provide feedback on a writing sample produced by a fourth-grade student who was not a strong writer. Later in the day, I asked them to do the same thing with a paper written two weeks later. After discussing the two writing samples, we reached consensus on four points:

- Too much feedback can be debilitating to students and too time consuming for teachers.
- Feedback should celebrate students' accomplishments and direct attention in a constructive manner to the aspects of text most in need of revision.
- Feedback may not always lead to instruction, but students will need instruction if they are to address some issues identified through feedback.
- Feedback for each paper should not be treated as a singular and unique event. It should be connected across papers where appropriate.

I would also like to add some additional recommendations made by Underwood and Tregido (2006), which extend the conclusions drawn by the teachers in my workshop:

- Survey students to determine what types of feedback they want (e.g., some students may want more directive versus facilitative feedback).
- Do not include an overall grade for writing when providing students with detailed feedback, as the overall impetus to make the paper better is eliminated.
- Provide feedback that is specific, as students may not understand what they need to do to make their paper better if the feedback is vague or general, such as "This part is unclear."
- Provide examples (when appropriate) that make feedback concrete by exemplifying the characteristics of the writing expected (e.g., provide an example of a well-organized paragraph to guide students' revision of a poorly written paragraph).
- If the same problem occurs repeatedly in text, draw the student's attention to it in a couple of places and suggest a possible solution (versus marking the problem every time it occurs).
- Provide feedback on content and surface-level features of text, but consider when each will be most helpful to students.
- Provide feedback in language that the student will understand and consider how much detail is appropriate given your knowledge of the writer.

I think Underwood and Tregido (2006) and the teachers in my workshop are on to something good. I hope scholars interested in instructional feedback in writing will consider these points when designing their own research. I also hope that teachers view these recommendations as useful too.

References

Abington, A. (1952). *Bigger and better boners*. New York: Viking Press.

Afflerbach, P. (2005). National Reading Conference policy brief: High stakes testing and reading assessment. *Reading Research Quarterly, 37*, 151–162.

Albertson, B. (2007). Organization and development features of grade 8 and grade 10 writers: A descriptive study of Delaware student testing program (DSTP) essays. *Research in the Teaching of English, 41*, 435–465.

Andrade, H., Wang, X., Du, Y., & Akawi, R. (2009). Rubric-referenced self-assessment and self-efficacy for writing. *Journal of Educational Research, 102*, 287–302.

Balzer, W., Doherty, M., & O'Connor, R. (1989). Effects of cognitive feedback on performance. *Psychological Bulletin, 106*, 410–433.

Bazerman, C. (2016). What do sociocultural studies of writing tell us about learning to write? In C. MacArthur, S. Graham, & J. Fitzgerald (Eds.), *Handbook of writing research* (2nd edn., pp. 11–23). New York: Guilford.

Beach, R., & Freidrich, T. (2006). Response to writing. In C. MacArthur, S. Graham, & J. Fitzgerald (Eds.), *Handbook of writing research* (pp. 222–233). New York: Guilford.

Beck, S., & Jeffrey, J. (2007). Genres of high-stakes writing assessments and the construct of writing competence. *Assessing Writing, 12*, 60–79.

Burdick, H., Swartz, C., Stenner, J., Fitzgerald, J., Burdick, D., & Hanlon, S. (2013). Measuring students' writing ability on a computer-analytic developmental scale: An exploratory validity study. *Literacy Research & Instruction, 52*, 255–280.

Callahan, S. (1999). All done with the best of intentions: One Kentucky high school after six years of State Portfolio tests. *Assessing Writing, 6*, 5–40.

Cho, K., & MacArthur, C. (2011). Learning by reviewing. *Journal of Educational Psychology, 103*, 73–84.

Coe, M., Hanita, M., Nishioka, V., & Smiley, R. (2011). *An investigation of the impact of the 6+1 Trait Writing model on grade 5 student writing achievement (NCEE 2012–4010)*. Washington, DC: National Center for Education Evaluation and Regional Assistance, Institute of Education Sciences, US Department of Education.

Coffman, W. (1966). On the validity of essay tests of achievement. *Journal of Educational Measurement, 3*, 151–156.

Coniam, D. (2009). Experimenting with a computer essay-scoring program based on ESL student writing scripts. *European Association for Computer Assisted Language Learning, 21*, 259–279.

Costa, P., & McCrae, R. (1992). Four ways five factors are basic. *Personality & Individual Differences, 13*, 653–655.

Crossley, S., & McNamara, D. (2017). *Adaptive educational technologies for literacy instruction*. New York: Routledge.

Culham, R. (2003). *6+1 traits of writing: The complete guide, grades 3 and up*. New York: Scholastic Professional Books.

Dappen, L., Isernhagen, J., & Anderson, S. (2008). A statewide writing assessment model: Student proficiency and future implications. *Assessing Writing, 13*, 45–60.

De La Paz, S., Swanson, P., & Graham, S. (1998). Contribution of executive control to the revising problems of students with writing and learning difficulties. *Journal of Educational Psychology, 90*, 448–460.

Deno, S. (1985). Curriculum-based measurement: The emerging alternative. *Exceptional Children, 52,* 219–232.

Elliott, S., Kurz, A., & Neergaard, L. (2012). Large-scale assessment for educational accountability. In K. R. Harris, S. Graham, & T. Urdan (Eds.), *APA educational psychology handbook: Application to learning and teaching* (vol. 3, pp. 111–138). Washington, DC: American Psychological Association.

Fitzgerald, J. (1987). Research on revision in writing. *Review of Educational Research, 57,* 481–506.

Galbraith, D. (1999). Writing as a knowledge-constituting process. In D. Galbraith & M. Torrance (Eds.), *Knowing what to write: Conceptual processes in text production* (pp. 139–159). Amsterdam: Amsterdam University Press.

Graham, S. (1997). Executive control in the revising of students with learning and writing difficulties. *Journal of Educational Psychology, 89,* 223–234.

Graham, S. (2014). The use of multiple forms of assessment in the service of writing. *Literacy Research & Instruction, 53,* 96–100.

Graham, S. (2018). A writer(s) within community model of writing. In C. Bazerman, V. Berninger, D. Brandt, S. Graham, J. Langer, S. Murphy, P. Matsuda, D. Rowe, & M. Schleppegrell, (Eds.), *The lifespan development of writing* (pp. 271–325). Urbana, IL: National Council of English.

Graham, S. (in press). Writers in community model: 15 recommendations for future research in using writing to promote science learning. In V. Prain & B. Hand (Eds.), *Future research in science education.* New York: Springer.

Graham, S., Bruch, J., Fitzgerald, J., Friedrich, L., Furgeson, J., Greene, K., Kim, J., Lyskawa, J., Olson, C. B., & Smither Wulsin, C. (2016). *Teaching secondary students to write effectively (NCEE 2017–4002).* Washington, DC: National Center for Education Evaluation and Regional Assistance (NCEE), Institute of Education Sciences, US Department of Education.

Graham, S., Harris, K. R., Bartlett, B., Popadopoulou, E., & Santoro, J. (2016). Acceptability of adaptations for struggling writers: A national survey with primary grade teachers. *Learning Disability Quarterly, 39,* 5–16.

Graham, S., Harris, K. R., & Hebert, M. (2011). *Informing writing: The benefits of formative assessment.* Washington, DC: Alliance for Excellence in Education.

Graham, S., Harris, K. R., & Mason, L. (2005). Improving the writing performance, knowledge, and motivation of struggling young writers: The effects of self-regulated strategy development. *Contemporary Educational Psychology, 30,* 207–241.

Graham, S., Harris, K. R., & Santangelo, T. (2015). Research-based writing practices and the common core: Meta-analysis and meta-synthesis. *Elementary School Journal, 115,* 498–522.

Graham, S., Hebert, M., & Harris, K. R. (2011). Throw 'em out or make 'em better? High-stakes writing assessments. *Focus on Exceptional Children, 44,* 1–12.

Graham, S., Hebert, M., & Harris, K. R. (2015). Formative assessment and writing: A meta-analysis. *Elementary School Journal, 115,* 524–547.

Graham, S., Hebert, M., Sandbank, M., & Harris, K. R. (2016). Credibly assessing the writing achievement of young struggling writers: Application of generalizability theory. *Learning Disability Quarterly, 39,* 72–82.

Graham, S., Kiuhara, S., McKeown, D., & Harris, K. R. (2012). A meta-analysis of writing instruction for students in the elementary grades. *Journal of Educational Psychology*, *104*, 879–896.

Harris, K. R., Graham, S., Mason, L., & Friedlander, B. (2008). *Powerful writing strategies for all students*. Baltimore, MD: Brookes.

Hattie, J., & Timperely, H. (2007). The power of feedback. *Review of Educational Research*, *77*, 81–112.

Hendrickson, R. (1994). *The literary life and other curiosities*. San Diego, CA: Harcourt Brace.

Heritage, M. (2010). *Formative assessment and next-generation assessment systems: Are we losing an opportunity?* Washington, DC: Council of Chief State School Officers.

Hillocks, G. (1986). *Research on written composition: New directions for teaching*. Urbana, IL: National Conference on Research in English.

Hillocks, G. (2002). *The testing trap: How state writing assessments control learning*. New York: Teachers College Press.

Horner, R., Carr, E., Halle, J., McGee, G., Odom, S., & Wolery, M. (2005). The use of single-subject research to identify evidence-based practice in special education. *Exceptional Children*, *71*, 165–180.

Hosp, J. (2012). Using assessment data to make decisions about teaching and learning. In K. R. Harris, S. Graham, & T. Urdan (Eds.), *APA educational psychology handbook: Application to learning and teaching* (vol. 3, pp. 87– 110). Washington, DC: American Psychological Association.

Huang, J. (2008). How accurate are ESL students' holistic writing scores on large-scale assessments? A generalizability theory approach. *Assessing Writing*, *13*, 201–218.

Jeffrey, J. (2009). Constructs of writing proficiency in US state and national writing assessments: Exploring variability. *Assessing Writing*, *14*, 3–24.

Jones, I., (1998). The effect of computer-generated spoken feedback on kindergarten students' written narratives. *Journal of Computing in Childhood Education*, *9*, 43–56.

Karask, H., Fer, S., & Orhan, F. (2014). The effect of using cooperative and individual weblog to enhance writing performance. *Educational Technology & Society*, *17*, 229–241.

Kiuhara, S., Graham, S., & Hawken, L. (2009). Teaching writing to high school students: A national survey. *Journal of Educational Psychology*, *101*, 136–160.

Kluger, A., & DeNisi, A. (1996). The effects of feedback interventions on performance: A historical review, a meta-analysis, and a preliminary feedback intervention theory. *Psychological Bulletin*, *119*, 254–284.

Kulik, J., & Kulik, C. (1988). Timing of feedback and verbal learning. *Review of Educational Research*, *58*, 79–97.

Lederer, R. (1993). *More anguished English*. New York: Dell.

Lederer, R. (2000). *The bride of anguished English*. New York: St. Martin's.

Linkletter, A. (1962). *Kids sure rite funny*. New York: Banard Geis Associates.

Lipnevich, A., & Smith, J. (2009a). "I really need feedback to learn": Students' perspectives on the effectiveness of the differential feedback message. *Educational Assessment, Evaluation, and Accountability*, *21*, 347–367.

Lipnevich, A., & Smith, J. (2009b). Effects of differential feedback on students' examination performance. *Journal of Experimental Psychology: Applied*, *15*, 319–333.

MacArthur, C. (2016). Instruction in evaluation and revision. In C. MacArthur, S. Graham, & J. Fitzgerald (Eds.), *Handbook of writing research* (2nd edn., pp. 272–287). New York: Guilford.

MacArthur, C., & Graham, S. (2016). Writing research from a cognitive perspective. In C. MacArthur, S. Graham, & J. Fitzgerald (Eds.), *Handbook of writing research* (2nd ed., pp. 24–40). New York: Guilford.

MacArthur, C., Graham, S., Schwartz, S., & Shafer, W. (1995). Evaluation of a writing instruction model that integrated a process approach, strategy instruction, and word processing. *Learning Disability Quarterly, 18*, 278–291.

Matsumura, L., Patthey-Chavez, G., Valdes, R., & Garnier, H. (2002). Teacher feedback, writing assignment quality, and third grade students' revisions in lower and higher-achieving urban schools. *Elementary School Journal, 103*, 3–25.

Moore, N., & MacArthur, C. (2016). Student use of automated essay evaluation technology during revision. *Journal of Writing Research, 8*, 149–175.

Nicolaidou, I. (2013). E-portfolios supporting primary students' writing performance and peer feedback. *Computers & Education, 68*, 404–415.

Parke, C., Lane, S., & Stone, C. (2006). Impact of a state performance assessment program in reading and writing. *Educational Research and Evaluation, 12*, 239–269.

Peterson, S. (2003). Peer response and students' revisions of their narrative writing. *LI – Educational Studies in Language and Literature, 3*, 239–272.

Rijlaarsdam, G., Baarksma, M., Couzijn, M., Janssen, T., Braaksma, M., Tillema, M., Steendam, E., & Raedts, M. (2012). Writing. In K. R. Harris, S. Graham, & T. Urdan (Eds.), *APA educational psychology handbook: Application to learning and teaching* (vol. 3, pp. 189–228). Washington, DC: American Psychological Association.

Rijlaarsdam, G., Van den bergh, H., Couzijn, M., Janssen, T., Raedts, M., Steendam, E., Rogers, L., & Graham, S. (2008). A meta-analysis of single subject design writing intervention research. *Journal of Educational Psychology, 100*, 879–906.

Sadler, D. R. (1989). Formative assessment and the design of instructional systems. *Instructional Science, 18*, 119–140.

Salovey, P., & Haar, M. (1990). The efficacy of cognitive-behavior therapy and writing process training for alleviating writing anxiety. *Cognitive Therapy and Research, 14*, 515–528.

Sanchez, C., Atkinson, K., Koenka, A., Moshontz, H., & Cooper, H. (in press). Self- and peer-grading of formative and summative assessments in 3rd through 12th grade classrooms: A research synthesis and meta-analysis. *Journal of Educational Psychology*.

Schunk, D. H., & Swartz, C. W. (1993a). Goals and progress feedback: Effects on self-efficacy and writing achievement. *Contemporary Educational Psychology, 18*, 337–354.

Schunk, D. H., & Swartz, C. W. (1993b). Writing strategy instruction with gifted students: Effects of goals and feedback on self-efficacy and skills. *Roeper Review, 15*, 225–230.

Smith, J., & Lipenvich, A. (2009). Formative assessment in higher education: Frequency and consequence. In D. McInerey, G. Brown, & G. Liem (Eds.), *Student perspectives on assessment: What students can tell us about assessments for learning* (pp. 279–296). Charlotte, NC: IAP.

Stiggins, R. (2005). From formative assessment to assessment for learning: A path to success in standards-based schools. *Phi Delta Kappan, 87*, 324–328.

Toorenaar, A., & Van den Bergh, H. (2008). Observations of peers learning to write. *Journal of Writing Research, 1*, 53–83.

Underwood, J., & Tregidgo, A. (2006). Improving student writing through effective feedback: Best practices and recommendations. *Journal of Teaching Writing, 22*, 73–98.

Welch, N. (1977). *Getting restless: Rethinking revision in writing instruction.* Portsmouth, NH: Boynton Cook.

Wiliam, D. (2006). Formative assessment: Getting the focus right. *Educational Assessment, 11*, 283–289.

Wilson, J., & Czik, A. (2015). Automated essay evaluation software in English language arts classrooms: Effects on teacher feedback, student motivation, and writing quality. *Computers & Education, 100*, 94–109.

Zheng, B., Lawrence, J., Warschauer, M., & Lin, C. (2015). Middle school students' writing and feedback in a cloud-based classroom environment. *Technology, Knowledge, Learning, 20*, 201–229.

Zumbrunn, S., Marrs, S., & Mewborn, C. (2016). Toward a better understanding of student perceptions of writing feedback: A mixed methods study. *Reading & Writing, 29*, 349–370.

8 Instructional Feedback in Mathematics

Marian Small and Amy Lin

Introduction

Just as for teachers in other disciplines, math teachers are beginning to recognize that formative assessment is a key element in improving the learning of mathematics for their students. Formative assessment needs to be integrated intentionally into classroom instruction at all grade levels. Black and Wiliam (1998) have affirmed that gains in student learning result from a variety of methods, all of which have the common feature of formative assessment. This type of assessment is about using evidence that is gathered from student responses to adapt instruction to meet the need of those students.

There is a long history of feedback focusing on whether a student is right or wrong, and *how* wrong he or she is. This is particularly prevalent in mathematics, which is regarded by many as a subject where the focus is on getting right answers to very direct questions. Roos and Hamiltion (2005) argued that this perspective is insufficient, and suggested that formative assessment in the form of feedback in mathematics can provide students the means to self-regulate and become more mindful and aware of what they have (or have not) learned. The main purpose of providing feedback to students should be to reduce the gap between current understandings and a desired learning goal (Hattie & Timperley, 2007).

How and under what conditions feedback in the discipline of mathematics affects learning has not been addressed extensively in research, but there have been some attempts. "Process-oriented" feedback in mathematics was investigated in a study to see if this type of feedback leads to higher achievement and whether learners perceive this feedback as useful and supportive (Rakoczy, Harks, Klieme, Blum, & Hochweber, 2013). This study explored the question of how and under what conditions feedback in mathematics impacts learning and students' perception of their abilities to reach their goals. The study of 146 ninth-grade students of mathematics compared process-oriented feedback with what the authors termed "social-comparative feedback." The students were completing a unit on the Pythagorean theorem and linear relations. Process-oriented feedback provided students with information about their strengths and weaknesses, as well as tips on how to improve and strategies on how to solve the problems, or structurally similar problems, for each reported weakness. However, social-comparative feedback consisted of a grade each for technical and modeling competencies. The results suggest that the implementation of process-oriented feedback when teaching mathematics could foster students' interest. Process-oriented feedback was perceived as more supportive and useful than social-comparative feedback, and the researchers observed an indirect effect on achievement development through perceived usefulness.

Nunez-Pena, Bono, and Suárez-Pellicioni (2015) studied the impact of feedback on students' mathematical performance by providing specific feedback on student errors made in a series of assignments throughout a course. Data were collected on students' level of math anxiety, their attitudes toward math, and their perceptions regarding the usefulness of feedback classes. Students who attended feedback classes were found to have increased final exam grades. Students' perceived usefulness of the feedback was the best predictor of student grades. The results suggested that feedback may have played an important role in reducing the effect of math anxiety on students' academic achievement. By gaining confidence through effective feedback, students with high math anxieties could show their real knowledge and understanding on various types of final assessments.

Researchers found gains in performance were greater in assessments that provided open-ended questions rather than multiple-choice questions. Smaller gains were made when no feedback was given and only correct responses were given to students. Feedback in the form of explanations was more beneficial than simply giving the correct response (Butler, Godbole, & Marsh, 2013; Attali, 2015).

There has been some investigation of feedback that focuses on mathematical misconceptions. It has been suggested that feedback is most powerful when it addresses a learning context and is targeted at addressing misconceptions (Hattie & Timperley, 2007). Bee and Kaur (2014) carried out research that showed that when written feedback was provided to students that was designed to clarify student misconceptions, students improved their strategies for processing knowledge and self-regulation of learning. Traditional feedback, in the form of grades, was compared with what the researchers called enhanced feedback, which specifically addressed student misconceptions. The results of the study suggested that the enhanced feedback improved student performance and seemed to motivate students to do better and to think more deeply about their work. Students indicated that with the mistakes and misconceptions highlighted, the comments helped them clarify their ideas and helped them understand why their own solutions did not work.

Many believe that the focus of feedback in mathematics should be on promoting thinking, on mathematical processes, on the quality of the accomplishments made in mathematical problem-solving, and on the documentation of the learning in mathematics (Hodgen & Wiliam, 2006), rather than on correctness of solutions. Some believe that it is more likely that students will respond to feedback if it is tied clearly to a learning goal and when students believe that they will eventually successfully reach their goal (Kluger & DeNisi, 1996). It has also been suggested that if a teacher responds to a student by

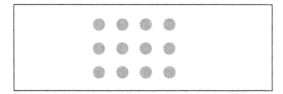

Figure 8.1 *An example of an array.*

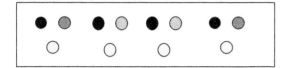

Figure 8.2 *An example of a student solution.*

asking a question with a particular answer in mind, it may actually inhibit the learning of the student by shutting down thought processes that could have been productive, preventing the student from coming up with his or her own answer (Black & Wiliam, 1998). To give effective feedback, teachers need to question purposefully and provide students with enough time to process their thoughts and respond.

Often, math teachers assume that students have and should use specific prior knowledge when asking them to work on a task or problem. For example, a third-grade teacher asks a student to draw a picture to show why $4 \times 3 = 3 \times 4$. The teacher is expecting an array as shown in Figure 8.1 to be drawn. Instead, the student draws what is shown in Figure 8.2. Although the immediate response might be that something is wrong, a teacher needs to realize that students might think differently from how he or she does, and ask:

> *So where in the picture do I see four times three?*

> *Where in the picture do I see three times four?*

Teachers can use questions in their feedback, rather than statements, to better understand how their students are thinking and to help those students move forward in their learning.

This chapter will explore various aspects of offering feedback to students who are learning mathematics. In particular, we will provide examples at a variety of grade levels of how to connect feedback to rich learning objectives and what math we should focus on when giving feedback, including attention to assumptions students do or do not make. We will consider various types of feedback. We will also discuss challenges for teachers when dealing with the need for immediate feedback and responding to student errors and misconceptions, which are particularly big problems in mathematics.

Feedback Linked to Learning Goals

If the only goal of math instruction was for students to determine the correct answer to a math question or a series of questions, then the feedback would not need to be much more than a checkmark or grade to indicate that the student had met the goal. The feedback process as an assessment for learning strategy can accomplish much more and can be used to engage students with more deeply understanding the mathematics, which is the focus of the learning goal.

Bangert-Drowns, Kulik, Kulik, and Morgan (1991) have shown that marking right or wrong answers and giving these scores to students negatively impacted the learning of students compared with an invested amount of time from students in analyzing their own work. The feedback that results in students reflecting on their mathematical thinking is the type that will increase their motivation and effort. It is particularly valuable if the learning goals developed by math teachers toward which feedback is given reflect deeper ideas about the math being learned and not just procedures.

Just as the current Common Core State Standards for Mathematics (CCSSI, 2010) focus on some big ideas, learning goals for individual lessons should highlight bigger ideas. The following paragraphs provide examples at different grade levels of what those bigger idea learning goals could be and what associated feedback might sound like. For example, in a lesson about multiplying multidigit numbers, the goal is not just getting the answer but understanding that we subdivide the computation into many simpler computations that can be accomplished mentally and put together to create the desired answer. The goal relates to how to best decompose the numbers being multiplied to accomplish this. That means the feedback would focus on why students decomposed and how they decomposed rather than on the actual product.

For a lesson about calculating surface area and volumes of cones and cylinders, the goal should be not only substituting numbers into formulas that are given or memorizing those formulas but also about the number and choices of linear measurements that are needed to determine particular surface areas and volumes; the relationships between volumes of similar cylinders and cones; the relationship, or lack of relationship, between volume and surface area of a given figure; or the value of formulas. That means the feedback would focus on one or more of these ideas rather than exclusively on the specific calculations of the measurement values.

For a primary-level lesson on money, there are specific things students must learn about how to count money, how to use the ¢ symbol, etc., but the big idea might be that there are relationships between coin values that help represent the same amount of money in different ways. The feedback from the teacher could then focus more on the big idea rather than a single answer. For example, the teacher might ask:

You have eight nickels. How many dimes do you need to represent the same amount?

or

>*Choose an amount in cents that you can have with only nickels. How could you represent it with fewer coins?*

Feedback could lead students to understand that fewer dimes are needed because they are worth more than nickels and that you can trade two nickels for one dime every time. For example, a teacher might say:

>*Would you probably trade for pennies or dimes? Why?*

In early years, children are comparing numbers, and one big idea is that sometimes you can compare numbers by just looking at them quickly but other times you need to match or count. If a student is looking at these two sets and is asked if there are more gray or more black counters (see Figure 8.3), feedback could be:

>*I noticed that you counted to decide that there were more gray counters than black ones. Did you have to count? What else could you have done?*

The feedback above is much more valuable to a student than the feedback below, which is evaluative:

>*You said there were eight gray counters and six black counters, but didn't tell me which was more.*

Students often have difficulty understanding operations with fractions. When dividing fractions, the learning goal may be: students will recognize that $a \div b$ means how many bs fit into an a, e.g., $\frac{4}{5} \div \frac{2}{3}$ asks how many $\frac{2}{3}$ s fit into a $\frac{4}{5}$.

So if students are asked to calculate $\frac{3}{8} \div \frac{3}{10}$ and simply apply a rule to get an answer, feedback could be:

>*How could you have known the answer is a little more than one before you even did the division?*

This is very different feedback from, for example, querying a student as to why he or she wrote $\frac{10}{8}$ as the answer instead of the simplified $\frac{5}{4}$.

In high school, students learn about quadratic functions. If the learning goal was narrow, for example, "Students learn how to write quadratic equations in standard form from the factored form," the feedback might be:

>*What was the first step you did?*

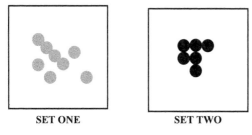

SET ONE   SET TWO

Figure 8.3 *An example of sets of counters.*

But a deeper learning goal could be students recognizing that different forms of a quadratic are useful for different purposes. The task could ask: "You want to determine the axis of symmetry of a quadratic. In what form would you want the quadratic to be given to you? Why?" The feedback in this case would be:

> *You chose vertex form and explained why. But could you have suggested factored form?*

These are just some of many possible examples to show that feedback that focuses on deeper learning goals is different from the feedback given when focusing on more procedural learning goals, and they should sound different.

Types of Feedback

If a task, whether a learning task or an assessment of learning task, has been carefully structured by the teacher to allow students more choice and is more open ended, it offers a greater opportunity than a narrower task to give meaningful feedback because more of the student's own thinking is revealed. The feedback can include responses to how a student arrives at an answer, the understanding of the strategies that were used, and/or how the student interpreted the task.

Feedback That Offers the Opportunity for Self-Correction

A response from a student may present itself as a solution with errors. Math teachers may be unsure as to how to direct the student to reevaluate the situation and try again. The feedback options presented here need to help the student move forward and to not give up. A response may require feedback to focus more on the strategies that the students used to solve the problem than on the solution itself.

For example, a primary student might work on a task that requires solving this problem:

> **You are on a number line at 5. You move forward some steps and back some steps. You end up at 9.**
>
> **How many forward and back steps might you have moved?**

A student says that she moved forward 6 and back 1 (an incorrect solution). Instead of talking about the solution being incorrect, the teacher might say:

> *Show me what strategy you used to figure that out.*

He might find out that the student said: 5, 6, 7, 8, 9, 10 and back 1 and counted the forward moves as six since she said six numbers, even though she moved only five spaces. This is important information to bring to a student's attention. The teacher might follow up by asking the student:

> *If you stand here on five, how many steps do you actually take to get to ten?*

Feedback on Choice of Strategy

Even if a correct answer is presented, whether the student used the most appropriate solution or an efficient or even insightful strategy could be the focus of the feedback.

For example, a student might respond to the task:

Which is greater: $-4 - (-5)$ or $-4 - (-6)$? Why?

A student might correctly indicate that $-4 - (-6)$ is more, having calculated the two answers as 1 and 2, but the teacher might ask:

> *How could you have predicted the second one would be more without doing the calculation?*

The teacher wants the student to realize that if you take away more, you are left with less and -5 is more than -6 or that you have to move farther to get from -6 to -4 than to get from -5 to -4.

Feedback That Encourages Perspective Taking

Sometimes, students may present solutions to problems that are unexpected due to their interpretation of a problem. In these cases, the teacher might respond to the student with feedback that encourages him or her to reconsider other ways of looking at the problem without dismissing the initial solution. For example, students are asked:

Which bank account grew more: one that grew from $100 to $250 or one that grew from $800 to $1000?

If the following solution was presented:

$250 - 100 = 150$
$1000 - 800 = 200$, so this account grew more.

Feedback could be:

> *I see your point. Why might someone say that the other account grew more and still be right?*

Feedback That Is Based on an Alternate Interpretation of the Problem

Students might be given a task such as this one:

A store sells donut holes only in packs of 6, 9, or 20.
What are some exact amounts of donut holes you could buy?
Are there amounts you cannot buy? If so, what are those amounts?

Some students read this problem and assume, maybe without even thinking about it, that you can only buy multiples of 6, multiples of 9, or multiples of 20 donut holes and never consider combinations. Their solution reflects this assumption. Feedback could be:

Do you think it might be possible to buy a box of six and a box of nine? How many donut holes would that be?

Would that change your answer to the problem?

Feedback That Encourages Creativity

Many adults, including teachers, do not see mathematics as a subject area where creativity needs to be encouraged. Even if teachers accept creative answers, they might not focus on pushing students in that direction. Other teachers feel differently and might deliberately encourage more creative responses through feedback, especially when student responses are correct, just traditional.

Students might be asked to respond to this task:

How are the numbers 10 and 20 alike?

A student might respond:

They are both ten numbers.
They are both friendly numbers.
They both have 0s in them.
They both are not that big.

Feedback could be:

Your answers make sense to me, but didn't really surprise me.

Can you think of a more unusual reason why you might think ten and twenty are alike?

Another example at a higher grade level might be one where students are asked to come up with an interesting problem involving composition of functions.

A student writes:

If $f(x) = 3x + 5$ and $g(x) = 2x - 8$, what is the value of $f(g(4))$?

This question is about composition, but is not very interesting, in contrast to something like *Can every function be written as the composition of at least three other functions?* Feedback could be:

Tell me what makes your problem an interesting one.

Feedback That Extends

Especially when students give completely correct answers, but the teacher wishes to encourage them to reflect even more on a problem, the teacher might provide feedback that extends the thinking of those students. For example, a task might be given:

List some equations with a solution of x = 8.

The student lists these equations:

$4x = 32; \quad x + 1 = 9; \quad \text{and} \quad 5x = 40$

Feedback could be:

> *All of your equations seem to work, but I noticed you only use addition and multiplication. Are there equations that involve division or subtraction or even multiple operations?*

Different Responses to Student Work on the Same Task

All teachers realize that when they assign a task to a group of students, the responses can vary a great deal. In this section, there are a number of examples of how a teacher might have to come up with different feedback for different students in the same teaching situation. In each case, the focus will still be on a big idea in mathematics.

Task 1

A big idea in number sense is that numbers can be compared in different ways, both to each other and to benchmarks. For example, students may be asked:

Which is closer to $\frac{1}{2}$: $\frac{3}{8}$ or $\frac{4}{10}$? How do you know?

Figures 8.4, 8.5, and 8.6 are some sample student solutions with suggested feedback.

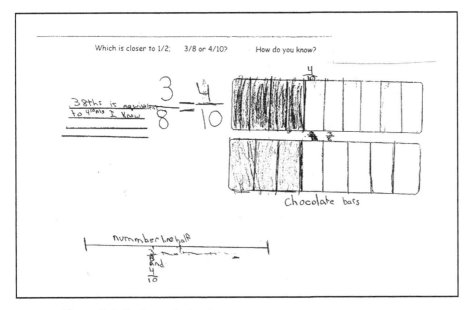

Figure 8.4 *Student solution 1.*

In Figure 8.4, the student believes that $\frac{3}{8}$ is the same as $\frac{4}{10}$ based on the drawings and number line he has made. This is, of course, an example of an incorrect solution. But the focus is less on the fact that it is incorrect than on how to improve it. The feedback could be:

> *It's a great strategy to draw pictures when solving problems involving fractions. Fraction strips can be hard to draw sometimes as they need to be exact.*
>
> *Are you sure that all the parts you've drawn in your chocolate bars are equal? Do you think it matters that they are equal parts? Why (or why not?)?*

In Figure 8.5, this student, too, provides an incorrect solution, but the nature of the thinking is different than in the previous case and requires different feedback. This student recognizes that $\frac{3}{8}$ and $\frac{4}{10}$ are both "1 away" from $\frac{1}{2}$ (meaning $\frac{1}{8}$ and $\frac{1}{10}$ away from $\frac{1}{2}$, respectively). The feedback to this student should help him to clarify an understanding of the denominator and how he used this to determine which fraction was closer to $\frac{1}{2}$.

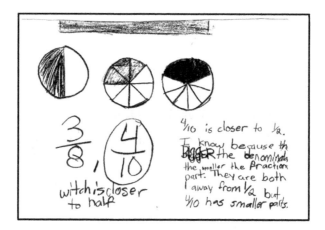

Figure 8.5 *Student solution 2.*

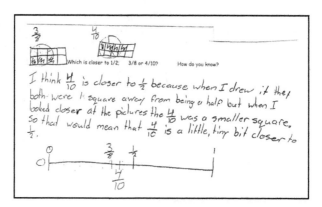

Figure 8.6 *Student solution 3.*

The feedback could be:

> *You say that they are both "one" away from one-half. Tell me, "one" what?*

In Figure 8.6, this solution is a good one, but still deserving of feedback. Often teachers do not give as much feedback to good answers as they might. In this case, the student uses an excellent strategy for deciding which fraction is closer to one half.

The feedback could be:

> *How did shading in the boxes in your pictures help you with figuring out which fraction was closer to one-half?*

> *Which helped you more to figure it out – the pictures you drew with the boxes or the number line you drew?*

Task 2

Another task involving proportional reasoning has students considering this question:

Four boxes of cookies cost $10.00. How much would 18 boxes cost?

The first student solution below is an example of nonproportional reasoning that led to an incorrect result (Figure 8.7). The feedback for this student could be:

> *It looks like you decided that one box costs ten dollars. How did you know that?*

This is in contrast to telling the student that she read it wrong and that four boxes cost $10.

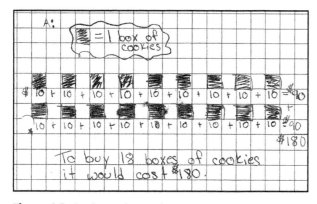

Figure 8.7 *Student solution demonstrating nonproportional reasoning.*

1 2 3 4 ① box
$10
$10 –
$10 – 5 6 7 8 ② boxes
$10 – 9 10 11 12 ③ boxes
$10 – 13 14 15 16 ④ boxes
$5 – 17 18 4.5 boxes
$10
$10
$10
$10
$5
$45.00 for 18 boxes.

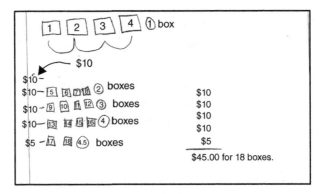

Figure 8.8 *Student solution demonstrating informal reasoning.*

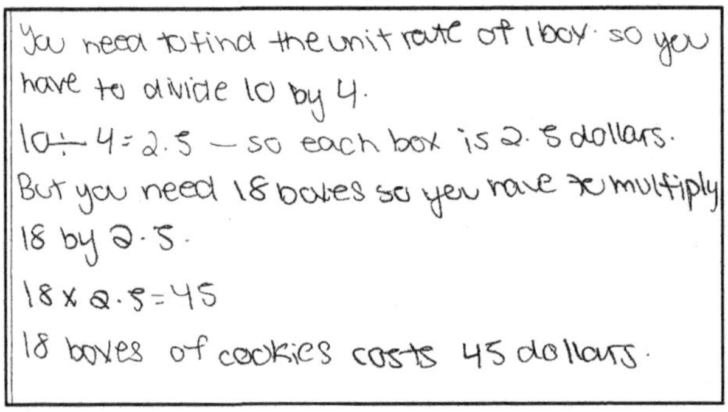

You need to find the unit rate of 1 box. so you
have to divide 10 by 4.
10 ÷ 4 = 2.5 – so each box is 2.5 dollars.
But you need 18 boxes so you have to multiply
18 by 2.5.
18 x 2.5 = 45
18 boxes of cookies costs 45 dollars.

Figure 8.9 *Student solution demonstrating formal solution.*

Figure 8.8 shows another student solution that shows informal reasoning leading to a correct solution. Here the feedback is more about strategy than solution. The feedback for this student could be:

Why is your last line five dollars instead of ten dollars?

Students may know about using unit rates, and another correct, but more formal solution, to the same problem may look like Figure 8.9. The feedback here could be:

You said "you need" to find the unit rate. It obviously helped.

But do you really have to find the unit rate?

In this particular case, an incorrect mathematical statement is made that does not affect the solution but still needs to be addressed.

Task 3

In high school, trigonometric ratios and the Pythagorean theorem are introduced and subsequently used to solve problems involving right-angled triangles. The big idea may be that a triangle can be described using different

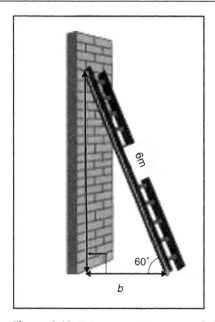

Figure 8.10 *Trigonometric ratios and the Pythagorean theorem.*

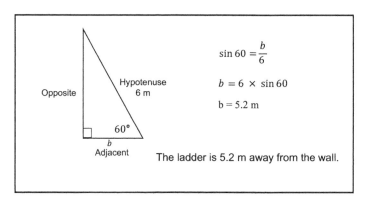

$$\sin 60 = \frac{b}{6}$$

$$b = 6 \times \sin 60$$

$$b = 5.2 \text{ m}$$

The ladder is 5.2 m away from the wall.

Figure 8.11 *Student solution 1.*

measurements and some of these measurements are related and can be used to determine missing measurements. A possible question could be finding the distance b, which is how far away from the wall the ladder is, given the height of the ladder, as shown in Figure 8.10.

In Figure 8.11, the student labels the sides of the right-angled triangle correctly as the opposite and adjacent side relative to the $60°$ angle and the hypotenuse. However, the student incorrectly uses the sine ratio to solve for b, the distance from the wall (Figure 8.11). The feedback here should help move the student forward to determining the correct solution and understanding where he made the error. So even though the teacher could tell the student that

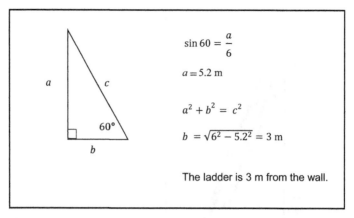

$$\sin 60 = \frac{a}{6}$$

$$a = 5.2 \text{ m}$$

$$a^2 + b^2 = c^2$$

$$b = \sqrt{6^2 - 5.2^2} = 3 \text{ m}$$

The ladder is 3 m from the wall.

Figure 8.12 *Student solution 2.*

it is the cosine that is $\frac{b}{6}$ or that he used the adjacent instead of the opposite, which does the error-finding for the student, a teacher might say:

> *How would you determine the length of the vertical side?*

> *When you get the answer, do the three numbers for the right triangle make sense?*

(They should not make sense since chances are the opposite side will end up smaller than the adjacent, and that will look wrong.)

In the second solution (Figure 8.12) the student uses the sine ratio to determine the height and then uses the Pythagorean theorem to determine the value of b. This solution is correct but not the most efficient way to solve this problem. The feedback provided to this student could help him see that. The feedback might be:

> *That looks great. I notice that you needed four lines to figure out the value of b.*

> *Is it possible to do it in fewer steps?*

The third solution (Figure 8.13) uses the cosine ratio to solve for b. Although this is the correct solution, the feedback from the teacher can still provide an opportunity to challenge and push student thinking further. The teacher might say:

> *I notice that three is half of six. I wonder if there are other right triangles where one side is half of the hypotenuse.*

> *I wonder what the angles are in those triangles?*

The last solution (Figure 8.14) is typical in that many students who are unsure of what they need to solve for simply do everything possible, hoping that the teacher will find whatever she wants in the solution. This solution determines all of the angles and side lengths of the given triangle and does not focus only on the question asked. The feedback to the student needs to guide the student into making decisions on what is important to know here and what the question is asking for. The teacher might say:

You gave me a LOT of information.

What part of what you did do you want me to focus on to answer the question I asked?

$$\cos 60 = \frac{b}{6}$$

$b = 3$ m

The ladder is 3 m away from the wall.

Figure 8.13 *Student solution 3.*

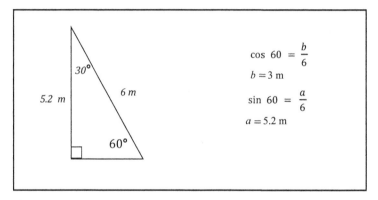

Figure 8.14 *Student solution 4.*

Immediacy of Feedback

The timing of feedback can vary. During a lesson, feedback might need to be immediate, for example, while teachers observe students working on a math problem. In this situation, teachers have very little reflection time. Feedback could be delayed if students submit written or recorded work that is returned to them on a subsequent day. This latter situation allows time for the teacher to carefully consider what to say and can be studied by the student and digested over time.

One advantage of delayed feedback, beyond allowing the time for the teacher to carefully consider what to say and the student to digest it, is that there is some evidence it may lead to better transfer (Schroth, 1992). Although this particular research was not in mathematics, it seems reasonable to apply to mathematics as well.

But an advantage of timely (or immediate) feedback is that students hear the feedback while they are still mindful of the problem and the learning goal. In many situations, students care less about a problem that is done and over with and are not interested in feedback later. Students can also benefit from immediate feedback as they work further on the problem. In addition, immediate feedback can attend to misconceptions and faulty assumptions made by students before those misconceptions or faulty assumptions become more firmly entrenched.

In mathematics classrooms, immediate responses can be challenging for elementary school teachers who may not have adequate background knowledge in mathematics to deal with unanticipated responses, or for some secondary school teachers who may be unfamiliar with alternative approaches to particular topics. The level of challenge can vary with the task; teachers may find open-ended tasks more challenging to respond to quickly since it is more likely that students will bring up ideas the teacher was not expecting.

Hadley and Doward (2011) carried out a study in which elementary school teachers completed a questionnaire that assessed their anxiety about teaching mathematics and their current mathematics instructional practices. Student mathematics achievement data were collected from their students and a relationship was found between teacher anxiety about mathematics and anxiety about teaching mathematics and student achievement; increased student math achievement related to lower levels of anxiety about teaching mathematics.

Karp (1991) found that elementary teachers with math anxiety and a fear of mathematics tended to use methods of teaching math where students listened to the teacher and used the teacher as the main source of information. The teaching in these situations tended to be more algorithmic and did not promote thinking or mathematical reasoning. This teacher-driven practice using prepared worksheets did not encourage student initiative or independence and did not promote questions from students or teachers. Similarly, elementary teachers who were anxious about math spent more time in class devoted to whole class instruction and did not field many questions during lessons, fearing the need to respond to the questions asked (Bush, 1989). Students who had teachers who were confident in mathematics asked twice as many questions in classes.

Research has suggested that there is an association between teachers' mathematical content knowledge including facts and procedures, understanding of concepts and connections, and understanding of mathematical models and generalizations and students' performance in the intermediate grades (Tchoshanov et al., 2017). Follow-up teacher interviews and students' problem-solving showed that teachers with higher content knowledge were more likely to emphasize problems that required higher levels of cognitive demand and could make a clearer connection between content and pedagogy. These types of questions allow for richer feedback.

In a math classroom, the learning environment must be able to support student discussions and participation that promotes reasoning and sense-making. Students should be explaining their thinking and the use of their chosen strategies (Lampert, 2010). This requires teachers to be able to analyze responses and products of their students, build on what has been presented, and then scaffold and provoke student thinking while keeping in mind the mathematical goals of the lesson. Teachers who engage in these tasks not only have their own knowledge of the mathematical reasoning but also a strong understanding of the pedagogical issues that might affect how students learn math (Ball, Thames, & Phelps, 2008).

An approach for some of this might be a realization that when a teacher is unsure of how a child has arrived at an answer, it is not always essential for the teacher to indicate immediately whether or not the answer is correct; instead, the teacher could probe further. For example, a child is figuring out how the perimeter of a square changes if the area is divided in half. The child says that the new perimeter is three-fourths the length of the old perimeter. The teacher is not sure if this is true. Instead of trying to figure it out herself, she might ask:

> *How many squares did you try?*

> *Was it three-fourths each time?*

> *How would you convince someone it would have to be three-fourths with a different square that you had not already tried?*

In another example, a student says that when you multiply numbers, the answer is always more than when you divide numbers. The teacher may think that it sounds right, but is unsure. The teacher might ask:

> *How many pairs of numbers did you try?*

> *What kinds of numbers did you try?*

> *Did you try little numbers?*

> *Did you try fractions?*

Teachers can slow down the questioning process, probe further into the thinking of the student, and give themselves time to figure out what the student has done and how to help that student.

Inappropriate Assumptions

When students are presented with a mathematical problem, they often have to decide which assumptions should be made, and sometimes they are not even aware that they had decisions to make or that they made decisions. Feedback might address these assumptions. For example, students are asked to determine the number of sections in a circle if the circle is cut by n lines. They try one, then two, and then three lines. The first values they get are 2, 4, 6. As shown in Figure 8.15, this student had decided that the lines always should go through the center, which was not actually indicated. Feedback could be:

> *I noticed all your lines meet at the center. What if they didn't? Would the strategy you used still work?*

In an example involving fractions, the teacher may ask students to multiply the number 4/5 by different fractions to determine if the product is less than 4/5 or not.

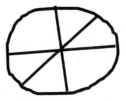

Figure 8.15 *Student solution for determining the number of sections in a circle, if a circle is cut by* n *lines.*

Some student may try only proper fractions and say yes. Feedback could be:

I noticed that all of the fractions you multiplied by were less than one. What if you had multiplied by five-fourths?

Generalizing Too Quickly and Overgeneralizing

Many times, students are asked to come to generalizations in mathematics. It might be generalizations about whether or not one can perform operations in any order; it might be about whether or not when multiples of a certain number are combined, one gets multiples of that same number. It might be about whether when one operates with negative numbers, the answers are positive or negative.

One of the difficulties students have is that they either generalize too quickly or overgeneralize and apply something that is true in one situation to the wrong situation. For example, if a pattern starts 2, 4, 6, students might, too quickly, assume that the next number has to be 8, when in fact it might not, e.g., 2, 4, 6, 12, 14, 16, 22, 24, 26, ... (add 2, add 2, add 6, repeatedly). They also overgeneralize. If, for example, they learn that multiplying two negatives make a positive, they might assume that –3 + (–4) = +7 since there are two negatives, so they should make a positive. Since many of these situations can be anticipated, teachers can be ready with feedback.

For example, teachers may ask students to determine two numbers whose sum is double their difference. A student figures out that 3 and 9 work since 3 + 9 = 12 and 9 – 3 = 6 and 12 is double 6, so the student suggests the numbers in general have to be six apart. It turns out that this is an incorrect generalization. Feedback could be:

Do four and ten work?
So what other relationship between three and nine might you have used?

A teacher working on areas and perimeters may ask two students if the number describing the area of a rectangle or the number describing the perimeter is usually more (Figure 8.16). They try three standard-looking rectangles and decide that since the area was greater in those three cases, it must always be greater. Feedback could be:

There are only three examples.
Are you sure it would be the same for other rectangles?
What if the rectangles were really long and skinny?

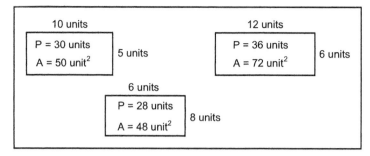

Figure 8.16 *An areas and perimeters problem.*

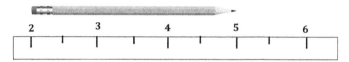

Figure 8.17 *Primary grades measurement problem.*

Misconceptions

There is considerable literature in mathematics on the common mathematical misconceptions that students hold and the difficulties in learning that result (Confrey, 1990; Fazio & Siegler, 2011; Welder, 2012). Some examples are shown below, and again, since these misconceptions can be anticipated, feedback can be planned. Many math education leaders suggest that it is critical for novice teachers to anticipate student responses to be prepared to give appropriate and timely feedback (Smith & Stein, 2011; Meikle, 2016).

For example, when children learn to measure in primary grades using a ruler, a number of misconceptions come to the fore (Figure 8.17). Children may read this measurement as five units or four units instead of the correct three units. They might suggest the length is 5 since the number that is under the end of the pencil tip is 5. They may say 4 since there are four numbers under the pencil even though there are only three spaces. Feedback could be:

How did you decide where to start measuring the pencil length from?
(move pencil to start at three) – How long is the pencil now?

Children, when learning subtraction, are usually taught that subtraction means "take away." However, subtraction is better understood when thinking about differences between numbers. For example, children may believe that when you subtract, you always end up with a smaller amount. This is not always true as in $10 - (-5) = 15$. Feedback could be:

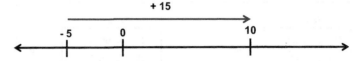

Figure 8.18 *A number line solution example.*

How do you take away negative five from ten?
How can you figure out five minus two by starting at two on a number line?
   Could that be useful here?

Students could start thinking about a number line and what you might need to add to –5 to reach +10 (Figure 8.18).

When it comes to solving equations, students learn ideas that may result in misconceptions. Students may learn that when they "change sides in an equation, they change signs," leading to bringing numbers and variables to the other side of the equal sign and changing the sign. For example, to solve

$$-4x = 8$$

a student may respond with:

$$x = 8 \div (+4)$$

(Bring the –4 over to the other side of the equal sign and change to +4.)
   Feedback for this could be:

Can you prove you are correct?
Does the value of two for x work?

Or, using the equation,

$$\frac{x+5}{3} = 6$$

a student may respond with

$$\frac{x}{3} = 6 - 5$$

Feedback for this could be:

So if x divided by three is one, what value is x?
But what happens when you divide the quantity three plus five by three? Is it six?
What could you divide by three to get six?
How does this help you with solving the equation?

Misconceptions also arise when children are learning about fractions. One common misconception among some students is their belief that the greater the number on the bottom (the denominator), the greater the fraction. For example,

$\frac{1}{10}$ is bigger than $\frac{1}{5}$ *because* 10 *is bigger than* 5.

The teacher could provide the following feedback:

Draw a picture that shows me what one-tenth looks like.
I think I also see one-fifth in your picture.
Where is it?
Is it more or less than one-tenth?

Summary

   Math teachers need to provide feedback in service of deep student learning that is formative; in this way, students use the feedback to improve their understanding and their performance. Feedback should always relate to rich learning goals. It can relate to

- strategies employed or
- interpretations of the task, as much as, if not more, than
- correctness of solution.

Even when addressing a correct solution, feedback might extend what a student does, and not only address what the student had already done. There are some issues that are frequent in mathematics including jumping to conclusions too quickly, overgeneralizing, or making faulty assumptions in problem-solving. Useful feedback can and must address these issues.

   The goal for feedback is always is to move students even further forward to a conceptual understanding of mathematics.

References

Attali, Y. (2015). Effects of multiple-try feedback and question type during mathematics problem solving on performance in similar problems. *Computers & Education, 86*, 260–267.

Ball, D. L., Thames, M. H., & Phelps, G. (2008). Content knowledge for teaching: What makes it special? *Journal of Teacher Education, 59*, 389–407.

Bangert-Drowns, R. L., Kulik, C. C., Kulik, J. A., & Morgan, M. (1991). The instructional effect of feedback in test-like events. *Review of Educational Research, 61*, 213–238.

Bee, S. N., & Kaur, B. (2014). Using enhanced feedback to improve the learning of mathematics. *The Mathematics Educator, 15*, 101–110.

Black, P., & Wiliam, D. (1998). Inside the black box: Raising standards through classroom assessment. *The Phi Delta Kappan, 80*, 139–44.

Bush, W. S. (1989). Mathematical anxiety in upper elementary school teachers. *School Science and Mathematics, 89*, 499–509.

Butler, A. C., Godbole, N., & Marsh, E. J. (2013). Explanation feedback is better than correct answer feedback for promoting transfer of learning. *Journal of Educational Psychology, 105*, 290–298.

Common Core State Standards Initiative. (2010). Common Core State Standards for Mathematics. Retrieved from www.corestandards.org/wp-content/uploads/Math_Standards1.pdf.

Confrey, J. (1990). A review of the research on student conceptions in mathematics, science, and programming. *Review of Research in Education, 1*, 3–55.

Fazio, L., & Siegler, R. (2011). *Teaching fractions.* Belley, France: Gonnet Imprimeur.

Hadley, K., & Dorward, J. (2011). The relationship among elementary teachers' mathematics anxiety, mathematics instructional practices, and student mathematics achievement. *Journal of Curriculum & Instruction, 5*(2), 27–44.

Hattie, J., & Timperley, H. (2007). The power of feedback. *Review of Educational Research, 77*, 81–112.

Hodgen, J., & Wiliam, D. (2006). *Mathematics inside the black box: Assessment for learning in the mathematics classroom.* London: NFER-Nelson.

Karp, K. S. (1991). Elementary school teachers' attitudes toward mathematics: The impact on students' autonomous learning skills. *School Science and Mathematics, 91*, 265–270.

Kluger, A. N., & DeNisi, A. (1996). The effects of feedback interventions on performance: A historical review, a meta-analysis and a preliminary feedback intervention theory. *Psychological Bulletin, 119*, 254–284.

Lampert, M. (2010). Learning teaching in, from, and for practice: What do we mean? *Journal of Teacher Education, 61*, 21–34.

Meikle, E. M. (2016). Selecting and sequencing students' solution strategies. *Teaching Children Mathematics, 23*, 226–234.

Núñez-Peña, M., Bono, R., & Suárez-Pellicioni, M. (2015). Feedback on students' performance: A possible way of reducing the negative effect of math anxiety in higher education. *International Journal of Educational Research, 70*, 80–87.

Rakoczy, K., Harks, B., Klieme, E., Blum, W., & Hochweber, J. (2013). Written feedback in mathematics: Mediated by students' perception, moderated by goal orientation. *Learning and Instruction, 27*, 63–73.

Roos, B., & Hamilton, D. (2005). Formative assessment: A cybernetic viewpoint. *Assessment in Education Principles Policy and Practice, 12*, 7–20.

Schroth, M. L. (1992). The effects of delay of feedback on a delayed concept formation transfer task. *Contemporary Educational Psychology, 17*, 78–82.

Smith, M. S., & Stein, M. K. (2011). *5 practices for orchestrating productive mathematical discussions.* Reston, VA: National Council of Teachers of Mathematics.

Tchoshanov, M., Cruz, M. D., Huereca, K., Shakirova, K., Shakirova, L., & Ibragimova, E. N. (2017). Examination of lower secondary mathematics teachers' content knowledge and its connection to students' performance. *International Journal of Science & Math Education, 15*, 683–702.

Welder, R. M. (2012). Improving algebra preparation: Implications from research on student misconceptions and difficulties. *School, Science and Mathematics, 112*, 255–264.

9 Looking Closely at Mathematics and Science Classroom Feedback Practices

Examining Artifacts, Students' Products, and Teachers' Communications

Maria Araceli Ruiz-Primo and Heidi Kroog

At the center of formative assessment, or assessment for learning, is feedback. Indeed, feedback has been considered one of the most powerful interventions in education (Hattie, 1999). However, we know that not all forms of feedback are equally effective. Evidence accumulated over the past twenty-five years shows a high degree of variability in effects (Bangert-Drowns, Kulik, Kulik, & Morgan, 1991; Kluger & DeNisi, 1996; Shute, 2008; Bennett, 2011; Van der Kleij, Feskens, & Eggen, 2015). Although meta-analyses (e.g., Kluger & DeNisi, 1996; Hattie & Timperley, 2007) and reviews (Black & Wiliam, 1998; Shute, 2008) have demonstrated positive effects of feedback on student learning outcomes (medium to large effect sizes), some studies have shown small effects (Bangert-Drowns, Kulik, Kulik, & Morgan, 1991) and even negative effects (Kluger & DeNisi, 1996; Shute, 2008).

Ruiz-Primo and Li (2013a) have offered some reasons for this disparity. One critical factor is how feedback is defined in different studies. These researchers identified different dimensions to characterize feedback across studies (e.g., who provides the feedback or the focus of the feedback) and found that the way feedback is defined varied so much from study to study that it was difficult to cluster many studies with similar definitions. Another variation is in the methodological quality of the studies. Characteristics of the measures used to evaluate the impact of feedback also vary considerably from study to study. In most of the meta-analyses these discrepancies are ignored, and studies are grouped together in hundreds as if they all focus on the same conceptualization of feedback.

Another important issue pointed out by Ruiz-Primo and Li (2013) relates to the particular tasks that students worked on for which they received feedback. Tasks tended to be artificial (e.g., puzzles) or deal with declarative knowledge (36% in science and 12% in mathematics). Still, it must be said, the overall effects of feedback on student performance were shown to be positive, although the magnitude of the effects varied according to the conceptual and methodological characteristics of the individual studies.

Regardless of the meta-analytic findings, feedback is often reported as one of the weakest components of teachers' classroom assessment practices (Black &

Wiliam, 1998; Askew, 2000; Ruiz-Primo & Li, 2004, 2013a, 2013b; Ruiz-Primo & Furtak, 2006, 2007; Li, Ruiz-Primo, & Thummaphan, 2014). The data used in this chapter were drawn from a project funded by the US Institute of Education Sciences. In this project, called DEMFAP (Developing and Evaluating Measures of Formative Assessment Practices) (Ruiz-Primo & Sands, 2009), we made daily observations of 26 classrooms as they implemented mathematics and science units. During this period, we collected 3,459 student products from 22 of the 26 classrooms (due to logistical issues, we could not collect student products in four classrooms). In this chapter, we provide descriptive information about teachers' written communication practices about these products, and we discuss strategies that can help to improve feedback practices. The purpose is to provide a map of what was observed in the students' products.

To analyze the students' products, we propose a coding system that focuses on three levels of analysis. Level 1 focuses on the *characteristics of the artifacts* collected, level 2 on *characteristics of teacher communications (feedback) found in individual students' products*, and level 3 on the *trends of comments across all the students' products*. We include information about several critical areas within the coding system.

We first provide some information about the DEMFAP project and describe the coding system we used to code the students' products. We then characterize the artifacts collected and describe the feedback observed in the students' products. We do not link these practices to students' learning. Rather, the intention is to reflect on the observed strategies. The chapter closes with some ideas that can contribute to improving teachers' feedback practices.

Context of the Study: The DEMFAP Project

The goal of the DEMFAP project was to develop reliable and valid instruments to measure formative assessment practices in the classroom, which could have *utility* in real contexts – e.g., for use by teacher leaders, instructional coaches, principals, and/or district-level administrators (Ruiz-Primo & Sands, 2009). We proposed the development of instruments that were efficient and practical and would facilitate quick feedback to teachers about their formative assessment practices. The DEMFAP project was organized into three phases: Phase I, Theory- and Research-Based Construct Definition; Phase II, Empirically Based Construct Refinement; and Phase III, Instrument Development and Evaluation.

Phase I: Defining the Construct. After conducting a literature review, we identified critical dimensions, aspects, and characteristics of formative assessment. The result of this phase was the development of a framework that could guide the project activities. The *DEMFAP formative assessment framework* characterized formative assessment practices based on four dimensions (Ruiz-Primo, 2010): (1) a *cycle of formative assessment*, (2) *formality of a formative*

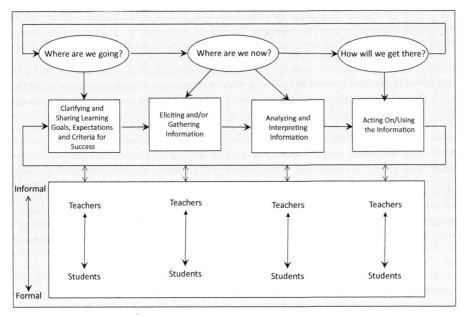

Figure 9.1 *Graphical representation of the formative assessment facets used in the DEMFAP project (adapted from Ruiz-Primo, 2010).*

assessment event, (3) *social participation in the formative assessment event*, and (4) *classroom context*. A simplified version of the framework that we used for the project is presented in Figure 9.1.

The *formative assessment activity cycle* is based on Ramaprasad's (1983) and Sadler's (1989) ideas about feedback, and Bell and Cowie's (2001) types of formative assessment. We identified four facets of formative assessment: clarifying learning goals and expectations, collecting information, analyzing and interpreting information, and acting on/using the information collected to move students closer to the learning goals. *Formality* refers to the ways in which the formative assessment practices are consistent with certain protocols or conventions. The formality or informality of a formative assessment event varies according to the planning involved (Ruiz-Primo & Furtak, 2006, 2007; Shavelson et al., 2008; Ruiz-Primo et al., 2010), the strategies used to collect information (e.g., based on raised hands or based on written responses to a question), and the strategies used to act on the information collected (e.g., discuss the approach used to solve a certain type of problem with the whole classroom or indicate approval or not with just a facial expression). *Social participation* refers to the teachers' and students' roles in a formative assessment event. This dimension reflects the social organization through which the assessment activity cycle can take place (e.g., one on one, pairs, small group, or whole class). Finally, *context* focuses on the nature of the social organization within which the assessment activity cycle occurs, and the norms and rules established for formative assessment to happen.

Phase II: Refining the Construct Defined. To refine the construct, we collected information from twenty teachers (ten in science, nine in mathematics, and one mathematics/science teacher) during the implementation of a complete mathematics and/or science unit. With some teachers, we observed the implementation of more than one unit: five teachers (three in science, two in mathematics) were observed during two separate units. As mentioned, one teacher taught a math and a science unit concurrently to the same group of students (she moved back and forth between the topics daily); therefore, we considered these two units separately although they occurred over the same time span. In total, we observed 26 entire units (14 science units and 12 mathematics units). We collected 429.5 hours of video across 420 days (an average of 1.02 hours per day) from the 26 units. Information about the teachers from whom we collected information is presented in Table 9.1.

When coding the collected videos for formative assessment practices, we applied a unique approach: we used *instructional tasks* – the basic structural component of a classday – as the unit of analysis. We coded each video twice: we first identified the instructional tasks (e.g., covering content, warm-up, reviewing students' work), then coded the formative assessment practices for each instructional task. After the videos had been coded, we used a statistical method of selecting variables (codes in the coding system) that could differentiate among teachers' formative assessment practices. Based on a set of codes, we applied a two-step cluster analysis to classify groups of instructional tasks. This particular analysis allowed us (1) to assess the usefulness of our codes (representing a conceptual scheme of formative assessment) for grouping and differentiating teachers' practices and (2) to identify variables that could be used in the development of the measurement tools. These tools focused on variables that were shown to distinguish teachers' practices relative to certain critical dimensions.

Phase III: Instrument Development. Based on the cluster analysis results, we developed and tested nine instruments in the pilot study. We developed *three sets of instruments* per facet of the formative assessment framework (clarifying learning goals/expectations, informal formative assessment, and formal formative assessment), and one instrument per source of information (an external observer, the teacher, and her students). The three instruments created for each facet were referred to as a "suite." In the pilot study, we tried out and revised the instruments guided by *small learning cycles* of trying→revising→adapting. School district personnel participated in the pilot study by using the observation protocols alongside a DEMFAP researcher. The pilot study involved forty-three teachers and was conducted over a twelve-week period. The final versions of the instruments were field-tested with fifty-eight teachers, each of whom was observed on three separate occasions by teams of district personnel and DEMFAP researchers.

In Phase II, the everyday data collection was carried out by a videographer and a DEMFAP researcher assigned to every classroom participating in the

Table 9.1 *Demographics and data collection information for the teachers in the DEMFAP study*

Teacher	Gender	Ethnicity	Experience (in years)	Grade Level	Year of the Project	Number of Units Observed	Number of Days Observed	Number of Hours of Video	Number of Daily Interviews	Number of Artifacts Collected	Number of Student Interviews
Mathematics Teachers											
TM1	Female	White	4	Elementary	2	1	11	11.26	11	149	9
TM2	Female	White	5	Middle	2	1	13	15.5	11	38	9
TM3	Female	White	6	Middle	2	2	18	27.2	19	111	20
TM4	Female	White	6	Middle	2	2	27	37.1	21	556	9
TM5	Female	White	6	Middle	2	1	7	9.0	8	25	5
TM6	Female	White	8	Elementary	2	1	12	13.2	8	251	12
TM7	Female	White	9	Middle	2	1	25	29.1	22	1175	9
TM8	Male	White	12	Middle	3	1	22	27.6	12	3	7
TM9	Female	Hispanic	17	Middle	2	1	17	14.0	11	17	8
Mathematics and Science Teachers											
TMS10	Female	White	18	Elementary	1–2	3	47	56.7	27	341	13
Science Teachers											
TS11	Female	White	3	Middle	1–2	2	44	36.7	22	156	9
TS12	Male	White	5	Elementary	2	1	19	10.4	16	325	7
TS13	Female	White	6	Elementary	4	1	24	22.1	0	0	0
TS14	Male	Hispanic	10	Middle	2	1	7	5.9	7	55	10
TS15	Female	White	12	Elementary	1	1	12	11.9	8	163	10
TS16	Female	White	16	Elementary	4	1	26	18.6	0	0	0
TS17	Female	White	17	Elementary	4	2	35	33.0	0	0	0
TS18	Female	Hispanic	18	Elementary	4	1	21	23.0	0	0	0
TS19	Female	White	19	Middle	2	1	21	19.5	15	94	9
TS20	Female	White	24	Elementary	4	1	12	7.7	0	0	0
Total						26	420	429.5	218	3459	146

study. The researcher's role was to record any information that could not be captured in the videos. One of their responsibilities was to collect any artifacts that were used that day and, when possible, to photocopy students' work. Handouts and other material used on a given day were referred to as *artifacts*, and students' work on those artifacts was referred to as *products*. We were usually able to collect artifacts, but not always the student work that resulted from the administration of the artifacts (i.e., the products). The artifacts were coded to capture the general characteristics of the activities in which students were involved, and the students' products were coded to capture the characteristics of the teachers' written comments on the students' products. This chapter focuses on the exploratory findings of the analysis of the artifacts and the students' products. We present information about the characteristics of the artifacts collected without considering disciplines – that is, without considering mathematics and science classrooms separately.

Issues on Feedback

Feedback constitutes the critical link between information collected about student learning or performance and the subsequent action(s) based on deliberate interpretation of that information. Feedback becomes the action as a result of the information collected (acting on or using the information collected). In this sense, when feedback is incorporated, assessment becomes *formative* – that is, feedback is viewed as a mechanism with the potential to influence student learning. We expect feedback to help students improve and build their learning resources by helping them to reach higher levels of understanding relative to where they were before the information was collected (Sadler, 1989; Hargreaves, McCallum, & Gipps, 2000). In the best-case scenario, feedback should help students to improve their strategies for grappling with a task, at the same time enhancing their self-regulation habits.

In our work we explicitly emphasized the importance of not considering feedback as a discrete and isolated event but, rather, being embedded in each formative assessment activity – from clarifying learning goals to gathering information, to analyzing and interpreting the information collected, and to acting on the information provided (to use the feedback to improve learning or performance). For example, feedback should be based on the learning goals being pursued or the criteria for success. Feedback becomes focused and contributes to the achievement of learning goals only if teachers and students are clear about what to look for in the students' responses (i.e., criteria).

Activities should make students' thinking explicit in order for feedback to be effective. As such, these activities should be carefully crafted, selected, or adapted. Identifying what students have learned is possible only when appropriate tasks are used and students' responses are analyzed relative to the learning goals or criteria for success. Such carefully designed and implemented feedback will illuminate students' struggles and strengths and suggest appropriate action to help them achieve the learning goals. This is the feedback that students provide to the teachers that helps to inform subsequent instructional decisions (Hattie, 2009). As a result, a critical aspect of the formative assessment process is acknowledging the teacher's role in designing, selecting, or adapting the tasks intended for students. We know that teachers should not rely solely on students' written responses as a source of information. They should also pay attention to students' oral responses, to what students make and create, to students' conversations, to the strategies they use when solving a problem, and to the observations they make of the students. That is, we believe that any daily classroom activity can be used as an assessment tool to gather evidence about student learning.

We recognize that there are several ways to respond to students to provide feedback (Ruiz-Primo, Iverson, & Sands, 2013; Ruiz-Primo & Li, 2013a). For example, teachers can respond with *instructional moves* such as modeling an approach to solve a problem with or without the help of the students (Ruiz-Primo, Iverson, & Sands, 2013). Both comments (oral or written) and instructional moves should have the same purpose (i.e., modifying students' thinking to improve learning) but employing different strategies and both should be considered feedback. In this chapter we focus only on feedback as *written comments* on students' products. Other forms of feedback have been addressed in other papers.

In our work we have recognized that the best feedback is that which is informative and readily usable by those who receive it – in this case, the students. Feedback that motivates students to take action to improve their learning and performance is the best possible but the least frequently implemented (Ruiz-Primo & Li, 2013b). Rather than referring to all teachers' written communications as *feedback*, we prefer to use the term *communications*. Also, instead of four general levels of comments (to the student as a person, to the student's work, to processes, and toward self-regulation; Hattie &Timperley, 2007), we considered more granular categories in which these four are embedded. We think about teachers' communications as having different forms, different foci, different tone, different levels of understanding (communicability to the students), different types of information, or different levels of eliciting actions (Ruiz-Primo & Li, 2013a, 2013b). Some of these communications will be informative and useful, while others will not. To capture the quality of the teachers' communications, we focus on different dimensions, some of which are presented in this chapter (e.g., the focus of the content of the teachers' comment).

We further recognize that it is critical, in all the formative assessment facets (e.g., clarifying learning goals), to involve students in the assessment process. As a result, we believe that, when provided with sound criteria, students can provide feedback as valuable as the teacher's feedback.

In the following section, we describe some of the codes used to capture information from the collected artifacts and students' products.

Classroom Artifacts and Students' Products: The DEMFAP Coding System

DEMFAP's coding system was developed based on previous studies conducted with students' work (Ruiz-Primo & Li, 2004, 2011, 2013b; Li, Ruiz-Primo, & Thummaphan, 2014). In the DEMFAP coding system, we distinguish between *products* (the students' work) and *artifacts* (handouts, worksheets, other similar formats) and *products*, which describe each individual student's work on an artifact where students responded. The coding system captures general characteristics of the activities in which students were engaged and the characteristics of the teachers' communications observed on students' products. As mentioned above, the coding system taps three levels of analysis: the artifact level, the student's products level, and the whole-class level, where we looked for trends or tendencies across all the students' products. In this chapter, we focus on only a few critical codes that are described below. The intercoder agreement among three coders was 88% for this analysis.

Characteristics of the Artifacts

For teachers to help students become successful learners, they need to identify students' special challenges and strengths, understand their thinking, and determine where they are in their learning. To be able to do all of this, teachers need appropriate tools or resources (questions, problems, or other types of tasks) that will help them gather the most relevant information about their students. Teachers will use these tools to learn how students are thinking while engaged in different tasks, whether oral or written, hands on, or digital. (In this chapter, we focus on artifacts that elicit written responses from all or most of the students in a classroom.)

The premise of the study was that the artifacts collected can provide at least some information about the quality of tasks in which students were engaged. We developed some codes, exploratory in nature, but which might potentially provide some insight into the characteristics of the artifacts. In this chapter, we focus on seven aspects of the artifacts:

- *Potential underlying purpose of the artifact* (Considering the artifact as a whole, what would be its intended purpose? e.g., making students' thinking explicit or practicing something)
- *Explicit goal of the artifact* (Does the artifact cite/mention a purpose, an objective, or a learning goal? If so, do the questions/tasks in the artifact correspond to the purpose or learning goal?) When providing instructions to the students, some teachers orally provide information about the purpose of what students are about to do (e.g., Ruiz-Primo, Sands, & Kroog, 2016). We still wanted to know whether, in their descriptions or instructions of the tasks, some teachers provided some kinds of information specific to its purpose.
- *Relationships among artifacts within the same unit* (Are the questions/problems/tasks in this artifact somehow linked in terms of content to the

previous day's artifacts? e.g., the artifact focuses on the same topic or skills; the questions/problems/tasks are more of the same or very similar)

- *Efficiency of the artifact* in providing critical information about the students (How time-consuming would it be for the teacher to review all the artifacts? For example, with just a quick glance an experienced teacher could immediately be aware of each student's struggles and strengths).

We further asked whether some type of criteria accompanied the artifacts. We focus on:

- *Evidence of use of a rubric* (How do you know the student's product was scored with a rubric?)
- *User of the rubric* (Who used the rubric – the teacher, a peer, the student?)
- *Focus of the rubric* (What aspects of the student's work does the rubric focus on, e.g., completeness, accuracy of work, presentation of work?)

Characteristics of the Communication in Students' Products

Our coding focused on the characteristics of the teachers' communications found on students' products. We acknowledge that the oral feedback that teachers could potentially provide to the students is absent from the students' products. Similarly, also missing is evidence about how the information teachers gained from reviewing the students' products affected their instruction. We believe, however, that the communications seen on the students' products constitute evidence of the written feedback practices in the classroom.

The following are examples of the coding questions we used to characterize the communications found on students' products:

- *Form of the communication* (scores, symbols, comments? Ruiz-Primo & Li, 2004, 2011, 2013b)
- *Type of comments* (as statements, questions, or both?)
- *Focus of comment* (What aspects of the student's work does the communication focuses on, e.g., content, meta-cognitive, disciplinary communication? Ruiz-Primo & Li, 2011, 2013b)
- *Type of information offered to the students in the comments* (evaluative on quantitative work? evaluative on qualitative work? editorial, descriptive, prescriptive? Ruiz-Primo & Li, 2011, 2013b)
- *Usability of comments* (Does the communication prompt students to take any action? Ruiz-Primo & Li, 2011, 2013b)
- *Provider of comments* (Are there comments from someone other than the teacher? If so, who provided them – the student, a peer, someone else, unknown?)

Trends across All of the Students' Products

At this level of analysis, we asked whether it would be possible to gather information across all the students' products. We focused on three kinds of information:

- *Missed questions/problems/tasks* (Looking at all of the students' products, were there any questions/problems/tasks that all or nearly all of the students missed?)
- *Repeated comments* (Looking at all of the students' products, were there comments that were repeated across all or almost all of the students' products, that is, was the same comment repeated across many products?)

Characterizing Artifacts and Teachers' Comments on Students' Products: Some Findings

We first describe the general characteristics of the artifacts collected, then the characteristics of the rubrics collected, followed by the characteristics of the teachers' communications added to the students' products. We conclude with trends observed across all of the students' products.

Characteristics of the Artifacts

Type of Artifacts. From the 3,459 students' products collected, we identified 498 unique artifacts. Table 9.2 provides information about the artifacts collected, by type. Overall, the majority (41%) were worksheets with problem sets, followed by notebook entries (15.9%), warm-up tasks (11.4%), and assessments (10%).

We identified three types of assessments: pre-test ($n=9$; 1.8%), post-test ($n=13$; 2.6%), and quizzes ($n=30$; 6.0%). In only about half of the classrooms in the sample, teachers administered a pre-test before implementing the unit in which there was a post-test to check students' learning at the end of the unit. The low frequency of quizzes, a formal strategy to collect information about students' level of understanding, may indicate that teachers use other sources (e.g., worksheet or notebook entries) to gather information about their students.

Table 9.2 *Type of unique artifact: Frequency and percentage*

Type of Artifacts	Frequency	Percentage
Assessments	52	10.4
Entrance/exit tickets	13	2.6
Homework	32	6.4
Investigation reports	23	4.6
Notebook entries	79	15.9
Problem sets/worksheets	204	41.0
Self-assessments	18	3.6
Warm-ups	57	11.4
Other	20	4.0
Total	498	100.0

Potential Underlying Purpose of Artifacts. We focused on five types of artifact purposes: (1) assess students in a summative manner; (2) identify issues students may face, such as misconceptions, misapplications, common errors; (3) provide practice; (4) push students to higher levels of understanding; and (5) accustom students to self-assess their own understanding of the content or their thinking strategies. Table 9.3 provides information from the coders about these possible purposes of the artifacts, grouped by type of artifact.

Most of the artifacts collected were coded as having as a purpose of practicing something (65%). Only 12% of the artifacts appeared to push students thinking to higher levels of understanding (i.e., productive struggle). Moreover, only about 9% of the artifacts appeared to explicitly reveal students' thinking (i.e., to identify misconceptions, misapplications, common errors). From this group, most of the artifacts fell into the category of warm-ups, followed by entrance/exit tickets. As artifacts, only five of the pre-tests and seven of the quizzes made students' thinking explicit. The majority of the assessments as artifacts ($n=37$) were designed for summative purpose. Two of the quizzes were designed for students to practice something, and only one gave some clear indication of students' areas of difficulty and struggle. Finally, just 4.6% of the collected artifacts focused on self-assessments. This finding reflects a lack of attention towards helping students develop self-regulation/monitoring strategies.

Table 9.3 *Potential underlying purpose of artifacts by type of artifact: Frequency*

Type of Artifacts	No Code Selected	Assess students in a Summative Way	Identify Potential Issues In Students' Understanding	Practice Something	Push Students' Thinking	For Students to Self-Assess Their Own Understanding
Assessments	0	37	12	2	1	0
Entrance/exit tickets	0	2	11	0	0	0
Homework	0	0	0	32	0	0
Investigation reports	0	0	0	13	10	0
Notebook entries	2	0	0	47	28	2
Problem sets/worksheets	2	0	4	180	18	0
Self-assessments	0	0	0	0	0	18
Warm-ups	1	0	17	37	2	0
Other	1	1	0	13	2	3
Total *	6	40	44	324	61	23
Total %**	1	8	9	65	12	5

* Total number of artifacts is 498.
**Total percentage across columns is 100.

Making the Purpose of Artifacts Explicit. We have argued that it is extremely important that students understand why they are doing something rather than just completing something for the sake of completion (Ruiz-Primo & Kroog, 2016). When students know what they need to focus on and how, their efforts contribute to achieving their learning goals. Unfortunately, our DEMFAP study (Ruiz-Primo & Kroog, 2016) showed that for about 70% of the 420 days that were coded, teachers did not share the relevant learning goals or expectations/criteria for success with students, or when they did very few teachers took visible steps to determine students' understanding of these. We know that one potential reason why formative assessment may not be as effective as possible is the ambiguity and vagueness with which learning goals are treated in the classroom (Nebelsick-Gullet, Hamen Farrar, Huff, & Pickman, 2013). Furthermore, feedback should be based on learning goals and criteria for success. In other DEMFAP studies we focused on how learning goals and criteria were shared during class time. In this study we focus on whether teachers share the purpose of the tasks in which students were engaged. We focus on finding out whether some type of learning goal, objective, or target was mentioned in the artifacts.

In only 38 (7.6%) of the 498 artifacts collected, we found evidence that students were provided with a purpose; 25 of the 38 were notebook entries. In seven of the artifacts, students were instructed to read the learning goal somewhere else (e.g., "Please read the learning target on the board before answering the question"). We found five artifacts with multiple learning goals. This practice can be potentially confusing for the student since it is hard to know on which of the multiple learning goals they need to focus. We did not find criteria or expectations for students in any of the artifacts themselves. However, some of the artifacts did have rubrics attached (see below).

We found ten different verbs used in the learning goals that were included in the artifacts: apply, demonstrate, describe, design, develop, identify, investigate, measure, prove, and understand. Of these, *describe* was the verb used most frequently (19%), followed by *apply, demonstrate, measure,* and *understand* (13%). Depending on how it is used, *describe* is a verb that can impose different cognitive demands (e.g., "I can describe the states of water," "I can describe how to find the area and perimeter of regular quadrilaterals and tringles," "I can describe the physical interactions in the path of a roller coaster"). In other cases, although the verbs may suggest high cognitive demands, indeed they are used in a vague manner (e.g., "I can apply my knowledge of measurement, speed, and forces").

Overall, it appears that the collected artifacts did not provide students with effective guidance about where to focus their efforts, why they were doing something, or how well they were doing it (criteria). The following discussion expands on this finding.

Rubrics. A necessary condition for sound feedback, based on the work by Ramaprasad (1983) and Sadler (1989), is the presence of a reference level for performance – that is, what constitutes quality in what students are asked to do? Having a reference, such as a rubric, helps students and teachers to know the characteristics of "good" work that they need to look for. This is the main reason that criteria have been referred to as "student look-fors" (Moss & Brookhart, 2012). We have argued that for students to develop self-regulation and monitoring habits, these kinds of criteria for quality should be shared with them. Therefore, we looked for evidence that could provide insight into the use of criteria to judge work as successful. More specifically, in this section we focus on artifacts for which there was evidence that a rubric had been used to review students' work.

Results indicated that a rubric was used in only 13 (2.6%) of the 498 artifacts. Of those, there was evidence that five were used by teachers to review the student products: in seven cases students used rubrics to review their own work, and in one case the rubric was used by both teacher and students. There was no evidence that rubrics were used by peers. This finding provides some insight into the degree to which students are engaged in reviewing their own work, which appears very little, given the 498 artifacts collected. Furthermore, only five cases show evidence that the rubrics led to some type of action by the students other than using it solely for reviewing purposes.

In examining the types of artifacts associated with the use of rubrics, we found that entrance/exit tickets and self-assessments showed the highest frequency of rubric use (six each). In only one post-test assessment was a rubric used.

We also sought to identify the main focus of the rubrics associated with the artifacts. For this purpose, we used twelve non-mutually exclusive codes such as content, completeness, accuracy, and meta-cognitive strategies. Therefore, a rubric could focus on more than one aspect (e.g., accuracy and meta-cognitive strategy). Our results showed that three of the rubrics focused on accuracy of students' work, eight on content, two on meta-cognitive strategies, five on motivation, and one on correct and incorrect responses. (The last item should be considered a "response key," but it was named as a rubric.)

Relationship among the Artifacts. To find out more about the connections among the artifacts collected within a unit, we coded the artifacts based on six categories: (1) hard to know the connection since the artifact was the first one coded for the unit; (2) the content of the artifact is unrelated to artifacts coded in previous days; (3) the artifact focuses on the same topic or skill, and the problems or questions are very similar to those found on previous days; (4) the artifact focuses on the same topic or skill but the problems or questions vary in difficulty compared with those found on previous days; (5) the artifacts can be described as forming a bridge between topics or skills because they include problems and questions familiar to the students as well as new content in the unit; and (6) the focus of the artifact is related to content of previous days but the problems and questions are an extension of what was found on those days.

Table 9.4 provides information about how artifacts were related to one another based on the type of artifact. The highest percentage of artifacts (34%) included problems or questions that were more difficult than those coded in previous artifacts. As expected, this characteristic appeared most frequently

Table 9.4 *Relationships among artifacts by type of artifact: Frequency*

Type of Artifacts	No Code Selected	Hard to Know, First Artifact of the Unit	Artifact Is Unrelated to Previous Ones	Questions Are Very Similar to Previous Ones	Question Seems More Difficult than Previous Ones	Some Questions Are Similar and Others Are More Difficult	Questions Extend to What Was Found Previously
Assessments	0	10	2	12	19	3	6
Entrance/exit tickets	0	1	2	3	6	0	1
Homework	0	0	3	10	13	5	1
Investigation reports	0	0	1	2	8	6	6
Notebook entries	4	10	7	12	11	21	14
Problem sets/worksheets	3	9	22	28	90	30	22
Self-assessments	0	3	3	2	2	0	8
Warm-ups	0	5	18	17	12	3	2
Other	0	2	4	3	6	2	3
Total*	7	40	62	89	167	70	63
Total %**	1	8	12	18	34	13	14

*Total number of artifacts is 498.
**Total percentage across columns is 100.

in worksheets with problem sets (18% of all the artifacts), followed by artifacts categorized as homework (3%), and then quizzes as a type of assessment (3%).

About 18% of the artifacts presented problems or questions very similar to those found in previously collected artifacts, which may suggest that students were simply practicing something; however, it is hard to determine if the practice was *deliberate* – practicing something that students needed help with (Ericsson, Krampre, & Tesch-Römer, 1993; Ericsson, 1996; Colvin, 2008). Still, we had another piece of information that could provide some insight about this result. That is, the coding system includes a specific code to identify evidence of whether the teacher indeed reviewed a given artifact. In at least 36% of the worksheets with sets of problems, there was no sign of any teacher review, and in 12% of these worksheets there was only a check of "completion." It can be inferred that students were practicing something, but it is also possible that the teacher did not know whether students' learning was actually improving. By asking students to practice something, teachers can focus on elements of students' performance that need improvement or correction, and work with them on those exact areas. As we have mentioned before, repetition for repetition's sake is not helpful, and it seems that some of these artifacts may have focused on *unpurposeful* practice (Syed, 2010).

Three categories have similar percentages: artifacts categorized as including problems or questions (tasks) that somehow extend from those on previous tasks (14%), artifacts with mixed types of questions (13%), and artifacts not related to previous ones (12%). Artifacts that include problems or questions that can extend students' thinking tend to encourage *productive struggle*. These are tasks that challenge students to think about and wrestle with ideas/concepts/ processes critical to their learning (Hiebert & Grouws, 2007).

Efficiency of the Artifacts. Clearly, most assessments, when embedded in the implementation of a unit, have the potential to function as formal formative assessment tools, if the information collected through them is used to improve student learning. It is less common for an artifact (e.g., a handout with a set of questions or problems) that elicits responses from all or most of the students to be considered by teachers as a formal source of information about what students know and can do. However, this type of artifact can still be as useful as any quiz or embedded assessment. Teachers frequently implement this type of artifact during the class period or after class (as homework). Regardless of the type of task, it takes teachers time and effort to fully review the artifacts if they are to be used for formative purposes. As such, teachers need to be strategic in gathering critical information, as quickly as possible, allowing them to move to the next instructional activity while incorporating the information they learned about the students. We believe curriculum developers or teachers should design artifacts in ways that illuminate students' thinking, thus making it easier to quickly gather information about the students' strengths and weaknesses. This is not about how many problems and questions are in a handout, but about having *certain* problems and questions that can quickly yield information that tells the teacher if students are on the right path.

In our coding system, we include codes about whether the artifacts were efficient in providing teachers with critical information related to the students' performance. Three codes were developed to discern the efficiency of the artifacts: (1) substantial time was required to read students' responses; (2) substantial time was required to review all the questions or problems in the artifact that helped reveal students' strengths and weaknesses; and (3) an experienced teacher, knowing what to look for, could quickly get a good sense of each student's level of understanding.

Table 9.5 provides information about how efficiently artifacts can be analyzed by type of artifact. A positive finding is that about 50% of the artifacts had the potential to immediately reveal students' issues. As would be expected, worksheets with sets of problems were the artifacts with the highest percentage in this category (15% of the 498 artifacts collected), followed by notebook entries (13%) and warm-ups (8%).

About 41% of the artifacts required more time to review due to the number of problems or questions in the artifacts. The highest percentage (23% of the 498 artifacts collected) in this category corresponded, again, to worksheets with sets of problems, followed by assessments (5%) and homework and warm-ups (3%). Only 7% of the artifacts required substantial time to read the students' responses.

Table 9.5 *Efficiency of artifacts by type of artifact: Frequency*

Type of Artifacts	No Code Selected	Good Deal of Time Required to Read Students' Responses	Good Deal of Time to Review All Problems or Questions	It Is Possible to Get a Good Sense of Each Student's Level
Assessments	2	15	26	9
Entrance/exit tickets	0	0	2	11
Homework	3	1	16	12
Investigation reports	0	4	10	9
Notebook entries	2	1	9	67
Problem sets/worksheets	4	8	115	77
Self-assessments	0	1	1	16
Warm-ups	0	0	16	41
Other	1	4	10	5
Total *	12	34	205	247
Total %**	2	7	41	50

*Total number of artifacts is 498.
**Total percentage is 100.

Characteristics of Teacher Communications in Student Products

In this section, we focus on the 3,459 student products collected from the twenty-two classrooms. To code students' products we developed rules to determine whether the comments were provided by the teacher or someone else, such as a peer or the student herself.

Type of Teacher' Communications. Seven different codes were developed to capture information about the teachers' communications: (1) nothing to code (e.g., the student product showed only the student's name with no responses and no teacher communication), (2) no communication (i.e., student completed the artifact tasks but there is no teacher communication), (3) rubric score (i.e., the level of performance is indicated in a structured format page with specific scoring criteria, rating, and/or evaluative information), (4) score (i.e., the communication indicates the performance level of the student work, which could be a grade or a numeric value), (5) symbol (e.g., checkmarks indicating correct/incorrect, completion stamps, emoticons), (6) comments (i.e., verbal communication in words, phrases, sentences, or questions), and (7) illegible (i.e., communication that was meaningless, could not be read, or did not make sense to the coders). It is important to note that students' products may have more than one type of communication. Therefore, categories are non-mutually exclusive: coders were allowed to select more than one code, if appropriate, for each student's product.

Table 9.6 *Type of communication in students' products: Frequency and Percentage**

Type of Communication	Frequency	Percentage**
Nothing to code	289	8.36
No communication	2051	59.29
Rubric score	178	5.15
Score	887	25.64
Symbol	698	20.18
Comment	700	20.24
Illegible	5	0.14

*Categories are non-mutually exclusive; therefore, frequencies do not add to 3,459 and percentages do not add to 100.
**Percentage calculated using the 3,459 students' products on each type of communication.

Table 9.6 provides information about the different types of communication in the students' products, but we focus only on those with teachers' comments. About 71% of the students' products exhibited some type of communication, but only 20% had teachers' comments (versus another type of communication, such as symbols). A rubric was used to review students' work in only 5% of the products. The majority of the students' products (59%) did not display any teacher communication. This finding is consistent with other studies in which teacher communication is rarely found (Ruiz-Primo & Li, 2004; 2013b).

Type of Comments. Our coding system distinguishes between two types of teachers' comments: statements and questions. Based on the coding of the 700 student products to identify teacher comments, 534 (76%) of the products exhibited comments only as statements, 110 (16%) products had both statements and questions as comments, and 45 (6%) had only questions as comments. A total of 155 of the students' products included questions as teacher comments and 644 included statements as comments. The coders applied the no category code to 11 (2%) of the products.

Questions as Comments. Table 9.7 presents information about the characteristics of the questions found in the teacher comments. Of these, we focused on two aspects: (1) whether the questions were formulated in such a way that students would not know exactly what they did correctly or incorrectly or that they were missing something, and/or how to improve the work (e.g., "What about *a*?"), and (2) whether the questions were formulated in a way that could inspire or guide student action (e.g., "Do you think you can organize your description in steps to make it clearer?").

The majority of the questions appearing in the students' products were judged by the coders as helpful (78%) and having the potential to motivate the students to act (93%). Notably, however, only in 1% of the cases did the coders find evidence (the criterion for selecting "Yes" in this code) that students visibly responded to the teacher's question. Despite the *potential* for acting, based on the information they received, students did not act on the feedback,

Table 9.7 *Characteristics of teachers' questions as comments by type: Frequencies*

| | | Characteristics of the Questions | | | | |
| | | Helpful | | Lead to a Student's Action | | |
	n	No	Yes	No	Potentially	Yes
Products with both questions and statements	110	21	89	6	102	2
Questions only	45	13	32	3	42	0
Total	155	34	121	9	144	2
Total %*		22	78	6	93	1

*Percentages are rounded and calculated using the 155 students' products with questions as comments.

because they were not given the opportunity to do so, were not appropriately coached, or simply because they ignored that feedback.

Statements as Comments. The analyses of the statements were completed while taking into account different dimensions. In this chapter we present only three: the type of information students received through the statements, the focus of the statements, and whether the statements were effectively formulated to inspire or guide students' actions.

For 644 student products, Tables 9.8 and 9.9 show the frequency of occurrence of the type and focus of the information observed in the statements as comments obtained from these products. Categories in both tables are non-mutually exclusive. That is, a student's product could have comments with statements of different types and focus; the coding system captured the presence of the different kinds of comments found in any given student's product. Frequencies reflect the number of products with a certain class of comment rather than just the number of comments found in the students' products. Therefore, percentages do not add to 100.

According to the results shown in Table 9.8, the majority (38%) of students' products displayed statements with information considered as *general evaluative* (e.g., WOW!, Good!, Awesome!, No!, Incorrect!). This type of information does not make clear to the student exactly what they did correctly or incorrectly and makes no reference to content. The second most frequently occurring comment on students' products (21%) were statements categorized as *evaluative in quality* – that is, statements that commented on student responses using more concrete attributes, such as accuracy or appropriateness, but still ambiguous and imprecise (e.g., "This is not accurate").

Showing similar frequencies are products with comments that were *evaluative on quantity statements* (21%), *descriptive statements* (19%), and *correct responses* (18%). *Evaluative on quantity statements* are those that signify incomplete work or responses (e.g., "need more") but, similarly, are also ambiguous and imprecise about what is needed to improve or correct the work. *Descriptive statements* provide concrete information about what was right or wrong, rather

Table 9.8 *Characteristics of the information observed in the teachers' comments as statements by type: Frequencies*

| | | Type of Information Provided in the Comment | | | | | | | |
	n	General Evaluative	Evaluative on Quantity	Evaluative on Quality	Editorial	Correct Answer	Descriptive Information	Prescriptive Information	Hard to Know
Products with both questions and statements	110	21	30	20	23	29	28	17	24
Statements only	534	223	78	117	35	89	92	77	58
Total	644	244	108	137	58	118	120	94	82
Total %*		38	17	21	9	18	19	15	13

*Percentages are rounded and calculated using the 644 students' products with statements as teachers' comments. Since categories are not mutually exclusive, percentages do not add to 100.

Table 9.9 *Focus of the teachers' comments as statements by type: Frequencies*

	n	Content	Meta-Cognitive Strategies	Motivational	General Communication	Disciplinary Communication	Transitional	Missing work	Unrelated	Other
Products with both questions and statements	110	61	6	2	28	14	4	7	18	0
Statements only	534	245	37	5	61	68	41	8	31	19
Total	644	306	43	7	89	82	45	15	49	19
Total %*		48	7	1	14	13	7	2	8	3

*Percentages are rounded and calculated using the 644 students' products with statements as teachers' comments. Since categories are non-mutually exclusive, percentages do not add to 100.

than editing the students' response or explaining how to improve it. When offering a detailed account of what is correct and incorrect, the comments assume "functional significance" (Deci & Ryan, 1985) for student learning. Statements that provide the complete correct response are basically doing all of the thinking for the students, eliminating their opportunity to take any active role in using the new information.

Appearing less frequently on students' products were comments considered *prescriptive* (15%) or *editorial* (9%). *Prescriptive statements* give students specific, concrete help on how they can improve their work. They prompt the students to act on the information provided, potentially encouraging a desired action. *Editorial statements* annotate, model, edit, correct, or show how to do the work or task, thus diminishing the role of the student as an active agent. The coders had difficulty categorizing comments on 13% of the students' products.

Although 19% and 15% do not seem to be very low percentages of students' products bearing descriptive and prescriptive statements, relative to the total number of students' products coded (n=3459), they are actually low (3.5% and 2.7%, respectively). This finding confirms what others have reported, that teachers' feedback practices are one of the weakest components of formative assessment (Black & Wiliam, 1998; Askew, 2000; Ruiz-Primo & Li, 2004, 2013a, 2013b; Ruiz-Primo & Furtak, 2006, 2007; Li, Ruiz-Primo, & Thummaphan, 2014).

Table 9.9 presents information about the focus of the statements. We considered nine categories: content, meta-cognitive strategies, motivational, general communication, disciplinary communication, transitional, missing work, unrelated, and other. The categories are non-mutually exclusive; therefore, a student's product could show different categories of comments. All categories were captured. As a result, percentages do not total 100.

The statement category most frequently found in students' products focused on content (48%). *Content statements* directly address students' conceptual understanding of the relevant topic (e.g., "You're getting better about identifying chemical and mechanical changes!"). The second highest percentage (14%) was students' products showing *general communication* statements, which focus on presentation of the work (e.g., grammar, neatness, clarity of paragraphs). The third highest percentage (13%) was *disciplinary communication*, where statements focus on rules that apply to the relevant discipline (e.g., "Remember that in science we always label our units").

We should not overlook the low percentages of certain categories such as *meta-cognitive strategies statements* (e.g., "Read carefully each question and try to understand first what you are asked to do") and *transitional statements*, which tell the students a face-to-face interaction is required (e.g., "See me after school to talk about question 5").

The type of information in the statements varies according to its focus. A cross-tabulation shows that the highest percentage of the students' products with statements focusing on content (n=306; see Table 9.9) had correct answers (36%), followed by statements with descriptive information (35%). The profile for students' products with statements focusing on communication (n=89; see Table 9.9) looks different. In this category, the highest percentage of students' products offered evaluative information on quantity (43%). In comparison, for students' products with statements focusing on disciplinary communication (n=82; see Table 9.9), the lowest percentage was found in the category of evaluative information on quantity (6%) but was much higher for descriptive information (34%) and prescriptive information (33%). Another key finding is that the highest percentage of students' products with statements focusing on meta-cognitive strategies (n=43; see Table 9.9) was found in the category of prescriptive information in their comments (51%). We have not done this type of analysis in other feedback studies, but it seems an area worth exploring.

Statements That Motivate Action. The coding system also focuses on whether statements in students' products were formulated in ways that might lead students to respond to the teachers' statements with overt action. As with questions, a high percentage of students' products (49.5%) were coded as displaying statements with the potential to help the students improve their work; but the coders found evidence that the students actually responded to the teacher's statement in only 7.0% of the students' products. Still, for students' products with statements as comments, 41% of them did not facilitate or favor an action by the students; that is, the students were not successfully prompted to do any additional work.

Final Note. This section mentions students' products in which we found comments made by someone other than the teachers. Of the 700 student products in which comments were discovered, only eleven products fell into this category. This finding also reflects minimal participation of students in self- and peer assessment.

Trends over All of Students' Products

The system of coding begins by first coding each student's product, then, in another section, focuses on questions that require reviewing all the students' products for the same artifact within the same class. We provide information about this process in the latter section of the coding system.

Table 9.10 presents information about trends across all students' products. The coding system focuses on two aspects: (1) whether there were artifacts in which students' responses were consistently missed in any problem or question and (2) the teachers' responses to this type of product. We found that of the

Table 9.10 *Artifacts in which problems or questions were missed by almost all students by type: Frequency and Percentage*

Type of Artifact	Frequency	Percentage*
Assessments	15	41.6
Entrance/exit tickets	1	2.8
Homework	8	22.2
Investigation reports	0	0.0
Notebook entries	0	0.0
Problem sets/worksheets	6	16.7
Self-assessments	5	13.9
Warm-ups	1	2.8
Other	0	0.0
Total	36	100.0

*Percentage was calculated using the 36 artifacts with problems missed by almost or all the students.

498 artifacts collected, 36 (7.2%) included questions or problems that most or almost all the students missed. Among the 36 artifacts, the most frequently occurring type were those classified as assessment (post-test=19.4% and quizzes=22.2%), followed by homework artifacts (22.2%), and then worksheets with problem sets (16.7%).

In 86% of these collected artifacts, teachers used the same or very similar comments from one student to the next (e.g., "Please explain your answer," "Show your work," "Watch for triangle properties that can help you"). We called these *recycled comments*. Writing comments on all or almost all the students' products takes time, and there is always a question of whether it is time well used.

We went further and asked if teachers tended to write similar comments on students' products despite the presence or absence of errors. We (Kroog, King Hess, & Ruiz-Primo, 2016) found that 92% of all students' products exhibited recycled comments.

Improving Teachers' Feedback Practices

The data presented in this chapter support some suggested changes with the potential for substantially improving feedback practices in mathematics and science classrooms. We organize the suggestions into the design of the artifacts and managing feedback to the artifacts.

Design, Selection, or Adaptation of Artifacts

In conducting formative assessment, it is critical that the students' tasks somehow tangibly/visibly/clearly elicit the students' thinking, as well as evidence of the students' learning. Further, there should be full clarity about the ways the task contributes to what students need to learn on any given day within any given lesson in order to achieve the learning goals. We believe these two criteria are fundamental to the design of appropriate artifacts that have a purpose in mind. Thinking deliberately about the artifacts that students will be engaging with is part of the complexity of creating quality learning experiences (Bennett, Desforges, Cockburn, & Wilkinson, 1984; Perrenoud, 1998; Kennewell, 2001; Marshall, Carmichael, & Drummond, 2007).

How can one know whether a task can actually reflect students' thinking? If the students' responses lead to conclusions about the student's strengths and weaknesses, then we can be reassured that the artifacts are reflecting students' thinking. If an artifact can tell us only which responses are correct and which are not, then they are not being optimally useful in helping teachers to identify the next instructional move or what type of comment the student needs. In the everyday classroom, well-designed tasks will allow the teacher to quickly and easily determine how well students are answering the problems and questions and making decisions about what is going right or wrong. We acknowledge that there are certain tasks that are implemented usually at critical junctures in a unit, and more time will be spent in reviewing students' responses. Everyday tasks, however, should allow teachers to readily decide what action needs to take place. Well-designed artifacts should be designed with feedback in mind. That means that as they design or select tasks, teachers have to know what they are looking for – What are the actions, the steps the procedures followed by the students that reflect misunderstandings or problems in reasoning? Being clear and knowledgeable about students' potential errors may facilitate analysis of the students' responses and provide appropriate and helpful feedback, even on the fly.

When designing, selecting, or adapting artifacts it is critical to keep the learning goals being pursued in mind. These goals should help determine the purpose of the artifact. Clarifying the role of the artifact for students helps them achieve learning goals – Is the purpose of the artifact to practice something, to identify errors in specific processes, or to introduce a new type of problem or apply a procedure? Describing an artifact as simply practicing something is not enough if it is not clear how practicing something helps students to improve their learning. It is important to remember that only 12% of the artifacts analyzed in the DEMFAP project pushed students' thinking to higher levels of performance and understanding.

Another consideration is that increasing the number of problems or questions does not necessarily improve an artifact. A few well-designed questions or problems are more effective than many superficial ones (Kroog, King Hess, & Ruiz-Primo, 2016). What matters is thinking carefully about what needs to be revealed/demonstrated in the artifacts. The most important criterion is that the artifact can illuminate information about student thinking and can allow a teacher to analyze the information accurately and efficiently.

Students are able to monitor their own performances when they know and understand the criteria aligned to the successful performance that was considered during the design, selection, or adaptation of the artifacts. It is a way to promote students' active participation in their own learning. Rubrics, if well designed, can be used as a tool to help students assume control during the production of their responses (Sadler, 1989). If well developed, the rubrics also help students to (1) understand the goal being pursued based on quality criteria, (2) have a benchmark to compare the quality of what they are producing with criteria, and (3) engage in concrete actions to reduce the difference between where they are and where they should and want to be. Based on the data collected from the DEMFAP project, the collected rubrics rarely showed these characteristics.

Managing Feedback of Artifacts

Providing feedback is usually seen as a time-consuming endeavor. Indeed, this is true if instructional tasks (including artifacts) are not well designed and if feedback is conceptualized as providing only written feedback to each student.

If teachers design or select tasks that are carefully designed or selected, the feedback can be more focused, helpful, and appropriate, because it is easier for teachers to recognize the type of error or faulty reasoning that the students are making. For example, as reported in a previous study (Kroog, King Hess, & Ruiz-Primo, 2016), an artifact with a single problem that required students to complete all the potential steps when multiplying mixed numbers (e.g., converting a mixed number in a fraction) made it possible for the teacher to quickly assess learning. As she reviewed the students' responses or as she walked around the classroom, the teacher could quickly identify students' problem areas. This type of task saves teachers a lot of unnecessary work, allowing them to provide almost all their students with immediate feedback while they are working. The following discussion explains more fully how artifacts can be successfully used both during class (e.g., worksheets) or outside the classroom (e.g., homework).

Implementation of Artifacts during Class. Data from the videos recorded from all twenty-six classrooms in the DEMFAP study showed that teachers very often assign individual work (i.e., students working by themselves, in pairs, or in small groups) merely to keep students on track. As such, they miss many opportunities to provide students with feedback that can improve their learning (Ruiz-Primo, Kroog, & Sands, 2015). Tasks that are appropriately designed or selected have the potential to improve teachers' ability to identify students' problems while observing them working independently, and then provide immediate feedback. We observed expert teachers in the DEMFAP project who knew exactly what to look for as they observed students who were still working on tasks. They provided quick individual verbal feedback (e.g., a brief question that could guide the student's thinking) or written feedback (in sticky notes). At times, teachers asked students to stop so they could address a problem being experienced by many of the students. The feedback process was very fluid and spontaneous but also highly purposeful and focused.

Implementation of Artifacts Outside the Class. If artifacts (tasks) are designed in ways that allow teachers to quickly review students' responses, the feedback process has already begun. For example, based on one glance at students' responses, is it possible to separate students' products into two, three, or four piles, each indicating a certain type of problem? How many students are struggling with a similar issue; i.e., are their products in one pile? Based on the number of students, what is the best course of action the next day? If most of the students missed the same question, it is better to discuss the questions with the whole classroom rather than repeating a comment with each student. The teacher can start the discussion by first identifying the difficult questions, then asking the students to deduce what these questions have in common (or not), and finally moving on to discuss possible strategies with the students to solve this type of problem (e.g., "Mimi, how would you start approaching this problem? What about John? What do these approaches have in common?"). She can model the solution strategies without students' help (e.g., "Let me go through the solution and let me know which step you find the most problematic"). We also observed teachers who asked students which problem or question from the artifact was the most difficult or troublesome – with more than one suggestion, students voted to pick one. Also, it is always possible to work with a small group of students who shared the same problems in the artifact, to create groups of students to help each other, or, when there is an opportunity, to meet with students individually.

At the end, *feedback* is not just providing written comments to all students' products; true and valuable feedback depends on the quality of the comments, the critical aspects of the artifact that the teacher selects to spend the time and thought on in addressing in a written comment. There are many strategies that seem to be more efficient and effective than recycling the comments (writing the same comment again and again).

Final Comments

This chapter offered information on an exploratory analysis of the data that we collected in the DEMFAP project. There is still so much to learn from the 3,459 classroom products that were collected for the project. Still, we hope that this chapter will inspire others to look for and even create new strategies that can give new visibility or stimulate new ideas about artifacts and the quality of the teachers' comments in classrooms.

References

Askew, S. (2000). *Feedback for learning*. London: Routledge Falmer.

Bangert-Drowns, R. L., Kulik, C.-L., Kulik, J. A., & Morgan, M. T. (1991). The instructional effect of feedback in test-like events. *Review of Educational Research, 61*(2), 213–238.

Bell, B., & Cowie, B. (2001). *Formative assessment and science education*. Dordrecht: Kluwer.

Bennett, N., Desforges, C., Cockburn, A., & Wilkinson, B. (1984). *The quality of pupil learning experiences*. London: Lawrence Erlbaum Associates.

Bennett, R. E. (2011). Formative assessment: A critical review. *Assessment in Education: Principles, Policy & Practice, 18*(1), 5–25.

Black, P., & Wiliam, D. (1998). Assessment and classroom learning. *Assessment in Education: Principles, Policy, & Practice, 5*(1), 7–74.

Colvin, G. (2008). *Talent is overrated: What really separates world-class performers from everybody else*. London: Nicholas Brealey.

Deci, E. L., & Ryan, R. M. (1985). *Intrinsic motivation and self-determination in human behavior*. New York: Plenum.

Ericsson, K. A. (1996). The acquisition of expert performance: An introduction to some issues. In K. A. Ericsson (Ed.), *The road to excellence: The acquisition of expert performance in the arts and science, sports, and games* (pp. 14–64). New York: Lawrence Erlbaum.

Ericsson, K. A., Krampe, R. T., & Tesch-Römer, C. (1993). The role of deliberate practice in the acquisition of expert performance. *Psychological Review*, *100*(3), 363–406.

Hargreaves, E., McCallum, B., & Gipps, C. (2000). Teacher feedback strategies in primary classrooms: New evidence. In S. Askow (Ed.), *Feedback for learning* (pp. 34–43). New York: Routledge.

Hattie, J. (1999, August). Influences on student learning. Inaugural lecture, professor of education, University of Auckland. Retrieved from www.arts.auckland.ac.nz/staff/index.cfm?P=5049.

Hattie, J. A. C. (2009). *Visible learning: A synthesis of over 800 meta-analyses relating to achievement*. London: Routledge.

Hattie, J. A. C., & Timperley, H. (2007). The power of feedback. *Review of Educational Research*, *77*(1), 81–112.

Hiebert, J., & Grouws, D. A. (2007). The effects of classroom mathematics teaching on students' learning. In J. F. K. Lester (Ed.), *Second handbook of research on mathematics teaching and learning* (pp. 371–404). Charlotte, NC: Information Age Publishing.

Kennewell, S. (2001). Using affordance and constraints to evaluate the use of information and communications technology in teaching and learning. *Journal of Information Technology for Teacher Education*, *10*(1–2), 101–116.

Kluger, A. N., & DeNisi, A. (1996). The effects of feedback interventions on performance: A historical review, a meta-analysis, and a preliminary feedback intervention theory. *Psychological Bulletin*, *119*, 254–284.

Kroog, H., King Hess, K., & Ruiz-Primo, M. A. (2016). Implement effective and efficient approaches to formal formative assessment that will save time and boost student learning. *Educational Leadership*, *73*(7), 22–25.

Li, M., Ruiz-Primo, M. A., & Thummaphan, P. (2014, April). Students' use of written feedback in science notebooks. Paper presented at the AERA annual meeting, Philadelphia.

Marshall, B., Carmichael, P., & Drummond, M.-J. (2007). Learning how to learn in classrooms. In M. James, R. McCormick, P. Black, P. Carmichael, M.-J. Drummond, A. Fox, J. MacBeath, B. Marshall, D. Pedder, R. Procter, S. Swaffield, J. Swann, & D. Wiliam (Eds.), *Improving learning how to learn: Classrooms, schools, and network* (pp. 56–71). New York: Routledge.

Moss, C. M., & Brookhart, S. M. (2012). *Learning targets: Helping students aim for understanding in today's lesson*. Alexandria, VA: ASCD.

Nebelsick-Gullett, L., Hamen Farrar, C., Huff, K., & Packman, S. (2013). Design of interim assessment for instructional purpose: A case study using evidence centered design in advanced placement. In R. W. Lissitz (Ed.), *Informing the practice of teaching using formative and interim assessments* (pp. 21–48). Charlotte, NC: Information Age Publishing.

Perrenoud, P. (1998). From formative evaluation to a controlled regulation of learning process: Towards a wider conceptual field. *Assessment in Education: Principles, Policy, & Practice*, *5*(1), 85–102.

Ramaprasad, A. (1983). On the definition of feedback. *Behavioral Science*, *28*, 4–13.

Ruiz-Primo, M. A. (2010). Developing and Evaluating Measures of Formative Assessment Practice (DEMFAP) theoretical and methodological approach. Manuscript, Laboratory of Educational Assessment, Research, and Innovation (LEARN), University of Colorado Denver.

Ruiz-Primo, M. A., & Furtak, E. M. (2006). Informal formative assessment and scientific inquiry: Exploring teachers' practices and student learning. *Educational Assessment, 11*(3–4), 205–235.

Ruiz-Primo, M. A., & Furtak, E. M. (2007). Exploring teachers' informal formative assessment practices and students' understanding in the context of scientific inquiry. *Journal of Research in Science Teaching, 44*(1), 57–84.

Ruiz-Primo, M. A., Furtak, E., Ayala, C., Yin, Y., & Shavelson, R. J. (2010). Formative assessment, motivation, and science learning. In G. J. Cizek & H. Andrade (Eds.), *Handbook of formative assessment* (pp. 139–158). New York: Routledge, Taylor & Francis.

Ruiz-Primo, M. A., Iverson, H., & Sands, D. (2013). Video logging approach. Document for Second Advisory Board Meeting, Laboratory of Educational Assessment, Research, and Innovation, University of Colorado Denver.

Ruiz-Primo, M. A., & Li, M. (2004). On the use of students' science notebooks as an assessment tool. *Studies in Educational Evaluation, 30*, 61–85.

Ruiz-Primo, M. A., & Li, M. (2011, April). Looking into the teachers' feedback practices: How teachers interpret students' work. Paper presented at the annual meeting of the American Educational Research Association, New Orleans, LA.

Ruiz-Primo, M. A., & Li, M. (2013a). Examining formative feedback in the classroom context: New research perspectives. In J. H. McMillan (Ed.), *Handbook on research on classroom assessment* (pp. 215–232). Los Angeles, CA: Sage.

Ruiz-Primo, M. A., & Li, M. (2013b). Analyzing teachers' feedback practices in response to students' work in science classrooms. Special Issue on Using Evidence to Take Action: Strategies Teachers Use to Deconstruct Student Work. *Applied Measurement in Education, 26*(3), 163–175.

Ruiz-Primo, M. A., & Kroog, H. (2016). The impact of observation sampling strategies on the accuracy of inferences about teacher's formative assessment practices. Paper submitted for publication.

Ruiz-Primo, M. A., Kroog, H., & Sands, D. (2015, August). Teachers' judgments on-the-fly: Teachers' response patterns to students' responses in the context of informal formative assessment. Paper presented at the Symposium "From Teachers' Assessment Practices to Shared Professional Judgment Cultures" at the European Association for Research on Instruction and Learning, Limassol, Cyprus.

Ruiz-Primo, M. A., & Sands, D. (2009). Developing and Evaluating Measures of Formative Assessment Practices (DEMFAP). Proposal submitted to the Institute of Education Sciences, Cognition and Student Learning. Award ID: R305A100571.

Ruiz-Primo, M. A., Sands, D., & Kroog, H. (2016). Developing and Evaluating Measures of Formative Assessment Practices (DEMFAP): Technical report on instrument development and evaluation. Technical report submitted to the Institute of Education Sciences, Washington, DC, IES Grant R305A100571.

Sadler, D. R. (1989). Formative assessment and the design of instructional systems. *Instructional Science, 18*, 119–144.

Shavelson, R. J., Yin, Y., Furtak, E. M., Ruiz-Primo, M. A., & Ayala, C. (2008). On the role and impact of formative assessment on science inquiry teaching and learning. In J. Coffey, R. Douglas, & C. Stearns (Eds.), *Assessing science learning: Perspectives from research and practice* (pp. 21–36). Arlington, VA: National Science Teachers Association Press.

Shute, V. J. (2008). Focus on formative feedback. *Review of Educational Research, 78*(1), 153–189.

Syed, M. (2010). *Bounce: Mozart, Federer, Picasso, Beckman, and the science of success.* New York: Harper.

Van der Kleij, F. M., Feskens, R. C. W., & Eggen, T. J. H. M. (2015). Effects of feedback in a computer-based learning environment on students' learning outcomes: A meta-analysis. *Review of Educational Research, 85*(4), 475–511.

10 Instructional Feedback in Music

Kelly A. Parkes

Introduction

Feedback is, of course, vital in any musical setting. In these settings feedback "can come from almost anywhere" (Duke, 2005, p. 124) and has been widely studied, with a variety of terminologies, by music performance and music education researchers. This chapter explores three main lines of inquiry: teacher behaviors, peer and student feedback (assessment), and sensory feedback in the performance of music. In the first example, feedback has predominantly been seen in music as teacher behavior in music classrooms where musicians are making music in groups. In the second case, peer and self-feedback are often utilized in the applied studio (also called individual, private, one-to-one) settings as peer and self-assessment where students take lessons individually with their music teacher. In the third setting, musicians actively listen to themselves and attend to their bodies, garnering feedback from their own musical performance as part of sensory feedback. Sensory feedback from both a musical instrument and a musician's body is gathered through the skin, muscles, and tendons.

Feedback as a teacher behavior is observed in several instructional settings in music education research. The first is the K-12 music classroom; the second is the university setting where music education students are learning to become teachers who use feedback with students in grades K-12. The third is in the applied studio where, until recently, the master–apprentice paradigm has persisted. Teachers in this setting have used almost constant informal formative feedback to guide learning; however, recently a move toward more structured and specific feedback has been seen. Professional musicians also provide themselves with feedback as they perform music, as part of auditory feedback. The way musicians learn to use this feedback is part of their education; it is instructional for, in fact essential to, the quality of the music performance they are able to produce. This chapter considers feedback as evidenced by teacher behaviors and as a student behavior that operates as peer assessment in several settings: K-12 music, music education preparation in universities, and applied music studio settings. Sensory feedback, as a proprioceptive and exteroceptive event, used in the performance of music is also explored.

Music creativity – the process of creating or composing new music – is another area where feedback can occur and has been described in terms of cognitive evaluation theory by Priest (2006), whereby the distinction is made between controlling and informational feedback. That means that when giving informational feedback, it can constrain the creative processes. In his study, when students either assessed their own compositions (controlling feedback) or took informational feedback from others, the results were seen in assessments of their musical compositions. Controlling feedback is said to lower levels of intrinsic motivation out of pressure to meet a specific behavioral outcome, whereas informational feedback should raise levels when it contains behaviorally relevant information (Priest, 2006, p. 48). Priest made the observation that self-evaluation might also be seen as controlling or informational; it seems that many music research investigations follow this line of thought, while not directly attributing the terms to cognitive evaluation theory. This contribution to the literature is important but outside the three main areas to be considered in the current chapter. Research studies in music examine the effects of different types of feedback with much variety in the lexicon – approval/disapproval, positive/negative, praise, conversations, verbalizations, directives, commands – with a view to measuring the resulting behaviors in students. Priest also made the point that internal feedback, which musicians give themselves, can also be seen as self-evaluation or self-assessment.

Music instruction is generally given by teachers who possess advanced music performance skills. For example, a music teacher who teaches a middle school band needs to know how to play all the instruments. Likewise, a music teacher teaching at the higher education level, in a music department or school at a university, would be, or may have been, a high-level professional musician working in an orchestra or other professional ensemble (such as a vocal soloist with the Metropolitan Opera or highly visible touring ensemble/band). Students who learn music might start with group lessons as beginners, but at some stage they usually have private individual lessons with an advanced teacher, either in a teacher's home or at a music conservatory or music school. Students studying to become music teachers must be proficient in a primary instrument (for example, voice, piano, or trumpet), and as they continue to study music at the baccalaureate level (university) they can engage in both private lessons and take part in ensembles (such as a band, chorus, or orchestra). For all music students at all levels, receiving feedback from teachers as to the quality of their performances is essential in one's development as a musician; however, musicians can also derive helpful feedback from their instruments and the sounds produced in addition to the feedback given by teachers and peers. This chapter explores three areas of feedback in music instruction: teacher behaviors, peer and student feedback (assessment), and sensory feedback in the performance of music.

Teacher Behaviors

Duke (2005) is highly experienced in this research, and his perspective on feedback is useful, given that he has conducted many of the studies that are explored in this chapter. Duke's view is that feedback in music settings is largely misunderstood. He successfully dispels the myths that many music educators believe about feedback. He noted that feedback can come from anywhere; it does not have to come only from the teacher. He argued that "the function of feedback can be independent of its intent" and that feedback might function differently for different learners and in different situations (p. 124). He suggested that the associations between feedback and behavior do not need to be overtly recognized in order for behavior to be changed. He offered an insightful and accessible essay discussing feedback in teaching, noting the types of feedback, the teacher's role, and when feedback can and should occur. His essay is recommended to individuals seeking an introduction to music feedback.

In general music education research, feedback has been approached in many different ways with notable differences in the way it is described. Researchers in music education examined feedback with a behavioral lens in early investigations. Feedback to students was observed and studied as a teacher behavior that could be categorized, counted, and rated. Schmidt and Zdzinski (1993) stated that teacher approval/disapproval rates (as given to students) were among the most frequently studied teacher behaviors in music education between 1975 and 1990. Studies from this time typically focused on specific or descriptive praise (Madsen & Madsen, 1983; Madsen & Yarbrough, 1985), negative corrective feedback (Salzberg & Salzberg, 1981), and corrective feedback (Yarbrough & Price, 1989). Somewhat later, the frequencies of feedback were also examined (for example, Younger, 1998). Many of these studies reported teachers giving specific information to students at varying rates and specificity. Moreover, these researchers viewed feedback as behaviors separate from approval/disapproval, seen rather as praise or corrective (negative) feedback (Salzberg & Salzberg, 1981) and corrective feedback with correct models (Yarbrough & Price, 1989, p. 185). Reinforcement behaviors (Madsen & Madsen, 1983; Madsen & Yarbrough, 1985) were also separately observed in teachers; however, there seemed a fair amount of interchangeability with the terms used as they cited each other in their studies. Salzberg and Salzberg (1981) compared praise and corrective negative feedback, determining that praise was as effective as corrective negative feedback, at least for the remediation of incorrect left-hand positions for young string (violin, etc.) players.

Carpenter (1988) used the term "verbal behaviors" to make the distinction between specific disapproval and general approval. Madsen and Duke (1985a, 1985b) reported that sometimes observers/trained raters could be inconsistent with rating positive and negative approval events and that often observers were more sensitive to negative teacher approvals than positive; their point was that perceptions of teacher praise (approval) should not be seen as reinforcement when they are not contingent on student behaviors. Praise and verbal approval seemed to be one and the same in the language of these early studies. Duke and Prickett (1987) also reported that observers who were focused on the teacher instead of the students significantly estimated more teacher disapproval than was actually given.

Most of these early studies examined instructional feedback, either directly or indirectly, using a variety of their own vocabulary such as approval/disapproval/praise. In the last decades of the twentieth century, it was clear in the wider educational literature that praise/feedback was important; however, it was also becoming clear that students perceived feedback from teachers differently, even if given at the same time and in the same way (Brophy, 1981). Later studies (e.g., Byo, 1994) generally concluded that positive feedback was preferred to negative feedback; negative feedback would reduce student motivation, reduce students' perceptions of achievement, and create more off-task behaviors. Music researchers at this time started using negative or positive feedback as the term of choice when examining the patterns of sequence in a music teacher's instruction. Feedback also came to be considered part of a music teacher's "style" (Wolfe & Jellison, 1990), and positive feedback was considered as the most effective, and most desirable, style by the university music education students in their study. Price (1989) asserted that more positive feedback yielded the best results, in particular, effective use of time in rehearsals/class, more attentive students, more highly performing students, and positive attitudes in students.

Price and Yarbrough, in a series of studies (1991, 1993/1994), illustrated that students prefer positive feedback and specific approval reinforcements. Specific approval reinforcements were seen when a teacher gives an approval contingently on a student behavior, such as playing the correct note. The teacher would say, "That's the right note, it sounds great!" Price (1992) examined feedback (along with instruction and teaching practica) within "sequential patterns" as an extension of the direct instruction model (Becker, Englemann, & Thomas, 1971; Becker & Englemann, 1976, as cited by Price, 1992). These patterns (first used by Yarbrough & Price, 1981) include a sequence of (1) presentation of material from the teacher, (2) interaction between student/teacher, and (3) specific praise or feedback about the task. Sequential patterns were the focus of many research studies in music education for nearly a decade (e.g., Maclin, 1993; Arnold, 1995; Goolsby, 1997). Feedback in this instance (Price, 1992) included approvals and disapprovals (both specific or unspecific). Bowers (1997) also used sequential patterns to examine if the individual components of the sequence (task presentation, interaction, teacher feedback) were connected to overall teaching effectiveness in music education students who were learning to teach elementary (grades K-6) music. Specific and nonspecific feedback behaviors were both noted in this research, but there were more instances of specific feedback use in teaching episodes than nonspecific feedback.

Interestingly, Duke and Blackman (1991) conducted a study to examine relationships among four feedback indicators, within the process of evaluation in music instruction in general. This was required in a teaching evaluation instrument used to determine teaching effectiveness with K-12 teachers in Texas as part of the state's requirement. The four indicators used by teachers were (1) reinforces correct responses, (2) gives corrective academic feedback, (3) reinforces appropriate behavior, and (4) gives correct social feedback. It is illustrative of the field in general that feedback was required as part of direct instruction in Texas in the last decade of the twentieth century. The researchers asked observers to watch a teaching episode and calculate totals of behaviors. Duke and Blackman reported that despite the observers recording both approvals and disapprovals, and the subsequent calculation of an approval/disapproval ratio for each teacher, there was only a low correlation with the summative teaching evaluation of the music instruction. They found that the observed frequencies of approval and disapproval ratios did not correlate with the overall teaching summative score. This raised the caution that there is more to teaching than simply providing the expected ratio of approvals to disapprovals.

What was termed "sequential patterns" in the late twentieth century shifted slightly in the twenty-first century when researchers moved to examine smaller "chunks" of musical rehearsals in classrooms. These chunks were called "rehearsal frames," originally characterized by Duke (1994) as segments within a musical rehearsal that accomplish specific goals. Cavitt (2003) worked with ten band ensemble directors to determine that, within rehearsal frames, teachers used twice as much negative feedback compared with positive feedback when trying to correct errors in student performances. Negative feedback is described as "dispassionate, businesslike ... and focused on very specific information regarding the performance rather than focusing on social behavior or the student personally" (Cavitt, 2003, p. 223). Negative feedback was focused specifically on correcting the musical problem, not on the student individually, and was seen as "error correction" as part of a musical rehearsal in Cavitt's work.

Some researchers (such as Montemayor & Moss, 2009) began identifying any teacher verbalization as feedback of some kind (positive, specific, negative). Montemayor and Moss reported the specific nature of verbalizations (in this instance, accuracy in student performance). The researchers gave some teachers auditory materials (CD recordings of the music to be taught) with which to prepare their lesson, while other teachers could prepare their lesson only with the musical written score. Montemayor and Moss (2009) found that neither preparatory method influenced the amount of verbalizations teachers gave to their students in the music rehearsal; however, the verbalizations given were focused on either accuracy or error correction. Whitaker (2011) illustrated the teaching behaviors of high school band teachers and found that "sequential pattern components" were still evident. In calculating ratios of approval/disapproval and specific/nonspecific feedback, she determined that teachers gave only 12% of their rehearsal time to reinforcement feedback. Reinforcement feedback was seen as verbal and nonverbal teacher behavior. During the 12% of time giving reinforcements, it was disapproving 79% of the time, with approving feedback occurring only 21% of the time. It seemed also that teachers gave specific feedback 83% of the time and nonspecific feedback 17% of the time. Feedback was observed being given verbally and with facial expressions (approving or disapproving). Students also reported (in interviews) that they got more disapproving feedback than approving; however, they reportedly recognized the necessity of the disapproving feedback as "constructive criticism" or "critical feedback" (Whitaker, 2011, p. 303).

Montemayor, Silvey, Adams, and Witt (2015) observed that music education students, those who are learning to teach, illustrated higher levels of specific/positive feedback when they had spent more time learning observable rehearsal behaviors prior to a teaching episode. Feedback is taught as an observable rehearsal teacher behavior in most music education programs. In a meta-analysis specifically targeting the instructional effects on singing in children ages five to eleven, Svec (2017) found that feedback was the most effective means of improving singing ability in the thirty-four studies she reviewed. She noted that several studies used feedback provided by computer programs (not as a teacher behavior), suggesting that now in an age of increased technology and information, information about singing can be transferred not only from teacher to student but also from technology to student.

Roesler (2017) noted that in classroom music settings, the specificity of teacher feedback preceded student problem-solving instances. Problem-solving in music classes occurs when teachers relinquish control of their classrooms and take more learner-centered approaches, posing musical problems for students to solve. This is in contrast to traditional music teacher–directed styles, where teachers give corrective feedback to students to correct their errors most of the time. Roesler (2017) observed three types of feedback given to students before they undertook problem-solving activities: (1) nonspecific feedback, (2) attention-directing negative feedback, and (3) specific negative feedback, with nonspecific feedback preceding more problem-solving activities than specific negative feedback. This seems to circle back to the late twentieth-century examinations of feedback; however, in Roesler's study it is being used not simply to identify rates of use but to locate usefulness in how students solve musical problems in classes. Musical problem-solving is a relatively new pedagogical element in the United States with respect to lesson content. Traditionally, in a rehearsal setting there is an expert (the teacher or ensemble director) and the learners (the students, musicians), which limits the degree to which students actively ask questions, seek answers to questions, or solve problems. The music to be learned has traditionally been chosen by the teacher and rehearsed to an expected level of proficiency. More recently, there has been somewhat of a modification in the pedagogies used in music classrooms. In some parts of the United States, traditional music rehearsal classrooms (band, chorus, orchestra) are seeing fewer enrollments, whereas more general music classes, designed for students with little or no music instrument experience, are being scheduled more often in some school districts. These classes often involve more activities related to creating music and responding to music. This may be due to the 2014 National Core Music Standards published by the National Coalition for Core Arts Standards (NCCAS, 2014). The new standards focus heavily on process-based music experiences with a view toward artistic literacy in the arts in four areas: creating, performing/presenting/producing, responding, and connecting. Importantly, there are Model Cornerstone Assessments that accompany the

Music Standards (see https://nafme.org/my-classroom/standards/mcas/). These were created in an attempt to give teachers models for providing instructional feedback to students with an authentic and curriculum-embedded process.

Student Perceptions of Feedback

Students' perceptions of feedback are considered important in the music classroom and have been studied to some degree since earlier investigations. Schmidt (1989, 1995), like his peers at the time, used the term "approvals and disapprovals" and reported that university students and K-12 students have mixed responses to approvals, but that approvals related to student improvement were the most highly rated by students in music settings. Dunn (1997) also reported that positive feedback garnered higher performance ratings and more positive student attitudes toward rehearsals. Students engaged in off-task activities more often than students receiving no feedback in choral classrooms. Yarbrough and Madsen (1998) reported that teachers received higher evaluations from students when they used approval feedback at least 80% of the time during teaching in choral classrooms (where teachers are instructing students to sing in a chorus setting). As discussed earlier, Whitaker's (2011) finding seems to indicate that music students are acutely aware of approving and disapproving feedback ratios in their classrooms. Droe (2012) examined praise as it exists in the "teaching-feedback loop" (p. 63). Fourth-grade music students who received verbal praise feedback for efforts in the music classroom illustrated higher attitudes toward task persistence, in this case tapping rhythms. However, there are few studies such as this that actually engage K-12 students in this way, in an effort to study their perceptions or attitudes toward feedback. In this case, specifically seating the effects of feedback in the frameworks of goal orientation, motivation, and performance attributions garnered a more complete understanding of feedback in learners.

When music teachers use feedback to improve their teaching, whether in professional practice or while learning to teach, the feedback format they had received proves to be salient. Early studies (such as Yarbrough, Wapnick, & Kelley, 1979) examined feedback given to teachers in the form of video information with respect to their teaching behaviors, in this case conducting.[1] Yarbrough et al. (1979) determined that when teachers were given feedback based on a video of their conducting, it was different depending on whether teachers had watched their video with an experienced professor and received feedback about their work or whether they had simply viewed their own videos with an observational form and checklist. In this case the teachers were learning to become ensemble directors and they were using the videotape feedback to improve their conducting skills. Their perceptions about feedback illustrated

---

1 A conductor is the individual at the front of the ensemble with the small white baton, sometimes referred to in professional settings as a "maestro," a somewhat gendered label. Regardless of gender, the skill of conducting is desirable for a middle or high school ensemble music teacher.

that videotape feedback proved to be as useful as traditional feedback from experienced teachers. Systematic self-observation did not seem to be markedly different from the feedback provided by experienced professors. Moore (1976) examined the effect that videotaped feedback and self-evaluation forms had on improving teaching with students learning to teach. He found that students who received teacher, peer, and self-evaluation on their videotapes were rated significantly better at teaching. The evaluation form included ratings for number of approvals, disapprovals, and reinforcement rates during the teaching episode. This study seems to be the first to incorporate self-assessment as feedback when learning to teach.

When learning to teach, novice teachers seem to associate positive feedback with higher-quality teaching. MacLeod and Napoles (2011) studied seventy-five music education students from two large music education schools to discover that, after watching episodes of teaching, beginning teachers rated teachers who used more positive feedback more highly than those who used less positive feedback. Teachers who included more displays of positive feedback were considered to have a positive demeanor and were considered to be higher in teaching effectiveness. Chaffin and Manfredo (2009) were interested in the perceptions of music education students, who were learning to become teachers, when they received feedback in written and verbal formats. The feedback was largely about the effectiveness of their pedagogical instruction. Interestingly, Chaffin and Manfredo used the terms "evaluation" and "feedback" synonymously and drew a parallel between feedback and formative assessment (p. 58). They reported that students were better able to reflect on their progress in learning to teach when they had received written feedback as well as verbal feedback in conjunction with modeling. More recently, in examining how students who are learning to teach respond to video feedback, Powell (2016) reported that while students are critical of their physical appearances after video feedback, their reflections illustrated greater detail and specificity about their teaching skills. Notably, these novice teachers also recognized their level of competence in how they themselves provided feedback to the students in the teaching episode captured in the videos.

Feedback in the Applied Studio Setting

The applied studio setting is a cornerstone of musical teaching. It has been labeled dyadic teaching, private teaching, studio teaching, one-to-one teaching, and the expert–novice dyad. It stems from the master–apprentice model where there is one master (the teacher) and one apprentice (the learner). This is the type of music lesson with which most readers may be familiar. Music conservatories around the world utilize this type of teaching for musicians wanting to increase their level of achievement and performance, and it has been in place for hundreds of years. Traditionally, high-level musicians teach aspiring musicians. This can occur privately, in the home of the teacher, and in higher education with students pursuing tertiary (undergraduate and graduate) education in music. Music degree study in the United States includes applied studio lessons, along with a variety of other coursework, as well as frequent opportunities to perform for the teacher and other students. Applied studio lessons are given by faculty teachers who usually have recognition in the field of music for their expertise in music performance. Many applied music teachers are expert performers but may be employed by the institution only at the adjunct, or part-time, level. Other applied music teachers are employed full time and are in tenure-track positions or hold tenured positions because they have a terminal degree in music, such as the Doctor of Musical Arts (DMA), PhD, or EdD. Teacher behaviors in this setting were not studied frequently for much of the twentieth century because it has traditionally been a largely unregulated setting (Burwell, 2016). As might be anticipated, early studies focused on feedback as the most readily observable teacher behavior. In the applied studio setting research, the term "feedback" is used with a variety of meanings and often seems to be interconnected to assessment. In some cases it refers to teacher behaviors but also to the information students share with each other and their teachers as part of the process of self-evaluation.

Benson (1989) used videotaped models and videotape feedback to affect the amount of time violin teachers spent giving specific feedback in the applied music setting. He found that the most experienced teacher gave the least amount of approving feedback to students in private violin lessons. The less-experienced teacher, who used the videotape feedback for her teaching, demonstrated an increase in specific feedback in subsequent teaching episodes. Kostka (1984) investigated reinforcement as a feedback behavior in the applied piano studio. She was able to determine approval and disapproval rates, along with some other teacher behaviors. She found that approvals and disapprovals were used relatively equally during piano lessons and that more reinforcements were given for academic performance rather than social behaviors. Interestingly, Kostka observed differences in the ratios of approvals and disapprovals given when the age of the student changed. Elementary students had more approvals than high school students, both of whom had more approvals than adult learners. Siebenaler (1997) found that in piano lessons, both specific positive and negative feedback elicited high evaluations from students about teacher effectiveness when compared with nonspecific feedback. However, it is important to observe that the perception of feedback behaviors may be different from the actual occurrence of those behaviors. Studies of feedback perceptions and their relationship to actual feedback have not been seen often in applied studio settings. Studies of feedback perceptions and their relatedness to the feedback given are typically not present in the applied studio setting research around feedback. A notable exception is Schmidt's (1989) study, which examined individual differences in the perception of music teaching feedback by asking students to rate different types of feedback given. The various types of feedback were (1) academic information, (2) student improvement, (3) norm-referenced feedback, (4) person praise, (5) personal approval by the teacher, and (6) approval as control. Schmidt was interested in identifying the causes for variability in student responses to teacher feedback, so he examined the personality characteristics (as outlined by the Myers–Briggs Type Indicator) of students to see if there were differences in their responses to different types of feedback. He found that the extraversion/introversion type student was a significant source of variance in the ratings of the teacher's behaviors. Introverted students rated teacher behaviors (such as academic information, student improvement, norm-referenced feedback, person praise, personal approval from the teacher, and approval as control) more highly than the extroverted subjects. Schmidt also found significant interactions between introvert/extrovert and judgment/perception with the variables of approval-control and approval-person praise. Speer (1994) found that more experienced teachers gave higher levels of disapprovals to more senior students, when compared with novice teachers; this study was conducted in the private piano studio when examining for sequential patterns in the applied studio. Previously, sequential patterns had been examined only in classroom music settings.

Duke and Henninger (1998) used the terms "negative feedback and specific directives," which then seemed to move the music education profession toward a more aligned use of vocabulary around the concept of feedback. They noted the wide and varied uses of the term "feedback" in their review of the literature. For the purposes of their study they defined feedback as "teachers' expressions of corrective information" (p. 486); however, the two conditions in their study involved a directive condition and a negative feedback condition. The directive condition involved the teacher only giving commands describing the desired outcome, and avoiding negative evaluative statements (e.g., "Try again and play softer next time," p. 487). The negative feedback condition involved teachers identifying what was wrong with a student's performance (such as "You played too loudly that time," p. 487). They discovered that regardless of whether the information was conveyed as a directive or as negative feedback, it was the successful accomplishment of the music goal that led students to feel positive about their learning experience in the applied studio setting. Duke and Henninger (2002) used objective observers to evaluate lessons. Lessons using specific directives or negative feedback were rated equally positively. What we start to see in Duke and Henniger's later work is that the use of feedback becomes interesting to researchers, such as Duke, who move between the classroom setting and the applied music setting.

McPhail (2010) explicitly shared action research from music teaching in the classroom to the applied studio and suggested that feedback is one of three main components that could be improved. He labeled feedback in this setting as specific (descriptive) and positive (evaluative) feedback. He noted that the student was observed to be more involved in the lessons over the course of the semester as the quality of feedback increased and improved in specificity.

Parkes (2010) examined how one applied studio teacher (of flute) provided formative feedback to students in the form of a criteria-specific rubric during weekly lessons. She found that the teacher and students had increased positive perceptions about the feedback format and that there was an increase over time in awareness of students about what they needed to do to improve their performance. Parkes reported that students developed a clearer understanding of what the teacher was expecting over the semester, as evidenced in their weekly reflections about the rubric feedback and their lesson progress. In examining the interactions between applied studio teachers and students, Ivaldi (2016) examined instances of feedback via a process of conversation analysis to illustrate how students learned in a music lesson as opposed to only performing. The conversational analysis identified sections of the lessons where students were engaged in learning – this is where the teacher is interrupting the student performing to give corrective feedback. The analysis also illustrated when students were simply performing the music, playing the piece of music through, which is usually the step prior to receiving feedback. When students were learning, they offered apologies and pauses, not wanting feedback or assessment, but when they were performing their piece of music through, they wanted assessment or feedback as soon as possible. Students were able to indicate to teachers when they wanted to receive feedback and assessment. By analyzing the two-way conversations between students and teachers, Ivaldi illustrates a rich form of feedback measurable in the applied studio setting.

Feedback as Assessment: Peer and Self

Applied Studio Teaching

In learning to become a performer, there are two types of techniques that have proven popular in music learning: peer interaction/feedback and observation of videotape/self-assessment (Bergee & Cecconi-Roberts, 2002). Daniel has a focused body of work (2001, 2004, 2006, 2007) that specifically investigated these phenomena as they appear in Australian conservatories (higher education music schools) where applied studio teaching occurs. In 2001, Daniel posited that the role of learner is affected by the relationship with the teacher, specifically how students respond to "comments made by the teacher" (p. 217). Students in this early study were tasked with reviewing a video recording of their performance and writing a critical self-reflection. Daniel found that although students were guided in providing themselves feedback, they still relied heavily on feedback from the teacher. Most students, however, were positive about the process of self-assessment, noting that it assisted their performance skills. In 2004, Daniel investigated the benefits of peer feedback (as peer assessment) and utilized a detailed evaluation sheet for students to use with each other. Students reported enjoying discussions more than the evaluation sheet. The students reported wanting more critical feedback from their peers. In a way, this supports the finding of Whitaker (2011) where students noted the need for critical specific feedback after a musical performance.

Daniel (2006) then found that technology, specifically video analysis, was a beneficial tool in closing the "feedback loop" and in providing a form of assessment to students. Teachers gave much more feedback in one-to-one lessons but less when lessons were held in groups. Daniel (2007) surveyed students to ascertain how assessment comments, provided by both faculty and peers, were different. He examined the differences of student comments between year levels and between faculty. He reported that the average number of comments increased in frequency as year level increased and that first-year students gave positive comments more often than senior students in second and third years of study. More detailed advice and direction given to peers was observed in second- and third-year students. He noted that faculty were more consistent with the substance of their comments, moving between positive, critical, and general advice. Faculty shared almost double the amount of feedback comments than the students, who typically gave half the amount of comments to their peers than the faculty did. Daniel reported that students valued the comments of faculty more so than that of their peers; however, the senior students (in their third or fourth year of study) were most accepting of critical evaluations from both peers and faculty.

In Sweden, Rostval and West (2003) conducted a study with guitar students and teachers, examining differences between one-to-one lessons and group lessons. They found (like Daniel, 2007) that the group lessons had less feedback from the teacher compared with the one-to-one lessons. The teachers' approaches to feedback seemed to be hierarchical; that is, their role was to share their mastery with students and not encourage responses from them. In the United States, Bergee (1993, 1997) examined the relationships between applied studio teachers, student/peer, and student/self-evaluations in music performances given by undergraduate students studying to become musicians. He found in both studies that self-evaluation correlated poorly with the evaluation of peers and teachers. Peer feedback and teacher feedback correlated more highly. In a later study, Bergee and Cecconi-Roberts (2002) explored the interactions of small groups of peers sharing feedback with each other after performances with two experiments. Students completed peer evaluations in groupings of similar instruments (woodwind, brass, etc.). They found again that self-evaluation did not correlate highly with the evaluations made by the teachers, which implies to some degree that teacher feedback is still the most highly valued in music-learning settings. This might explain, again to some degree, why feedback was initially examined only as a teacher behavior in the music education research literature.

In a move that embraced the notion of peer feedback in the music classroom, Napoles (2008) investigated the relationships among self-ratings, teacher ratings, and peer ratings with student teachers who were learning to teach in a university setting in music education. She suggested that if novice teachers could remember peer feedback, they would be more likely to implement it in their future practice and teaching episodes. She required that the music education students give each other four positive feedback comments and one improvement suggestion after a demonstration teaching episode. She cited the early work of Madsen and Yarbrough (1985), who determined that the most effective ratio of positive to negative feedback was 4:1. She found that her participants' self-comments were often in agreement with peer comments (feedback) and that the action of recalling feedback was unique. Her participants tended to recall feedback more effectively when they heard the same information from both the instructor and peer(s). Peer feedback seemed particularly useful in this instance of novice teachers learning to teach in a classroom music setting.

Feedback from Music Performance Itself

Some of the earliest research regarding sensory feedback in music can be seen in the work of Havlicek (1968). He argued that skilled movements (such as the kind found in producing musical performances) were "controlled by kinesthetic cues along with exteroceptic cues depending on the situation" (p. 309). Exteroceptic cues are generally characterized as being cues from outside the body, received and perceived through our senses. In this case, Havlicek examined our auditory system – hearing – to see the effect on musicians when they heard a delayed version of what they were performing. In his study he delayed the auditory feedback (via headphones) to the musicians as they performed, which resulted in statistically significantly more errors than when musicians heard their performance synchronously. Obviously, musicians need to hear the sound they are producing simultaneously as they are performing so that they can adjust and keep synchronized with their collaborating performers. In the 1990s, music perception researchers started to consider these types of cues as feedback, somatosensory feedback (vibrotactile, sensory information from skin such as the vibrating of a violin string under a finger), and kinesthetic feedback (sensory information from muscles and tendons) (Sundberg & Verillo, 1992; Todd, 1993). The most recent definitions of these terms use the word "interoceptive"; interoceptive cues are internal to the body, such as sweating or an increase in body temperature or heart rate. Kinesthetic feedback comes from our movements (such as fingers on a keyboard). Ellis and Thayer (2010) also described that music and the autonomic nervous system are intricately related whether we are listening to music, entraining to music (for example, synchronizing breathing to music), or engaged in making music.

In musical settings, performers typically try to be synchronized with others, particularly with pitch and with rhythm in their music-making. Pitch refers to the notes and rhythm indicates that they are in time with each other. If one is not producing the correct pitch to match another musician playing the same pitch it is often described as being "out of tune" and conversely if one is playing exactly the correct pitch it is considered to be "in tune." Duke (1985) discovered that verbal feedback and the use of headphones actually did not have any significant effect on how well high school and university musicians played in tune. In music performances, musicians need to adjust their instruments and voices to match notes with other musicians or to keep the correct distances between notes; this process is called "intonating" and allows them to have correct intonation (to be "in tune"). Duke found that what predicts how well musicians can keep good intonation is the direction from which the musician approaches the note. Simplified, this means that if a musician plays from a higher-pitched note down to a lower-pitched note, it is likely that the note will be sharp – this means the musician is playing a little higher than the note should be. The effect of verbal feedback telling musicians this fact seemed not to mediate their intonation at all, nor did the provision of other aural information via headphones.

Welch, Howard, and Rush (1989) created a real-time visual feedback system designed to give feedback to vocalists about the accuracy of their singing. In testing the system with seven-year-old children, they found that the young singers who received visual feedback while singing made significant improvement between the pre- and post-tests of pitch accuracy. This work grew out of Welch's original (1985) study where he meticulously described the feedback loop involved when children try to sing a note to match another vocally produced stimulus. He described the motor response schema, with expected proprioceptive feedback, and the voice mechanism (which, along with the environment, provides exteroceptive feedback). Proprioceptive feedback comes from within the body and exteroceptive feedback comes from the environment (such as sound). The bones in a singer's head conduct feedback to the singer (proprioceptive information), as does the surrounding air, which conducts sound waves (exteroceptive information) informing the singer as to whether he or she is singing the correct note or not. His schema theory of how children learn to sing in tune incorporates proprioceptive feedback (information provided by sense receptors in the musculature of the singer), exteroceptive feedback (information provided by the major sense organs such as eyes and ears), knowledge of results (the information about the performance provided by an external source such as a teacher), and subjective reinforcement (a subjective evaluation). This study was a major landmark in music perception research, specifically determining which methods of feedback are best in a teaching and learning setting. This type of work can also be seen most recently in France with Bella's (2015) work. She described the mechanics that underlie all singing as the vocal sensorimotor loop (p. 273). She noted that it is a closed-loop system, that the vocal output is fed back to the singer (via perceptual processing). The vocal output is quite complex and is different from instrumentalist musical output. Vocalists use physical mechanisms (breath, larynx, vocal folds) to create sound. Her model used both physical and auditory feedback and also includes motor planning/implementation and auditory motor-mapping.

Todd (1993) speculated that in addition to somatosensory feedback and kinesthetic feedback, there is a third system of feedback that musicians may rely on. He suggested that the vestibular system is equally important for musicians. The vestibular responses to music can be seen in movement and dance, as performers often move as they play, in time with the music, as part of what

Todd described as the vestibuloocular reflex and the otolith spinal reflex – he suggested that music with "a strong regular pulse gives rise to strong compulsion to dance or move" (p. 381). Goebl and Palmer (2009) found that when pianists are performing together as a duet, and auditory feedback is removed, visual cues such as movement (raised fingers and head movements) increased and became more synchronized, so while Todd's idea was not widely utilized in the research in this area, it seems that there may be some evidence for his ideas in Goebl and Palmer's work. Goebl and Palmer used twenty-first-century motion-capture technology that gave rise to their findings in a way that was not possible in the last decade of the twentieth century.

Auditory feedback is essential for all musicians to perform at high levels but especially so for instrumentalists. Finney (1997) conducted a study using electronic keyboards and manipulated auditory feedback (both timing and pitch). He included a condition where there was no auditory feedback. It would seem intuitive that musicians need to hear what they are doing in order to do it well. However, Finney also found that the condition that caused the most error in the keyboard performances was delayed auditory feedback. When the pitch was altered, there were not nearly as many errors, and when there was no auditory feedback at all, performances were not impacted. Finney noted, however, that the reason for this could be that the musicians were using sheet music – meaning they literally had a map of what to play and it could simply be reproduced in their hands on the keyboard. Banton (1995) studied the roles of both aural and visual feedback in the performance of piano music when musicians were reading the music for the first time, or "sight-reading." Not surprisingly, Banton found that pianists made more mistakes when they could not see the keyboard. The missing visual feedback for pianists limited their ability to move their hands across the keyboard. When the pianists could not hear themselves, they did not suffer any loss of accuracy, indicating that when playing a piece of music for the first time, the visual feedback is important for pianists. Two decades later, Duke, Cash, and Allen (2011) found that musicians are more accurate when they focus on the effects or outcomes of their performance, such as the sound produced, rather than the movements producing the sound (fingers, piano keys, piano hammers). Duke et al. were interested in seeing what elements might distract performers as they played a piece of music with which they already were familiar, whereas Banton was concerned with elements involved in the specific activity of sight-reading. The two studies are quite different in their experimental goals: when sight-reading, most musicians typically focus on "getting the notes correct," and the secondary goal is to communicate the music with expression. When musicians play music they are familar with, there is a greater sense of ease – they know the notes and can focus on expressive intent and content of the music.

Sensory feedback, the kind that comes from the senses, is especially important for instrumental musicians because the feedback comes from touching the instrument itself. Musicians garner extensive information, processing it very quickly, from their instruments. Palmer, Koopmans, Loehr, and Carter (2009) studied sensory feedback in clarinet performance. Clarinet players need to move their fingers very quickly, and the rate at which their fingers contact and release the keys can impact their performance. Tactile information is important to the musician in this instance. Palmer and her colleagues found that sensory information given at the finger-key contact point improves the accuracy of musical performance.

Byo and Schlegel (2016) reported that university musicians are able to use the sound of their instruments as feedback, bringing them in tune as they play. Their study examined what advanced instrumentalists perceived during the process of tuning that informs their pitch adjustment. Students explained their understanding of the feedback from their instrument as "I can just tell," "I feel the vibrations," or "I can feel it in my mouthpiece; I feel the waves" (p. 354). Students were describing the physical and auditory sensations of being in tune as opposed to being out of tune. This referential information came from what they heard and felt in their bodies and in the tones being produced by their instrument. This is formally recognized in other studies (such as Welch, 1985) as exteroceptive and proprioceptive feedback.

In examining other feedback processes that musicians encounter, Spahn, Walther, and Nusseck (2015) discovered some critical influences on music performance anxiety (MPA), which in turn can impact the performance outcome for musicians. MPA can cause "cognitive distractions, unwanted emotions, and impaired behaviors that can negatively affect performance quality" (p. 894). Cognitive distractions usually mean musicians have a series of negative thoughts competing in their mind while they are trying to perform. Spahn et al. (2015) found that by providing video feedback to performers suffering from MPA, their anxiety lessened over time. Video feedback provided to performers included autogenic training, body awareness, mental techniques, imaginative techniques, and an exercise where performers compared their first and second performances in an effort to recognize successful strategies for overcoming MPA. These strategies assisted in keeping sensory feedback related to music, rathen than unwanted distractions, emotions, and behaviors when students performed after the intervention.

In a loosely related but more theoretical line of inquiry, Hargreaves, McDonald, and Miell (2005) proposed that feedback is musical communication. They presented a reciprocal feedback model of music processing that takes into account the three main influences on musical response (physiological, cognitive, affective) for individuals listening to music. They proposed that in music communication, there are reciprocal feedback loops among these three main variables. Hargreaves (2012) revised this earlier work to include musical production (which includes performance, interpretation, expression, etc.) and imagination (which includes internal mental representations, schemas, and cultural frames). He retained perception (physiological, cognitive, affective responses) from his earlier model, arguing that by combining it with production and imagination, the cognitive processes and communications utilized with feedback can be illustrated.

Viewed more pragmatically, it is well known that professional musicians utilize auditory acoustical feedback from the concert halls they perform in, but there do not seem to be any formal empirical studies of this particular phenomenon. For example, the acoustics in the Orchestra Hall at Symphony Center in Chicago are quite different from those of the David Geffen Hall at Lincoln Center in New York. Highly expert musicians rely on how their sound carries back to them in their specific locations in order for them to give extraordinarily high-quality performances.

Summary

This chapter has explored three major positions with respect to feedback in musical settings. Teacher behaviors were viewed with a behavioral lens in early work, and the lexicon varied widely. Feedback in K-12 classrooms is largely seen as a teacher behavior, rated and counted, whereas peer and self-assessment has been examined more thoroughly in the applied studio setting. Although not necessarily instructional in the pedagogical sense, the sensory feedback that expert musicians use while performing is critical for high levels of performance. There is less research examining how sensory feedback operates for novice musicians, such as those in K-12 classrooms and universities, but further research in this area would provide value for music educators in the future.

References

Arnold, J. A. (1995). Effects of competency-based methods of instruction and self-observation on ensemble directors' use of sequential patterns. *Journal of Research in Music Education, 43*, 127–138.

Banton, L. J. (1995). The role of visual and auditory feedback during the sight-reading of music. *Psychology of Music, 23*, 3–16.

Becker, W. C., & Englemann, S. (1976). Analysis of achievement data on six cohorts of low-income children from 20 school districts in the University of Oregon direct instruction follow through model. College of Education, Oregon University. ERIC Document Reproduction Service No. ED 145 922.

Bella, S. D. (2015). Defining poor-pitch singing: A problem of measurement and sensitivity. *Music Perception: An Interdisciplinary Journal, 32*, 272–282.

Benson, W. L. (1989). The effect of models, self-observation, and evaluation on the modification of specified teaching behaviors of an applied music teacher. *Update: The Applications of Research in Music Education, 7*(2), 28–31.

Bergee, M. J. (1993). A comparison of faculty, peer, and self-evaluation of applied brass jury performances. *Journal of Research in Music Education, 41*, 19–27.

Bergee, M. J. (1997). Relationships among faculty, peer, and self-evaluations of applied performances. *Journal of Research in Music Education, 45*, 601–612.

Bergee, M. J., & Cecconi-Roberts, L. (2002). Effects of small-group peer interaction on self-evaluation of music performance. *Journal of Research in Music Education, 50*, 256–268.

Bowers, J. (1997). Sequential patterns and the music teaching effectiveness of elementary education majors. *Journal of Research in Music Education, 45*, 428–443.

Brophy, J. (1981). Teacher praise: A functional analysis. *Review of Educational Research, 51*, 5–32.

Burwell, K. (2016). *SEMPRE studies in the psychology of music: Studio-based instrumental learning.* Abingdon, UK: Routledge.

Byo, J. L. (1994). Tracing the evolution of a research line: The role of sequential patterns in structuring the rehearsal. *Journal of the World Association of Symphonic Bands and Ensembles, 1*, 67–79.

Byo, J. L., & Schlegel, A. L. (2016). Effects of stimulus octave and timbre on the tuning accuracy of advanced college instrumentalists. *Journal of Research in Music Education, 64*, 344–359.

Carpenter, R. A. (1988). A descriptive analysis of relationships between verbal behaviors of teacher-conductors and ratings of selected junior and senior high school band rehearsals. *Update: Applications of Research in Music Education, 7*, 37–40.

Cavitt, M. E. (2003). A descriptive analysis of error correction in instrumental music rehearsals. *Journal of Research in Music Education, 51*, 218–230.

Chaffin, C., & Manfredo, J. (2009). Perceptions of preservice teachers regarding feedback and guided reflection in an instrumental early field experience. *Journal of Music Teacher Education, 19*(2), 57–72.

Daniel, R. (2001). Self-assessment in performance. *British Journal of Music Education, 18*, 215–226.

Daniel, R. (2004). Peer assessment in music performance: The development, trial and evaluation of a methodology for the Australian tertiary environment. *British Journal of Music Education, 21*, 89–110.

Daniel, R. (2006). Exploring music instrument teaching and learning environments: Video analysis as a means of elucidating process and learning outcomes. *Music Education Research, 8*, 161–215.

Daniel, R. (2007, July). Closing the feedback loop: An investigation and analysis of student evaluations of peer and staff assessments in music performance. Paper presented at the XXIXth meeting of the Australian Association for Research in Music Education, Music Values, Research, and Initiatives, Melbourne, Australia.

Droe, K. L. (2012). Effect of verbal praise on achievement goal orientation, motivation, and performance attribution. *Journal of Music Teacher Education, 23*, 63–78.

Duke, R. A. (1985). Wind instrumentalists' intonational performance of selected musical intervals. *Journal of Research in Music Education, 33*, 101–111.

Duke, R. A. (1994). Bringing the art of rehearsing into focus: The rehearsal frame as a model for prescriptive analysis of rehearsing conducting. *Journal of Band Research, 30*, 78–95.

Duke, R. A. (2005). *Intelligent music teaching: Essays on the core principals of effective instruction.* Austin, TX: Learning and Behavior Resources.

Duke, R. A., & Blackmail, M. D. (1991). The relationship between observers' recorded teacher behavior and evaluation of music instruction. *Journal of Research in Music Education, 39*, 290–297.

Duke, R. A., Cash, C. D., & Allen, S. E. (2011). Focus of attention affects performance of motor skills in music. *Journal of Research in Music Education, 59*, 44–55.

Duke, R. A., & Henninger, J. C. (1998). Effects of verbal corrections on student attitude and performance. *Journal of Research in Music Education, 46*, 482–495.

Duke, R. A., & Henninger, J. C. (2002). Teachers' verbal corrections and observers' perceptions of teaching and learning. *Journal of Research in Music Education, 50*, 75–87.

Duke, R. A., & Prickett, C. A. (1987). The effect of differentially focused observation on evaluation of instruction. *Journal of Research in Music Education, 35*, 27–37.

Dunn, D. E. (1997). Effect of rehearsal hierarchy and reinforcement on attention, achievement, and attitude of selected choirs. *Journal of Research in Music Education, 45*, 547–567.

Ellis, R. J., & Thayer, J. F. (2010). Music and autonomic nervous system (dys)function. *Music Perception: An Interdisciplinary Journal, 27*(4), 317–326.

Finney, S. A. (1997). Auditory feedback and musical keyboard performance. *Music Perception: An Interdisciplinary Journal, 15*, 153–174.

Goebl, W., & Palmer, C. (2009). Synchronization of timing and motion among performing musicians. *Music Perception: An Interdisciplinary Journal, 26*, 427–438.

Goolsby, T. W. (1997). Verbal instruction in instrumental rehearsals: A comparison of three career levels and preservice teachers. *Journal of Research in Music Education, 45*, 21–40.

Hargreaves, D. J. (2012). Musical imagination: Perception and production, beauty and creativity. *Psychology of Music, 40*, 539–557.

Hargreaves, D. J., MacDonald, R. A. R., & Miell, D. E. (2005). How do people communicate using music? In D. E. Miell, R. A. R. MacDonald, & D. J. Hargreaves (Eds.), *Musical communication* (pp. 1–25). Oxford: Oxford University Press.

Havlicek, L. L. (1968). Effect of delayed auditory feedback on musical performance. *Journal of Research in Music Education, 16*, 308–318.

Ivaldi, A. (2016). Students' and teachers' orientation to learning and performing in music conservatoire lesson interactions. *Psychology of Music, 44*, 202–218.

Kostka, M. J. (1984). An investigation of reinforcements, time use, and student attentiveness in piano lessons. *Journal of Research in Music Education, 32*(2), 113–122.

MacLeod, R. B., & Napoles, J. (2011). Preservice teachers' perceptions of teaching effectiveness during teaching episodes with positive and negative feedback. *Journal of Music Teacher Education, 22*, 91–102.

Maclin, J. P. (1993). The effect of task analysis on sequential patterns of music instruction. *Journal of Research in Music Education, 41*, 48–56.

Madsen, C. H., & Madsen, C. K. (1983). *Teaching/discipline: Behavioral principles toward a positive approach.* Raleigh, NC: Contemporary Publishing.

Madsen, C. K., & Duke, R. A. (1985a). Observation of teacher/student interactions in music: Observer perceptions versus actual events. *Journal of Research in Music Education, 33*, 205–214.

Madsen, C. K, & Duke, R. A. (1985b). Perception of approval/disapproval in music. *Bulletin of the Council for Research in Music Education, 85*, 119–130.

Madsen, C. K., and Yarbrough, C. (1985). *Competency-based music education.* Raleigh, NC: Contemporary Publishing.

McPhail, G. J. (2010) Crossing boundaries: Sharing concepts of music teaching from classroom to studio. *Music Education Research, 12*, 33–45.

Montemayor, M., & Moss, E. A. (2009). Effects of recorded models on novice teachers' rehearsal verbalizations, evaluations, and conducting. *Journal of Research in Music Education, 57*, 236–251.

Montemayor, M., Silvey, B. A., Adams, A. L., & Witt, K. L. (2015). Effects of internal and external focus of attention during novices' instructional preparation on subsequent rehearsal behaviors. *Journal of Research in Music Education, 63*, 455–468.

Moore, R. S. (1976). The effects of videotaped feedback self-evaluation forms on teaching skills, musicianship, and creativity of prospective elementary teachers. *Bulletin for the Council of Research in Music Education, 47*, 1–15.

Napoles, J. (2008). Relationships among instructor, peer, and self-evaluations of undergraduate music education majors' micro-teaching experiences. *Journal of Research in Music Education, 56*, 82–91.

NCCAS. (2014). National Music Standards. Retrieved from www.nationalartsstandards.org/.

Palmer, C., Koopmans, E., Loehr, J. D., & Carter, C. (2009). Movement-related feedback and temporal accuracy in clarinet performance. *Music Perception: An Interdisciplinary Journal, 26*, 439–449.

Parkes, K. A. (2010). The use of criteria specific performance rubrics for student self-assessment: A case study. In T. Brophy (Ed.), *The practice of assessment in music education: Frameworks, models, and designs* (pp. 453–458). Chicago, IL: GIA Publications.

Powell, S. R. (2016). The influence of video reflection on preservice music teachers' concerns in peer- and field-teaching settings. *Journal of Research in Music Education, 63*, 487–507.

Price, H. E. (1989). An effective way to teach and rehearse: Research supports using sequential patterns. *Update: Applications of Research in Music Education, 8*, 42–46.

Price, H. E. (1992). Sequential patterns of instruction and learning to use them. *Journal of Research in Music Education, 40*, 14–29.

Price, H. E., & Yarbrough, C. (1991). Validation of sequential patterns of instruction in music. *Canadian Music Educator, Research Edition, 33*, 165–174.

Price, H. E., & Yarbrough, C. (1993/1994). Effect of scripted sequential patterns of instruction in music rehearsals on teaching evaluations by college non-music students. *Bulletin of the Council for Research in Music Education, 119*, 170–178.

Priest, T. (2006) Self-evaluation, creativity, and musical achievement. *Psychology of Music, 34*, 47–61.

Roesler, R. A. (2017) Independence pending: Teacher behaviors preceding learner problem solving. *Journal of Research in Music Education, 64*, 454–473.

Rostvall, A.-L., & West, T. (2003). Analysis of interaction and learning in instrumental teaching. *Music Education Research, 5*, 213–226.

Salzberg, R. S., & Salzberg, C. L. (1981). Praise and corrective feedback in the remediation of incorrect left-hand positions of elementary string players. *Journal of Research in Music Education, 29*, 125–133.

Schmidt, C. P. (1989). Individual differences in the perception of applied music teaching feedback. *Psychology of Music, 17*, 110–122.

Schmidt, C. P. (1995). Attributions of success, grade level, and gender as factors in choral students' perceptions of teacher feedback. *Journal of Research in Music Education, 43*, 313–329.

Schmidt, C. P., & Zdzinski, S. F. (1993). Cited quantitative research articles in music education research journals, 1975–1990: A content analysis of selected studies. *Journal of Research in Music Education, 41*, 5–18.

Siebenaler, D. J. (1997). Analysis of teacher–student interactions in the piano lessons of children and adults. *Journal of Research in Music Education, 45*, 6–20.

Spahn, C., Walther, J. C., & Nusseck, M. (2015). The effectiveness of a multimodal concept of audition training for music students in coping with music performance anxiety. *Psychology of Music, 44*, 893–909.

Speer, D. R. (1994). An analysis of sequential patterns of instruction in piano lessons. *Journal of Research in Music Education, 42*, 14–26.

Sundberg, J., & Verrillo, R. T. (1992) Editorial. *Music Perception: An Interdisciplinary Journal, 9*(3), 277–280.

Svec, C. L. (2017). The effects of instruction on the singing ability of children ages 5 to 11: A meta-analysis. *Psychology of Music*, advance online publication. Retrieved from https://doi.org/10.1177/0305735617709920.

Todd, N. P. (1993). Vestibular feedback in musical performance: Response to somatosensory feedback in musical performance. *Music Perception: An Interdisciplinary Journal, 10*, 379–382.

Welch, G. F. (1985). A schema theory of how children learn to sing in tune. *Psychology of Music, 13*, 3–18.

Welch, G. F., Howard, D. M., & Rush, C. (1989). Real-time visual feedback in the development of vocal pitch accuracy in singing. *Psychology of Music, 17*, 146–157.

Whitaker, J. A. (2011). High school band students' and directors' perceptions of verbal and nonverbal teaching behaviors. *Journal of Research in Music Education, 59*, 290–309.

Wolfe, D. E., & Jellison, J. A. (1990). Music and elementary education students' evaluations of music-teaching scripts. *Journal of Research in Music Education, 38*, 311–321.

Yarbrough, C., & Madsen, K. (1998). The evaluation of teaching in choral rehearsals. *Journal of Research in Music Education, 46*, 469–481.

Yarbrough, C., & Price, H. E. (1981). Prediction of performer attentiveness based on rehearsal activity and teacher behavior. *Journal of Research in Music Education, 29*, 209–217.

Yarbrough, C., & Price, H. E. (1989). Sequential patterns of instruction in music. *Journal of Research in Music Education, 37*, 179–187.

Yarbrough, C., Wapnick, J., & Kelley, R. (1979). Effect of videotape feedback techniques on performance, verbalization, and attitude of beginning conductors. *Journal of Research in Music Education, 27*, 103–112.

Younger, K. G. (1998). An observational analysis of instructional effectiveness in intermediate level band and orchestra rehearsals. Doctoral dissertation, University of Texas at Austin.

11 Feedback and Noncognitive Skills

From Working Hypotheses to Theory-Driven Recommendations for Practice

Dana Murano, Jonathan E. Martin, Jeremy Burrus, and Richard D. Roberts

The Importance of Noncognitive Skills

Cognitive ability is undeniably important for life success. Measures of cognitive ability (sometimes referred to as the g-factor, other times hushed to make it seem venerable in conversations like the present one) predict a broad range of desirable outcomes, including academic success (e.g., Adelman, 1999; Hezlett et al., 2001; Kobrin, Patterson, Shaw, Mattern, & Barbuti, 2008), college grades (Mattern & Patterson, 2011), job performance (e.g., Schmidt & Hunter, 1998), health (e.g., Deary, Whalley, & Starr, 2003), and marital stability (e.g., Roberts, Kuncel, Shiner, Caspi, & Goldberg, 2007). Each of these predictive relationships, however, is far from perfect. Correlations of cognitive ability with the outcomes listed above range from $r = 0.06$ (mortality) to $r = 0.51$ (job performance), leaving a large amount of variance unaccounted for. That's exactly what science suggests; there is no alchemist solution, and no Holy Grail. Indeed, while arguably one can never completely explain any single outcome, we suggest that accounting for a set of skills/attributes commonly known as *noncognitive skills* can provide substantial predictive power over and above the unholy g-factor. In this chapter, we use the term "noncognitive skills" to describe a larger set of individual difference variables that are not typically assessed with intelligence or achievement tests. Although all skills clearly have a cognitive component, we use the term "noncognitive" here to indicate this set of skills that differs from the traditional cognitive skills that are generally taught and tested in K-12 education.

It should be noted that this domain is subject to *jingle* (calling different things the same name) and *jangle* fallacies (calling the same things different names; Kelley, 1927). In addition, there is also controversy about the most appropriate

* We would like to thank colleagues working with us in the Center for Social, Emotional, and Academic Learning for their inspiration, guidance, and assistance in the writing of this chapter. It truly is a next-generation SEAL team, cutting across so many organizations it has touched upon and/or been supported by: RAD Science, ARC, CUNY, USyd, Asia Society, ACT, ETS, ProExam, ERB, SSAT-B, NNSTOY, and NWEA, to name a few. All statemenets expressed in this chapter are the authors' and do not reflect the official opinions or policies of the authors' host affiliations. Correspondence concerning this chapter should be addressed to: Dana.Murano@act.org.

nomenclature to use in referring to these constructs (e.g., Duckworth & Yeager, 2015). Whereas some researchers use the label "noncognitive skills" to describe trait-level differences in personality and motivation, others use the term "psychosocial skills." Scholars in the field of business often gravitate toward the label of "soft skills," whereas educational researchers often prefer the label of "social and emotional skills." Despite different labels, these terms are essentially used to describe the same underlying constructs. In order to avoid either fallacy, we use the term "noncognitive skills" consistently throughout the rest of the chapter to refer to the underlying skill set of interest. We also use the distinction of "skills" in order to stress, in a student-centered context, that noncognitive constructs are malleable to intervention via deliberate practice, as reviewed below.

Noncognitive variables include constructs such as personality, attitudes, motivation, time management, engagement, and anxiety (Kyllonen, Lipnevich, Burrus, & Roberts, 2014). Noncognitive skills can be broadly organized using the Big Five framework (e.g., Kyllonen et al., 2014; John & DeFruyt 2015; Roberts, Martin, & Olaru, 2015; Lipnevich, Preckel, & Roberts, 2016). The Big Five model, consisting of the personality traits of openness to experience, conscientiousness, extraversion, agreeableness, and neuroticism (commonly reversed to emotional stability in the literature) has been widely accepted as a way to characterize and organize various interpersonal and intrapersonal competencies (e.g., National Research Council, 2012). In using this taxonomy, we can organize discrete noncognitive skills by aligning them to their respective Big Five traits. In a sense, more specific skills can be considered *facets* of these higher-order traits. For example, organization and responsibility are facets of conscientiousness; empathy and cooperation are facets of agreeableness; and emotional control and stress resistance are facets of emotional stability. Primi, Santos, John, and DeFruyt (2016) confirmed this crosswalk at the item level between commonly identified social and emotional skills and the Big Five factors. For a full review of the use of the Big Five as an organizing framework for noncognitive skills, see Roberts, Martin, and Olaru (2015).

Noncognitive skills are valued both by the workforce and in education. For example, several large-scale surveys have found that employers highly value noncognitive skills in their new employees, often prioritizing these skills over traditional cognitive skills such as mathematical ability (e.g., Casner-Lotto & Barrington, 2006; Hart Research Associates, 2010). In education, noncognitive skills are highly valued; these skills have been cited as skills that many colleges and universities aim to develop in their mission statements (Stemler, 2012). These skills are valued for a reason: they are highly predictive of important outcomes. To provide just a few examples, noncognitive skills predict:

- Academic performance (Poropat, 2009)
- Behavioral problems (Ge & Conger, 1999)
- Peer relationships (Jensen-Campbell et al., 2002)
- Happiness (Diener & Lucas, 1999)

- Health (Bogg & Roberts, 2004) and longevity (Roberts et al., 2007)
- Job performance (Barrick, Mount, & Judge, 2001)
- Job satisfaction (Judge, Heller, & Mount, 2002).

These skills have also been shown to be predictive of desirable outcomes longitudinally over the course of several decades (e.g., Damian, Su, Shanahan, Trautwein, & Roberts, 2014).

Is It Possible to Learn Noncognitive Skills?

In addition to being highly predictive of desirable outcomes, a critical component of the equation is that noncognitive constructs are malleable to intervention. In other words, they can be improved through deliberate instruction, effort, and practice. Recent empirical evidence suggests that noncognitive constructs, such as personality, do indeed change over the life span. Roberts, Walton, and Viechtbauer (2006) conducted a meta-analysis of ninety-two studies, which demonstrated that people tend to increase in social dominance, agreeableness, conscientiousness, and emotional stability as they age. This research indicates that noncognitive skills related to personality may be more malleable than once thought, correcting William James's famous adage: "Personality is set like plaster" (James, 1890/1981). More recent work has confirmed this finding and shows that while rank order remains relatively stable over time, individuals can change in mean levels of personality (Walton & Billera, 2016). The increasing recognition of the fact that noncognitive skills are important has led to an increase in programs deliberately designed to teach them. Students who develop such skills are thought to be well rounded and demonstrate effectiveness in interpersonal and intrapersonal domains (Kyllonen et al., 2014).

One vehicle through which noncognitive skills are taught in K-12 schools is through social and emotional learning (SEL) programs. Social and emotional skills are defined by the Organisation for Economic Cooperation and Development (OECD) as "individual capacities that (a) are manifested in consistent patterns of thought, feelings, and behaviors, (b) can be developed through formal and informal learning experiences, and (c) influence important socio-economic outcomes throughout the individual's life" (John & De Fruyt, 2015, p. 4). The OECD organizes these skills using the Big Five personality framework as an organizing taxonomy (John & De Fruyt, 2015). The Collaborative for Social and Emotional Learning (CASEL) also offers a definition for SEL: "Social and emotional learning (SEL) is the process through which children and adults acquire and effectively apply the knowledge, attitudes, and skills necessary to understand and manage emotions, set and achieve positive goals, feel and show empathy for others, establish and maintain positive relationships, and make responsible decisions" (CASEL, 2017). These five competency areas identified by the definition can be bolstered in classrooms via SEL curriculum and instruction, in schools through schoolwide practices and policies, and in homes and communities through family and community partnerships. Whereas CASEL does not have their competencies grounded in the Big Five framework, John and De Fruyt (2015) have crosswalked CASEL's competency framework with the Big Five in order to demonstrate near-perfect correspondence. SEL programs are designed to bolster critical social and emotional skills, which then facilitate various other dimensions of school success, including improvements in school behaviors, school attitudes, and school performance (Zins et al., 2004).

Evidence on the effectiveness of interventions in increasing social and emotional skills continues to accumulate. Durlak, Weissberg, Dymnicki, Taylor, and Schellinger (2011) present meta-analytic findings of SEL programs; their review includes 213 school-based, universal SEL programs involving K-12 students and shows that students receiving SEL programming demonstrated significant improvements in social and emotional skills, school attitudes, school behavior, and academic performance. These results demonstrate that SEL interventions are indeed effective in increasing student noncognitive skills. Meta-analytic evidence also shows that these positive effects can last weeks, months, and even years after intervention delivery (Taylor, Oberle, Durlak, & Weissberg, 2017). Kautz et al. (2014) examined the effects of interventions throughout the life span on cognitive and noncognitive skill development. They found that early childhood interventions yielded the most cognitive skill gains, but interventions targeting noncognitive skills were effective throughout the life span. Their results suggest that noncognitive skills are actually more malleable than cognitive skills in adolescence, implying that noncognitive skill interventions can be fruitful throughout secondary schooling. In their review, various noncognitive skill interventions yielded gains in noncognitive skills, as well as increased academic performance and retention. Additionally, society benefits greatly when it invests in SEL programming. A recent cost–benefit analysis of six individual SEL interventions shows that for every dollar invested in SEL programming, there is a return of $11 to society (Belfield, Bowden, Klapp, Levin, Shand, & Zander, 2015). As evidence accumulates, more schools, districts, and states are including SEL standards in their student learning outcomes (e.g., Dusenbury, Weissberg, Goren, & Domitrovich, 2014).

Other interventions in schools, not necessarily nestled under the label of "social and emotional learning," have also demonstrated promise in improving noncognitive skills. Classroom interventions designed to improve critical thinking skills have been shown to be effective in improving metacognitive awareness and monitoring of one's learning of reading passages (Haller, Child, & Walberg, 1988). Furthermore, study skills interventions have been found to improve both student motivation and academic performance (Dignath, Buettner, & Langfeldt, 2008). Finally, interventions designed to reduce the negative emotionality and worry that comes with test anxiety have been demonstrated to improve test performance (Hembree, 1988). The work of these researchers, and others, demonstrates that it is possible to improve noncognitive skills.

Intervention programs at the college level have also been shown to be effective in improving student motivation and emotional control (Robbins,

Oh, Le, & Button, 2009). For instance, a recent meta-analysis revealed that taking part in a self-management program, which typically attempts to improve emotional and self-regulation skills such as anxiety reduction, self-control, and self-management, was associated with greater motivational and emotional control. Consistent with the meta-analyses of SEL programs described above and the theoretical groundwork of SEL curricula, greater motivational and emotional control was, in turn, associated with improved academic performance. Together, this combination of evidence shows that noncognitive skills can explicitly be taught in K-20 classrooms, yielding positive effects for students across age ranges.

Will Teaching Noncognitive Skills Detract from the Teaching of Cognitive Skills?

Importantly, the addition of these programs did not seem to impede on students' learning of traditional academic content. In fact, academic performance improved for students who took part in SEL programs. Students who participated in SEL programs showed an 11% increase in academic achievement, measured by school-reported GPA (Durlak et al., 2011). Whereas several critics of SEL programs suggest that these programs take away from traditional cognitive skill development and may lead to lags in learning (e.g., Ecclestone & Hayes, 2009), much more research supports the notion that SEL interventions indirectly increase academic performance. Some of these indirect paths operate via reducing behavioral infractions, raising attendance rates, and reducing dropout rates (e.g., Zins, Weissberg, Wang, & Walberg, 2004; Brackett & Rivers, 2014). Past studies have also embedded social and emotional learning skills with cognitive skill development. In a large-scale randomized control trial with third-grade students, a one-year intervention program was implemented that combined social and emotional learning with literacy development. At the end of the intervention period, students showed gains in components of literacy development and reductions in problem behaviors (Jones, Brown, Hoglund, & Aber, 2010).

Though not all mean effect differences were statistically significant – an important point – they were generally in the predicted direction, demonstrating an increase in skill. This suggests there is potential for both cognitive and noncognitive skills to be cultivated simultaneously through carefully designed intervention curricula. It remains a very important point – all the same – whether or not programs ratified by opinion or weak evidentiary bases over gold-standard science, such is the case with groups like CASEL, should be considered acceptable (i.e., while incredibly influential in the education sector, there seems to be some incongruence between their standards and standards established by, for example, the What Works Clearinghouse). The principals of do no harm apply here, and it is fortunate a recent meta-analysis (Corcoran, Cheung, Kim, & Chen, 2017) reminds us of this fact.

Best Practices for the Development of Noncognitive Skills

Putting aside the previous concerns, which are relatively trivial (though worth stating), let us assume all is well with SEL interventions. Because non-cognitive skills are critical for attaining desirable life outcomes, are malleable to intervention, and can (and should) be taught in schools, the next logical step is to consider what are the best practices for teaching noncognitive skills. Non-cognitive skills can be taught in a variety of settings, throughout the life span, in disparate settings: in school, in after-care programs, in the home, within and across any given community, to the individual and in spite of the individual. For the purpose of this chapter, we focus on recommendations that apply to classroom settings at the K-12 level.

We posit that, much like cognitive skill development, noncognitive skill development stems from frequent and deliberate practice, which eventually enables the transition from controlled processing (requires deliberate effort) to automatic processing (e.g., Sweller, 1994; Willingham, 2009). When these complex noncognitive skills are first acquired, they require considerable cognitive effort to process, which taxes working memory. With time and practice, skills become automatic and require very little processing for them to operate. Therefore, practice is a good first step in the development of noncognitive skills. Increased practice will lead to increased automaticity of processing, enabling the individual to demonstrate skills without putting an extensive burden on a limited working memory capacity (e.g., Miller, 1956).

Eccles and Gootman (2002) provide general guidelines for youth development programs that support the development of noncognitive skills. First, they recommend that all curricula should be developmentally, culturally, and ecologically appropriate for students. Next, supportive relationships are critical. In order for development to occur, students must have healthy and supportive relationships in the classroom with their teachers and peers. Students must also be given a sense of belonging that accompanies the intervention (i.e., feel that they matter). To bolster skill development within these programs, Eccles and Gootman suggest that instruction involve: (1) active construction of knowledge; (2) disciplined inquiry, which requires deep cognitive work and learning for understanding; (3) culturally relevant material; (4) regular feedback; (5) opportunities to modify understanding; (6) ongoing reflective opportunities; (7) differentiated instruction that provides multiple ways of learning; and (8) cooperative and highly interactive learning activities. According to their review, these practices best promote the development of noncognitive skills in students.

Guidelines for the effective teaching of noncognitive skills are also put forth by Durlak, Weissberg, and Pachan (2010), in a measured perspective, often however lacking a solid empirical basis, likely because this is an emerging field (but see our previous point; the time is nigh to make this more scientific). The first recommendation is that programs are sequenced. Maximally effective interventions employ a coordinated and connected set of curricular units that center on learning objectives. The teaching of more complex skills cannot come before more basic skills are mastered first, and then pieced together to enable higher-order skill learning. The second guideline is that active forms of learning are employed. In alignment with principles from cognitive psychology, practice is a necessary component of skill acquisition. Furthermore, didactic instruction should be accompanied by more hands-on forms of learning, such as role-playing and behavioral rehearsal. Next, Durlak et al. (2010) recommend that instructors must spend a sufficient amount of time and attention on development of a particular skill. Last, students need clear and explicit learning objectives. It is not enough for teachers to say that they are working on "social skills" within a particular unit; instead, more specific skill labels, such as "communication skills" or "self-regulatory" skills, are more conducive to learning.

Feedback in the Development of Noncognitive Skills

Largely missing from the conversation about the teaching of noncognitive skills is the role of feedback (for a notable exception, see Eccles and Gootman, 2002). And even when articulated, to the knowledge of the present set of authors, no experimental studies yet exist that focus on feedback and the development of noncognitive skills; we know very little about what optimal feedback looks like.

But two theoretical papers do exist, which will be reviewed later in this chapter. From these sources, we expect that many general guidelines for feedback in the development of cognitive skills also apply to the development of noncognitive skills. In some ways, noncognitive skills can be seen as similar to cognitive skills. They both involve procedural and declarative knowledge (Marzano, 2015); are to be taught in scaffolded, progressive sequences in order to maximize effective learning (Schunk, 2008; Durlak et al., 2010); and can be improved through deliberate practice (Durlak et al., 2010; Kyllonen et al., 2014). While we are not claiming an absolute parallel between cognitive and noncognitive skill development, using the evidentiary basis of cognitive skill feedback remains a better option than using no evidentiary basis at all. In the following section, we review some literature on effective feedback principles in the development of cognitive skills. Many of these principles outlined below guided our development of recommendations for feedback in noncognitive skills.

Feedback in Cognitive Skills

Decades of research on feedback in the fields of psychology and education have demonstrated that feedback can lead to significant improvements in cognitive performance (e.g., Kluger & DeNisi, 1996; Hattie & Timperley, 2007; Shute, 2008; Lipnevich & Smith, 2009). Typically, this research has focused on feedback that is provided in the classroom. An overarching theme is that not all feedback is created equal. Hattie and Timperley (2007) reviewed twelve meta-analyses and found that feedback had a large effect on student outcomes, with a mean effect size of 0.79 over 196 studies. Effect sizes varied greatly, ranging from 0.12 for teacher praise to 0.60 for extrinsic feedback rewards to 1.24 for feedback given to special education students. Lower effect sizes were commonly found in studies where feedback was related to praise, rewards, and punishment, whereas studies showing higher effect sizes involved feedback about how tasks could be done most effectively. Clearly, the type of feedback matters. Despite the average effect size for feedback being quite large, one should not conclude that feedback *always* has a positive effect on student performance. In fact, another meta-analysis on feedback (Kluger & DeNisi, 1996) found that 32% of the effects of feedback were negative.

In classrooms, there are many different ways for teachers to use feedback effectively to promote learning. Beginning in early childhood education and spanning throughout the early elementary school years, feedback should be a means through which children can develop a dynamic-learning frame, as opposed to a fixed-performance frame. Johnston's (2012) dynamic-learning frame parallels an incremental theory of intelligence, in which intelligence is not fixed and can be improved through effort and practice, whereas the fixed-performance frame aligns with entity theories, in which intelligence is a fixed quality that cannot be changed (e.g., Dweck, 2000). As Johnston (2012) describes, there are major differences between telling a child "It's a very good score, you must have worked hard" and "It's a very good score, you must be smart" (p. 12). Feedback that praises effort, rather than intelligence, will help children adopt the notion that achievement is based on effort, rather than innate ability, enabling them to develop a dynamic-learning frame and growth mindset.

Johnston (2012) also cautions against the use of person-centered criticism and praise in kindergarten classrooms. This recommendation echoes Hattie and Timperley's (2007) review, which also cautions teachers against giving feedback based on the person. Person-oriented praise or criticism introduces judgments of self-worth, value, and importance as confounds into the evaluation of academic work. Person-oriented feedback can also engender a fixed-performance mindset. Instead, it is suggested that teachers use process-oriented feedback, particularly focusing on effort. Last, Johnston (2012) argues that causal process statements, such as "when you added dialogue to your piece, I really understood how the character felt" (p. 42), are particularly effective pieces of feedback that can build agency in young children. Schunk (2012) also discusses the importance of effort-based feedback in the development of self-regulatory skills. Feedback promoting effort, rather than ability, can promote self-regulation learning by increasing and sustaining motivation, enabling accurate perceptions of students' own progress, and increasing their efficacy for future learning.

As children reach adolescence and gain the ability to think abstractly, effective feedback becomes more complex as well. Feedback for high school and university students is most effective when it helps students understand each of the following: (1) the level of quality of their current work, (2) the desired level of quality, and (3) the changes required to bridge the gap between the current and desired level of the quality of their work (Lipnevich, McCallen, Miles, & Smith, 2014). Feedback following this premise can take several forms. First, descriptive feedback, or comments pertaining specifically to the student's work and suggesting specific steps toward improvement, can be highly effective. This type of descriptive feedback is preferred to evaluative feedback (e.g., a letter grade). Evaluative feedback is not as effective in helping students improve the quality of their work and can even depress student performance (Lipnevich & Smith, 2009). These recommendations that follow a developmental trajectory are important considerations for educators to take into account.

The results of systematic reviews on feedback have also contributed to the recommendations made for effective feedback. Kluger and DiNisi (1996) present a feedback intervention theory (FIT), which consists of five basic arguments: "(a) Behavior is regulated by comparisons of feedback to goals or standards, (b) goals or standards are organized hierarchically, (c) attention is limited and therefore only feedback-standard gaps that receive attention actively participate in behavior regulation, (d) attention is normally directed to a moderate level of the hierarchy, and (e) feedback interventions change the locus of attention and therefore affect behavior" (Kluger & DeNisi, 1996, p. 259). Following another systematic review, Hattie and Timperley (2007) present a model of feedback based on current research in the field. Their model ultimately states that feedback works by reducing a discrepancy between current performance and a desired outcome. Three questions guide the purpose of feedback in this framework: "Where am I going?," "How am I going?," and "Where to next?" Within this context, feedback should focus on goals and goal-monitoring and exists at four independent levels: feedback about the task, feedback about process, feedback about self-regulation, and feedback about the self as a person. Shute (2008) also presents a model of formative feedback, along with specific guidelines for giving formative feedback in instructional settings. She argues that in order for formative feedback to be effective, it must be supportive, timely, nonevaluative, and specific. She provides specific guidelines for feedback, including the following: "(a) focus feedback on the task, not the learner, (b) provide elaborated feedback to enhance learning, in manageable units, (c) be specific and clear with feedback, (d) keep feedback as simple as possible, based on learner needs and constraints, (e) reduce uncertainty between performance and goals, (f) give unbiased, objective feedback, (g) promote a 'learning goal' orientation, and (h) provide feedback after learners have attempted a solution" (Shute, 2008, pp. 177–178).

Best Practices for Noncognitive Skills Feedback

To the knowledge of the present authors, no empirical studies to date have focused on factors related to feedback in the development of noncognitive skills. Despite the lack of experimental research in the area, two pieces of theoretical work exist that have guided our recommendations for noncognitive feedback. It should be acknowledged that neither of the two works represents original research in this field, but both are reviews of the fields of social emotional learning that include recommendations for best practices on SEL and feedback.

Robert Marzano has twice addressed this topic, first in materials prepared for the CASEL (Marzano, 2010), and then more formally in a 2015 book chapter discussing formative assessment in social and emotional learning skills (Marzano 2015). In both works, Marzano used Hattie and Timperley's (2007) framework as a theoretical foundation for his recommendations. Specifically, Marzano's statement that "the research on feedback does provide the foundations for developing a clear and focused approach to one manifestation of formative assessment – a manifestation that focuses on clear learning goals, tracking student progress toward these goals, and helping students identify the next steps they might take to attain these goals" (p. 338) embodies Hattie and Timperley's (2007) three guiding questions that should shape feedback. Marzano (2015) provides four key recommendations based on this framework. First, it is essential to communicate to students they have the power to change and moreover that they are capable of making positive changes, both in their own lives and in the lives of others. Second, students should know what is expected of them. To ensure this outcome, teachers should spend ample time informing students of their expectations and how they can meet them. Moreover, these expectations should be conveyed in student-friendly language that all students can easily understand. Third, data used for feedback should derive from a variety of sources and assessments, and not a single source. Fourth, and most heavily emphasized in Marzano (2015), feedback should empower students to conduct their own self-assessments and to use these as well as other assessment sources for their goal-setting and monitoring. Self-assessment can be conducted by having students track their own progress on SEL skills using visuals, such as charts or bar graphs.

The second set of guidelines comes from a 2016 book entitled *The Other Side of the Report Card: Assessing Students' Social, Emotional, and Character Development* (Elias, Ferrito, & Moceri, 2016). Elias and his coauthors draw on decades of work (again, this does not necessarily make this science; we need to work with better procedures and practice to make this a true science) with schools developing social and emotional learning programs to provide nine recommendations for effective SEL (i.e., noncognitive skills) feedback. Their recommendations are as follows:

- Clearly define constructs being assessed and align assessment of them to observable behaviors.
- Ensure items are developmentally appropriate to the students being assessed.
- Ensure feedback is based on what is clearly and consistently observed.
- Ensure students and parents can understand the nature of the feedback.
- Ensure that feedback is not viewed as an indicator of a child's fixed personality, but rather how the child acts and behaves in specific situations.
- Feedback should emphasize that all children can improve their skill sets.

- Feedback should be used as part of a system, in that it is a vehicle through which to plan interventions and also to monitor progress.
- In the feedback, a clear connection should be made between noncognitive skills and success in school, careers, and in life.
- The child should be involved in a cooperative project of SEL skill development between and among teachers and parents and not be seen as a passive recipient of this information.

These advisements for noncognitive skills feedback are well aligned to the much broader research in cognitive skills feedback, reviewed earlier. Based on these premises from the cognitive feedback literature and on frameworks set forth by others in the SEL field, we present our own six recommendations for feedback in noncognitive skills development.

Six Recommendations for Noncognitive Skills Feedback

Drawing on the above sources, the following are identified as key recommendations for quality noncognitive skills feedback to students, to which every such program should be held accountable for meeting as best practice.

Recommendation 1: *Feedback should focus on effort and actions of the student and not on any permanent personal qualities. The feedback should convey to students that all students can improve their skills, since they are indeed malleable entities, as opposed to fixed qualities.*

Recommendation 2: *Feedback should be framed in student-friendly language and terms that students can easily understand and act on.*

Recommendation 3: *Feedback should be provided after multiple student actions or performances and should be related to those actions or performances.*

Recommendation 4: *Feedback should effectively identify and communicate critical "gaps" between the students' actions/performances and developmentally appropriate goals, standards, or benchmarks for their skills.*

Recommendation 5: *Feedback should provide suggested steps or interventions for the student to close identified gaps.*

Recommendation 6: *Feedback should be provided to students in a way that enlists and empowers them as participants in the process of better self-knowledge and agents of their own growth. It should intrinsically motivate students to want to grow. The feedback should furthermore seek to avoid messages entailing or connoting rewards or punishment, as this may result in extrinsic motivation, versus the desired intrinsic desire to improve.*

Although this set of six recommendations draws heavily on the two identified substantial treatments of noncognitive skills feedback (Marzano, 2015; Elias, Ferrito, & Moceri, 2016), these six recommendations are not mutually exclusive with respect to noncognitive skills. While they can be applied to cognitive skills as well, these six recommendations are particularly salient in the development of noncognitive skills.

More insight on these standards in the context of noncognitive skill assessment can be found by applying them to three sample noncognitive skills assessment systems: Marzano's rubrics for CASEL, the Character Lab Character Growth Card, and the ACT® Tessera® Social and Emotional Learning Assessment System (for full disclosure, the authors of this chapter have each been involved in the development of the Tessera system). These three systems were chosen because they are representative of three major ways feedback can be generated and provided: (1) in the context of a classroom lesson or unit on the completion of a task or series of tasks (CASEL rubrics), (2) at the end of a quarter or semester on a student's report card for work of that time period (Character Lab Character Growth Card), and (3) in a standardized testing and reporting system that is widely used in cognitive assessment but less often in noncognitive assessment (ACT Tessera). Note that these three systems stand as a valuable "trinity" of feedback levels, because when the approaches they represent are used together, they form the kind of aligned systems of assessment – classroom, school level, external/standardized – that is recommended by Hammond and Conley (2013). However, though these three types or levels form such a system, each uses a different framework for noncognitive skills. They are simply independent representatives of each level. We should add that because they are situated differently, we are not comparing them with each other, but only evaluating each through the lens of our six recommendations.

Applying the Six Recommendations to Three Systems

Rubrics for Social Emotional Learning. These were prepared in 2010 by the Marzano Research Lab for CASEL and tied to the Illinois state SEL standards. The purpose of this project was to design a comprehensive assessment system for SEL standards that could (1) focus school and/or district-level instruction on specific areas of knowledge, referred to as measurement topics, and (2) provide a tool enabling teachers to track individual student progress on each measurement topic using teacher-designed formal and informal assessments (Marazano 2010). In order to achieve these goals, rubrics were developed for teacher use (see Figure 11.1 for an example rubric). Teaches can easily use these rubrics after a specific lesson or class activity in order to deliver formative feedback to students.

Character Growth Card. This tool was developed by the Character Lab, an organization cofounded by Angela Duckworth, a researcher at the University of Pennsylvania. These report cards are intended to be completed at the end of each grading period for each student. In rating students' noncognitive skill development, teachers enable researchers to track how closely behaviors predict positive school outcomes and how students change in their behaviors over time. Users of the system report that in addition to monitoring student growth, staff members and students have the goal of strengthening internal motivation. At the top of the Growth Card it is stated "Adults and students can use the Character Growth Card to discuss differences and similarities between self-scores and teacher-scores, changes and progress over time, and/or variations in scores in different environments, situations, or class settings. After that conversation, students and adults can set goals together. It's important to note

Topic: Behaviors		
Level: 5th		
Score 4.0	**In addition to Score 3.0, in-depth inferences and applications that go beyond what was taught.**	**Sample Tasks**
	3.5	In addition to score 3.0 performance, in-depth inferences and applications with partial success.	
Score 3.0	• **The student articulates how one's behavior affects others** • **The student exhibits no major errors or omissions.**	Reflect in a journal or with a peer on how your behavior affected your work with a group or work with a partner.
	2.5	No major errors or omissions regarding 2.0 content and partial knowledge of the 3.0 content	
Score 2.0	**There are no major errors or omissions regarding the simpler details and processes as the student performs basic processes, such as:** • **Recognizes or recalls examples of behaviors and how the behaviors affect others** • **However, the student exhibits major errors or omissions regarding the more complex ideas and processes.**	After watching a role play, students identify specific behaviors and how the behaviors affected others.
	1.5	Partial knowledge of the 2.0 content but major errors or omissions regarding the 3.0 content	
Score 1.0	**With help, a partial understanding of some of the simpler details and processes and some of the more complex ideas and processes.**	
	0.5	With help, a partial understanding of the 2.0 content but not the 3.0 content	
Score 0.0	**Even with help, no understanding or skill demonstrated.**	

Figure 11.1 *Rubric for the measurement topic of behaviors at the fifth grade.*

that this tool should not be used to diagnose or compare children, nor to compare schools or programs. Please use it to help children focus on their own growth and development in these areas, and as a positive conversation starter" (Character Lab, 2017). The skills that can be measured using the Character Growth Cards are curiosity, growth mindset, gratitude, grit, self-contol, and optimism. For more information on Character Lab Character Growth Cards, visit www.characterlab.org/character.

ACT Tessera Noncognitive Assessment System. This tool is a comprehensive assessment system that measures noncognitive skills in middle and high school students. The assessment is structured on the Big Five framework and captures a norm-referenced score for individual students on each of the following noncognitive skills: tenacity/grit, organization/responsibility, teamwork/cooperation, composure/resilience, curiosity/ingenuity, and leadership/communication style. The ACT Tessera assessment is computer based and uses a triangulation of three methods to measure individual differences in these six noncognitive skills: self-report items, situational judgment test items, and forced choice items. Both situational judgment and forced choice items are used to reduce several biases inherent in self-report items, the foremost of which is faking. It is relatively easy for a student to "fake," or inaccurately portray themselves in an effort to look more desirable, on the self-report items, but it is much more difficult to do so on the two latter item types (Stark, Chernyshenko, & Drasgow, 2005; Hooper, Cullen, & Sackett, 2006; Ziegler, MacCann, & Roberts, 2011). This multitrait,

Tenacity / Grit: Where are you now?

The extent to which you try hard to reach your goals and fill your potential

How do you currently see yourself?

DEVELOPING

What would you do in a real-world situation? One Example:

In English class, you write a paper about a book that you did not enjoy and receive a barely passing grade on your first assignment. Your teacher has explained the areas to work on in order to improve your grade on the next paper.

Here you can see how experts in Tenacity/Grit rated the options in comparison to how you responded. The more likely you were to say that you would choose a response that the experts rated as effective, the better.

Response Option	How likely did you say you were to choose this option?	How effective is each response as rated by experts?
Hope that the next book you have to write about is one that you like.	(Student Response)	Somewhat ineffective
Ask the teacher to read your paper again to see if they might give you a better grade.	(Student Response)	Somewhat ineffective
Try harder and make sure to address the teacher's concerns when writing the next paper.	(Student Response)	Very effective
Do the best you can on the next paper without really thinking about the comments from the teacher.	(Student Response)	Somewhat ineffective
Decide that you will probably not get a very good grade in that class, since the teacher is too picky.	(Student Response)	Very ineffective

Tenacity / Grit: What is it?

The extent to which you try hard to reach your goals and fill your potential

People with 1 star like you currently tend to

- Not always try their hardest to learn everything in school
- Stop trying after they have failed once
- Not always do what is expected of them

People with 3 stars tend to

- Try extremely hard to learn everything in school
- Only stop trying after they have failed many times
- Do more than what is expected of them

Figure 11.2 *ACT Tessera sample student score report.*

multimethod design provides a robust measurement of the student's noncognitive skill profile. A student can have three possible scores on each noncognitive skill: developing, approaching, and demonstrating. Individual student score reports, roster reports, and school-level reports are generated for all schools in which students take the assessment. Student score reports are intended to give students a "snapshot" of where they currently are in their skill development and are intended to be used to direct intervention (see Figure 11.2 for an example).

Table 11.1 *Summary of six feedback recommendations applied to each SEL system*

	Marzano's CASEL Rubrics	Character Lab Character Growth Card	ACT Tessera SEL Assessment System
1. Focus on actions, not character	Yes	Yes	Yes
2. Clear student language	Not as is without adaptation, but calls for that	Yes	Yes
3. Response and related to multiple actions	Yes, with caveats	Yes, with caveats	Yes, with caveats
4. Identify gaps	Yes	Not clearly	Yes
5. Provide steps	Yes	Not clearly	Yes
6. Involve students	Unclear	Unclear	Yes

An additional component of the system, the ACT Tessera Teacher Playbook, is a four-part tool designed to give teachers specific lessons, units, and additional resources that aid the development of noncognitive skills in students.

We now turn to evaluating the three systems using each of the six recommendations. Table 11.1 outlines how each of our six feedback recommendations applies to each of the three systems.

Recommendation 1: *Feedback should focus on effort and actions of the student and not on any permanent personal qualities. The feedback should convey to students that all students can improve their skills, since they are indeed malleable entities, as opposed to fixed qualities.*

All three systems well reflect adherence to the first recommendation. The rubrics from Marzano consistently entail teachers preparing feedback to evaluate students not on their personal qualities but on their actions; in the example provided, the rubrics reads that the student "articulates how one's behavior affects others" and "recognizes or recalls examples of behaviors." This is very different from language that might have stated the student "has the capacity to articulate how one's behavior affects others" or "knows how behavior affects others," which would have spoken more to the student's personal qualities than to his or her effort and actions. Similarly, the Character Lab Character Growth Card uses language such as "showed appreciation," "remained calm," and "show that s/he cared" rather than "is appreciative," "has good composure," or "cares about others." ACT Tessera too works to focus attention on actions, not attributes, by stating on its report, for each skill area, "Where are you now?" and "How do you currently see yourself?" rather than stating something like "your capacity" or "your skill level." Tessera's three performance level descriptors are also intended to reinforce this understanding among students: the terms "developing, approaching, and demonstrating" were intentionally chosen to convey and emphasize that these performance levels are about actions, things students do, and not attributes or personality qualities.

Recommendation 2: *Feedback should be framed in student-friendly language and terms that students can easily understand and act on.*

This recommendation is well met by both the Character Lab Character Growth Card and ACT Tessera. Each of the eight terms on the Growth Card is illustrated with three to four specific practices, and they appear to have been worded in a way to take care to be student friendly. Under "gratitude," for instance, a term that might be abstract to some middle school students, one of the items is "did something nice for someone else as a way of saying thank you." In another example, for "optimism," again a term not used universally among twelve-year-olds, one example is "when bad things happened, s/he thought about things they could do to make it better next time."

In ACT Tessera, we find the same approach. Tessera is built on the research framework of the Big Five (see ACT Inc., 2017, for a full theory of action document) but has adapted those not-so-friendly-to-student terms, such as "conscientiousness, agreeableness, openness, neuroticism, and extraversion" into far more recognizable terms such as grit, teamwork, and curiosity. We can see this also in the section at the bottom of each skill report, where the term is defined more thoroughly. "Grit," for instance, is explained as "the extent to which you try hard."

The Marzano SEL Rubrics do not meet this recommendation very well. The behaviors themselves are only partially transparent to a student's eyes; the wording "performs basic processes such as recognizes examples of behaviors" may not be hugely complex, but will not be easy to understand or visualize for many young adults. The rubric also uses for some levels language like "in-depth inferences" and "partial understanding of some of the simpler details," which will not be of great help to some students. In fairness, the memo accompanying these rubrics acknowledges that they were written for teachers, not students, and that schools and educators should consider adapting them into more student-friendly versions if distributing them.

Recommendation 3: *Feedback should be provided after multiple student actions or performances and should be related to those actions or performances.*

This recommendation is reasonably well met by the SEL rubrics; they are written to be used by teachers or other raters of student behaviors, and could not easily be used except during a student performance. The accompanying material also urges that they be used for rating a series of behaviors, and never just a single event, though it remains possible that a teacher or observer might deploy these rubrics for feedback after only a single activity, thereby falling short on this recommendation.

For ACT Tessera, the feedback follows the student-taken assessment, and the linkage from performance on the assessment to feedback is very clear. Furthermore, unlike many other standardized SEL assessments, Tessera uses three different types of items, so student feedback is based not only on what they self-report (a single assessment) but also on how they would act in certain types of described scenarios (situation judgment tests). This covers a far wider range of performances than the usual such system, and the use of situational judgment test items and forced choice items also make the assessment less prone to faking, as reviewed previously. Some could quibble, however, about whether student responses to Tessera questions and items actually reflect true actions and performances; a counterargument could be made that it reflects only what students think about their actions. There is a gap between one's thoughts about how one behaves and what one actually does, after all. Indeed, the Tessera feedback form underscores this, explaining that this is based on "how you currently see yourself," and not "how you currently act or behave."

As for the Character Lab Character Growth Card, it certainly is designed for use at the end of a term, whatever length that term may be, and is clearly intended to reflect on the breadth of student actions in that term. There is no space provided, however, nor clarity about methodology, to demonstrate how students will come to understand that their ratings on this form are connected to particular events, moments, or behaviors during what may be a matter of several months. Surely, some teachers use this in a way, perhaps accompanied by a conference or narrative, to tie these ratings to those specific actions, which would clearly meet this recommendation. But without such elaboration, the Growth Card alone might fall short on this recommendation.

Recommendation 4: *Feedback should effectively identify and communicate critical "gaps" between the students' actions/performances and developmentally appropriate goals, standards, or benchmarks for their skills.*

The SEL Rubrics meet the fourth recommendation very well. Using the Illinois state standards, they differentiate the rubrics by many different grade level or grade groupings, in order to establish developmentally appropriate targets for students. For each different developmental standard, they also, by using a rubric format, report on where students stand along a continuum of proficiency, and the student, on receiving this feedback, can easily identify the gaps between his or her performance and what the appropriate standard for that performance would be. It should be said, though, that the rubric provides true descriptive performance indicators at only two levels, 3.0 and 2.0, and the others follow a formulaic wording that is less descriptive and will provide far less information than would be ideal about what those higher- or lower-level performances contain.

ACT Tessera also meets this recommendation fairly well. Students are rated on their performance with one, two, or three stars (the system is expected to expand to five star ratings in the near future), and so students get a clear sense of where they stand relative to the standard. The report also goes far beyond the star rating to include information about one of the situation judgment test items they completed, communicating how their responses compare to an expert rating. Tessera also provides developmental differentiation by rating middle school students on a scale different from that of high school students.

The Character Lab Character Growth Card, however, provides no communication of developmental differentiation, nor any clarity about different levels of performance for its eight skills. Raters are asked to use a numerical indicator to communicate frequency of student behaviors, so students can learn where they stand vis-à-vis the expected regularity of these actions, but they do not get any descriptive insight into what different levels of proficiency would entail.

Recommendation 5: *Feedback should provide suggested steps or interventions for the student to close identified gaps.*

Both the SEL Rubrics and the Tessera system meet this recommendation very well. As can be seen in the sample SEL rubric, embedded within each rubric are suggested tasks to develop and strengthen each proficiency described in the rubric. Tessera provides at the bottom of each report information to students on the actions of people with three stars, and so gives them steps they can take to improve performance. Tessera also provides as an accompaniment to its assessment a 168-page Teacher Playbook with more than forty lesson plans and activities.

The Character Lab Character Growth Card meets this expectation only partially. It does not provide on its form any additional information for students or teachers to guide students' improved performances, but on the website it does provide for each of the assessed skills some additional information and links to resources on how they can be developed and improved.

Recommendation 6: *Feedback should be provided to students in a way that enlists and empowers them as participants in the process of better self-knowledge and agents of their own growth.*

This would appear to be a recommendation less easy to meet, or at least less frequently attained. Neither the SEL Rubrics nor the Character Lab Character Growth Card on their face seems to go to any length in engaging students in the work of participating in the process of self-assessment, goal-setting, or progress monitoring, though materials accompanying the SEL rubrics encourage that schools and districts adapt them for this use and purpose. Tessera goes a bit further; its reports are designed to "speak to" students, using the second-person voice and, as noted, it gives more guidance on what improved performance would look like. Accompanying material also informs educators on how the system can be used for student self-understanding, goal-setting, and progress monitoring.

Conclusion

It cannot be ignored that there is no empirical research currently on the role feedback plays in the development of noncognitive skills and that though our model draws on published scholarship for social and emotional skills feedback and formative assessment, the underpinning research is derived from studies on feedback in cognitive skills. It is likely that many guidelines for feedback for cognitive skill development do transfer to noncognitive skill development, particularly since noncognitive skills have a similar pattern of knowledge structure (i.e., declarative knowledge precedes procedural knowledge, which both precede self-regulatory strategies for skill demonstration).

Using the suggested six recommendations to evaluate available systems for noncognitive skills feedback, we can see that some are easier to achieve than others. Providing student-friendly language that focuses on actions and behaviors, not inherent personal qualities, and that responds to multiple actions is something that, for the most part, the systems reviewed accomplish fairly well. Using a developmental model and ensuring students can see the gaps between their performance and the desired standard, and then providing them with steps they can take and involving them as co-constructors of their self-understanding and progress are taller orders for feedback systems of all kinds and are only partially met in these three examples. We invite others to use our recommendations in evaluating other noncognitive assessment systems they may have used or come across in schools.

Future research can and should focus on the role feedback plays specifically in the development of noncognitive skills; studies could consider each of the six suggested recommendations in this chapter and evaluate their effectiveness and impact in comparison to other feedback conditions. Researchers could also aim to validate the claims that recommendations for cognitive feedback can indeed be applied to noncognitive skill development. We invite contributors and readers of this volume alike to consider such studies, as they have great potential for creating maximally effective feedback to foster noncognitive skill development. The more equipped we are with effective teaching practices for the development of noncognitive skills, the greater potential we have to change children's lives for the better.

References

ACT, Inc. (2017). ACT Tessera social and emotional learning assessment: Comprehensive theory of action. Retrieved from: https://pages2.act.org/rs/035-EZR-959/images/Tessera_Theory_of_Action.pdf?aliId=62500134.

Adelman, C. (1999). *Answers in the tool box: Academic intensity, attendance patterns, and bachelor's degree attainment*. Washington, DC: US Department of Education.

Barrick, M. R., Mount, M. K., & Judge, T. A. (2001). Personality and performance at the beginning of the new millennium: What do we know and where do we go next? *International Journal of Selection and Assessment, 9*, 9–30.

Belfield, C., Bowden, A. B., Klapp, A., Levin, H., Shand, R., & Zander, S. (2015). The economic value of social and emotional learning. *Journal of Benefit-Cost Analysis, 6*, 508–544.

Bogg, T., & Roberts, B. W. (2004). Conscientiousness and health behaviors: A meta-analysis. *Psychological Bulletin, 130*, 887–919.

Brackett, M. A., & Rivers, S. E. (2014). Transforming students' lives with social and emotional learning. In R. Pekrun & L. Linnebrink-Gracia (Eds.), *International handbook of emotions in education*. New York: Routledge.

CASEL. (2015). Effective social and emotional learning programs: Middle and high school edition. Collaborative for Academic, Social, and Emotional Learning. Retrieved from: https://casel.org/middle-and-high-school-edition-casel-guide/.

CASEL. (2017). What is SEL? Retrieved from: https://casel.org/what-is-sel/.

Casner-Lotto, J., & Barrington, L. (2006). *Are they really ready to work? Employers' perspectives on the basic knowledge and applied skills of new entrants to the 21st century U.S.* New York: Conference Board. Retrieved from www.conference-board.org/pdf_free/BED-06-Workforce.pdf.

Character Lab. (2017). Character Growth Card. Retrieved from https://cdn.characterlab .org/assets/Character-Growth-Card-cad815b0b3ba79c794bcfd3a89e2a8d5ac30 57963fff02cee539d8d9af1b9777.pdf.

Conley, D. T., & Darling-Hammond, L. (2013). *Creating systems of assessment for deeper learning.* Stanford, CA: Stanford Center for Opportunity Policy in Education.

Corcoran, R. P., Cheung, A., Kim, E., & Chen, X. (2017). Effective universal school-based social and emotional learning programs for improving academic achievement: A systematic review and meta-analysis of 50 years of research. *Educational Research Review.* Retrieved from http://dx.doi.org/10.1016/j.edurev.2017.12.001.

Damian, R. I., Su, R., Shanahan, M., Trautwein, U., & Roberts, B. W. (2014). Can personality traits and intelligence compensate for background disadvantage? Predicting status attainment in adulthood. *Journal of Personality and Social Psychology, 109,* 473–489.

Deary, I. J., Whalley, L. J., & Starr, J. M. (2003). IQ at age 11 and longevity: Results from a follow-up of the Scottish Mental Survey 1932. In C. E. Finch, J.-M. Robine, & Y. Christen (Eds.), *Brain and longevity: Perspectives in longevity* (pp. 153–164). Berlin: Springer.

Diener, E., & Lucas, R. E. (1999). Personality and subjective well-being. In D. Kahneman, E. Diener, & N. Schwarz (Eds.), *Well-being: The foundations of hedonic psychology* (pp. 213–229). New York: Russel Sage Foundation.

Dignath, C., Buettner, G., & Langfeldt, H.-P. (2008). How can primary school students learn self-regulated learning strategies most effectively? A meta-analysis on self-regulation training programs. *Educational Research Review, 3,* 101–129.

Duckworth, A. L., & Yeager, D. S. (2015). Measurement matters: Assessing personal qualities other than cognitive ability for educational purposes. *Educational Researcher, 44,* 237–251.

Dunesbury, L., Weissberg, R. P., Goren, P., & Domitrovich, C. (2014). State standards to advance social and emotional learning: Findings from CASEL's state scan of social and emotional learning standards, preschool through high school, 2014. Collaborative for Academic, Social, and Emotional Learning. Retrieved from www.casel.org/wp-content/uploads/2016/06/casel-brief-on-state-standards-january-2014.pdf.

Durlak, J. A., Weissberg, R. P., Dymnicki, A. B., Taylor, R. D., & Schellinger, K. B. (2011). The impact of enhancing students' social and emotional learning: A meta-analysis of school-based universal intervention. *Child Development, 82,* 405–432.

Durlak. J. A., Weissberg, R. P., & Pachan, M. (2010). A meta-analysis of after-school programs that seek to promote personal and social skills in children and adolescents. *American Journal of Community Psychology, 45,* 294–309.

Dweck, C. S. (2000). *Self-theories: Their role in motivation, personality, and development.* New York: Taylor & Francis.

Eccles, J., & Gootman, J. A. (2002). *Community programs to promote youth development.* Washington, DC: National Research Council and Institute of Medicine. Retrieved from www.nap.edu/download/10022.

Ecclestone, K., & Hayes, D. (2009). Changing the subject: The educational implications of developing emotional wellbeing. *Oxford Review of Education, 35,* 371–389.

Elias, M. J., Ferrito, J. J., & Moceri, D. C. (2016*). The other side of the report card: Assessing students' social, emotional, and character development.* Newbury Park, CA: Corwin Press.

Ge, X., & Conger, R. D. (1999). Adjustment problems and emerging personality characteristics from early to late adolescents. *American Journal of Community Psychology, 27,* 429–459.

Haller, E. P., Child, D. A., & Walberg, H. J. (1988). Can comprehension be taught? A quantitative synthesis of "metacognitive" studies. *Educational Researcher, 17,* 5–8.

Hart Research Associates. (2010). *Raising the bar: Employers' views on college learning in the wake of the economic downturn.* Washington, DC. Retrieved from www.aacu.org/sites/default/files/files/LEAP/2009_EmployerSurvey.pdf.

Hattie, J., & Timperley, H. (2007). The power of feedback. *Review of Educational Research, 77,* 81–112.

Hembree, R. (1988). Correlates, causes, effects, and treatment of test anxiety. *Review of Educational Research, 58,* 7–77.

Hezlett, S., Kuncel, N., Vey, M., Ahart, A., Ones, D., Campbell, J., & Camara, W. (2001). The effectiveness of the SAT in predicting success early and late in college: A comprehensive meta-analysis. Paper presented at the annual meeting of the National Council of Measurement in Education, Seattle, WA.

Hooper, A. C., Cullen, M. J., & Sackett, P. R. (2006). Operational threats to the use of situational judgment tests: Faking, coaching, and retesting issues. In J. Weekley and R. Ployhart (Eds.), *Situational judgment tests* (pp. 205–323). Mahwah, NJ: Lawrence Erlbaum.

James, W. (1981). *The principles of psychology.* Vol. 1. Cambridge, MA: Harvard University Press. (Originally published in 1890.)

Jensen-Campbell, L. A., Adams, R., Perry, D. G., Workman, K. A., Furdella, J. Q., & Egan, S. K. (2002). Agreeableness, extraversion, and peer relationships in early adolescents: Winning friends and deflecting aggression. *Journal of Research in Personality, 36,* 224–251.

John, O. P., & De Fruyt, F. D. (2015). Framework for the Longitudinal Study of Social and Emotional Skills in Cities. Retrieved from www.oecd.org/officialdocuments/publicdisplaydocumentpdf/?cote=EDU/CERI/CD(2015)13&docLanguage=En.

Johnston, P. H. (2012). *Opening minds.* Portland, ME: Stenhouse.

Jones, S. M., Brown, J. L., Hoglund, W. L. G., & Aber, J. L. (2010). A school-randomized clinical trial of an integrated social-emotional learning and literacy intervention: Impacts after 1 school year. *Journal of Consulting and Clinical Psychology, 78,* 829–842.

Judge, T. A., Heller, D., & Mount, M. K. (2002). Five-factor model of personality and job satisfaction: A meta-analysis. *Journal of Applied Psychology, 87,* 530–541.

Kautz, T., Heckman, J. J., Diris, R., ter Weel, B. T., & Borghans, L. (2014). Fostering and measuring skills: Improving noncognitive skills to promote lifetime success. OECD, Educational and Social Progress. Retrieved from www.oecd.org/edu/ceri/Fostering-and-Measuring-Skills-Improving-Cognitive-and-Non-Cognitive-Skills-to-Promote-Lifetime-Success.pdf.

Kelley, T. L. (1927). *The interpretation of educational measurements.* Yonkers-on-Hudson, NY: World Book.

Kluger, A. N., & DeNisi, A. (1996). The effects of feedback interventions on performance: A historical review, a meta-analysis, and a preliminary feedback intervention theory. *Psychological Bulletin, 119*, 254–284.

Kobrin, J. L., Patterson, B. F., Shaw, E. J., Mattern, K. D., & Barbuti, S. M. (2008). *Validity of the SAT® for predicting first-year college grade point average.* College Board Research Rep. No. 2008-5. New York: College Board.

Kyllonen, P. C., Lipnevich, A. A., Burrus, J., & Roberts, R. D. (2014). Personality, motivation, and college readiness: A prospectus for assessment and development. *ETS Research Report Series, 2014*, 1–48.

Lipnevich, A. A., McCallen, L. N., Miles, K. P., & Smith, J. K. (2014). Mind the gap! Students' use of exemplars and detailed rubrics as formative assessment in writing. *Instructional Science, 42*, 539–559.

Lipnevich, A. A., Preckel, F., & Roberts, R. D. (2016). Psychosocial constructs: Knowns, unknowns, and future directions. In A. A. Lipnevich, F. Preckel, and R. D. Roberts (Eds.), *Psychosocial skills and school systems in the 21st century: Theory, research, and practice.* Springer.

Lipnevich, A. A., & Smith, J. K. (2009). Effects of differential feedback on students' examination performance. *Journal of Experimental Psychology: Applied, 15*, 319–333.

Marzano, R. J. (2010). Final topic assessment rubric. Social and emotional learning standards rubric assessment system and the scales, the handbook, and implementation. Unpublished documents prepared for the Collaborative for Academic, Social, and Emotional Learning (CASEL).

Marzano, R. J. (2015). Using formative assessment with SEL skills. In J. A. Durlak, C. E. Domitrovich, R. P. Weissberg, & T. P. Gullotta (Eds.), *Handbook of social and emotional learning: Research and practice* (pp. 336–347). New York: Guilford.

Mattern, K. D., & Patterson, B. F. (2011).*The validity of the SAT for predicting fourth-year grades: 2006 SAT validity sample.* College Board Statistical Report 2011-7. New York: College Board.

Miller, G. A. (1956). The magical number seven, plus or minus two: Some limits on our capacity for processing information. *Psychological Review, 63*, 81–97.

National Research Council. (2012). *Education for life and work: Developing transferable knowledge and skills in the 21st century.* Report by the Committee on Defining Deeper Learning and 21st Century Skills. Washington, DC: National Academies Press.

Payton, J., Weissberg, R. P., Durlak, J. A., Dymnicki, A. B., Taylor, R. D., Schellinger, K. B., & Pachan, M. (2008). *The positive impact of social and emotional learning for kindergarten to eighth-grade students: Findings from three scientific reviews.* Chicago, IL: Collaborative for Academic, Social, and Emotional

Learning. Retrieved from www.casel.org/wp-content/uploads/2016/08/PDF-4-the-positive-impact-of-social-and-emotional-learning-for-kindergarten-to-eighth-grade-students-executive-summary.pdf.

Poropat, A. E. (2009). A meta-analysis of the five factor model of personality and academic performance. *Psychological Bulletin, 135*, 322–338.

Primi, R., Santos, D., John, O. P., & De Fruyt, F. (2016). Development of an inventory assessing social and emotional skills in Brazilian youth. *European Journal of Psychological Assessment, 32*, 5–16.

Robbins, S. B., Allen, J., Casillas, A., Peterson, C. H., & Le, H. (2006). Unraveling the differential effects of motivational and skills, social, and self-management measures from traditional predictors of college outcomes. *Journal of Educational Psychology, 98*(3), 598–616.

Robbins, S. B., Lauver, K., Le, H., Davis, D., Langley, R., & Carlstrom, A. (2004). Do psychosocial and study skill factors predict college outcomes? A meta-analysis. *Psychological Bulletin, 130*, 261–288.

Robbins, S. B., Oh, I., Lee, H., & Buton, C. (2009). Intervention effects on college performance and retention as mediated by motivational, emotional, and social control factors: Integrated meta-analytic path analyses. *Journal of Applied Psychology, 94*, 1163–1184.

Roberts, B. W., Kuncel, N. R, Shiner, R., Caspi, A., & Goldberg, L. R. (2007). The power of personality: The comparative validity of personality traits, socio-economic status, and cognitive ability for predicting important life outcomes. *Perspectives on Psychological Science, 2*, 313–345.

Roberts, B. W., Walton, K., & Viechtbauer, W. (2006). Patterns of mean-level change in personality traits across the life course: A meta-analysis of longitudinal studies. *Psychological Bulletin, 132*, 1–25.

Roberts, R. D., Martin, J. E., & Olaru, G. (2015). A Rosetta stone for noncognitive skills: Understanding, assessing, and enhancing noncognitive skills in primary and secondary education. Asia Society and Professional Examination Service. Retrieved from: https://pages2.act.org/rosetta-stone-for-noncognitive-skills.html.

Schmidt, F., & Hunter, J. (1998). The validity and utility of selection methods in personnel psychology: Practical and theoretical implications of 85 years of research findings. *Psychological Bulletin, 124*, 262–274.

Schonfeld, D. J., Adams, R. E., Fredstrom, B. K., Weissberg, R. P., Gilman, R., Voyce, C., Tomlin, R., & Speese-Linehan, D. (2015). Cluster-randomized trial demonstrating impact on academic achievement of elementary social emotional learning. *School Psychology Quarterly, 30*, 406–420.

Schunk, D. H. (2008). Cognition and instruction. In *Learning theories: An educational perspective* (pp. 278–323). Upper Saddle River, NJ: Pearson.

Schunk, D. H. (2012). *Learning theories: An educational perspective* (6th edn.). Boston: Pearson.

Shute, V. J. (2008). Focus on formative feedback. *Review of Educational Research, 78*, 153–189.

Stark, S., Chernyshenko, O. S., & Drasgow, F. (2005). An IRT approach to constructing and scoring pairwise preference items involving stimuli on different dimensions: An application to the problem of faking in personality assessment. *Applied Psychological Measurement, 29*, 184–201.

Stemler, S. E. (2012). What should university admissions tests predict? *Educational Psychologist, 47*, 5–17.

Sweller, J. (1994). Cognitive load theory, learning difficulty, and instructional design. *Learning and Instruction, 4*, 295–312.

Taylor, R. D., Oberle, E., Durlak, R. A., & Weissberg, R. P. (2017). Promoting positive youth development through school-based social and emotional learning interventions: A meta-analysis of follow-up effects. *Child Development, 88*, 1156–1171.

Walton, K. E., & Billera, K. A. (2016). Personality development during the school-aged years: Implications for theory, research, and practice. In A. A. Lipnevich, F. Preckel, & R. D. Roberts (Eds.), *Psychosocial skills and school systems in the 21st century: Theory, research, and practice*. Switzerland: Springer.

Willingham, D. T. (2009). *Why don't students like school? A cognitive scientist answers questions about how the mind works and what it means for the classroom*. San Francisco, CA: Jossey-Bass.

Ziegler, M., MacCann, C., & Roberts, R. D. (Eds.) (2011). *New perspectives on faking in personality assessment*. New York: Oxford University Press.

Zins, J., Weissberg, R. P., Wang, M. C., & Walberg, H. J. (2004). *Building academic success on social and emotional learning: What does research say?* New York: Teachers College, Columbia University.

12 Feedback in Tertiary Education

Challenges and Opportunities for Enhancing Current Practices

Jacques van der Meer and Phillip Dawson

Introduction

Feedback is one of the most powerful influencers of student learning in higher education. However, university students in Australia and the United Kingdom have been more dissatisfied with assessment and feedback than any other aspect of their studies for more than a decade (Carroll, 2014; Higher Education Funding Council for England, 2014).

Some of the largest meta-analyses in education have focused on feedback, and as a result we have very strong evidence that feedback underpins learning in schools and higher education (Hattie & Timperley, 2007; Hattie, 2009a, 2009b). Furthermore, meta-analyses of the variables most likely to influence student achievement found that feedback is the "active ingredient" behind most of the top ten to twenty correlates with student achievement (Hattie, 2009b).

However, feedback has different meanings to different tertiary teachers and researchers. Popular use of the term (e.g., "I left feedback on their final essay which they never collected") does not always align with its usage by feedback researchers (Sadler, 2010; Carless, Salter, Yang, & Lam, 2011; Boud & Molloy, 2013). In current definitions of feedback, comments on student work are not feedback unless they lead to change in the learner (Boud & Molloy, 2013). In these definitions, feedback is not "given to" or "done to" the learner; instead, it is a participatory process.

Inconsistent understandings of feedback in tertiary education have a negative effect on research and practice (Adcroft, 2011; Evans, 2013). For example, the mismatch between how much feedback higher education teachers think they "give" and how much students think they "receive" leads to dissatisfaction on both sides (Orrell, 2006; Adcroft, 2011). National surveys in the United Kingdom and Australia tell us that student dissatisfaction with higher education feedback stretches back at least a decade (Carroll, 2014; Higher Education Funding Council for England, 2014). However, these surveys are still rooted in a discourse of asking students if they receive sufficient comments from their teachers. The conceptual legacy of old understandings of feedback seems almost as powerful as feedback itself. A recent review of thirty-seven studies found that university students want feedback that is objective, personal, timely, explicable, criterion-referenced, and actionable for future improvement (Li & De Luca, 2014). The same review found that the student experience of feedback often does not meet these aspirations.

Alongside tertiary student demands for improvements to feedback, new models of effective feedback are emerging. Feedback "Mark 2" (Boud & Molloy, 2013) sees students as key players in the feedback process, who are engaged in a series of activities to improve the quality of their work. Sustainable feedback (Carless et al., 2011) privileges learning for the long term and uses feedback to develop student self-regulation. Peer feedback models (Nicol, Thomson, & Breslin, 2014) emphasize that students learn much from active engagement with each other in reviewing their peers' work. Tertiary education thus has a specific body of evidence and theory to guide educators in improving feedback in this context.

Focus of This Chapter

This chapter is focused on the questions of what the particular purposes and the specific challenges and opportunities of feedback processes are in tertiary education. We will argue that effective feedback processes that go beyond the notion of a corrective purpose could contribute to students' developing dispositions, perspectives, and skills for life beyond academia.

In considering the challenges and opportunities, we will use a systems view to reveal complex interconnections at the various levels, "micro, meso, and macro." In discussing the challenges, we will explicitly move away from a discourse of "blaming" students for not understanding assessment expectations or not using feedback. Instead, we focus on the responsibility of academic staff to explicitly communicate expectations and to purposefully engage and involve students in feedback processes. We will be drawing in particular on a more dialogical participatory focus of feedback that is aimed at developing students as self-regulating learners (see, e.g., Hattie & Timperley, 2007; Boud & Molloy, 2013).

We will finish the chapter with a possible agenda for change in practices and for future research into feedback processes in tertiary education.

We do not claim to cover the complexity of feedback process across the whole tertiary education sector. The tertiary education sector comprises a wide range of educational institutions, both institutions of "higher" education, such as universities, and institutions of "further" education. As the diversity in the latter category worldwide is so vast, comprising both degree-granting and subdegree courses, it would be difficult to write a general chapter on feedback in tertiary education that does justice to this diversity. Hence, this chapter focuses mainly on the higher education sector. Even though there is a considerable diversity within this sector as well, there is more accepted commonality as evidenced by the general mutual recognition of degree structures and awards granted at institutions of higher education across the world.

We admit that the majority of feedback research we are familiar with has been published in English from a limited range of contexts: North America, the United Kingdom, Australia, New Zealand, and Hong Kong. We acknowledge the need to study feedback cultures beyond these contexts as they may have much to teach us.

The Purpose of Feedback in Higher Education

Whereas some of the purposes of student feedback in the tertiary sector are similar to those in other sectors (such as the importance of communicating to students how they are doing and what they are to do next with regard to the work they are producing), there are also roles and purposes of feedback in higher education that are distinctly different from those in other sectors.

First, especially as students transition into the first year of tertiary education, feedback can help students to understand their progress and their acculturation to a new education environment and their grasp of disciplinary differences and requirements (Lea & Street, 2006; Blair, 2017). Interpretation of course and assessment requirements may be a challenge for students at any level of education. However, in tertiary education, as students often take courses/units of study in different disciplines and/or coordinated by different academic staff, expectations and formats in which assessment requirements are communicated may vary considerably.

We argue that effective feedback processes in tertiary education can also contribute significantly to outcomes beyond those directly related to students' academic work. There is a worldwide interest in the function of tertiary education with regard to preparing students for life beyond the walls of academia. The outcomes of this preparation are variously referred to as "graduate outcomes," "graduate attributes," "employability skills," or variations thereof (Harvey, 2000; Barrie, 2006, 2007; Cassidy, 2006). Furthermore, we argue that effective feedback processes that go beyond this notion of a corrective purpose could also contribute to students developing dispositions and perspectives that may result in a "better world," with more graduates with a greater tolerance for diversity and respect for difference.

However, feedback processes do not always figure prominently as one of the "vehicles" that can contribute to graduate outcomes. This, we argue, is because of a restricted understanding of what feedback is, and how feedback processes can be more than simply corrective comments on students' work. The purpose of feedback in higher education is related not just to a one-off event related to a particular assignment but also to life beyond the institution once students have graduated. This is not just in the context of professional courses where students may have to maintain portfolios but also in the context of particular aimed-for graduate outcomes as espoused by many institutions, such as students as self-regulated independent lifelong learners. Self-regulation in this context includes students being able to self-assess and self-correct as well as being able to act on feedback from others (Nicol, 2006; Nicol & Macfarlane-Dick, 2006; Hattie & Timperley, 2007; Boud & Molloy, 2013; Evans, 2013). A specific aspect of this is students' ability to make decisions about the quality of their work and the work of others, which is referred to as evaluative judgment (Tai, Canny, Haines, & Molloy, 2016). Approaches like Boud and Molloy's (2013) "Feedback Mark 2" seek to develop evaluative judgment through students being oriented to criteria and standards for their discipline, students engaging in feedback conversations with their peers about the work they have produced, and focusing feedback conversations with staff around the differences in understandings of quality in the work the student has produced.

Other graduate outcomes can also be considered in this context. Most universities, for example, articulate the importance of students' skills of communication and collaboration and the value of diversity and global connectedness. They seek to develop these through curricular and extracurricular activities (Lehtomäki, Moate, & Posti-Ahokas, 2016). Development of these graduate outcomes could also be facilitated through feedback processes. This could be the case where the feedback process is considered not just a unidirectional action of a single lecturer in providing information on a piece of assessment but a complex set of processes that involve engagement/dialogue with multiple sources of information, especially through involvement of peers (Nicol & Macfarlane-Dick, 2006; Boud & Molloy, 2013; Carless, 2013, 2017; Evans, 2013; Nicol, Thomson, & Breslin, 2014)

A Systems View of Feedback in Higher Education

In order to better understand what the particular challenges are, where the challenges are, and to identify opportunities for enhancing practices, we need to have a better understanding of the typical processes of feedback in the higher education context. These processes, however, cannot be considered in isolation, but need to be considered in the broader institutional context in which academic staff develop and teach their courses.

Assessment and feedback at universities can be considered through multiple perspectives. Macdonald and Joughin (2009) advocated a systems perspective, noting:

> Well-founded statements of assessment principles fail to work their way down from the committees which draft them; individual lecturers' innovative assessment practices take hold within their immediate sphere of influence without infiltrating a whole programme.   (p. 193)

By viewing assessment through a variety of levels, they reveal complex interconnections. In this section we explore systems of feedback, adopting the "micro, meso, and macro" levels used by Boud and colleagues' recent work on assessment practices (Boud et al., 2016).

Macro Level

Educators and students engage in feedback in a context that is typically resourced, regulated, and standardized by forces outside their control. Most notable among these is the influence of institutional policy – or the lack of such an influence. Orrell's (2006) study of students and higher education teachers focused on the thinking and beliefs they had around feedback. Her educator participants made no reference to institutional policy around feedback. However, in a later study of assessment and feedback, educators discussed policy as somewhat of a constraint on their assessment design work (Bearman et al., 2016). In particular, the often bureaucratic and arduous processes required to make changes to assessment designs inhibited some educators from implementing significant changes to their assessment and feedback practices.

Academic workloads have a very significant influence on the feedback practices enacted by staff and students. For example, in a typical Australian university, the time provided for marking and feedback is usually around one hour per student per course unit. In New Zealand this varies considerably between universities. Orrell (2006) wrote about formative feedback as being seen as an unpaid "add-on" to such responsibilities. This may lead to academics consciously conducting their feedback design work to minimize time required while simultaneously attempting to maximize learning; this is a challenging task (Bearman et al., 2016). Although individual academics may find clever ways to achieve this balance, on a whole the macro concern of workload management may trump many otherwise evidence-based efforts to improve feedback. Higher education academics have to satisfy multiple demands other than teaching. In many jurisdictions, academics are rewarded more for their research output than for their teaching achievements. Hence, time available for extensive feedback processes may be reduced (Bearman et al., 2016).

When issues of workload come up, often class sizes in higher education are considered a major challenge and a distinct difference compared with education at the elementary and secondary levels. Whereas class sizes at the latter levels typically do not exceed forty (at most), in higher education class sizes have increased considerably over the last few decades. With the expansion of higher education, or "massification" (Scott, 1995; Evans, 2013), class sizes in some cases exceed 2,000. Evans (2013) argued that issues related to the quality of feedback need to be considered against the backdrop of massification of higher education and an increased conception of students as consumers.

Although it could be argued that staffing will typically be adjusted to class size, small group teaching (e.g., tutorials, sections, workshops, etc.), especially at the lower undergraduate levels, is often carried out by teaching assistants, graduate students, or part-time staff who may be less well versed in educational practices around providing feedback. Academic work is increasingly becoming unbundled (Macfarlane, 2011), and the work of feedback is no longer primarily conducted by 'all-rounder' academics.

Unlike the elementary and secondary sectors, not all institutions of higher education require staff to have formal teaching qualifications. Although there has been an increase in staff development opportunities and focus on enhancing teaching practices in higher education (even making these opportunities a requirement in some cases), feedback processes may not necessarily receive prominent attention. Even those academic staff with formal education qualifications and sophisticated understandings of feedback may not necessarily be implementing them. There is evidence of a dissonance between teachers' espoused theories of feedback and their everyday practice (Orrell, 2006). In assessment more broadly, it has been found that changing teacher 'thinking' about assessment does not necessarily lead to changed assessment practice (Offerdahl & Tomanek, 2011). Given all of this complexity, higher education teachers may tend to focus on local contextual issues, rather than accessing higher-level notions of theory (Eley, 2006).

The system of higher education feedback interacts with other educational systems in ways that may not be optimal. It has been well documented that especially first-year students experience a considerable challenge in understanding what is expected of them (Lea & Street, 1998, 2000; van der Meer, 2006). They are typically not familiar with assessment practices in higher education and may not always be able to 'tune in' to disciplinary differential expectations. These challenges of students in transition are not always recognized by staff that teach in first-year courses. It could be argued that this makes feedback even more important (van der Meer, 2006, 2012). Feedback practices in higher education suggest that academics may expect more independence of the learner than the more structured processes in the schools sector. In response, interventions have been developed specifically to improve transitioning students' skill with using feedback as part of their development toward becoming self-regulated learners (see, e.g., Carless, 2013). Micro-level attempts to improve feedback are likely limited or enabled by the broader macro-level policies and support structures that recognize the particular transition challenges.

Meso Level

The meso-level matters we find most influential are those related to the overarching design of programs of study, their individual course units, and the degree to which technology is used.

Where course units are designed in an overly modular fashion, as a set of independent packages without connection, feedback is less likely to occur. This is because students have less opportunity to demonstrate what they are capable of within a domain, get helpful information from teachers or peers, and then demonstrate improvement. At a bare minimum, course units need to be designed to integrate connections between tasks and require action on feedback information (Boud & Molloy, 2013). The effectiveness of innovations like improvements to feedback comments will be limited if they are not undertaken as part of coherent meso-level designs.

Feedback systems exist within the context of a program of study, such as a degree or diploma structure. Well-designed programs of study can support programmatic feedback as part of programmatic approaches to assessment. Such approaches aim to build student capability in degree-level outcomes through feedback that spans multiple course units. Rather than being told the same corrective information multiple times in isolation, markers are made aware of how students have performed in previous units and the feedback comments they have received before. Students are directed toward relevant sources of prior feedback. When receiving traditionally 'summative' comments at the end of a course unit, students are instead required to reflect on the utility of this feedback for work in future course units. Such approaches require complex logistical planning in mapping out the connections between tasks across units and year levels, which may be assisted by technology. However, the payoff for this meso-level work is intended to be increased feedback utilization and subsequent improvements to learning. A focus on ongoing programmatic feedback is often a feature of portfolios or e-portfolios. Students enrolled in some professional courses (in some countries), for example, in the health sciences and teaching, are often required to maintain a portfolio in which they demonstrate their acquired competencies and learning. This demand offers some particular opportunities for use of feedback processes (Naumann, Yang, Thai, Ford, & Polly, 2016; Roberts, Maor, & Herrington, 2016).

Decisions to use technology in the design of programs of studies could have considerable influence on feedback practices. In many countries, higher education is increasingly conducted online, in a mix of blended courses, wholly online courses, and massive open online courses (MOOCs). Many institutions offer whole degrees by distance education, with no opportunities for in-person feedback conversations; however, new approaches to rich media feedback may mitigate this loss of social presence (see, e.g., Henderson & Phillips, 2015). While online learning offers many opportunities for improved learning (Means, Toyama, Murphy, Bakia, & Jones, 2009) it also poses problems for higher education staff. A recent qualitative study in the United Kingdom found even the relatively mundane switch to online assignment submission resulted in unintended consequences: double-handling of student assignments (printing out assignments, hand-writing comments on them, typing those comments), slower marking, resistance to the change, and technical skill difficulties (Tomas, Borg, & McNeil, 2015). There is a complex relationship between technological affordances and the feedback designs ultimately implemented by educators (Bennett, Dawson, Bearman, Molloy, & Boud, 2016).

Technology, however, has shown that some higher education feedback practices are able to be scaled up in a nonlinear fashion. The success of some MOOC feedback approaches, such as peer feedback and multiple-choice questions, and their clever integration into sophisticated feedback designs, indicates that it is possible to provide feedback for tens of thousands of students without significantly more resources than for a few hundred (Dawson & Henderson, 2017).

A decentralized approach and the relative autonomy of faculty to design their own courses and make decisions about use of technology may be considered a challenge for academic staff developers who consider that feedback processes in academic departments could be improved. Faculty claims to "academic freedom" are sometimes advanced to deter discussions about improvements in their area of teaching and learning. In other words, the tension between autonomy and accountability in higher education (Berdahl, 1990; Alexander, 2000) can be a complicating factor that is not present to the same degree in other education sectors.

Micro Level

At the micro level, we consider the actual practices and processes involved in making sense of expectations, providing and receiving feedback, and ultimately students interpreting feedback.

Particularly at the micro level, fundamental differences come to the fore with regard to views of academic staff about what they should be expected to do and where the responsibility lies for students' performance on assessment. This has a major influence on the feedback process related to assessment tasks. Also at this level, differences arise with regard to the purpose and aim of feedback in higher education. These too influence decisions on feedback processes.

It would be difficult to propose changes in the feedback processes at this level without a comprehensive understanding about the challenges and opportunities. We argue that there are three main processes that need to be considered, related to (1) making sense of and interpreting assessment expectations/specifications, (2) the actual process of generating feedback, and (3) the receiving and interpretation of feedback. See Figure 12.1 for a diagrammatic overview of these processes.

Feedback too often functions as retrospective clarification of expectations. Closing the gap between lecturers' interpretation of assessment requirements and students' interpretation is an important step in the feedback process. However, we argue that this needs to occur before lecturers start the marking process. Ideally, no effort and time should have to be spent on this retrospective clarification of expectations if the assessment and feedback design decisions include steps for this to occur as an integral and productive step in students' engagement with assessment tasks.

First-year students face particular challenges in understanding what is expected of them. This is especially the case in the area of academic writing (Cartwright, Ryan, Hacker, Powell, & Reidy, 2000; Ecclestone, 2001; Elwood & Klenowski, 2002; Chanock, 2004; O'Donovan, Price, & Rust, 2004; Lea & Street, 2006; O'Donovan, Rust, & Price, 2016). There are often vastly divergent views on what should be expected of students and what teaching at the first-year level should be about when it comes to particular skills, such as writing (Craigie, 1998).

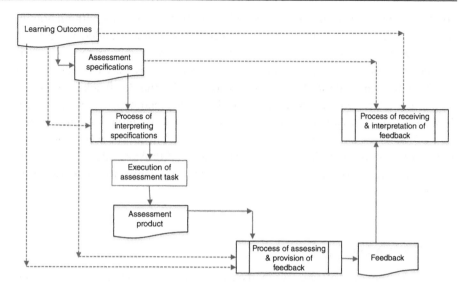

Figure 12.1 *The process of interpreting assessment specifications.*

The debate relating to this area of contestation provides a good insight into the challenges related to effective feedback practices. The social practice perspective (Lea & Street, 1998, 2000; Gee, 2000; Lea & Stierer, 2000; Lillis & Turner, 2001; Lankshear & Knobel, 2003) is particularly pertinent in this context. Lea and Street (1998) contended:

> Viewing literacy from a cultural and social practice approach (rather than in terms of educational judgements about good and bad writing) and approaching meanings as contested can give us insights into the nature of academic literacy in particular and academic learning in general.   (p. 158)

Essential to the social practice perspective is that students learn literacy skills in the context of particular academic disciplinary communities. Proponents of this perspective argue that academic skills need to be learned within the ongoing negotiation of what counts as acceptable practice in these communities (Lea & Street, 1998).

In this context, the notion of "academic literacies" was developed (Ivanic, 1998; Lea & Street, 1998, 2000; Pardoe, 2000b; Lillis & Turner, 2001; Lillis, 2003). In the academic literacies perspective, the experiences of students and staff are viewed as inextricably related to the wider context of developments in higher education. Lea and Street (1998, 2006) considered it important that the literacy practices of both staff and students are investigated. This, they said, is important if we want to understand how anyone becomes academically literate. In their seminal 1998 article, Lea and Street formulated the notion of academic literacies and distinguished three models. The first model, the "skills model," is the "fix it" model, where academic literacy is considered as comprising different atomistic skill elements and students as having deficits that need to be addressed. They pointed out that, although these skills are important, they are just one aspect of academic writing. Lea (1994) argued that language structure and form is the traditional category that staff and students refer to when concerns about student writing are discussed. Feedback on students' writing, she said, often focuses on this level.

The second model is the "academic socialization model," which recognizes that students have to be acculturated into a new culture. An example of framing students' problems within the academic socialization model can be seen in Graff (2003). Graff argued that he views his role as teacher essentially as one where he helps students to enter the academic "club" by helping students to understand what the rules of this club are. Graff, however, seemed to assume, somehow paradoxically, that there is one club, albeit one that needs to be held together through command of a meta-language or meta-discourse that can help to make sense of the diversity of arguments and discourse styles. He recognized that many first-year students spend their entire first year figuring out what the different teachers want from them. As an English scholar, Graff considered that his contribution could be in providing first-year students in his composition classes with a meta-language that could help students with making sense of other subjects. Although his book *Clueless in Academe* (Graff, 2003) has much to contribute and is to be recommended, we would argue that the assumption that it is "just" about the command of argument literacy, about a language that can be used across a range of disparate subjects, does not sufficiently recognize diversity among disciplines. It assumes that students can be taught discourse styles that they can hold more or less constant, irrespective of the course for which they are producing work. Students, however, are still faced with differential requirements across different courses.

Lea and Street's third model, the "academic literacies model," recognizes that both skills development and acculturation are important. However, it rejects the notion of a homogeneous culture; they pointed at various contested heterogeneous discourse communities with varying practices, conventions, and communicative repertoires. They considered student learning and writing as having to do with the process of meaning-making and contestations around that, rather than just a skill to be learned. The degree to which teachers consider disciplinary conventions within their own discipline as "normal," then, could affect students' understanding of disciplinary expectations.

For first-year students, then, making sense of expectations across various disciplines is a major challenge. Clerehan and Walker's (2003) study into students' perceptions of their preparedness for university writing refers to students having to "decode the guidelines." They found that students had trouble decoding the assessment requirements, such as fully understanding the question, guidelines, presentation requirements, and how much detail was required. Students in their study also had difficulty starting to write without an example and did not always understand the required focus of the work and the meaning of key instruction words, such as "recommend," "describe," and "analyze."

Various studies point at the seemingly "taken for granted" attitude by academic staff toward expectations. Some writers refer to students being expected to acquire an understanding of university expectations and requirements by "osmosis" (Skillen, Merten, Trivett, & Percy, 1998; Levin, 2000; Francis, 2005). One of the students in the study by van der Meer (2006) referred to "mind-reading." Metaphors of a similar kind also came through in other literature. Read, Francis, and Robson (2001), in reporting on a study with undergraduate students, referred to students trying to "crack the code" and "scrambling in the dark." By this they mean that expectations are seldom made explicit and that students have to find out about "the rules of the game" (Norton, 2004) in different ways. One of the academics who was interviewed by Gair and Mullins (2001) remarked: "When you are trying to belong to ... [a] club ... there are rules and it takes you a while to learn the rules" (2001, p. 35) Their interviewee saw this as a description of the "hidden curriculum," a set of rules that are not made obvious.

Tacit and Explicit Knowledge

Feedback on assessed work appears to be one of the ways in which students sometimes find out what they were supposed to have done. The students that Sambell and McDowell (1998) interviewed commented regularly on feedback from tutors as a way of "discovering" what would satisfy tutors and what they expected. However, students' lack of clear understanding of requirements does not imply that teachers deliberately obfuscate expectations related to assignments. One of the key issues is that of "tacit" knowledge. Tacit knowledge can be defined as knowledge that one has but that is not necessarily recognized as knowledge by those who possess it, and that therefore is not explicitly communicated. This tacit knowledge may have become an integral part of how academics "think and breathe." This may be something that is so obvious to them (Pardoe, 2000a) that it does not occur to them that it is a learned way of "thinking and breathing." They may be so immersed in the conventions and requirements of their own discipline that they cannot see that they too at one stage had to learn these conventions and requirements. It could be argued, then, that it is 'normal' that students do not understand straight away what is expected of them; learning a new language takes time. It is also 'normal,' then, that teachers sometimes have difficulty explicating their expectations.

Tacit knowledge is problematic not only in communicating assessment expectations but also in the area of assessment feedback (see, e.g., Boud, 1995; Ecclestone, 2001; Norton, 2004; Sadler, 2005). Expert, tacit knowledge is often used intuitively (Ecclestone, 2001; Greatorex, 2003). Ecclestone (2001), in discussing the intuitive way by which academics arrive at judgments about assessed work, emphasized that the claim by academics that they "know a 2-1 [a UK term for a particular grade] when I see it" (2001, p. 305), is not to be taken as a deliberate effort to obfuscate. Experts, she argued, do become more intuitive and less able to articulate the tacit knowledge on which their marking depends. Lea and Street (1998) found that staff recognized what good work looked like but that they were unable to describe what a well-developed argument looked like (see, e.g., Ecclestone, 2001; O'Donovan et al., 2004). Although expertise is important and necessary, a lack of awareness is problematic if it leads to ignoring students' needs for greater clarity.

On the other hand, there may be an issue of a lack of tacit knowledge. Ecclestone (2001) suggested that changes in higher education may have contributed to teachers not always having an "intuitive" understanding of marking standards. These changes included increased numbers of students and staff, changes in course and curricular structures, and a blurring of disciplinary boundaries and involvement of multiple departments in courses. She argued that these have changed the environment in which course organization, marking, and providing feedback occurs. She further argued that whereas once there may have been a close-knit academic community where professional judgment was taken for granted, this assumption could now be challenged. Teachers, then, are not necessarily clear among each other about assessment standards. This inevitably would make it more difficult to communicate these clearly to students.

Possible Approaches to Communicating Expectations

Teachers have a responsibility for creating an environment and processes in which students have a fair chance of understanding assessment requirements and standards as teachers intend students to understand them. Various approaches can be used to close gaps in understanding. The authors of this chapter, for example, have used class exercises whereby teachers engage students in discussion about assessment requirements. These exercises typically entail a process of individual meaning-making, followed by students in groups discussing their understanding, and sharing group understanding with the whole class.

The use of exemplars is an approach favored by some higher education teachers to address the issue of clarifying assessment requirements and engaging students in feedback dialogues about work (Yang & Carless, 2013; Carless & Chan, 2016). Exemplars can provide students with models to emulate or orient themselves toward. Exemplars can be described as artifacts that highlight the salient features required of particular assessment pieces, often annotated by means of written or verbal commentary. "Exemplars are key examples of products or processes chosen so as to be typical of designated levels of quality or competence" (Sadler, 2005, p. 192). Exemplars, however, can also consist of verbal exemplification of processes such as group work (James, Skillen, Percy, Tootell, & Irvine, 2003) and are not just artifacts. Read et al. (2001) used the concept of "communities of practice" to point at the importance of transfer of knowledge from tacit knowledge, or implicit knowledge, to explicit knowledge. Furthermore, exemplars could play a role in socialization of both students and staff (Ecclestone, 2001; Sadler, 2005). Sadler (2005) argued for the convenience of using exemplars because they "are more concrete than abstract, they are specially convenient for direct 'viewing' by academic colleagues and students" (p. 192).

Marking schedules can also play a role in communicating assessment expectations, both before assessment exercises and in providing feedback afterward. Marking schedules can be understood as a generic term referring to a list of assessment criteria with accompanying grade descriptors. However, the use of marking schedules has also been contested. Biggs (2003), for example, suggested that the use of some marking schedules may result in atomistic or fragmented marking, adding up disjointed aspects of the work rather than judging whether a piece of assessment as a whole demonstrates achievement of particular learning objectives. In this context, Biggs (2003) distinguished between quantitative and qualitative views of learning. However, the helpfulness of marking schedules is that they can contribute something to students' need for clarity and can signal expectations. Rubrics are a particular type of marking schedule, typically represented as a set of quality indicators expected for particular criteria at particular levels (Popham, 1997). However, there is considerable variation in rubric use, ranging from secret scoring sheets never seen by students to holistic articulations of quality used for formative purposes to rubrics that are co-created with students (Dawson, 2015). The utility of different types of rubrics for feedback thus varies greatly.

Some higher education researchers, however, have pointed at possible disadvantages of explicit communication of criteria. Norton (2004), for example, argued that being too explicit may cause students to become overly mechanistic and concentrate on satisfying specific assessment requirements rather than engaging more with the learning process; similar arguments have also been put forward by others (Torrance, 2007). Some students in the study by Bloxham and West (2004) on peer assessment reported similar sentiments from their perspectives. Some participants felt that making criteria too specific stopped them from thinking. Norton's solution, however, was to reconceptualize assessment criteria as learning criteria. It is difficult to judge from the description of a case study that this substantially changed her approach to explicit communication. She also made suggestions about how to stimulate students' engagement in their learning through closely aligning assessment tasks and learning criteria. The instructions to her students provided them with a clear understanding of what was expected of them. What her article highlights is that making the language about criteria less prescriptive does not have to result in less clarity for students. What her article also highlights, however, are the confusing semantics and technicalities around communicating expectations to students.

We argue that recognizing the difficulty of communicating expectations is a first step to clarifying expectations to students. What we mean by this is that it is normal that students who come into new environments or communities are unfamiliar with the ways of thinking, doing, and writing in these environments. It is equally normal that those who have been in these communities for some time are so familiar with how to read, write, and argue in these communities that this may have become "second nature," taken for granted, "tacit," difficult to explain. Recognition of this, we argue, is therefore important. Academics need to regularly engage in a process of "defamiliarization" (O'Regan, 2005), in other words, to remind themselves of the normality of first-year students' challenges and the role that they as teachers play in the familiarization process. Also, intentional engagement with colleagues who work in other disciplines or contexts could be helpful (James et al., 2003; Chanock, 2007). Discussion of what "good" academic writing or "good" arguments mean may bring to the fore the divergent and even contested nature of what we often take for granted. O'Regan (2000) gives an interesting example of this with regard to divergent understandings of a literature review. Not everyone, she says, has the same understanding of how this should be approached.

Engaging Students in Dialogue

Intentionally initiating a dialogue among students about their understanding of expectations can be an effective practice. A study by Krause (2001) focused particularly on the first essay that first-year students have to write in their university career. Apart from a need for clear expectations and clear instructions, her students wanted examples and time during tutorials to discuss assignments. Lea (2004), in discussing using an academic literacies approach for course design, argues that some of the significant features of this approach specifically recognize the gaps between students' and tutors' understandings. She advocates creating space to explore these differences. In exploring differences in understanding, we contend, not only do students benefit but also teachers. It will not only highlight and make more transparent the complexities of academic assignments for both parties but also help teachers to identify students' possible needs for further explication of particular features of an assignment.

Active engagement of students in discussing assessment requirements can also highlight the problematic and contested nature of assessment. This may encourage students in questioning their own and others' literacy conventions and approaches, and thereby more clearly recognize, for example, how writing is approached in a particular discipline, and even perhaps the contested nature of writing within their discipline (Loads, 2005; Lea & Street, 2006). It also may emphasize to first-year students that writing is different across disciplines and that adopting academic "appropriate" writing in these different disciplines is a learned skill. Such dialogue can be conducted with students' own work or with exemplars (Carless & Chan, 2016).

Engaging first-year students in dialogue with other students through peer assessment can also help them to gain an understanding of expectations and the discourse of academia (Bloxham & West, 2004; Liu & Carless, 2006; Nicol et al., 2014). Topping (1998) defined peer assessment as "an arrangement in which individuals consider the amount, level, value, worth, quality, or success of the products or outcomes of learning of peers of similar status" (p. 250). Elwood and Klenowski (2002) advocated for creating communities of shared understanding or shared practice. They recommended that this can be achieved through explicating both criteria and standards, discussing with students what their understanding of these criteria and standards are, working with past examples, getting students to assess their own and other's work, and providing students with feedback that clearly explains what students have to do to reach the next stage. Bloxham and West (2004) found in their research that most students were able to apply the assessment schedule within a suitable range of accuracy. Liu and Carless (2006), after conducting a study in Hong Kong on staff and student attitudes toward peer assessment, described peer feedback as the "learning element" of peer assessment. Ballantyne, Hughes, and Mylonas (2002), in summarizing the benefits of peer assessment for student learning, pointed out that it encourages students to engage with the purpose and objectives of assessments, as well as the standards and requirements. In other words, it takes the mystery out of the assessment process. They pointed out that the benefit of peer assessment with first-year students is that they have fewer preconceived ideas of peer assessment and therefore are likely to be more open. They emphasized, however, that the process needs to be structured very carefully. A more in-depth discussion of the mechanisms and issues around peer feedback are discussed elsewhere in this book.

Process of Assessing and Providing Feedback

The next step at the micro level is generation of feedback. This feedback could be formative and/or summative, provided by teaching staff and/or peers. With regard to the focus of feedback, Hattie and Timperley (2007) argued that three main questions need to guide provision of feedback to students: "Where am I going?," "How am I doing?," and "Where to from here?" They referred to the importance of ensuring that feedback closely relates to the goals of feedback. They also identified four different levels at which feedback can be provided, related to (1) the correctness of performance and amount of information required of the task, (2) the process students may want to attend to in order to enhance their performance, (3) self-regulation processes that students could engage in, and (4) the person of the student (feedback on "self").

Much feedback typically is at the level of the task. Boud and Molloy (2013) referred to this "corrective" feedback. Feedback at the process level, according to Hattie and Timperley, is more likely to enhance deeper learning as it provides students with suggestions about alternative strategies and processes to enhance the aimed-for outcomes of the assessment tasks. Self-regulation feedback "addresses the way students monitor, direct, and regulate actions towards the learning goal" (Hattie & Timperley, 2007, p. 93). This includes self-assessment processes through the seeking of feedback information and creating internal feedback:

> When students have the metacognitive skills of self-assessment, they can evaluate their levels of understanding, their effort and strategies used

on tasks, their attributions and opinions of others about their
performance, and their improvement in relation to their goals
and expectations.   (Hattie & Timperley, 2007, p. 94)

Process of Interpreting Feedback

The process of students' engagement with and interpretation of feedback is
the most critical aspect of the feedback loop. Boud and Molloy (2013)
remarked that assumptions are often made that information provided was
"unambiguous and would be interpreted the same way by the students as was
intended by the teacher" (p. 701). They continued by making the point that if
teachers do not monitor the impact of information provided on students'
performance, we cannot really speak of feedback: "If the term *feedback* is
used, rather than simply *information*, there needs to be a way of detecting
that there has been an effect in the direction desired. The cycle of feedback,
therefore, needs to be completed"(p. 702). They argued that "if there is no
discernible effect, the feedback has not occurred" (pp. 701–702). For this
basic process of closing the feedback loop, they argued, there needs to be at
least one subsequent task on which the student can demonstrate a change in
performance.

The practicalities of using a basic format of feedback that is more than
providing information but consists of closing of the feedback loop, however,
may pose considerable challenges in higher education considering class sizes
and typical course unit structures (modules) of typical short duration. Apart
from resource constraints in providing sufficient information to affect a change
in subsequent performance, Boud and Molloy (2013) also pointed out another
constraint: "the tradition and expectation of not 'spoon feeding' students"
(p. 703). Van der Meer (2006), too, pointed out that this concern to not
"spoon-feed" first-year students often results in students not knowing what is
expected of them, which casts them into the role of attempting to be "mind-
readers" of their lecturers' intention. To address the resource constraints, Boud
and Molloy proposed a more sustainable approach to feedback, which they
refer to as "Feedback Mark 2."

The distinguishing characteristic of a more sustainable model of feedback is
one whereby students are involved as active agentic participants in identifying
what they need to do to enhance future performance and thereby prepare them
for life beyond university. "It shifts feedback from a notion of telling followed
by identifiable utilisation to one of seeking followed by judgment and identifiable utilisation" (Boud & Molloy, 2013, p. 704).

Possible Directions for Enhancing Feedback Practices

Feedback researchers are wary of appearing to promote a generic
model of good feedback. No single feedback model can be applied to all

learners in all situations (Boud & Molloy, 2013). On reading four review studies on the topic, Sadler (2010) notes: "At the risk of glossing over the complexities of what is known about feedback, the general picture is that the relationship between its form, timing and effectiveness is complex and variable, with no magic formulas" (p. 536).

In attempting to enhance feedback practices in our institutions, therefore, we may need to come back over and over again to the central focus: What is the purpose of feedback in tertiary education and how do we know that we have achieved this purpose? Focusing discussions in the first instance on the purpose of feedback, and leading this discussion to broader goals than that of "corrective" only, may then lead to ways to achieve those broader goals.

An overarching concern is the importance of developing students' metacognitive/self-regulation skills if we want them to be more active participants in the feedback process and if we want them to be able to carry forward these skills beyond their time at university, that is, "feed-up" (Evans, 2013). Students' active help-seeking and information-seeking skills are especially important in this context. Hattie and Timperley (2007) pointed out that students may not seek help because of fear of embarrassment or threat to their self-esteem. We would argue that this may be particularly the case at the first-year level. Strategies that would involve opportunities for students to engage with peers therefore may be more effective at that level. Evans (2013), who has written one of the more recent systematic reviews on feedback in higher education that includes 460 studies, suggested that a "new culture of assessment within higher education has been identified with evidence of peer assessment being used to promote student self-regulatory practices" (p. 73). Nicol (2010), for example, made the argument that not only are peers able to provide feedback in a "student-centred discourse," but when they act as an assessor they learn how to evaluate the work of others, and consequently also their own. Sadler (2010) argued that if we want students to develop their ability to evaluate their own work, then peer processes should become the main pedagogical strategy. We would add that for this to be successful and effective, sufficient attention should be given to structure these strategies purposefully and with due recognition of the research around peer processes, including careful preparation of students.

One program that operates in many universities at the first-year level is the Peer Assisted Study Sessions (PASS) program, also known as Supplemental Instruction (SI). Research evidence suggest that this program is effective for students' learning (Dawson, van der Meer, Skalicky, & Cowley, 2014). To our knowledge there is no research about this program that looks specifically at issues of feedback. However, the design of the program and its processes are likely to contribute to peer interactions that relate to students' development of understanding about assessment expectations and engagement with feedback. Furthermore, the program

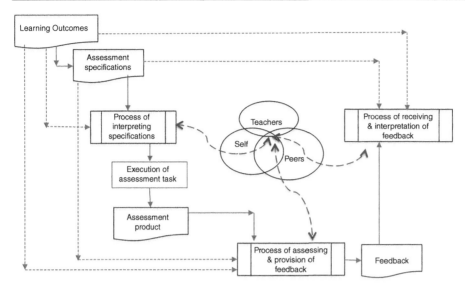

Figure 12.2 *Dialogical processes.*

is intentionally designed to support students' metacognitive skills and help-seeking behavior.

Boud and Molloy (2013) suggested that academic staff be encouraged to take a curriculum perspective to developing the role of feedback, starting with the purpose of feedback. They identified eight main curriculum features (Boud & Molloy, 2013, p. 707):

- Learners are oriented to the purpose of feedback.
- Learners participate in activities that promote self-regulation.
- Learner disposition for seeking feedback is developed.
- Opportunities are provided for students to produce work that is central to the learning outcomes.
- Regular opportunities are provided for students to calibrate their judgment against the work of experts and peers.
- Assessment tasks provide progressively incremental challenges.
- The sequencing and timing of tasks is such that input from others (teachers, peers) can be utilized for subsequent tasks.
- Opportunities are provided for students to orient themselves to the dimensions of the expected task performance and practice both receiving and giving feedback.

In Figure 12.2 we depict this dialogical approach whereby students are actively involved in the three key feedback processes as discussed in the micro-level section.

These above ideas fall under the banner of "Feedback Mark 2." Ideally, they are implemented not just at the level of an individual course unit but at the level of a program. Unfortunately, we have been unable to find evidence of programmatic feedback in mass higher education contexts in the literature; this is understandable given the logistical challenges of implementing even subelements of programmatic assessment approaches like curriculum mapping (Lawson et al., 2015).

We suggest that a new approach, the "feedback portfolio," may also be a way to facilitate programmatic feedback. In such an approach, all feedback information provided to a student is required to be criterion referenced and stored inside the students (e)portfolio alongside the assessed work. When students undertake a new task, the feedback portfolio presents the most recent feedback information they have been provided with on the relevant criteria from across their programs of study. Then, when the students submit their work they are required to mention how they have responded to this previous feedback. This feedback information, and students' responses to it, are then provided to markers when marking student work so they can provide comments that are contextualized within the student's entire feedback journey. Such an approach provides the opportunity for ipsative feedback, that is, feedback on student achievement not just against the criteria but against their previous performance. Although there would be initial investment in implementing such an approach, on an ongoing basis it would shift the feedback burden over to students, leading them to draw additional value from past feedback information rather than discarding it.

Possible Directions for Further Research

Research on feedback in higher education needs to develop a greater focus on the effects of feedback. For many new feedback approaches, such as audio feedback, there are many studies showing that students like the particular approach. However, there are no robust studies showing that many alternative approaches actually produce better feedback (Dawson & Henderson, 2017). If feedback is intended to lead to learning, feedback researchers have a responsibility to demonstrate in some way that the novel approaches they advocate actually lead to better learning.

The benefits of more dialogical feedback processes, including peer feedback processes, on outcomes beyond "straight" academic benefits, are underresearched. These could include noncognitive benefits, such as enhancing students' skills of collaboration, communication, self-regulation, enhanced tolerance of difference, and greater connectedness to other students. For this to occur, some structured programs need to be developed for research to have a greater chance to assess the multitude of factors that could influence the range of outcomes.

Longitudinal research exploring the effects of feedback practices on life beyond academia may be ambitious but may be worthwhile in order to make the higher education sector more credible as an educational environment that can demonstrate its contribution to society.

References

Adcroft, A. (2011). The mythology of feedback. *Higher Education Research & Development*, *30*(4), 405–419.

Alexander, F. (2000). The changing face of accountability: Monitoring and assessing institutional performance in higher education. *Journal of Higher Education*, *71*(4), 411–431.

Ballantyne, R., Hughes, K., & Mylonas, A. (2002). Developing procedures for implementing peer assessment in large classes using an action research process. *Assessment & Evaluation in Higher Education*, *27*(5), 427–441.

Barrie, S. (2006). Understanding what we mean by the generic attributes of graduates. *Higher Education*, *51*(2), 215–241.

Barrie, S. (2007). A conceptual framework for the teaching and learning of generic graduate attributes. *Studies in Higher Education*, *32*(4), 439–458.

Bearman, M., Dawson, P., Boud, D., Bennett, S., Hall, M., & Molloy, E. (2016). Support for assessment practice: Developing the Assessment Design Decisions Framework. *Teaching in Higher Education*, *21*(5), 545–556.

Bennett, S., Dawson, P., Bearman, M., Molloy, E., & Boud, D. (2017). How technology shapes assessment design: Findings from a study of university teachers. *British Journal of Educational Technology*, *48*(2), 672–682.

Berdahl, R. (1990). Academic freedom, autonomy and accountability in British universities. *Studies in Higher Education*, *15*(2), 169–180.

Biggs, J. (2003). *Teaching for quality learning at university: What the student does* (2nd edn.). Buckingham: Society for Research into Higher Education and Open University Press.

Blair, A. (2017). Understanding first-year students' transition to university: A pilot study with implications for student engagement, assessment, and feedback. *Politics*, *37*(2), 215–228.

Bloxham, S., & West, A. (2004). Understanding the rules of the game: Marking peer assessment as medium for developing students' conceptions of assessment. *Assessment & Evaluation in Higher Education*, *29*(6), 721–733.

Boud, D. (1995). *Enhancing learning through self-assessment*. London: Kogan Page.

Boud, D., Dawson, P., Bearman, M., Bennett, S., Joughin, G., & Molloy, E. (2016). Reframing assessment research through a practice perspective. *Studies in Higher Education*, *41*(1), 1–12.

Boud, D., & Molloy, E. (2013). Rethinking models of feedback for learning: The challenge of design. *Assessment & Evaluation in Higher Education*, *38*(6), 698–712.

Carless, D. (2013). Sustainable feedback and the development of student self-evaluative capacities. In S. Merry, M. Price, D. Carless, & M. Taras (Eds.), *Reconceptualising feedback in higher education: Developing dialogue with students* (pp. 113–122). Abingdon: Routledge.

Carless, D. (2016). Feedback as dialogue. In M. Peters (Ed.), *Encyclopedia of educational philosophy and theory* (pp. 1–6). Singapore: Springer Science and Business Media.

Carless, D., & Chan, K. (2017). Managing dialogic use of exemplars. *Assessment & Evaluation in Higher Education*, *42*(6), 930–941.

Carless, D., Salter, D., Yang, M., & Lam, J. (2011). Developing sustainable feedback practices. *Studies in Higher Education*, *36*(4), 395–407.

Carroll, D. (2014). *Graduate course experince 2013: A report on the course experience perceptions of recent graduates*. Melbourne: Graduate Careers Australia.

Cartwright, P., Ryan, J., Hacker, P., Powell, E., & Reidy, J. (2000, November). Collaboration and interaction: Modelling explored. Paper presented at the Third National Language and Academic Skills Conference: Sources of Confusion. La Trobe University, Bundoora.

Cassidy, S. (2006). Developing employability skills: Peer assessment in higher education. *Education+Training, 48*(7), 508–517.

Chanock, K. (2004). *Introducing student to the culture of enquiry in an arts degree*. Milperra (NSW): HERDSA.

Chanock, K. (2007). What academic language and learning advisers bring to the scholarship of learning and teaching: Problems and possibilities for dialogue with the disciplines. *Higher Education Research and Development, 26*(3), 269–280.

Clerehan, R., & Walker, I. (2003). Student perceptions of preparedness for first-year university assignment writing: The discipline of marketing. *Arts and Humanities in Higher Education, 2*(1), 37–46.

Craigie, D. (1998, July). Hold on now! What are universities about anyway? Paper presented at the Third Pacific Rim First Year in Higher Education Conference: Strategies for Success in Transition Years. Auckland Institute of Technology in conjunction with Queensland University of Technology, Auckland.

Dawson, P. (2015). Assessment rubrics: Towards clearer and more replicable design, research and practice. *Assessment & Evaluation in Higher Education*, 1–14.

Dawson, P., & Henderson, M. (2017). How does technology enable scaling up assessment for learning? In D. Carless, S. Bridges, C. Chan, & Rick Glofcheski (Eds.), *Scaling up Assessment for Learning in Higher Education* (pp. 209–222). Singapore: Springer.

Dawson, P., van der Meer, J., Skalicky, J., & Cowley, K. (2014). On the effectiveness of supplemental instruction: A systematic review of supplemental instruction and peer-assisted study sessions literature between 2001 and 2010. *Review of Educational Research, 84*(4), 609–639.

Ecclestone, K. (2001). "I know a 2:1 when I see it": Understanding criteria for degree classifications in franchised university programmes. *Journal of Further and Higher Education, 25*(3), 301–313.

Eley, M. (2006). Teachers' conceptions of teaching, and the making of specific decisions in planning to teach. *Higher Education, 51*(2), 191–214.

Elwood, J., & Klenowski, V. (2002). Creating communities of shared practice: The challenge of assessment use in learning and teaching. *Assessment & Evaluation in Higher Education, 27* (3), 243–256.

Evans, C. (2013). Making sense of assessment feedback in higher education. *Review of Educational Research, 83*(1), 70–120.

Francis, G. (2005, April). An approach to report writing in statistics courses. Paper presented at the IASE/ISI Satellite Conference on Statistics Education and Communication of Statistics. University of Technology Sydney.

Gair, M., & Mullins, G. (2001). Hiding in plain sight. In E. Margolis (Ed.), *The hidden curriculum in higher education* (pp. 21–41). New York: Routledge.

Gee, J. P. (2000). The New Literacy Studies: From "socially situated" to the work of the social. In D. Barton, M. Hamilton, & R. Ivanic (Eds.), *Situated literacies: Reading and writing in context* (pp. 180–196). London: Routledge.

Graff, G. (2003). *Clueless in academe: How schooling obscures the life of the mind*. New Haven, CT: Yale University.

Greatorex, J. (2003). Developing and applying level descriptors. *Westminster Studies in Education, 26*(2), 125–133.

Harvey, L. (2000). New realities: The relationship between higher education and employment. *Tertiary Education & Management, 6*(1), 3–17.

Hattie, J. (2009a). The black box of tertiary assessment: An impending revolution. In L. H. Meyer, S. Davidson, H. Anderson, R. Fletcher, P. M. Johnston, & M. Rees (Eds.), *Tertiary assessment and higher education student outcomes: Policy, practice and research* (pp. 259–275). Wellington: Ako Aotearoa.

Hattie, J. (2009b). *Visible learning: A synthesis of 800+ meta-analyses on achievement*. Oxford: Routledge.

Hattie, J., & Timperley, H. (2007). The power of feedback. *Review of Educational Research, 77*(1), 81–112.

Henderson, M., & Phillips, M. (2015). Video-based feedback on student assessment: Scarily personal. *Australasian Journal of Educational Technology, 31*(1), 51–66.

Higher Education Funding Council for England. (2014). *UK review of the provision of information about higher education: National Student Survey results and trends analysis 2005–2013*. HEFCE.

Ivanic, R. (1998). *Writing and identity: The discoursal construction of identity in academic writing*. Amsterdam: John Benjamins.

James, B., Skillen, J., Percy, A., Tootell, H., & Irvine, H. (2003, November). From integration to transformation. Paper presented at the Fifth National Language and Academic Skills Conference: Challenges, Initiatives, Evaluations and Consequences. Flinders University, Adelaide.

Krause, K. (2001). The university essay writing experience: A pathway for academic integration during transition. *Higher Education Research and Development, 20*(1), 147–168.

Lankshear, C., & Knobel, M. (2003). *New literacies: Changing knowledge and classroom learning*. Buckingham: Open University Press.

Lawson, R., Kift, S., Wilson, K., Boud, D., Lee, N., & Deem, R. (2015). Whole of degree curriculum design: Transitioning students in, through and out of higher education. Retrieved from http://researchrepository.murdoch.edu.au/33277/1/whole%20degree.pdf.

Lea, M. (1994). "I thought I could write until I came here": Student writing in higher education. In G. Gibb (Ed.), *Improving student learning* (pp. 216–225). Oxford: Oxford Centre for Staff Development.

Lea, M. (2004). Academic literacies: A pedagogy for course design. *Studies in Higher Education, 29*(6), 739–756.

Lea, M., & Stierer, B. (2000). Introduction. In M. Lea & B. Stierer (Eds.), *Student writing in higher education: New contexts* (pp. 1–13). Buckingham: SRHE and Open University Press.

Lea, M., & Street, B. (1998). Student writing in higher education: An academic literacies approach. *Studies in Higher Education, 23*(2), 157–172.

Lea, M., & Street, B. (2000). Student writing and staff feedback in higher education: An academic literacies approach. In M. Lea & B. Stierer (Eds.), *Student writing in higher education: New contexts* (pp. 32–46). Buckingham: SRHE and Open University Press.

Lea, M., & Street, B. (2006). The "academic literacies" model: Theory and applications. *Theory into Practice, 45*(4), 368–377.

Lehtomäki, E., Moate, J., & Posti-Ahokas, H. (2016). Global connectedness in higher education: Student voices on the value of cross-cultural learning dialogue. *Studies in Higher Education, 41*(11), 2011–2027.

Levin, E. (2000, November). Making expectations clear. Paper presented at the Third National Language and Academic Skills Conference: Sources of Confusion. La Trobe University, Bundoora.

Li, J., & De Luca, R. (2014). Review of assessment feedback. *Studies in Higher Education, 39*(2), 378–393.

Lillis, T. (2003). Student writing and "academic literacies": Drawing on Bakhtin to move from critique to design. *Language and Education, 17*(3), 192–207.

Lillis, T., & Turner, J. (2001). Student writing in higher education: Contemporary confusion, traditional concerns. *Teaching in Higher Education, 6*(1), 57–68.

Liu, N., & Carless, D. (2006). Peer feedback: The learning element of peer assessment. *Teaching in Higher Education, 11*(3), 279–290.

Loads, D. (2005). Signposts to success: An academic literacies approach to orientation. Paper presented at the Napier University staff conference: Using the Curriculum to Address the Needs of Individual Students. Napier University.

Macdonald, R., & Joughin, G. (2009). Changing assessment in higher education: A model in support of institution-wide improvement. In *Assessment, learning and judgement in higher education* (pp. 193–213). Dordrecht: Springer.

Macfarlane, B. (2011). The morphing of academic practice: Unbundling and the rise of the para-academic. *Higher Education Quarterly, 65*(1), 59–73.

Means, B., Toyama, Y., Murphy, R., Bakia, M., & Jones, K. (2009). Evaluation of evidence-based practices in online learning: A meta-analysis and review of online learning studies. US Department of Education.

Naumann, F., Yang, J., Thai, T., Ford, C., & Polly, P. (2016). Virtual patient consultations and the use of an ePortfolio assessment to support student learning of integrated professional skills. *Focus on Health Professional Education: A Multi-Disciplinary Journal, 17*(3), 69.

Nicol, D. (2006, December). Increasing success in first year courses: Assessment re-design, self-regulation and learning technologies. Paper presented at ASCILITE, Sydney.

Nicol, D. (2010). From monologue to dialogue: Improving written feedback processes in mass higher education. *Assessment & Evaluation in Higher Education, 35*(5), 501–517.

Nicol, D., & Macfarlane-Dick, D. (2006). Formative assessment and self-regulated learning: A model and seven principles of good feedback practice. *Studies in Higher Education, 31*(2), 199–218.

Nicol, D., Thomson, A., & Breslin, C. (2014). Rethinking feedback practices in higher education: A peer review perspective. *Assessment & Evaluation in Higher Education, 39*(1), 102–122.

Norton, L. (2004). Using assessment criteria as learning criteria: A case study in psychology. *Assessment & Evaluation in Higher Education, 29*(6), 687–702.

O'Donovan, B., Price, M., & Rust, C. (2004). Know what I mean? Enhancing student understanding of assessment standards and criteria. *Teaching in Higher Education, 9*(3), 325–335.

O'Donovan, B., Rust, C., & Price, M. (2016). A scholarly approach to solving the feedback dilemma in practice. *Assessment & Evaluation in Higher Education, 41*(6), 938–949.

Offerdahl, E., & Tomanek, D. (2011). Changes in instructors' assessment thinking related to experimentation with new strategies. *Assessment & Evaluation in Higher Education, 36*(7), 781–795.

O'Regan, K. (2000, November). We all know what an article review is ... or do we? Paper presented at the Third National Language and Academic Skills Conference: Sources of Confusion. La Trobe University, Bundoora.

O'Regan, K. (2005). Theorising what we do: Defamiliarise the university. Paper presented at the Critiquing and Reflecting LAS 2005 Conference. Australian National University, Canberra.

Orrell, J. (2006). Feedback on learning achievement: Rhetoric and reality. *Teaching in Higher Education, 11*(4), 441–456.

Pardoe, S. (2000a). A question of attribution: The indeterminacy of learning from experience. In M. Lea & B. Stierer (Eds.), *Student writing in higher education: New contexts* (pp. 125–146). Buckingham: SRHE and Open University Press.

Pardoe, S. (2000b). Respect and the pursuit of "symmetry" in researching literacy and student writing. In D. Barton, M. Hamilton, & R. Ivanic (Eds.), *Situated literacies: Reading and writing in context* (pp. 149–166). London: Routledge.

Popham, W. (1997). What's wrong – and what's right – with rubrics. *Educational Leadership, 55,* 72–75.

Read, B., Francis, B., & Robson, J. (2001). Playing it safe: Undergraduate essay writing and the presentation of the student "voice." *British Journal of Sociology, 22*(3), 387–399.

Roberts, P., Maor, D., & Herrington, J. (2016). ePortfolio-based learning environments: Recommendations for effective scaffolding of reflective thinking in higher education. *Journal of Educational Technology and Society, 19*(4), 22–33.

Sadler, D. (2005). Interpretations of criteria-based assessment and grading in higher education. *Assessment & Evaluation in Higher Education, 30*(2), 175–194.

Sadler, D. (2010). Beyond feedback: Developing student capability in complex appraisal. *Assessment & Evaluation in Higher Education, 35*(5), 535–550.

Sambell, K., & McDowell, L. (1998). The construction of the hidden curriculum: Messages and meaning in the assessment of student learning. *Assessment and Evaluation in Higher Education, 23*(4), 391–402.

Scott, P. (1995). *The meanings of mass higher education.* Buckingham: SRHE.

Skillen, J., Merten, M., Trivett, N., & Percy, A. (1998, July). The IDEALL approach to learning development: A model for fostering improved literacy and learning outcomes for students. Paper presented at the Australian Association for Research in Education Annual Conference, Adelaide.

Tai, J., Canny, B., Haines, T., & Molloy, E. (2016). The role of peer-assisted learning in building evaluative judgement: Opportunities in clinical medical education. *Advances in Health Sciences Education, 21*(3), 659–676.

Tomas, C., Borg, M., & McNeil, J. (2015). E-assessment: Institutional development strategies and the assessment life cycle. *British Journal of Educational Technology, 46*(3), 588–596.

Topping, K. (1998). Peer assessment between students in colleges and universities. *Review of Educational Research, 68*(3), 249–276.

Torrance, H. (2007). Assessment as learning? How the use of explicit learning objectives, assessment criteria and feedback in post-secondary education and training can come to dominate learning. 1. *Assessment in Education, 14*(3), 281–294.

van der Meer, J. (2006). Spoon-feeding or mind-reading? First year students' need for explicit communication of expectations. In *Proceedings of the 2005 Annual International Conference of the Association of Tertiary Learning Advisors,* Aotearoa/New Zealand (ATLAANZ), Dunedin.

van der Meer, J. (2012). "I don't really see where they're going with it": Communicating purpose and rationale to first-year students. *Journal of Further and Higher Education, 36*(1), 81–94.

Yang, M., & Carless, D. (2013). The feedback triangle and the enhancement of dialogic feedback processes. *Teaching in Higher Education, 18*(3), 285–297.

13 Instructional Feedback in Medical Education

Joan Sargeant and Christopher Watling

Medical education aims to prepare its learners for the real-life work of health care – to enable them to develop and maintain their skills against a backdrop of ever-changing knowledge. Typically, medical education unfolds in undergraduate, postgraduate, and continuing professional development phases. Undergraduate medical education combines classroom and small group learning to build knowledge with increasing forays into clinical environments to apply that knowledge to authentic clinical problems. Postgraduate (residency) training is workplace based; learners hone their knowledge and skills in specific domains of medicine by doing clinical work while following defined curricula that move them through gradually increasing levels of responsibility and independence. And continuing professional development – the longest phase of medical education – comprises a career-long process of identifying and filling knowledge gaps, keeping up with advances in knowledge and practice, and adapting to a moving target of competent performance.

Today, medical education is in flux. Traditional medical education, like most professional education, has focused on time and on process; learners spend predetermined periods of time in a range of different specialty areas or learning settings, with the goal of learning what they need to know about that domain during the allotted time. This traditional approach assumes that if time and process requirements are met in a curriculum, then competence will (likely) be reached (Hodges, 2010). But, increasingly, medical educators are acknowledging the central flaw of this approach: some individuals graduate with gaps in their knowledge and skills, despite completing the required curriculum successfully (Mattar et al., 2013).

In response, medical schools around the world are embracing competency-based medical education (CBME) models. CBME stresses outcomes over process; its assessment strategies focus on what doctors can do, rather than on what they know (Iobst et al., 2010). Competency-based curriculum design begins with desired outcomes (Frank et al., 2010), often framed as entrustable professional activities (EPAs) (ten Cate & Scheele, 2007). EPAs are the core elements of medical practice that require mastery; once learners can demonstrate that mastery, they can be entrusted to take on that task without supervision. The path to entrustment is studded with milestones – developmentally appropriate checkpoints or building blocks (Caraccio et al., 2016).

Navigating the road to competence constitutes a central challenge for educators and learners. While the CBME philosophy lifts time out of the equation altogether, medical schools cannot afford to ignore pragmatic questions about how long a learner will require to complete their program, or how much funding will be required to support their training. Loosening our grip on time requires that we strengthen our hold on learning efficiency. For this reason, feedback figures prominently in the CBME approach (Holmboe, 2015). Without feedback, we risk learners meandering through a competency-based curriculum at their own pace, potentially increasing the time required for them to develop competence. Feedback is thus the catalyst – facilitating learners' development, allowing learners to gauge their progress against appropriate milestones, and enabling course correction when necessary to maintain learning momentum.

Promises and Problems

Feedback has been referred to as a cornerstone of clinical teaching (Cantillon & Sargeant, 2008). Such is the faith in feedback as a promoter of learning that accreditation standards for undergraduate and postgraduate medical programs in North America explicitly demand that learners be provided with regular feedback. (Royal College of Physicians and Surgeons of Canada, 2011; Accreditation Committee on Graduate Medical Education, 2016; Liaison Committee on Medical Education, 2016). Without feedback, Ende suggested that "mistakes go uncorrected, good performance is not reinforced, and clinical competence is achieved empirically, or not at all" (Ende, 1983, p. 778). Feedback in medical training aims to identify specific strengths and weaknesses in a learner's performance, to calibrate the gap between actual and desired performance, and to offer motivation and direction for addressing that gap. Deployed effectively, credible feedback from trusted sources should enhance the meaning contained in learning experiences and facilitate efficient learner progress.

Evidence from sources outside medicine supports medicine's faith in feedback – to a point. Kluger and DeNisi's 1996 meta-analysis of 131 studies of feedback interventions showed that feedback has a beneficial effect on performance overall, albeit a modest one. A sobering finding of this meta-analysis was that some feedback was even detrimental to performance. From this work, Kluger and DeNisi derived what they termed "feedback intervention theory." We will explore this useful theory in greater depth later in this chapter, but at its core is a simple notion: feedback that threatens self-esteem is less likely to be effective, and risks being harmful. One critique of this meta-analysis is that most of the included studies did not examine feedback in educational settings. Bangert-Drowns, Kulik, Kulik, and Morgan's (1991) meta-analysis of feedback around test-like events was situated in the educational realm, and its findings were strikingly similar: feedback had a modestly positive impact overall but was harmful to performance in one-third of the studies considered. Hattie and

Timperley (2007) have rather more optimistically identified feedback as one of the strongest facilitators of achievement; while they identified an average high effect size for feedback (0.70 compared with 0.07 for other teaching interventions), they warned that the effect size for feedback was highly variable and subject to a wide range of influences.

Feedback research in the medical education realm sounds similar notes of caution. Bing-You and Patterson (1997), for example, found that residents might reject feedback if they felt that the feedback provider was not credible. Similarly, Watling, Driessen, van der Vleuten, and Lingard (2012b) found that feedback was just one of an array of sources of information learners might use to calibrate and make sense of their own performance. Feedback had to compete with other "learning cues" for learners' attention, including patient and family responses, clinical outcomes, comparisons with peers, and the standards demonstrated by role models, and whether feedback became a meaningful influence on learning depended largely on learners' judgments about its credibility. Feedback from supervisors was subjected to particularly critical judgment about its credibility and was often ultimately discarded as a result. (Watling, 2012a; Watling et al., 2012b)

This minefield appears to persist past the formal educational phase of medical training and well into practice. In Sargeant, Mann, and Ferrier's (2005) work exploring the responses of practicing family physicians to receiving multisource feedback, they found a strong tendency for negative feedback to be perceived as inaccurate or lacking in credibility; as a result, feedback perceived as negative tended not to be useful. As Brett and Atwater (2001) concluded, people who need feedback the most because of performance problems may be least receptive to it; their research, although done outside medicine, nonetheless resonates with medical educators. Taken together, these studies suggest that feedback can meaningfully shape learning but that its benefits cannot be assumed. Rather, it must be employed with great care.

Challenges in Medical Education

Challenges confront medical educators at every turn in their efforts to offer consistently meaningful feedback to learners, especially in clinical settings. The difficulties inherent in the feedback exchange are not unique to medicine, of course. Higgins and colleagues, writing about feedback in the higher education setting, recognized that "the process of feedback as communication is inherently problematic" (Higgins, Hartley, & Skelton, 2001, p. 272). Feedback, simply put, is a tricky form of human communication. But medicine faces distinct challenges that are rooted in its learning settings, its pedagogical routines, and its professional culture.

Experts on feedback in medical education have called for feedback to be treated as a conversation rather than as a commodity (Lefroy, Watling, Teunissen, & Brand, 2015). The conversation metaphor provides a useful starting point for better understanding the challenges of feedback in medical education and for strategizing about approaches that will generate more consistently meaningful feedback. Many elements make a conversation tick: the words and content of the conversation, the players and their relationship to one another, and the context in which the conversation occurs. Increasingly, medical education is critically examining each of these elements in an effort to understand how feedback conversations can become derailed, and how more consistently meaningful feedback can be fostered.

Content and Credibility

Feedback in medical education suffers chronically from deficient content. It veers toward the vague and superficial, often lacking substance. In one review of feedback comments written on senior medical students' evaluations, the most frequently appearing comment was "a pleasure to work with" (Lye, Biernat, Bragg, & Simpson, 2001). Virtually all medical learners have a file bursting with platitudes such as "good job" or with empty efforts at constructive feedback such as "read more." Furthermore, medical learners often receive feedback long after the fact, sometimes days or weeks after the feedback-generating event occurred. Frequently, feedback arrives at the end of a clinical placement of multiple weeks, after the opportunity to apply the feedback has passed. To be effective, feedback should be specific, elaborated, timely, and grounded in authentic clinical work (Lefroy et al., 2015). It should be well informed, ideally by direct observation of the task. It should be accompanied by an action plan that charts a course for the learner to follow in order to improve performance. In short, it should be both credible and constructive. Credible feedback is feedback a learner can trust. Constructive feedback is feedback a learner can act on. Training of medical faculty to provide good feedback has tended to focus on these core quality markers.

Credibility deserves particular attention, as feedback's impact seems to depend on it (Watling et al., 2012b). A teacher needs to be a credible source of feedback in order for their words to hit the mark. How do medical teachers earn credibility? They do so first and foremost by demonstrating clinical expertise; in medicine, those individuals who are the most clinically adept are most likely to be perceived as credible sources of feedback (Watling et al., 2012b). Clinical expertise is often insufficient, however: credibility also requires teachers to actively engage in the process of generating feedback by making clear efforts to observe the learner in action and to understand their strengths and weaknesses. Learners, in turn, must engage as feedback recipients (Watling et al., 2008). A learner's receptivity to feedback is influenced by a number of factors, including their trust in the fairness of the process. Learners who perceive that the process by which their performance is judged is fundamentally unfair may be less receptive to feedback generated as a result of that performance (Duffield & Spencer, 2002; Barclay et al., 2005;

Sargeant et al., 2011; Telio, Regehr, & Ajjawi, 2016). The interaction between external feedback and learner self-assessment is another complicating factor; feedback that misaligns with self-assessment often proves challenging for learners to integrate and use (Sargeant, Mann, Sinclair, van der Vleuten, & Metsemakers, 2008; Sargeant et al., 2010).

A learner's perception of the authenticity of the performance on which feedback is based further influences their trust in that feedback. Recent research has shown that learners may "stage a performance" in the presence of a physician observer, striving to successfully tick off the boxes on an assessment checklist rather than to perform as they naturally would without the observer present (LaDonna et al., 2017). As a result, feedback provided on that performance may be discarded as unhelpful if the learner's perception is that the performance does not reflect how they actually do the work (Sargeant et al., 2011).

Like credibility, emotion modulates feedback, from both sides of the table. Teachers may temper negative feedback out of fear of harming learners or discomfort with challenging conversations (Dudek, Marks, & Regehr, 2005; Watling et al., 2010). Learners may struggle to incorporate feedback that engenders a strong negative emotional response (Sargeant et al., 2008, 2010). Feedback in medical education aims to nurture and develop the desired attributes of a competent physician. But many of these attributes – compassion, exemplary communication, a capacity to collaborate, an ability to advocate for others – are easy to conceptualize as elements of the self, rather than as collections of trainable skills. Kluger and DeNisi's (1996) warning that feedback that threatens a learner's self-esteem might prove destructive rather than constructive resonates here: while medical learners may not have more fragile self-esteem than any other learners, they perhaps are more frequently confronted with feedback that can feel as though it is directed at them as individuals, rather than at the tasks that they undertake.

Finally, feedback that conflicts with a learner's self-assessment may be particularly challenging. Self-assessment has long been touted as a professional value in medicine. Medical students and residents are told that they must be lifelong learners and that to do so they must develop an ability to self-assess. As evidence has mounted that physicians, like most people, are relatively poor at self-assessment (Davis et al., 2006), calls for a more sophisticated concept of self-assessment have emerged – one in which self-assessment includes a systematic and routine process of seeking and acting on feedback from trusted external sources (Eva & Regehr, 2005). But when that feedback contradicts a learner's self-assessment, that conflict may provoke questions about credibility, may test self-esteem, and may unleash strong emotions – all of which complicate the hoped-for path to performance improvement (Sargeant et al., 2010). Enhancing clinical teachers' understanding of these complications and providing them with communication techniques to effectively address and resolve them remain challenges.

Relationship Challenges

Trusting relationships between teachers and learners create safety in feedback conversations, facilitating the exchange of feedback even when the conversation is a difficult one (Sargeant et al., 2011; Telio et al. 2015). Medical training, however, affords only inconsistent opportunities for longitudinal teacher–learner relationships to develop. During clerkship – an extended phase of undergraduate medical training that occurs entirely in clinical settings – medical students typically rotate through a series of clinical settings, spending from one to eight weeks in a range of venues representing various fields of medicine. While this approach emphasizes a breadth of experience, it also fosters brief interactions with supervisors; it is not uncommon for a medical student's sole experience with a particular supervisor to occur in the context of a single day's clinic. Certain residency training programs offer similar curricula; internal medicine residents, for example, typically rotate through dozens of medical subspecialty areas over the course of their training, potentially working with different supervisors every week or two. In such contexts, the lack of longitudinal relationships can conspire against efforts to provide meaningful feedback.

Efforts to make space for relationship building within medical curricula are gathering momentum. Longitudinal integrated clerkships, for example, situate medical students with one preceptor for the duration of their clerkship, with exposure to a range of medical and surgical specialties arising naturally in the course of providing care for the patients in that individual's practice (Hirsh, Walters, & Poncelet, 2012). Within this approach, feedback appears to flourish; research indicates the quality of feedback in longitudinal integrated clerkships is enhanced (Bates, Konkin, Suddards, Dobson, & Pratt, 2013). Even in the revolving door of an internal medicine residency, longitudinal educational relationships can be introduced. One group, for example, paired residents with one faculty teacher who spent a few hours three to four times per year observing them at work, then offering formative feedback on what they observed. Compared with feedback arising from their typical fleeting supervisory relationships, residents found the quality, credibility, and impact of the feedback much higher (Voyer et al., 2016).

System and Culture Challenges

Medical education's context and culture create distinctive challenges to the exchange of meaningful feedback. First, much education in medicine occurs in real clinical settings; competent performance is not just an aspiration for learners but also a necessity for patients and families. Second, the organization of clinical training often limits opportunities for teachers to directly observe the performance of their learners, compromising efforts to create well-informed feedback (Holmboe, 2004). Third, medicine blurs the lines between feedback as instruction and feedback as assessment, complicating the feedback conversation, whose intent and consequences may be unclear for the players (Watling, 2016).

For the latter part of medical school, and for essentially all the training that follows graduation from medical school, learning occurs primarily in real clinical settings. Clinician teachers supervise learners in the settings where clinical work occurs – hospital inpatient wards, ambulatory clinics, operating rooms, family physicians' offices, medical laboratories, public health units. And these clinician teachers, for the most part, do not view teaching as their primary responsibility. Rather, they are first and foremost physicians responsible for patient care and other clinical tasks. From moment to moment, then, supervisors may shift roles, moving from teacher to health-care provider and back again depending on the needs of the patient. Feedback may fall by the wayside as the intensity and the stakes of the clinical situation rise.

Feedback may further suffer from a lack of direct observation of learners in clinical settings (Holmboe, 2004; Kogan, Holmboe, & Hauer, 2009). Consistently, research has identified direct observation as a necessary precursor for credible feedback (Lefroy et al., 2015). Observation provides the performance data that form the foundation for the feedback conversation – data such as how a learner performed a physical examination or executed a procedure, for example. When learners have not been observed performing the task on which feedback is offered, they tend to distrust and discard that feedback (Watling et al. 2012b). Although accreditation guidelines for medical schools now require that medical students receive a minimal level of direct observation during their training (Association of Faculties of Medicine of Canada graduate questionnaire), the quantity and quality of observation varies across clinical settings, raising questions about the quality of the feedback that is exchanged.

The organization of clinical work in training settings offers insights into the challenge of routinely observing learners. In many clinical settings, teachers and learners work in parallel rather than together. Supervisors delegate tasks to learners, such as taking histories, performing physical examinations, obtaining informed consent, and performing minor procedures. Their assessment of a learner's performance of those tasks is often based on proxy measures of performance rather than direct observation. For example, a learner's ability to present a clinical case concisely and coherently may serve as a proxy measure for their ability to take a history and perform a physical examination.

The reasons for these organizational decisions that limit direct observation are complex and are embedded in both pragmatism and culture. Observation can be time consuming, which can render it difficult to routinely incorporate into clinical settings. In an ambulatory clinic, for example, the practice of teachers and learners working in parallel and seeing patients concurrently allows more patients to be seen than could occur if the supervisor sat in with the learner as they did their work. Efficiency is in fact a cultural value in medicine (Watling, 2016). Teachers, learners, hospitals, governments, and the public value timely and efficient patient care. Learners often receive praise from their supervisors for their efficiency, reinforcing the value the culture places on this attribute (Watling, 2016). More regular use of direct observation may be viewed as a threat to this cultural value. Medicine as a profession also values autonomy and independence. Learners aspire to practice independently and to graduate from the need to be supervised or observed (Watling, 2016). Learning itself may be perceived as more influential when it occurs in the absence of a supervisor – when a learner has to sink or swim. And virtually no tradition exists of independent, practicing physicians asking for observation and coaching (Gawande, 2011). Observation may undermine learners' sense of autonomy and corrode their confidence, as it may be viewed as a threat to the cultural value of independent work (Watling, 2016). Little wonder, then, that ambivalence about direct observation has been found among both learners and teachers (Madan, Conn, Dubo, Voore, & Wiesenfeld, 2012; Ross, Mauksch, Huntington, & Beard, 2012). This ambivalence mirrors the conflicted relationship many learners have with the acts of seeking and receiving feedback (Teunissen et al., 2009; Mann et al., 2011).

Finally, medicine has organized its curricula in such a way that the lines between assessment and feedback are often blurred (Watling, 2016b). Assessment and feedback are, of course, inextricably linked. Teachers observing a learner's performance use the data they gather to make a judgment – an *assessment* – about the quality of that performance compared with a desired standard. What happens next – what is done with that initial assessment – may be more summative in nature or more formative, depending on the intended purpose of the encounter. With summative assessments, teachers ask whether the learner's level of performance measures up, whether it is at the required level. With formative assessments, teachers ask how the observation data can be used to inform a feedback conversation that will help the learner to develop and improve. These two purposes are fundamentally different: summative assessment is about judgment, while formative assessment is about learner development.

The problem in medicine is that the same individuals are routinely required to take on both summative assessment and formative feedback tasks for the same learners, sometimes simultaneously. This situation occurs in part because faculty resources may be limited; many educational programs do not have the luxury of having separate cadres of coaches and assessors. The situation also reflects medicine's pact with society. Clinical teachers are accountable not only to their learners but also to the profession and to the public. They must not only prepare their learners for competent practice but also assure the public that their graduates are safe and skilled.

This dual responsibility complicates the feedback dynamic. Feedback flounders when the intent of the conversation is unclear and when the goals of the teacher and learner fail to align. When formative feedback and summative assessment coalesce, learners can be left uncertain as to what to make of the information they receive (Cavalcanti & Detsky, 2011). When a conversation intended as coaching for improvement is instead perceived as summative assessment, a learner's ability to use the information productively may be impaired.

Theoretical Perspectives

In this section we explore five theoretical perspectives on learning that are being used, to varying degrees, in medical education to inform and guide feedback interactions. In particular, we address those that especially contribute to our understanding of the individual, relationship, and system factors identified in the preceding sections. For each we briefly describe the perspective, provide a brief statement about why it matters in feedback, and provide a couple of examples of how it is or might be applied.

Cognitivist Learning

Prominent for decades in the field of education, the cognitivist learning perspective enables us to understand how individuals make sense of the information presented to them. It studies internal mental processes including how information is received, processed, stored, accessed, responded to, and applied. It seeks to understand how data are stored in the brain, retrieved, and synthesized with both new and existing data.

Cognitivist perspectives help us to understand several features that we know make feedback effective, such as timeliness, relevance, and specificity. These features enable the learner to connect the feedback data to the specific situation and to data already stored in the brain about the situation and similar situations, thereby enhancing the accessibility and usefulness of the feedback.

Further, as noted in the above sections, providing and responding to feedback are complex processes, and feedback is not consistently accepted and used. Cognitive perspectives also aid understanding of the internal influences that moderate responses to feedback. We describe two theories in particular: feedback intervention theory (Kluger & Denisi 1996, 1998; Denisi & Kluger 2000) and regulatory focus theory (Higgins, 1997; Kluger & van Dijk, 2010).

Feedback intervention theory considers the locus or point of attention for the feedback and suggests that it influences the response to feedback. The authors propose three points or levels of attention for feedback: self, task, and task process. Feedback that is perceived as being directed at the "self" level is often interpreted as a threat to self-esteem and can evoke an emotional response. As the focus of feedback moves away from the task and toward the self, the likelihood that feedback will result in improved performance diminishes, and the risk of harming performance increases. To be more effective, therefore, feedback should be directed toward the task or task process level. For example, if a medical student or resident is engaged in teaching a patient about their condition, the feedback on the teaching needs to be directed to the task, in this case to the characteristics of good teaching and the process used by the learner. However, due to the sensitive nature of performance assessment and the tendency to view feedback in a negative rather than a positive light, even feedback offered at the task level (e.g., "I noticed you spoke quickly and didn't ask the patient if they understood your explanation") can be perceived by the learner as being directed to the self level and being critical of them as a novice practitioner.

Perceiving feedback as criticism and a threat to self-esteem generates negative emotional responses that can get in the way of being able to use the feedback. However, in their original description of feedback intervention theory, Kluger and DeNisi (1996) also acknowledged a gap in understanding: feedback's influence on performance appeared to be unrelated to its "sign." That is, positive feedback, which provides information about success, and negative feedback, which provides information about failure, had similar effects on performance (Kluger & DeNisi, 1996). This finding appeared paradoxical, given that negative feedback would seem to pose a greater potential threat to self-esteem.

Recently, Kluger and van Dijk (2010) invoked *regulatory focus theory* to explain this phenomenon. Regulatory focus theory distinguishes two systems of self-regulation that underlie human motivation: promotion focus and prevention focus (Higgins, 1997). Promotion focus concerns goals and aspirations – things we do because we *want* to do them. Prevention focus, on the other hand, concerns responsibility and safety – things we do because we *ought* to do them (Higgins, 1997). Linking regulatory focus and feedback response, Kluger and van Dijk (2010) predicted that when individuals are operating in promotion focus, positive feedback will be motivating and enhance performance while negative feedback will be discouraging and harmful. In prevention focus, they predicted the opposite would be true: negative feedback would improve performance while positive feedback would be detrimental. Indeed, these predictions held true in a variety of experimental settings. In a study exploring regulatory focus theory's utility in explaining feedback responses in naturalistic clinical settings, Watling, Driessen, van der Vleuten, Vanstone, and Lingard (2012a) found that while the theory offers considerable insights into the feedback responses of medical learners, its explanatory power is limited. Regulatory focus around clinical learning tasks is often unclear, may contain elements of both promotion and prevention focus, and may shift over time. Furthermore, other factors may trump regulatory focus; feedback from a highly credible source, for example, may influence a learner even if not optimally aligned with regulatory focus (Watling et al., 2012a).

Cognitivist Learning Perspectives: Theory to Practice

Cognitivist learning perspectives usefully direct our attention away from how feedback is given and toward how it is received. Using these perspectives, we can better understand – and in some cases predict – how and why learners respond to feedback in the way that they do. Armed with this understanding of the influences on individual receptivity, we can begin to offer more tailored feedback that is more likely to be perceived by learners as meaningful.

Sociocultural Perspectives

Sociocultural theories are less concerned with internal cognitive processes and more concerned with external factors and influences. They direct the attention of educators away from the minds of individual learners and toward the social and organizational elements, some of which are within educators' control. Learning is considered a social and cultural process, inseparable from context, and feedback is situated within that social and cultural context. Learning occurs through social interaction; cognitive functioning of individuals is inseparable from the social milieu in which it takes place and the activities that occur. Knowledge is constructed and reconstructed between participants in specific situated activities and within the specific culture (Vygotsky, 1978). Feedback, then, is inseparably linked to the context in which it takes place.

Lave and Wenger's (1991) work on learning has particular resonance in clinical medical education. They suggested that learning occurs as individuals gradually become part of a professional community, along the way adopting the practices, beliefs, and values of that community. Clinical learning in medicine is workplace learning, and students and residents develop as they become integral participants in the real work of providing health care. This sociocultural perspective on learning offers a lens through which to critically examine our feedback practices. To understand how feedback succeeds or fails, we must consider not only the cognitive processes of the individuals involved but also the culture and setting in which the feedback exchange is situated and the norms, routines, and values of that culture. As noted above, medical education's traditions of limited direct observation of performance and patchy opportunities for teacher–learner relationship building conspire against its efforts to improve feedback. Similarly, traditional beliefs and values held within the medical profession also confound attempts to cast feedback in a more favorable light, for example, the belief that being observed and requiring feedback is inconsistent with perceptions of professional competence and independence. These challenges are cultural and organizational, rather than individual, and cannot be overcome simply by training learners to be eager feedback receivers or seekers or by training teachers to be adept feedback givers.

Watling's research on feedback in medical education has been strongly influenced by the sociocultural perspective. In work exploring how professional cultures influence feedback practices, he found that while learners consistently value feedback that is credible and constructive, the very meanings of credibility and constructiveness are culturally determined. In medicine, for example, learners tend to look to outstanding clinicians as the most credible sources of feedback; in music, learners instead gravitate to the best teachers – rather than best performers – when seeking credible feedback (Watling, Driessen, van der Vleuten, Vanstone, & Lingard, 2013). Furthermore, culture drives organizational and pedagogical practices in ways that can support or constrain the exchange of meaningful feedback. Teacher training, for example, embeds opportunities for supervisors to observe student teachers in action in the classroom over extended periods of time, facilitating the exchange of detailed and constructive feedback. Medicine, in contrast, organizes its learning settings so that teachers and learners work in parallel, limiting the direct observation of learners and complicating the creation of constructive feedback (Watling, Driessen, van der Vleuten, Vanstone, & Lingard, 2014). As Eraut (2007) has pointed out, individual and sociocultural theories of learning are complementary rather than competing. Individual learners bring much to the table – motivation, orientation toward feedback, preferences around feedback style – that shapes how they respond to feedback. But culture acts as a catalyst, creating (or constraining) opportunities for meaningful feedback to be exchanged and for learners to respond.

Sociocultural Perspectives: Theory to Practice

Sociocultural perspectives remind us of the system, organizational, and cultural influences on the feedback conversation. Using these perspectives, we can better understand how the quality of feedback is as much a product of the setting and the culture as it is of the individuals involved. Improving feedback thus depends not only on training participating individuals to have good feedback conversations but also on creating the conditions and opportunities that will facilitate those conversations. Changing a clinic's scheduling practices to afford routine opportunities for clinical teachers to directly observe learners in action, for example, may enhance the quality of the resulting feedback more than any individually directed interventions that fail to address this organizational issue.

Perspectives on Informed Self-Assessment and Reflection

Although medicine is a self-regulated profession and physicians are considered to be self-directed professionals, they, like everyone, are subject to the limitations of personal self-assessment undertaken without the benefit of guidance from external sources of data (Eva & Regehr, 2005, 2008; Davis et al., 2006). "Informed" or "guided" self-assessment recognizes that individuals can and should seek out and use external data (e.g., feedback) to generate an appraisal of their own performance (Eva & Regehr, 2005, 2008; Sargeant et al., 2010). We now know that external data and feedback are essential to informed self-assessment and to accurate self-monitoring, i.e., to knowing how one is performing. In medical education, external data and feedback take many forms ranging from informal verbal feedback from peers, patients, and other health care professionals to formal assessment formats used by supervisors in clinical teaching in the workplace. Personal, internal data need also be considered and include self-perceptions of one's performance and one's emotional state in relation to that performance, e.g., "Am I feeling anxious? Surprised? Confident?"

However, as noted above, recipients of performance feedback do not always accept and use the feedback. One reason for this is that the feedback can evoke emotional reactions if it disconfirms the recipient's self-perceptions. Emotional reactions occur because one's performance is integrally linked to one's sense of self, and disconfirming feedback can be difficult to accept. Earlier research demonstrated that physicians receiving performance feedback first compared that feedback with how they saw themselves (Sargeant et al., 2008). If the feedback confirmed their self-perceptions, they tended to react more favorably and accept it more readily than if it disconfirmed their views. These findings were surprising and problematic. While the purpose of providing the feedback was for the physicians to use it to improve their practice, feedback that was corrective and offered direction for change was often not accepted.

These findings led to an international qualitative study to understand more fully how physicians, residents, and students self-assess and self-monitor their performance in their practice and education. Participants confirmed the need for external feedback to inform their self-assessments and guide future performance, yet described diverse factors and complex interactions that influenced their interpretation of feedback and their decisions about whether or not to accept and use it. Self-assessment appeared as dynamic and fluid, and external feedback was used variably. Similar to the tenets of other perspectives, influences are both individual and social and include the perceived quality and authenticity of the feedback, individual emotional state and self-efficacy, relationships, the opportunity to reflect, and the context and culture (Sargeant et al., 2010; Lockyer et al., 2011; Mann et al., 2011; Eva et al., 2012). Understanding this complicated manner in which one perceives one's own performance and the dynamic interactions between one's self-perceptions and external feedback can provide further insight into strategies for enhancing the positive impact of feedback.

Reflection is understood as a learning strategy and as integral to feedback acceptance and use, especially when feedback data are perceived as disconfirming of one's own assessment of one's performance (Goodstone & Diamnate, 1998; Mann, Gordon, & MacLeod, 2009; Sargeant et al., 2009). "Reflection in the context of learning is a generic term for those intellectual and affective activities in which individuals engage to explore their experiences in order to lead to new understandings and appreciations" (Boud, Keough, & Walker, 1985, p. 18). It is through the process of reflecting on and considering one's experiences that one learns from them. Similarly, it is through reflecting on the feedback that one receives and what it means, that one gains the insight into one's performance that may be a necessary precursor for performance improvement. Receiving feedback presents a dual opportunity for reflection: first, for reflection on the performance data provided by the supervisor in the feedback conversation and, second, for reflection on one's self-assessment of the performance receiving the feedback and how the two data sources compare. Discrepancy between the external feedback and one's self-assessment creates an opportunity for further reflection to understand each other's views and reasons for them and the approaches required to reduce the discrepancy. In some cases, hearing the learner's perspective on a situation – for example, their rationale for doing a procedure in a particular way – may alter the supervisor's assessment and feedback. More often, encouraging the learner's reflection on the performance and feedback can lead to new insights on the part of the learner. As an example, the learner in the patient teaching example above may not have realized that they were speaking too quickly or didn't ask the patient's views, due to anxiety or for another reason. Encouraging learners to pause and reflect can give them space to see their own performance and feedback in a different light and can offer an opportunity for self-critique. Through thoughtful facilitation by the instructor, learners can gain insight and come to the self-realization that there may be gaps in their performance and clear ways to use the feedback being offered and to improve. Reflection also enables the learner to consider how they will use the feedback. Facilitating reflection can be an effective strategy for promoting both feedback acceptance and use.

Perspectives on Informed Self-Assessment and Reflection: Theory to Practice

Perspectives on informed self-assessment remind us that while external feedback is a prerequisite for accurate self-assessment, constructive feedback is often not readily accepted and used, especially when it disconfirms one's own views of performance. It actually creates a challenging conundrum in medical education; i.e., the feedback is needed but often not taken on. Practically, these perspectives guide us to consider the various factors that influence acceptance of feedback and assimilation with perceptions of self. They also direct us to give careful thought to communication strategies in feedback conversations to enable learners to gain insight and assimilate and make use of external feedback. One such strategy is fostering their reflection on their performance and the feedback offered.

Learner/Person-Centeredness, Humanism, and Relationships

Humanistic perspectives are person centered and address individuals' needs, capabilities, and potential. Maslow (1954) introduced the notion of a hierarchy of human needs comprised of five levels with basic biologic and safety needs as the first two. The next two levels are psychological needs for belongingness and affiliation, and esteem and self-respect. The highest level is for self-fulfillment and personal growth. Carl Rogers (1969) developed a more complete theory of person-centeredness, describing the need for individuals to strive for self-actualization and explaining that behavior is generally driven by achieving one's goals. He suggested that the best way to understand behavior is from the internal perspective of the individual. Finally he highlighted that the heart of education is *learning*, not teaching, with the focus on the learner and what happens to them.

Humanism encourages us to take a learner-centered focus in feedback and to consider how best to promote learning while also meeting learners' higher-level needs for belonging, self-esteem, and self-actualization. Meeting these needs is integrally linked to relationships with learners. Such relationships have a profound impact on the learner and what is learned, including how feedback is perceived and responded to (Sargeant et al., 2011; Molloy & Boud, 2013; Telio et al., 2015).

Insights into the impact of a person-centered relationship on development and learning were first gained in the fields of psychotherapy and therapeutic counseling (Goodstone & Diamante, 1998; Telio et al., 2015). In counseling settings, the nature of the therapeutic relationship and the degree to which it explored and supported the goals of the person being counseled were found to influence whether or not the expert advice being offered was accepted (Gabbard & Westen, 2003). Goodstone and Diamante (1998) demonstrated a similar influence of person-centeredness and therapeutic relationships on the acceptance and use of corrective feedback in business settings. More recently, Telio and colleagues (2015) suggested that reorienting feedback discussions in medical education toward developing a supportive learner-centered relationship between teacher and learner – what they called an "educational alliance" – fostered learner appreciation of feedback and its use for development.

Similar to the doctor–patient relationship, which influences patient satisfaction and health outcomes, the supervisor–learner relationship influences learner satisfaction and can influence education outcomes. The positive influence of an educational alliance between supervisors and learners in which learners' best interests are explicitly pursued is now recognized. Although positive relationships over longer periods of time are most beneficial, they are not always possible. Ultimately, the quality of the relationship may matter more than its duration. For example, a supervisor who has a learner for only a short time can build an effective learning relationship using communication and feedback techniques in a very efficient yet sincere and engaged manner (Telio et al., 2015).

The supervisor–learner relationship is pivotal in learning; meaningful feedback conversations depend on it. Learners' perceptions of the relationship – and particularly of the supervisors' authenticity, interest, sincerity, and engagement – impact their willingness to engage in meaningful conversations about their performance and to accept and use their feedback. The acceptability and impact of feedback can be increased if it relates to personally meaningful goals set by the recipient (Goldman, 2009; Archer, 2010).

Perspectives on Learner-Centeredness, Humanism, and Relationships: Theory to Practice

These perspectives direct our attention away from considering the content and nature of the feedback toward taking into account the relationship between teacher and learner. Relationships directly impact how feedback is heard and whether it will be taken on. A supportive, trusting relationship with the teacher, one in which the learner perceives that the teacher is engaged and has the learner's best interests at heart, enhances perceptions of the credibility and usefulness of the feedback. Practically speaking, providing system supports in medical education to enable the development of longer-term relationships between teachers and learners – for example, lengthening clinical placements or providing a longitudinal coach or mentor – are suggested. Another approach is to remember that it is the quality of the relationship that matters, and even in a very short clinical placement of a day or less, a teacher can demonstrate their engagement with the learner and their learning.

Developmental Approaches to Learning and Feedback

Developmental models position instruction and feedback as integral to learning and the development of competence. We will briefly take a look at two approaches, and then consider "coaching" through the lens of feedback and development. Dreyfus (2004) offered a five-stage model for developing competence and expertise. These include advancement from novice to advanced beginner, competent practitioner, proficient practitioner, and expert, each with significant features. Feedback and instruction are integral to enabling the learner to develop the technical, cognitive, and affective skills required to advance from one level to the next and to perform a task competently. For example, think of the developmental levels in learning to drive a car.

Ericsson (2004, 2008, 2015) studied in detail the influence of deliberate practice on the development of expertise. He describes deliberate practice as being "designed and implemented by teachers and coaches and focused on improving particular tasks. It involves the provision of immediate feedback, time for problem-solving and evaluation, and opportunities for repeated performance to refine behavior" (Ericsson 2008, p. 988). Ericsson's premise is that deliberate practice allows an individual's knowledge and performance to develop gradually. Deliberate practice with feedback and reflection is necessary for the development of expertise. More specifically, from a review of studies of learning and skill acquisition, he found evidence for consistent gradual improvement of performance under the following three conditions: (1) participants were instructed to improve some aspect of performance for a well-defined task; (2) they received immediate detailed feedback on their performance; and (3) they were expected to and were given ample opportunity to improve their performance gradually by performing the same or similar tasks repeatedly, reflecting on and integrating the feedback they had received.

Such developmental models give reason to pause and consider traditional medical education. In contrast to the developmental model, medical educators and physicians refer to the traditional model of learning in clinical settings as "see one, do one, teach one." This model lacks integration of notions of feedback or development. As discussed in an earlier section, such a model has developed over time for several reasons, among them the culture of medicine in which physicians need to be seen as being competent, and the logistically complicated interaction of clinical education and the health-care system that limit opportunities for ideal learning and teaching. However, also of note in clinical medical education and at variance with the developmental models described is the culture and practice in which feedback appears to be linked, integrally at the system level and intuitively at the personal level, to assessment and judgment of a learner and not to learning and development.

Viewing feedback through a developmental and learning lens casts a fresh light on it. Feedback is seen as part of and in fact integral to learning and not part of assessment. The question then is: How to change the culture in medical education so that feedback becomes a natural component of learning? One hope is that adoption of such a developmental model may be enabled by the move toward competency-based education, which proposes development of learners in their achievement of outcomes.

Another developmental approach being explored is coaching, which has long been accepted as an integral approach to developing successful athletes and musicians (Heen & Stone, 2014). It is understood to be directive, developmental, person centered, and outcome oriented. Recently, the notion of coaching is being considered within other contexts, including medicine, and indeed the question is being asked as to whether physicians should also consider having coaches to help them maintain and fine-tune their skills and approaches, through observation, feedback, and reflective conversations (Gawande, 2011). Similarly, in the business world, executive coaching is recognized as an approach for managers to continue their development. Within education, one helpful perspective views coaching in education as "a one-to-one conversation focused on the enhancement of learning and development through increasing self-awareness and a sense of personal responsibility, where the coach facilitates the self-directed learning of the coachee through questioning, active listening, and appropriate challenge in a supportive and encouraging climate" (Van Niewerburgh, 2012, p. 19). Such a definition seems in keeping with the goals of medical education.

As can be seen, coaching in education contrasts with the more traditional directive model of coaching – i.e., telling the learner what to do – in that the coach engages the learner actively in reflection on the feedback, self-direction, and planning for change. However, the goal is the same: to enable the learner to become the very best they can be. It is proposed that having feedback conversations with learners about their performance data and coaching them on opportunities for improvement could be valuable activities for enabling them to learn from their clinical performance and develop their competence.

Informed by the notions inherent in developmental perspectives and the others described above, a multisite qualitative study developed an evidence- and theory-informed reflective model for facilitating performance feedback conversations and coaching for improvement (Sargeant et al., 2015). The model includes four phases: (1) Relationship building, (2) exploring Reactions to the feedback, (3) exploring understanding of feedback Content, and (4) Coaching for performance change, referred to as the R2C2 feedback model.

Each of the four phases has a particular goal guided by theoretical perspectives:

1. Relationship building: To engage the learner, build relationship, build respect and trust, understand their context
2. Exploring reactions to the feedback: For the learner to feel understood and that their views are heard and emotions are respected
3. Exploring understanding of feedback content: For the learner to be clear about what the assessment data mean for their practice and/or learning and the opportunities identified for change and development
4. Coaching for performance change: For the learner to engage in developing an achievable learning and change plan.

While the phases are seen to proceed in a linear way, the model is iterative and earlier phases can be revisited as required based on how the conversation is unfolding. An overall goal of the model is to promote reflection at each phase, and to this end, specific open-ended questions are provided to foster reflection (Sargeant et al., 2015). The R2C2 model has been tested with physicians and residents and found to be helpful in various ways (Sargeant et al., 2015, 2016). It provides structure and content for supervisors for engaging learners in the feedback conversation and in their performance data, and it enhances learners' understanding, acceptance, and use of feedback. Learners and supervisors report that it is valuable in a CBME environment to enable learner development and progression from one level to the next and that coaching is the most novel phase and particularly helpful for enabling this progression. Moreover, participants describe it as contributing to a supportive learner–teacher relationship in which the two collaborate and co-create the plan for improvement.

Developmental Approaches to Learning and Feedback: Theory to Practice

Drawing on developmental perspectives enables us to view feedback through a fresh lens. Traditionally within medical education, feedback has been associated with assessment, even to the point of the two being inextricably connected. Feedback is seen as part of assessment, and somehow it has become almost forgotten that feedback is also part of learning. Seeing feedback in the light of development reminds us that feedback is indeed part of learning. It is an instructional strategy to help learners learn, develop, and progress from one level to the next. It is also a positive activity for teachers, enabling them to facilitate learning and the progression of their learners. While this makes sense and is grounded in good education practices, turning the thinking around in medical education to uncouple feedback from assessment and instead connect it to learning will benefit from various change strategies. Examples included identifying champions to lead the transition, promoting practical and explicit models for having developmental feedback conversations, and developing procedures preventing individual formative feedback interactions being used for summative decisions.

In summary feedback vexes teachers and learners alike in medical education. While its value is widely endorsed, its effective application often proves difficult. The challenges are legion: learning tasks are often charged with emotion and linked with burgeoning professional identity; instructional skills are underdeveloped in teachers whose primary roles are as clinicians; organizational decisions limit opportunities for trusting relationships to develop between teachers and learners; and "competent performance" may be an ill-defined moving target. Against this backdrop, much progress has been made in understanding why feedback succeeds or fails in influencing learners. Theoretically grounded research on feedback is helping educators to avoid the trap of oversimplifying the problem. Feedback is a complex conversation; the individuals involved, the words they use, the emotions they experience, the relationship they have, and the culture in which the conversation occurs all contribute to the meaning that emerges. With a holistic approach, real progress is on the horizon – and just in time.

References

Accreditation Council for Graduate Medical Education. (2016). *Common Program Requirements*. Retrieved from www.acgme.org.

Archer J. C. (2010). State of the science in health professional education: Effective feedback. *Medical Education, 44*, 101–108.

Association of Faculties of Medicine of Canada. (2015). *Graduation Questionnaire National Report*. Retrieved from www.afmc.ca/sites/default/files/documents/en/Publications/AFMC%20Graduation%20Questionnaire%20National%20Report%202015.pdf.

Bangert-Drowns, R. L., Kulik, C.-L. C., Kulik, J. A., & Morgan, M. T. (1991). The instructional effect of feedback in test-like events. *Review of Educational Research, 61*, 213–238.

Barclay, L. J., Skarlicki, D. P., & Pugh, S. D. (2005). Exploring the role of emotions in injustice perceptions and retaliation. *Journal of Applied Psychology, 90*, 629–643.

Bates, J., Konkin, J., Suddards, C., Dobson, S., & Pratt, D. (2013). Student perceptions of assessment and feedback in longitudinal integrated clerkships. *Medical Education, 47*, 362–374.

Bing-You, R. G., & Paterson, J. (1997). Feedback falling on deaf ears: Residents' receptivity to feedback tempered by sender credibility. *Medical Teacher, 19*, 40–44.

Boud, D., Keough, R., & Walker. D. (Eds.). (1985). *Reflection: Turning experience into learning*. Oxon, UK: Routledge.

Brett, J. F., & Atwater, L. E. (2001). 360° feedback: Accuracy, reactions, and perceptions of usefulness. *Journal of Applied Psychology, 86*, 930–942.

Cantillon, P., & Sargeant, J. (2008). Giving feedback in clinical settings. *British Medical Journal, 337*, a1961.

Carraccio, C., Englander, R., Gilhooly, J., Mink, R., Hofkosh, D., Barone, M. A., & Holmboe, E. S. (2016). Building a framework of entrustable professional activities, supported by competencies and milestones, to bridge the educational continuum. *Academic Medicine, 92*. Advance online publication.

Cavalcanti, R. B., & Detsky, A. S. (2011). The education and training of future physicians: Why coaches can't be judges. *Journal of the American Medical Association, 306*, 993–994.

Davis, D. A., Mazmanian, P. E., Fordis, M., Van Harrison, R., Thorpe, K. E., & Perrier, L. (2006). Accuracy of physician self-assessment compared with observed measures of competence: A systematic review. *Journal of the American Medical Association, 296*, 1094–1102.

DeNisi, A., & Kluger, A. (2000). Feedback effectiveness: Can 360-degree appraisals be improved? *Academy of Management, 14*, 129–139.

Dreyfus, S. E. (2004). The five-stage model of adult skills acquisition. *Bulletin of Science, Technology and Society, 24*, 177–181.

Dudek, N., Marks, M., & Regher. G. (2005). Failure to fail: The perspectives of clinical supervisors. *Academic Medicine, 80*(Suppl. 10), S84–S87.

Duffield, K. E., & Spencer, J. A. (2002). A survey of medical students' views about the purposes and fairness of assessment. *Medical Education, 36*, 879–886.

Ende, J. (1983). Feedback in clinical medical education. *Journal of the American Medical Association, 250*, 777–781.

Eraut, M. (2007). Learning from other people in the workplace. *Oxford Review of Education, 33*, 403–422.

Ericsson, K. A. (2004). Deliberate practice and the acquisition and maintenance of expert performance in medicine and related domains. *Academic Medicine, 79*(Suppl. 10), S70–S81.

Ericsson, K. A. (2008). Deliberate practice and acquisition of expert performance: A general overview. *Academic Emergency Medicine, 15*, 988–999.

Ericsson, K. A. (2015). Acquisition and maintenance of medical expertise: A perspective from the expert-performance approach with deliberate practice. *Academic Medicine, 90*, 1471–1486.

Eva, K. W., Armson, H., Holmboe, E., Lockyer, J., Loney, E., Mann, K., & Sargeant, J. (2012). Factors influencing responsiveness to feedback: On the interplay between fear, confidence, and reasoning processes. *Advances in Health Sciences Education, 17*, 15–26.

Eva, K. W., & Regehr, G. (2005). Self-assessment in the health professions: A reformulation and research agenda. *Academic Medicine, 80*(Suppl. 10), S46–54.

Eva, K. W., & Regehr, G. (2008). "I'll never play professional football" and other fallacies of self assessment. *Journal of Continuing Education in the Health Professions, 28*, 14–19.

Frank, J. R., Snell, L. S., Cate, O. T., Holmboe, E. S., Carraccio, C., Swing, S. R., . . . & Harris, K. A. (2010). Competency-based medical education: Theory to practice. *Medical Teacher, 32*, 638–645.

Gabbard, G. O., & Westen, D. (2003). Rethinking therapeutic action. *International Journal of Psychoanalysis, 84*(Part 4), 823–841.

Gawande, A. (2011, October 3). Personal best: Top athletes and singers have coaches. Should you? *The New Yorker*.

Goldman, S. (2009). The Educational Kanban: Promoting effective self-directed adult learning in medical education. *Academic Medicine, 84*, 927–934.

Goodstone, M., & Diamante, T. (1998). Organizational use of therapeutic change: Strengthening multisource feedback systems through interdisciplinary coaching. *Consulting Psychology Journal: Practice and Research*, *50*, 152–163.

Hattie, J., & Timperley, H. (2007). The power of feedback. *Review of Educational Research*, *77*, 81–112.

Heen, S., & Stone, D. (2014). Managing yourself – finding the coaching in criticism: The right way to receive feedback. *Harvard Business Review*, *92*(1–2), 108–111.

Higgins, E. T. (1997). Beyond pleasure and pain. *American Psychologist*, *52*, 1280–1300.

Higgins, R., Hartley, P., & Skelton, A. (2001). Getting the message across: The problem of communicating assessment feedback. *Teaching in Higher Education*, *6*, 269–274.

Hirsh, D., Walters, L., & Poncelet, A. N. (2012). Better learning, better doctors, better delivery system: Possibilities from a case study of longitudinal integrated clerkships. *Medical Teacher*, *34*, 548–554.

Hodges, B. D. (2010). A tea-steeping or i-Doc model of medical education? *Academic Medicine*, *85*(Suppl. 9), S34–S44.

Holmboe, E. S. (2004). Faculty and the observation of trainees' clinical skills: Problems and opportunities. *Academic Medicine*, *79*, 16–22.

Holmboe, E. S. (2015). Realizing the promise of competency-based medical education. *Academic Medicine*, *90*, 411–413.

Iobst, W. F., Sherbino, J., Cate, O. T., Richardson, D. L., Dath, D., Swing, S. R., ... & Frank, J. R. (2010). Competency-based medical education in postgraduate medical education. *Medical Teacher*, *32*, 651–656.

Kluger, A. N., & DeNisi, A. (1996). The effects of feedback interventions on performance: A historical review, a meta-analysis, and a preliminary feedback intervention theory. *Psychological Bulletin*, *119*, 254–284.

Kluger, A. N., & DeNisi, A. (1998). Feedback interventions towards an understanding of a double-edged sword. *Current Directions in Psychological Sciences*, *7*(3), 67–72.

Kluger, A. N., & Van Dijk, D. (2010). Feedback, the various tasks of the doctor, and the feedforward alternative. *Medical Education*, *44*, 1166–1174.

Kogan, J. R., Holmboe, E. S., & Hauer, K. E. (2009). Tools for direct observation and assessment of clinical skills of medical trainees: A systematic review. *Journal of the American Medical Association*, *302*, 1316–1326.

LaDonna, K., Hatala, R., Lingard, L., Voyer, S., & Watling, C. (2017). Staging a performance: Learners' perceptions about direct observation during residency. *Medical Education* (in press).

Lave, J., & Wenger, E. (1991). *Situated learning: Legitimate peripheral participation*. Cambridge: Cambridge University Press.

Lefroy, J., Watling, C., Teunissen, P. W., & Brand, P. (2015). Guidelines on feedback for clinical education: The dos, don'ts, and don't knows of feedback for clinical education. *Perspectives in Medical Education*, *4*, 284–299.

Liaison Committee on Medical Education. (2016). Functions and structure of a medical school: Standards for accreditation of medical education programs leading to the MD degree. Retrieved from www.lcme.org.

Lockyer, J., Armson, H., Chesluk, B., Dornan, T., Holmboe, E., Loney, E., ... & Sargeant, J. (2011). Feedback data sources that inform physician self assessment. *Medical Teacher, 33*(2), e113–e120.

Lye, P. S., Biernat, K. A., Bragg, D. S., & Simpson, D. (2001). A pleasure to work with: An analysis of written comments on student evaluations. *Ambulatory Pediatrics, 1,* 128–131.

Madan, R., Conn, D., Dubo, E., Voore, P., & Wiesenfeld, L. (2012). The enablers and barriers to the use of direct observation of trainee clinical skills by supervising faculty in a psychiatry residency program. *Canadian Journal of Psychiatry, 57,* 269–272.

Mann, K., Gordon, J., & MacLeod, A. (2009). Reflection and reflective practice in health professions education: A systematic review. *Advances in Health Science Education, 14,* 595–621.

Mann, K., van der Vleuten, C., Eva, K., Armson, H., Chesluk, B., Dornan, T., ... & Sargeant, J. (2011). Tensions in informed self-assessment: How the desire for feedback and reticence to collect/use it create conflict. *Academic Medicine, 86,* 1120–1127.

Maslow, A. H. (1954). *Motivation and personality.* New York: Harper & Row.

Mattar, S. G., Alseidi, A. A., Jones, D. B., Jeyarajah, D. R., Swanstrom, L. L., Aye, R. W., ... & Minter, R. M. (2013). General surgery residency inadequately prepares trainees for fellowship: Results of a survey of fellowship program directors. *Annals of Surgery, 258,* 440–449.

Molloy, E., & Boud, D. (2013). Changing conceptions of feedback. In D. Boud & E. Molloy (Eds.), *Feedback in higher and professional education: Understanding it and doing it well* (pp. 11–33). New York: Routledge.

Rogers, C. (1969). *Freedom to learn (studies of the person).* Columbus, OH: Charles E. Merrill.

Ross, V., Mauksch, L., Huntington, J., & Beard, J. M. (2012). Interdisciplinary direct observation: Impact on precepting, residents, and faculty. *Family Medicine, 44,* 318–324.

Royal College of Physicians and Surgeons of Canada. (2011). *General standards of accreditation applicable to all residency programs.* Retrieved from www.royalcollege.ca.

Sargeant, J., Armson, H., Chesluk, B., Dornan, T., Holmboe, E., Eva, K., ... & Loney, E. (2010). Processes and dimensions of informed self-assessment: A conceptual model. *Academic Medicine, 85,* 1212–1220.

Sargeant, J., Armson, H., Holmboe, E., Lockyer, J., Mann, K., Silver, I., ... & Boudreau, M. (2016). Evidence-informed facilitated feedback: The R2C2 feedback model. *MedEdPORTAL Publications, 12,* 10387. Retrieved from www.mededportal.org/publication/10387/.

Sargeant, J., Eva, K. W., Armson, H., Chesluk, B., Dornan, T., Holmboe, E., ... & van der Vleuten, C. (2011). Features of assessment learners use for informed self-assessments of clinical performance. *Medical Education, 45,* 636–647.

Sargeant, J., Lockyer, J., Mann, K., Holmboe, E., Silver, I., Armson, H., ... & Power, M. (2015). Facilitated reflective performance feedback: Developing an evidence- and theory-based model that builds relationship, explores reactions and content, and coaches for performance change (R2C2). *Academic Medicine, 90,* 1698–1706.

Sargeant, J., Mann, K., & Ferrier, S. (2005). Exploring family physicians' reactions to multisource feedback: Perceptions of credibility and usefulness. *Medical Education*, *39*, 497–504.

Sargeant, J., Mann, K., Sinclair, D., van der Vleuten, C., & Metsemakers, J. (2008). Understanding the influence of emotions and reflection upon multi-source feedback acceptance and use. *Advances in Health Science Education*, *13*, 275–288.

Sargeant, J., Mann, K., van der Vleuten, C., & Metsemakers, J. (2009). Reflection: A link between receiving and using assessment feedback. *Advances in Health Science Education Theory Practice*, *3*, 399–410.

Telio, S., Ajjawi, R., & Regehr, G. (2015). The "educational alliance" as a framework for reconceptualizing feedback in medical education. *Academic Medicine*, *90*(5), 609–614.

Telio, S., Regehr, G., & Ajjawi, R. (2016). Feedback and the educational alliance: Examining credibility judgments and their consequences. *Medical Education*, *509*, 933–942.

ten Cate, O., & Scheele, F. (2007). Competency-based postgraduate training: Can we bridge the gap between theory and clinical practice? *Academic Medicine*, *82*, 542–547.

Teunissen, P., Stapel, D., van der Vleuten, C., Scherpbier, A., Boor, K., & Scheele, F. (2009). Who wants feedback? An investigation of the variables influencing residents' feedback-seeking behavior in relation to night shifts. *Academic Medicine*, *84*, 910–917.

Van Niewerburgh, C. (2012). *Coaching in education: Getting better results for students, educators and parents*. London: Karnac Books.

Voyer, S., Cuncic, C., Butler, D. L., MacNeil, K., Watling, C., & Hatala, R. (2016). Investigating conditions for meaningful feedback in the context of an evidence-based feedback program. *Medical Education*, *50*, 943–954.

Vygotsky, L. S. (1978). *Mind in society: The development of higher psychological processes*. Cambridge, MA: Harvard University Press.

Watling, C. (2016). The uneasy alliance of assessment and feedback. *Perspectives in Medical Education*, *5*, 262–264.

Watling, C., Driessen, E., van der Vleuten, C., & Lingard, L. (2014). Learning culture and feedback: An international study of medical athletes and musicians. *Medical Education*, *48*, 713–723.

Watling, C., Driessen, E., van der Vleuten C., Vanstone, M., & Lingard, L. (2012a). Understanding feedback responses: The potential and limitations of regulatory focus theory. *Medical Education*, *46*, 593–602.

Watling, C., Driessen, E., van der Vleuten, C., Vanstone, M., & Lingard, L. (2013). Music lessons: Revealing medicine's learning culture through comparison with that of music. *Medical Education*, *47*, 842–850.

Watling, C., LaDonna, K., Lingard, L., Voyer, S., & Hatala, R. (2016b). "Sometimes the work just needs to be done": Sociocultural influences on direct observation in medical training. *Medical Education*, *50*, 1054–1064.

Watling, C. J., Driessen, E., van der Vleuten, C., & Lingard, L. (2012b). Learning from clinical work: The roles of learning cues and credibility judgments. *Medical Education*, *46*, 192–200.

Watling C. J., Kenyon, C. F., Schulz, V., Goldszmidt, M. A., Zibrowski, E., & Lingard, L. (2010). An exploration of faculty perspectives on the in-training evaluation of residents. *Academic Medicine, 85,* 1157–1162.

Watling, C. J., Kenyon, C., Zibrowski, E., Schulz, V., Singh, I, Goldszmidt, M., . . . & Lingard, L. (2008). Rules of engagement: Residents' perceptions of the in-training evaluation process. *Academic Medicine, 83*(Suppl. 10), S97–S100.

14 360-Degree Feedback at the Workplace

A Transformative Learning Perspective

Vidya S. Athota and Ashish Malik

Introduction

For an organization to be successful in the long term, it should be able to manage its resources and deliver products and services in the most effective and efficient manner. Although technical and other resources are invaluable in the delivery of products and services, in this chapter we focus on performance assessment and feedback in order to have effective management of human resources. There is an extensive body of literature that points to the significant and positive impact of human resources in building a firm's sustained competitive advantage (Barney, 1991; Wright, Dunford, & Snell, 2001; Boxall & Purcell, 2016). Several studies have highlighted the fact that managing people requires attention to three key factors that significantly impact performance (Vroom, 1964; Blumberg & Pringle, 1982): ability, motivation, and opportunity – popularly known as the AMO framework (Appelbaum, Bailey, Berg, & Kalleberg, 2000). First, employees must have the ability (the relevant knowledge, skills, and competencies) to carry out their jobs productively. Second, employees must be motivated to apply their ability in a productive manner in a workplace context. Third, they should be able to do so in a work context that is supportive and provides them with the opportunity to apply the skills and knowledge for productive activities. It is not surprising then to see an extensive interest by organizations in investing in performance and productive capacity of individuals.

The performance appraisal system is the most widely used practice in firms for assessing and determining whether an employee has delivered the performance required for a given role. It is also used as a tool to develop employee and organizational capabilities and forms the basis for distributing rewards for expected or above-expected levels of performance (Fletcher, 2001). In a similar vein, Hermel-Stanescu (2015) has highlighted why managers in organizations must not ignore opportunities in human resource management practice. Effective human resource management helps to explore an employee's potential. By engaging with employees in a constructive manner and providing feedback using the performance appraisal process, firms can deliver on performance improvements and administer a well-designed rewards and benefits program (Obisi, 2011).

There are several elements in performance management and appraisal process that, if not attended to in the design and implementation stage, can become sore points for managers and employees. A key element is objective measurement of performance by employees, managers, and other stakeholders, which is fundamental in the design of the system. Feedback, along with positive reinforcement and open and frequent exchange of views and agreements between the employees and their managers, is also important (Rusu, Avasilcai, & Hutu, 2016). Firms must also pay special attention to the alignment issues between what the business needs are and what the employees want. Therefore, a candid appraisal between the employee and the supervisor is highly recommended (Campbell & Lee, 1988; Farh, Werbel, & Bedeian, 1988). Managers must also engage in constant monitoring in a way that is not too intrusive and must also not permit the performance of an individual to fall back to such a level that there are only disciplinary recourses left to them. Campion, Campion, and Campion (2015) highlighted the role of ongoing feedback and informal conversations with employees to improve performance rather than waiting for the annual or biannual review to occur. The employees should be in little doubt through this process and during planning what their targets and goals are, and these should be set in a transparent manner to avoid aspects of surprise at a later stage (Luffarelli, Goncalves, & Stanatoginannakis, 2016). This often leads to breaches in psychological contract between the manager and the employees (Franceschini & Turina, 2013).

Despite the importance and prevalence of this human resource management practice, there are a number of deficiencies apparent in its design and implementation. Even in the best-designed feedback systems, problems arise in the form of discord among employees that affects the rater–ratee relationship. In most cases these problems arise due to a lack of perceived fairness and objectivity in the system. Pichler (2012) suggested that such dissent in relationships can be reduced by reinforcing and building aspects of trust and mutual support between the employee and manager, a view that was also held by DeNisi and Pritchard (2006). The researchers note that an ideal appraisal process is one that is fair, efficient, and delivers on the strategic and horizontal alignment of goals. Errors in appraisal can arise due to an inaccurate assessment of performance against objective criteria or from focusing only on providing feedback and developing their competencies in a narrow range (Decotiis & Petit, 1978). Gorman, Meriac, Roch, Ray, and Gamble (2017) surveyed performance management practices in 101 US-based firms to assess whether their performance management systems, as perceived by the firms' human resources managers, were comparable with industry best practices. Their findings revealed that while most of the practices are perceived to be fair by human resources managers, there are areas where improvements are needed. These include aspects such as preparatory training for users and paying greater attention to contextual factors. Changes in business and institutional environment context are extremely important as these have been noted to impact a firm's human resource management practices (Malik, 2013). In brief, a good performance feedback system must attend to issues such as building employees' trust and providing managerial support (Pichler, 2012). Feedback must also serve as an opportunity to clarify expectations and remove any misunderstandings employees may have about their own knowledge and expectations of their job (Gruman & Saks, 2011). A well-designed and well-implemented feedback system must not be susceptible to manipulation by either party. Even prior to dealing with the procedural aspects of this practice, management must look at creating a culture of trust and confidence between their managerial staff and their employees (Mayer & Davis, 1999). Although there are several design approaches available to managers in organizations for providing feedback to employees, in this chapter we focus our attention on the 360-degree feedback system, a widely used approach for providing an opportunity for holistic development to employees and managers in organizations and in achieving effective organizational leadership.

The 360-degree feedback system is an approach that has been associated with improved performance and productivity of employees in a workplace context (Rai & Singh, 2013). This approach is also called "multidirectional feedback" as it focuses on collecting data from multiple sources rather than only from the traditional employee–manager dyad. The main goal of 360-degree feedback is to gather data about an individual's performance and effectiveness at work from various sources to provide feedback insights for improvement and development. According to Bracken, Rose, and Church (2016), the goal of 360-degree feedback is the "creation of sustainable individual, group, and/or organizational change in behaviors valued by the organization" (p. 764). This approach has been found to be effective in understanding individual strengths and competencies and identifying areas of development of human capital (Baker, 2010). The 360-degree feedback system has been effectively used in various organizations, including international health-care systems (Swing, 2007; Zhao, Zhang, Chang, & Sun, 2013; Hageman, Ring, Gregory, Rubash, & Harmon, 2015). Hageman et al. (2015) assessed perceptions of a physician's leadership and outcome of clinical practice style by using the Physicians Universal Leadership-Teamwork Skills Education (PULSE) 360. The assessment outcome helped to improve physicians' leadership abilities. Longitudinal studies have shown that behavioral changes were achieved over time through 360-degree feedback (Nowack, Hartley, & Bradley, 1999). Many Fortune 500 companies are using the 360-degree feedback mechanism to increase employee performance. Generally, individuals are assessed once a year; some companies are using this system twice a year. This approach has been quite well known in Europe and the United States and has proliferated in a number of emerging market economies, although not so much in some of the less-developed countries. This approach is not very common in Australia nor New Zealand, although there are some organizations that successfully employ it.

This chapter provides an overview of the key drivers, benefits, and challenges in implementing 360-degree feedback for individuals and groups in organizations. More specifically, it provides an in-depth account of the theoretical bases and applications employing transformative adult learning approaches. The rest of the chapter is organized as follows. We begin by providing a review of the literature on the topic. This is followed by a critical review of the approach through the theoretical lens of transformative adult learning theory, followed by some future research themes for theory and practice.

360-Degree Feedback: A Review

The study and practice of 360-degree feedback is grounded largely in the human resource management functional area of performance management and improvement (McKenna, Richardson, & Manroop, 2011), and its effective use may serve to help multiple companies achieve their goals, such as employee job satisfaction, talent management, employee retention, and reduction of attrition (McKenna et al., 2011; Smith, Oczkowski, & Sellby-Smith, 2011). Hence, many companies are using the 360-degree feedback mechanism as the key for effective employee performance and productivity. Recently, DeNisi and Murphy (2017) reviewed the research on performance management spanning 100 years (incorporating performance appraisal) and noted that much of the scholarship on this topic tends to fall into eight major streams of research: (1) employing appropriate measurement scales for measuring performance of individuals, (2) developing objective criteria for assessing performance evaluation scores, (3) training and development of employees, (4) dealing with positive and negative emotions and reactions to the performance appraisal process, (5) studying the purpose of performance scores, (6) focusing on the use of different sources of performance ratings, (7) focusing on population differences in performance scores, and (8) focusing on the varied cognitive processes involved in the area of performance management. They also highlighted the areas that were deemed successful as well as those that inhibited its success. All eight points cover key elements of 360-degree feedback and promote productivity in organizations (DeNisi and Murphy, 2017). These have direct implications for job satisfaction, performance, and retention of talent (McKenna et al., 2011; Smith et al., 2011). Therefore, a thorough understanding of 360-degree feedback is pivotal.

A number of definitions have been given to understand the 360-degree feedback. According to Ward (1997), 360-degree feedback is a process of systematically collecting performance data from a number of stakeholders for the purposes of providing feedback to an individual for his or her development. It was found that a 360-degree feedback system plays a vital role in providing constructive feedback and individual development (Dalton, 1998). According to Bracken et al. (2016), "360 Feedback is a process for collecting, quantifying, and reporting coworker observations about an individual (i.e., a rate) that facilitates/enables three specific data-driven/based outcomes: (a) the collection of rater perceptions of the degree to which specific behaviors are exhibited; (b) the analysis of meaningful comparisons of rater perceptions across multiple rates, between

Table 14.1 *Sample 360-degree items*

Administrative Skills
- Delegates responsibilities appropriately
- Manages meetings effectively

Communication Skills
- Speaks clearly in front of groups
- Conveys information clearly in written documents

Interpersonal Skills
- Works with others to effectively resolve conflicts
- Develops cooperative working relationship

Leadership and Coaching Skills
- Leads by example
- Provides specific constructive feedback in a timely manner

Political Skills
- Understands the agendas and perspectives of others
- Recognizes key stakeholders related to important decisions

Motivation Skills
- Persists in the face of obstacles
- Establishes challenging goals

Service Skills
- Anticipates customers' needs
- Shows a concern for customer satisfaction

Source: Bommer, Rubin, & Bartels (2005, p. 119).

specific groups of raters for an individual ratee, and for ratee changes over time; and (c) the creation of sustainable individual, group, and/or organizational changes in behaviors valued by the organization" (p. 364). In 360-degree feedback, collecting feedback from various sources is crucial for effective analysis of individual and organizational issues. There can be biased perception in feedback from one source, but collecting data from various sources tends to provide a more balanced view. Therefore, multi-prospective feedback is vital in an effort to bring sustainable change in individual and organizational levels.

There are different aspects of 360-degree feedback. The most commonly discussed in the literature is *peer review*, which describes feedback provided by peers or colleagues other than a supervisor. Typically, peer review is based on the observation by a peer on the overall performance of a colleague. In the process of *self-review*, the employees are given an opportunity to evaluate themselves by using some of the 360-degree scales or measures. Table 14.1 presents some of these items. Research shows that self-review works best when the supervisor and the employee together come to an understanding of future performance goals (Ward, 1997; Dalton, 1998; Bracken, et al. 2016). During *upward review*, employees provide feedback on how the top management is performing or how people are viewing them (McKenna et al., 2011; Smith et al., 2011; Bracken et al., 2016).

There are some precautions that should be taken in utilizing the peer review, self-review, and upward review processes. Specifically, self-review can be positive when pay and promotion are involved. Generally, confidentiality should be ensured to the raters and participants in all types of organizations. It would be hard to provide confidential peer feedback in small teams. There is a potential to know who provided the feedback. Time and resources are another major part in overall 360-degree feedback. Managers who were given negative feedback might take it personally, potentially creating tension and withdrawing support for the subordinates. Therefore, extra caution should be taken to provide feedback on behaviors, tasks, and situations rather than personal characteristics. The 360-degree feedback ideally should be used as part of development plan rather than being used to terminate an employee.

Reviewing studies from 1995 to 2013, Mohapatra (2015) offered a detailed review of 360-degree feedback with a particular focus on job satisfaction scores. She argued that 360-degree feedback is mainly used for individuals' performance assessment and their development, both personally and within the organizations. An individual is assessed by peers, superiors, and self. Individual strengths and weaknesses are explored throughout the process. The goal of 360-degree feedback is to reduce weaknesses and increase strengths of an employee. The review highlighted the benefits of 360-degree feedback in improved communication, reassurance of assessment, and building better relationships among different parties. Additionally, the success of 360-degree feedback is underpinned by communicating clearly its purpose and scope and ensuring there is genuineness in the process as perceived by the recipient of the feedback.

Al Ansari, Donnon, Al Khalifa, Darwish, and Violato (2014) undertook a meta-analysis of construct and criterion validity of multirater feedback to assess its impact on the performance of physicians and surgeons. Focusing on studies concentrated in the health-care domain, the authors analyzed thirty-five studies from January 1975 to November 2012. The study found support for multisource feedback systems' construct validity when this was administered to surgeons and physicians and studied over a period of time. The study confirmed the positive impacts of multisource feedback on surgeons' and physicians' clinical performance, communication skills, professionalism, teamwork, productivity, and building trusting relationships with their patients. Overall, physician performance in relation to their clinical communication, professionalism, teamwork, and clinical performance effectively was found through multisource feedback.

Personality Traits and Cultural Factors Influencing 360-Degree Feedback

Individual personality traits play an important role in providing and receiving 360-degree feedback. Some individuals may negatively react to the feedback based on their personality traits. Individuals who score high on narcissism may not respond well to the negative feedback (Dweck, 1986). According to Conger (2002), "Narcissistic leaders can lose touch with reality, promote self-serving and grandiose aims and use the company as a vehicle for personal gain. A strong sense of self-importance may blind them to divergent points of view or to whistle-blowers, leading to poor strategic and organizational decision-making. This can end in catastrophe" (p. 4). Therefore, providing appropriate feedback in a tactful way can be very helpful for organizational productivity. Subclinical traits of narcissism, psychopathy, and Machiavellianism have been identified as the "dark triad" (Paulhus & Williams, 2002). Similar to persons who score high on narcissism, high scorers on psychopathy and Machiavellianism also may not react positively to negative 360-degree feedback. Research suggests that individuals who score high on Machiavellianism appear charming but are driven by self-centeredness (O'Connor & Athota, 2013). Dark triad personality traits of narcissism, psychopathy, and Machiavellianism were also found to have a negative relationship with task (e.g., core technical skills) and contextual performance (e.g., psychological climate for individual's performance) (Moscoso & Salgado, 2004). Individuals with dark triad personality traits can be charismatic and charming but with deceitful intensions (Paulhus & Williams, 2002; O'Connor & Athota, 2013; de Silva, 2014). The qualities of being charismatic, charming, and self-promoting open the doors into leadership positions. Therefore, additional care is required when conducting 360-degree analysis and feedback for individuals who score high on the dark triad.

Feedback plays a pivotal role in developmental of individuals in organizations. Brett and Atwater (2001) pointed out that negative feedback is counterproductive to individuals who rate themselves higher in terms of perceptions of their performance: "negative feedback (i.e., ratings that were low or that were lower than expected) was not seen as accurate or useful, and it did not result in enlightenment or awareness but rather in negative reactions such as anger and discouragement" (p. 938). Contrary to narcissistic leaders, effective leaders are high in extraversion and openness to experience and are proactive in gaining more feedback in order to change their behavior (Bell & Arthur, 2008). We suggest that there may be other positive benefits of the combination of these two traits. That is, people who are high on extraversion and openness to experience may be more likely to be more creative (Athota & Roberts, 2015).

Positive and negative evaluations in the 360-degree feedback generally help to explore individuals' strengths and weaknesses. People tend to take positive and negative evaluations personally, and this influences their motivation to change through 360-degree feedback (Bono & Colbert, 2005). Research suggests that the significant gap between peer ratings and self-evaluation can lead to psychological dissonance (Festinger, 1957). The gap between peer ratings and self-evaluation is counterproductive and individuals may lose the motivation to fill it. Conversely, a small gap between peer ratings and self-evaluation might provide motivation fill the gap (Carver & Scheier, 1982). Therefore, caution must be exercised in providing 360-degree feedback to individuals in the workplace.

Culture has been found to influence 360-degree feedback. The majority of the Fortune 500 countries operate in both individualistic (e.g., United States, United Kingdom, and Australia) and collectivistic (India, China, Dubai, and Japan) societies. Power distance is high in collectivist societies like India and China. Exploring cultural dimensions is critical for understanding the process of providing and receiving 360-degree feedback (Hofstede & McRae, 2004; Atwater, Waldman, Ostroff, Robie, & Johnson, 2005). Atwater et al. (2005) conducted a large study (n=3793) focused on leadership skills with reference to self and other ratings. A second investigation (n=2732) was conducted to understand how performance impacts self–other agreement. These studies were conducted in the United States and Europe, and differences by country were found. We suggest that a review is less likely to be accepted in collectivistic countries where power distance is high. More research needs to be conducted to understand cultural differences and 360-degree feedback.

Despite positive benefits, much of the literature points to limits in the 360-degree analysis and feedback (Hofstede & McRae, 2004; Atwater et al. 2005). Research on the use of this approach in expatriation contexts shows that cultural and linguistic differences may have an adverse impact on the effectiveness of this practice. Kossek, Huang, Piszczek, Fleenor and Ruderman (2017) employed social categorization and relational demography theories and analyzed data from 360-degree performance ratings of expatriates from thirty-six countries. The authors investigated the impact of cultural distance and suggested that firms should propose solutions for minimizing the adverse impacts of cultural distance on subordinate and peer ratings, specifically among expatriate managers.

Contextualization is also important. Contextually grounded application of this approach has been noted recently by scholars who have applied the concept of national business systems to understand the challenges faced by multinational firms operating in developing economies (Pereira, Malik, & Froese, 2017). Their review of the impact of national business systems (which includes influences of culture and business practices and institutions) on human resource management practices highlighted the importance of national business systems in shaping the effectiveness of human resource management practices. This approach also brings to the focus the importance of, and differences between, cultural influences in actors in an institutional and cultural context. In developing economies such as India and its relatively less understood cultural context (Pereira & Malik, 2013, 2015a, 2015b, 2015c, 2015d, 2016a; Malik & Pereira, 2015a, 2015b, 2016a, 2016b), implementing a best-practice 360-degree feedback approach using a Western cultural lens would only result in an ineffective design. Malik and Pereira (2015a, 2015b, 2016a, 2016b) therefore stressed the importance of disengaging from a popular Hofstedian approach to cultural understanding (i.e., power distance individualism vs. collectivism, uncertainty

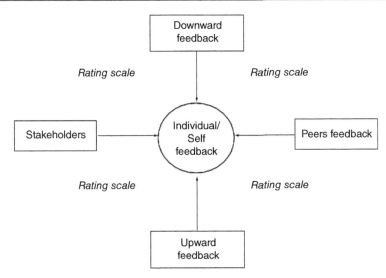

Figure 14.1 *Individual 360-degree feedback from self, peer, upward, and downward.*

avoidance, masculinity vs. femininity, long-term vs. short-term orientation, indulgence vs. restraint) and instead focusing on ten cultural and business singularities of Indianness (Laleman, Pereira & Malik, 2015) to develop a deeper contextual and cultural understanding. Such an approach would help design and implement a more relevant 360-degree feedback system.

Feedback can be collected from other sources, such as customers and suppliers, in addition to the commonly discussed peer review, self-review, upward review, and downward review. Feedback is most useful when there are many sources of data. Multiple data sources, as opposed to only the immediate supervisor, are pivotal to understanding and analyzing the behavior of a person. Including external stakeholders and other members in the value chain who may be indirectly affected is a highly desirable aspect of its design. Figure 14.1 depicts the influence of multiple sources of information.

Among several goals noted in the literature for 360-degree feedback, a number of studies suggested that the main goal of 360-degree feedback is leadership development. Organizational support is necessary in order to have a supportive environment for 360-degree analyses. The 360-degree feedback is most effective when the wider organizational cultural and values system supports a better understanding of the process, which in turn supports the achievement of consistent feedback ratings. The feedback must be job-related and exclude commentary on personal issues pertaining to faith, family situation, and cultural background.

Research has established that 360-degree feedback is effective in bringing behavioral and organizational change (Bracken & Rose, 2011). There are several design aspects that need to be considered in developing a robust 360-degree feedback system. The key areas of best practices of the 360-degree

Table 14.2 *Fifteen key questions about 360-degree feedback*

Purpose and Goals
1. Does 360-degree feedback do more harm than good?
2. Under what conditions and for whom does 360-degree feedback become beneficial?

Methodology and Psychometric Properties
3. What type and how many raters should be included?
4. Do ratings between rater groups agree with each other?
5. Do ratings within rater groups agree with each other?
6. Which response scale is best for 360-degree feedback?
7. How many rating points should be on a 360-degree feedback scale?
8. Should a 360-degree feedback report contain a mix of graphs, charts, and responses to open-ended questions to maximize understanding?

Process and Implementation
9. Can open-ended questions be emotionally damaging to clients?
10. Does personality impact how people respond to 360-degree feedback?
11. How do you manage the feedback of underestimators and overestimators?
12. What kind of training or certification is required by coaches to help clients understand and interpret 360-degree feedback reports?
13. Are there cultural differences to be considered in the use of 360-degree feedback?
14. Does 360-degree feedback require debriefing?
15. How can you leverage the impact of 360-degree feedback to ensure successful behavior change?

Source: Nowack (1999) and Nowack & Mashihi (2012, p. 158).

feedback can be grouped into three categories: purpose and goals this approach seeks to deliver, the design principles in terms of a robust methodology and the psychometric properties of this system, and key questions on which to focus in the implementation stage (see Table 14.2; Nowack, 1999). Much of the groundwork for these questions was done by previous research conducted by Fleenor, Taylor, and Chappelow (2008). Note also that there is no suggestion that this a prescription; rather, this is a guide that will require some further contextualization to the specific needs of the designers and implementers. Nowack and Mashihi (2012) reviewed extensive literature in addressing fifteen questions and ways to change behavior, as shown in Table 14.2.

These questions explore important issues in conducting the assessment process and outcome. Some of the questions are specific; for example, the question "Does 360-degree feedback do more harm than good?" deals with purpose and goal of the feedback, and "Which response scale is best for 360-degree feedback?" explores the type of scale that needs to be used. Further, "Can open-ended questions be emotionally damaging to clients?" and "What kind of training or certification is required by coaches to help clients understand and interpret 360-degree feedback reports?" explore the emotional component of the 360-degree feedback assessment. Effectively answering these questions may help in the preparation for overall 360-degree feedback and subsequent outcome.

Why Do We Need 360-Degree Feedback?

Dysfunctional managers can have a negative impact on the morale of coworkers and fail to deliver desired business results; therefore, it is pivotal for organizations to provide opportunities for development (Bunker, Kram, & Ting, 2002; Hogan, Hogan, & Kaiser, 2011). Functional managers can positively influence the morale of individuals at the workplace. There are numerous reasons highlighted in the literature to support the use of 360-degree feedback. The main reasons include talent management, developing leadership, and facilitating opportunity for organizational growth through human capital. Employing a management skills profile inventory comprising nineteen dimensions, Hazucha, Hezlett, and Schneider (1993) investigated the impact of the implementation of 360-degree feedback on changes in managers' skills profiles. The study included forty-eight participants who provided their responses both pre- and post-360-degree feedback intervention programs. The authors hypothesized that following the intervention there would be an increase in participants' skills and greater agreement in the self–other dyad. Specifically, the researchers hypothesized that feedback would increase participants' skills and that management skills would influence future advancement. The study found strong support for these hypotheses. The researchers also noted that environmental support was related to skill development. There was an association between self-ratings and environmental support. Similarly, in their study of two organizations, Atwater and Brett (2006) found support for improvements in performance orientation, leader consideration and cooperation, and employee development following a 360-degree feedback intervention. In total, 174 leaders took part in this study, where the majority of participants (70%) were male. Surveys from subordinates and peers were kept anonymous. Results may have been slightly different if the study had been done in a predominantly female sample. This study found that improved leaders' behaviors in a post-feedback scenario may lead to direct changes in the employees' attitudes toward work.

Longitudinal studies also support the use of 360-degree feedback in organizations. Smither, London, and Reilly (2005) conducted a meta-analysis of twenty-four longitudinal studies and showed small positive effects of 360-degree feedback on performance. The authors suggested that "Practitioners should not expect large, widespread performance improvements after employees receive multi-source feedback" (p. 33). But their key finding was an improvement, albeit small, in overall performance. Smither et al. (2005) also found that performance is likely to improve if the feedback highlights the need for change, when the receiver of the feedback has a favorable orientation toward feedback, and when he or she perceives there is a need to undertake behavioral changes. Furthermore, the nature of expected change must be achievable; individual perceptions play a pivotal role in the overall change process. Much effort is needed to facilitate evidence-based feedback in order to bring positive change.

Challenges for 360-Degree Feedback

The popularity of 360-degree feedback has been widespread in English-speaking contexts. Waldman, Atwater, and Antonioni (1998) noted that its success could largely be attributed to evaluations emerging from the human relations movement of the early 1950s and 1960s, in particular Mayo's human relations movement, which valued the role of developing relational contracts with people. However, adopting best-practice approaches may not always work as they do not take into account contingency and contextual influences. Managers need to receive contextualized feedback about their self-perception, making them personally more effective in their day-to-day management of employees.

Although the appeal of the 360-degree feedback process is evident in several reviews of literature, there are many implementation, validation, and perception challenges that may render this approach less effective. For example, Waldman et al. (1998) noted the paucity of objective and verifiable data or, in some cases, even a total lack of data and excessive reliance on anecdotes in the 360-degree process. They further noted the use of political agendas resulting in adverse performance outcomes against certain managers. These researchers highlighted the need to make consultants implementing programs more accountable and transparent in the process. Some of the problems can be averted through the use of pilot studies and training of the raters, as well as the use of focus group sessions for clarifying the expectations (Waldman et al., 1998). In a similar vein, DeNisi and Kluger (2000) stressed that clear and frequent feedback on complex tasks often results in positive outcomes for individual performance and development.

When organizations change the stated purpose of 360-degree feedback from developmental purposes to others such as imposing punitive and disciplinary measures or restricting access to certain resources for people, its effectiveness comes into question. Therefore, it is vital that consistency and transparency of purpose prevails to avoid potential harm to employees who partake in this feedback activity. We contend that coaching and training in the use of the instruments for 360-degree feedback and its genuine implementation through getting feedback on different aspects of performance from different groups are critical in realizing its full potential. Despite the novelty of 360-degree feedback in some countries, this approach has been used for the past thirty years. Church (2016) suggested that the popularity of 360-degree feedback may decline. Despite feedback, some managers may be reluctant to give up control of the review process. Personal prejudices might complicate giving and receiving feedback and there might be retaliation following low ratings. Overall, parties partaking in the 360-degree feedback enterprise should understand the purpose of this activity and appreciate the potential value thereof. Only in such circumstances can 360-degree feedback be effective.

Health implications also need to be considered when giving feedback. Positive or negative feedback influences feelings and there may be a biological response to it. For example, negative feedback can increase blood pressure (Lehman & Conley, 2010). The ratio of positive to negative feedback is critical in reducing negative emotions (Losada & Heaphy, 2004). It was found that a ratio of 3:1 positive to negative feedback may result in optimal performance, emotional well-being, and positive work ethic in workplace settings (Losada & Heaphy, 2004; Fredrickson & Losada, 2005). Well-being is pivotal for employee workplace performance (Athota, 2016). Therefore, negative feedback should be used cautiously and balanced with positive feedback.

High-quality instruments should be utilized to conduct 360-degree feedback assessment. Viswesvaran, Ones, and Schmidt (2016) highlighted the problems associated with interrater reliability of the measures. Problems with scales have also been noted by Bracken et al. (2016) in their work on undertaking meaningful comparisons of raters. To begin, the criterion validity (the accuracy of measures using clear indicators of performance) needs to be clearly agreed on in the design stage. Relevance of performance standards (construct validity) and its representativeness (content validity) are also important. The related issues of reliability of such measures in terms of consistency and accuracy by raters and ratees then become the focus of attention. We suggest that to deal with such problems, an attempt should be made to examine the differences between the raters' perceptions. Interrater reliabilities can also be compared, and, if necessary, training for the raters should be offered to improve the reliability of the process. More recently, Brown, Inceoglu, and Lin (2017) studied how rater biases can be prevented in a 360-degree feedback context by using forced choice items. Analyzing the effects of response biases in 360-degree feedback, they examined a data set of 4,765 observations of appraisal data of 922 managers. The researchers analyzed sixteen competencies of managers as assessed by peers, bosses, and subordinates as well as a self-assessed managerial skills inventory. Their analysis suggested that firms should use multidimensional forced choice models for preventing biases in rating.

360-Degree Feedback: A Transformational Learning Theory Perspective

The above review points to two core applications of the 360-degree feedback: assessment of performance and development of targeted individuals. Our focus here is more on the latter, and we argue that there is always an element of learning needed in developing adults in a workplace or other contexts. This view is widely recognized in a number of studies on adult learning as applied to the study and practice of developing human resources in a workplace context (Delahaye, Limmerick, & Hearn, 1994; Delahaye, 2004). As 360-degree feedback occurs in a workplace context and involves learning for adults in this setting, we consider Mezirow's theory of transformational learning to be a useful framework for making the 360-degree feedback process more effective (Mezirow, 1981, 1994a, 1994b). Mezirow (1981, 1994a), building on

Haberman's ideas, developed a critical theory of adult learning and suggested three main domains of learning for adults in the workplace: instrumental learning, communicative learning, and emancipatory learning. While instrumental learning focuses on learning where individuals can manipulate the environment, communicative learning is concerned with developing an understanding of the values and beliefs others have in order for the learner to be able to understand them and interact with them more effectively. Finally, emancipatory learning, which is the highest order of learning, focuses on learning that challenges the premises and assumptions that we as individuals hold very closely to our hearts. These are the mental models and routines that we develop over a long period of time and that may affect our performance at the workplace.

The above domains of learning are relevant to the discussion here as these also appear as workplace competencies that people are expected to deliver in their day-to-day roles. For example, knowledge of and ability to perform a technical operation is central to all forms of instrumental learning. Similarly, adults in the workplace have to interact and work with others not just at a technical level but also at a relational and emotional level. This is the domain of communicative learning. It concerns how we interact and communicate with others. Our understanding of the expressed and emotional messages that are explicit or implicit in our interactions with other people is a key part of developmental learning. Similarly, for emancipatory learning to happen, we must challenge our preconceived values, belief systems, and paradigms. There are many critiques of Mezirow's work as well as responses to those critiques (e.g., Mezirow, 1992, 1994b; Newman, 1994; Tennant, 1994). The reader may find these exchanges informative.

We argue that the above three domains of learning are relevant to the 360-degree feedback process. We note that because of the inadequate development of people in all of the above domains of learning, we often see major gaps in capabilities of managerial staff as well as in leaders' soft skills for effective management of people. For example, we see deficits in skills and knowledge aspects such as *administrative skills of planning, organizing,* and *time management,* which are well within the scope of instrumental learning. Similarly, skills pertaining to communication such as *informing, listening, oral communication, inter- and intrapersonal skills, human relations,* and so on are well within the umbrella or domain of communicative learning. Finally, higher-order skills, such as *leadership development* and those focusing on individuals' *world views* about running a business, *orientation toward workers,* and *management* require skills and strategies that are germane to emancipatory learning.

We also note that 360-degree feedback can be used as a groundwork for making decisions and has been found to be useful for talent management and succession planning (Bracken et al., 2016). Unfortunately, if one looks at the approach taken by most organizations in dealing with training and development themes, they rarely scratch the surface in terms of either the topics covered or the depth in which they are delivered. There are numerous reasons for this.

In most cases, the cost involved in delivering such interventions is so high that this exercise is often reduced to a compliance activity. Additionally, in other cases, there may not be enough managerial and employee bandwidth or managers and employees are reluctant to deal with developmental issues when there are pressing operational issues at hand.

As the problems with implementing effective 360-degree feedback extend beyond instrumental learning approaches, there is therefore a need in practice to engage with both managers and raters in communicative and emancipatory forms of learning if the 360-degree approach is to realize its full potential. This would require a significant commitment from the organizational development practitioners' community to work closely with human resource management practitioners as well as line managers. This would redesign the 360-degree feedback model to incorporate an integrated approach wherein elements of learning are embedded in the design. Similarly, there should be aspects of the above approach embedded in the implementation at various stages. Traditional approaches to reliability and validity may fail to capture the complexity in assessing the effectiveness of the rating process as such approaches cannot capture the vast and complex nature of development necessary for managers in dealing with today's complex, interrelated, and interdependent environment. The wider business environment today has been classified by many as volatile, uncertain, chaotic, and agile. This would suggest that all three levels of learning intervention should be integrated in the approach to promote individual and organizational development. The 360-degree feedback approach should incorporate input from people who are qualified to comment. The focus of such assessments for developing feedback should provide detailed and accurate descriptors by involving leaders from the organization rather than using a generic inventory profile.

Conclusion

In conclusion, the existing evidence suggests that 360-degree feedback is vital to enhancing leaders' performance in the workplace and that sustainable individual, group, and organizational change is possible through 360-degree feedback. It is pivotal to use appropriate high-quality scales for assessing performance. Personality traits and emotional reactions also should be taken into account when conducting and delivering 360-degree feedback assessment. Cultural factors also play an important role in receiving and delivering 360-degree feedback. As with any complex assessment, challenges are inevitable in conducting 360-degree feedback analysis and providing feedback. Therefore, future research should continue to devise new scales and methods for implementing 360-degree feedback assessment in addition to advancing theory and research. In sum, we contend that 360-degree feedback can be used effectively to bring change through a transformational learning opportunity.

References

Al Ansari, A., Donnon, T., Al Khalifa, K., Darwish, A., & Violato, C. (2014). The construct and criterion validity of the multi-source feedback process to assess physician performance: A meta-analysis. *Advances in Medical Education and Practice, 5*, 39.

Appelbaum, E., Bailey, T., & Berg, P. Kalleberg, A. (2000). *Manufacturing advantage: Why high-performance work systems pay off*. New York: ILR Press.

Athota, V. S. (2016). Foundations and future of well-being: How personality influences happiness and well-being. In *Impact of organizational trauma on workplace behavior and performance* (pp. 279–293). Business Science Reference Press.

Athota, V. S., & Roberts, R. D. (2015). How extraversion + leads to problem-solving ability. *Psychological Studies, 60*, 332–338.

Atwater, L. E., & Brett, J. F. (2006). 360-degree feedback to leaders: Does it relate to changes in employee attitudes? *Group & Organization Management, 31*(5), 578–600.

Atwater, L., Waldman, D., Ostroff, C., Robie, C., & Johnson, K. M. (2005). Self–other agreement: Comparing its relationship with performance in the U.S. and Europe. *International Journal of Selection and Assessment, 13*, 25–40.

Baker, N. (2010). Employee feedback technologies in the human performance system. *Human Resource Development International, 13*(4), 477–485.

Barney, J. (1991). Firm resources and sustained competitive advantage. *Journal of Management, 17*(1), 99–120.

Bell, S. T., & Arthur, W. A. (2008). Feedback acceptance in developmental assessment canters: The role of feedback message, participant personality, and affective response to the feedback session. *Journal of Organizational Behavior, 29*, 681–703.

Blumberg, M., & Pringle, C. D. (1982). The missing opportunity in organizational research: Some implications for a theory of work performance. *Academy of Management Review, 7*(4), 560–569.

Bommer, W. H., Rubin, R. S., & Bartels, L. K. (2005). Assessing the "unassessable": Interpersonal and managerial skills. In K. Martell & T. Calderon (Eds.), *Assessment of student learning in business schools: Best practices each step of the way* (pp. 103–130). Tallahassee, FL: Association for Institutional Research and AACSB International.

Bono, J., & Colbert, A. (2005). Understanding responses to multi-source feedback: The role of core self-evaluations. *Personnel Psychology, 58*, 171–203.

Boxall, P., & Purcell, J. (2016). *Strategy and human resource management* (4th edn.). Houndmills: Palgrave Macmillan.

Bracken, D. W., & Rose, D. S. (2011). When does 360-degree feedback create behaviour change? And how would we know it when it does? *Journal of Business and Psychology, 26*(2), 183–192.

Bracken, D. W., Rose, D. S., & Church, A. H. (2016). The evolution and devolution of 360 degree feedback. *Industrial and Organizational Psychology: Perspectives on Science and Practice, 9*(4), 761–794.

Brett, J., & Atwater, L. (2001). 360-degree feedback: Accuracy, reactions and perceptions of usefulness. *Journal of Applied Psychology, 86*, 930–942.

Brown, A., Inceoglu, I., & Lin, Y. (2017). Preventing rater biases in 360-degree feedback by forcing choice. *Organizational Research Methods, 20*(1), 121–148.

Bunker, K. A., Kram, K. E., & Ting, S. (2002). The young and the clueless. *Harvard Business Review, 80*(12), 80–87.

Campbell, D. J., & Lee, C. (1988). Self-appraisal in performance evaluation: Development versus evaluation. *Academy of Management Review, 13*(2), 302–314.

Campion, M. C., Campion, E. D., & Campion, M. A. (2015). Improvements in performance management through the use of 360 feedack. *Industrial and Organizational Psychology: Perspectives on Science and Practice, 8*(1), 85–93.

Carver, C. S., & Scheier, M. F. (1982). Control theory: A useful conceptual framework for personality–social, clinical, and health psychology. *Psychological Bulletin, 92*, 111–135.

Church, A. H. (2016). Is engagement overrated? Five questions to consider before doing your next engagement survey. *Talent Quarterly, 9*, 1–7.

Conger, J.A. (2002, November 29). The danger of delusion. *Financial Times*, pp. 1–4.

Dalton, M. A. (1998). Best practices: Five rationales for using 360-degree feedback in organizations. In W. W. Tornow & M. London (Eds.), *Maximizing the value of 360-degree feedback: A process for successful individual and organizational development* (pp. 59–77). San Francisco, CA: Jossey-Bass.

Decotiis, T., & Petit, A. (1978). The performance appraisal process: A model and some testable propositions. *Academy of Management Review, 3*(3), 635.

Delahaye, B. L. (2004). *Human resource development: Adult learning and knowledge management*. Milton, Australia: John Wiley & Sons.

Delahaye, B. L., Limerick, D. C., & Hearn, G. (1994). The relationship between andragogical and pedagogical orientations and the implications for adult learning. *Adult Education Quarterly, 44*(4), 187–200.

DeNisi, A. S., & Kluger, A. N. (2000). Feedback effectiveness: Can 360-degree appraisals be improved? *The Academy of Management Executive, 14*(1), 129–139.

DeNisi, A., & Pritchard, R. (2006). Performance appraisal, performance management and improving individual performance: A motivational framework. *Management and Organization Review, 2*(2), 253–277.

DeNisi, A. S., & Murphy, K. R. (2017). Performance appraisal and performance management: 100 years of progress? *Journal of Applied Psychology, 102*(3), 421–433.

de Silva, P. (2014). Tackling psychopathy: A necessary competency in leadership development? *Progress in Neurology and Psychiatry, 5*, 4–6.

Dweck, C. S. (1986). Motivational processes affecting learning. *American Psychologist, 41*, 1040–1048.

Farh, J. L., Werbel, J. D., & Bedeian, A. G. (1988). An empirical assessment of self-appraisal based performance evaluation. *Personnel Psychology, 41*, 141–156.

Festinger, L. (1957) *A theory of cognitive dissonance*. Stanford, CA: Stanford University Press

Fleenor, J., Taylor, S., & Chappelow, C. (2008). *Leveraging the impact of 360-degree feedback*. New York: Wiley.

Fletcher, C. (2001). Performance appraisal and management: The developing research agenda. *Journal of Occupational and Organizational Psychology, 74*(4), 473–487.

Franceschini, F., & Turina, E. (2013). Quality improvement and redesign of performance measurement systems an application to the academic field. *Quality and Quantity, 47*, 465–483.

Fredrickson, B. L., & Losada, M. (2005). Positive affect and the complex dynamics of human flourishing. *American Psychologist, 60*, 678–686.

Gorman, C. A., Meriac, J. P., Roch, S. G., Ray, J. L., & Gamble, J. S. (2017). An exploratory study of current performance management practices: Human resource executives' perspectives. *International Journal of Selection and Assessment, 25*(2), 193–202.

Gruman, J. A., & Saks, A. M. (2011). Performance management and employee engagement. *Human Resource Management Review, 21*(2), 123–136.

Hageman, M. G. J. S., Ring, D. C., Gregory, P. J., Rubash, H. E., & Harmon, L. (2015). Do 360-degree feedback survey results relate to patient satisfaction measures? *Clinical Orthopaedics and Related Research, 473*(5), 1590–1597.

Hazucha, J. F., Hezlett, S. A., & Schneider, R. J. (1993). The impact of 360-degree feedback on management skills development. *Human Resource Management, 32*(2–3), 325–351.

Hermel-Stanescu, M. (2015). The role of performance appraisal in the context of performance management systems. *SEA-Practical Application of Science, 3*(1), 275–278.

Hofstede, G., & McRae, R. R. (2004). Personality and culture revisited: Linking traits and dimensions of culture. *Cross-Cultural Research, 38*, 52–88.

Hogan, J., Hogan, R., & Kaiser, R. B. (2011). Management derailment: Personality assessment and mitigation. In S. Zedeck (Ed.), *American Psychological Association handbook of industrial and organizational psychology* (pp. 555–575). Washington, DC: American Psychological Association.

Kossek, E. E., Huang, J. L., Piszczek, M. M., Fleenor, J. W., & Ruderman, M. (2017). Rating expatriate leader effectiveness in multisource feedback systems: Cultural distance and hierarchical effects. *Human Resource Management, 56*(1), 151–172.

Laleman, F., Pereira, V., & Malik, A. (2015). Understanding cultural singularities of "Indianness" in an intercultural business setting. *Culture and Organization, 21*(5), 427–447.

Lehman, B. J., & Conley, K. M. (2010). Momentary reports of social-evaluative threat predict ambulatory blood pressure. *Psychological Science and Personality Science, 1*, 51–56.

Losada, M., & Heaphy, E. (2004). The role of positivity and connectivity in the performance of business teams: A nonlinear dynamics model. *American Behavioral Scientist, 47*, 740–765.

Luffarelli, J., Goncalves, D., & Stanatoginannakis, A. (2016). When feedback interventions backfire: Why higher performance feedback may result in lower self-percieved competence and satisfaction with performance. *Human Resource Management, 55*, 591–614.

Malik, A. (2013). Post-GFC people management challenges: A study of India's information technology sector. *Asia Pacific Business Review, 19*(2), 230–246.

Malik, A., & Pereira, V. (2015). Culture research in India: Critical issues and future research opportunities. In Vijay Pereira and Ashish Malik (Eds.), *Investigating cultural aspects in Indian organizations* (pp. 185–197). Cham, Switzerland: Springer.

Malik, A., & Pereira, V. (2016a). *Indian culture and work organisations in transition*. New Delhi: Routledge.

Malik, A., & Pereira, V. (2016b). India: A culture in transition. In A. Malik & V. Pereira (Eds), *Indian culture and work organisations in transition* (pp. 1–13). New Delhi: Routledge.

Mayer, R. C., and Davis, J. H. (1999). The effect of the performance appraisal system on trust for mnagement: A field quasi-experiment. *Journal of Applied Psychology*, *84*(1), 123–136.

McKenna, S., Richardson, J., & Manroop, L. (2011). Alternative paradigms and the study and practice of performance management and evaluation. *Human Resource Management Review*, *21*, 148–157.

Mezirow, J. (1981). A critical theory of adult learning and education. *Adult Education Quarterly*, *32*(1), 3–24.

Mezirow, J. (1992). Transformation theory: Critique and confusion. *Adult Education Quarterly*, *42*(4), 250–252.

Mezirow, J. (1994a). Understanding transformation theory. *Adult Education Quarterly*, *44*(4), 222–232.

Mezirow, J. (1994b). Response to Mark Tennant and Michael Newman. *Adult Education Quarterly*, *44*(4), 243–244.

Mohapatra, M. (2015). 360 degree feedback: A review of literature. *Research Scholar of Management KIIT University Bhubaneswar Orissa*, *2*(1), 112–116.

Moscoso, S., & Salgado, J. (2004). "Dark side" personality styles as predictors of task, contextual, and job performance. *International Journal of Selection and Assessment*, *12*, 356–362.

Newman, M. (1994). Response to understanding transformation theory. *Adult Education Quarterly*, *44*(4), 236–242.

Nowack, K. (1999). 360 degree feedback. In D. G. Langdon, K. S. Whiteside, & M. M. McKenna (Eds.), *Intervention: 50 performance technology tools* (pp. 34–46). San Francisco, CA: Jossey-Bass.

Nowack, K., Hartley, J., & Bradley, W. (1999). Evaluating results of your 360-degree feedback intervention. *Training and Development*, *53*, 48–53.

Nowack, M. K., & Mashihi, S. (2012). Evidence-based answers to 15 questions about leveraging 360-degree feedback. *Consulting Psychology Journal: Practice and Research*, *64*(3), 157–182.

Obisi, C. (2011, December). Employee performance appraisal and its implication for individual and organizational growth. *Australian Journal of Business and Management Research*, *1*(9), 92–97.

O'Connor, P. J., & Athota, V. S. (2013). The intervening role of agreeableness in the relationship between trait emotional intelligence and Machiavellianism: Reassessing the potential dark side of EI. *Personality and Individual Differences*, *55*, 750–754.

Paulhus, D. L., & Williams, K. (2002). The dark triad of personality: Narcissism, Machiavellianism, and psychopathy. *Journal of Research in Personality*, *36*, 556–568.

Pereira, V., & Malik, A. (2013). East is East? Understanding aspects of Indian culture(s) within organisations. *Culture and Organization*, *19*(5), 453–456.

Pereira, V., & Malik, A. (2015a). *Human capital in the Indian IT/BPO industry*. London: Palgrave Macmillan.

Pereira, V., & Malik, A. (2015b). *Investigating cultural aspects in Indian organizations: Empirical evidence*. Cham, Switzerland: Springer.

Pereira, V., & Malik, A. (2015c). Culture in Indian organisations: Evidence-based research and practice. In V. Pereira & A. Malik (Eds.), *Investigating cultural aspects in Indian organizations: Empirical evidence* (pp. 1–10). Cham: Springer.

Pereira, V., & Malik, A. (2015d). Making sense and identifying aspects of Indian culture(s) in organisations: Demystifying through empirical evidence. *Culture and Organization, 21*(5), 355–365.

Pereira, V., & Malik, A. (2016a). Conclusion and future research directions. In *Indian culture and work organisations in transition* (pp. 220–232). Abingdon, UK: Routledge and Taylor & Francis.

Pereira, V., Malik, A., & Froese, F. (2017). Mapping the impact of Asian business systems on HRM and organisational behaviour: Multi-level comparative perspectives. *Journal of Asia Business Studies, 11*(3), 253–261.

Pichler, S. (2012). The social context of performance appraisal and appraisal reactions: A meta-analysis. *Human Resource Management, 51*(5), 709–732.

Rai, H., & Singh, M. (2013). A study of mediating variables of the relationship between 360 feedback and employee performance. *Human Resource Development International, 66*(1), 56–73.

Rusu, G., Avasilcai, S., & Hutu, C.-A. (2016). Employee performance appraisal: A conceptual framework. *Annals of the University of Oradea*, 53–58.

Smith, A., Oczkowski, E., & Sellby-Smith, C. (2011). To have and to hold: Modelling the drivers of employee turnover and skill retention in Australian organisations. *International Journal of Human Resource Management, 22*(2), 395–416.

Smither, J. W., London, M., & Reilly, R. R. (2005). Does performance improve following multisource feedback? A theoretical model, meta-analysis, and review of empirical findings. *Personnel Psychology, 58*(1), 33–66.

Swing, S. R. (2007). The ACGME outcome project: Retrospective and prospective. *Medical Teacher, 29*(7), 648–654.

Tennant, M. (1994). Response to understanding transformation theory. *Adult Education Quarterly, 44*(4), 233–235.

Viswesvaran, C., Ones, D. S., & Schmidt, F. L. (2016). Comparing rater groups: How to disentangle rating reliability from construct-level disagreements. *Industrial and Organizational Psychology, 9*(4), 800–806.

Vroom, V. H. (1964). *Work and motivation*. New York: Wiley

Waldman, D. A., Atwater, L. E., & Antonioni, D. (1998). Has 360 degree feedback gone amok? *Academy of Management Executive, 12*(2), 86–94.

Ward, P. (1997). *360 Feedback*. London: Institute of Personnel and Development.

Wright, P., Dunford, B., & Snell, S. (2001). Human resources and the resource-based view of the firm. *Journal of Management, 6*, 701–721.

Zhao, Y., Zhang, X., Chang, Q., & Sun, B. (2013). Psychometric characteristics of the 360 feedback scales in professionalism and interpersonal and communication skills assessment of surgery residents in China. *Journal of Surgical Education, 70*, 628–635.

PART III

Contexts and Sources of Feedback

15 Technology-Enhanced Feedback

Cassim Munshi and Christopher C. Deneen

Introduction

Technology-enhanced assessment (TEA) and technology-enhanced feedback (TEF) are growing areas of development and research. TEA, as the name suggests, may be understood as assessment of, for, and as learning where technology is leveraged to benefit assessment experience or outcomes (Jordan, 2013). TEF may be understood within that context. Benefit focuses on engagement with feedback and the impact of that engagement (Gomez et al., 2013). The acronym TEF may also stand for "technology-enabled feedback," which suggests that technology makes possible an approach to feedback. It became apparent during this review, however, that there is an absence of reliable evidence that what people call enabling actually enables. Several studies, for example, claimed to examine technology as an enabler for feedback; it was clear, however that the feedback approaches under examination were still entirely feasible to enact absent of technology. This chapter therefore focuses on and frames technology using a more reliable benchmark: how technology may enhance feedback processes.

Much progress has been made in TEF research and practice. We have seen growth in the use of instructional designers to assist in redesigning curricula and learning experiences, particularly in higher education. Benefit of learning and assessment are increasingly common benchmarks for evaluating efficacy of instructional design. This has positively influenced development of backbone architecture for universities and schools as well as enhancement of learning management systems. Corresponding practices in TEF are increasingly identified and discussed in terms of success, scalability, and applicability in educational contexts. We have also witnessed the emergence of educational data mining, which builds on TEA and TEF and carries larger scale formative potential for program and institutional evaluation and improvement. Accompanying this has been gradual progress toward conducting critical and empirical research into TEF and away from using showcasing of success as a substitute for critical inquiry.

The potential of TEF is tempered by chronic problems, however. The use of technology to support feedback is marked by cycles of technology adoption and abandonment (Deneen, Brown, & Carless, 2017). Unresolved issues of validity and reliability related to the interpretation of students' achievement not only have impact on the sustainability of an initiative but may call into question the value of that initiative (Deneen & Shroff, 2014). Research on TEF continues to place a disproportionate emphasis on showcasing, with less inquiry into the significant challenges of adopting and sustaining these practices. This research issue applies to TEF and more generally TEA (Deneen et al., 2017). As this review discusses, even highly reputable peer-reviewed publications routinely publish research that emphasizes showcasing at the expense of critical inquiry. Assuming research informs practice, a clear connection may be suggested: problems in TEF research contribute to the scarcity of sustained adoption, integration, and scaling-up of TEF. Examining issues within the research may, therefore, have implications for critical areas of TEF practice.

This chapter aims to explore issues in TEF through a systematic review of the literature and make suggestions on ways forward. We first provide some historical context on TEF, which includes a discussion of the impetus for TEF, how it has progressed into modern use, and several unresolved issues. We then present our methodology for the review process, focusing on issues of scope, evaluation, and analysis. Next, we discuss the results of the review in terms of core, emergent themes, and their relationships to one another. We then discuss these results as current trends and issues in TEF research and practice. Key points include the implications of who is driving the dialog around TEF, what we know works well in TEF, and where there seem to be persistent and significant gaps in research and practice. Finally, we present suggestions for researchers and practitioners wishing to explore and utilize TEF, and in doing so move forward the connected fields of research and practice.

Historical Context of TEF

This section provides some background on the progressive development and implementation of TEF systems over the past few decades and the corresponding research that has been conducted.

TEF Development

Early emphasis in TEF was directed toward automation and enhanced scoring efficiency. As early as the 1960s, automated marking systems were promoted as saving time and resources, while reducing the drudgery associated with staff marking and generating performance indicators (Dikli, 2006; Warschauer & Ware, 2006). Limitations of technology, however, imposed boundaries on sophistication. This resulted in an emphasis on scoring as a primary means of feedback. While a score or letter grade may technically be considered feedback, its function is principally summative and of limited value toward advancing achievement (Lipnevich & Smith, 2008; Jackson & Marks, 2016). Beyond scores, automated interpretations of quality were limited to surface-level judgments. Even provision of this rudimentary feedback carried a high risk of error and therefore required carefully constrained user responses.

Developments in hardware and software led to the affordance of deeper and broader automated performance indicators. The Writers Workbench software, introduced in the early 1980s, used algorithms to provide narrative feedback based on the quality of students' writing with fewer constraints on students' inputs. Writers Workbench went beyond surface judgment limitations of prior software and was able to offer more sophisticated interpretations of appropriate language use in less constrained user responses (Warschauer & Ware, 2006).

These enhancements represent a seminal moment in TEF – developments in input and output allowed the focus of TEF to shift from score provision toward more formative provision of feedback (Warschauer & Ware, 2006). This also allowed the orientation of TEF development to change – from TEF near-exclusively serving as workload-reducing tools for teachers to formatively oriented, student-centered systems that facilitated students' academic development. By the turn of the twenty-first century, this change in orientation had allowed development of software engines capable of providing immediate and diagnostic feedback to students on specific features of writing, including grammar, style, organization, and development (Attali, 2004; Dikli, 2006).

Advances in artificial intelligence have enabled further TEF capabilities. Natural language processing technology, for example, has been used to train computers to analyze essays and provide feedback designed to promote understanding and use of best writing practices (Attali, 2004). Machines could be trained to learn from input and analysis of large sets of human-annotated essays (Attali, 2004; Shermis, Burstein, & Bursky, 2013) and adapt their analysis of individual responses before providing feedback. These advances, accompanied by increased computational power and efficiency, have led to the development of systems with enhanced sophistication and reliability. The remarkable progress made within this sphere has moved TEF development beyond automated scoring and multimodal feedback types toward the development of computers as intelligent agents of feedback. Intelligent tutoring systems and adaptive testing engines are increasingly able to provide specific and directed feedback in response to students' ongoing interactions with computers. Today, these systems are even capable of making data-informed recommendations on follow-up tasks intending to consolidate learning efforts.

These developments accelerated larger-scale adoption of TEF by the testing industry. Companies like Educational Testing Service (ETS) were able to significantly enhance the reliability of their automated feedback engines. This led to their deployment in large-scale, high-stakes tertiary tests such as the GMAT. During this time, ETS's e-rater engine went into widespread use in the United States. Thousands of students from sixth through twelfth grade were interacting with it as an essay feedback mechanism (Burstein et al., 1998). The increasing sophistication and formative potential of TEF had by then become apparent; TEF was, however, still not commonly framed as an instructional tool for teachers nor was it frequently seen in classrooms.

The Internet changed this. The rapid expansion of the web during the early 2000s gave birth to a plethora of TEF applications. Web portals, online discussion forums, and learning management systems afforded teachers opportunities to directly interface with TEF systems and deliver feedback more quickly to students (Warschauer & Ware, 2006). This also marked a shift in emphasis in what constituted enhancement. Until this point, TEF systems emphasized feedback automation. With the development of the web as a platform for communication came TEF systems that utilized technology to enhance transmission and mode of instructor and peer feedback. By the late 2000s, these applications were supplemented with alternative modes of feedback creation and delivery. Audio and video feedback and screencasts of instructional feedback could now be utilized through increased connectivity. Through these developments, TEF became more prevalent in classroom settings while continuing to evolve toward systems supporting formative student development through increasingly complex and multimodal engagement.

TEF Research

TEF has been a constant subject of research over the past few decades. Some findings are encouraging – three meta-analyses investigating the effects of TEF on student writing all found significant positive effects on quality (Cochran-Smith, 1991; Bangert-Drowns, 1993; Goldberg, Russell, & Cook, 2003). Attali (2004) in discussing these analyses reported that through regularized TEF usage, students demonstrated enhanced capabilities in correcting errors and effectively improving their work in subsequent submissions.

Persistent and unresolved concerns have surfaced, however. One issue is quality of computer-generated feedback, much of which is derived from pre-programmed banks of questions and generic statements. Warschauer and Ware (2006) expressed concern when they observed that none of the feedback provided by automated scoring engines was "remotely similar to what a trained instructor can provide" (p. 160). They further questioned the ability of students to understand, let alone act on, any form of computer feedback other than "the most simple of computer-generated feedback" (p. 172). This perspective was published over a decade ago, yet similar issues persist today.

Another concern lies with acceptance and sustained use of technology as a facilitator of the feedback provision process. TEF and more generally TEA systems have allowed feedback from tutors and peers to be delivered more efficiently. In addition to its widely reported benefits of this efficiency on student achievement, such systems have been shown to improve other aspects of student development such as their competencies in self-regulated learning (Van den Boom, Paas, Van Merrienboer, & Van Gog, 2004). Despite substantial benefits that have been reported over the past few decades, it appears that TEF systems have not found their way into mainstream schooling systems.

Some problems lie within the approach to researching TEF. Many studies on TEF over the past few decades have been directed toward demonstrating high levels of agreement between computer and human feedback (Burstein et al., 1998; Attali & Burstein, 2006; Warschauer & Ware, 2006). There are at least two concerns over such an approach. First, using agreement with human scores as a measure of TEF quality does not directly evaluate specific content and merits of the actual feedback. Second, such an approach downplays the importance of students taking up and responding to feedback.

Another concern is that much of TEF research is funded or even carried out by companies that produce commercial TEF products. Warschauer and Ware (2006) bring attention to one particularly harmful consequence of this: inherent biases in such research may compromise use of research to further evidence-based practices. Implementers are left with doubts regarding results on whether TEF systems are able to provide accurate and usable information and on the degree to which TEF contributes to positive learning outcomes. The authors advocated for increased objectivity and criticality in the evaluation of these TEF systems.

Advances in TEF over the past half-century have certainly been remarkable; avenues of improvement must, however, address concerns within both use of and research into TEF systems. Through conducting a systematic review of substantive published research, this chapter explores current trends and issues in TEF and make evidence-based recommendations for research and practice. To that end, the remainder of the chapter is organized into the following sections:

1. Methodology applied to search and analyze the literature
2. Key constructs and concepts associated with technology-enhanced feedback
3. Synthesis of key findings that indicates current trends and issues
4. Discussion of implications and suggestions for how practice and research into TEF may be improved and guided.

Methodology

This section describes the approaches adopted by the authors during the review process and highlights some of the considerations that took place during the processes of scoping, searching, abstraction, and analysis.

Setting the Scope

The core term that sets the scope of this literature review is technology-enhanced feedback. Research uses terms such as enabled, assisted, or enhanced. These are more than semantic distinctions; each term suggests a different threshold must be met. We chose "enhanced" as a balanced term – it suggests that technology plays a central role for the feedback, unlike the term "assisted," but feedback may in fact still be possible in the absence of technology, unlike the term "enabled."

The scope of our search included relevant studies that did not specifically use the terms technology-assisted/enabled/enhanced assessment but were nonetheless relevant. Terms like assessment (inclusive of assessment of, as, and for learning) and feedback (inclusive of feed forward) were used to manipulate search strings and obtain relevant sources. "Technology" was also used as a search string modifier and was treated as inclusive of key areas such as smartphones and mobile technology.

Conducting the Search

Search strings derived from the set scope were used to conduct an extensive search with multiple passes. A first pass was conducted using Google Scholar and restricted search terms. The initial search yielded a massive number of results representing a wide range of quality, even when excluding pieces not purporting to be research. The initial results sustain a point raised in our introduction: there is a vast body of publications on TEF (and more generally, TEA) labeled as scholarship but lacking empirical research components, sound theoretical frameworks, accounts of bias and limitations, or some combination thereof.

The search was narrowed and refined through several standard methods. Search strings were manipulated; more narrowly defined search strings were used as recommended by Fink (2005). A core group of relevant, high-impact journals were identified and hand searches were conducted within these journals. Reference lists of identified high-impact publications were examined and compared for articles that appear in multiple reference lists and are themselves high impact. Finally, expert consultation on sources was sought from two scholars in the fields of educational technology and educational assessment.

Abstracting the Articles

Out of this process, we assembled an initial list of thirty-five articles meeting basic criteria of admission. The authors split the articles and engaged in a two-pass system for determining quality and eliminating unqualified articles (Fink, 2005). The first pass was for relevance. Although the initial list of articles already met a basic threshold, an additional set of relevance benchmarks was applied. Specifically, we excluded articles that did not address what was identifiably TEF, regardless of terms used.

A second pass was conducted for methodological soundness with a scale score given to articles. A soundness threshold was established. Articles not meeting this were excluded. Assuming articles came from credible sources, further inclusion thresholds were set liberally. This supports the function of this chapter as a critical review and supports several key points raised later in this chapter regarding research impact and quality.

The authors then conducted a reliability exercise (Fink, 2005). A selection of five articles was abstracted by each author. Results were compared, discussed, and adjusted. Once sufficient interreader reliability had been established, the articles were divided between the two authors and full abstracting was systematically conducted. This consists of setting a priori categories according to typology, context, methodology, and findings. An additional holistic judgement was made regarding article quality, as noted earlier.

Conducting Analysis

Our approach utilized principles of meta-synthesis. Within the established a priori categories, emergent categories and codes were derived. This was accomplished through a multistage progress involving the authors and an external research assistant. Emergent categories and codes were established separately by each author. Then, the authors and research assistant came together to stabilize categories, codes, and axial relationships between and among both.

Ironically, this analytical process was conducted using nothing more technologically sophisticated than sticky notes, pens, a few dry erase markers, and a whiteboard. In a chapter concerning technology as process-enhancer, the authors chose to forgo "enhancing" their analysis through technology. Certainly, options exist – software packages such as NVivo are visually alluring and marketed as flexible solutions. The authors share Saldaña's (2015) perspective, however, that the sophistication of qualitative analysis lies in the human decision-making process rather than any particular technology. For this project, the low-tech activities of physically arranging codes on a white board, stepping back, evaluating, discussing, and then rearranging presented a superior advantage. We conducted our analytical process according to the same standard for technology under examination: enhancement.

Current Trends and Issues

Results from our analysis indicated three primary areas that may be explored in the TEF literature: (1) how feedback processes are enhanced by technology, (2) the effects of different types of TEF systems on students, and (3) how TEF systems are evaluated.

How Does Technology Enhance Feedback?

We may understand how technology enhances feedback by identifying three distinct processes during feedback provision. These are (1) *acquiring* information from the student during some learning activity, (2) *transforming* the acquired information into a feedback message, and (3) *conveying* the feedback message to the student. Technology may enhance feedback if it can perform at least one of these three processes. Table 15.1 summarizes how feedback may be enhanced by several types of TEF systems.

Table 15.1 *Processes where technology enhances feedback*

TEF System	Reported by	Technology Enhances Feedback by		
		Acquiring	Transforming	Conveying
Websites that host feedback	Harrison et al. (2013)			✓
Audio feedback	Cann (2014); Henderson & Phillips (2014); Hennessy & Forrester (2014); McCarthy (2015)	✓		✓
Video and screencast feedback	Barry (2012); Crook et al. (2012); Marriott & Teoh (2012); Henderson & Phillips (2014, 2015); McCarthy (2015); Yuan & Kim (2015); Phillips et al. (2016); West & Turner (2016);	✓		✓
Discussion forums	Shroff & Deneen (2011); Coll et al. (2013); Huang & Hung (2013)	✓		✓
Messaging systems and learning management systems	Burrows & Shortis (2011); Hovardas et al. (2014); Lai & Hwang (2015)	✓		✓
Adaptive grade release	Hepplestone et al. (2011); Parkin et al. (2012); Irwin et al. (2013)	✓		✓
e-Learning applications	Shute & Towle (2003); Timmers et al. (2013); Van der Kleij et al. (2015)	✓	✓	✓
Automated marking systems	Dikli (2006); Warschauer & Ware (2006); Jordan & Mitchell (2009); Chodorow et al. (2010); Jordan (2012); Jordan (2013)	✓	✓	✓
Intelligent tutoring systems	Narciss et al. (2014)	✓	✓	✓
Computer games	Shute (2011); Shute & Ke (2012); Nino & Evans (2015)	✓	✓	✓

Most TEF systems are able to convey information to and from students; only a handful engage in transforming information. Two categories of TEF systems are thus identified: systems that enhance feedback processes without transforming acquired information and systems that do.

Enhancing Feedback without Transforming Information

This category of TEF focuses on acquisition and presentation of information as feedback. Technology is not involved in modifying or processing the information; thus, human action is necessary. For example, a tutor who receives a student's essay through email must construct the feedback before replying via email. While technology affords instant essay submission and instant feedback delivery, the analysis of work product and subsequent generation of feedback remains human. TEF systems in this category include those that deliver feedback messages through audiovisual modalities, email, text messages sent over web portals, and forums on learning management systems.

These are not simply vehicles for feedback, however. Audio, video, and screencast modalities allow for enhanced capture, distribution, and storage of digital information by both tutors and students. Feedback processes are also enhanced as tutors can quickly self-record feedback and comments on students' work, and then host these audio and video files on an online portal for students to access (Crook et al., 2012; Marriott & Teoh, 2012; McCarthy, 2015; Phillips, Henderson, & Ryan, 2016; West & Turner, 2016). Of great importance is the ability of students to self-regulate their engagement with audio, video, and screencast feedback. This may account for the high demonstrated impact of these modes of feedback on student achievement (Hattie & Timperley, 2007). This allows for use of students' own performance to serve as a self-regulated feedback mechanism as well; for example, by students recording their own presentations for later viewing and reflection (Barry, 2012). Other studies have also investigated the utility of video modalities in relationship to other feedback-related activities, such as online discussion forums. Huang and Hung (2013), for example, observed that students regarded such activities as being highly promising and beneficial in their development.

Design principles play an important role in using audiovisual technologies for feedback. Hennessy and Forrester (2014) developed a conceptual framework that highlights best practices for academic staff utilizing audio feedback. Cann (2014) assessed the effectiveness of various approaches in creating and delivering audio feedback. Barry (2012) studied the use of a video-recording protocol for group presentations and examined its effects on students' self-reflections. Other studies (Henderson & Phillips, 2014; Yuan & Kim, 2015) have developed design principles and guidelines that academic staff can use to create and deliver feedback, using these technologies. These speak to the importance of research principles in the design of audiovisual TEF systems. It is encouraging that the development and implementation of some of these systems, particularly those with audiovisual modalities, have been informed by design principles and frameworks.

Another type of TEF system within this category is textual feedback by tutors, delivered through online portals. A key focus here is in ensuring student engagement with feedback. Approaches include requiring students to respond to feedback messages before they were given access to view their grades – a practice that was reported to have substantially enhanced student engagement with feedback (Hepplestone, Holden, Irwin, Parkin, & Thorpe, 2011; Parkin, Hepplestone, Holden, Irwin, & Thorpe, 2012; Irwin, Hepplestone, Holden, Parkin, & Thorpe, 2013). Other studies explored the effects of allowing students to send textual feedback to their peers based on their work through online desktop applications (Hovardas, Tsivitanidou, & Zacharia, 2014) and mobile devices (Lai & Hwang, 2015). Textual feedback has also been used by tutors participating in computer-supported collaborative learning environments and online discussion forums (Coll, Rochera, de Gispert, & Barriga, 2013).

What these systems all have in common is that technology enhances conveyance of and interaction with information without changing the information itself.

Enhancing Feedback by Transforming Information

The systems in this category change the information through a mediating technology. A key characteristic of these systems is autonomous action. These systems are able to create and convey feedback rather than rely on human actors to do so. These systems include adaptive e-learning applications, automated marking and scoring systems, intelligent tutoring systems, and educational games.

Shute and Towle (2003) discussed the use of adaptive e-learning applications and proposed a framework to guide the design of adaptive engines that form the core of such applications. These systems, which today run as web, desktop, and mobile applications, typically operate by first administering tasks such as multiple-choice questions to students. Information collected from the student's responses to these tasks is processed and used by the application to either generate feedback messages or select them from a preprepared statement bank. Depending on each individual student's responses, these TEF systems are able to recommend appropriate follow-up tasks. Students may be assigned tasks similar to earlier ones in order to check if they have internalized the feedback messages or may even be given the opportunity to resubmit their previously incorrect responses after receiving feedback (Jordan, 2013).

A widely documented drawback of these systems is that their operation is often limited to the context of selected-response types of questions, or short numerical answers typically keyed into a text field (Jordan, 2013). As previously discussed, progress has been made in pushing the boundaries of this limitation. Approaches include TEF systems that employ certainty-based marking (Nicol, 2007; Jordan, 2013), where students indicate their responses together with an associated level of confidence on the correctness of their answer. Credit and penalties are then awarded based on their response and level of certainty (Nicol, 2007), thereby reducing the occurrence of guesswork.

Although this technique is helpful, it operates within the boundaries of selected-response items. Other approaches that step outside these boundaries include computational algorithms based on natural-language processing.

These allow computers to assess free-text responses from students and provide corresponding responses (Chodorow, Gamon, & Tetreault, 2010; Jordan, 2012). These systems are able to check for language use in free-text responses and automatically provide subsequent feedback in the form of suggested corrections that students can use to improve and resubmit their work (Jordan & Mitchell, 2009; Chodorow et al., 2010).

Even automated marking systems have now achieved a level of sophistication that allows the provision of targeted, formative feedback at each step of a multistage task. Such systems are frequently referred to as intelligent tutoring systems. The ActiveMath application (Narciss et al., 2014), for example, allows students to attempt multistep mathematical problems. As students interact with this system, they receive feedback in the form of flagged errors, directed prompts, and explanations. Each provision of feedback then feeds forward into the next step of the problem.

Another development within this category is game-based learning. These systems retain adaptive feedback provision but also include elements of conflict or challenge, governed by a set of rules (Shute, 2011). As students engage with the game, data are collected. Students' levels of competency may then be inferred from this data. Shute (2011) refers to this as "stealth assessment" and advocates for its use in making inferences about student knowledge and providing them with feedback. She notes that the design and evaluation of these games may also be informed by a principled assessment design framework called evidence-centered design, which supports constructing explicit links between collected stealth data and students' knowledge and skills (Shute & Ke, 2012).

The TEF systems discussed in this section share a common goal – they attempt to harness technology to process acquired data into feedback messages, and do so autonomously using computational algorithms and machine intelligence. These affordances are in contrast with TEF systems where technology is harnessed for efficiency, convenience, and enhanced interaction with feedback.

Effects of TEF Systems on Students

Different types of TEF systems enhance different aspects of the feedback process. In this section, we discuss the various effects that four types of TEF systems have, particularly on students.

Audiovisual Feedback Modalities

Audio, video, and screencast feedback are well received by both students and academic tutors (Crook et al., 2012; Cann, 2014; Henderson & Phillips, 2014). Students perceive digitally recorded feedback and comments as clearer, more useful, more personalized, more constructive, and more satisfying than text-based comments (Crook et al., 2012; Henderson & Phillips, 2014; Phillips et al., 2016). They also view these modalities as helpful for emphasizing key subject matter points and aiding visualization of information (Crook et al., 2012) and appreciate the opportunity to review and reflect on audiovisual feedback messages. This suggests that audio, visual, and screencast modalities may foster repeated and self-regulated engagement with the feedback (Barry, 2012; Crook et al., 2012). Barry (2012) found that these could provoke deeper insights into outcomes and performance in group presentations.

Video feedback in particular has led to greater levels of student engagement (Barry, 2012; Crook et al., 2012) as students have been observed to take greater notice of generic video feedback instead of other feedback types (Crook et al., 2012). Further, TEF systems offering audiovisual modalities have led to savings in staff time (Henderson & Phillips, 2014) and positively changed staffs' approach to feedback provision (Crook et al., 2012). Some video TEF systems have features that allow students to respond to tutor feedback; tutors may then determine if students have correctly understood the feedback (Gomez et al., 2013). Phillips et al. (2016) find that this iterative mode of feedback provision positively correlates with improved student experience.

These modalities, however, are not without problems. While Phillips et al. (2016) note a positive correlation with student experience, they also point out that this effect is not a given; other factors may hinder positive impact. Henderson and Phillips (2014) also found that students encounter difficulties anchoring video feedback to specific sections of their assignments. Further, video modalities can induce anxiety among students (Henderson & Phillips, 2014), which can negatively impact their motivation to use them (Huang & Hung, 2013).

Online Portals and Learning Management Systems

Online portals allow for convenient uploading and access of feedback information (Parkin et al., 2012) as well as tracking of access statistics. Some online portals allow for separation of feedback from marks. Research on withholding marks using online portals indicates that doing so may encourage students to reflect on feedback, thereby enhancing their engagement and uptake (Parkin et al., 2012; Cann, 2014). Parkin et al. (2012) further noted that this affordance was more effective than attempts to link feedback to assessment criteria. Students also expressed appreciation of the benefits offered by such a design facility (Parkin et al., 2012).

Online portals are also used to obtain student access statistics (Cann, 2014). This data help determine frequency of students accessing online feedback, providing insights into access patterns. Harrison et al. (2013) conducted a study where norm and criterion-referenced feedback was published on a website. Higher-performing students were found to have accessed the website feedback more frequently. However, it was found that these students did not access the website for diagnostic feedback information. Instead, access patterns indicated that they did so mainly for positive affirmation of their level of competence. This suggests that even when students were aware that the feedback message came directly from a human tutor and was not transformed by technology, they sometimes did not engage with the feedback as expected. This speaks to the need for a more nuanced understanding of students' perceptions of feedback.

e-Learning Applications

e-Learning applications provide feedback to students autonomously by processing student responses to a specific task. The degree of student engagement generally depends on the type of feedback provided with each task. Narciss et al. (2014), for example, observed that students who were given conceptual feedback messages were less likely to sustain engagement with their tasks than students who were provided with procedurally oriented feedback.

The effects of such systems on students have been found to be largely positive. Timmers, Braber-Van Den Broek, and Van Den Berg (2013) measured the effects that an e-learning application had on students' motivation, task-value beliefs, and expectancy of success. They found positive correlations between each characteristic and the amount of effort students reported expending in seeking feedback. Likewise, Narciss et al. (2014) observed increases in students' intrinsic motivation as they used an e-learning application. The effects on learning were also positive with some variation depending on type of feedback provided and subject matter. Timmers et al. (2013), for example, observed that students who received elaborated feedback through an e-learning application demonstrated higher levels of achievement than those who received simple feedback.

Automated Marking Systems

Automated marking systems provide feedback based on unconstrained free-text responses such as essays. Students may demonstrate different levels of engagement, however. Chodorow et al. (2010) observed that students engaged positively with computer-suggested corrections and were sufficiently discerning in their uptake. In contrast, Jordan and Mitchell (2009) noted that students do not read feedback from these systems as carefully as they would read human-generated feedback and that some students were unconvinced that the system had correctly understood their responses. There are also concerns whether students take computer feedback seriously. Some students may see such feedback as being neither accurate nor helpful, but others may respond to it the same way they would with human feedback (Lipnevich & Smith, 2009) and act on it similarly.

Jordan and Mitchell (2009) observed that many students entered their responses as discrete phrases instead of complete sentences, assuming that the system was able to mark their responses based on only the presence or absence of certain key words (Jordan & Mitchell, 2009). The effectiveness of automated marking systems in terms of students' uptake of feedback thus appears to be largely dependent on the different assumptions and perceptions that students have about the TEF systems they are using. These perceptions dictate not only how they construct their responses but also how the system constructs feedback for them. These examples further speak to the need for a deeper understanding of students' attitudes, perceptions, and behavior when interacting with computer feedback.

There is evidence, however, that the use of automated marking and feedback systems contributes to learning. Chodorow et al. (2010) found that suggested corrections to responses can help students make informed decisions when resubmitting their work, leading to a significant reduction in the number of errors in their final essays. In addition, where effective use of feedback had taken place, students were able to increase their proportion of valid corrections (Chodorow et al., 2010). Different types of feedback seem to produce differences in level of effectiveness. Elaborated feedback generated by automated systems was strongly associated with improvement in essay scores (Chodorow et al., 2010); greater effectiveness was demonstrated when the systems provided feedback tailored to the mistakes made and when it prompted students for a response, rather than simply providing an answer (Jordan, 2012).

The effects of these four TEF systems on students appear to be positive, but there are possibilities for improvement. From the observations made in this section, it appears that a deeper understanding of students as recipients of feedback would significantly help realize the potential of these systems.

How TEF Systems Are Evaluated

TEF systems are typically evaluated within three areas: facilitating feedback, transforming feedback, and affecting the student. In this section, we discuss some of the specifics within these three areas as well as the sources of data employed to make these evaluations.

Many studies evaluate the merits of TEF systems on technical functionality, especially in terms of increasing efficiency. Among these are attributes such as how quickly and conveniently feedback can be created, stored, and accessed through online portals (Barry, 2012; Crook et al., 2012; Parkin et al., 2012; Cann, 2014; Henderson & Phillips, 2014). Studies reporting on these characteristics investigate TEF systems that are primarily designed to acquire and convey information rather than transform it. Methodologically, these studies typically use interviews and focus group discussions to understand perceptions of students and academic staff on the affordances of these TEF systems (Burrows & Shortis, 2011; Crook et al., 2012; Parkin et al., 2012). It is worth noting then that the data used to interpret quality are largely perceptual in nature; that is, most of these studies rely wholly on users reporting their perceptions of functionality rather than attempting to establish objective benchmarks of, for example, increased efficiency.

TEF systems are also evaluated in terms of quality of feedback and degree of student engagement with the feedback. Specific foci include clarity and usefulness of the TEF messages (Jordan & Mitchell, 2009; Burrows & Shortis, 2011; Crook et al., 2012; Henderson & Phillips, 2014; Phillips et al., 2016) and the level of confidence students invest in feedback, either mediated by or originating from a technological system (i.e., human generated versus computer generated) (Lipnevich & Smith, 2009; Jordan, 2012). As with functionality-based evaluation, most of these studies target the perceptions of those interacting with the systems. Data are typically collected through interviews, focus groups, and self-report questionnaires.

Noting the potential limitations of such approaches, Jordan (2012) asserts that students' self-reported behavior should not be assumed to correlate highly with observable engagement. She provides this critique as a rationale for integrating an observational approach in her study. Her study employs observations of students' online activity and their use of verbal think-aloud protocols to collect data on student engagement. These modes of data collection are then supplemented by interviews that attempt to identify reasons for specific student actions during their interaction with the TEF system (Jordan, 2012).

There have been other approaches to evaluating TEF systems that extend beyond self-report. These include analysis of digitally acquired information from student interactions, such as the amount of time and effort spent on feedback messages (Timmers et al., 2013) and the number of hits received by a site providing feedback (Harrison et al., 2013). Chodorow et al. (2010) used data logs to identify students' activities relating to feedback suggestions made by a TEF system. Similar methods have also been reported (Hepplestone et al., 2011; Parkin et al., 2012; Irwin et al., 2013; Narciss et al., 2014).

Some studies are concerned with quantifying the effects of TEF systems on students. These include latent characteristics such as motivation, self-efficacy, goal-orientation, self-regulation, confidence, control of learning beliefs, and attitudes to feedback (Harrison et al., 2013). As with the other two areas, data are most often derived from self-report; a common example is use of survey questionnaires to report quantitative results. Some exceptions include Narciss et al.'s (2014) use of scores on tests and examinations to examine effects of TEF systems on learning and achievement and Van der Kleij, Feskens, and Eggen's (2015) meta-analysis evaluating effects of feedback in computer-based learning environments on students' achievement.

Discussion

Reported results of TEF have been largely positive, but the adoption of TEF systems is seldom sustained (Deneen et al., 2017). This presents a paradox; TEF is demonstrably beneficial and yet widely abandoned. Understanding this paradox requires looking at the quality and characteristics of TEF research.

Affordances and Benefits of TEF

This review has established a typology of TEF systems ranging from audio-visual to heuristic-driven adaptive computer systems. Regardless of the type of

TEF system, a significant trend within the reviewed studies is to highlight the substantial benefits of TEF systems.

TEF systems have been lauded for their efficiency, intelligence, and substantial benefits to students and instructors. In terms of efficiency, benefits include being able to quickly and conveniently create, store, and access feedback artifacts (Barry, 2012; Crook et al., 2012; Parkin et al., 2012; Cann, 2014; Henderson & Phillips, 2014). These new affordances have resulted in positive experiences for both students and staff. In terms of intelligence, TEF systems have been found to be able to generate feedback information that closely matches what academic tutors are able to provide (Jordan & Mitchell, 2009), demonstrating their potential in relieving staff workload, among other benefits. Further, TEF systems have been shown to bring substantial benefit to students, particularly in terms of motivation and self-regulation (Barry, 2012; Harrison et al., 2013; Timmers et al., 2013; Narciss et al., 2014). For e-learning applications and automated marking systems, where TEF has a transformative role, positive results were reported in terms of learning and academic achievement (Chodorow et al., 2010; Jordan, 2012; Timmers et al., 2013).

The benefits described here seem to reflect what their researchers consider to be of merit – TEF facilitates feedback, transforms it, and impacts the student. These are all defensible priorities. Equally important, however, is the quality of the research that speaks to if and how these priorities are met.

Data Collection Procedures in TEF Research

The majority of the reviewed studies rely on self-report as the principal mechanism for evaluating TEF. This approach is not inherently flawed; there are limitations, however, to evaluating a system solely through the perceptual filter of a user (most often, the student). Self-report should not be taken as synonymous with observed impact. Within the studies relying on self-report, rarely was this acknowledged, let alone positioned as a limitation. In fact, we found a common theme of implicitly and sometimes explicitly positioning findings derived from self-report as synonymous with observed impact within the three areas of facilitating feedback, transforming feedback, and affecting the student.

The use of such procedures has led to overly generic conclusions in many cases, such as "learners felt that the feedback was clearer and more useful" and "the majority seemed to appreciate video feedback." In fact, very few studies reported on rigorous follow-up procedures that could have absolved themselves of any suspicion of bias. Commendably, those that did so reported on alternative methods of observation, such as think-aloud protocols, video recordings of student activity (Jordan & Mitchell, 2009), and the use of data logs (Chodorow et al., 2010), in order to more objectively examine students' interactions with TEF systems. Without such approaches, TEF research may lack the necessary levels of rigor and soundness and, consequently, may risk making unjustified claims that do little more than showcase potential.

The prevalent use of self-report in TEF research raises further concerns when the researchers themselves are the developers of technology. Any lack of objectivity can result in claims that are favorably skewed toward the merits of one's own innovation.

TEF Innovators Conducting TEF Research

A research focus typically reflects a particular perspective on what matters most. For TEF research, great effort has been made to showcase affordances. Interestingly, such efforts have been confined to illustrations of what actually works in TEF, instead of attempting to uncover reasons for why they work, when they work, and whom they best work for. TEF research places an overemphasis on technological development, affordances, and overly generic effects on students without much consideration for principles in feedback and assessment. This observation is perhaps a consequence of TEF studies being conducted by researchers whose primary focus lies in technological development and not in education research. Further, as the discourse in TEF development is driven and dominated by technologists and instructional designers, it is inevitable that there are extensive and sophisticated discussions from the perspective of what technology can offer and not what educational institutions require.

Most TEF design and modalities do not reflect sound feedback theories or frameworks. There is little discussion on the types of feedback that work best for the different TEF modalities. Research principles are occasionally used when developing TEF systems but are almost never used when evaluating them. At best, there is a fragmented and superficial allusion to principles of feedback provision, and this adversely affects theoretical development and utilization.

As technologists are not responsible for developing assessment and feedback principles within the various disciplines, they may not appreciate specific disciplinary variations when applying their innovations in different contexts and levels of schooling. Contextual nuances such as academic discipline and stages of learning have been afforded little attention in the discussion of TEF performance. Without adequate contextualization, it becomes difficult for education researchers to critically examine and evaluate these innovations in relation to well-established feedback principles. In terms of practice, the absence of critical evaluation in specific contexts makes adoption difficult to justify. TEF systems are undeniably used in multiple contexts, but when results of TEF research are not discussed in relation to these contexts, the possibilities of dissemination of best practices for continued development are limited.

Further, few papers discussed the reasons for the purported benefits in consideration of students' behaviors and characteristics. There is little objective consideration of students' perceptions and thought processes – factors that necessarily influence their response and uptake. Without such an understanding, it is difficult for academic staff, practitioners, and students to fully appreciate the benefits of TEF. It appears that despite great technological advances, the focus in TEF "has not been on using technologies to address fundamental educational issues" as Nicol and Milligan (2006, p. 11) pointed out more than a decade ago. Robust relationships between research and practice have not been sufficiently established. As these fundamental requirements are not met, it is perhaps unsurprising that sustained TEF adoption is rare.

Worse, yet, those who adopt such systems might not question the value of such research. Through this review, we found many instances of highly regarded journals publishing articles in which the researchers had a clear stake (in some cases financial) in reporting success based on self-report data. These published articles usually did not contain provisos or limitations sections acknowledging potential bias or conflict of interest. While this is damaging to credibility at the scale of the individual article, the larger picture is alarming: journals with significant impact are failing to apply a necessary and anticipated critical filter to published research. The implications for furthering research and evidence-based practice in TEF are deeply troubling. We may well wonder if some of the extraordinarily high rates of technology rejection and abandonment in TEF and more generally TEA may be attributed to the promulgation of findings that should have been challenged by reviewers and journals.

Technologists and instructional designers certainly possess the much-needed expertise and have contributed significantly toward TEF development and deployment. Nevertheless, their present approach toward the research and development of TEF systems has led to doubts over the true value of TEF systems to the stakeholders in the educational fraternity. Until these issues are resolved, the promise of TEF is unlikely to be fulfilled.

Future Directions in TEF Research

In this section, we propose several research directions for the advancement of TEF research. Although the research directions proposed here may benefit education and technology researchers, they are worthy of consideration by instructors, instructional designers, and educational leaders, particularly when evaluating TEF research and development.

There are several potential avenues of research to TEF development. One worthwhile route is to investigate the role of sophisticated models of assessment and feedback in TEF development and evaluation, such as those proposed by leading researchers in these fields (Sadler, 1989; Nicol & Macfarlane-Dick, 2006; Hattie & Timperley, 2007; Black & Wiliam, 2010). In particular, we strongly recommend that TEF systems that involve the automated transformation of acquired information into feedback are evaluated using feedback and assessment principles and models that are espoused by these authors and have been widely used in assessment and feedback research.

Research and development of TEF systems must relate clearly with contexts and disciplines. It is unreasonable to expect that TEF systems perform equally well in all contexts; the existence of disciplinary variation must be acknowledged as part of any scientific investigation of TEF systems. A clearly defined context offers guidance for instructors and academic staff in making well-informed decisions on the applicability and relevance of the TEF system to their respective disciplines. This further allows them to be fully aware of the potential pitfalls during the adoption of these TEF systems. At present, disciplinary variation in performance of TEF systems has been only nominally discussed. Therefore, this is an area of research requiring attention.

There is also substantial room for research on student perceptions and uptake of feedback. Many TEF systems are designed based on technological affordances from the perspective of instructional designers or instructors themselves. There is insufficient consideration of students as recipients of feedback in both transformative and nontransformative TEF systems. Students' perceptions of TEF can influence their response to and uptake of the feedback message (Harrison et al., 2013; Deneen et al., 2017). At present, there is little to no discussion on student perceptions and behaviors that influence their uptake of feedback in TEF research.

Sound research requires cogent framing of problems, collecting appropriate data, conducting transparent analyses, and reporting defensible results. There is an onus as well on researchers to account for limitations and acknowledge potential conflicts of interest. Research into TEF demonstrates widespread evidence of deviation from these principles. This pattern holds true across sources of varying quality, including highly respected "tier one" journals.

If TEF and more generally TEA are to be research-informed enterprises, then we must target not only gaps in areas of understanding but also gaps in quality. The great threat to TEF is a lack of sustained adoption; we may see some of this problem originating in the quality of research meant to inform adoption. The opportunity for progress in TEF then is interconnected – improve the quality and scope of the research so that the sustaining and scaling of TEF becomes a better realized possibility.

References

Attali, Y. (2004). *Exploring the feedback and revision features of Criterion.* National Council on Measurement in Education (NCME), Educational Testing Service, Princeton, NJ.

Attali, Y., & Burstein, J. (2006). Automated essay scoring with e-rater® V. 2. *Journal of Technology, Learning and Assessment, 4*(3).

Bangert-Drowns, R. L. (1993). The word processor as an instructional tool: A meta-analysis of word processing in writing instruction. *Review of Educational Research, 63,* 69–93.

Barry, S. (2012). A video recording and viewing protocol for student group presentations: Assisting self-assessment through a Wiki environment. *Computers & Education, 59*(3), 855–860.

Black, P., & Wiliam, D. (2010). Inside the black box: Raising standards through classroom assessment. *Phi Delta Kappa, 92*(1), 81–90.

Burrows, S., & Shortis, M. (2011). An evaluation of semi-automated, collaborative marking and feedback systems: Academic staff perspectives. *Australasian Journal of Educational Technology*, *27*(7), 1135–1154.

Burstein, J., Kukich, K., Wolff, S., Lu, C., Chodorow, M., Braden-Harder, L., & Harris, M. D. (1998, August). Automated scoring using a hybrid feature identification technique. In *Proceedings of the 36th Annual Meeting of the Association for Computational Linguistics and 17th International Conference on Computational Linguistics*, vol. 1 (pp. 206–210). Montreal: Association for Computational Linguistics.

Cann, A. (2014). Engaging students with audio feedback. *Bioscience Education*, *22*(1), 31–41.

Chodorow, M., Gamon, M., & Tetreault, J. (2010). The utility of article and preposition error correction systems for English language learners: Feedback and assessment. *Language Testing*, *27*(3), 419–436.

Cochran-Smith, M. (1991). Word processing and writing in elementary classrooms: A critical review of related literature. *Review of Educational Research*, *61*, 107–155.

Coll, C., Rochera, M. J., de Gispert, I., & Barriga, F. D. (2013). Distribution of feedback among teacher and students in online collaborative learning in small groups. *Digital Education Review*, *23*, 27–45.

Crook, A., Mauchline, A., Maw, S., Lawson, C., Drinkwater, R., Lundqvist, K., ... & Park, J. (2012). The use of video technology for providing feedback to students: Can it enhance the feedback experience for staff and students? *Computers & Education*, *58*(1), 386–396.

Deneen, C. C., Brown, G. T. L., & Carless, D. (2017). Students' conceptions of eportfolios as assessment and technology. *Innovations in Education and Teaching International*, 1–10. Online prepublication, retrieved from http://dx.doi .org/10.1080/14703297.2017.1281752.

Deneen, C. C., & Shroff R. (2014). Understanding successes and difficulties in program-level eportfolios: A case study of two professional degree programs. *Review of Higher Education and Self-Learning*, *7*(24), 145–160.

Dikli, S. (2006). An overview of automated scoring of essays. *Journal of Technology, Learning and Assessment*, *5*(1).

Fink, A. (2005). *Conducting research literature reviews: From the Internet to paper*. Thousand Oaks, CA: Sage.

Goldberg, A., Russell, M., & Cook, A. (2003). The effect of computers on student writing: A meta-analysis of studies from 1992 to 2002. *Journal of Technology, Learning, and Assessment*, *2*(1).

Gomez, S., Andersson, H., Park, J., Maw, S., Crook, A., & Orsmond, P. (2013). A digital ecosystems model of assessment feedback on student learning. *Higher Education Studies*, *3*(2), 41–51.

Harrison, C. J., Könings, K. D., Molyneux, A., Schuwirth, L. W., Wass, V., & van der Vleuten, C. P. (2013). Web-based feedback after summative assessment: How do students engage? *Medical Education*, *47*(7), 734–744.

Hattie, J., & Timperley, H. (2007). The power of feedback. *Review of Educational Research*, *77*(1), 81–112.

Henderson, M., & Phillips, M. (2014). Technology enhanced feedback on assessment. In Australian Computers in Education Conference, Adelaide, SA, September 30–October 3, 2014 (pp. 1–11). Retrieved from http://acec2014.acce .edu.au/session/technology- enhanced- feedback-assessment.

Henderson, M., & Phillips, M. (2015). Video-based feedback on student assessment: Scarily personal. *Australasian Journal of Educational Technology*, *31*(1), 51–66.

Hennessy, C., & Forrester, G. (2014). Developing a framework for effective audio feedback: A case study. *Assessment & Evaluation in Higher Education*, *39*(7), 777–789.

Hepplestone, S., Holden, G., Irwin, B., Parkin, H. J., & Thorpe, L. (2011). Using technology to encourage student engagement with feedback: A literature review. *Research in Learning Technology*, *19*(2), 117–127.

Hovardas, T., Tsivitanidou, O. E., & Zacharia, Z. C. (2014). Peer versus expert feedback: An investigation of the quality of peer feedback among secondary school students. *Computers & Education*, *71*, 133–152.

Huang, H. T. D., & Hung, S. T. A. (2013). Exploring the utility of a video-based online EFL discussion forum. *British Journal of Educational Technology*, *44*(3), E90–E94.

Irwin, B., Hepplestone, S., Holden, G., Parkin, H. J., & Thorpe, L. (2013). Engaging students with feedback through adaptive release. *Innovations in Education and Teaching International*, *50*(1), 51–61.

Jackson, M., & Marks, L. (2016). Improving the effectiveness of feedback by use of assessed reflections and withholding of grades. *Assessment & Evaluation in Higher Education*, *41*(4), 532–547.

Jordan, S. (2012). Student engagement with assessment and feedback: Some lessons from short-answer free-text e-assessment questions. *Computers & Education*, *58*(2), 818–834.

Jordan, S. (2013). E-assessment: Past, present and future. *New Directions*, *9*(1), 87–106.

Jordan, S., & Mitchell, T. (2009). e-Assessment for learning? The potential of short answer free text questions with tailored feedback. *British Journal of Educational Technology*, *40*(2), 371–385.

Lai, C. L., & Hwang, G. J. (2015). An interactive peer-assessment criteria development approach to improving students' art design performance using handheld devices. *Computers & Education*, *85*, 149–159.

Lipnevich, A. A., & Smith, J. K. (2008). Response to assessment feedback: The effects of grades, praise, and source of information. *ETS Research Report Series*, *2008*(1).

Lipnevich, A. A., & Smith, J. K. (2009). Effects of differential feedback on students' examination performance. *Journal of Experimental Psychology: Applied*, *15*(4), 319.

Marriott, P., & Teoh, L. K. (2012). Using screencasts to enhance assessment feedback: Students' perceptions and preferences. *Accounting Education*, *21*(6), 583–598.

McCarthy, J. (2015). Evaluating written, audio and video feedback in higher education summative assessment tasks. *Issues in Educational Research*, *25*(2), 153–169.

Narciss, S., Sosnovsky, S., Schnaubert, L., Andrès, E., Eichelmann, A., Goguadze, G., & Melis, E. (2014). Exploring feedback and student characteristics relevant for personalizing feedback strategies. *Computers & Education*, *71*, 56–76.

Nicol, D. (2007). E-assessment by design: Using multiple-choice tests to good effect. *Journal of Further and Higher Education*, *31*(1), 53–64.

Nicol, D. J., & Macfarlane-Dick, D. (2006). Formative assessment and self-regulated learning: A model and seven principles of good feedback practice. *Studies in Higher Education*, *31*(2), 199–218.

Nicol, D. J., & Milligan, C. (2006). Rethinking technology-supported assessment in terms of the seven principles of good feedback practice. In C. Bryan and K. Clegg (Eds.), *Innovative assessment in higher education* (pp. 64–77). London: Taylor & Francis Group.

Nino, M., & Evans, M. A. (2015). Fostering 21st-century skills in constructivist engineering classrooms with digital game-based learning. *IEEE Revista Iberoamericana de Tecnologias del Aprendizaje, 10*(3), 143–149.

Parkin, H. J., Hepplestone, S., Holden, G., Irwin, B., & Thorpe, L. (2012). A role for technology in enhancing students' engagement with feedback. *Assessment & Evaluation in Higher Education, 37*(8), 963–973.

Phillips, M., Henderson M., & Ryan, T. (2016). Multimodal feedback is not always clearer, more useful or satisfying. In S. Barker, S. Dawson, A. Pardo, & C. Colvin (Eds.), *Show me the learning: Proceedings ASCILITE 2016 Adelaide* (pp. 512–522).

Sadler, D. R. (1989). Formative assessment and the design of instructional systems. *Instructional Science, 18*(2), 119–144.

Saldaña, J. (2015). *The coding manual for qualitative researchers.* Thousand Oaks, CA: Sage.

Shermis, M. D., Burstein, J., & Bursky, S. A. (2013). Introduction to automated essay evaluation. In M. D. Shermis, J. Burstein, & S. A. Bursky (Eds.), *Handbook of automated essay evaluation: Current applications and new directions* (pp. 1–15). New York: Routledge.

Shroff, R. H., & Deneen, C. C. (2011). Assessing online textual feedback to support student intrinsic motivation using a collaborative text-based dialogue system: A qualitative study. *International Journal on E-Learning, 10*(1), 87–104.

Shute, V., & Towle, B. (2003). Adaptive e-learning. *Educational Psychologist, 38*(2), 105–114.

Shute, V. J. (2011). Stealth assessment in computer-based games to support learning. *Computer Games and Instruction, 55*(2), 503–524.

Shute, V. J., & Ke, F. (2012). Games, learning, and assessment. In *Assessment in game-based learning* (pp. 43–58). New York: Springer.

Timmers, C. F., Braber-Van Den Broek, J., & Van Den Berg, S. M. (2013). Motivational beliefs, student effort, and feedback behaviour in computer-based formative assessment. *Computers & Education, 60*(1), 25–31.

Van den Boom, G., Paas, F., Van Merrienboer, J. J., & Van Gog, T. (2004). Reflection prompts and tutor feedback in a web-based learning environment: Effects on students' self-regulated learning competence. *Computers in Human Behavior, 20*(4), 551–567.

Van der Kleij, F. M., Feskens, R. C., & Eggen, T. J. (2015). Effects of feedback in a computer-based learning environment on students' learning outcomes: A meta-analysis. *Review of Educational Research, 85*(4), 475–511.

Warschauer, M., & Ware, P. (2006). Automated writing evaluation: Defining the classroom research agenda. *Language Teaching Research, 10*(2), 157–180.

West, J., & Turner, W. (2016). Enhancing the assessment experience: Improving student perceptions, engagement and understanding using online video feedback. *Innovations in Education and Teaching International, 53*(4), 400–410.

Yuan, J., & Kim, C. (2015). Effective feedback design using free technologies. *Journal of Educational Computing Research, 52*(3), 408–434.

16 Digital Games as Tools for Embedded Assessment

Bruce D. Homer, Teresa M. Ober, and Jan L. Plass

With decreased cost and increased portability, digital technologies have become ubiquitous in nearly all aspects of our lives, including education. During the past decade, one of the promising uses of digital technologies in education has been the use of video games for learning. There are now thousands of educational games, ranging from casual games intended to teach simple concepts (or, more commonly, to reinforce existing knowledge) to more complex and involved games intended to teach deeper knowledge, support the development of complex cognitive skills, and change attitudes or increase awareness. Although a majority of the work in this area has investigated learning outcomes, there is also a growing interest in the use of digital games as tools for assessing learners.

Assessment is a critical component of the education process. Ideally, meaningful assessment provides feedback to students, teachers, parents, and administrators that can be used to improve educational outcomes or, in the case of standardized assessments, allow learners to compare their skills with one another. However, both the development and the implementation of traditional methods of assessment (i.e., paper-based testing) require significant time and resources. In part, this has led to passionate critiques of the current state of standardized testing in our schools, and arguments that the time used to prepare for and administer standardized tests is significantly reducing valuable time that could be devoted to better teaching students (e.g., Ravitch, 2016).

One possible solution to this problem that has been offered is the use of digital technologies with assessment embedded into the learning process. Combining the learning and assessment processes not only allows for more instructional time but also enables the possibility of more authentic assessment and more informed instruction. This view is reflected in the most recent supplement to the National Education Technology Plan, in which the US Department of Education (2017) argues that digital forms of assessment can help to "reduce the time, resources, and disruption to learning" caused by traditional modes of assessment. Standard paper-and-pencil forms of assessment are external to the learning process; that is, they are added to the instructional process without providing any clear benefit to learners. In contrast, digital technologies, including video games, can have assessments embedded into the learning context. Using assessment that is embedded into digital learning environments can provide educators with insight into what students are actually thinking while engaging in the learning process and can provide near real-time feedback so that appropriate action can be taken in the moment to support students' learning (US Department of Education, 2017).

As we describe later, these advantages can be particularly true for video games, which have assessment as an essential component. However, in spite of the potential of game-based assessment, there is still only a limited body of research exploring the use of games as assessment tools. In this chapter, we consider the ways in which digital games can be used to authentically evaluate learners' knowledge and skills. Specifically, this chapter aims to accomplish the following goals:

1. Provide a summary of the research to date on the use of games as tools for assessment
2. Describe models of game-based assessment used to evaluate learning in an authentic manner
3. Present examples from the research literature of successful implementation of game-based learning and assessment
4. Make recommendations for advancing the future of game-based assessment for learning.

Assessment Is Integral to Digital Games

In contrast to the limited work on games as tools for assessment, there is now a substantial body of work on how and why digital games can be effective tools for learning. In the influential book, *What Video Games Have to Teach Us about Learning and Literacy*, Gee (2003) argues that video games embody many of the principles of good learning. These include *agency*, or the fact that players have control over their environment in digital games; *well-ordered problems*, which refers to the fact that players typically solve interconnected problems of increasing complexity in video games (or at least in certain genres of video games); and *customization*, which refers to the fact that games can become easier or more difficult based on the success (or failure) of the player in order to keep the player challenged, but still succeeding. Plass, Homer, and Kinzer (2015) similarly suggest that video games have the potential to embody the best practices of different approaches to learning, and argue that to fully understand the educational potential of video games requires adopting an "overarching, learning sciences perspective" that considers cognitive, motivational, affective, and sociocultural factors.

Arguably, the feature of video games that is most relevant for assessment is their affordance to be adaptive and personalized for individual learners. In order to successfully adapt, an accurate estimate of the learner must be created that informs the game system's adaptation. Commercial entertainment games need only model whether or not the player is successful in the game. If "yes" (i.e., if the player is successful), then the game can "level up" (e.g., by increasing speed, decreasing player resources, providing additional obstacles, etc.), and if "no," then the game can "level down" (e.g., by decreasing speed, increasing player resources, removing obstacles, etc.) in order to keep the player challenged and engaged. For learning games, wider and more complex assessments are required. In a paper arguing that games are the "future of assessment," Gee and Shaffer (2010) point out that games must be good "assessment engines" in order to be effective tools for learning. The authors claim that video games can effectively evaluate students' current knowledge and skills as well as their broader "twenty-first century skills," which is then used to adapt the difficulty or content of the learning game.

From very early on, video games have been used to educate and evaluate users' knowledge in a wide range of domains. For example, classic and popular educational games such as the *Oregon Trail*, which dates back to 1971, and *Where in the World Is Carmen Sandiego?*, released in 1985, utilize the game context to promote learning, requiring users to apply their knowledge, monitor their understanding, and solve in-game problems using domain-specific knowledge (e.g., information from history or geography). Within the context of these games (versions of which are still available today), users discover consequences resulting from their choices as the game tracks the users' decisions and progress throughout the duration of game play. To succeed in the games requires users to apply their knowledge of history and geography – success or failure in the game is a direct assessment of users' knowledge in these areas. If players fail, they are encouraged to "try again" – in other words, to go back and learn the information that is needed in order to succeed.

In this regard, the concept of evaluating and responding to users' performance while playing a game is not novel. Even early computer games were designed with what could be considered to be some sort of basic formative assessment. *Formative assessment* is a technique where a learner's mastery of a concept or skill is regularly evaluated and instruction is adjusted to accommodate their needs (Black & Wiliam, 1998). The immediacy of feedback provided by these early educational games allowed the learner to know whether or not specific concepts or skills had been acquired and, if not, to learn them in order to succeed at the game.

As the technology has developed, so too has the quantity and detail of the data gathered by games. Most games now collect logs of some sort that not only assess whether or not the player succeeded but also collect details about how the player progressed through the game. This information is typically used to inform revisions to the game. For example, if there is a spot in the game where many players are dying in a way that was not intended by the game designers (e.g., falling off a cliff because it is not visually clear that the road curves), then the next version of the game can be modified to remove this issue (e.g., putting up a barricade to keep players from walking off the cliff). In this way, the game industry has been at the cutting edge of research involving the collection of users' information to understand and evaluate behaviors while playing a game (or using an application). For learning games, log data can provide a detailed record of learners' activities within the context of the game, and insight into the learning process. As such, the structure, ease of data collection on learning, and the immediacy of feedback that is provided to learners can make games an ideal medium for assessing learning.

Challenges for Game-Based Assessment

Although there is a long history of assessment in games, there is still limited use of video games as tools for assessment. In part, this is due to the need for more systematic research on how best to design in-game assessments that adequately estimate learners' knowledge and skills. However, there are still a number of broader challenges that need to be addressed stemming from the gaming context, as well as how games may be perceived. Specifically, challenges to the adoption of game-based assessments include the following:

1. *A lack of general acceptance of games as assessment tools.* Even with more open-ended areas of learning, there is still some resistance to the idea that something involving "play" can be a serious tool for learning. It has taken a while – and considerable empirical evidence – for there to be a general acceptance that games can be effective tools to support student learning. For assessment, which has the potential to be even more "high stakes," the skepticism can be even greater that games can be useful tools for assessment. Overcoming this issue will involve ensuring that any game-based assessment is grounded in a robust theory of assessment and providing empirical support for the efficacy of game-based assessment.

2. *Games often violate requirements of test theory.* Most games are designed in ways that the player advances a story by progressively solving problems that build on one another, where later challenges may require knowledge acquired in earlier parts of the game. This is in conflict with classical test theory, which assumes independence of test items, and often also with item response theory, which assumes local independence of items. This needs to be taken into consideration when designing games for assessment (Mislevy, Behrens, Dicerbo, Frezzo, & West, 2012).

3. *The gaming context can create excessive extraneous cognitive load.* Traditional assessments will often just ask children to say or write the information that is being assessed – or perhaps use the information in a simple way (e.g., "In the triangle presented below, solve the missing angle"). Alternative modes of assessment often ask for a more in-depth use of the content of what has been taught, for example, through solving of complex problems. Although this approach can tap into a "deeper" understanding, it also has the potential to underestimate students' knowledge, because a small mistake early on in the solution can derail the entire process. Additionally, there is a possibility that the way the problem is presented (e.g., to provide challenge and/or authenticity) can add to complexity in ways that are not germane to the problem (i.e., they can add to the "extraneous cognitive load" in the

assessment). This is also a potential issue when students are asked to apply knowledge to solve problems within the context of a game – in addition to the knowledge that is being assessed, additional knowledge or gaming skills may be required. Avoiding this particular issue involves paying close attention to the game mechanic being used for assessment to ensure that it is not adding unnecessary cognitive complexity.

4. *Games are meant for playing.* One of the first things experienced gamers will do when playing a new game is test the limits of the game. They will see how far off the path they can drive, or how they can "blow up" the system. Even if the game is intended as a form of assessment, learners may intentionally not solve a problem in the most efficient way in order to explore or play. Conversely, players may find a novel way to solve an in-game problem that does not require them to use the knowledge that is being assessed (i.e., they may find ways to "game" the system). There is a long tradition in games of both intentionally failing in order to test the limits of the system (e.g., finding out "how many hits will it take before my character dies?") as well as one of "cheats and hacks" (i.e., finding ways to "win" that the programmers did not originally intend). Good design and playtest can help reduce the likelihood of either intentionally failing or "hacks." It is also important to examine game logs to ensure that there were no unintended activities in the game.

In spite of these possible difficulties, the potential of game-based assessment is still great. To do it well, however, requires a grounding in established assessment theory, careful design of the in-game activities being used for assessment, and reviewing and evaluating the relations between in-game activities and assessments to determine their validity.

Foundations of Game-Based Assessment

A useful first step in understanding how to create reliable and effective assessment in video games is to examine how assessment has been conducted in other related digital systems. Thelwall (2000) argues that computerized assessments have passed through four distinct technological phases. The first generation of computerized testing began with the administration of conventional tests in a computerized format. The second generation included features that supported adaptive processes, attempting to tailor difficulty, content, or timing features of the subsequent item on the basis of examinees' responses. During the third generation, advances in technology were influenced by item-response theory, resulting in adaptive measurement, including an automatic calibrated measurement system that continuously and unobtrusively estimated dynamic changes in the student's achievement trajectory and profile. The fourth generation built on previous achievements in the adaptive computerized testing field by incorporating intelligent measurement, interpreting users' profiles, and providing advice to learners and teachers based on performance, which in turn is based on knowledge and inferencing procedures. Arguably, the body of research in which these advances in digital assessment have been most well developed and that has implication for game-based assessment is in the area of intelligent tutoring systems.

Assessment in Intelligent Tutoring Systems (ACT-R)

Research on assessments within the context of computer applications began decades ago, based on early information-processing models of human cognition (e.g., Koedinger, Anderson, Hadley & Mark, 1997). The Adaptive Control of Thought – Rational (ACT-R) theory was developed as a model of human thought that attempted to simulate how complex cognitive processes could arise through an interaction of more basic procedural and declarative knowledge (Anderson, Boyle, Corbett, & Lewis, 1990; Anderson, 1996). According to the ACT-R theory, human learning and cognition can be successfully modeled using computer language containing a set of procedural rules, composed of simple "if" and "then" statements. The ACT-R model is a network model that distinguishes between procedural knowledge, which involves a set of production rules, and declarative knowledge, which involves a database containing many units forming chunks of information (Miller, 1956; Servan-Schreiber, 1991; Anderson, 1996). The original ACT model followed a computationally plausible model of learning and memory, based on the theory that human memory is associative (Anderson & Bower, 1974). A major premise of the original ACT and revised ACT-R model is that all knowledge can be broken down into units of information, and a set of rules dictates how those units relate to one another. Unlike its predecessor, the ACT-R model accounts for the adaptive nature of learning by incorporating statistical structures better suited to explain the adaptive performance necessary to more accurately model human learning and memory processes.

In addition to modeling actual student learning and cognition, the ACT-R model was used to inform adaptive, or "intelligent," tutoring systems that would respond to student responses within the system. The ACT-R model was originally tested on knowledge acquisition related to problem-solving skills involved in mathematical or spatial reasoning (Anderson, Corbett, Koedinger, & Pelletier, 1995). In addition to predicting knowledge-acquisition processes, the model accounts for memory retrieval, or "knowledge deployment," processes and uses a method known as rational analysis (Anderson et al., 1995). According to the rational analysis framework, the availability of learned information can be predicted by the odds of it being used in a certain context and, therefore, depends on a set of conditional probabilities (Anderson, Boyle, Corbett, & Lewis, 1990; Anderson et al., 1995). The likelihood of correctly remembering some piece of information can be modeled using Bayesian inference to calculate the odds of the information being remembered given certain context and task-specific a priori probabilities. The ACT-R model predicts that human cognition tracks the overall usefulness of knowledge and assesses whether to apply the knowledge given a certain context. The likelihood of correctly retrieving information is therefore predicted by the effects of contextual priming. Based on the premises of this rational analysis framework proposed by Anderson and colleagues, a game environment context may increase the likelihood of knowledge being retrieved and applied correctly.

Research with these early cognitive tutoring programs indicates that the success of tutoring programs is largely due to the construction of separate models used to assess learning within the context in which knowledge is meant to be applied (e.g., Corbett, Anderson & O'Brien, 1995). Corbett and Anderson (1995) describe how the ACT Programming Tutor, intended to teach coding, constructs an *ideal student model* of knowledge in the domain (i.e., a "complete, executable model of procedural knowledge," p. 256). Students' actions are interpreted in light of this idealized model (a process termed "model tracing"), and if the actions indicate an understanding that falls short of the ideal model, then the system intervenes to support the students' learning. This discrepancy between the students' performance and the hypothesized learning model reveals the skills that the learner has mastery over and those that they have yet to develop.

This rational analysis framework proposed by Anderson and colleagues has been effectively used in tutoring specific academic skills; however, it also applies well to more general game contexts for learning. Many computer games have a prespecified set of goals that the player must accomplish before a game-play session is considered successful. In most educational games, the achievement of these goals is evidence of the acquisition of a specific skill. When a player does not achieve the desired goals, much like the cognitive tutoring programs, the game allows them to continue by replaying segments that caused a discrepancy between their performance and mastery (i.e., the learning model). Given digital computer games' unobtrusive means of capturing students' performance within a contextually enriched learning environment, and considering earlier efforts (e.g., ACT-R tutoring programs), games as mediums for assessing learning seem to be a natural progression to create adaptive learning systems.

Theoretical Methods of Game-Based Assessment: Evidence-Centered Design

The approach to assessment within intelligent tutoring systems such as ACT-R provides some insight into how best to undertake game-based assessment. Further insight can be provided by considering appropriate models of assessment, one of the most promising of which is *evidence-centered design* (ECD; Mislevy & Haertel, 2006). ECD is a framework for developing assessment (Mislevy, Steinberg, & Almond, 2002) that asks two key questions: What knowledge, skills, etc. should be assessed, and what behaviors provide evidence of the knowledge, skills, etc.? As an approach for developing assessments, the

ECD framework consists of interrelated components that describe the process of creating a conceptual assessment framework incorporating abstract knowledge aspects of the domain being assessed (i.e., *learning model*), paradigms for gathering information about domain proficiency (i.e., *performance model*), and the operational assessment whereby an instructor or administrator provides information and expectations necessary for completing the assessment as well as summary feedback to reciprocally improve the learner's future thinking and learning processes.

According to this framework, measuring proficiency involves consideration of at least three distinct paradigms that relate to standards of proficiency, evidence of proficiency, and the assessment task itself. Proficiency paradigms contain claims and aspects of proficiency; evidence paradigms consist of rubrics and means to identify evidence of proficiency in student work; task paradigms describe how students produce work relevant to the domain proficiency in question. The ECD framework promoted assessment validity and generalizability to measure aspects of learning, regardless of the content domain. In this regard, the ECD framework was based on an evidentiary perspective where criteria for proficiency is viewed as an argument and students' proficiency is determined by a body of logic-based evidence. In contrast to more traditional standardized forms of assessment, the ECD framework acknowledges the role of the assessment context and additional interrelated cognitive processes once considered peripheral to the proficiency domain. More recently, the *evidence-centered game design* (ECgD), a modified ECD framework for a game-based learning environment, has been developed (Mislevy, Orange, Bauer, von Davier, Hao, Corrigan, et al., 2014). Similar to the original ECD framework, ECgD defines targeted real-world competencies, aligns the game-world to the real-world competencies, unobtrusively integrates formative feedback systems into games, and engages the learner in iterative design processes that support meaningful learning.

Within ECgD, there are four main components: (1) definition of real-world target competencies, (2) alignment of game-world competencies with those in the real-world context, (3) integration of unobtrusive formative feedback into the game, and (4) engagement in an iterative process to further develop engaging games with embedded assessment to deep learning.

Considering that the general ECD framework effectively measures student proficiency, integrating assessments into game-based contexts seems sensible. The ECD framework acknowledges that mental and cognitive process of learning, students' activity, and observed performance are distinct aspects of the assessment framework. Digital computer games' affordance to monitor learners' activity enables such systems to collect evidence of domain proficiency on a continuous basis, allowing educators to better understand learner proficiency through documentation of the assessment context as well as learners' knowledge construction and application processes as documented through their actions and decisions within the game context.

Sources of Evidence for Assessment

When using ECD (or other assessment models) to guide game-based assessment, two fundamentally different approaches can be used regarding the activities that learners engage in to provide evidence for the assessment. One approach is to build activities into the game that are intended to evoke actions by the players that are to be used for assessment, and the other approach is to consider activities in the game after the fact, to look for evidence in game log files of the knowledge, skills, etc. that are being assessed. Both approaches have strengths and limitations, but either can be an effective source of assessment data.

Building Assessment into the Game: Assessment Mechanics. The term "game mechanics" refers to the specific actions, behaviors, and control mechanisms available to a player within the game (Hunicke, LeBlac, & Zubek, 2004). Building on the concept of game mechanics, Plass, Homer, Kinzer, Frye, and Perlin (2011) identify three discrete mechanics that impact the efficacy of educational games: *game mechanics*, *learning mechanics*, and *assessment mechanics*. The concept of game mechanics has the same meaning as it does in nonlearning games; however, learning and assessment mechanics are considered "meta-mechanics" – they describe activities within the game designed with the intention of either supporting student learning or assessing the student (or both). A single learning mechanic or assessment mechanic may be instantiated as several different game mechanics, depending on game genre, platform, context, and users.

In an educational game, a learning mechanic may be a single activity or a set of coordinated activities that form the essential learning activities. Learning mechanics include high-level cognitive activities that describe how learning is presented to students, much like the task model in ECD. Depending on the educational content and type of game, the specific learning mechanic may vary. Nevertheless, it should always be grounded in the learning sciences and reflect activities that support student learning. For example, a learning mechanic might be that the player needs to apply specific math rules to solve a problem. This describes the learning function, but not the specific action within the game (i.e., the game mechanic). How this learning mechanic will be instantiated as a game mechanic could vary, similar to the presentation model in ECD. In a text-based game, the player may have to type out a response to a question in the game that requires using the math rule. If the game uses an Angry Birds–type "slingshot" game mechanic, then the player may need to fling the correct rule to the proper spot in a puzzle to solve the problem. In both cases, it is the same learning mechanic (use a rule to solve a math problem), but uses a different game mechanic (type a response versus "fling" a response).

Similarly, assessment mechanics involve an in-game activity or coordinated set of activities that is used to have players demonstrate knowledge or skills, similar to the task model in ECD. In the same way that the design of effective learning mechanics should be grounded in the learning sciences, the design of effective assessment mechanics should be grounded in theories of assessment, such as ECD or ECgD (Mislevy et al., 2014). Within the ECgD framework, the competency model assumes criteria indicative of certain competencies that are considered unobservable latent variables to be assessed. Meanwhile, the evidence model may collect and analyze behavioral evidence that is essentially observable variables to support users' relative understanding of the content or mastery of the skill. The evidence model also quantifies observable variables by establishing scoring systems to align evidence alongside claims statistically. Within this framework, designing assessment mechanics entails deciding what in-game activities can be created to provide data for the evidence model. Assessment mechanics may require the learner to apply rules to solve problems, to arrange items in time or space for solving problems, or to select items that are contiguous with either time or space (Plass, Homer, et al., 2013). For example, *Light Lanes*, a game developed by the NYU CREATE lab to teach about reflection and refraction and to promote systems thinking, asks users to direct a beam of light emitted from a fixed source into a vessel using reflectors that can be repositioned on a two-dimensional playing field. For this game, the positioning of the reflectors in space and the number of moves required to do so provide an opportune assessment mechanic. Other games may afford additional measures of performance (see Reese, Seward, Tabachnick, Hitt, Harrison, & Mcfarland, 2012). For example, multiple scores may measure different performance areas such as total number of problems solved correctly, timed reports (Reese et al., 2012), or more complex performance indicators such as an "efficiency" score derived from a combined score of the proportion of items correct and the average response time (e.g., Homer, Plass, Raffaele, Ober, & Ali, 2018). Assessment mechanics in games may also serve as diagnostic instruments for complex cognitive and neurological disorders, such as dyslexia (Kyle, Kujala, Richardson, Lyytinen, & Goswami, 2013), dyscalculia (Wilson, Revkin, Cohen, Cohen, & Dehaene, 2006), and attention deficit/hyperactivity disorder (Rizzo, Buckwalter, Bowerly, Van Der Zaag, Humphrey, Neumann, et al., 2000).

When designing an assessment mechanic, a number of issues must be considered to assure its validity. Care must be taken to ensure that the mechanic does not depend too heavily on other factors that may confound the assessment. For example, a game-based math assessment could be embedded into a baseball simulation that might then require a knowledge of baseball. If the student fails the assessment, it could be due to either not knowing the math or not knowing enough about baseball to understand the demands of the assessment. Similarly, depending on the gaming mechanic used, a player may fail the assessment because of a lack of gaming skills, rather than a lack of knowledge about the content being taught. For example, in one popular math game, learners are required to tilt their tablets to direct a ball to the correct answer. While this game mechanic is fun for the players, it is a poor assessment mechanic because failure on this task could be due to either a misconception in math or a lack of hand-eye coordination.

Conversely, it is also important to ensure that the task being used as an assessment cannot be passed in a way that does not require use of the knowledge of skill being assessed (e.g., through a "hack" or "cheat"). An example of this is reported in Shute, Ventura, and Kim (2013), who were studying *Newton's Playground*, a video game that teaches physics to students. In the game, students must guide the path of a balloon by drawing simple machines (e.g., ramps, levers, pendulums). Shute et al. (2013) describe how they found in playtesting that students were initially able to pass some tasks just by drawing and stacking many small objects rather than using the simple machines that were supposed to be used for the tasks. The authors eliminated this problem by imposing a limit on the number of items students could draw to solve any one problem.

Another issue to consider is that mechanics that have been designed to optimize learning may not be ideal for assessment. For example, the *Alien Game* has been shown to be effective for developing high school students' executive functions (Parong, Mayer, Fiorella, McNamara, Homer & Plass, 2017; Homer et al., 2018). However, because the game is adaptive, there is too much variability in performance demands within the game for any simple metrics in the game to serve as an effective assessment mechanic.

A final issue to consider when developing assessment mechanics is the role of emotion. Good games are intended to elicit emotions from players, and in part, it is this emotional engagement that allows games to be excellent tools for learning and assessment (Plass et al., 2015). However, too much emotional arousal in an educational game can result in excessive cognitive load and interfere with learning and assessment (Fraser, Ma, Teteris, Baxter, Wright, & McLaughlin, 2012). Assessments within games, then, should be emotionally engaging but not excessively emotionally arousing.

Assessing In-Game Activities after the Fact: Computer Log Data. A second source of data for in-game assessment comes from log data (Shute, 2011; Plass, Homer, et al., 2013; All, Nunez Castellar, & Van Looy, 2016). In this case, the specific assessment activities may not be predefined. Instead, to use the ECgD framework, data from the game are examined statistically to create an evidence model for certain target competencies (Mislevy et al., 2014). The best examples of this approach come from work by Shute and her colleagues in the "stealth assessment" approach (Shute, 2011; Shute & Ventura, 2013; Shute & Sun, in press). This method uses Bayesian network analysis (de Klerk, Veldkamp, & Eggen, 2015, 2016) in order establish conditional relationships among in-game indicators and the competency variables. Each of these conditional relationships is determined by a set of statistical probabilities assigned based on the user's previous course of action. The use of advanced statistical methods for analyzing computer log data may allow researchers to draw more accurate inferences of the user's competency model based on the information available about the user's performance model. The stealth-assessment approach has been used to successfully evaluate learner's creativity, problem-solving, spatial skills, and persistence (Shute, 2011; Buelow, Okdie, & Cooper, 2015).

Analyses of game log data can also be used to enhance the effectiveness of an educational intervention. For example, Baker, Clarke-Midura, and Ocumpaugh (2016) studied log data collected from 2,000 middle school students as they explored a virtual world intended to support science education. The authors then examined models of behavior in the virtual world that predicted science inquiry and achievement. The virtual environment featured many characteristics of an exploration game with personalized avatars and opportunities for goal-setting and served as a virtual performance assessment, extracting information about students' sequence of actions and response times to build a probabilistic model of student performance in relation to target competencies indicative of science inquiry. This probabilistic model was then applied to a new scenario or "virtual world" to test users' skills of scientific inquiry based on parameters that had been operationalized in the previous scenario. The results indicated that the probabilistic model, when applied to a new scenario that featured similar structural components of the original one, reliably predicted student performance in the new scenario. Furthermore, the probabilistic model of performance also identified students unable to demonstrate scientific inquiry skills, allowing for early intervention. The model was capable of identifying learners with poor self-regulation: those demonstrating off-task behavior, inadequate or extended amount of time spent on a certain task, or behaviors indicative of frustration, boredom, or lack of perseverance.

While computer log data provides the learner teacher, and researcher with invaluable information, such an abundance of data may be challenging to interpret. Solutions to this problem include generating log files that record only information of interest (see Shute, Wang, Greiff, Zhao, & Moore, 2016) or developing a generic log file structure applicable to different games to manage the more tedious aspects of data storage and extraction (see Hao, Smith, Mislevy, von Davier, & Bauer, 2016).

Validation of Game-Based Assessments

As with any new assessment tool, game-based assessments need to be validated. Three main approaches for such a validation include: (1) comparing game-based assessments to established assessment tools administered outside the context of the game, (2) having experts evaluate in-game activities and comparing expert evaluation with the in-game assessment, or (3) examining how well the game-based assessments predict some sort of future learning performance or outcome in the domain.

The most common approach is to give external measures of the knowledge, skills, etc. that are being assessed within the game. For example, the game *Factor Reactor* was created to help develop math fluency in middle school children (see Plass, O'Keefe, et al., 2013). The game presents users with a center number surrounded by two rings of other numbers. The objective is to transform the center number into one of the outer "goal" numbers by adding, subtracting, multiplying, or dividing it by one of the numbers in the inner ring.

Players are rewarded for both speed and using the fewest possible number of steps to transform the target number. In a study examining the effects of different play conditions (individual, competitive, or collaborative), Plass, O'Keefe, et al. (2013) used the Woodcock–Johnson III Math Fluency subtest (McGrew & Woodcock, 2001) as an external measure of math fluency and found that a number of game metrics, including levels completed, were correlated with students' scores on the standardized assessment of math fluency, suggesting that the game could be a valid assessment tool (Plass, Homer et al., 2013; Plass, O'Keefe, et al., 2013).

Another example of using external validation of game-based assessment comes from a study by Shute et al. (2016), who sought to design, develop, and validate a game-based assessment to measure problem-solving abilities with a group of middle school students playing a custom-designed game, *Use Your Brainz*. The students played the game on a mobile tablet for three hours over the course of three consecutive days. On the fourth day, they participated in a series of post-tests to assess transfer of knowledge attained during game play. The game *Use Your Brainz*, which was closely modeled on the structure of the popular game *Plants vs. Zombies 2*, had been previously used as an instrument for inquiry into the efficacy of game-based stealth assessment (Shute, Moore, & Wang, 2015). In designing the game, the researchers constructed a competency model based on previous research on problem-solving. Aspects of problem-solving included analyzing game constraints, planning a course of action toward a solution, using resources efficiently, and monitoring progress along the way toward a solution. In addition, a set of actions was identified that indicated either the acquisition or application of a certain rule by the learner, necessary for achieving a solution. Bayesian network analysis was used to evaluate the progress of learners while playing the game to construct an evidence model with respect to the desired competency model. The results from the in-game measures were then compared with two external measures, MicroDYN (Wüstenberg, Greiff, & Funke, 2012) and Raven's Progressive Matrices (Raven, 1941, 2000). A multiple regression model revealed that both external measures predicted some of the variability within game measures, with the MicroDYN subscore for knowledge application significantly predicting various within-game measures such as planning, tool usage, and evaluation progress. This research suggests that the greater complexity that games afford assessment mechanics may make them ideal environments to test abstract constructs that require cognitive flexibility and creative problem-solving.

Practical Implications for Education

Assessment in the context of games holds much promise for improving testing practices, especially for formative assessments. Game-based assessment may promote mastery learning with students while simultaneously allowing teachers and researchers to close the gap between the desired competency model and the individual student's performance model by collecting detailed information about their progress. Furthermore, with quality design, game-based assessments may promote a more authentic form of knowledge construction, whereby the learner can acquire practical knowledge that utilizes skills such as problem-solving (Kiili, 2007) and spatial reasoning (De Lisi & Wolford, 2002). These authentic forms of learning may ultimately promote knowledge transfer, while stimulating long-term retention and retrieval processes through sustained attention and engagement within the game learning environment.

Limitations of Game-Based Assessments

In order for game-based assessments to be practical and achieve the desired aims of assessing students within a dynamic learning environment, they must be well designed and cater to learners and researchers, teachers, or administrators. Data points must be relevant and easily interpretable (Leighton & Chu, 2016). Unfortunately, the cost of developing a high-quality game-based assessment system can be difficult to justify. Additional concerns revolve around the issue of fairness, particularly as testing is involved. Most games afford users a context to learn and explore content; however, if a learner is unfamiliar with the context or setting of the game, it may place them at an unfair disadvantage for learning the material (Kim & Shute, 2015). Conversely, learners who are avid gamers may have an advantage within the context of the game that does not serve them well in a real-world setting.

An open question concerns the usefulness of games as standardized assessments. A fully developed game may introduce too many confounds, as discussed above, but it seems clear that current approaches to standardized assessments would benefit from insights resulting from game-based learning and assessment, such as their affordance to provide meaningful contexts for performance, to incorporate emotional design considerations, and to motivate the learner or test taker (Plass & Kaplan, 2016).

Future Research

While the findings described above are ultimately promising, further research is necessary to understand the full implications and possibilities for game-based assessment. Future research on game-based assessment should consider three basic questions as outlined by Mayer (2015) with respect to educational games in general. The first question seeks to address the value-added nature of "game as embedded assessment tool" and attempts to identify the underlying benefits of using games for assessment purposes, such as optimizing instructional time, instantaneous formative feedback, and facilitating engagement. The second question addresses the cognitive consequences of using games for assessment. For example, is a student in fact learning the content that is relevant for long-term achievement, or is the student merely demonstrating optimal performance in the game because of an understanding of the game design? The third question addresses the issue of media comparison and whether digital or traditional forms of media are more suitable for certain content. For example, would students benefit more from playing the game in a digital or traditional context? Also, which format is most likely to lead to sustained near or far transfer?

While these three broad questions provoke long-term consideration of the use of games as assessment tools, an understanding of games as assessment tools may benefit from the integration of methods to detect learners' cognitive, affective, and motivational responses. The inclusion of emotion recognition along with assessment may allow future digital technologies to mirror human interactions and positively influence the learner's performance. Referred to as affective computing (Picard, 1997), such technologies could detect and respond accordingly to human emotions that may serve as effective means to mitigate negative affect (e.g., frustration and anxiety induced during the learning and testing process) and optimize long-term learning by adapting the game environment to provide a context that induces positive emotions such as confidence and fascination (Novak & Johnson, 2012). Positive affect is associated with improved long-term memory outcomes that support working memory, storage, and retrieval processes (Erez & Isen, 2002), often viewed as indicators of actual learning (Chen & Wang, 2011). In addition to research on affective computing, augmented and virtual reality are rapidly becoming more accessible to a broader set of users and may serve as means to further develop models for authentic and engaging assessment.

Conclusions

In this chapter, we examined the ways in which digital games can be used to authentically evaluate learners' knowledge and skills. Challenges to the use of game-based assessment include lack of general acceptance of games as assessment tools, potential for extraneous cognitive load caused by the gaming environment, concerns related to test theory regarding item independence, and a culture of exploration and "cheats/hacks" in games. To overcome these challenges, we have argued that game-based assessments need to be grounded in existing assessment practice and theory (e.g., ECD/ECgD), undergo thorough playtesting (including evaluation of the activities being used to assess learners' knowledge, i.e., the assessment mechanics), and be validated through external evaluations and examination of game log data. The integration of assessment into the context of games offers the promise of constructing a high-quality dynamic system that is engaging and adaptive to the learner while assessing student knowledge in order to enhance student learning. Though game-based assessments hold much promise with future implications for education, more research is needed to fully address current limitations and questions regarding its practical usage.

References

All, A., Castellar, E. P. N., & Van Looy, J. (2016). Assessing the effectiveness of digital game-based learning: Best practices. *Computers & Education*, *92–93*, 90–103.

Anderson, J. R. (1996). ACT: A simple theory of complex cognition. *American Psychologist*, *51*(4), 355–365.

Anderson, J. R., & Bower, G. H. (1974). A propositional theory of recognition memory. *Memory & Cognition*, *2*(3), 406–412.

Anderson, J. R., Boyle, C. F., Corbett, A. T., & Lewis, M. W. (1990). Cognitive modeling and intelligent tutoring. *Artificial intelligence*, *42*(1), 7–49.

Anderson, J. R., Corbett, A. T., Koedinger, K. R., & Pelletier, R. (1995). Cognitive tutors: Lessons learned. *Journal of the Learning Sciences*, *4*(2), 167–207.

Azevedo, R., Cromley, J. G., Moos, D. C., Greene, J. A., & Winters, F. I. (2011). Adaptive content and process scaffolding: A key to facilitating students' self-regulated learning with hypermedia. *Psychological Testing and Assessment Modeling*, *53*(1), 106–140.

Baker, R. S., Clarke-Midura, J., & Ocumpaugh, J. (2016). Towards general models of effective science inquiry in virtual performance assessments. *Journal of Computer Assisted Learning*, *32*, 267–280.

Black, P., & Wiliam, D. (1998). Assessment and classroom learning. *Assessment in Education: Principles, Policy & Practice*, *5*(1), 7–74.

Black, P., & Wiliam, D. (2009). Developing the theory of formative assessment. *Educational Assessment, Evaluation and Accountability* (formerly Journal of Personnel Evaluation in Education), *21*(1), 5.

Buelow, M. T., Okdie, B. M., & Cooper, A. B. (2015). The influence of video games on executive functions in college students. *Computers in Human Behavior*, *45*, 228–234.

Chen, C. M., & Wang, H. P. (2011). Using emotion recognition technology to assess the effects of different multimedia materials on learning emotion and performance. *Library & Information Science Research*, *33*(3), 244–255.

Corbett, A. T., Anderson, J. R., & O'Brien, A. T. (1995). Student modeling in the ACT programming tutor. *Cognitively Diagnostic Assessment*, 19–41.

Csapó, B., Lörincz, A., & Molnár, G. (2012). Innovative assessment technologies in educational games designed for young students. In *Assessment in game-based learning* (pp. 235–254). New York: Springer.

De Lisi, R., & Wolford, J. L. (2002). Improving children's mental rotation accuracy with computer game playing. *Journal of Genetic Psychology*, *163*(3), 272–282.

de Klerk, S., Veldkamp, B. P., & Eggen, T. J. H. M. (2015). Psychometric analysis of the performance data of simulation-based assessment: A systematic review and a Bayesian network example. *Computers & Education*, *85*, 23–34.

de Klerk, S., Veldkamp, B. P., & Eggen, T. J. H. M. (2016). A methodology for applying students' interactive task performance scores from a multimedia-based performance assessment in Bayesian network. *Computers in Human Behavior*, *60*, 264–279.

DeLoache, J. S. (1987). Rapid change in the symbolic functioning of very young children. *Science*, *238*, 1556–1557.

Domagk, S., Schwartz, R. N., & Plass, J. L. (2010). Interactivity in multimedia learning: An integrated model. *Computers in Human Behavior*, *26*(5), 1024–1033.

Fraser, K., Ma, I., Teteris, E., Baxter, H., Wright, B., & McLaughlin, K. (2012). Emotion, cognitive load and learning outcomes during simulation training. *Medical Education*, *46*(11), 1055–1062.

Erez, A., & Isen, A. M. (2002). The influence of positive affect on the components of expectancy motivation. *Journal of Applied Psychology*, *87*(6), 1055.

Gee, J. P. (2003). *What video games have to teach us about learning and literacy*. New York: Macmillan.

Gee, J. P., & Shaffer, D. W. (2010). Looking where the light is bad: Video games and the future of assessment. *Phi Delta Kappa International EDge*, *6*(1), 3–19.

Hao, J., Smith, L., Mislevy, R., von Davier, A., & Bauer, M. (2016). Taming log files from game/simulation-based assessments: Data models and data analysis tools. Research Report ETS RR-16-10. Retrieved from http://onlinelibrary .wiley.com/doi/10.1002/ets2.12096/epdf.

Homer, B. D., Plass, J. L., Raffaele, C., Ober, T. M., & Ali, A. (2018). Improving high school students' executive functions through digital game play. *Computers & Education*, *117*, 50–58.

Hoffman, B., & Nadelson, L. (2010). Motivational engagement and video gaming: A mixed methods study. *Educational Technology Research and Development*, *58*(3), 245–270.

Hunicke, R., LeBlanc, M., & Zubek, R. (2004, July). MDA: A formal approach to game design and game research. In *Proceedings of the AAAI Workshop on Challenges in Game AI* (vol. 4, no. 1, pp. 1–5). San Jose, CA: AAAI Press.

Kiili, K. (2007). Foundation for problem-based gaming. *British Journal of Educational Technology*, *38*(3), 394–404.

Kim, B. (2015). Game mechanics, dynamics, and aesthetics. *Library Technology Reports*, *51*(2), 17.

Kim, Y. J., & Shute, V. J. (2015). The interplay of game elements with psychometric qualities, learning, and enjoyment in game-based assessment. *Computers & Education*, *87*, 340–356.

Koedinger, K. R., Anderson, J. R., Hadley, W. H., & Mark, M. A. (1997). Intelligent tutoring goes to school in the big city. In *Proceedings of the 7th World Conference on Artificial Intelligence in Education*. Charlottesville, VA: Association for the Advancement of Computing in Education.

Kyle, F., Kujala, J., Richardson, U., Lyytinen, H., & Goswami, U. (2013). Assessing the effectiveness of two theoretically motivated computer-assisted reading interventions in the United Kingdom: GG Rime and GG Phoneme. *Reading Research Quarterly*, *48*(1), 61–76.

Leighton, J. P., & Chu, M. W. (2016). First among equals: Hybridization of cognitive diagnostic assessment and evidence-centered game design. *International Journal of Testing*, *16*(2), 164–180.

Mayer, R. E. (2003). The promise of multimedia learning: Using the same instructional design methods across different media. *Learning and Instruction*, *13*(2), 125–139.

Mayer, R. E. (2015). On the need for research evidence to guide the design of computer games for learning. *Educational Psychologist*, *50*(4), 349–353.

McGrew, K. S., & Woodcock, R. W. (2001). *Technical manual: Woodcock–Johnson III*. Itasca, IL: Riverside.

Meyer, B., & Sørensen, B. H. (2009). Designing serious games for computer assisted language learning: A framework for development and analysis.

In M. Kankaanranta & P. Neittaanmäki (Eds.), *Design and use of serious games* (pp. 69–82). Dordrecht: Springer.

Miller, G. A. (1956). The magical number seven, plus or minus two: Some limits on our capacity for processing information. *Psychological Review, 63*(2), 81.

Mislevy, R. J., Behrens, J. T., Dicerbo, K. E., Frezzo, D. C., & West, P. (2012). Three things game designers need to know about assessment. In *Assessment in game-based learning* (pp. 59–81). New York: Springer.

Mislevy, R. J., & Haertel, G. D. (2006). Implications of evidence-centered design for educational testing. *Educational Measurement: Issues and Practice, 25*(4), 6–20.

Mislevy, R. J., Orange, A., Bauer, M. I., von Davier, A., Hao, J., Corrigan, S., ... & John, M. (2014). Psychometric considerations in game-based assessment. White paper. Retrieved from www.ets.org/research/policy_research_reports/publications/white_paper/2014/jrrx.

Mislevy, R. J., Steinberg, L. S., & Almond, R. G. (2002). Design and analysis in task-based language assessment. *Language Testing, 19*(4), 477–496.

Novak, E., & Johnson, T. E. (2012). Assessment of student's emotions in game-based learning. In *Assessment in game-based learning* (pp. 379–399). New York: Springer.

Parong, J., Mayer, R. E., Fiorella, L., MacNamara, A., Homer, B. D., & Plass, J. L. (2017). Learning executive function skills by playing focused video games. *Contemporary Educational Psychology, 51*, 141–151.

Piaget, J. (1962). *Play, dreams and imitation in childhood.* New York: W. W. Norton.

Picard, R. W. (1997). *Affective computing.* Cambridge: MIT Press.

Plass, J. L., Chun, D. M., Mayer, R. E., & Leutner, D. (1998). Supporting visual and verbal learning preferences in a second-language multimedia learning environment. *Journal of Educational Psychology, 90*(1), 25.

Plass, J. L., Homer, B. D., & Kinzer, C. K. (2015). Foundations of game-based learning. *Educational Psychologist, 50*, 258–283.

Plass, J. L., Homer, B. D., Kinzer, C. K., Chang, Y. K., Frye, J., Kaczetow, W., ... & Perlin, K. (2013). Metrics in simulations and games for learning. In M. Seif El-Nasr, A. Drachen, & A. Canossa (Eds.), *Game analytics* (pp. 697–729). London: Springer.

Plass, J. L., Homer, B. D., Kinzer, C. K., Frye, J., & Perlin, K. (2011). Learning mechanics and assessment mechanics for games for learning. G4LI White Paper, 1.

Plass, J. L., & Kaplan, U. (2016). Emotional design in digital media for learning. In *Emotions, technology, design, and learning* (pp. 131–161).

Plass, J. L., O'Keefe, P. A., Homer, B. D., Case, J., Hayward, E. O., Stein, M., & Perlin, K. (2013). The impact of individual, competitive, and collaborative mathematics game play on learning, performance, and motivation. *Journal of Educational Psychology, 105*(4), 1050–1066.

Raven, J. (2000). The Raven's progressive matrices: Change and stability over culture and time. *Cognitive Psychology, 41*, 1–48.

Raven, J. C. (1941). Standardization of progressive matrices, 1938. *British Journal of Medical Psychology, 19*(1), 137–150.

Ravitch, D. (2016). *The death and life of the great American school system: How testing and choice are undermining education.* Basic Books.

Reese, D. D., Seward, R. J., Tabachnick, B. G., Hitt, B. A., Harrison, A., & Mcfarland, L. (2012). Timed report measures learning: Game-based embedded assessment. In *Assessment in game-based learning* (pp. 145–172). New York: Springer.

Rizzo, A. A., Buckwalter, J. G., Bowerly, T., Van Der Zaag, C., Humphrey, L., Neumann, U., ... & Sisemore, D. (2000). The virtual classroom: A virtual reality environment for the assessment and rehabilitation of attention deficits. *CyberPsychology & Behavior*, *3*(3), 483–499.

Servan-Schreiber, E. (1991). The competitive chunking theory: Models of perception, learning, and memory. Doctoral dissertation, Carnegie-Mellon University.

Shute, V., & Sun, C. (in press). Game-based assessment: What it is and does it work? In J. Plass, R. Mayer, & B. D. Homer (Eds.), *Handbook of game-based learning*. MIT Press.

Shute, V., & Ventura, M. (2013). *Stealth assessment: Measuring and supporting learning in video games*. Cambridge, MA: MIT Press.

Shute, V. J. (2011). Stealth assessment in computer-based games to support learning. *Computer Games and Instruction*, *55*(2), 503–524.

Shute, V. J., Moore, G. R., & Wang, L. (2015). Measuring problem solving skills in Plants vs. Zombies 2. *International Educational Data Mining Society: Proceedings of the 8th International Conference on Educational Data Mining* (pp. 428–431). Madrid, Spain.

Shute, V. J., Ventura, M., & Ke, F. (2015). The power of play: The effects of Portal 2 and Lumosity on cognitive and noncognitive skills. *Computers & Education*, *80*, 58–67.

Shute, V. J., Ventura, M., & Kim, Y. J. (2013). Assessment and learning of qualitative physics in Newton's Playground. *Journal of Educational Research*, *106*(6), 423–430.

Shute, V. J., Wang, L., Greiff, S., Zhao, W., & Moore, G. (2016). Measuring problem solving skills via stealth assessment in an engaging video game. *Computers in Human Behavior*, *63*, 106–117.

Thelwall, M. (2000). Computer-based assessment: A versatile educational tool. *Computers & Education*, *34*(1), 37–49.

US Department of Education (2017). Reimagining the role of technology in education: 2017 National Education Technology Plan Update. Retrieved from https://tech.ed.gov/files/2017/01/NETP17.pdf.

Wilson, A. J., Revkin, S. K., Cohen, D., Cohen, L., & Dehaene, S. (2006). An open trial assessment of "The Number Race," an adaptive computer game for remediation of dyscalculia. *Behavioral and Brain Functions*, *2*(1), 20.

Wüstenberg, S., Greiff, S., & Funke, J. (2012). Complex problem solving more than reasoning? *Intelligence*, *40*, 1–14.

17 Feedback in the Context of Self-Assessment

Heidi L. Andrade

This is a good time to be writing about self-assessment. My colleagues, especially Ernesto Panadero, Lois Harris, and Gavin Brown, have recently produced thoughtful analyses of the topic (Brown & Harris, 2013; Panadero & Alonso-Tapia, 2013). Drawing on their work, as well as my own and others', I can provide an updated overview of theory and research. The treatment of theory presented here involves articulating a refined definition and operationalization of self-assessment. The review of the small but growing body of empirical research provides a critical perspective, in the interest of provoking new investigations into neglected areas.

Defining and Operationalizing Student Self-Assessment

Without exception, recent reviews of self-assessment (Sargeant, 2008; Brown & Harris, 2013; Panadero, Brown, & Strijbos, 2016) call for clearer definitions: What is self-assessment, and what is not? This question is surprisingly difficult to answer, as the term *self-assessment* has been used to describe a diverse range of activities, such as assigning a happy or sad face to a story just told, estimating the number of correct answers on a math test, graphing scores for dart throwing, indicating understanding (or the lack thereof) of a science concept, using a rubric to identify strengths and weaknesses in one's persuasive essay, writing reflective journal entries, and so on. Each of those activities involves some kind of assessment of one's own functioning, but they are so different that distinctions among types of self-assessment are needed. In this chapter I will draw those distinctions in terms of the purposes of self-assessment, which, in turn, determine its features: a classic form-fits-function analysis.

What Is Self-Assessment?

Brown and Harris (2013) defined self-assessment in the K-16 context as a "descriptive and evaluative act carried out by the student concerning his or her own work and academic abilities" (p. 368). Panadero, Brown, and Strijbos (2016) defined it as a "wide variety of mechanisms and techniques through which students describe (i.e., assess) and possibly assign merit or worth to (i.e., evaluate) the qualities of their own learning processes and products" (p. 804). Referring to physicians, Epstein, Siegel, and Silberman (2008) defined "concurrent self-assessment" as "ongoing moment-to-moment self-monitoring" (p. 5). Self-monitoring "refers to the ability to notice our own actions, curiosity to examine the effects of those actions, and willingness to use those observations to improve behavior and thinking in the future" (p. 5). Taken together, these definitions include self-assessment of one's *abilities*, *processes*, and *products* – everything but the kitchen sink. This very broad conception might seem unwieldy, but it works because each object of assessment – competence, process, and product – is subject to the influence of feedback from oneself.

What is missing from each of these definitions, however, is the purpose of the act of self-assessment. Their authors might rightly point out that the purpose is implied, but a formal definition requires us to make it plain: Why do we ask students to self-assess? I have long held that self-assessment is feedback (Andrade, 2010) and that the purpose of feedback is to inform adjustments to processes and products that deepen learning; hence the purpose of self-assessment is to generate feedback that promotes learning and improvements in performance. This learning-oriented purpose of self-assessment implies that it should be formative: if there is no opportunity for adjustment and correction, self-assessment is almost pointless.

Why Self-Assess?

Clarity about the purpose of self-assessment allows us to interpret what otherwise appear to be discordant findings from research, which has produced mixed results in terms of both the accuracy of students' self-assessments and their influence on learning and/or performance. I believe the source of the discord can be traced to the differences between summative and formative self-assessment. This issue will be taken up again in the review of current research that follows this overview. For now, consider a study of the accuracy and validity of summative self-assessment in teacher education conducted by Tejeiro et al. (2012), which showed that students' self-assigned marks tended to be higher than marks given by professors. All 122 students in the study assigned themselves a grade at the end of their course, but half of the students were told that their self-assigned grade would count toward 5% of their final grade. In both groups, students' self-assessments were higher than grades given by professors, especially for students with "poorer results" (p. 791) and those for whom self-assessment counted toward the final grade. In the group that was told their self-assessments would count toward their final grade, no relationship was found between the professor's and the students' assessments. Tejeiro et al. concluded that although students' and professor's assessments tend to be highly similar when self-assessment did not count toward final grades, overestimations increased dramatically when students' self-assessments do count. Interviews of students who self-assigned highly discrepant grades revealed (as you might guess) that they were motivated by the desire to obtain the highest possible grades.

Studies like Tejeiro et al.'s (2012) are interesting in terms of the information they provide about the relationship between consistency and honesty, but the purpose of the self-assessment, beyond addressing interesting research questions, is unclear. There is no feedback purpose. This is also true for another example of a study of summative self-assessment of competence, during which elementary school children took the Test of Narrative Language and then were asked to self-evaluate "how you did in making up stories today" by pointing to one of five pictures, from a "very happy face" (rating of 5) to a "very sad face" (rating of 1) (Kaderavek, Gillam, Ukrainetz, Justice, & Eisenberg, 2004, p. 37). The usual results were reported: older children and good narrators were more accurate than younger children and poor narrators, and males tended to more frequently overestimate their ability.

Typical of clinical studies of accuracy in self-evaluation, this study rests on a definition and operationalization of self-assessment with no value in terms of instructional feedback. If those children were asked to rate their stories and then revise or, better yet, if they assessed their stories according to clear, developmentally appropriate criteria before revising, the valence of their self-assessments in terms of instructional feedback would skyrocket. I speculate that their accuracy would too. In contrast, studies of formative self-assessment suggest that when the act of self-assessing is given a learning-oriented purpose, students' self-assessments are relatively consistent with those of external evaluators, including professors (Lopez & Kossack, 2007; Barney, Khurum, Petersen, Unterkalmsteiner, & Jabangwe, 2012; Leach, 2012), teachers (Bol, Hacker, Walck, & Nunnery, 2012; Chang, Tseng, & Lou, 2012; Chang, Liang, & Chen, 2013), researchers (Panadero & Romero, 2014; Fitzpatrick & Schulz, 2016), and expert medical assessors (Hawkins, Osborne, Schofield, Pournaras, & Chester, 2012).

My commitment to keeping self-assessment formative is firm. However, Gavin Brown (personal communication, April 2011) is fond of reminding me that summative self-assessment exists and we cannot ignore it, try as I might: any definition of self-assessment must acknowledge and distinguish between formative and summative forms of it. Thus the taxonomy in Table 17.1, which depicts self-assessment as serving formative and/or summative purposes, and focuses on competence, processes, and/or products.

Fortunately, a formative view of self-assessment seems to be taking hold in various educational contexts. For instance, Sargeant (2008) noted that all seven authors in a special issue of the *Journal of Continuing Education in the Health Professions* "conceptualize self-assessment within a formative, educational perspective, and see it as an activity that draws upon both external and internal data, standards, and resources to inform and make decisions about one's performance" (p. 1). Sargeant also stresses the point that self-assessment should be guided by evaluative criteria: "Multiple external sources can and should inform self-assessment, perhaps most important among them performance standards" (p. 1). Now we are talking about the *how* of self-assessment, which demands an operationalization of self-assessment practice. Let us examine each object of self-assessment (competence, processes, and/or products) with an eye for what is assessed and why.

What Is Self-Assessed?

Monitoring and self-assessing *processes* are practically synonymous with self-regulated learning (SRL), or at least central components of it such as goal-setting and monitoring, and research on SRL has clearly shown that self-generated feedback on one's approach to learning is associated with academic gains (Zimmerman & Schunk, 2011). Self-assessment of the *products*, such as papers and presentations, are the easiest to defend as instructional feedback, especially when those self-assessments are grounded in explicit, relevant, evaluative criteria and followed by opportunities to relearn and/or revise (Andrade, 2010).

Including the self-assessment of *competence* in this definition is a little trickier. I hesitated to include it because of the risk of sneaking in global assessments of one's overall ability, self-esteem, and self-concept ("I'm good enough, I'm smart enough, and doggone it, people like me," Franken, 1992), which do not seem relevant to a discussion of instructional feedback. Research on global self-assessment, or self-perception, is popular in the medical education literature, but even there, scholars have begun to question its usefulness in terms of influencing learning and professional growth (e.g., see Sargeant, Mann, van der Vleuten, & Metsemakers, 2008). Eva and Regehr (2008) seem to agree in the following passage, which states the case in a way that makes it worthy of a long quotation:

> Self-assessment is often (implicitly or otherwise) conceptualized as a personal, unguided reflection on performance for the purposes of generating an individually derived summary of one's own level of knowledge, skill, and understanding in a particular area. For example, this conceptualization would appear to be the only reasonable basis for studies that fit into what Colliver (2005) has described as the "guess your grade" model of self-assessment research, the results of which form the core foundation for the recurring conclusion that self-assessment is generally poor.
>
> This unguided, internally generated construction of self-assessment stands in stark contrast to the model put forward by Boud (1999), who argued that the phrase self-assessment should not imply an isolated or individualistic activity; it should commonly involve peers, teachers, and other sources of information. The conceptualization of self-assessment as enunciated in Boud's description would appear to involve a process by which one takes personal responsibility for looking outward, explicitly seeking feedback and information from external sources, then using these externally generated sources of assessment data to direct performance improvements. In this construction, self-assessment is more

of a pedagogical strategy than an ability to judge for oneself; it is a habit that one needs to acquire and enact rather than an ability that one needs to master. (p. 15)

As in the K-16 context, self-assessment is coming to be seen as having value as much in terms of pedagogy as in assessment (Silver, Campbell, Marlow, & Sargeant, 2008; Brown & Harris, 2014). In the end, however, I decided that self-assessing one's competence to successfully learn a particular concept or complete a particular task (which sounds a lot like self-efficacy – more on that later) might be useful feedback because it can inform decisions about how to proceed, such as the amount of time to invest in learning how to play the flute, or whether or not to seek help learning the steps of the jitterbug. An important caveat, however, is that self-assessments of competence are useful only if students have opportunities to do something about their perceived low competence – that is, it serves the purpose of formative feedback for the learner.

How to Self-Assess?

Panadero et al. (2016) summarized five very different taxonomies of self-assessment and called for the development of a comprehensive typology that considers, among other things, its purpose, the presence or absence of criteria, and the method. In response, I propose the taxonomy depicted in Table 17.1, which focuses on the *what* (competence, process, or product), the *why* (formative or summative), and the *how* (methods, including whether or not they include standards, e.g., criteria) of self-assessment. The collections of examples of methods in the table is wildly inexhaustive.

I put the methods in Table 17.1 where I think they belong, but many of them could be placed in more than one cell. Take *self-efficacy*, for instance, which is essentially a self-assessment of one's competence to successfully undertake a particular task (Bandura, 1997). Summative judgments of self-efficacy are certainly possible but they seem like a silly thing to do – what is the point, from a learning perspective? Formative self-efficacy judgments, on the other hand, can inform next steps in learning and skill-building. There is reason to believe that monitoring and making adjustments to one's self-efficacy (e.g., by setting goals or attributing success to effort) can be productive (Zimmerman, 2000), so I placed self-efficacy in the formative row.

It is important to emphasize the fact that self-efficacy is task specific, more or less (Bandura, 1997). This taxonomy does not include general, holistic evaluations of one's abilities, for example, "I am good at math." Global assessment of competence does not provide the leverage, in terms of instructional feedback, that is provided by task-specific assessments of competence, that is, self-efficacy. Eva and Regehr (2008) provided an illustrative example: "We suspect most people are prompted to open a dictionary as a result of encountering a word for which they are uncertain of the meaning rather than out of a broader assessment that their vocabulary could be improved" (p. 16). The exclusion of global

Table 17.1 *A taxonomy of self-assessment*

	Competence	Processes		Products	
		Standards		Standards	
		Yes	No	Yes	No
Formative	Task-specific self-efficacy ratings	Judgments of progress toward specific targets	• Traffic lights • Comprehension checks • Self-monitoring, metacognition • Reflective journal writing	• Rubric- or checklist-referenced self-assessment • Self-testing	
Summative	Post-task judgments of ability based on performance		Post-task judgments of effectiveness of procedures	• Self-grading	• Self-grading

evaluations of oneself resonates with research that clearly shows that feedback that focuses on aspects of a task (e.g., "I did not solve most of those math problems") is more effective than feedback that focuses on the self (e.g., "I am bad at math") (Kluger & DeNisi, 1996; Dweck, 2006; Hattie & Timperley, 2007). Hence, global self-evaluations of ability or competence do not appear in Table 17.1.

Another approach to student self-assessment that could be placed in more than one cell is *traffic lights*. The term *traffic lights* refers to asking students to use green, yellow, or red objects (or thumbs up, sideways, or down – anything will do) to indicate whether they think they have good, partial, or little understanding (Black, Harrison, Lee, Marshall, & Wiliam, 2003). It would be appropriate for traffic lights to appear in multiple places in Table 17.1, depending on how they are used. Traffic lights seem to be most effective at supporting students' reflections on how well they understand a concept or have mastered a skill, which is line with their creators' original intent, so they are categorized as formative self-assessments of one's learning processes – which sounds like metacognition.

In fact, several of the methods included in Table 17.1 come from research on metacognition, including *self-monitoring*, *self-testing* (checking one's performance on test items), and checking one's *reading comprehension*. These last two methods have been excluded from some taxonomies of self-assessment (e.g., Boud & Brew, 1995) because they do not engage students in explicitly considering relevant standards or criteria. However, new conceptions of self-assessment are grounded in theories of the self- and co-regulation of learning (Andrade & Brookhart, 2016), which includes self-monitoring of learning processes with and without explicit standards.

However, my research favors self-assessment with regard to standards (Andrade & Boulay, 2003; Andrade & Du, 2007; Andrade, Du, & Wang, 2008; Andrade, Wang, Du, & Akawi, 2009; Andrade, Du, & Mycek, 2010), as does related research by Panadero and his colleagues (see later). I have involved students in self-assessment of stories, essays, or mathematical word problems according to *rubrics* or *checklists* with criteria. For example, two studies investigated the relationship between elementary or middle school students' scores on a written assignment and a process that involved them in reading a model paper, co-creating criteria, self-assessing first drafts with a rubric, and revising (Andrade et al., 2008; Andrade et al., 2010). The self-assessment was highly scaffolded: students were asked to underline key phrases in the rubric with colored pencils (e.g., underline "clearly states an opinion" in blue), then underline or circle in their drafts the evidence of having met the standard articulated by the phrase (e.g., his or her opinion) with the same blue pencil. If students found they had not met the standard, they were asked to write themselves a reminder to make improvements when they wrote their final drafts. This process was followed for each criterion on the rubric. There were main effects on scores for every self-assessed criterion on the rubric, suggesting that guided self-assessment according to the co-created criteria helped students produce more effective writing.

Panadero and his colleagues have also done quasi-experimental and experimental research on standards-referenced self-assessment, using rubrics or lists of assessment criteria that are presented in the form of questions (Panadero, Alonso-Tapia, & Huertas, 2012; Panadero, Alonso-Tapia, & Reche, 2013; Panadero, Alonso-Tapia, & Huertas, 2014; Panadero & Romero 2014). Panadero calls the list of assessment criteria a "script" because his work is grounded in research on scaffolding (e.g., Kollar, Fischer, & Hesse, 2006); I call it a "checklist" because that is the term used in classroom assessment contexts. Either way, the list provides standards for the task. Here is a script for a written summary that Panadero et al. (2014) used with college students in a psychology class:

- Does my summary transmit the main idea from the text? Is it at the beginning of my summary?
- Are the important ideas also in my summary?
- Have I selected the main ideas from the text to make them explicit in my summary?
- Have I thought about my purpose for the summary? What is my goal?

Taken together, the results of the studies cited above suggest that students who engaged in self-assessment using scripts or rubrics were more self-regulated, as measured by self-report questionnaires and/or think aloud protocols, than were students in the comparison or control groups. Effect sizes were very small to moderate ($\eta2 = 0.06$–0.42), and statistically significant. Most interesting, perhaps, is one study (Panadero & Romero, 2014) that demonstrated an association between rubric-referenced self-assessment activities and all three phases of SRL: forethought, performance, and reflection.

There are surely many other methods of self-assessment to include in Table 17.1, as well as interesting conversations to be had about which method goes where and why. In the meantime, I offer the taxonomy in Table 17.1 as a way to define and operationalize self-assessment in instructional contexts and as a framework for the following overview of current research on the subject.

An Overview of Current Research on Self-Assessment

Several recent reviews of self-assessment are available (Brown & Harris, 2013; Brown, Andrade, & Chen, 2015; Panadero, Jonsson, & Botella, 2017), so I will not summarize the entire body of research here. Instead, I chose to take a bird's-eye view of the field, with the goal of reporting on what has been sufficiently researched and what remains to be done. I used the references lists from reviews, as well as other relevant sources, as a starting point. In order to update the list of sources, I directed a new search of the ERIC database.[1] Two search terms, "self-assessment" or "self-evaluation," were the subject descriptors. Advanced search options had four delimiters: (1) peer-reviewed, (2) January 2013–October 2016, (3) English, and (4) full text. Because the focus was on K-20 educational contexts, sources were excluded if they were about adult or early childhood education.

The search yielded 347 hits. Research that was unrelated to instructional feedback was excluded, such as studies of self-estimates of performance before or after taking a test, guesses about whether a test item was answered correctly, and estimates of how many tasks could be completed in a certain amount of time. Although some of the excluded studies might be thought of as useful investigations of self-monitoring, as a group they seemed too unrelated to theories of self-generated feedback to be useful for this chapter. Thirteen studies were selected for inclusion in Table 17.2, which also contains studies published before 2013 that were not included in key reviews, and studies solicited directly from authors.

The "type" column in Table 17.2 indicates whether the study focused on formative or summative self-assessment. This distinction was often difficult to make, given a lack of information in some articles. For example, Memis and Seven (2015) frame their study in terms of formative assessment, and note that the purpose of the self-evaluation done by the sixth-grade students is to "help students improve their [science] reports" (p. 39), but they do not indicate how the self-assessments were done nor whether students were given time to revise their reports based on their judgments or supported in making revisions. A sentence or two of explanation about the process of self-assessment in the procedures sections of published studies would be most useful.

Table 17.2 lists fifty-two studies. Of those, thirty were inquiries into the consistency of students' self-assessments with other judgments (e.g., a test score

---

1 Many thanks to my graduate assistant, Joanna Weaver, for conducting the search.

Table 17.2 *Summary of reviewed studies of student self-assessment (SA)*

	Topic	Source	Type[a]	Sample	Context	N	Research Design	Results
1	Achievement	Birjandi & Hadidi Tamjid, 2012	F	TEFL juniors	Iran	157	Quasi-experimental	The groups in which the students employed SA and peer assessment (PA), together with teacher assessment, produced the maximum improvements in writing.
2	Achievement	Fastre et al., 2012	F	Secondary vocational	Netherlands	68	Experimental	Students in the relevant-criteria group outperformed the students in the all-criteria group but experienced higher mental effort in self-assessing their performance.
3	Achievement	Fastre et al., 2010	F	Secondary vocational	Netherlands	39	Quasi-experimental	Performance-based criteria group outperformed the competence-based group on test task performance, and did so with lower mental effort.
4	Achievement	Kitsantas & Zimmerman, 2006	F	Undergraduates	United States	70	Experimental	Students who used graduated self-evaluative standards surpassed those with absolute or no standards in skill and motivation. Graphing outcomes resulted in higher skill and stronger motivation than not graphing.
5	Achievement	Memis & Seven, 2015	F	Grade 6	Turkey	108	Quasi-experimental	Students in the Science Writing Heuristic (SWH) and self-evaluation SWH groups scored significantly higher than the students in the control group on post-tests and retention tests of science knowledge (electricity unit).

#	Focus	Study	F	Sample	Country	N	Design	Findings
6	Achievement	Ross & Starling, 2008	F	Grade 9	Canada	164	Quasi-experimental	Controlling for pretest computer self-efficacy, the treatment group outscored a comparison group on the production of a map using software, a report on problem-solving strategies, and an exam.
7	Achievement and SRL	Glaser & Brunstein, 2007	F	Ten-year-olds	Germany	113	Quasi-experimental	Students in the SRL with SA condition wrote more complete and qualitatively better stories than two comparison conditions, at post-test, at maintenance (five weeks), and on a transfer task
8	Achievement and SRL	Panadero, Tapia, & Huertas, 2012	F	High school	Spain	120	Experimental	Students who used scripts reported more self-regulation than those who used rubrics and were in the control group. Script and rubric groups learned more than the control group.
9	Achievement and SRL	Panadero, Tapia, & Huertas, 2014	F	Undergraduates	Spain	85	Quasi-experimental	The use of rubrics related to increased learning but decreases in SRL more than the use of scripts. Students preferred rubrics, reporting they focus more on learning when using them.
10	SRL	Al-Rawahi & Al-Balushi, 2015	F	Grade 10 females	Oman	62	Quasi-experimental	Participants in the treatment (reflective journal writing) group significantly outperformed participants in the comparison group with respect to self-reported self-regulation strategies.
11	SRL	Meusen-Beekman et al., 2016	F	Grade 6	Netherlands	695	Experimental	SA and PA affected self-reported self-regulation and motivation in students. No significant differences were found between PA and SA.

Table 17.2 (cont.)

	Topic	Source	Type[a]	Sample	Context	N	Research Design	Results
12	SRL	Panadero, Alonso-Tapia, & Huertas, 2013	F	Preservice teachers	Spain	69	Experimental	Students using scripts had higher postintervention levels of **SRL**; rubrics decreased performance/ avoidance self-regulation. Students preferred rubrics to scripts.
13	SRL	Punhagui & de Souza, 2013	F	Grade 8	Brazil	25	Case study	SA encourages the use of strategic planning and monitoring of learning only if joined to teacher intervention and motivational strategies.
14	Achievement, consistency, and SRL	Panadero & Romero, 2014	F	Preservice teachers	Spain	218	Quasi-experimental	Rubric group reported more use of learning strategies than nonrubric group, performed better on task, and were more accurate. Rubric group reported higher performance/ avoidance self-regulation.
15	Achievement and student perceptions	Huang & Gui, 2015	F	Undergraduates	China	61	Quasi-experimental	SA with rubrics associated with improvements in discourse length, discourse organization, and linguistic flexibility but not linguistic accuracy. Students perceived rubrics as facilitating practice and SA.
16	Achievement, consistency, and student perceptions	Lopez & Kossack, 2007	F	Undergraduate and graduate	United States	79	Quasi-experimental	Grades for students who used continuous SA increased more consistently and were higher than for no or pre-/post- SA groups. End-of-course SA correlations with actual course grades were more significantly aligned for the continuous SA group. Students reported placing a greater emphasis on the nature of and responsibility

#		Author		Population	Country	N	Design	Findings
17	Achievement and consistency	Barney, Khurum, Petersen, et al., 2012	F	Graduate students	Sweden	40	Pre-/post-treatment only	for their own learning when SA occurred throughout the term. Rubric-based SA was accurate to within one grade level for 85% of cases. SA was associated with statistically significant improvements in grades and a significant decrease in the number of complaints regarding grades.
18	Achievement and consistency	Fitzpatrick & Schulz, 2016	F	Grade 4	Canada	80	Quasi-experimental	Treatment students' SA aligned more closely with teacher/researcher ratings. Treatment was associated with improvements in the clarity of students' writing, and their discussions of the standards for their work and how they improved it.
19	Achievement and consistency	Lin-Siegler, Shaenfield, & Elder, 2015	F	Grade 6	United States	63	Quasi-experimental	Students who read contrasting cases (well- and poorly written stories) created stories of better quality, developed a deeper understanding of the assessment criteria, and became better able to identify areas in need of improvement.
20	Achievement and consistency	Miller & Geraci, 2011	S	Undergraduates	United States	211	Experimental	Students' predictions were almost always higher than the grade they earned, particularly low-performing students. Incentives with minimal feedback failed to improve accuracy. When feedback was concrete, accuracy improved for low performing students, but exam scores did not.

Table 17.2 (*cont.*)

	Topic	Source	Type[a]	Sample	Context	N	Research Design	Results
21	Consistency	Admiraal, Huisman, & Pilli, 2015	S	Online learners	MOOCs	2711	Correlational	SAs had low correlations with final exam grades as well as with other assessment forms and did not significantly explain variance in students' final exam scores.
22	Consistency	Alaoutinen, 2012	S	Undergraduates	Finland	145	Correlational	Students placed their knowledge along the taxonomy-based scale quite well and the scale seemed to fit engineering students' learning styles. Advanced students assessed themselves more accurately than novices.
23	Consistency	Baars, Vink, van Gog, de Bruin, & Paas, 2014	S	Secondary education students	Netherlands	373	Experimental	Two experiments showed no effect of training on SA or judgments of learning (JOL) accuracy, but SA and JOLs were positively correlated with each other and negatively with effort. Providing standards improves SA and JOL accuracy on identical problems, and performance on all problems.
24	Consistency	Baxter & Norman, 2011	S	Nursing students	Canada	27	One group pre-test, post-test	All but one of sixteen correlations between SA and the objective, structured clinical examination total scores were negative. SA was also unrelated to several indices of experience in critical care settings.
25	Consistency	Blanch-Hartigan, 2011	S	Medical students	Multiple locations	4,305	Three meta-analyses of thirty-five studies	Students were moderately able to self-assess performance and were more accurate later in medical school.

#	Construct	Author(s)	F/S	Level	Country	N	Design	Findings
								Students were more likely to overestimate on communication-based, standardized patient encounters than on objective, knowledge-based performance measures. Female students underestimated more than male students, but gender analyses are often unreported.
26	Consistency (calibration)	Bol, Hacker, Walck, & Nummery, 2012	F and S	High school	United States	82	Quasi-experimental; 2x2 factorial design	The use of guidelines and group settings was associated with calibration accuracy and achievement in four intact IB biology classes.
27	Consistency	Chang, Liang, & Chen, 2013	F	High school seniors	Taiwan	72	Correlational	SAs and teacher assessments were highly consistent, as were SAs and end-of-course examination scores.
28	Consistency	Chang, Tseng, & Lou, 2012	F	High school seniors	Taiwan	72	Correlational	Teacher-raters adopted the most rigorous scoring standards, while peer-raters tended to use the most lax standards; self- and teacher-assessment were consistent.
29	Consistency	De Grez, Valcke, & Roozen, 2012	S	Undergraduates	Belgium	57	Correlational	SA scores were generally higher than marks given by teachers.
30	Consistency	Gonida & Leonardi, 2011	S	Grades 9 and 10	Greece	6,119	Survey	(1) Underestimation of performance, even with regard to a single school subject, was associated with costs and no benefits; (2) realistic self-appraisals were associated with benefits and no costs; and (3) overestimation was more likely to be associated with more costs but not necessarily fewer benefits than realistic self-beliefs.

Table 17.2 (*cont.*)

	Topic	Source	Type[a]	Sample	Context	N	Research Design	Results
31	Consistency (calibration)	Hacker, Bol, Horgan, & Rackow, 2000	F	Undergraduates, teacher prep	United States	96	Correlational	High-performing students were accurate; accuracy improved over multiple exams. Low-performing students had moderate predication accuracy but good postdiction accuracy. Lowest performers had gross overconfidence in predictions and postdictions. Judgments were influenced by prior judgments, not prior performance. Performance and judgments had little influence on subsequent test preparation behavior.
32	Consistency	Harding & Hbaci, 2015	S	Preservice teachers	United States	32	Observational, survey	Students' self-evaluations of teaching performance were higher than professors' in areas of assessment and time management. There were similarities in evaluation regarding student engagement, inquiry teaching, and scaffolding.
33	Consistency	Hawkins et al., 2012	F	Final-year medical students	United Kingdom	31	Correlational	The demonstration of a video benchmark performance in combination with video feedback was associated with accuracy of students' SAs.
34	Consistency	Karnilowicz, 2012	S	Undergraduates	Australia	64	Correlation	Higher-achieving students underestimated their performance, while lower-achieving students overestimated.

#	Category	Author	F/S	Level	Country	N	Method	Findings
35	Consistency (calibration)	Kolovelonis, Goudas, & Dermitzaki, 2012	S	Grades 5 and 6	Greece	100	Experimental	Students who practiced dribbling under different self-regulatory conditions (i.e., receiving feedback, setting goals) did not differ in calibration bias and accuracy. Regardless of the group, students were overconfident. Sixth-grade students were more accurate than fifth-grade students.
36	Consistency	Kostons et al., 2012	S	Secondary students	Netherlands	80 and 90	Experimental	Students who studied SA modeling examples were more accurate than participants who had not.
37	Consistency (calibration)	Labuhn et al., 2010	F	Grade 5	Germany	90	Experimental	Graphed feedback on accuracy led to more accurate self-evaluation; in overconfident students, feedback also increased prediction accuracy.
38	Consistency	Leach, 2012	F and S	Under- and postgraduate	New Zealand	472	Secondary analysis of assessment data	No statistically significant difference between the self-assessed and teacher-assessed grades. Higher-achieving students tended to underrate and lower-achieving to overrate.
39	Consistency	Lew, Alwis, & Schmidt, 2010, study 1	S	Freshmen	Singapore	3,588	Correlational	More academically competent students self-assessed with higher accuracy than their less competent peers.
40	Consistency	Lew, Alwis, & Schmidt, 2010, study 2	S	Freshmen	Singapore	936	Survey	No association between student beliefs about the utility of SA and the accuracy of their SAs.
41	Consistency	Lopez-Pastor et al., 2012	S	Undergraduates	Spain	187	Correlation	Reliability correlations among students' self-grades, professors' grades, and negotiated final grades were high. The grade differences were never greater than 1.5 on a scale of 0–10.

Table 17.2 (cont.)

	Topic	Source	Type[a]	Sample	Context	N	Research Design	Results
42	Consistency	Nowell & Alston, 2007	S	Undergraduates	United States?	715	Survey	Male students and those with lower GPAs exhibited greater overconfidence; professors' grading practices related to overconfidence.
43	Consistency	Tejeiro et al., 2012	S	Undergraduates	Spain	122	Quasi-experimental	Students' SAs were higher than marks given by professors, especially for students with poorer results. In the group in which SA counted toward the final mark, no relationship was found between the professors' and the students' assessments.
44	Consistency	Van Loon, de Bruin, van Gog, et al., 2014	F	Grade 9	Netherlands	123	Experimental	Accuracy of predictions of performance was highest for learning following delayed diagram completion. When selecting texts for restudy, participants followed their predictions of performance to the same degree, regardless of monitoring accuracy.
45	Student perceptions	Andrade & Du, 2007	F	Undergraduates	United States	14	Focus groups	Students reported they can self-assess when they know the teachers' expectations; they used SA to check their work and revise; and they believed SA leads to improvements in grades, quality of work, motivation, and learning.
46	Student perceptions	Bourke, 2014	F	Tertiary professional students	New Zealand	157	Qualitative	Three functions of SA were reported by students: (1) to analyze self, (2) to understand others, and (3) to

#	Focus	Study	Type	Participants	Country	N	Method	Findings
47	Student perceptions	Bourke, 2016	F	Eleven to twelve-year-olds	New Zealand	28	Ethnography	understand learning. When students developed their own criteria for an effective SA response, they actively engaged in all SA exercises.
48	Student perceptions	Harris & Brown, 2013	F	Primary, middle, secondary	New Zealand	68	Case studies	The majority of students held the least sophisticated conceptions of learning and SA in school-based settings. Students with more sophisticated conceptions of SA often already knew when they had learned without an external source, but external assessments provided messages about what constituted a valued outcome. Primary students did not see an improvement purpose for SA; comments were superficial and did not diagnose weaknesses. Students thought the SA was for the teachers. Honesty was compromised by social interactions.
49	Student perceptions	Murakami et al., 2012	S	Undergraduates	Japan	99	Survey	Regular SA and peer assessment, in addition to teacher assessment, was associated with self-reported increases in the frequency of spoken English in the class and engagement with English learning outside the classroom.
50	Student perceptions	Siow, 2015	F	Undergraduates	Malaysia	62	Qualitative	Both SA and PA were perceived as enabling students to think more critically and deeply, and work in a more structured way.

Table 17.2 (*cont.*)

	Topic	Source	Type[a]	Sample	Context	N	Research Design	Results
51	Student perceptions	Van Helvoort, 2012	S	Adult undergraduates	Netherlands	10	Online survey, focus group	Students reported using a rubric for SA to become more critical of their own and others' writing throughout the course and in subsequent courses. They appreciated SA but said it was not a substitute for teacher feedback.
52	Student perceptions	Wang, 2017	F and S	Undergraduates	China	80	Qualitative	The rubric was perceived as useful for fostering the students' self-regulation by guiding them to set goals, plan, self-monitor, and reflect.

[a]F, formative; S, summative.

or teacher's grade). Sixteen studies investigated the relationship between self-assessment and achievement. Ten explored students' perceptions of self-assessment. Eight studies focused on the association between self-assessment and self-regulated learning. The sum ($n = 64$) of the list of research topics is more than fifty-two because several studies had multiple foci. In the next section, I review each topic of research in turn.

Consistency

Table 17.2 reveals that much of the recent research on self-assessment has investigated the accuracy or, more accurately, consistency, of students' self-assessments. The term *consistency* is more appropriate in the classroom context because the quality of students' self-assessments is often determined by comparing them with their teachers' assessments and then generating correlations. Given the evidence of the unreliability of teachers' grades (Falchikov, 2005), the assumption that teachers' assessments are accurate might not be well founded (Leach, 2012; Brown et al., 2015). Ratings of student work done by researchers are also suspect, unless evidence of the validity and reliability of the inferences made about student work by researchers is available. Consequently, much of the research on classroom-based self-assessment should use the term *consistency*, which refers to the degree of alignment between students' and expert raters' evaluations, not necessarily the purer, more rigorous term *accuracy*.

In their review, Brown and Harris (2013) reported that correlations between student self-ratings and other measures tended to be weakly to strongly positive, ranging from $r \approx 0.20$–0.80, with few studies reporting correlations greater than 0.60. But their review included results from studies of any self-appraisal of school work, including summative self-rating/grading, predictions about the correctness of answers on test items, and formative, criteria-based self-assessments, a combination of methods that makes the correlations they reported difficult to interpret. Qualitatively different forms of self-assessment, especially summative and formative types, cannot be lumped together without obfuscating important aspects of self-assessment as instructional feedback.

Given my concern about combining studies of summative and formative assessment, you might anticipate a call for research on consistency that distinguishes between the two. I will make no such call for three reasons. One is that we have enough research on the subject, including the thirty studies found in Table 17.2 that were published after Brown and Harris's review (2013). Drawing only on studies included in Table 17.2, we can say with confidence that summative self-assessment tends to be inconsistent with external judgments (Baxter & Norman, 2011; De Grez, Valcke, & Roozen, 2012; Admiraal, Huisman, & Pilli, 2015), but there are exceptions (Alaoutinen, 2012; Lopez-Pastor, Fernandez-Balboa, Santos Pastor, & Aranda 2012) as well as mixed results, with students being consistent regarding some aspects of their learning but not others (Blanch-Hartigan, 2011; Harding & Hbaci, 2015). We can also say that older, more academically competent learners tend to be more consistent

(Hacker, Bol, Horgan, & Rackow, 2000; Lew, Alwis, & Schmidt, 2010; Alaoutinen, 2012). There is evidence that consistency can be improved through experience (Lopez & Kossack, 2007), the use of guidelines (Bol et al., 2012), and the use of standards (Baars, Vink, van Gog, de Bruin, & Paas, 2014), perhaps in the form of rubrics (Panadero & Romero, 2014). Modeling and feedback also help (Labuhn, Zimmerman, & Hasselhorn, 2010; Miller & Geraci, 2011; Hawkins et al., 2012; Kostons, van Gog, & Paas, 2012).

An outcome typical of research on the consistency of summative self-assessment can be found in row 43, which summarizes the study by Tejeiro et al. (2012) discussed earlier: students' self-assessments were higher than marks given by professors, especially for students with poorer results, and no relationship was found between the professors' and the students' assessments in the group in which self-assessment counted toward the final mark. Students are not stupid: if they know that they can influence their final grade and that their judgment is summative rather than intended to inform revision and improvement, they will be motivated to inflate their self-evaluation. I do not believe we need more research to demonstrate that phenomenon.

The second reason I am not calling for additional research on consistency is that a lot of it seems somewhat irrelevant. This might be because the interest in accuracy is rooted in clinical research on calibration, which has very different aims. Calibration accuracy is the "magnitude of consent between learners' true and self-evaluated task performance. Accurately calibrated learners' task performance equals their self-evaluated task performance" (Wollenschläger, Hattie, Machts, Möller, & Harms, 2016). Calibration research often asks study participants to predict or postdict the correctness of their responses to test items. I caution about generalizing from clinical experiments to authentic classroom contexts because the dismal picture of our human potential to self-judge was painted by calibration researchers *before* study participants were effectively taught how to predict with accuracy, provided with the tools they needed to be accurate, or motivated to do so. Calibration researchers know that, of course, and have conducted intervention studies that attempt to improve accuracy, with some success (e.g., Bol et al., 2012). Studies of formative self-assessment also suggest that consistency increases when it is taught and supported in many of the ways any other skill must be taught and supported (Lopez & Kossack, 2007; Labuhn et al., 2010; Chang, 2012; Hawkins et al., 2012; Chang et al., 2013; Panadero & Romero, 2014; Lin-Siegler, Shaenfield, & Elder, 2015; Fitzpatrick & Schulz, 2016).

Finally, I remain unconvinced that consistency is a necessary condition for useful self-assessment. Although it seems obvious that accurate evaluations of their performance positively influence students' study strategy selection, which should produce improvements in achievement, I have not seen any research that tests those conjectures. The closest I have seen are two studies of calibration, one of which suggested that performance and judgments of performance had little influence on subsequent test preparation behavior (Hacker et al., 2000), and another that showed that study participants followed their predictions of performance to the same degree, regardless of monitoring accuracy (van Loon, de Bruin, van Gog, van Merriënboer, & Dunlosky, 2014). Some claim that inaccurate estimates of learning lead to the selection of inappropriate learning tasks (Kostons et al., 2012), but they cite research that does not support their claim. For example, Kostons et al. cite studies that focus on the effectiveness of SRL interventions but do not address the accuracy of participants' estimates of learning, nor the relationship of those estimates to the selection of next steps.

Eva and Regehr (2008) believe that

> research questions that take the form of "How well do various practitioners self-assess?" "How can we improve self-assessment?" or "How can we measure self-assessment skill?" should be considered defunct and removed from the research agenda [because] there have been hundreds of studies into these questions and the answers are "Poorly," "You can't," and "Don't bother."   (p. 18)

I almost agree. A study that could change my mind about the importance of accuracy of self-assessment would be an investigation of the relearning/revision behaviors of accurate and inaccurate self-assessors: Do students whose self-assessments match the valid and reliable judgments of expert raters make better decisions about what they need to do to deepen their learning and improve their work? Here, I admit, is a call for research related to consistency: I would love to see a high-quality investigation of the relationship between accuracy in formative self-assessment, students' subsequent study behaviors, and their learning. For example, a study that closely examines the revisions to writing made by accurate and inaccurate self-assessors, and the resulting outcomes in terms of the quality of their writing, would be most welcome.

Student Perceptions

Ten of the studies listed in Table 17.2 focused on students' perceptions of self-assessment. The studies of children suggest that they tend to have unsophisticated understandings of its purposes (Harris & Brown, 2013; Bourke, 2016), which might lead to shallow implementation of related processes. In contrast, results from the studies conducted in higher education settings suggested that college and university students understand the function of self-assessment and found it to be useful for guiding and revision (Andrade & Du, 2007), understanding how to take responsibility for learning (Lopez & Kossack, 2007; Bourke, 2014), prompting them to think more critically and deeply (van Helvoort, 2012; Siow, 2015), applying newfound skills (Murakami, Valvona, & Broudy, 2012), and fostering self-regulated learning by guiding them to set goals, plan, self-monitor, and reflect (Wang, 2017).

Not surprisingly, positive perceptions of self-assessment were developed by students who actively engaged the formative type by, for example, developing their own criteria for an effective self-assessment response (Bourke, 2014) or using a rubric or checklist to guide their assessments and then revising their work (Andrade & Du, 2007; Huang & Gui, 2015; Wang, 2017). Earlier research suggested that children's attitudes toward self-assessment can become negative if it is summative (Ross, Rolheiser, & Hogaboam-Gray, 1998). However, even summative formative assessment was reported by adult learners to be useful in helping them become more critical of their own and others' writing throughout the course and in subsequent courses (van Helvoort, 2012).

Achievement

Sixteen of the studies in Table 17.2 investigated the relation between self-assessment and achievement. Fifteen of the sixteen employed the formative type. Without exception, those fifteen studies demonstrated a positive association between self-assessment and learning. All but one of the studies (Barney et al., 2012) were quasi-experimental or experimental, providing relatively rigorous evidence that their treatment groups outperformed their comparison or control groups in terms of everything from writing to dart-throwing, map-making, speaking English, and exams in a wide variety of disciplines. The one experiment about summative self-assessment (Miller & Geraci, 2011), in contrast, resulted in no improvements in exam scores.

It would be easy to overgeneralize and claim that the question about the effect of self-assessment on learning has been answered, but this is a limited review, not a meta-analysis. There are plenty of unanswered questions about the key components of effective self-assessment, especially social-emotional components related to power and trust (Andrade & Brown, 2016). The trends are pretty clear, however: it appears that formative forms of self-assessment can promote knowledge and skill development. This is not surprising, given that it involves many of the processes known to support learning, including practice, feedback, revision, and especially the intellectually demanding work of making complex, criteria-referenced judgments (Panadero, Brown & Strijbos, 2014). Boud (1995a, 1995b) predicted this trend when he noted that many self-assessment processes undermine learning by rushing to judgment, thereby failing to engage students with the standards or criteria for their work.

Self-Regulated Learning

The association between self-assessment and learning has also been explained in terms of self-regulation (Andrade, 2010; Panadero & Alonso-Tapia, 2013; Andrade & Brookhart, 2016; Panadero, Jonsson, & Strijbos, 2016). Self-regulated learning occurs when learners set goals and then monitor and manage their thoughts, feelings, and actions to reach those goals. SRL is moderately to highly correlated with achievement (Zimmerman & Schunk, 2011). Research suggests that formative assessment is a potential influence on SRL (Nicol & Macfarlane-Dick, 2006). The eight studies in Table 17.2 that focus on SRL demonstrate the recent increase in interest in the relationship between self-assessment and SRL.

Conceptual and practical overlaps between the two fields are abundant. In fact, Brown and Harris (2014) recommend that student self-assessment no longer be treated as an assessment, but as an essential competence for self-regulation. Butler and Winne (1995) introduced the role of self-generated feedback in self-regulation years ago:

> [For] all self-regulated activities, feedback is an inherent catalyst. As learners monitor their engagement with tasks, internal feedback is generated by the monitoring process. That feedback describes the nature of outcomes and the qualities of the cognitive processes that led to those states.   (p. 245)

The outcomes and processes referred to by Butler and Winne are many of the same *products* and *processes* I referred to earlier in the definition of self-assessment and in Table 17.1.

In general, research and practice related to self-assessment has tended to focus on judging the products of student learning, while scholarship on self-regulated learning encompasses both processes and products. The very practical focus of much of the research on self-assessment means it might be playing catch-up, in terms of theory development, with the SRL literature, which is grounded in experimental paradigms from cognitive psychology (de Bruin & van Gog, 2012), while self-assessment research is ahead in terms of implementation (E. Panadero, personal communication, October 21, 2016). One major exception is the work done on self-regulated strategy development (Glaser & Brunstein, 2007; Harris, Graham, Mason, & Friedlander, 2008), which has successfully integrated SRL research with classroom practices, including self-assessment, to teach writing to students with special needs.

Nicol and Macfarlane-Dick (2006) have been explicit about the potential for self-assessment practices to support self-regulated learning:

> To develop systematically the learner's capacity for self-regulation, teachers need to create more structured opportunities for self-monitoring and the judging of progression to goals. Self-assessment tasks are an effective way of achieving this, as are activities that encourage reflection on learning progress.   (p. 207)

The studies of SRL in Table 17.2 provided encouraging findings regarding the potential role of self-assessment in promoting achievement, self-regulated learning in general, and metacognition in particular. The studies also represent a solution to the "methodological and theoretical challenges involved in bringing metacognitive research to the real world, using meaningful learning materials" (Koriat, 2012, p. 296).

Future Directions for Research

An important aspect of research on self-assessment that is not explicitly represented in Table 17.2 is practice, or pedagogy: Under what conditions does self-assessment work best, and how are those conditions influenced by context? Fortunately, the studies listed in the table, as well as others (see especially

Andrade & Valtcheva, 2009; Nielsen, 2014; Panadero et al., 2016), point toward an answer. But we still have questions about how best to scaffold effective formative self-assessment. One question is about the characteristics of the standards or criteria used by learners.

Influence of Types of Standards or Criteria

There is now some evidence that it is important that the criteria used to self-assess are concrete, task-specific, and graduated. For example, Fastre, van der Klink, and van Merrienboer (2010) revealed an association between self-assessment according to task-specific criteria and task performance: In a quasi-experimental study of thirty-nine novice vocational education students studying stoma care, they compared concrete, task-specific criteria ("performance-based criteria") such as "Introduces herself to the patient" and "Consults the care file for details concerning the stoma" to vaguer, "competence-based criteria" such as "Shows interest, listens actively, shows empathy to the patient" and "Is discrete with sensitive topics." The performance-based criteria group outperformed the competence-based group on test task performance, presumably because "performance-based criteria make it easier to distinguish levels of performance, enabling a step-by-step process of performance improvement" (p. 530).

This finding echoes the results of a study of self-regulated learning by Kitsantas and Zimmerman (2006), who argued that "fine-grained standards can have two key benefits: They can enable learners to be more sensitive to small changes in skill and make more appropriate adaptations in learning strategies" (p. 203). In their study, seventy college students were taught how to throw darts at a target. The purpose of the study was to examine the role of graphing of self-recorded outcomes and self-evaluative standards in learning a motor skill. Students who were provided with graduated self-evaluative standards surpassed "those who were provided with absolute standards or no standards (control) in both motoric skill and in motivational beliefs (i.e., self-efficacy, attributions, and self-satisfaction)" (p. 201). Kitsantas and Zimmerman hypothesized that setting high absolute standards would limit a learner's sensitivity to small improvements in functioning. This hypothesis was supported by the finding that students who set absolute standards reported significantly less awareness of learning progress (and hit the bull's-eye less often) than students who set graduated standards. "The correlation between the self-evaluation and dart-throwing outcomes measures was extraordinarily high ($r = 0.94$)" (p. 210). Classroom-based research on specific, graduated self-assessment criteria would be informative.

Cognitive and Affective Mechanisms of Self-Assessment

There are many additional questions about pedagogy, such as the hoped-for investigation mentioned above of the relationship between accuracy in formative self-assessment, students' subsequent study behaviors, and their learning. There is also a need for research on how to help teachers give students a central role in their learning by creating space for self-assessment (e.g., see Hawe & Parr, 2014) and the complex power dynamics involved in doing so (Tan, 2004, 2009; Taras, 2008; Leach, 2012). However, there is an even more pressing need for investigations into the internal mechanisms experienced by students engaged in assessing their own learning. Angela Lui and I call this the *next black box* (Lui, 2017).

Black and Wiliam (1998) used the term *black box* to emphasize the fact that what happened in most classrooms was largely unknown: all we knew was that some inputs (e.g., teachers, resources, standards, and requirements) were fed into the box and that certain outputs (e.g., more knowledgeable and competent students, acceptable levels of achievement) would follow. But what, they asked, is happening inside, and what new inputs will produce better outputs? Black and Wiliam's review spawned a great deal of research on formative assessment, some but not all of which suggests a positive relationship with academic achievement (Bennett, 2011; Kingston & Nash, 2011). To better understand why and how the use of formative assessment in general and self-assessment in particular is associated with improvements in academic achievement in some instances but not others, we need research that looks into the next black box: the cognitive and affective mechanisms of students who are engaged in assessment processes (Lui, 2017).

The role of internal mechanisms has been discussed in theory but not yet fully tested. Lui (2017) noted that Crooks (1988) argued that the impact of assessment is influenced by students' internalization of their interpretation of the tasks and results, and Butler and Winne (1995) theorized that both cognitive and affective processes play a role in determining how feedback is internalized and used to self-regulate learning. Other theoretical frameworks about the internal processes of receiving and responding to feedback have been developed (e.g., Nicol & MacFarlane-Dick, 2006; Draper, 2009; Andrade, 2013; Lipnevich, Berg, & Smith, 2016). Yet Shute (2008) noted in her review of the literature on formative feedback that "despite the plethora of research on the topic, the specific mechanisms relating feedback to learning are still mostly murky, with very few (if any) general conclusions" (p. 156). This area is ripe for research.

Conclusion

Self-assessment is the act of monitoring one's processes and products in order to make adjustments that deepen learning and enhance performance. Although it can be summative, the evidence presented in this chapter strongly suggests that self-assessment is most beneficial, in terms of both achievement and self-regulated learning, when it is used formatively. That much is pretty clear.

What is not yet clear is why and how self-assessment works. Those of you who like to sink your teeth into phenomena that are maddeningly difficult to measure will rejoice to hear that the cognitive and affective mechanisms of self-assessment are the next black box. Studies of the ways in which learners think and feel, the interactions between their thoughts and feelings and their context, and the implications for pedagogy will make major contributions to our field.

References

Admiraal, W., Huisman, B., & Pilli, O. (2015). Assessment in massive open online courses. *Electronic Journal of e-Learning, 13*, 207–216.

Alaoutinen, S. (2012). Evaluating the effect of learning style and student background on self-assessment accuracy. *Computer Science Education, 22*, 175–198.

Al-Rawahi, N. M., & Al-Balushi, S. M. (2015). The effect of reflective science journal writing on students' self-regulated learning strategies. *International Journal of Environmental and Science Education, 10*, 367–379.

Andrade, H. (2010). Students as the definitive source of formative assessment: Academic self-assessment and the self-regulation of learning. In H. Andrade & G. Cizek (Eds.), *Handbook of formative assessment* (pp. 90–105). New York: Routledge.

Andrade, H. (2013). Classroom assessment in the context of learning theory and research. In J. H. McMillan (Ed.), *Sage handbook of research on classroom assessment* (pp. 17–34). New York: Sage.

Andrade, H., & Boulay, B. (2003). The role of rubric-referenced self-assessment in learning to write. *Journal of Educational Research, 97*, 21–34.

Andrade, H., & Brookhart, S. M. (2016). The role of classroom assessment in supporting self-regulated learning (pp. 293–309). In D. Laveault & L. Allal (Eds.), *Assessment for learning: Meeting the challenge of implementation*. Heidelberg: Springer.

Andrade, H. L., & Brown, G. T. L. (2016). Student self-assessment in the classroom. In G. T. L. Brown & L. R. Harris (Eds.), *Handbook of human and social conditions in assessment* (pp. 319–334). New York: Routledge.

Andrade, H., & Du, Y. (2007). Student responses to criteria-referenced self-assessment. *Assessment and Evaluation in Higher Education, 32*, 159–181.

Andrade, H., Du, Y., & Mycek, K. (2010). Rubric-referenced self-assessment and middle school students' writing. *Assessment in Education, 17*, 199–214.

Andrade, H., Du, Y., & Wang, X. (2008). Putting rubrics to the test: The effect of a model, criteria generation, and rubric-referenced self-assessment on elementary school students' writing. *Educational Measurement: Issues and Practices, 27*(2), 3–13.

Andrade, H., & Valtcheva, A. (2009). Promoting learning and achievement through self-assessment. *Theory into Practice, 48*, 12–19.

Andrade, H., Wang, X., Du, Y., & Akawi, R. (2009). Rubric-referenced self-assessment and self-efficacy for writing. *Journal of Educational Research, 102*, 287–302.

Baars, M., Vink, S., van Gog, T., de Bruin, A., & Paas, F. (2014). Effects of training self-assessment and using assessment standards on retrospective and prospective monitoring of problem solving. *Learning and Instruction, 33*, 92–107.

Bandura, A. (1997). *Self-efficacy: The exercise of control*. New York: Freeman.

Barney, S., Khurum, M., Petersen, K., Unterkalmsteiner, M., & Jabangwe, R. (2012). Improving students with rubric-based self-assessment and oral feedback. *IEEE Transactions on Education, 55,* 319–325.

Baxter, P., & Norman, G. (2011). Self-assessment or self deception? A lack of association between nursing students' self-assessment and performance. *Journal of Advanced Nursing, 67,* 2406–2413.

Bennett, R. E. (2011). Formative assessment: A critical review. *Assessment in Education: Principles, Policy, and Practice, 18,* 5–25.

Birjandi, P., & Hadidi Tamjid, N. (2012). The role of self-, peer and teacher assessment in promoting Iranian EFL learners' writing performance. *Assessment & Evaluation in Higher Education, 37,* 513–533.

Black, P., Harrison, C., Lee, C., Marshall, B., & Wiliam, D. (2003). *Assessment for learning: Putting it into practice.* Berkshire, UK: Open University Press.

Black, P., & Wiliam, D. (1998). Inside the black box: Raising standards through classroom assessment. *Phi Delta Kappan, 80,* 139–144, 146–148.

Blanch-Hartigan, D. (2011). Medical students' self-assessment of performance: Results from three meta-analyses. *Patient Education and Counseling, 84,* 3–9.

Bol, L., Hacker, D. J., Walck, C. C., & Nunnery, J. A. (2012). The effects of individual or group guidelines on the calibration accuracy and achievement of high school biology students. *Contemporary Educational Psychology, 37,* 280–287.

Boud, D. (1995a). *Implementing student self-assessment* (2nd edn.). Australian Capital Territory: Higher Education Research and Development Society of Australasia.

Boud, D. (1995b). *Enhancing learning through self-assessment.* London: Kogan Page.

Boud, D. (1999). Avoiding the traps: Seeking good practice in the use of self-assessment and reflection in professional courses. *Social Work Education, 18,* 121–132.

Boud, D., & Brew, A. (1995). Developing a typology for learner self-assessment practices. *Research and Development in Higher Education, 18,* 130–135.

Bourke, R. (2014). Self-assessment in professional programmes within tertiary institutions. *Teaching in Higher Education, 19,* 908–918.

Bourke, R. (2016). Liberating the learner through self-assessment. *Cambridge Journal of Education, 46,* 97–111.

Brown, G., Andrade, H., & Chen, F. (2015). Accuracy in student self-assessment: Directions and cautions for research. *Assessment in Education, 22*(4), 444–457.

Brown, G. T., & Harris, L. R. (2013). Student self-assessment. In J. H. McMillan (Ed.), *Sage handbook of research on classroom assessment* (pp. 367–393). Los Angeles, CA: Sage.

Brown, G. T. L., & Harris, L. R. (2014). The future of self-assessment in classroom practice: Reframing self-assessment as a core competency. *Frontline Learning Research, 3,* 22–30.

Butler, D. L., & Winne, P. H. (1995). Feedback and self-regulated learning: A theoretical synthesis. *Review of Educational Research, 65,* 245–281.

Chang, C.-C., Liang, C., & Chen, Y.-H. (2013). Is learner self-assessment reliable and valid in a web-based portfolio environment for high school students? *Computers & Education, 60,* 325–334.

Chang, C.-C., Tseng, K.-H., & Lou, S.-J. (2012). A comparative analysis of the consistency and difference among teacher-assessment, student self-assessment and peer-assessment in a web-based portfolio assessment environment for high school students. *Computers & Education, 58*, 303–320.

Crooks, T. J. (1988). The impact of classroom evaluation practices on students. *Review of Educational Research, 58*, 438–481.

de Bruin, A. B. H., & van Gog, T. (2012). Improving self-monitoring and self-regulation: From cognitive psychology to the classroom, *Learning and Instruction, 22*(4), 245–252.

De Grez, L., Valcke, M., & Roozen, I. (2012). How effective are self- and peer assessment of oral presentation skills compared with teachers' assessments? *Active Learning in Higher Education, 13*, 129–142.

Draper, S. W. (2009). What are learners actually regulating when given feedback? *British Journal of Educational Technology, 40*, 306–315.

Dweck, C. (2006). *Mindset: The new psychology of success.* New York: Random House.

Epstein, R. M., Siegel, D. J., & Silberman, J. (2008). Self-monitoring in clinical practice: A challenge for medical educators. *Journal of Continuing Education in the Health Professions, 28*, 5–13.

Eva, K. W., & Regehr, G. (2008). "I'll never play professional football" and other fallacies of self-assessment. *Journal of Continuing Education in the Health Professions, 28*, 14–19.

Falchikov, N. (2005). *Improving assessment through student involvement: Practical solutions for aiding learning in higher and further education.* London: Routledge Falmer.

Fastre, G. M. J., van der Klink, M. R., Sluijsmans, D., & van Merrienboer, J. J. G. (2012). Drawing students' attention to relevant assessment criteria: Effects on self-assessment skills and performance. *Journal of Vocational Education and Training, 64*, 185–198.

Fastre, G. M. J., van der Klink, M. R., & van Merrienboer, J. J. G. (2010). The effects of performance-based assessment criteria on student performance and self-assessment skills. *Advances in Health Sciences Education, 15*, 517–532.

Fitzpatrick, B., & Schulz, H. (2016, April). Teaching young students to self-assess critically. Paper presented at the annual meeting of the American Educational Research Association, Washington DC.

Franken, A. S. (1992). *I'm good enough, I'm smart enough, and doggone it, people like me! Daily affirmations by Stuart Smalley.* New York: Dell.

Glaser, C., & Brunstein, J. C. (2007). Improving fourth-grade students' composition skills: Effects of strategy instruction and self-regulation procedures. *Journal of Educational Psychology, 99*, 297–310.

Gonida, E. N., & Leondari, A. (2011). Patterns of motivation among adolescents with biased and accurate self-efficacy beliefs. *International Journal of Educational Research, 50*, 209–220.

Hacker, D. J., Bol, L., Horgan, D. D., & Rakow, E. A. (2000). Test prediction and performance in a classroom context. *Journal of Educational Psychology, 92*, 160–170.

Harding, J. L., & Hbaci, I. (2015). Evaluating pre-service teachers' math teaching experience from different perspectives. *Universal Journal of Educational Research, 3*(6), 382–389.

Harris, K. R., Graham, S., Mason, L. H., & Friedlander, B. (2008). *Powerful writing strategies for all students.* Baltimore, MD: Brookes.

Harris, L. R., & Brown, G. T. L. (2013). Opportunities and obstacles to consider when using peer- and self-assessment to improve student learning: Case studies into teachers' implementation. *Teaching and Teacher Education, 36*, 101–111.

Hattie, J., & Timperley, H. (2007). The power of feedback. *Review of Educational Research, 77*, 81–112.

Hawe, E., & Parr, J. (2014). Assessment for learning in the writing classroom: An incomplete realization. *Curriculum Journal, 25*, 210–237.

Hawkins, S. C., Osborne, A., Schofield, S. J., Pournaras, D. J., & Chester, J. F. (2012). Improving the accuracy of self-assessment of practical clinical skills using video feedback: The importance of including benchmarks. *Medical Teacher, 34*, 279–284.

Huang, Y., & Gui, M. (2015). Articulating teachers' expectations afore: Impact of rubrics on Chinese EFL learners' self-assessment and speaking ability. *Journal of Education and Training Studies, 3*(3), 126–132.

Kaderavek, J. N., Gillam, R. B., Ukrainetz, T. A., Justice, L. M., & Eisenberg, S. N. (2004). School-age children's self-assessment of oral narrative production. *Communication Disorders Quarterly, 26*, 37–48.

Karnilowicz, W. (2012). A comparison of self-assessment and tutor assessment of undergraduate psychology students. *Social Behavior and Personality: An International Journal, 40*, 591–604.

Kingston, N. M., & Nash, B. (2011). Formative assessment: A meta-analysis and a call for research. *Educational Measurement: Issues and Practice, 30*(4), 28–37.

Kitsantas, A., & Zimmerman, B. J. (2006). Enhancing self-regulation of practice: The influence of graphing and self-evaluative standards. *Metacognition and Learning, 1*, 201–212.

Kluger, A. N., & DeNisi, A. (1996). The effects of feedback interventions on performance: A historical review, a meta-analysis, and a preliminary feedback intervention theory. *Psychological Bulletin, 119*, 254–284.

Kollar, I., Fischer, F., & Hesse, F. (2006). Collaboration scripts: A conceptual analysis. *Educational Psychology Review, 18*, 159–185.

Kolovelonis, A., Goudas, M., & Dermitzaki, I. (2012). Students' performance calibration in a basketball dribbling task in elementary physical education. *International Electronic Journal of Elementary Education, 4*(3), 507–517.

Koriat, A. (2012). The relationships between monitoring, regulation and performance. *Learning and Instruction, 22*, 296–298.

Kostons, D., van Gog, T., & Paas, F. (2012). Training self-assessment and task-selection skills: A cognitive approach to improving self-regulated learning. *Learning and Instruction, 22*, 121–132.

Labuhn, A. S., Zimmerman, B. J., & Hasselhorn, M. (2010). Enhancing students' self-regulation and mathematics performance: The influence of feedback and self-evaluative standards *Metacognition and Learning, 5*, 173–194.

Leach, L. (2012). Optional self-assessment: Some tensions and dilemmas. *Assessment & Evaluation in Higher Education, 37*, 137–147.

Lew, M. D. N., Alwis, W. A. M., & Schmidt, H. G. (2010). Accuracy of students' self-assessment and their beliefs about its utility. *Assessment & Evaluation in Higher Education, 35*, 135–156.

Lin-Siegler, X., Shaenfield, D., & Elder, A. D. (2015). Contrasting case instruction can improve self-assessment of writing. *Educational Technology Research and Development, 63*, 517–537.

Lipnevich, A. A., Berg, D. A. G., & Smith, J. K. (2016). Toward a model of student response to feedback. In G. T. L. Brown & L. R. Harris (Eds.), *The handbook of human and social conditions in assessment* (pp. 169–185). New York: Routledge.

Lopez, R., & Kossack, S. (2007). Effects of recurring use of self-assessment in university courses. *International Journal of Learning, 14*, 203–216.

Lopez-Pastor, V. M., Fernandez-Balboa, J.-M., Santos Pastor, M. L., & Aranda, A. F. (2012). Students' self-grading, professor's grading and negotiated final grading at three university programmes: Analysis of reliability and grade difference ranges and tendencies. *Assessment & Evaluation in Higher Education, 37*, 453–464.

Lui, A. (2017). Validity of the Responses to Feedback Survey: Operationalizing and measuring students' cognitive and affective responses to teachers' feedback. Doctoral dissertation, University at Albany, State University of New York.

Memis, E. K., & Seven, S. (2015). Effects of an SWH approach and self-evaluation on sixth grade students' learning and retention of an electricity unit. *International Journal of Progressive Education, 11*(3), 32–49.

Meusen-Beekman, K. D., Joosten-ten Brinke, D., & Boshuizen, H. P. A. (2016). Effects of formative assessments to develop self-regulation among sixth grade students: Results from a randomized controlled intervention. *Studies in Educational Evaluation, 51*, 126–136.

Miller, T. M., & Geraci, L. (2011). Training metacognition in the classroom: The influence of incentives and feedback on exam predictions. *Metacognition and Learning, 6*, 303–314.

Murakami, C., Valvona, C., & Broudy, D. (2012). Turning apathy into activeness in oral communication classes: Regular self- and peer-assessment in a TBLT programme. *System: An International Journal of Educational Technology and Applied Linguistics, 40*, 407–420.

Nicol, D., & Macfarlane-Dick, D. (2006). Formative assessment and self-regulated learning: A model and seven principles of good feedback practice. *Studies in Higher Education, 31*, 199–218.

Nielsen, K. (2014), Self-assessment methods in writing instruction: A conceptual framework, successful practices and essential strategies. *Journal of Research in Reading, 37*, 1–16.

Nowell, C., & Alston, R. M. (2007). I thought I got an A! Overconfidence across the economics curriculum. *Journal of Economic Education, 38*(2), 131–142.

Panadero, E., & Alonso-Tapia, J. (2013). Self-assessment: Theoretical and practical connotations. When it happens, how is it acquired and what to do to develop it in our students. *Electronic Journal of Research in Educational Psychology, 11*, 551–576.

Panadero, E., Alonso-Tapia, J., & Huertas, J. A. (2012). Rubrics and self-assessment scripts effects on self-regulation, learning and self-efficacy in secondary education. *Learning and Individual Differences, 22*, 806–813.

Panadero, E., Alonso-Tapia, J., & Huertas, J. A. (2014). Rubrics vs. self-assessment scripts: Effects on first year university students' self-regulation and performance. *Journal for the Study of Education and Development, 3*(7), 149–183.

Panadero, E., Alonso-Tapia, J., & Reche, E. (2013). Rubrics vs. self-assessment scripts effect on self-regulation, performance and self-efficacy in pre-service teachers. *Studies in Educational Evaluation*, *39*, 125–132.

Panadero, E., Brown, G. L., & Strijbos, J.-W. (2016). The future of student self-assessment: A review of known unknowns and potential directions. *Educational Psychology Review*, *28*, 803–830.

Panadero, E., Jonsson, A., & Botella, J. (2017). Effects of self-assessment on self-regulated learning and self-efficacy: Four meta-analyses. *Educational Research Review, 22*, 74–98.

Panadero, E., Jonsson, A., & Strijbos, J. W. (2016). Scaffolding self-regulated learning through self-assessment and peer assessment: Guidelines for classroom implementation. In D. Laveault & L. Allal (Eds.), *Assessment for learning: Meeting the challenge of implementation* (pp. 311–326). New York: Springer.

Panadero, E., & Romero, M. (2014). To rubric or not to rubric? The effects of self-assessment on self-regulation, performance and self-efficacy. *Assessment in Education: Principles, Policy & Practice, 21*, 133–148.

Punhagui, G. C., & de Souza, N. A. (2013). Self-regulation in the learning process: Actions through self-assessment activities with Brazilian students. *International Education Studies, 6*(10), 47–62.

Ross, J. A., Rolheiser, C., & Hogaboam-Gray, A. (1998, April). Impact of self-evaluation training on mathematics achievement in a cooperative learning environment. Paper presented at the annual meeting of the American Educational Research Association, San Diego, CA.

Ross, J. A., & Starling, M. (2008). Self-assessment in a technology-supported environment: The case of grade 9 geography. *Assessment in Education: Principles, Policy & Practice, 15*(2), 183–199.

Sargeant, J. (2008). Toward a common understanding of self-assessment. *Journal of Continuing Education in the Health Professions, 28*, 1–4.

Sargeant, J., Mann, K., van der Vleuten, C., & Metsemakers, J. (2008). "Directed" self-assessment: Practice and feedback within a social context. *Journal of Continuing Education in the Health Professions, 28*, 47–54.

Shute, V. (2008). Focus on formative feedback. *Review of Educational Research, 78*(1), 153–189.

Silver, I., Campbell, C., Marlow, B., & Sargeant, J. (2008). Self-assessment and continuing professional development: The Canadian perspective. *Journal of Continuing Education in the Health Professions, 28*, 25–31.

Siow, L.-F. (2015). Students' perceptions on self- and peer-assessment in enhancing learning experience. *Malaysian Online Journal of Educational Sciences, 3*(2), 21–35.

Tan, K. (2004). Does student self-assessment empower or discipline students? *Assessment & Evaluation in Higher Education, 29*(6), 651–662.

Tan, K. (2009). Meanings and practices of power in academics' conceptions of student self-assessment. *Teaching in Higher Education, 14*, 361–373.

Taras, M. (2008). Issues of power and equity in two models of self-assessment. *Teaching in Higher Education, 13*, 81–92.

Tejeiro, R. A., Gomez-Vallecillo, J. L., Romero, A. F., Pelegrina, M., Wallace, A., & Emberley, E. (2012). Summative self-assessment in higher education: Implications of its counting towards the final mark. *Electronic Journal of Research in Educational Psychology, 10,* 789–812.

van Helvoort, A. A. J. (2012). How adult students in information studies use a scoring rubric for the development of their information literacy skills. *Journal of Academic Librarianship, 38,* 165–171.

van Loon, M. H., de Bruin, A. B. H., van Gog, T., van Merriënboer, J. J. G., & Dunlosky, J. (2014). Can students evaluate their understanding of cause-and-effect relations? The effects of diagram completion on monitoring accuracy. *Acta Psychologica, 151,* 143–154.

Wang, W. (2017). Using rubrics in student self-assessment: Student perceptions in the English as a foreign language writing context. *Assessment & Evaluation in Higher Education, 42*(8), 1280–1292.

Wollenschläger, M., Hattie, J., Machts, N., Möller, J., & Harms, U. (2016). What makes rubrics effective in teacher-feedback? Transparency of learning goals is not enough. *Contemporary Educational Psychology, 44–45,* 1–11.

Zimmerman, B. J. (2000). Self-efficacy: An essential motive to learn. *Contemporary Educational Psychology, 25,* 82–91.

Zimmerman, B. J., & Schunk, D. H. (2011). Self-regulated learning and performance: An introduction and overview. In B. J Zimmerman & D. H. Schunk (Eds.), *Handbook of self-regulation of learning and performance.* New York: Routledge.

18 Providing Formative Peer Feedback

What Do We Know?

Ernesto Panadero, Anders Jonsson, and
Maryam Alqassab

Starting from the seminal work of Dewey, Piaget, Vygotsky, and Bruner (Falchikov, 2007), peers have been conceptualized as potential mediators in students' learning and development. In recent decades, there has been an increasing interest in how students' learning can be fostered through involving them in assessment via self- and peer assessment (Topping, 1998; Dochy, Segers, & Sluijsmans, 1999; van Zundert, Sluijsmans, & van Merriënboer, 2010; Brown & Harris, 2013). Both self- and peer assessment are now well-established fields of research with the following main lines of work: (1) the reliability/validity of self- and peer assessment scores (Falchikov & Boud, 1989; Falchikov & Goldfinch, 2000) and (2) the effects of such assessment on students' learning, which have mostly been studied after the emergence of research on formative assessment (Black & Wiliam, 1998; Wiliam, 2011). Two more topics that have recently received more interest are (3) the effects of self- and peer assessment on self-regulated learning and metacognition (Panadero, Jonsson, & Strijbos, 2016; Panadero, Jonsson, & Botella, 2017) and (4) the role of psychological and social factors in self- and peer assessment (van Gennip, Segers, & Tillema, 2009; Panadero, 2016; Yan & Brown, 2016).

Consequently, researchers have become interested in the type of information that students exchange in peer assessment situations, with research focused on whether the quality of such information can lead to improved learning compared with just providing a score (i.e., peer scoring). This information is known as peer feedback. There has been an increased interest in peer feedback – a trend reflected in the publication of dissertations that focus on various aspects of peer feedback (Gielen, 2007; Gan, 2011; Alqassab, 2016; Gielen, 2016; Rotsaert, 2017). The aim of this chapter is to explore the concept of peer feedback, presenting the results of the main dissertations and discussing the key empirical themes that have been investigated.

Introduction to the Peer Feedback Concept

Simply put, peer feedback is feedback that comes from a peer. Nevertheless, "peer" and "feedback" need further clarification as both are multifaceted constructs. A peer is an equal in one or more of the following aspects: age, educational level, or level of expertise. Feedback in an educational context refers to any information provided to students about their performance. This information may take different forms ranging from a single grade/score to very detailed qualitative information (e.g., explaining in detail how to improve an essay). There are tensions regarding the summative and formative purposes of feedback, and peer feedback is not excluded from this controversy (see next section, also Brookhart, Chapter 3, this volume). For the purposes of this chapter, we will adhere to the definition of formative feedback offered by Shute (2008): "information communicated to the learner that is intended to modify his or her thinking or behavior for the purpose of improving learning" (p. 154). This definition includes the original idea that feedback is information routed back to an original source of action, in our case the student. It also situates the formative use of feedback within a learning context: it aims to improve students' learning. Furthermore, this definition allows feedback to take different forms when provided in different learning contexts (Lipnevich, Berg, & Smith, 2016), and covers different types of feedback that can be directed to the task, process, self-regulation, or personal levels (Hattie & Timperley, 2007). What students do with that information and their reactions to it will depend on some features of feedback but also on personal variables (Lipnevich et al., 2016; Jonsson & Panadero, Chapter 24, this volume). In other words, students' decisions to act or not act on the received feedback in order to close the gap between their actual performance and the desired one go beyond our conceptualization of what constitutes feedback.

Disentangling Uses of Peers: Assessment and Learning

The tensions mentioned above between feedback for summative and formative purposes have also been translated into research around students' involvement in evaluating a peer's piece of work (Liu & Carless, 2006). As proposed by Gielen et al. (2011, figure 1), peer assessment can serve five purposes: as a social control tool, assessment tool, learning tool, learning-how-to-assess tool, and active participation tool. This diversity of purposes has led to inconsistencies in the terminology. For instance, research focusing on peer feedback may be labeled as peer assessment (e.g., Sluijsmans, Brand-Gruwel, & van Merriënboer, 2002) and, vice versa, research on peer scoring and assessment may be labeled as peer feedback (e.g., Cho, Chung, King, & Schunn, 2008). Some studies have used a combination of these terms to differentiate between different purposes (e.g., Rotsaert, Panadero, Schellens, & Raes, 2018a). This confusion can be explained by the fact that the two main areas of research into peer involvement in assessment have revolved around either accuracy/validity/reliability of scoring (Falchikov & Goldfinch, 2000; Panadero, Romero, & Strijbos, 2013) or effects of students' involvement with assessment on students' learning (Dochy et al., 1999; van Zundert et al., 2010). Due to the interchangeability in the use of the terms *peer assessment* and *peer feedback*, it can be difficult to separate different purposes of using peer feedback in the literature.

It is therefore important to start using a more precise terminology. We are not the first to issue such a call (Liu & Carless, 2006; McCarthy, 2016). In this chapter, we will operationalize peer feedback and *formative* peer assessment as referring to the provision of qualitative information about student performance (e.g., strengths and weaknesses), but without a peer-awarded score or grade. Peer assessment, on the other hand, will refer to situations in which the assessor provides qualitative feedback *and* a score or grade (Liu & Carless, 2006). We also propose a third category, referring to situations in which a score is given without being accompanied by any type of qualitative feedback. In the latter case the term *peer scoring* will be used, similar to what has been done in the field of self-assessment (for a review, see Panadero, Brown, & Strijbos, 2016).

These distinctions are important in order to promote a more unified use of terms in the field, but also because students are likely to approach the task differently depending on whether they are asked to score or grade a peer's piece of work or not, which affects their social interactions (for a review, see Panadero, 2016). Similarly, students could be expected to react to feedback provided by peers differently compared with feedback coming from a teacher (Gielen, Dochy, Onghena, et al., 2011).

Peer assessment and peer feedback can be seen as forms of either formative assessment (Topping, 1998) or collaborative learning (van Gennip, Segers, & Tillema, 2010). However, depending on the purpose, the actual implementation would differ. In collaborative learning activities, students provide peer feedback to each other in order to achieve a shared learning goal. This situation is not the same as providing qualitative feedback to a peer working on his or her own individual task. Even if peer feedback is an integral part of collaborative learning situations, it is still a different feedback situation than providing peer feedback from an "assessor position." The collaborative learning feedback situation represents a more "natural" (or neutral) interaction, which is more balanced in terms of roles and processes through which feedback is delivered. One example of these different voices and roles can be found in the study by Gan and Hill (2014). In this study, the characteristics of verbal peer feedback were explored during a collaborative task using a scheme that included two dimensions of interactive/noninteractive and dialogic/authoritative. This study will be presented in greater detail later.

The main message from this section is that the purpose of the activity and the type of feedback expected from students make a difference in how students approach the activity. Furthermore, the instructions that they receive on how feedback should be formulated and delivered are crucial for what students actually provide to their peers. Therefore, the act of providing feedback to a peer will be different if students are asked to score, to provide qualitative feedback, or to collaborate with their team. All of these possibilities need to be considered when investigating the effect of peer feedback on learning.

Conditions Influencing the Effectiveness of Peer Feedback

A significant number of reviews and meta-analyses conducted on the most effective characteristics of teachers' feedback for student learning and performance (e.g., Kluger & DeNisi, 1996; Hattie & Timperley, 2007; Shute, 2008) revealed that the effect of feedback is shaped by (1) characteristics of the feedback, (2) characteristics of instruction, and (3) characteristics of students. The interaction among these three factors determines students' reactions to the feedback received and whether or not they will engage with it (Jonsson & Panadero, Chapter 24 in this volume). The same factors are equally relevant for peer feedback. Nevertheless, there are some aspects that are more likely to influence peer feedback that are not always included in teacher feedback models. These are interpersonal variables, which we describe in the forthcoming section.

Peer Feedback Characteristics

Drawing on the literature on teachers' feedback, the characteristics of peer feedback include such categories as content, function, and presentation (see Narciss & Huth, 2004). According to Narciss and Huth (2004), examples of content aspects are level of performance, accuracy, focus, level of detail, and comprehensibility. Regarding aspects of function, two different models have been proposed. Narciss and Huth (2004) suggested that the characteristics of function are cognitive, metacognitive, and motivational aspects of feedback. Hattie and Timperley (2007) suggested the following aspects (or levels): (1) the task, (2) the processes that produce successful performance on the task, (3) self-regulation, and (4) the self. Finally, regarding feedback presentation, the following aspects have been discussed: frequency, timeliness, elaborated feedback in manageable units, and tone (e.g., Narciss & Huth, 2004; Shute, 2008).

Characteristics of Instruction

Narciss and Huth (2004) proposed several factors related to the instructional context that can contribute to the effects of feedback on learning. These include learning goals, characteristics of the learning task, and possible sources of learning difficulties or problems. When it comes to peer feedback, these factors are important as they can hinder or facilitate the success of peer feedback activities. For instance, the complexity of the learning task can influence the accuracy of peer assessment (see van Zundert, Sluijsmans, et al., 2012). Additionally, the amount of instructional support that students receive during peer feedback activities (e.g., scaffolds, rubrics, training) and the purpose of peer feedback activities (e.g., to teach domain knowledge or to teach assessment skills) can be regarded as important aspects of the learning context.

Individual Characteristics

Narciss and Huth (2004) proposed that students' individual characteristics that can influence the effect of feedback are students' cognitive factors (e.g., prior knowledge), metacognitive factors, and motivational factors (e.g., beliefs, academic self-efficacy). Due to the reciprocal nature of peer feedback, we stress that individual characteristics of the recipient and the provider are equally important for peer feedback and can influence the provision and the reception of peer feedback (see Strijbos & Müller, 2014).

Social and Interpersonal Variables

Several researchers stressed the role of social factors in peer assessment and peer feedback activities and acknowledged the importance of these aspects beyond controlling for peer assessment validity or reliability (Strijbos, Ochoa, Sluijsmans, Segers, & Tillema, 2009; van Gennip et al., 2009; Strijbos & Sluijsmans, 2010; Panadero, 2016). These are variables that determine interpersonal communication among peers that can also influence processes and outcomes of peer assessment or peer feedback. In a recent review, Panadero (2016) identified ten research themes that appear in the peer assessment literature, grouped into three categories: intraindividual, interpersonal, and cognitive aspects. Among those ten themes are friendship marking (e.g. Panadero et al., 2013), psychological safety (e.g., van Gennip et al., 2010), trust in the other as an assessor (e.g., Lin, Liu, & Yuan, 2002), and trust in the self as an assessor (Sluijsmans et al., 2002). The main conclusion of Panadero's (2016) review was that formative approaches seemed to help alleviate some of the interpersonal tensions that can occur during peer assessment.

In sum, although a number of factors mentioned in this section are frequently found in the teacher's feedback literature, they can also affect peers as a source of feedback. Some of them are even more important for peer feedback because of its egalitarian nature. Next, we will explore the main lines of research on peer feedback.

Empirical Evidence on Peer Feedback

Research with a focus on peer feedback characteristics is relatively recent. Searching for peer feedback in databases reveals that the vast majority of studies have been published from 2005 and onward. A significant percentage of these publications are based on students' perceptions of peer feedback implementation (e.g., Chesney & Marcangelo, 2010; Gikandi & Morrow, 2016). They consist of studies seeking students' or teachers' opinions about the implementation of peer feedback, many times without a more objective dependent variable (e.g., performance). This research can be problematic, as some studies do not acknowledge the limitations of such methodology.

Despite certain methodological concerns, the main focus of this chapter is on specific characteristics of peer feedback that enhance learning. We present five dissertations that examined peer feedback in the realm of formative peer assessment. The goal behind the presentation of these dissertations is to explore in detail the rich type of empirical evidence that represents a coherent line of work. Further, after discussing the dissertations, we identify seven major themes in the peer feedback literature.

Five Dissertations on the Topic of Peer Feedback

Sarah Gielen (2007): "Peer Assessment as a Tool for Learning"

This dissertation was published in 2007, defended at the University of Leuven (Belgium), and completed under the supervision of Filip Dochy and Patrick Onghena. The work of Dochy in the 1990s onward was seminal in the formative assessment field, and Gielen's dissertation is an example of his influence. The six publications in this dissertation made both theoretical and empirical contributions. The three theoretical publications were crucial in exploring the formative use of peer assessment. In the first publication, Gielen, Dochy, and Dierick (2003) examined the role of peer assessment in the larger assessment system of a learning environment and discussed its impact on the learning processes of students. Peer assessment is shown to enhance the consequential validity (what happens as a consequence of a particular assessment, see Messick, 1998) of the larger assessment system. By introducing peer assessment, the contribution of an assessment system to a powerful learning environment can be strengthened.

The second publication (Gielen, Dochy, Onghena, et al., 2011) has already been cited earlier, and it explored the different goals that peer assessment may have. Identifying these goals is important to accurately evaluate the success of a peer assessment implementation. The study identified five types of goals: assessment tool, learning, social control, preparation of self-monitoring and self-regulation, and students' active participation. Additionally, the researchers found that most of the research had been conducted with peer assessment as an assessment tool, but its use as a means to increase students' learning was increasing, mostly as a result of the emergence of research on formative assessment. Finally, in her third theoretical contribution, Gielen developed a tool to analyze features of peer assessment, thereby providing a framework to capture and categorize the diversity of peer assessment in education (Gielen, Dochy, & Onghena, 2011). Her inventory expanded the one by Topping (1998) and includes twenty categories organized around five clusters (see Gielen et al., 2011).

Regarding Gielen's empirical contributions, three publications explored the following themes: (1) Is peer feedback as effective as teacher (expert) feedback? (2) What are the strengths and weaknesses of both peer feedback and teacher feedback? (3) How to design an effective (peer) feedback system? and (4) What constitutes effective peer feedback and who benefits from it? These themes are explored, alone and in combination, in the different dissertation studies. The first theme is addressed in two studies – one in secondary education and the other in higher education. The study conducted in the seventh-grade writing class (Gielen, Tops, Dochy, Onghena, & Smeets, 2010) showed that there were no significant differences between teacher and peer feedback in terms of students' progress. Another publication from Gielen's dissertation (Gielen et al., 2007) further explored this area by studying first-year university students' perceptions about (collective) staff versus (individualized) peer feedback. This was done not only in terms of effects (theme 1) but also in terms of feedback characteristics (theme 2). Because this study examined an assessment system in which both themes were combined, it also addressed the design question (theme 3). The authors reached the following conclusions: (1) half of the participants were willing to trade in the credibility of staff feedback for the specificity of peer feedback, (2) peer and staff feedback were shown to be complementary, and (3) they each provided the conditions under which the complementary source became better. By involving peers in providing specific individualized feedback, educators focused on more general aspects of their feedback, such as misconceptions. Most importantly, according to students, both types of feedback were needed. Furthermore, because peers took care of the individual feedback, staff could save time (by providing their feedback only collectively), which, in turn, was invested in facilitating a good peer feedback system that provided useful individualized feedback. This investment resulted in opportunities for personal coaching among students and lively discussions leading to deep and cooperative learning and metacognitive growth as measured via self-report.

The study in the secondary education context that was discussed earlier addresses the third theme. Gielen, Tops, et al. (2010) examined the additional value of peer feedback using an intervention study. More specifically, they looked at the effects of adding a priori and a posteriori questions aimed at supporting the assessee's response to peer feedback. Their findings showed that the extended peer feedback system (i.e., in which students were encouraged to react to the feedback they had received) was superior to both the "simple" peer feedback condition and the teacher feedback condition, in terms of students' progress in writing. However, in another empirical study, conducted in a seventh-grade writing class (Gielen, Peeters, Dochy, Onghena, & Struyven, 2010) that focused only on these different configurations of peer assessment, the superiority of an extended peer feedback system (i.e., including interventions to enhance the assessee's reflection after receiving the feedback) could not be replicated.

Finally, the latter study also investigated peer feedback at the micro level (theme 4). Gielen et al. (2010) examined differences in the quality of feedback provided by different peer assessors and its effects on the learning gains of both assessors and assessees after the peer feedback phase. Although the quality (in terms of constructiveness) of feedback in this study was low overall, receiving "better" feedback was associated with higher performance gains, while providing better feedback was not.

Why is this contribution important? This dissertation provided a strong theoretical exploration of the use of peer assessment for formative purposes that was later followed by two other important dissertations focusing on similar topics (van Gennip, 2012; van Zundert, 2012). Further, Gielen's work identified different peer assessment purposes and examined differences and similarities in peer and expert/teacher feedback and its effects on student learning and other meaningful outcomes (e.g., Cho, Schunn, & Charney, 2006).

Mark Gan (2011): "The Effects of Prompts and Explicit Coaching on Peer Feedback Quality"

This dissertation was published in 2011, defended at the University of Auckland (New Zealand), and was conducted under the supervision of John Hattie and Mary Hill. Hattie's research focuses on the effects of feedback on students' achievement among others, whereas Hill's main areas of research are educational assessment and teacher professional learning.

Gan's dissertation explored characteristics of peer feedback and instructional scaffolding effects on the peer feedback quality. Parts of the theoretical framework were already published in Hattie and Gan (2011), which provides an overview of perspectives of learning and the nature of feedback, including the following psychological and educational theories: objectivism, information processing, socioculturalism, and visible learning and teaching. Additionally, they further developed the three questions proposed by Hattie and Timperley (2007) (i.e., where am I going, how am I doing, where to next). While there is some information about peer feedback at the end of the chapter, the main focus of this publication was on the review of instructional feedback.

The empirical part of Gan's dissertation is composed of three studies. The first study (Gan & Hill, 2014) used a descriptive methodology to explore what types of verbal peer feedback students use in a chemistry task. Gan and Hill analyzed feedback along two dimensions: dialogic/authoritative and interactive/noninteractive and found that the participants predominantly used an "interactive/authoritative communicative approach, with peer feedback as confirmation or evaluation. Furthermore, the participants are also capable of a more interactive/dialogic exchange, characterised by elaborative peer feedback" (p. 727).

The second study (Gan & Hattie, 2014) explored the use of a scaffolding framework provided to the feedback givers in the form of question prompts on how to provide feedback. They found that this intervention increased the number of comments related to knowledge of errors, suggestions for improvement, and process-level feedback (as defined by Hattie and Timperley, 2007). A key finding was that "prompting peer feedback in the use of criteria, feedback specificity, and feedback levels" increased the quality of feedback. The third study (unpublished) built on the two previous studies to increase the features of the intervention (e.g., graphic organizer with feedback levels) received by the feedback givers. Findings were aligned with the second study: scaffolding tools enhanced the quality of the peer feedback produced.

Why is this contribution important? This dissertation explored the nature of peer feedback content and used scaffolding elements to improve the quality of the feedback following Gielen et al.'s (2010) work. In particular, Gan's studies built on the model of Hattie and Timperley (2007) to devise a peer feedback framework to allow students to engage in productive discursive interactions within a collaborative and visible learning context.

Mario Gielen (2016): "The Impact of Structuring Peer Feedback in a Wiki-Based CSCL Environment on Performance and Feedback Content"

This dissertation was published in 2016, defended at the Ghent University (Belgium), and conducted under the supervision of Bram De Wever, who is a specialist in computer-supportive collaborative learning, technology-enhanced learning, and the role of scripting in promoting better collaboration.

Gielen's dissertation focuses on exploring how peer assessment practices can be enhanced to improve students' learning by structuring the peer feedback process for both assessors and assessees. This dissertation contains five empirical studies extracted from three different interventions. The first intervention and empirical study (Gielen & De Wever, 2012) explored the effects of structured peer feedback on student performance. The study found no significant effects. There was, however, a significant effect of practice: both the experimental and the control group created better wiki products from pre- to post-tests. Additionally, participants in the structured peer feedback condition were more critical as providers and receivers of feedback and perceived the received feedback as more valuable, compared with their counterparts in the control group.

In the second intervention, the focus was on intervening in the assessor (feedback provider) alone, with the first study exploring the impact on peer feedback quality and performance, and the second study exploring the effects on more specific feedback characteristics (e.g., elaboration, verification, etc.). In their investigation Gielen and De Wever (2015a) explored the effects on feedback quality and student performance of two levels of intervention: elaborate structure peer feedback versus basic structure, against a control condition. For both experimental conditions, a significant effect was found for feedback quality and performance, compared with the control condition. Additionally, after several rounds of practice, peer feedback quality was higher in the elaborate condition as compared with the control, and both experimental conditions surpassed the control on performance. The second published study from this intervention (Gielen & De Wever, 2015b) reported a detailed analysis of the peer feedback content based on the different levels of structuring. They found that all conditions provided a balanced proportion of verifications and elaborations but also that the assessors receiving a peer feedback scaffold produced more general elaborations focusing on specific criteria and negative verifications. The authors emphasized the importance of such "negative" feedback as it might generate an increased effort in those who are on the receiving side of feedback.

Finally, in the third intervention, both the assessor and assessee underwent interventions to increase the quality of the feedback provided and the level of detail of the feedback requested. Additionally, the two studies from this intervention had a similar structure as the ones in the second intervention: the first one explored the effects of experimental manipulation on performance and peer feedback quality, whereas the second explored in detail specific characteristics of the peer feedback given. In the first published empirical study (Gielen & De Wever, 2015c), participants were assigned to one of four experimental conditions with scaffolds of varying degree of elaboration. The quality of the peer feedback and performance increased in all four conditions over time, possibly due to a practice effect. Additionally, when the assessee was scaffolded to request specific peer feedback from the assessor, this had a positive effect on peer feedback scores. In the second study (Gielen, 2016) the researchers found that all conditions showed a balanced proportion of "mostly positive verifications and equally informative and suggestive elaborations" (p. 135). No significant differences were found among conditions.

Why is this contribution important? This contribution explored differential effects of feedback scaffolds for both assessors and assessees. Additionally, it explored these effects on three main outcome variables: performance, feedback quality, and feedback content categories. Finally, it continued the exploration of peer feedback content, creating a sophisticated coding scheme.

Maryam Alqassab (2016): "Peer Feedback Provision and Mathematical Proofs: Role of Domain Knowledge, Beliefs, Perceptions, Epistemic Emotions, and Peer Feedback Content"

This dissertation was published in 2016, defended at the Ludwig-Maximilians University (Munich, Germany), and conducted under the supervision of Jan-Willem Strijbos, a specialist in peer assessment, peer feedback, collaborative learning, and computer supported collaborative learning (CSCL), and Stefan Ufer, a specialist in mathematics education. Additionally, John Hattie was an international advisor.

Alqassab's dissertation consisted of two empirical studies that focus on the individual characteristics that might influence peer feedback provision such as domain knowledge, beliefs about peer feedback provision, peer feedback providers' perceptions of peer feedback, and epistemic emotions. The sample comprised preservice mathematics teachers who participated in two studies.

In the first study, all participants received a structured peer feedback training based on Hattie and Timperley's (2007) model with four levels of feedback. Before the training, the participants were grouped into low, medium, and high domain knowledge groups based on their knowledge in geometry.

The participants' peer feedback skills and beliefs were measured pre and post using a coding scheme based on Hattie and Timperley's (2007) model. The study revealed that the training was beneficial for peer feedback provision skills but that their domain knowledge moderated the effect. Groups with medium and high levels of domain knowledge produced more self-regulation-level feedback, whereas the participants with lower levels of domain knowledge produced more task-level feedback. For the other two categories (process and self) no significant differences were found. Alqassab (2016) also found that the participants' beliefs about peer feedback became more realistic as these beliefs were less positive after the intervention, regardless of participants' domain knowledge.

Regarding the second study, the participants provided peer feedback in two conditions: one with a near-correct mathematical problem and the other with an incorrect solution to the same problem. There were five dependent variables. The first variable was participants' eye movements, which were tracked and analyzed based on the proportional total dwell time (PTDT) (i.e., the time the participant spent looking at the figure or text, also called fixation time). The second variable measured how well the participants understood the proof, called "proof comprehension."[1] The third variable was the feedback content provided to the fictional peers. The quality of this feedback was analyzed based on type (cognitive surface, cognitive verification, cognitive elaboration, self-efficacy, and affective function) and accuracy. The fourth variable was three emotions as experienced by the participants: curiosity, confusion, and anxiety. Finally, the fifth variable was beliefs about peer feedback and the participants' perceptions about the quality of peer feedback.

First, regarding PTDT, Alqassab (2016) reported that error in the peer solution led to reliance on a text-based (analytical) approach, whereas the absence of errors facilitated reliance on figure (i.e., a figure-based mental model). Second, regarding proof comprehension, those participants who provided peer feedback on the near-correct peer solution had a better understanding of the mathematical proof as compared with those who provided peer feedback on the incorrect peer solution, after controlling for their domain knowledge. The researcher suggested that errors in the peer solution hindered students' understanding of the proof during peer feedback provision. Third, the study revealed that the feedback content was not affected in the type category since participants in both conditions provided similar types of feedback. However, there was a significant difference in terms of accuracy[2] with preservice

---

1 Proof comprehension means the understanding of a proof. In mathematics education, there are several frameworks that describe the assessment of the understanding of different components of a proof. It is typical in mathematics education to measure students' proof comprehension (understanding of an already performed proof). This was used as a learning outcome.
2 Accuracy was determined in terms of the identification of errors and correct statements regarding the peer solution. The authors developed a coding scheme that noted whether each part of the peer solution was correct or incorrect. And if the student got any of that correct, they awarded one point for that.

teachers in the near-correct solution condition providing more accurate feedback. Fourth, regarding the experienced emotions, participants in the erroneous condition experienced more curiosity, but there were no differences in confusion. Additionally, the correlation between emotions and feedback accuracy was explored, revealing that confusion and anxiety were negatively related to accuracy in the near-correct condition. Fifth, regarding the peer feedback perceptions, the study found that the participants' perceptions about the quality of their feedback were positively correlated with their confidence in providing peer feedback. Finally, the researcher concluded that the participants' confidence regarding the feedback they provided, their perceptions of their peer feedback,[3] confusion, and anxiety were possible indicators of accuracy.

Why is this contribution important? This dissertation made a number of significant contributions. First, it explored the role of the feedback provider in terms of a number of variables (e.g., emotions and perceptions). Second, it explored the effect of domain knowledge on peer feedback provision. Although this effect had previously been studied, it was investigated from a different angle (Sluijsmans et al., 2002) and only in the domain of writing (Patchan, Hawk, Stevens, & Schunn, 2013; Patchan & Schunn, 2015). Third, this dissertation was a pioneer study on the use of eye tracking and exploring the role of emotions in peer feedback. Finally, it explored the effects of peer feedback on learning outcomes (i.e., proof comprehension), an aspect overlooked in previous research.

Tijs Rotsaert (2017): "The Social Nature of Peer Assessment in Secondary and Higher Education"

This dissertation was published in 2017, defended at Ghent University (Belgium), and was conducted under the supervision of Tammy Schellens, a specialist in educational technology and teaching methods. Additionally, the first author of this chapter was also involved as an international collaborator.

Rotsaert's dissertation addressed three main topics: the social and interpersonal nature of peer assessment, the quality of peer feedback, and the organization and management of peer assessment practices with a special focus on the role of anonymity. The dissertation contains five empirical studies. The first three mostly related to peer assessment and will be presented only briefly. The last two explored peer feedback.

The first study (Rotsaert, Panadero, Estrada, & Schellens, 2017) was conducted via a survey distributed to 3,680 Flemish secondary students and explored their perceptions of peer assessment interpersonal variables (e.g., trust) and their beliefs on the educational value of peer assessment. The results revealed that the educational value could be predicted by trust in the self and

---

3 *Confidence regarding feedback provided* is similar to what other researchers have called *trust in the self as an assessor; perceptions of their peer feedback* is specific to the very peer feedback that the participants provided in this activity.

the other, awareness of negative interpersonal processes that might affect peer assessment (e.g., fear of disapproval and friendship marking), and beliefs about peer assessment accuracy. Additionally, the importance that students attributed to anonymity was found to be a negative predictor of peer assessment conceptions. The second study (Rotsaert, Panadero, & Schellens, 2018b) explored the effects of 225 teacher conceptions of peer assessment and students' interpersonal processes on the educational value of peer assessment. The researchers found that teachers were moderately aware of students' concerns about the influence of interpersonal processes on peer assessment and the importance that students attributed to anonymity. No significant relation was found between the educational value of peer feedback as perceived by the teachers and interpersonal variables or anonymity. The third study explored the effect of a technological tool (mobile response technology) to provide anonymity for the assessors in a face-to-face peer assessment activity. Apart from a number of relationships among different peer assessment conceptions and interpersonal variables, the researchers found that students preferred nonanonymous teacher feedback and assessment.

The fourth study (Rotsaert et al., 2018a) investigated the effects of (1) practice (ten occasions) and (2) a scaffolding tool to filter out relevant information for feedback receivers on three dependent variables. The participants worked in groups, both providing and receiving peer feedback. The first dependent variable, peer feedback quality, was gauged by analyzing the feedback content considering different characteristics as verifications and elaborations. Results showed that only the practice effect was significant for the improvement of the quality of the feedback through an increase of negative verifications ("a dichotomous judgment to indicate that a response is right or wrong"), and informative and suggestive elaborations ("relevant information to help the learner in error correction," Hattie & Gan, 2011, p. 253). The second variable, perceived peer feedback skills, also improved with practice. Finally, the third variable, perceived usefulness of the received feedback, was rated highly by all participants at all measurement occasions.

The fifth study (Rotsaert et al., 2018c) explored the role of anonymity in peer feedback quality and students' perceptions. The forty-six undergraduate participants organized in working groups went through four cycles of peer assessment with the initial two cycles being anonymous and the last two not. The results showed that peer feedback quality increased based on the practice effects and that moving into the nonanonymous cycle continued this increase. Additionally, the change in the anonymity status did not negatively affect the perceptions of peer feedback skills, which increased as a result of practice, nor did it affect the conceptions of peer assessment. Furthermore, although students did find anonymity to be an important factor within peer assessment, they strongly acknowledged the value of a rich and interactive, nonanonymous feedback environment.

Why is this contribution important? This dissertation discusses practice and anonymity as moderators of the quality of peer feedback. The results show that practice is a crucial factor to increase the quality of the feedback students give to each other. Additionally, it has a more refined version of Gielen's feedback content categories, which could be used in future research. Furthermore, this dissertation adds to the peer assessment literature by exploring the role of interpersonal variables in both teachers and students, as well as the effects of feedback anonymity on students' perceptions of feedback and quality of their performance.

Features of Peer Feedback That Contribute to Students' Learning

From the dissertations summarized above and the existing peer feedback literature, we have identified seven central themes of research related to four main aspects influencing the effectiveness of peer feedback. In this section, we will present these themes, then discuss the effect of peer feedback on achievement. The themes are presented under headings that describe the general area of research, and are numbered one through seven.

Peer Feedback Characteristics

Regarding the characteristics of peer feedback, we have identified two themes of research, namely, differences between peer and teacher feedback, and the nature and quality of peer feedback content.

1. Differentiation between peer and teacher feedback. This line of work explores the pros and cons of peer feedback as compared with feedback from teachers as experts. Multiple publications by Cho and colleagues (Cho, Schunn, & Charney, 2006; Cho et al., 2008; Cho & MacArthur, 2010) extend the earlier work by Paulus (1999). Among the above-mentioned dissertations, research on the differentiation between peer and teacher feedback was taken up by Gielen, both empirically (Gielen, Dochy, et al., 2007; Gielen, Tops, et al., 2010), and theoretically (Gielen, Peeters, et al., 2010). One of the most salient differences between teacher and peer feedback is that teachers are supposed to be experts in the domain. However, Gielen's research found that peer feedback has distinct features that can also be beneficial for the recipients of peer feedback. Previous research has shown that, when they do not know the source of the feedback, students considered peer feedback as useful as teacher feedback (Cho et al., 2006). The work by Cho and colleagues has also shown that peer feedback can be as productive as feedback from the teacher, because (1) peers struggle with the same learning objectives and difficulties and can sometimes aid in addressing them better than an expert; (2) peers might share the same "language"; and (3) peer feedback may contain more nondirective comments, which may lead to more complex revisions and higher quality performance (Cho, Cho, & Hacker, 2010).

2. Nature and quality of peer feedback content. A strong line of research explored the types of feedback students produce when asked to provide peer feedback. All of the aforementioned dissertations have studied the content of peer feedback either in a descriptive way (e.g., Gan, 2011, found that students used predominantly an interactive/authoritative communicative approach) or as a dependent variable (e.g., Gielen, 2016, explored the effects of scaffolding peer feedback on the content of the feedback). Regarding Alqassab's (2016) dissertation, both empirical studies used peer feedback content as a dependent variable. In the first study, the groups with medium and high domain knowledge showed differential effects providing more self-regulation level feedback, and the students in the low domain knowledge group provided more task feedback. In the second study, there was no effect of the experimental conditions. Last, Rotsaert (2017) also used peer feedback content as a dependent variable in the fourth and fifth studies. These studies showed that the peer feedback content quality increased due to the practice effect, but the intervention did not have an effect in the first investigation. Additionally, the change in the anonymity status did not affect the quality of the peer feedback (Rotsaert et al., 2018c). Additionally, Strijbos, Narciss, and Dünnebier (2010) used experimental design to show that the participants were able to differentiate between peer feedback of different quality. This study showed that students are capable of identifying the quality of feedback as received by a peer. In conclusion, research shows us that (1) the quality of peer feedback can be increased via interventions; (2) students are well aware of, and are able to identify, peer feedback of different quality; and (3) peer feedback, although having different characteristics as compared with teacher feedback (e.g., research by Cho and colleagues) can be of high quality, but other factors such as domain knowledge can influence that.

Instructional Characteristics

Research related to instructional characteristics is mainly concerned with the amount or type of instructional support that the students receive during the peer feedback activity, such as scaffolding and practice effect and training.

Scaffolding Peer Feedback. This line of work concerns providing different scaffolds either to help feedback providers to produce better quality feedback or to help feedback receivers to ask for feedback or assimilate it better. This research has connections with studies in collaborative learning settings in which students are scaffolded for better interactions (Ge & Land, 2003). Examples of this type of research can be found in the aforementioned dissertations. Gan (2011) explored the effects of question prompts and graphic organizers provided to the persons delivering feedback. Such scaffolding increased the quality of peer feedback (Gan, 2011; Gan & Hattie, 2014). The main aim of Gielen's dissertation was to explore how providing scaffolding to both providers and receivers of feedback would increase peer feedback quality and performance. The scaffold was based on "scripting," which showed significant effects on peer feedback and on performance in one of the three studies exploring this (Gielen & De Wever, 2015a). In the other two studies, only the effect of practice was significant (Gielen & De Wever, 2012, 2015c). Finally, Rotsaert et al. (2018a) found that the effects of a tool for filtering out information that intended to help assessees identify the most important information in the peer feedback quality were not statistically significant. Instead, only the practice effect made a significant difference. As one can see, the use of scaffolds seems to have mixed results, with the researchers suggesting different reasons for nonsignificant results, such as lack of time or practice effect for all conditions neutralizing the effects of the intervention. Nevertheless, the use of scaffolds to help provide better peer feedback should, when the implementation conditions are optimal, enhance peer feedback quality and, thus, students' performance.

Practice Effect and Training. Regarding practice, five studies analyzed from the dissertations found a significant effect of practice on the quality of peer feedback (Gielen & De Wever, 2012, 2015a, 2015c; Rotsaert et al., 2018a, 2018c) and on perceived peer feedback skills (Rotsaert et al., 2018c). All these results show that it is important to consider previous experience and practice on improving the quality of peer feedback. Additionally, Panadero and Brown (2017) found that one of the main predictors of teachers' implementation of peer assessment is previous peer assessment experience. This would indicate that for peer assessment or peer feedback to be a successful instructional activity, it is important to consider the influence of practice for both students and teachers. Therefore, we would like to suggest that, as proposed by Panadero et al. (2016) in relation to self-assessment, a *developmental approach to the training of peer feedback* is needed. In other words, students need practice to actually master the skill necessary for providing and interpreting peer feedback.

Another aspect that is closely related to the practice effect is training. Gan (2011) showed that training students resulted in improvement in their peer feedback content compared with a control group – an effect that was also previously found with preservice teachers (see Sluijsmans et al., 2002; Sluijsmans et al., 2004). Accordingly, it seems that the degree to which students receive instructional support (scaffolding, training, and opportunities to practice) can facilitate the development of better peer feedback delivery skills.

Individual Characteristics

Despite the importance of students' individual characteristics, we have identified only two main research topics: domain knowledge and students' emotions, beliefs, and perceptions.

Domain Knowledge. Whereas practice refers to individuals' expertise pertaining to the process of peer feedback, domain knowledge is expertise pertaining to the task at hand. Regarding domain knowledge, the work by Alqassab (2016, first study) showed that students with different levels of domain knowledge (high, medium, and low) provided different types of peer feedback, a result supporting previous research (Patchan et al., 2013; Patchan & Schunn, 2015). Panadero et al. (2016) questioned why the self-assessment field has not considered domain knowledge as a key variable determining the effectiveness of self-assessment. Due to some of the similarities between self-assessment and peer assessment, it could be assumed that a similar call should be made here to explore this crucial variable for the quality of peer feedback in more detail. In addition, the work by Strijbos et al. (2010) also considered the role of domain knowledge by investigating how concise general or elaborated specific peer feedback provided from high or low competence peers influenced recipients' perceptions of peer feedback and their performance.

Beliefs, Perceptions, and Emotions. These variables are likely to influence the processes and outcomes of peer assessment and peer feedback, yet their role is still widely ignored. Due to the limited empirical evidence and the fact that available studies tend to explore these constructs together, we also clustered them in one theme. Once the corpus of knowledge increases, they should be presented separately. In the first study, Alqassab (2016) investigated the impact of peer feedback training on students' beliefs about peer feedback provision, including learning from peer feedback provision, having confidence regarding peer feedback provision, and engaging in reasoning during peer feedback provision. She found that such beliefs became less positive. In study 2, relations among these beliefs, students' perceptions of peer feedback message, and peer feedback content were investigated. The accuracy of peer feedback was found to relate to confidence beliefs and perceptions. In addition, emotions were investigated, revealing that the quality of peer solutions might result in the recipient experiencing more curiosity during peer feedback provision. Confusion and anxiety were negatively related to peer feedback accuracy, but only for the near-correct peer solution condition. Students' affect in peer feedback from the recipients' perspective was investigated by Strijbos et al. (2010), who showed that students who received elaborated specific peer feedback from a high competent peer experienced more negative affect.

Interpersonal Variables

There were two interpersonal variables investigated in the current research: social aspects (e.g., trust) and anonymity. This is still an understudied area in peer feedback. However, interest in the peer assessment field in the social aspects and effects of anonymity has been increasing in the last decade. A significant milestone was the publication of the review from van Gennip et al. (2009), followed by an updated review that summarized the results from an increased number of studies (Panadero, 2016). This last review concluded that formative approaches to peer assessment, the ones that are focused on providing more informative feedback than a score, might have better interpersonal results and seemed to be better received by the students. This represents an argument in favor of peer feedback and formative peer assessment rather than peer scoring. To our knowledge, only the work by Rotsaert (2017) has explicitly explored the effects of social aspects and anonymity on peer feedback in peer assessment situations. Even though the first and second study of Rotsaert's dissertation explored interpersonal factors, it was done in relation to other peer assessment features; we will not explore them further here. The fifth study (Rotsaert et al., 2018c) explored anonymity effects, finding that there were no differences in the peer feedback quality in the anonymous phase as compared with the nonanonymous one. Additionally, the third study (Rotsaert, 2017) found that students preferred nonanonymous teacher feedback. With all this in mind we want to bring forward an important reflection and leave the reader with it:

> the use of anonymity has to be considered carefully in terms of the learning benefits, if any, that it could produce (i.e., while anonymity may help assessors focus more on the content than the person who created the work, potentially decreasing bias, it is unknown if feedback written anonymously without much consideration of the recipient is as effective at connecting with the person and inspiring appropriate action to improve).   (Panadero, 2016, pp. 262–263)

Effects of Peer Feedback on Achievement

A limited number of studies has explored whether implementing peer feedback has an effect on students' performance. The results from the abovementioned dissertations are mixed. One study showed no effects of peer feedback intervention on performance (Gielen, Peeters et al., 2010). Two studies reported that it was the effect of peer feedback practice that enhanced performance rather than the scaffolding itself (Gielen & De Wever, 2012, 2015c). Finally, one study illustrated differential effects of the quality of the peer solution provided on their comprehension of the mathematical proof (Alqassab, 2016). Other studies have also found support for peer feedback effects on students' performance (e.g., Cho, Cho, & Hacker, 2010; Cho & MacArthur, 2010). Li, Liu, and Steckelberg (2010) found that the quality of the feedback provided by the assessor increased students' performance. This relationship was not found when the quality of feedback received by the assessee was explored. In this case, providing feedback (i.e., being an assessor) had a positive effect that receiving (i.e., being an assessee) had not. Therefore, it seems that peer feedback has a positive effect on achievement amplified by practicing peer feedback provision[4] and adequately implemented interventions.

Conclusions

In this chapter, we performed a thematic review of the field that is growing exponentially, as shown by the five dissertations' publication dates. Peer feedback is a field that is promising for enhancing students' achievement, as providing effective feedback can be of benefit to both the provider and the

---

4 Though probably peer feedback reception also benefits from practice, there is not solid empirical evidence yet. More attention needs to be paid by future research.

receiver of feedback. From the seven identified themes, a number of conclusions can be drawn. First, studies demonstrate that peer feedback can be of similar quality to teachers' feedback because it includes features that are not present in teachers' feedback. Peer feedback covers innovative aspects and is written in an easier language and by a nonexpert who faces the same challenges. Second, peer feedback quality can be enhanced by scaffolding interventions (e.g., scripting the steps for an assessor), even though these interventions have not been always successful and future work is needed on when and how they work. Third, as proposed here, the domain knowledge should be considered using a developmental skill approach, in which students are given several opportunities for practice (Panadero et al., 2016). This approach has shown to be effective in providing better-quality peer feedback as the effect of practice does make a difference in the existing literature. Fourth, areas that need more attention are the role of beliefs and emotions on peer feedback content, social aspects of peer feedback, and disentangling the effects of anonymity. For these research purposes, peer feedback could benefit from the growing body of knowledge from peer assessment literature and the existent empirical reviews (e.g., van Gennip et al., 2009; Panadero, 2016). Fifth, there is a significant number of studies on students' perceptions of peer feedback. While this research has important implications, it would be crucial to incorporate more objective measures of peer feedback impact that do not just ask for students' perceptions to move the field forward. Finally, and most importantly, the research shows that peer feedback does not per se have an effect on students' achievement and that the conditions for its implementation are crucial to obtain positive outcomes. In conclusion, it is clear that we have achieved some promising results in the incipient peer feedback research. Now is the time to increase our knowledge on peer feedback to determine key variables that affect its efficacy or, simply put, to understand when, how, and for whom it works.

References

Alqassab, M. (2016). Peer feedback provision and mathematical proofs: Role of domain knowledge, beliefs, perceptions, epistemic emotions, and peer feedback content. Doctoral thesis, Ludwig-Maximilians University.

Black, P., & Wiliam, D. (1998). Assessment and classroom learning. *Assessment in Education: Principles, Policy and Practice, 5*, 7–73.

Brown, G. T. L., & Harris, L. R. (2013). Student self-assessment. In J. McMillan (Ed.), *The SAGE handbook of research on classroom assessment* (pp. 367–393). Thousand Oaks, CA: SAGE.

Chesney, S., & Marcangelo, C. (2010). "There was a lot of learning going on": Using a digital medium to support learning in a professional course for new HE lecturers. *Computers & Education, 54*, 701–708.

Cho, K., Cho, M., & Hacker, D. J. (2010). Self-monitoring support for learning to write. *Interactive Learning Environments, 18*(2), 101–113.

Cho, K., Chung, T. R., King, W. R., & Schunn, C. D. (2008). Peer-based computer-supported knowledge refinement: An empirical investigation. *Communications of the ACM, 51*(3), 83–88.

Cho, K., & MacArthur, C. A. (2010). Student revision with peer and expert reviewing. *Learning and Instruction, 20*, 328–338.

Cho, K., Schunn, C. D., & Charney, D. (2006). Commenting on writing. *Written Communication, 23*, 260–294.

Dochy, F., Segers, M., & Sluijsmans, D. (1999). The use of self-, peer- and co-assessment in higher education: A review. *Studies in Higher Education, 24*, 331–350.

Falchikov, N. (2007). The place of peers in learning and assessment. In D. Boud & N. Falchikov (Eds.), *Rethinking assessment for higher education: Learning for the longer term* (pp. 128–143). London: Routledge.

Falchikov, N., & Boud, D. (1989). Student self-assessment in higher education: A meta-analysis. *Review of Educational Research, 59*, 395–430.

Falchikov, N., & Goldfinch, J. (2000). Student peer assessment in higher education: A meta-analysis comparing peer and teacher marks. *Review of Educational Research, 70*, 287–322.

Gan, J. S. M. (2011). The effects of prompts and explicit coaching on peer feedback quality. Doctoral thesis, University of Auckland.

Gan, M. J. S., & Hattie, J. (2014). Prompting secondary students' use of criteria, feedback specificity and feedback levels during an investigative task. *Instructional Science, 42*, 861–878.

Gan, M. J. S., & Hill, M. (2014). Using a dialogical approach to examine peer feedback during chemistry investigative task discussion. *Research in Science Education, 44*, 727–749.

Ge, X., & Land, S. M. (2003). Scaffolding students' problem-solving processes in an ill-structured task using question prompts and peer interactions. *Educational Technology Research and Development, 51*, 21–38.

Gielen, M. (2016). The impact of structuring peer feedback in a wiki-based CSCL environment on performance and feedback content. Dissertation, Faculty of Psychology and Educational Sciences, Ghent University.

Gielen, M., & De Wever, B. (2012). Peer assessment in a wiki: Product improvement, students' learning and perception regarding peer feedback. *Procedia – Social and Behavioral Sciences, 69*, 585–594.

Gielen, M., & De Wever, B. (2015a). Structuring the peer assessment process: A multilevel approach for the impact on product improvement and peer feedback quality. *Journal of Computer Assisted Learning, 31*, 435–449.

Gielen, M., & De Wever, B. (2015b). Structuring peer assessment: Comparing the impact of the degree of structure on peer feedback content. *Computers in Human Behavior, 52*, 315–325.

Gielen, M., & De Wever, B. (2015c). Scripting the role of assessor and assessee in peer assessment in a wiki environment: Impact on peer feedback quality and product improvement. *Computers & Education, 88*, 370–386.

Gielen, S. (2007). Peer assessment as a tool for learning. Doctoral thesis, University of Leuven.

Gielen, S., Dochy, F., & Dierick, S. (2003). Evaluating the consequential validity of new modes of assessment: The influence of assessment on learning, including pre-, post-, and true assessment effects. In M. Segers, F. Dochy, & E. Cascallar (Eds.), *Optimising new modes of assessment: In search of qualities and standards* (pp. 37–54). Dordrecht: Springer Netherlands.

Gielen, S., Dochy, F., & Onghena, P. (2011). An inventory of peer assessment diversity. *Assessment & Evaluation in Higher Education, 36,* 137–155.

Gielen, S., Dochy, F., Onghena, P., Janssens, S., Schelfhout, W., & Decuyper, S. (2007). A complementary role for peer feedback and staff feedback in powerful learning environments. Manuscript submitted for publication.

Gielen, S., Dochy, F., Onghena, P., Struyven, K., & Smeets, S. (2011). Goals of peer assessment and their associated quality concepts. *Studies in Higher Education, 36,* 719–735.

Gielen, S., Peeters, E., Dochy, F., Onghena, P., & Struyven, K. (2010). Improving the effectiveness of peer feedback for learning. *Learning and Instruction, 20,* 304–315.

Gielen, S., Tops, L., Dochy, F., Onghena, P., & Smeets, S. (2010). Peer feedback as a substitute for teacher feedback. Manuscript submitted for publication.

Gikandi, J. W., & Morrow, D. (2016). Designing and implementing peer formative feedback within online learning environments. *Technology, Pedagogy and Education, 25,* 153–170.

Hattie, J., & Gan, M. (2011). Instruction based on feedback. In R. E. Mayer & P. A. Alexander (Eds.), *Handbook of research on learning and instruction* (pp. 249–271). New York: Routledge.

Hattie, J., & Timperley, H. (2007). The power of feedback. *Review of Educational Research, 77,* 81–112.

Kluger, A. N., & DeNisi, A. (1996). The effects of feedback interventions on performance: A historical review, a meta-analysis, and a preliminary feedback intervention theory. *Psychological Bulletin, 119,* 254–284.

Li, L., Liu, X., & Steckelberg, A. L. (2010). Assessor or assessee: How student learning improves by giving and receiving peer feedback. *British Journal of Educational Technology, 41,* 525–536.

Lipnevich, A. A., Berg, D. A. G., & Smith, J. K. (2016). Toward a model of student response to feedback. In G. T. L. Brown & L. R. Harris (Eds.), *Handbook of human and social conditions in assessment* (pp. 169–185). New York: Routledge.

Lin, S. S. J., Liu, E. Z. F., & Yuan, S. M. (2002). Student attitudes toward networked peer assessment: Case studies of undergraduate students and senior high school students. *International Journal of Instructional Media, 29,* 241–254.

Liu, N. F., & Carless, D. (2006). Peer feedback: The learning element of peer assessment. *Teaching in Higher Education, 11,* 279–290.

McCarthy, J. M. (2016). Global learning partnerships in the café: Peer feedback as a formative assessment tool for animation students. *Interactive Learning Environments, 24,* 1298–1318.

Messick, S. (1998). Test validity: A matter of consequence. *Social Indicators Research, 45,* 35–44.

Narciss, S., & Huth, K. (2004). How to design informative tutoring feedback for multimedia learning. In H. M. Niegemann, R. Brünken, & D. Leutner (Eds.), *Instructional design for multimedia learning. Proceedings of the 5th International Workshop of SIG 6 Instructional Design of the European Association for Research on Learning and Instruction (EARLI)* (pp. 181–195). Münster: Waxmann.

Panadero, E. (2016). Is it safe? Social, interpersonal, and human effects of peer assessment: A review and future directions. In G. T. L. Brown & L. R. Harris (Eds.), *Handbook of human and social conditions in assessment* (pp. 247–266). New York: Routledge.

Panadero, E., & Brown, G. T. L. (2017). Teachers' reasons for using peer assessment: Positive experience predicts use. *European Journal of Psychology of Education, 32*, 133–156.

Panadero, E., Brown, G. T. L., & Strijbos, J. W. (2016). The future of student self-assessment: A review of known unknowns and potential directions. *Educational Psychology Review, 28*, 803–830.

Panadero, E., Jonsson, A., & Botella, J. (2017). Effects of self-assessment on self-regulated learning and self-efficacy: Four meta-analyses. *Educational Research Review, 22*, 74–98.

Panadero, E., Jonsson, A., & Strijbos, J. W. (2016). Scaffolding self-regulated learning through self-assessment and peer assessment: Guidelines for classroom implementation. In D. Laveault & L. Allal (Eds.), *Assessment for learning: Meeting the challenge of implementation* (pp. 311–326). New York: Springer.

Panadero, E., Romero, M., & Strijbos, J. W. (2013). The impact of a rubric and friendship on construct validity of peer assessment, perceived fairness and comfort, and performance. *Studies in Educational Evaluation, 39*, 195–203.

Patchan, M. M., Hawk, B., Stevens, C. A., & Schunn, C. D. (2013). The effects of skill diversity on commenting and revisions. *Instructional Science, 41*, 381–405.

Patchan, M. M., & Schunn, C. D. (2015). Understanding the benefits of providing peer feedback: How students respond to peers' texts of varying quality. *Instructional Science, 43*, 591–614.

Paulus, T. M. (1999). The effect of peer and teacher feedback on student writing. *Journal of Second Language Writing, 8*, 265–289.

Rotsaert, T. (2017). The social nature of peer assessment in secondary and higher education: Examining students' perceptions on interpersonal processes and peer feedback quality in anonymous face-to-face settings using mobile response technology. Doctoral thesis, Ghent University.

Rotsaert, T., Panadero, E., Estrada, E., & Schellens, T. (2017). How do students perceive the educational value of peer assessment in relation to its social nature? A survey study in Flanders. *Studies in Educational Evaluation, 53*, 29–40.

Rotsaert, T., Panadero, E., Schellens, T., & Raes, A. (2018a). "Now you know what you're doing right and wrong!" Peer feedback quality in synchronous peer assessment in secondary education. *European Journal of Psychology of Education, 33*(2), 255–275. doi:10.1007/s10212-017-0329-x

Rotsaert, T., Panadero, E., & Schellens, T. (2018b). Peer assessment use, its social nature challenges and perceived educational value: a teachers' survey study. Accepted for publication in Studies in Educational Evaluation.

Rotsaert, T., Panadero, E., & Schellens, T. (2018c). Anonymity as an instructional scaffold in peer assessment: Its effects on peer feedback quality and evolution in students' perceptions about peer assessment skills. *European Journal of Psychology of Education, 33*, 75–99. doi:10.1007/s10212-017-0339-8

Shute, V. J. (2008). Focus on formative feedback. *Review of Educational Research, 78*, 153–189.

Sluijsmans, D. M. A., Brand-Gruwel, S., & van Merriënboer, J. J. G. (2002). Peer assessment training in teacher education: Effects on performance and perceptions. *Assessment & Evaluation in Higher Education, 27*, 443–454.

Sluijsmans, D. M. A., Brand-Gruwel, S., van Merriënboer, J. J. G., & Martens, R. L. (2004). Training teachers in peer-assessment skills: Effects on performance and perceptions. *Innovations in Education and Teaching International, 41*, 59–78.

Strijbos, J. W., & Müller, A. (2014). Personale faktoren im feedbackprozess. In H. Ditton & A. Müller (Eds.), *Feedback und rückmeldungen: Theoretische grundlagen, empirische befunde, praktische anwendungsfelder [Feedback and evaluation: Theoretical foundations, empirical findings, practical implementation]* (pp. 87–134). Münster: Waxmann.

Strijbos, J. W., Narciss, S., & Dünnebier, K. (2010). Peer feedback content and sender's competence level in academic writing revision tasks: Are they critical for feedback perceptions and efficiency? *Learning and Instruction, 20*, 291–303.

Strijbos, J. W., Ochoa, T. A., Sluijsmans, D. M. A., Segers, M., & Tillema, H. H. (2009). Fostering interactivity through formative peer assessment in (web-based) collaborative learning environments. In C. Mourlas, N. Tsianos, & P. Germanakos (Eds.), *Cognitive and emotional processes in web-based education: Integrating human factors and personalization* (pp. 375–395). Hersey, PA: IGI Global.

Strijbos, J. W., & Sluijsmans, D. (2010). Unravelling peer assessment: Methodological, functional, and conceptual developments. *Learning and Instruction, 20*(4), 265–269.

Topping, K. J. (1998). Peer assessment between students in colleges and universities. *Review of Educational Research, 68*, 249–276.

van Gennip, N. (2012). Assessing together: Peer assessment from an interpersonal perspective. Doctoral thesis, Universiteit Leiden.

van Gennip, N., Segers, M., & Tillema, H. H. (2009). Peer assessment for learning from a social perspective: The influence of interpersonal variables and structural features. *Educational Research Review, 4*, 41–54.

van Gennip, N., Segers, M., & Tillema, H. H. (2010). Peer assessment as a collaborative learning activity: The role of interpersonal variables and conceptions. *Learning and Instruction, 20*, 280–290.

van Zundert, M. (2012). Conditions of peer assessment for complex learning. Doctoral thesis, Maastrich University.

van Zundert, M., Sluijsmans, D. M. A., Könings, K. D., & van Merriënboer, J. J. G. (2012). The differential effects of task complexity on domain-specific and peer assessment skills. *Educational Psychology: An International Journal of Experimental Educational Psychology, 32*, 127–145.

van Zundert, M., Sluijsmans, D., & van Merriënboer, J. (2010). Effective peer assessment processes: Research findings and future directions. *Learning and Instruction, 20*, 270–279.

Wiliam, D. (2011). What is assessment for learning? *Studies in Educational Evaluation, 37*, 3–14.

Yan, Z., & Brown, G. T. L. (2016). A cyclical self-assessment process: Towards a model of how students engage in self-assessment. *Assessment & Evaluation in Higher Education*, 1–16.

19 Feedback, Correctives, and the Use of Pre-Assessments

Thomas R. Guskey

The most significant advances in education today all build on ideas and principles developed by earlier scholars and researchers. As Sir Isaac Newton reminded us in the seventeenth century, we "stand on the shoulders of giants." Too often in education, however, we fail to acknowledge the contribution of the true giants on whose work we build. Instead, we reinvent or rename the principles they developed and then take credit for creating them (Guskey & DeWitt, 2017). This seems to be particularly true in the case of the feedback aspects of classroom formative assessments.

Most educators today recognize the importance of classroom formative assessments. They understand how assessments *for* learning can be used to improve a wide variety of student learning outcomes. But many of those same educators think that using assessments as learning tools, rather than simply as evaluation devices that mark the end of instruction, is a relatively new idea. They believe the powerful effects of classroom formative assessments on student learning have been recognized for only a couple of decades, perhaps dating back to the work of Black and Wiliam (1998).

The truth of the matter is that the value of formative assessments was identified nearly five decades ago by a true giant in the field of education. In his seminal 1968 article, *Learning for Mastery*, Benjamin Bloom described the benefits of offering students regular feedback on their learning progress through classroom formative assessments. Bloom went on to outline specific strategies teachers could use to implement formative assessments as part of regular classroom routines, both to improve student learning and to reduce achievement gaps among different subgroups of students (Bloom, 1971a). It was Bloom who introduced the term "formative" assessment to education and provided practical guidance on how teachers could use these learning tools in modern classrooms (Guskey, 2007a, 2012).

In this chapter we will explore the contribution of Benjamin Bloom, and particularly his work on classroom formative assessments, through the instructional strategies he labeled "mastery learning." We will then review the application of Bloom's theory and consider the vital nature of both feedback and correctives in the formative assessment process. In a volume dedicated to examining all facets of instructional feedback, it is essential we go back to its roots and consider the thinking of those who introduced these ideas to our field. Benjamin Bloom described all the things that are critical to us today: making expectations clear, using assessment data *for* learning, and developing an instructional model (i.e., mastery learning) dedicated to the notion of closing gaps in learning (Guskey, 2007b). In addition to this review, we will revisit and reexamine the use of pre-assessments in classroom instruction.

The Contribution of Benjamin S. Bloom

In the 1960s, Benjamin Bloom and his graduate students at the University of Chicago were engaged in a series of studies on individual differences in school learning. Although significant evidence showed that many factors outside school affect how well students learn (see Bloom, 1964), Bloom was convinced that teachers have potentially strong influence as well.

While observing classrooms, Bloom noted that most teachers teach in very similar ways. He found the majority of teachers engage all students in the same instructional activities and offer all the same amount of time to learn. Students for whom these instructional methods and time are ideal learn excellently. The largest number of students finds these methods and time only moderately appropriate and learn less well. Students for whom the instruction and time are inappropriate due to differences in their backgrounds or previous learning experiences tend to learn very little. In other words, little variation in teaching results in great variation in student learning. Under these conditions, the pattern of student achievement typically resembles a normal, bell-shaped curve distribution.

To attain better results and *reduce* the variation in student achievement, Bloom reasoned that teachers would have to *increase* variation in their teaching. Because students vary in their aptitudes and preferred approaches to learning, Bloom suggested that educators differentiate instruction to better meet students' individual learning needs. The challenge was to find practical ways to do this within group-based classrooms so that *all* students learn well.

In searching for such a strategy, Bloom considered two different sources of evidence. First, he explored research on the ideal teaching and learning situation where an excellent tutor is paired with each student. Bloom was particularly impressed by the work of early pioneers in individualized instruction, especially Washburne (1922) and his Winnetka Plan, and Morrison (1926) and his University of Chicago Laboratory School experiments. In examining this evidence, Bloom tried to determine what critical elements in one-to-one tutoring and individualized instruction could be applied in group-based classroom settings.

Second, Bloom looked at studies of the learning strategies of academically successful students, particularly the work of Dollard and Miller (1950). From this research he tried to identify the activities of high-achieving students in group-based classrooms that distinguish them from their less successful classmates.

Bloom saw the utility of teachers' traditional practice of organizing the concepts and skills to be learned into instructional units. He believed this offered students a valuable framework for organizing their learning. He also thought it vital for teachers to assess student learning at the end of each instructional unit. But to Bloom, most teachers' classroom assessments did little more than verify for whom their initial instruction was and was not appropriate.

A far better approach, according to Bloom, would be for teachers to use their classroom assessments as *learning tools*, both to provide students with *feedback* on their learning progress and to guide the *correction* of learning errors. In other words, instead of using assessments only as evaluation devices that mark the end of a unit, Bloom recommended they be used as an integral part of the instructional process to *identify* individual learning difficulties and to *prescribe* remediation procedures.

This is precisely what takes place when an excellent tutor works with an individual student. If the student makes an error, the tutor first points out the error (feedback) and then offers further explanation and clarification (correctives) to ensure the student's understanding. Similarly, academically successful students typically follow up the mistakes they make on quizzes and assessments. They ask the teacher about the items they missed, search for answers using various resources, or rework problems or tasks so that they do not repeat those errors.

Bloom's Mastery Learning

Benjamin Bloom then outlined a specific instructional strategy to make use of this feedback and corrective procedure, labeling it "learning for mastery" (Bloom, 1968), and later shortening the name to simply "mastery learning" (Bloom, 1971b). To use mastery learning, teachers first organize the concepts and skills they want students to learn into instructional units that typically involve approximately a week or two of instructional time. Following initial instruction on the unit, Bloom suggested teachers administer a brief "formative" assessment based on the unit's learning goals. "Formative" means simply "to provide information" or "to inform." Bloom borrowed the term "formative" from Michael Scriven (1967), who used it to describe program evaluation activities performed *during* the implementation of a program in order to inform developers of potential problems. Similarly in classrooms, rather than signifying the end of the unit, a formative assessment is part of the instructional process within the unit, designed to give students information, or "feedback," on their learning. It helps students identify what they have learned well to that point and what they need to learn better (Bloom, Hastings, & Madaus, 1971; Bloom, Madaus, & Hastings, 1981). Careful inspection of the items missed or the criteria not met on a well-constructed formative assessment shows students precisely where they need to focus their attention in order to meet the learning goals and achieve success. It also helps teachers identify where their instruction was effective in helping students learn and where new methods or an alternative approach may be needed.

Bloom believed that classroom formative assessments could closely resemble the performance checks or unit quizzes that teachers typically administer after a week or two of instruction, so long as those checks or quizzes closely align with the specified student learning goals. This view differs from some current interpretations of formative assessments, however, which offer a much broader definition.

Several recent authors describe formative assessments as also including "in-the-moment" checks, such as having students write answers on small whiteboards and hold them up, so the teacher can determine students' current level of understanding, or use electronic clickers that gather instant data on questions posed to the class by the teacher (Black & Wiliam, 1998; Leahy, Lyon, Thompson, & Wiliam, 2005). Bloom referred to these in-the-moment observations as "checking for understanding" (Bloom, 1971b) and stressed they are a vital part of teacher-directed learning activities. They allow teachers to adapt their instruction during lessons to determine which concepts are understood by students and which need further explanation.

But while these quick checks can be valuable instructional tools, Bloom envisioned formative assessments to be more formal examinations of the learning goals specified for an instructional unit. More than a single question or prompt, Bloom saw formative assessments in their various forms as providing evidence on the broader learning goals, crucial understandings, and higher-level skills students are expected to achieve from the collection of lessons that make up an instructional unit.

To improve student learning, Bloom further stressed that the feedback gain from formative assessments must be paired with specific "corrective" activities that help students remedy identified learning difficulties. The correctives are typically matched to each item or set of prompts within the assessment so that students need work on only those concepts or skills not yet mastered. In other words, the correctives are "individualized." They may point out sources of information on a particular concept, such websites, books, or workbooks where that concept is discussed. They may identify alternative learning resources such as learning kits, instructional materials, videos, or computerized instructional lessons. Or they may simply suggest sources of additional practice, such as study guides, independent or guided practice activities, or collaborative group activities (Guskey, 2008).

Bloom emphasized, however, that correctives will be effective *only* if they are qualitatively different from the original instruction. Having students repeat a process that has already proven unsuccessful is unlikely to yield any better results the second time around. Effective corrective activities provide students with alternative pathways to learning success, adapted to meet their individual learning needs and interests (see Duffy & Kear, 2007).

With the feedback and corrective information gained from a formative assessment, each student has a detailed prescription of what more needs to be done to master the concepts or skills from the unit. This "just-in-time" correction prevents minor learning difficulties from accumulating and becoming major learning problems. It also gives teachers a practical means to vary and differentiate their instruction in order to better meet students' individual learning needs. As a result, more students will learn well, master the important learning goals in each unit, and gain the necessary prerequisites for success in subsequent units.

When students complete their corrective work after a class period or two, Bloom recommended they take a *second* formative assessment. This second, "parallel" assessment covers the same concepts and skills as the first, but includes slightly different problems, questions, or prompts. As such, it serves two important purposes. First, it verifies whether or not the correctives truly helped students overcome their individual learning difficulties. Second, it offers students a second chance at success and, hence, has powerful motivational value.

Bloom also recognized that some students are likely to perform well on the first formative assessment, demonstrating their mastery of the unit concepts and skills. For these students, the teacher's initial instruction was highly appropriate, and they have no need for corrective work. To ensure their continued learning progress, Bloom recommended that teachers provide these students with special "enrichment" or "extension" activities to broaden their learning experiences. Enrichment activities often are self-selected by students and might involve special projects or reports, academic games, or a variety of complex but engaging problem-solving tasks. Figure 19.1 illustrates Bloom's mastery learning instructional sequence.

Through this process of regular classroom formative assessments designed to offer both students and teachers specific feedback on learning progress, combined with the correction of individual learning errors, Bloom believed all students could be provided with a more appropriate quality of instruction than is possible under more traditional approaches to teaching. As a result, nearly all might be expected to learn well and truly master the unit concepts or learning goals (Bloom, 1976, 1977). This, in turn, would drastically reduce the variation in students' achievement levels, eliminate achievement gaps, and help nearly all students learn excellently (Bloom, 1978, 1981).

In all of his descriptions of mastery learning, however, Bloom emphasized that reducing variation in students' achievement does not imply making all students the same. Even under these more favorable learning conditions, some students undoubtedly will learn more than others, especially those involved in

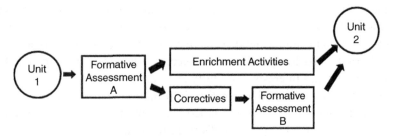

Figure 19.1 *The mastery learning instructional process.*

enrichment activities. But by recognizing relevant, individual differences among students and then adapting instruction to better meet these diverse learning needs, Bloom believed the variation among students in how well they learn specific concepts or master a set of well-articulated learning goals could eventually reach a "vanishing point" (Bloom, 1971a). In other words, *all* students would be helped to learn well the knowledge and skills prescribed in the curriculum. As a result, gaps in the achievement of different groups of students would be closed (see Guskey, 2007b).

Essential Elements of Mastery Learning

After Benjamin Bloom described his ideas, numerous programs based on mastery learning principles sprung up in schools throughout the United States and around the world. Although varying significantly from setting to setting, the programs true to Bloom's ideas maintained his emphasis of three essential elements: *feedback*, *corrective*, and *enrichment* (Guskey, 1997).

Teachers who use mastery learning provide students with frequent and specific *feedback* on their learning progress through regular classroom formative assessments. This feedback is both diagnostic and prescriptive (Hattie & Timperley, 2007). It reinforces precisely what students were expected to learn, identifies what they learned well, and describes what needs to be learned better (Guskey, 2003). By reviewing the questions they answered incorrectly or the criteria they did not meet, students gain individualized information about their learning progress. In other words, the feedback they receive is item or criterion specific. Two students might attain exactly the same score on the formative assessment and yet receive very different feedback depending on the items or criterion missed. As a result, the steps they take to remedy those problems might differ as well.

Likewise, by analyzing the items most frequently answered incorrectly or the criteria most frequently missed, teachers gain highly specific information about the effectiveness of their original instruction. They know precisely what skills or concepts were taught well and which ones might require a different approach. In this way, classroom formative assessments not only help students improve their learning; they also help teachers improve the quality of their instructional strategies. The research of Smith, Smith, and DeLisi (2001); Ainsworth and Viegut (2006); and Stiggins (2008) similarly emphasizes the vital nature of feedback from assessments *for* learning.

By itself, however, the feedback offered through regular classroom formative assessments does little to improve student learning. In other words, *formative assessments alone yield little if any improvement*. Regardless of their form, structure, or quality, formative assessments simply measure student learning – they do not improve it. Measuring something more often and more accurately does nothing to make it better. If that were the case, then all that would be required in a successful weight-loss program would be a better scale. Clearly, that is not enough. Just as being weighed more often and more accurately does not help a person lose weight, the use of regular classroom formative assessment alone does not improve student learning. It is what happens *after* the formative assessment that makes the difference.

Significant improvement requires the feedback gained from a formative assessment to be paired with *correctives*: activities that offer guidance and direction to students on how to remedy their learning problems (Guskey, 2008). Because of individual differences among students, no single method of instruction works best for all. To help every student learn well, therefore, teachers must differentiate their instruction, both in the initial teaching and especially through the corrective activities (Bloom, 1976). In other words, to *decrease* variation in results, teachers must *increase* variation in their teaching.

Effective corrective activities possess three essential characteristics (see Guskey, 1997). First, they *present the concepts differently.* For example, if a language arts unit initially taught the use of metaphors in poetry with a deductive approach (presenting the general concept and then giving specific examples), the corrective activity might use an inductive approach (presenting a variety of specific examples and building an understanding of the general concept from these examples). The best corrective activities involve a change in format, organization, or method of presentation.

Second, effective corrective activities *engage students differently in learning.* They consider different learning preferences or modalities (Sternberg, 1994; Lawrence, 1997; Given, 2000) or different forms of intelligence (Armstrong, 2000; Silver, Strong, & Perini, 2000; Gardner, 2006). If science students initially learned about cell structure through a group activity, for example, a good corrective might involve an individual activity, such as reviewing an informative website and then using the computer to write and illustrate a report. If students originally learned the events of the American Revolutionary War in social studies by reading passages in their textbook and studying maps and charts (linguistic and visual intelligences), a useful corrective might employ a group discussion of the events (auditory learning style and interpersonal intelligence). To make a corrective strategy effective, students' engagement in learning must be qualitatively different from what took place during the initial instruction.

Finally, effective corrective activities *provide students with successful learning experiences.* If an activity does not help students overcome their learning difficulties and experience success, the teacher should abandon it for another option. Corrective experiences should make students better prepared, more confident, and more motivated for future learning tasks.

The best ideas for effective corrective activities generally come from fellow teachers. Teaching colleagues often can offer new ways of presenting concepts, different examples, and alternative materials. Professional development opportunities that provide teachers with time for such sharing reduce the workload of individual teachers and typically yield higher-quality activities (Guskey, 1998, 2000, 2001). Faculty meetings devoted to examining classroom formative assessment results and developing corrective strategies also work well. Such meetings might involve district-level personnel or content experts from local colleges and universities.

On any given classroom formative assessment, some students will demonstrate their mastery of unit concepts and skills on the first try and have no need for corrective activities. Rather than sitting around, biding their time while other students engage in corrective work, these students need opportunities to extend their learning through *enrichment* or *extension* activities.

Effective enrichment activities provide students with valuable, challenging, and rewarding learning experiences. As described earlier, enrichment activities offer students opportunities to broaden and expand their learning. They reward students for their learning success and challenge them to go further. If students see enrichment as busy work or as simply more, harder tasks, however, they will have no incentive to perform well on formative assessments. So rather than narrowly restricted to the content of specific instructional units, enrichment activities should be broadly construed to cover a wide range of related topics.

Students also should have some degree of choice in selecting enrichments. For example, if a particular student has special interest in some aspect of the subject, using enrichment time to prepare a report on that topic not only provides a unique learning opportunity but also enhances this student's motivation to do well in subsequent formative assessments so that he or she can return to working on the report. Other examples of enrichment include advanced learning activities designed for creative expression, challenging academic games and exercises, various multimedia projects, and serving as a peer tutor for a classmate.

Some creative teachers find it easy to develop different types of enrichment activities for their students. Others struggle to create such learning experiences. Besides consulting with colleagues, many teachers turn to materials designed for gifted and talented students as their primary resource for enrichment. Certain publishers focus specifically on activities that genuinely extend students' learning by involving them in higher-order skills (e.g., Critical Thinking Press & Software in Pacific Grove, CA; Dale Seymour Publications in Palo Alto, CA; and Thinking Works in St. Augustine, FL). Further, the game-like nature of many of these activities motivates students to want to take part. Most teachers use class time in early instructional units to engage all students in enrichment activities, both to encourage participation and to enhance students' motivation on future formative assessments.

Feedback, corrective, and enrichment procedures are crucial to mastery learning, for it is through these procedures that mastery learning differentiates and individualizes instruction. In every instructional unit, students who need extended time and opportunity to remedy learning problems receive these through the correctives. Students who learn quickly and find the initial instruction highly appropriate have opportunities to extend their learning through enrichment. As a result, all students experience more favorable learning conditions and more appropriate, higher-quality instruction (Bloom, 1977). Similar elements provide the foundation for developing instructional approaches including differentiated instruction (Tomlinson, 2003) and understanding by design (Wiggins & McTighe, 2005).

Feedback through Pre-Assessments

Although Benjamin Bloom was the first to describe the importance of offering both students and teachers crucial feedback on learning progress through classroom formative assessments, he paid little attention to the use of pre-assessments as a source of feedback for students or teachers. In later work, Bloom et al. (1981) described the use of "diagnostic pretests and placement tests" to measure students' "cognitive entry behaviors." But due to the typically poor psychometric properties of these instruments, Bloom and his colleagues cautioned teachers against using such assessments on a regular basis. With the current popularity of pre-assessments as tools for instructional planning, however, it is important for us to consider their utility as another source of feedback on student learning.

Practitioners and educational researchers have long debated the benefits of pre-assessments. Advocates claim pre-assessments provide essential data about the knowledge, skills, and dispositions students bring to learning tasks. They contend teachers need this information to plan effective instructional activities (Hockett & Doubet, 2014). Critics counter that most pre-assessments simply confirm what teachers already know – that is, students don't know things they haven't yet been taught. In addition, beginning learning activities with a failure experience for most students, demonstrating how little they know, may instill a negative disposition toward upcoming content. Detractors further assert that little research evidence shows successful teachers consistently use pre-assessments in planning instruction or that the use of pre-assessments leads to improved student learning (Guskey & McTighe, 2016).

What makes this debate all the more confounded are the many nuances of the pre-assessment process. Pre-assessments vary widely in their purpose, form, and content. What works for one purpose in a particular context may not be effective for another purpose or in a different context. To ensure the most appropriate and efficient use of pre-assessments to improve learning for all students, teachers need to understand these differences and their implications for practice.

Theoretical Underpinnings of Pre-Assessments

Interest in pre-assessments has surged in recent years largely because they are considered integral in efforts to personalize learning and differentiate instruction (Tomlinson & Moon, 2013). But the theoretical basis for pre-assessments can be traced to a much earlier time. In his classic book, *Experience and Education*, renowned educational philosopher John Dewey (1938) argued that educators must provide students with learning experiences that are immediately valuable and enable students to contribute to society in meaningful ways. Most traditional approaches to education fail to do this. According to Dewey, this is because they focus exclusively on content rather than on the integration of content and process. But progressive approaches to education also fail, Dewey claimed, because they are too reactionary and emphasize student freedom and choice without really knowing why or how freedom and choice can be most useful in helping students learn.

To move beyond this dichotomy, Dewey stressed that educators must understand the nature of human experience, which he believed is explained by two principles. The first principle is *interaction*, which describes how present experiences arise out of the relationship between the situation and individuals' stored past. In other words, what we learn from a new experience depends a lot on the connection between that experience and our past experiences. The second principle Dewey labeled *continuity*, which states that all experiences are carried forward and influence future experiences. That is, as we change with each new experience, those changes become a part of us and affect how we address the new experiences we encounter in the future.

To provide effective learning interactions, therefore, teachers must find ways to relate learning tasks with students' past experiences. A thoughtfully designed pre-assessment could offer teachers critical insights into the experiences students bring to learning tasks and furnish the basis for planning truly meaningful instruction.

Defining Pre-Assessment

Despite a long history in education, few sources clearly define the meaning of pre-assessment. In fact, the term "pre-assessment" cannot be found in any modern dictionary. The Wikipedia definition states that "pre-assessment" is "a test students can take before a new unit to find out what the students need more instruction on and what they may already know" (see https://en.wikipedia.org/wiki/Pre-assessment). But this definition is problematic. Besides including a cringe-worthy dangling preposition (i.e., "on"), a pre-assessment need not be limited to a "test."

A more accurate (and grammatically correct) definition of pre-assessment would be: "Any means used by teachers to gather information about students prior to instruction." In other words, a pre-assessment might be a formal, pencil-and-paper instrument that asks students questions about certain academic content, much like a typical pre-test. It might even involve having students develop "concept maps" to illustrate their ideas connected to a topic. But a pre-assessment also could be an informal discussion or survey in which teachers ask students about their past experiences with a particular subject. These discussions could take the form of "think-pair-share" or "turn and talk" activities where students share their thoughts and understandings of specific concepts with classmates and the teacher. A pre-assessment also could be a simple "thumbs up/thumbs down" survey where students indicate whether or not they know the answer to the teacher's questions about vocabulary terms or facts that may be needed to begin a particular unit of study.

Research on Pre-Assessments

Surprisingly, research on pre-assessments has been scant, with most studies focusing on the use of pre-assessments for two primary purposes. The first purpose is to identify exceptional learners for placement into alternative instructional programs (Kastner & Gottlieb, 1991; Myles, Ormsbee, & Simpson, 1997). Exceptional learners include especially gifted or talented students who can readily demonstrate their proficiency on the learning goals of an upcoming instructional unit and need to be engaged in other, more challenging learning experiences that extend and enrich their learning. Exceptional learners also include students with learning deficits or disabilities who, given their previous learning history, are unlikely to achieve the learning goals of an upcoming instructional unit. These students need modified learning goals paired with different forms of engagement and alternative instructional strategies (Jenkins & Sekayi, 2016).

The second purpose of pre-assessments in research studies is to establish a baseline of performance from which student growth or learning gain can be gauged (Wagner, Sasser, & DiBiase, 2002; Lazarowitz & Lieb, 2006). This typically requires development of "parallel forms" of assessments that measure the same knowledge and skills at the same level of complexity, but use slightly different questions or prompts. One of the parallel forms is used as a pre-test and administered before instruction begins. A second form is used as the post-test, administered at the completion of instructional activities. Comparing differences in scores between the pre-test and post-test provides an indication of how much students gained and what improvements were made.

One exception to the "parallel forms" approach would be if the learning goals involve the demonstration of a particular skill or set of skills. In that case, identical criteria would be used to judge students' performance both before and after instruction. If the learning goals focused on developing students' skills in oral reading, presenting a persuasive argument in an essay, or shooting basketball free-throws, for example, the same, identical criteria would be used to judge performance both pre- and post-instruction.

Pre-assessments can be designed to measure any type of learning goal, including cognitive, affective, or behavioral goals. Cognitive pre-assessments address achievement or academic goals and focus on what students know and are able to do. They may consider what students can recall, illustrate, or explain. They also may reflect students' ability to transfer or apply what they have learned in new and different contexts. Cognitive pre-assessments are the most common form used in classrooms today.

Affective pre-assessments tap students' attitudes, beliefs, dispositions, or interests. They might consider students' confidence in learning situations, their sense of efficacy, their perceptions of the amount of effort they put into school-work, or the degree to which they see themselves as hard-working and conscientious (Mattern, Sanchez, & Ndum, 2017). Behavioral pre-assessments address physical skills such as the performance of particular athletic proficiencies, dance movements, or playing a musical instrument. They also may assess students' ability to work collaboratively with classmates or demonstrate engagement by actively participating in class discussions. Because each of these types of learning can vary in the level of complexity (see Bloom, Englehart, Furst, Hill, & Krathwohl, 1956; Krathwohl, Bloom, & Masia, 1964; Simpson, 1966), so too can the pre-assessments that measure them.

Forms of Pre-Assessment

Pre-assessments come in three different forms that differ in their purpose, structure, and content. These forms address different questions, provide different information, and are used by teachers in different ways to help student learn. The three forms include: *prerequisite*, *present*, and *preview pre-assessments*.

Prerequisite

Prerequisite pre-assessments focus on what students need to know and be able to do in order to get started. These pre-assessments often measure concepts or skills presented in previous grade levels, courses, or lessons. The prerequisites for understanding the equation of a line in algebra, for example, would include knowledge of the coordinate system along with the concepts of intercept and slope. In other instances, prerequisites may be experiences that teachers might assume all students have had because they plan to build on those experiences in forthcoming lessons or learning activities. To build on students' past experience in teaching personal responsibility, for example, teachers might ask students if they have ever had to care for a family pet or watch over a younger sibling. To better understand students' dispositions about learning, teachers might ask students about their past struggles in learning a new skill or their nervousness in a new and unfamiliar situation.

Present

Present pre-assessments address students' current knowledge, skills, dispositions, and interests. They seek to determine where students are right now and their existing level of skill or understanding. Teachers use this type of pre-assessment when they introduce a new instructional unit by asking students questions such as, "Tell me what you know about . . .," "What have you learned before about . . .?" or "Show me how you do . . .." Present pre-assessments often are used to place students appropriately in an instructional sequence. They also may be used to gather information on students' current attitudes, beliefs, or feelings so that teachers may target specific affective aspects of learning.

Preview

Preview pre-assessments measure the knowledge, skills, and dispositions that make up the learning goals of a forthcoming unit or task. They identify for students what they will be learning and perhaps why it is important. In some cases they also pinpoint specific student misunderstandings or misconceptions that may need to be addressed, although numerous resources are available to help teachers anticipate these (e.g., science misconceptions: http://undsci.berkeley .edu/teaching/misconceptions.php; mathematics misconceptions: www.counton .org/resources/misconceptions/; social studies misconceptions: www.historians .org/publications-and-directories/perspectives-on-history/may-2012/possibilities- of-pedagogy/preparing-history-teachers-to-develop-young-peoples-historical- thinking). Assessments used to measure student growth by comparing pre- and post-test results typically fall into this category. So do the pre-assessments used to determine if some students have already acquired the intended learning goals and can be moved on to more advanced material. These three forms of pre- assessment are illustrated in Figure 19.2.

Prerequisite, present, and preview pre-assessments can be designed to measure any type of learning: cognitive, affective, or behavioral. In addition, differences between these forms of pre-assessment can sometimes be blurred. In certain instances, for example, a present pre-assessment may include several items that measure specific prerequisite knowledge and skills.

Pre-assessments of any of the three forms may involve formal strategies such as an instrument or survey administered to the entire class or informal procedures such as class discussions or cooperative group activities. To use pre-assessments effectively, however, teachers must first determine the purpose and form that will provide the information they most need to plan and guide students in appropriate learning activities.

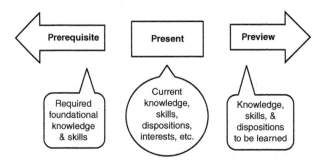

Figure 19.2 *The forms of pre-assessments.*

The Leyton Study

As described earlier, little research evidence currently shows that the regular use of pre-assessments leads to more effective instructional practices or improved student learning. One striking exception, however, is an early study by Leyton (1983), a student of Benjamin Bloom, on the use of prerequisite pre-assessments.

Leyton (1983) wanted to determine if taking time to teach students specific prerequisite skills at the beginning of a course or instructional sequence might influence how well they learn more advanced concepts. To test this idea, he chose high school courses in which prerequisite knowledge and skills crucial to students' success were easily identified. Specifically, he selected second courses in mathematics and foreign languages. The prerequisites for Algebra II, for example, come from Algebra I. The prerequisites for French II come from French I, and so on.

Leyton helped the teachers of these second-level courses in an inner-city school district develop brief pre-assessments to measure students' prerequisite knowledge and skills. Half of the teachers, randomly selected, used the first two weeks of the semester to teach students these prerequisites to a mastery level, while the other half offered only a brief review and began instruction on the new course material as usual. Leyton then helped half of the teachers in each of these groups, randomly selected, to implement mastery learning instructional strategies that included the regular administration of formative assessments follow by individualized corrective activities to help students remedy identified learning difficulties.

This "crossed" design gave Leyton four groups among which to compare results: (1) teachers who did not address prerequisites and taught with traditional methods, (2) teachers who taught the prerequisites but followed with their traditional instructional methods, (3) teachers who did not address the prerequisites but used mastery learning strategies, and (4) teachers who both addressed the prerequisites and implemented mastery learning strategies. To determine the differences among these four groups, Leyton used the percentage of students who achieved a mastery level (i.e., a grade of A or B) on a common course final examination. His results are shown in Figure 19.3.

Leyton's results showed that using pre-assessments to identify and then teach students specific prerequisite skills resulted in 20% more students (8% to 28%) achieving mastery on a comprehensive course exam. Using mastery learning strategies led to a 35% increase (8% to 43%). But when combined, the effects were cumulative. The percentage of students who achieved a mastery level on the comprehensive course examination rose to 61%. Viewed another way, the combination of teaching the prerequisites plus mastery learning resulted in more than *seven times* the number of students reaching the mastery standard than were able to under more traditional methods of instruction.

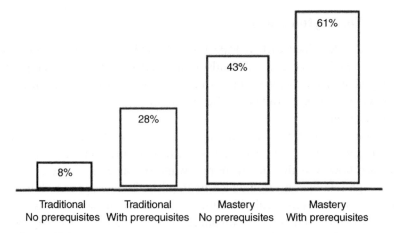

Figure 19.3 *Percentage of students reaching mastery level performance on a comprehensive final examination (from Leyton, 1983).*

Leyton's study was conducted in only a few subject areas and under tightly controlled conditions, so caution is necessary in interpreting the results and in making generalizations. Nevertheless, the findings are extremely promising.

Implications and Summary

Classroom formative assessments offer educators a valuable tool to improve student learning. The regular use of formative assessments helps students identify their individual learning errors so that specific steps can be taken to remedy those difficulties before they accumulate and become major learning problems. Such assessments also help teachers improve the quality of their instruction by identifying the particular concepts and skills their original instruction helped most students attain and those that may need to be revisited and revised. What must always be kept in mind, however, is that simply gathering accurate information on student learning through well-designed classroom formative assessments is not enough. What students and teachers do with that information is what counts.

To realize the true benefits of formative classroom assessments, teachers at all levels need to focus attention on how best to use assessment results to close achievement gaps and help all students learn well. Specifically, they must provide students with alternative pathways to learning success through thoughtfully constructed and carefully managed corrective activities. Engaging students through a mastery learning approach in either diverse corrective activities or exciting and challenging enrichment activities based on their performance on well-designed classroom formative assessments, offers teachers the practical means to accomplish that.

Research on the formative aspects of classroom pre-assessments is more mixed and justifies cautious optimism as well as prudent skepticism

(Guskey & McTighe, 2016). Pre-assessments vary widely in their purpose, form, and content, as does their usefulness in improving the effectiveness of teaching and learning. The benefits and drawbacks of pre-assessments also differ depending on the context. In some settings pre-assessments can guide teachers to more effective instruction and higher levels of student learning, while in others they waste valuable instructional time and simply confirm what teachers already know. In addition, by demonstrating to students how little they know, pre-assessments may even impart in students a negative disposition toward upcoming content.

To use pre-assessments effectively for feedback purposes, teachers must keep in mind the distinction in purpose of prerequisite, present, and preview pre-assessments. Important research evidence supports the use of prerequisite pre-assessments at the beginning of a course or instructional sequence, but only when teachers use results to engage students in learning activities that bring them to a mastery level on specific prerequisite knowledge and skills. The use of short and informal prerequisite pre-assessments at the start of learning units, followed by brief reviews, holds potential but has yet to be thoroughly investigated.

Although students' misconceptions and potential misunderstandings with regard to specific concepts can generally be anticipated (e.g., Wandersee, Mintzes, & Novak, 1994), present pre-assessments could help teachers identify which particular students have these misconceptions. In addition, present pre-assessments may offer teachers valuable information on students' interests, current involvements, and preferred ways of learning that could be useful in designing instructional activities.

Preview pre-assessments provide teachers with the basis for monitoring students' progress and for measuring growth or improvement. They also can help focus students' attention on specific learning goals as well as communicate expectations for students' performance. Teachers must assure students, however, that results are intended to guide learning activities and do not reflect any lack or deficiency on their part.

In summary, a clear focus on individualized corrective activities can help teachers take advantage of the feedback gained from well-designed classroom formative assessments. Careful consideration of the purpose, form, and content of pre-assessments can guide teachers in taking advantage of the potential benefits of the feedback gained from prerequisite, present, and preview pre-assessments, while avoiding potential drawbacks. In combination, these two assessment formats offer teachers powerful tools in their efforts to help all students learn excellently and gain the many benefits of that success.

True giants in the field of education established the groundwork of our knowledge base on effective pre-assessments and classroom formative assessments decades ago. The insights and research evidence they offered provide a solid foundation on which we can build to advance their work. Reinventing their ideas or renaming the principles they developed will not further our cause. Instead, we need to extend their work, add to their ideas in meaningful ways, and find new and better strategies for implementing those ideas in modern classrooms to achieve excellence in learning for all.

References

Ainsworth, L., & Viegut, D. (2006). *Common formative assessments: How to connect standards-based instruction and assessment.* Thousand Oaks, CA: Corwin Press.

Armstrong, T. (2000). *Multiple intelligences in the classroom* (2nd edn.). Alexandria, VA: Association for Supervision and Curriculum Development.

Black, P., & Wiliam, D. (1998). Inside the black box: Raising standards through classroom assessment. *Phi Delta Kappan, 80,* 139–144.

Bloom, B. S. (1964). *Stability and change in human characteristics.* New York: John Wiley & Sons.

Bloom, B. S. (1968). Learning for mastery. *Evaluation Comment (UCLA-CSIEP), 1*(2), 1–12.

Bloom, B. S. (1971a). *Individual differences in school achievement: A vanishing point?* Bloomington, IN: Phi Delta Kappan International.

Bloom, B. S. (1971b). Mastery learning. In J. H. Block (Ed.), *Mastery learning: Theory and practice* (pp. 47–63). New York: Holt, Rinehart & Winston.

Bloom, B. S. (1976). *Human characteristics and school learning.* New York: McGraw-Hill.

Bloom, B. S. (1977). Favorable learning conditions for all. *Teacher, 95*(3), 22–28.

Bloom, B. S. (1978). New views of the learner for instruction and curriculum. *Educational Leadership, 35,* 563–576.

Bloom, B. S. (1981). *All our children learning: A primer for parents, teachers, and other educators.* New York: McGraw-Hill.

Bloom, B. S., Englehart, M. D., Furst, E. J., Hill, W. H., & Krathwohl, D. R. (1956). *Taxonomy of educational objectives, Handbook 1: The cognitive domain.* New York: McKay.

Bloom, B. S., Hastings, J. T., & Madaus, G. (1971). *Handbook on formative and summative evaluation of student learning.* New York: McGraw-Hill.

Bloom, B. S., Madaus, G. F., & Hastings, J. T. (1981). *Evaluation to improve learning.* New York: McGraw-Hill.

Dewey, J. (1938). *Experience and education.* New York: Macmillan.

Dollard, J., & Miller, N. E. (1950). *Personality and psychotherapy.* New York: McGraw-Hill.

Duffy, G. G., & Kear, K. (2007). Compliance or adaptation: What is the real message about research-based practices? *Phi Delta Kappan, 88,* 579–581.

Gardner, H. (2006). *Multiple intelligences: New horizons.* New York: Basic Books.

Given, B. K. (2000). *Learning styles* (rev. edn.). Oceanside, CA: Learning Forum Publications.

Guskey, T. R. (1997). *Implementing mastery learning* (2nd edn.). Belmont, CA: Wadsworth.

Guskey, T. R. (1998). Making time to train your staff. *School Administrator, 55*(7), 35–37.

Guskey, T. R. (2000). *Evaluating professional development.* Thousand Oaks, CA: Corwin.

Guskey, T. R. (2001). Mastery learning. In N. J. Smelser & P. B. Baltes (Eds.), *International encyclopedia of social and behavioral sciences* (pp. 9372–9377). Oxford: Elsevier Science.

Guskey, T. R. (2003). How classroom assessments improve learning. *Educational Leadership, 60*(5), 6–11.

Guskey, T. R. (2007a). Formative classroom assessment and Benjamin S. Bloom: Theory, research, and practice. In J. H. McMillan (Ed.), *Formative classroom assessment: Theory into practice* (pp. 63–78). New York: Teachers College Press.

Guskey, T. R. (2007b). Closing achievement gaps: Revisiting Benjamin S. Bloom's "Learning for Mastery." *Journal of Advanced Academics, 19,* 8–31.

Guskey, T. R. (2008). The rest of the story. *Educational Leadership, 65*(4), 28–35.

Guskey, T. R. (Ed.) (2012). *Benjamin S. Bloom: Portraits of an Educator* (2nd edn.). Lanham, MD: Rowman & Littlefield Education.

Guskey, T. R., & DeWitt, P. (2017, June 1). Why do we recycle and sometimes misuse educational words? *Education Week Blog.* Retrieved from http://blogs.edweek.org/edweek/finding_common_ground/2017/06/educational_words_wh_they_are_recycled_and_sometimes_misused.html.

Guskey, T. R., & McTighe J. (2016). Pre-assessment: Promises and cautions. *Educational Leadership, 73*(7), 38–43.

Hattie, J., & Timperley, H. (2007). The power of feedback. *Review of Educational Research, 77,* 81–112.

Hockett, J. A., & Doubet, K. J. (2014). Turning on the lights: What pre-assessments can do. *Educational Leadership, 71*(4), 50–54.

Jenkins, J. K., & Sekayi, D. (2016, Winter). Teacher perceptions of response to intervention implementation in light of IDEA goals. *Journal of the American Academy of Special Education Professionals,* 66–86.

Kastner, J., & Gottlieb, J. (1991). Classification of children in special education: Importance of pre-assessment information. *Psychology in the Schools, 28,* 19–27.

Krathwohl, D. R., Bloom, B. S., & Masia, B. B. (1964). *Taxonomy of educational objectives, Handbook 2: The affective domain.* New York: McKay.

Lawrence, G. D. (1997). *Looking at type and learning styles.* Gainesville, FL: Center for Applications of Psychological Type.

Lazarowitz, R., & Lieb, C. (2006). Formative assessment pre-test to identify college students' prior knowledge, misconceptions and learning difficulties in biology. *International Journal of Science and Mathematics Education, 4,* 741–762.

Leahy, S., Lyon, C., Thompson, M., & Wiliam, D. (2005). Minute-by-minute and day-by-day. *Educational Leadership, 63*(3), 18–24.

Leyton, F. S. (1983). The extent to which group instruction supplemented by mastery of initial cognitive prerequisites approximates the learning effectiveness of one-to-one tutorial methods. Doctoral dissertation, University of Chicago.

Marzano, R. J. (2017). *The new art and science of teaching.* Bloomington, IN: Solution Tree Press.

Mattern, K., Sanchez, E., & Ndum, E. (2017). Why do achievement measures under-predict female academic performance? *Educational Measurement: Issues and Practice, 36,* 47–57.

Morrison, H. C. (1926). *The practice of teaching in the secondary school.* Chicago, IL: University of Chicago Press.

Myles, B. S., Ormsbee, C. K., & Simpson, R. L. (1997). Reflections on "General and special educators' perceptions of preassessment-related activities and team members." *Exceptionality*, *7*, 193–197.

Pendergrass, E. (2013). Differentiation: It starts with pre-assessment. *Educational Leadership*, *71*(4).

Scriven, M. S. (1967). The methodology of evaluation. In R. W. Tyler, R. M. Gagne, & M. Scriven (Eds.), *Perspectives of curriculum evaluation* (pp. 39–83). Chicago, IL: Rand McNally.

Silver, H. F., Strong, R. W., & Perini, M. J. (2000). *So each may learn: Integrating learning styles and multiple intelligences*. Alexandria, VA: Association for Supervision and Curriculum Development.

Simpson, E. J. (1966). *The classification of educational objectives: Psychomotor domain*. Urbana: University of Illinois.

Smith, J. K., Smith, L. F., & DeLisi, R. (2001). *Natural classroom assessment: Designing seamless instruction and assessment*. Thousand Oaks, CA: Corwin Press.

Sternberg, R. J. (1994). Allowing for thinking styles. *Educational Leadership*, *52*(3), 36–40.

Stiggins, R. (2008). *An introduction to student-involved assessment for learning* (5th edn.). Upper Saddle River, NJ: Merrill, Prentice Hall.

Tomlinson, C. (2003). *Fulfilling the promise of the differentiated classroom: Strategies and tools for responsive teaching*. Alexandria, VA: Association for Supervision and Curriculum Development.

Tomlinson, C. A., & Moon, T. R. (2013). *Assessment and student success in a differentiated classroom*. Alexandria, VA: Association for Supervision and Curriculum Development.

Wagner, E. P., Sasser, H., & DiBiase, W. J. (2002). Predicting students at risk in general chemistry using pre-semester assessments and demographic information. *Journal of Chemical Education*, *79*, 749–755.

Wandersee, J. H., Mintzes, J. J., & Novak, J. D. (1994). Research on alternative conceptions in science. In D. Gabel (Ed.), *Handbook of research in science teaching and learning* (pp. 177–210). New York: Macmillan.

Washburne, C. W. (1922). Educational measurements as a key to individualizing instruction and promotions. *Journal of Educational Research*, *5*, 195–206.

Wiggins, G., & McTighe, J. (2005). *Understanding by design* (2nd edn.). Alexandria, VA: Association for Supervision and Curriculum Development.

20 Teacher Expectations and Feedback Practices in South African Schools

Anil Kanjee

Introduction

Effective feedback is regarded as integral to the teaching and learning process and critical for supporting improvements in learning (Clark, 2003; Hattie & Timperly, 2007; Brookhart, 2008; Engelsen & Smith, 2010; Brown, Harris, & Harnett, 2012; Hattie, 2012; Chan, Konrad, Gonzalez, Peters, & Ressa, 2014). Hattie and Timperley (2007) defined feedback as "information provided by an agent (e.g., teacher, peer, book, parent, self, experience) regarding aspects of one's performance or understanding" (p. 81). Extending this definition to the classroom context, the Education Endowment Foundation (2016) noted that "feedback is information given to the learner and/or the teacher about the learner's performance relative to learning goals. It should aim to (and be capable of) producing improvement in students' learning" (p. 1). The Foundation further stated that feedback can come from learners or teachers and that it can be provided verbally, through written text, and/or through digital technology. Within this context, the primary purpose of providing feedback is to reduce the gap between what the learner currently knows and can do and the desired curriculum learning outcomes.

Research indicates that there are many factors that impact on teacher feedback practices, including the classroom and policy context within which learning and teaching take place, teacher knowledge and understanding of assessment, and teacher beliefs and expectations. In her review of research studies conducted in South Africa, Hoadley (2012) listed the following key factors that describe the average classroom and are associated with improved learning outcomes for students: lack of print material in classrooms, especially textbooks; lack of opportunities for reading and writing; classroom interaction patterns that privilege the collective (chorusing); limited coverage of the curriculum; and weak forms of assessment and lack of feedback on students' responses. Regarding the policy context, Kanjee and Sayed (2013) described the current policies as *"assessment focused and measurement driven"* given the advocacy of formative assessment practices but prescription of formal testing, recording, and reporting. The authors noted that while clear guidelines, time frames, and templates were provided for the number and types of summative assessments (tests, assignments, projects) that teachers must administer across the different subjects and grades, no information is provided on how informal, formative assessment should be conducted.

While the benefits of providing effective feedback to learners are well documented, teachers need to be highly skilled to provide effective feedback given the practical complexities that impact on the teaching and learning process. Hattie and Timperley (2007) noted that teachers are required to have

> high proficiency in developing a classroom climate, the ability to deal with the complexities of multiple judgments, and deep understandings of the subject matter to be ready to provide feedback about tasks or the relationships between ideas, willingness to encourage self-regulation, and having exquisite timing to provide feedback before frustration takes over. (p. 103)

In their review of feedback practices among New Zealand teachers, Irving, Harris, and Peterson (2011) found that teacher feedback practices were largely determined by different understandings of the purpose of feedback, which teachers identified as "improvement," "reporting," "encouragement," and "irrelevance." The authors reported that their data suggested a "large variability in the ways formative assessments were viewed and conducted. These differing conceptions may help to explain the diverse and at times ineffective implementations of AfL [assessment for learning]" (p. 425). In their study on teacher knowledge, capacity, and skill in the effective use of assessment in selected South African schools, Kanjee and Mthembu (2015) found all teachers demonstrated very low levels of formative assessment knowledge. The authors argued that the practical implication of this is that teachers are unable to effectively use assessment to support their learners and, in particular, to provide effective feedback that addresses specific learning needs. Brown et al. (2012) noted that the quality of feedback provided by teachers is also affected by their beliefs about the nature and purpose of feedback. The authors found that the content and timing of the feedback, as well as the reasons and manner in which it is provided, also impacts on the value and use of feedback. Similarly, McDonald et al. (2016) reported that teacher expectations impact on how they engage with learners in the classroom and that teachers with high expectations provide more detail feedback aimed at supporting improvements in learning.

While many studies have been conducted on teacher feedback practices and their impact on learning and learner performance (Clark, 2003; Hattie & Timperly, 2007; Brookhart, 2008; Engelsen & Smith, 2010; Brown et al., 2012; Hattie, 2012; Chan et al., 2014), and a number of studies have been conducted on teacher expectations and their impact on student performance, motivation, and classroom practices (Rubie-Davies, 2014), no information was found on what expectations teachers had when providing (written) feedback to their learners. In addition, limited information was found on teacher (written) feedback practices across developing nations and, in particular, South Africa, where most studies were based on small samples. To address this gap and to obtain information for use in the planning of a capacity development program to enhance teachers' formative assessment knowledge and skills, this chapter focuses on the following key questions in a South African context: (1) What are the different types of feedback that teachers provide to learners? (2) What are teacher expectations when providing the different types of feedback? (3) Are there any differences in feedback practices between teachers in no-fee versus fee-paying schools?

Value and Use of Feedback for Improving Learning

From their research on how effective feedback should be understood and applied in practice, Hattie and Timperley (2007) noted that the primary purpose of effective feedback is to reduce the discrepancy between current and desired understanding, and argued that any strategies applied in this regard must "address three major questions: Where am I going? (What are the goals?), How am I going? (What progress is being made toward the goal?), and Where to next? (What activities need to be undertaken to make better progress?)" (p. 86). Furthermore, the authors contend that the effectiveness of the feedback in addressing learning discrepancies is dependent on the level at which the feedback is provided, that is, level of the task performance, level of process of understanding how to do a task, the regulatory or metacognitive process level, and the self or personal level.

Hargreaves, McCullum, and Gipps (2000) noted that while the form of teacher feedback can be verbal, nonverbal, written, or a combination of these, the content of the feedback could be either evaluative or descriptive. Evaluative feedback refers to teacher judgments about the performance of learners that are either positive or negative and focus on implicit or explicit norms, while descriptive feedback refers to feedback based on specific references to the learners' actual achievement or competence that focus on improving performance (Hargreaves et al., 2000). Earl (2013) noted that evaluative feedback usually takes the form of grades and short, nonspecific comments, often praise or censure, which tells "students that they are 'ok' or not and affects their sense of themselves and their position in relation to learning, but offers very little direction for moving their learning" (p. 99). Descriptive feedback is directly linked to learning as it "addresses faulty interpretations and lack of understanding. It provides the student with visible and manageable next steps based on an assessment of the work at hand, and an image of what '*good work looks like*' so they can begin to take on the responsibility of self-assessing and self-correcting" (p. 99).

Written Feedback in Practice

Within the context of classroom practice, the notion of written feedback is generally understood and/or interpreted by teachers as "marking

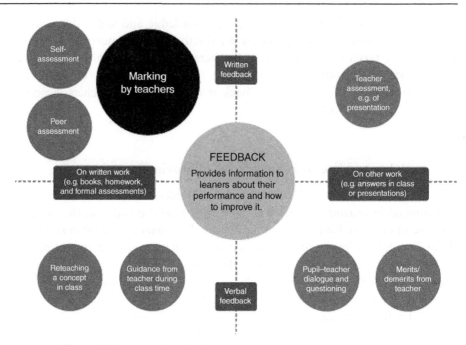

Figure 20.1 *Examples of different types of feedback (from Elliot et al., 2016).*

learners' work," which in practice has two meanings: reviewing learners' work or evaluating learners' work. When reviewing learners' work, usually found in an A4 exercise book where all written work produced by the learner is contained, the main purpose is to determine if the specific piece of work was correctly completed. Teachers usually append their signature and date at the end of the exercise as evidence that the work was "checked," use ticks and crosses to indicate correct and incorrect work, and sometimes provide comments (e.g., well done, good, incomplete), and/or correct errors, for example, inserting a comma or rewriting a word with the correct spelling. The same practices are applied when evaluating learners' work; the key difference is the allocation of a numerical value, for example, 6/10, or 60%, to a piece of written work being reviewed. In their review of evidence on written marking, Elliott et al. (2016) noted that marking is only one form of feedback and listed different types of written and verbal feedback (see Figure 20.1). The authors highlighted several findings to improve marking practices: (1) Awarding grades for every piece of work may reduce the impact of marking; (2) benefit from marking can be realized only if teachers set aside time for learners to consider and respond to the feedback provided; (3) careless mistakes should be marked differently from errors resulting from misunderstanding. To this end, the authors noted that "the latter may be best addressed by providing hints or questions which lead pupils to underlying principles; the former by simply marking the mistake as incorrect, without giving the right answer" (Elliot et al., 2016, p. 5). And they noted that (4) not all forms of marking can enhance pupil progress, and thus the authors

Table 20.1 *Type of written feedback provided by UK primary school teachers (from Eliot el al., 2016)*

How much, if at all, do you use the following marking practices?	Number of pieces of work that I mark (%)					
	All	Most	Some	Few	None	No response
(a) Correcting mistakes in pupils' work.	24	29	29	11	5	2
(b) Writing a qualitative/descriptive comment about the work.	14	34	33	11	7	23
(c) Putting a mark on work (e.g., 7/10).	2	2	10	32	51	3
(d) Writing praise on pupils' work (e.g., What went well).	28	42	21	4	3	1
(e) Giving pupils time in class to write a response to previous marking comments.	22	33	24	8	13	1

argue that "schools should mark less in terms of the number of pieces of work marked, but mark better" (p. 5).

Elliot et al. (2016) also surveyed teachers regarding their marking practices and reported that only a minority of primary teachers surveyed indicated that they provided marks (i.e., numerical scores) to most or all of the pieces of work that they review (14%). However, the majority of teachers, approximately 80%, also reported that they provided a descriptive or motivational comment, while also providing learners with time to respond to teacher comments (see Table 20.1). Notwithstanding their findings, the authors lamented the limited research on the topic of marking and/or written feedback, noting that "Despite its centrality to the work of schools and teachers, there is in fact little high-quality research related to marking" (p. 7).

Teacher Expectations and Feedback Practices

Teacher expectations are defined as "the judgements teachers make about the amount of academic progress they believe students will make by the end of a specific time frame" (Rubie-Davies, Flint, & McDonald, 2012, p. 271). The expectations of teachers have been shown to have a significant impact on learner performance as these expectations determine how teachers prepare and present lessons and how teachers behave toward students for whom they hold high or low expectations. As noted by Rubie-Davies (2014):

> Such expectations may be exemplified in the learning opportunities provided, in the affective climate created and in the interactional content and context of the classroom. These experiences may differ for students within the same classroom environment, or they may differ for students across different classrooms and may lead to differential learning. (p. 67)

In practice, teacher expectations can vary for different learners within a specific classroom, or for different groups of learners within and/or between different classrooms. From a whole-class perspective, Rubie-Davies et al. (2012) noted that high-expectation teachers anticipate learner performance to improve among all learners, while low-expectation teachers do not anticipate improvements in performance among their learners. Furthermore, the authors noted that the different beliefs of high and low expectations of teachers resulted in very different learning and teaching environments for learners. Specifically, they found that high-expectation teachers believe that learners should work in flexible ability grouping for reading, should be exposed to challenging tasks, and should have clear learning goals. Low-expectation teachers, the authors reported, believe that learners learned best when grouped by ability and when teachers planned specific activities for high- and low-ability learners.

In reporting on the practices of high-expectation teachers, McDonald et al. (2016) highlighted three key areas where practices and teaching strategies differed from other teachers: (1) when working with mixed-ability groupings, (2) in fostering a positive class climate, (3) and in motivation, evaluation, feedback, and promotion of student autonomy. The result of this, the authors argued, is the creation of positive learning and socioemotional classroom environments. Within this context, McDonald et al. (2016) noted that teachers with high expectations "appear to give students more feedback about their learning, and as a result the partnership between student and teacher in developing student learning is clearer" (p. 291). Furthermore, Rubie-Davis (2014) found that the feedback provided by high-expectation teachers was intended not only to reinforce learning but also to provide direction on what learners needed to do to improve and/or attain the next skills. The author provided the following example of this type of feedback: "Nice addition and I like the way you have kept all your numbers in straight columns so you didn't get the tens and hundreds muddled" (p. 87). On the other hand, Rubie-Davis (2014) noted that the feedback provided by low-expectation teachers tended to be in the form of praise or criticisms like "Well done," "No, you don't do it like that," or "You should know that by now" (p. 87). It needs to be noted that the nature and type of feedback provided, in this context, is a result of teacher's expectations of their learners and not how teachers expected their learners to react if provided with specific types of feedback. A review of the literature found no information on this specific topic.

Teacher Feedback: Policy Stipulations and Classroom Practice in South Africa

Teacher and school assessment practices in South Africa are stipulated in a number of key policy documents, the most recent being the Curriculum and Assessment Policy Statements (CAPS) for the different subject areas (DBE, 2011a) and the National Protocol for Assessment Grades R-12 (DBE, 2011b). The policy noted that "Informal (assessment for learning) or daily assessment is the monitoring and enhancing of learners' progress. This is done through

Table 20.2 *Number of formal assessments prescribed for foundation phase (DBE, 2011a)*

Learning Area	Term 1	Term 2	Term 3	Term 4	Total
Grade 1	2	2	2	1	7
Grade 2	2	2	2	2	8
Grade 3	2	3	3	2	10

teacher observation and teacher-learner interactions, which may be initiated by either teachers or learners" (DBE, 2011b, p. 3). "Formal assessment is noted as being synonymous with assessment of learning and is regarded as a process that provides teachers with a systematic way of evaluating how well learners are progressing in a particular subject and in a grade" (p. 3). The policy further noted that teachers must ensure that assessment criteria are very clear to the learners before the assessment process and that feedback should be provided to the learners after assessment. The CAPS document further stipulated the number and type of formal assessments to be conducted for each term for each of the different subject areas, the weighting between school-based assessment (continuous) tasks and the end-of-year examinations, and the cognitive levels and percentage that each level should contribute, and provided a scale for how scores should be reported. Table 20.2 specifies the number of formal assessment tasks that teachers must undertake for mathematics across the different Foundation Phase grades.

Teacher Feedback Practices

It is within this policy context that several research studies have been undertaken to investigate the use of teacher feedback practices in South African schools (Naroth, 2010; Kanjee & Croft, 2012; Kanjee & White, 2014; Mkhwanazi, Joubert, Phatudi, & Fraser; 2014; Kanjee & Mthembu 2015). Although most of the studies can be regarded as small scale with sample sizes of teachers ranging from two to thirty, they do provide some indication of how teachers understand the notion of feedback and how feedback is provided to learners in the classroom. Naroth's (2010) study examined the feedback strategies used by two mathematics teachers and the factors that impacted on their ability to provide constructive feedback to learners. Naroth (2010) reported that both teachers used ticks for correct answers and crosses for wrong answers, while one of the teachers also gave learners marks and wrote comments such as "Excellent" for learners who achieved the most on the test and posted stars and stickers in their workbooks.

Similarly, in their study of formative assessment practices of seven grade 3 teachers, Mkhwanazi et al. (2014) found that teachers lacked basic information about feedback. Specifically, the authors reported that teachers in their study considered feedback to be merely the corrections that teachers and learners engaged in after the written tasks and did not see feedback as an intervention to support learners' improvement. Consequently, few teachers made effective comments, with most of them simply giving the learners ticks, marks, and evaluative comments such as "good," "very good," and "You are a star." Furthermore, Mkhwanazi (2013) reported that evidence of feedback was primarily in the form of ticks for right answers and crosses for incorrect answers, while smiley faces and stickers were used to indicate good achievement. In addition, Mkhwanazi (2013) noted that feedback practices varied among teachers where some circled incorrect answers, others wrote the correct answer on top of the learners' work, and one teacher just wrote question marks next to the wrong answer with no other comment. In their study investigating formative assessment practices of teachers selected from eight primary schools across all poverty quintiles, Kanjee and Croft (2012) conducted observations and interviews with thirty teachers and obtained questionnaire responses from 115 teachers. Regarding the type and frequency of feedback provided to learners, an overwhelming majority of teachers (92%) reported that they always attached their signatures at the end of the learners' work that is reviewed; more than three-quarters indicated that they always used ticks and crosses (78%) and provided marks (85%); while 70% indicated that they always provided written comments. In addition, 76% of teachers also reported that they always focused on identifying learners' incorrect understanding when marking work, while 24% reported they do this only sometimes.

Most schools in South Africa require learners to record their written work in A4 size exercise books, referred to as learner workbooks. When reviewing learners' workbooks, Kanjee and Croft (2012) reported that while classwork was being regularly marked, teacher responses were comprised primarily of signatures to indicate that work has been checked, ticks and crosses to indicate correct or incorrect work, and motivational comments, for example, "great improvement," "well done," "too many mistakes," "don't copy," "be neat," and "pull up your socks," a colloquial term indicating the need to put more effort. No comments were found that provided learners with information on the errors made nor how to correct these. Similar findings were reported by Kanjee and White (2014) in their study of feedback practices of 339 teachers. The authors reported that all the learner books they reviewed (an average of between two and four per teacher) contained primarily or exclusively ticks or crosses and/or teacher signatures. Where written feedback was provided, this was mainly in the form of motivational comments, the most common of which was "good," "well done," and "try harder." No comments that indicated why errors were made, nor how to address these errors once found.

Linking Teacher Expectations to Their Feedback Practices

While several studies have focused on the different types of feedback that teachers provided to learners, and the feedback practices of teachers with high versus low expectations, there is limited information that directly links teacher feedback practices to their expectations regarding responses of their learners. To address this dearth of information, this section reports results of a study conducted to determine how teachers expected their learners to respond to written feedback, and whether teachers' expectations differ according to the type of written feedback provided.

Method

Data were obtained from teachers who participated in the Formative Assessment Professional Development Programme (FAPDP). The purpose of the program was to enhance teachers' formative assessment knowledge and skills for improving learning and teaching in general, and specifically to address the learning needs of poor and marginalized learners. The FAPDP was implemented as a randomized control trial in one hundred primary schools selected from two education districts. The intervention comprised a series of workshops conducted for teachers in the treatment group, while the evaluation was conducted by an external agency based on a pre- and post-design, collecting data using a reflection exercise in the form of a questionnaire, classroom observations, document reviews, teacher interviews, and learner tests. Data for this study were obtained from the baseline evaluation, conducted before the intervention program began, to determine participating teachers' knowledge and understanding of formative assessment and to obtain information on their current assessment practices in the classroom. In addition, focus group interviews were conducted with teachers and with district officials to obtain further information and explanations regarding teacher responses. This chapter reports on one aspect of the baseline evaluation, that is, on teachers' feedback practices and exceptions.

Sample

Data presented in this chapter were obtained from a sample of 217 primary school teachers from 83 primary schools randomly selected from two districts in Gauteng Province. Of these, there were 40 no-fee schools (i.e., schools that are usually underresourced, with poor facilities and with an overwhelming majority of learners from low socioeconomic backgrounds) and 43 fee-paying schools (i.e., schools that are usually well resourced, with excellent facilities and in which the overwhelming majority of learners are from middle to high socioeconomic backgrounds), representing 121 and 96 teachers, respectively. Regarding their experience in the teaching profession, 12% of the teachers indicated 1–5 years experience, 10% indicated 6–10 years, 22% noted 11–20 years, 21% noted 21–30 years, 10% listed more than 31 years, while 25% did not respond to the question. Seventy-two percent of the teachers indicated that they taught in the Foundation Phase (i.e,. grades 1–3), 20% taught mathematics in the Intermediate and/or Senior Phase (i.e., grades 4–7), while data were missing for 8%. All but one of teachers in the study were female. The number of teachers and schools by fee-paying status is given in Table 20.3.

Table 20.3 *Teacher sample by school category*

Fee Paying Status	Number of Schools	Number of Teachers
No fee	40	121
Fee paying	43	96

Instruments

Before the FAPDP program was implemented, all participating teachers were required to complete a reflection exercise questionnaire. The questionnaire was developed to obtain information on teachers' current assessment knowledge, skills, and practice; their understanding and use of the assessment policy; their views of learning and teaching; and their classroom management practices. Examples of questions used include: What are YOUR views on how children learn? What role does the learner have in the teaching and learning process? Define formative assessment. What is the difference between formative and summative assessment? For this study, four key questions were used to determine teachers' written feedback practices and expectations:

1. What kind of written feedback do you provide on learners' work and how often do you do this? Teachers were required to respond to the following options using a scale that ranged from "Almost always" to "Almost never"; teacher's signature; ticks and crosses (e.g., ✗, ✓); symbols (e.g., A, B, C); marks (e.g., 60% or 6/10); motivational comments (e.g., well done, work harder); written explanations that detail the errors made and how to correct the errors.
2. How do YOU expect learners to respond after they get the following types of feedback? Ticks, crosses (✗, ✓), letter grade (A, B), marks (6/10).
3. How do you expect your learners to respond after they get motivational comments? (e.g., good work, well done, good effort, try harder).
4. How do you expect your learners to respond after they get *detailed comments* on how they can improve their work?

Analysis

For question 1, no significant differences were found between teachers in the Foundation and Intermediate Phases; thus, results are reported only for fee versus no-fee schools. Thematic analysis was used to identify key themes emerging from teacher responses to questions 2–4 (Braun and Clarke, 2006). For each question, teacher responses were independently coded by two experienced researchers into specific categories to present the range of practical expectations listed. A third researcher then reviewed the coding and, through a process of mediation and consensus with the two researchers who compiled the original codes, revised any codes that did not correspond. The coded responses were then aggregated to identify common themes emerging from the responses of teachers (see the Appendix to this chapter for a detailed list of responses to questions 2–4).

The results for both the codes and the common themes were also disaggregated by fee and no-fee schools to identify any similarities or differences in the response patterns of teachers across the two school types.

Results and Discussion

Teacher Feedback Practices

Teachers were asked to respond to the type of written feedback provided as well as the frequency of providing this type of feedback. As presented in Table 20.4, responses indicated that teachers provide a range of different types of feedback, with appending their signature to learners' work listed as the most common type, followed by ticks and crosses, motivational comments, and marks. Symbols in the form of A, B, or C were reported as the type of feedback least provided. Responses from teacher interviews reveal that the primary reason for signing and, to a large extent, ticking learner's work was to provide evidence to parents, learners, and school leaders, specifically the head of department and district officials, that the work had been reviewed. The other forms of feedback were provided to indicate to learners where they went wrong, to provide support and motivation for correcting their errors, and/or to provide a mark as required for formal assessments. These findings are similar to those reported by Kanjee and Croft (2012) and Kanjee and White (2014).

In terms of frequency of the feedback provided (see Table 20.4), approximately 94% of the teachers reported that they either signed learners' work or provided ticks and crosses more than 75% of the time; 88% reported that they provided motivational comments more than 75% of the time; 78% noted that they provided detailed written explanations; 70% reported that they provided marks; while 23% noted that they provided symbols. The relatively lower frequency regarding the awarding of marks can be explained by policy

Table 20.4 *Types and frequency of written feedback*

Type of Written Feedback	Almost always	About 75% of the Time	About 50% of the Time	Less than 50%
(a) Teacher's signature	83.1%	11.1%	4.8%	1.1%
(b) Ticks and crosses (✗, ✓)	73.8%	19.8%	3.5%	2.9%
(c) Symbols (e.g., A, B, C)	13.4%	9.4%	12.6%	64.6%
(d) Marks (e.g., 60% or 6/10)	47.8%	22.3%	21.7%	8.3%
(e) Motivational comments (e.g., well done, work harder)	68.1%	19.8%	11.0%	1.1%
(f) Written explanations that detail the errors made and how to correct them	49.7%	28.1%	15.2%	7.0%

stipulations that require teachers to provide marks only for a fixed number of assessments, which are also reported to parents and, in the higher grades, used to contribute to the final examinations marks of learners. Similarly, the low frequency for awarding symbols can be explained by current "assessment cultures or practices" in the South African schools where symbols are generally used only for reporting results of the final matriculation examinations, while all marks in other grades are reported using percentage scores.

A clear message communicated during the interviews was that teachers spent too much time on marking; that huge variations exist between schools and, in some instances, within schools across different subject areas; and that this is a major contributor to their high workloads. Yet most teachers continue to ensure that they spend large amounts of their time marking. In exploring the reasons for the high frequency of marking, no clear evidence could be found in any official documents. Aside from the formal assessment tasks listed in the policy documents (DBE, 2011b), there are no specific regulations nor guidelines on the nature, amount, or type of feedback that teachers should provide when marking learner work. Personal communication with senior district subject advisors, district officers responsible for assessment, as well as members of a school management team confirmed this. Interviewees reported that in practice, the amount and frequency of marking was largely determined by school policies, which usually were derived from the specifications of the head of department (HoD), the person responsible for teaching, learning, monitoring, and supporting teachers within a specific phase (e.g., Foundation Phase) or for specific subject areas. The current system, guidelines, or most apt understanding in practice is summed up by the following response of an HoD: "Each school has its own marking policy. The district subject advisors normally give guidelines on how and how many times marking must take place. Each school also develops their own system and control forms. Each subject policy must have the marking process in it" (Mathematics HoD, personal communication, May 2017).

Additional analysis was also conducted to identify differences between fee-paying and no-fee schools. As noted in Table 20.5, significant differences were noted only for feedback provided in the form of marking. This finding, however, is not unexpected given the emphasis that fee-paying schools placed on marks as well as the substantial pressure that parents, most of whom are from middle and high socioeconomic backgrounds, exerted on schools and teachers regarding the performance of their children. As one teacher reported when explaining her challenges in implementing a "comment only" approach in her classroom: "Because we are regarded as a good school, as a high performing school, parents want to see their children's marks, and they want to see their kids get high marks. Our HoDs also want to see the marks, and district officials also regularly visit us to see if our marks have improved" (grade 2 teacher, August 2016). In her research on how teacher beliefs about teaching and learning influenced their instructional practices, Deemer (2004) noted that in

Table 20.5 *Type and frequency of written feedback aggregated for teachers in fee versus no-fee schools*

Type of Feedback	School Type	Almost always	About 75%	About 50%	Less than 50%	Chi sq	p
(a) Teacher's signature	No fees	79.6%	14.2%	4.4%	1.8%	4.158	.245
	Fee paying	88.2%	6.6%	5.3%	0		
(b) Ticks and crosses (✗, ✓)	No fees	75.9%	19.4%	3.7%	0.9%	4.144	.246
	Fee paying	70.3%	20.3%	3.1%	6.3%		
(c) Symbols (A, B, C)	No fees	12.0%	8.4%	8.4%	71.1%	5.456	.141
	Fee paying	15.9%	11.4%	20.5%	52.3%		
(d) Marks (60% or 6/10)	No fees	38.2%	30.4%	20.6%	10.8%	16.467	.001*
	Fee paying	65.5%	7.3%	23.6%	3.6%		
(e) Motivational comments (well done, work harder)	No fees	70.9%	19.1%	9.1%	0.9%	1.384	.709
	Fee paying	63.9%	20.8%	13.9%	1.4%		
(f) Written explanations that detail the errors made and how to correct them	No fees	46.2%	32.1%	14.2%	7.5%	2.589	.459
	Fee paying	55.4%	21.5%	16.9%	6.2%		

*Indicates significant associations.

schools that promoted a competitive environment, teachers were likely to do the same in their classrooms. However, Deemer also noted that "where teachers believe that they have opportunities to learn new things and will be recognized for doing so, they may also provide students with meaningful, challenging and creative work that promotes learning" (p. 86). For all other types of feedback, no significant differences were noted. For the South African context, this finding is especially important as it indicates the similar practices of teachers across the different school types despite the huge variations between these schools regarding facilities, teaching and learning resources, and teacher qualifications and socioeconomic status of learners attending these schools. Similar findings were reported by Kanjee and Croft (2012) in their study on teacher assessment practices and by Kanjee and Mthembu (2014) in their study on assessment literacy of foundation phase teachers.

Teacher Expectations of Learners

Teachers were asked to respond to three questions to determine how they expected their learners to respond when providing feedback to written work in the form of marks, ticks and crosses, motivational comments, and detailed comments. Initial analysis of teacher responses identified key themes that were categorized into four expectation dimensions: (1) an affective dimension, which refers to expectations related to emotional responses of learners, for example, to "feel excited," "happy," or "sad"; (2) a cognitive dimension, which refers to expectations of an intellectual or cognitive response, for example, "to follow instructions" or "to see the errors"; (3) a behavioral dimension, which refers to expectation of a practical nature, for example, "to work harder," "to do corrections," or "to ask questions"; and (4) a general dimension that was used to categorize those expectations that could be not classified into any of the three above, for example, "to improve," "to take notice," or "to show interest." However, a review of this categorization scheme did not prove fruitful in providing further insights into teacher expectations, and it was decided to revise the themes identified.

The revised categorization was based on adaptations of studies conducted by Hargreaves et al. (2000) and Eriksson, Björklund Boistrup, and Thornberg (2017). It should be noted that both sets of authors focused on feedback provided to learners and not on how teachers expected their learners to respond to their written feedback. In their study, Eriksson et al. (2017) generated five main categories of teacher feedback strategies. One of the categories developed was "*expecting*," which refers to "teachers' pre-evaluation of student perform-ance and communicates teachers' expectations of what a student or a group of students are able to perform" (p. 6). Within this category, Eriksson et al. identified "*ability improvement expecting*" as a type of feedback that they defined as expectations communicated to indicate that the student or group of students *can* improve their ability. For this study, this feedback type was adapted to an "*improvement response*," referring to teacher expectations that the learner would respond to their written feedback in a manner that would lead to some improvement. In this context, neither the nature and form of the improvement nor the process by which the improvement will take place was an area of focus. Responses listed under this theme include "to work harder," "to ask for help," or "to follow instructions."

From the Hargreaves et al. (2000) study, the concept of "evaluative feedback strategies" was used to refer to "giving rewards and punishments, and express-ing approval or disapproval" (p. 23). This was adapted to create a category called "*motivational response*," referring to teacher expectations that their writ-ten feedback would result in some form of affective response. In the analysis, no distinction was made between a positive or negative response, as it was assumed that all affective expectations were intended to motivate learners to improve their performance. A third category was created called "*generic response*," which was used to categorize teacher comments that could not be classified into any of the two categories above. These include "to take notice," "to understand," and "to respond." In reporting the results, only those expectations that yielded a response rate greater than 5% are discussed and disaggregated to compare differences between fee-paying and no-fee schools (see the Appendix to this chapter for a detailed list of responses to questions 2–4).

The next question was "How do YOU expect learners to respond after they get the following types of feedback: Ticks, crosses (✗, ✓), letter grade (A, B),

Table 20.6 *Teacher expectations by fee status when providing ticks, crosses, and marks*

Teacher Response	No Fees		Fee Paying		Total		z-ratio	p-value	sig
	n	%	n	%	n	%			
Improve	27	14.00	27	17.60	55	15.90	−1.089	0.275	p <0.05
Work harder	19	9.80	16	10.50	35	10.10	−0.188	0.849	p <0.05
Do corrections	28	14.50	6	3.90	34	9.80	3.285	0.001	p <0.05
Be motivated	9	4.70	14	9.20	23	6.60	−1.664	0.097	p <0.05
Be happy	16	8.30	7	4.60	23	6.60	1.378	0.168	p <0.05

marks (6/10)?" Half of the responses listed expectations that focused on the "improvement," with 21% focusing on the "motivation," while 4% were generic, and 25% of the responses were missing. However, significantly more teachers from no-fee schools than from fee-paying schools (57%) listed improvement expectations (p <.01). No differences were noted in the other two categories. Approximately 16% of the responses indicated expectations for learners "to improve their work," followed by "to work harder" (10%), "to do corrections" (10%), and "to be motivated" and "to be happy" (see Table 20.6). When comparing response rates by fee-paying status, differences were found only for "to do corrections" with significantly more teachers in no-fee schools listing this option (p< .01).

These findings indicate that expectations of teachers might be unrealistic given the view that the provision of ticks, crosses, and/or marks should spur learners to be motivated and improve or work harder. However, focus group interviews with teachers provided additional information on these findings. Many teachers noted that it was acceptable to provide ticks, crosses, and marks, as learners always get an opportunity to interact with them regarding the work that they have marked. Specifically, the teachers noted that this occurred when they did revision of the work or when they reviewed work with learners. It is during this time that teachers provided learners with explanations and/or support for understanding and/or corrected work marked with ticks or crosses. However, in practice, teachers have limited time during school hours and are often rushing to cover the curriculum. Usually, only work related to formal tests was revised, with other work mostly left unattended. These practices, according to Kanjee and Sayed (2013), are indicative of a measurement-driven system and reflective of what is promoted in the current assessment policies.

Another common practice among teachers is to write "corrections" for learners. That is, in instances where errors were noted, teachers generally corrected the work themselves, almost always using a red pen to write the correct text or calculations above or next to learner's work, and did this consistently for all learners in the class. Despite the significant increase in their workload, teachers felt this practice was necessary as it "showed learners what errors they made and how to correct these errors" (grade 2 teacher, August 2016). When

Table 20.7 *Teacher expectations by fee status when providing motivational comments*

Response	No Fees		Fee Paying		Total		z-ratio	p-value	Sig level
	n	%	n	%	n	%			
Work harder	44	25.0	33	25.2	77	25.1	−0.038	0.970	p<0.05
To be motivated	34	19.3	19	14.5	53	17.3	1.104	0.270	p<0.05
To be happy	18	10.2	26	19.8	44	14.3	−2.379	0.017	p<0.05
To improve	15	8.5	12	9.2	27	8.8	−0.195	0.842	p<0.05
To keep up their work	17	9.7	8	6.1	25	8.1	1.126	0.260	p<0.05

questioned on the value and practicality of this practice, teachers noted that they assumed that it was useful and helped learners but were uncertain as to whether the time invested for writing the corrections was the most effective way for providing relevant feedback that addressed specific learning gaps.

In response to the question "How do you expect your learners to respond after they get comments to encourage learners? (e.g. "Good work," "Well done," "Good effort," "Try harder"), 47% of the responses listed expectations that focused on the "improvement," with 39% noting the "motivation" aspect, 3% generic, and 11% of the responses were missing. No significant differences were noted when comparing responses by school status. As noted in Table 20.7, the most common expectation listed was "to work harder" (25%), followed by "to be motivated" (17%), "to be happy" (14%), "to improve" (9%), and "to keep up their work" (8%). A comparison of expectations by school status reveals significantly more teachers in fee-paying schools noting that they expected their learners "to be happy" (p ~<.01).

Teacher expectations that their learners will respond to their comments by being more motivated and working harder to improve their performance seem realistic. Motivational feedback is intended to stimulate an emotional response, such as the learners feeling good, and focuses specifically on comments like "well done" and "excellent work." Fishbach, Eyal, and Finkelstein (2010) noted that "positive feedback increased people's confidence that they are able to pursue their goals, leading people to expect successful goal attainment" (p. 517). However, according to Tunstall and Gipps (1996), this type of feedback, which they termed "evaluative feedback," is not helpful to learners as no information is provided on how to address gaps in their learning. Black and Wiliam (1998) noted that evaluative feedback can have a negative impact on learning, as teacher comments that are focused on characteristics of the learner rather than on the characteristics of the work can have the opposite of the intended effect. Davies and Le Mahieu (2003) also reported that evaluative feedback is especially problematic for learners who are struggling as this type of feedback not only failed to help learners address specific learning gaps but also impacted negatively on their motivation to learn. Learners with low marks were more likely to see themselves as failures and thus were less motivated and less likely to succeed. As summarized by Lipnevich and Smith (2008), "detailed, specific, descriptive feedback, which focuses students' attention on their work rather than the self,

Table 20.8 *Teacher expectations by fee status when providing comments to improve learner work*

Q56 Response	No Fee		Fee Paying		Total		z value	p-value	sig
	n	%	n	%	n	%			
To improve	37	24.50	13	11.40	50	19	2.698	0.006	p<0.05
To work harder	23	15.20	27	23.70	50	19	−1.741	0.082	p<0.05
To follow instructions	32	21.20	7	6.10	39	15	3.424	0.000	p<0.05
To ask for help	16	10.60	8	7.00	24	9	1.005	0.317	p<0.05
To be motivated	10	6.60	7	6.10	17	6	0.158	0.872	p<0.05

is the most advantageous kind of information that should be provided to students" (p. 39). For feedback to be useful, Earl (2013) noted that it must be linked to the learning that is expected, highlight key issues like faulty interpretations and lack of understanding, provide learners with visible and manageable "next steps," and provide exemplars of what "good work" looks like.

In response to the question "How do you expect your learners to respond after they get *detailed comments* on how they can improve their work?," 68% of the responses listed expectations that focused on "improvement," with 14% expecting learners to be "motivated," while 1% of the responses were categorized as generic and 18% of the responses were missing. However, significantly more teachers from no-fee schools (75%) compared with fee-paying schools (57%) listed "improvement expectations" (p < .01). A review of the specific expectations (see Table 20.8) revealed the most common expectation listed was "to improve" and "to work harder" (19%), followed by "to follow instructions" (15%), "to ask for help" (9%), and "to be motivated" (6%). Significantly more teachers in no-fee schools noted that they expected their learners "to improve" (p < .01) and "to follow instructions" (p < .01).

Here too, the expectations teachers noted were in line with the literature on feedback. Studies on the formative function of feedback reported that descriptive feedback helped students to learn by providing information about their current achievement (Where am I now?) with respect to a goal (Where am I going?) and identifying appropriate next steps (How can I close the gap?) (Sadler, 1989; Stiggins, Arter, Chappuis, & Chappuis, 2004). Similarly, Black, Harrison, Lee, Marshall, and Wiliam (2003) noted that comment-only feedback is more valuable in enhancing learning than other forms of feedback such as a percentage score or a letter grade. However, given that no reviews of learner workbooks were undertaken, the nature, type, and frequency of feedback provided and its relevance to the subject matter could not be determined. With regard to the value and impact of descriptive feedback, Wiliam (2011) cautions that the best-designed feedback is useless if it is not acted on, and noted that feedback cannot be evaluated without also considering the instructional context in which it is provided and used. Wiliam (2011) recommended that the most useful feedback for improving learning is that which provided learners with detailed information on how to improve performance, and noted that

> if teachers are providing careful diagnostic comments and then putting a score or grade on the work, they are wasting their time. They might as well give a score or a grade – the learners won't learn anything as a result, but the teacher will save a great deal of time. (p. 109)

Similarly, Lipnevich and Smith (2009) found that feedback was more helpful when grades or marks were not provided. However, if a grade was coupled with praise, the negative effects of a grade were somewhat ameliorated.

Conclusion

This study explored teachers' written feedback practices across the different types of schools that characterize the education system in South Africa. In addition, teachers' expectations regarding the responses of their learners to the different types of written feedback provided was also investigated using accepted feedback categories adapted to encompass feedback expectations. Teachers reported providing a range of different types of feedback, with the most common and frequent being ticks, crosses, and signatures. When comparing teacher responses by school status, significantly more teachers from fee-paying schools reported providing marks, a phenomenon that could be explained by the greater focus on competition and learner performance in these schools. While teacher expectations when providing ticks, crosses, and marks were found to be unrealistic and out of sync with the feedback provided, significantly more teachers in no-fee schools still listed an "improvement expectation." However, this result could be explained by reported teacher practices of engaging with learners after the teacher has marked the work. With regard to the provision of "motivational comments to encourage learners" and "detailed comments on how they can improve their work," most teachers listed an "improvement expectation." Across these two questions, comparisons by school status found that significantly more teachers in fee-paying schools expected their learners to "be happy" when they received motivational comments, while significantly more teachers in no-fee schools expected their learners "to improve" when provided with detailed comments. The reasons for these differences are not immediately apparent and would require additional research. A limitation of this study pertains to the use of self-reported data regarding the frequency of feedback practices. This limitation should be addressed in future studies by reviewing learner workbooks to obtain valid and reliable evidence on the nature, type, and frequency of feedback provided. The findings from this study provide valuable insights into how teachers view their written feedback practices, insights that could prove useful when planning programs for supporting teachers to develop their knowledge and skills for effectively using formative assessment in the classroom. However, there is a need for additional research regarding the relationship between teachers' beliefs of learning and teaching and their reported feedback practices and expectations, as well as current feedback practices based on evidence in learner workbooks.

Appendix to Chapter 20

Table 20.A1 *Teacher expectations when providing ticks, crosses, and marks*

Q54 Code	Teacher Response	Total n	Total %		Category
99	Missing	88	25.40%	–	Missing
I	Improve	55	15.90%	I	G
WH	Work hard(er)	35	10.10%	I	P
C	Do corrections	34	9.80%	I	P
H	Be motivated	23	6.60%	M	A
M	Be happy	23	6.60%	M	A
UNDER	Understand	14	4.00%	I	C
SEE	See the errors	12	3.50%	I	C
S	Be sad	11	3.20%	M	A
AH	Ask for help	9	2.60%	I	P
EX	Be excited	9	2.60%	M	A
AQ	As questions	3	0.90%	I	P
IG	Ignore comment	3	0.90%	G	P
PRD	Be proud	3	0.90%	M	A
DEMOV	Be demotivated	2	0.60%	M	A
FI	Follow instructions	2	0.60%	I	P
IDSW	Identify strengths and weaknesses	2	0.60%	I	C
PUS	Pull up your socks	2	0.60%	G	G
RES	Respond	2	0.60%	G	P
TN	Take notice	2	0.60%	G	G
AP	Appreciate what is written	1	0.30%	G	A
DW	Do well	1	0.30%	I	G
DWR	Do what is required	1	0.30%	G	P
EXPLAIN	Explain	1	0.30%	I	P
INTRO	Introspection	1	0.30%	I	G
KT	Know themselves	1	0.30%	I	G
LM	Learn more	1	0.30%	I	G
PAR	Inform parents	1	0.30%	M	P
Q	Query	1	0.30%	I	P
SA	Self-assessment	1	0.30%	I	C
STUDY	Study more	1	0.30%	I	P
SUPPORT	Ask for support	1	0.30%	I	P
Total		**346**	**100%**		

Table 20.A2 *Teacher expectations when providing motivational comments*

Q55 Code	Teacher Response	Total n	Total %		Category
WH	Work hard(er)	77	25.10%	I	P
M	Be motivated	53	17.30%	M	A
H	Be happy	44	14.30%	M	A

Table 20.A2 (*cont.*)

Q55 Code	Teacher Response	Total n	Total %		Category
99 Missing	Missing	33	10.70%	–	
I	Improve your work	27	8.80%	I	G
KUW	Keep up your work	25	8.10%	I	G
PRD	Be proud	15	4.90%	M	A
DW	Do well	6	2.00%	I	G
GW	Do good work	6	2.00%	I	G
CON	Confront	4	1.30%	I	P
RES	Respond	4	1.30%	G	P
AH	Ask for help	3	1.00%	I	P
PAR	Inform parents	2	0.70%	M	P
TN	Take notice	2	0.70%	G	G
CB	Change behavior	1	0.30%	G	p
PUS	Pull up your socks	1	0.30%	G	G
SHM	Shame	1	0.30%	M	A
TELL	Share	1	0.30%	G	P
Thank me	Thank me	1	0.30%	G	P
UNDER	Understand	1	0.30%	I	G
Total		**307**	**100%**		

Table 20.A3 *Teacher expectations when providing detail comments on how to improve work*

Q56 Code	Teacher Response	Total n	Total %		Category
I	Improve	50	18.90%	I	G
WH	Work hard(er)	50	18.90%	I	P
99	Missing	47	17.70%	–	
FI	Follow instructions	39	14.70%	I	C
AH	Ask for help	24	9.10%	I	C
M	Be motivated	17	6.40%	M	A
C	Do corrections	8	3.00%	I	P
PAR	Tell parents	7	2.60%	M	A
DW	Do well	4	1.50%	I	G
H	Happy	4	1.50%	M	A
CON	Consult	3	1.10%	I	P
S	Sad	3	1.10%	M	A
IGNORE	Ignore	2	0.80%	G	P
IN	Show interest	1	0.40%	M	G
IND	Work independently	1	0.40%	I	P
KUW	Know themselves	1	0.40%	G	G
LM	Learn more	1	0.40%	I	G
PRACTICE	Practice more	1	0.40%	I	P
PRD	Be proud	1	0.40%	M	A
RES	Respond	1	0.40%	G	P
Total		**265**	**100%**		

References

Black, P., Harrison, C., Lee, C., Marshall, B., & Wiliam, D. (2003). *Assessment for learning: Putting it into practice*. Buckingham, UK: Open University Press.

Black, P., & Wiliam, D. (1998). Assessment and classroom learning. *Assessment in Education: Principles, Policy & Practice*, *5*, 70–74.

Braun, V., & Clarke, V. (2006). Using thematic analysis in psychology. *Qualitative Research in Psychology*, *3*, 77–101.

Brookhart, S. M., (2008). *How to give to effective feedback to your students*. Alexandria, VA: Association for Supervision and Curriculum Development.

Brown, G. T., Harris, L. R., & Harnett, J. (2012). Teacher beliefs about feedback within an assessment for learning environment: Endorsement of improved learning over student well-being. *Teaching and Teacher Education*, *28*, 968–978.

Chan, P. E., Konrad, M., Gonzalez, V., Peters, M. T., & Ressa, V. A. (2014). The critical role of feedback in formative instructional practices. *Intervention in School and Clinic*, *50*, 96–104.

Clarke, S. (2003). *Unlocking formative assessment: Practical strategies for enhancing pupils' learning in the primary classroom*. London: Hodder & Stoughton.

Davies, A., & LeMahieu, P. (2003). Assessment for learning: Reconsidering portfolios and research evidence. In M. Segers, F. Dochy, & E. Cascallar (Eds.), *Optimising new modes of assessment: In search of qualities and standards* (pp. 141–169). Dordrecht: Springer.

Deemer, S. (2004). Classroom goal orientation in high school classrooms: Revealing links between teacher beliefs and classroom environments. *Educational Research*, *46*, 73–90.

Department of Basic Education (DBE). (2011a). *National Curriculum Statement (NCS): Curriculum and Policy Statement – Foundation Phase 6*. Pretoria, South Africa: Department of Basic Education.

Department of Basic Education (DBE). (2011b). *National Protocol for Assessment Grades R-12*. Pretoria, South Africa: Department of Education.

Earl, L. M. (2013). *Assessment as learning: Using classroom assessment to maximize student learning*. Thousand Oaks, CA: Corwin Press.

Education Endowment Foundation (2016). *Technical Appendix: Feedback*. London: Education Endowment Foundation. Retrieved from https://educationendowment foundation.org.uk/public/files/Toolkit/Technical_Appendix/EEF_Feedback_ Technical_Appendix.pdf.

Elliott, V., Baird, J. A., Hopfenbeck, T. N., Ingram, J., Thompson, I., Usher, N., & Coleman, R. (2016). *A marked improvement? A review of the evidence on written marking*. London: Education Endowment Foundation.

Engelsen, K., & Smith, K. (2010). Is "excellent" good enough? *Education Inquiry*, *1*(4), 415–431.

Eriksson, E., Björklund Boistrup, L., & Thornberg, R. (2017). A categorisation of teacher feedback in the classroom: A field study on feedback based on routine classroom assessment in primary school. *Research Papers in Education*, *32*, 316–332.

Fishbach, A., Eyal, T., & Finkelstein, S. R. (2010). How positive and negative feedback motivate goal pursuit. *Social and Personality Psychology Compass*, *4*, 517–530.

Hargreaves, E., McCallum, B., & Gipps, C. (2000). Teacher feedback strategies in primary classrooms: New evidence. In S. Askow (Ed.), *Feedback for learning* (pp. 21–31). New York: Routledge.

Hattie, J. (2012). *Visible learning for teachers: Maximizing impact on learning*. New York: Routledge.

Hattie, J., & Timperley, H. (2007). The power of feedback. *Review of Educational Research, 77,* 81–112.

Hoadley, U. (2012). What do we know about teaching and learning in South African primary schools? *Education as Change, 16,* 187–202.

Irving, S. E., Harris, L. R., & Peterson, E. R. (2011). "One assessment doesn't serve all the purposes" or does it? New Zealand teachers describe assessment and feedback. *Asia Pacific Education Review, 12,* 413–426.

Kanjee, A., & Croft, C. (2012, April). Enhancing the use of assessment for learning: Addressing challenges facing South African teachers. Paper presented at the annual American Educational Research Conference, Vancouver, Canada.

Kanjee, A., & Mthembu, J. (2015). Assessment literacy of Foundation Phase teachers: An exploratory study. *South African Journal of Childhood Education, 5,* 142–168.

Kanjee, A., & Sayed, Y. (2013). Assessment policy in post-apartheid South Africa: Challenges for improving education quality and learning. *Assessment in Education: Principles, Policy & Practice, 20,* 442–469.

Kanjee, A., & White, C. J. (2014). Evaluation of a national professional development programme to improve teacher formative assessment practices. Unpublished report, Department of Educational Studies, Tshwane University of Technology, Pretoria, South Africa.

Lipnevich, A. A., & Smith, J. K. (2008). Response to assessment feedback: The effects of grades, praise, and source of information. Report No. 08-30. Educational Testing Service.

Lipnevich, A. A., & Smith, J. K. (2009). Effects of differential feedback on students' examination performance. *Journal of Experimental Psychology: Applied, 15,* 319–333.

McDonald, L., Flint, A., Rubie-Davies, C. M., Peterson, E. R., Watson, P., & Garrett, L. (2016). Teaching high-expectation strategies to teachers through an intervention process. *Professional Development in Education, 42,* 290–307.

Mkhwanazi, H. N. (2013). Teachers' use of formative assessment in the teaching of reading comprehension in grade 3. PhD thesis, University of Pretoria.

Mkhwanazi, H. N., Joubert, I., Phatudi, N. C., & Fraser, W. J. (2014). Teachers' use of formative assessment for the teaching of reading comprehension in Grade 3. *Mediterranean Journal of Social Sciences, 5,* 468–475.

Naroth, C. (2010). Constructive teacher feedback for enhancing learner performance in mathematics. Master's thesis, University of the Free State.

Rubie-Davies, C. (2014). *Becoming a high expectation teacher: Raising the bar*. Abingdon, UK: Routledge.

Rubie-Davies, C. M., Flint, A., & McDonald, L. G. (2012). Teacher beliefs, teacher characteristics, and school contextual factors: What are the relationships? *British Journal of Educational Psychology, 82,* 270–288.

Sadler, D. R. (1989). Formative assessment and the design of instructional systems. *Instructional Science, 18*(2), 119–144.

Sadler, R. D. 2010. Beyond feedback: Developing student capability in complex appraisal. *Assessment & Evaluation in Higher Education, 35,* 535–550.

Stiggins, R. J., Arter, J. A., Chappuis, J., & Chappuis, S. (2004). *Classroom assessment for student learning: Doing it right, using it well.* Portland, OR: Assessment Training Institute.

Tunstall, P., & Gipps, C. (1996). Teacher feedback to young children in formative assessment: A typology. *British Educational Research Journal, 22,* 389–404

Wiliam, D. (2011). *Embedded formative assessment.* Bloomington, IN: Solution Tree Press.

21 Interactive Assessment

Cultural Perspectives and Practices in the Nexus of "Heart or Mind"

Masahiro Arimoto and Ian Clark

This chapter introduces the reader to an alternative perspective of feedback and formative assessment. We contrast the Western perspective of the child as a "student" or "pupil" with the Japanese practice of "*zenjin*-education," translated most closely as "whole-child education." Hiroshi Sugita (2012), Director for Special Curriculum Subjects at the Japanese Ministry of Education (MEXT), delineated the Japanese perspective on *zenjin* into three broad and interconnected curricular areas: (1) personal interrelationships, (2) social duty and responsibility, and (3) autonomous decision-making. The overall purpose of the Japanese curriculum is to nurture well-rounded (*zenjinteki*) and mature young learners. Schools that pursue a *zenjin* curriculum do so in order to address the question "What does society expect of its schools?" The answer goes beyond levels of academic achievement. *Zenjin* ideas permeate the entire continuum of Japanese history and were enshrined into Japan's national policy framework in the late 1960s. In doing so, the Japanese political establishment recognized that traditional ideologies alone do not provide an adequate basis for local and global sustainability and development. Twenty-first-century Japanese schools are therefore encouraged to organize in ways that nurture well-rounded young people with open hearts, who are capable of mature analysis without prejudice.

The chapter discusses this fundamentally holistic process, which involves a balance among the six basic values that correspond with the cultural activities of mankind: truth, goodness, beauty, holiness, soundness, and wealth. Further, we look at how the communal norms of Japanese society, steeped in Buddhist thought and thousands of years of historical precedent, result in a unique yet globally exportable model for instruction and assessment. This chapter draws on cultural philosophy, historical events, twenty-first-century "social neuroscience," and the ideas of social-cognition and constructivist theorists. Our aim is to provide a unique sociocultural geometry, a review of the often deeply inlaid shapes, patterns, and relationships that support interactive styles of classroom assessment. Insofar as interactive assessment encompasses formative assessment, we offer perhaps the most quoted conception of classroom assessment, as provided by Black and Wiliam (1998). Their conception includes a "what" element and a "when" element. What? "All those activities undertaken by teachers – and by their students in assessing themselves – that provide information to be used as feedback to modify the teaching and learning activities" in which they are engaged. And when? "Such assessment becomes formative assessment when the evidence is used to adapt the teaching work to meet the needs" (Black & Wiliam, 1998, p. 2). We hope that this approach will resolve some issues on its way to raising many more questions in the minds and hearts of the "whole reader."

In the final years of the twentieth century, Wiliam and his colleagues published their meta-analysis of classroom assessment gathered from European contexts (Black & Wiliam, 1998). The original name for this body of work was "formative assessment" (now also known as assessment for learning, or AfL). The nascent systematic and creative aspects of formative assessment created a kind of new and somewhat contentious educational movement (Young & Kim, 2010; Clark, 2011). It was a movement that claimed the potential to prepare students for the unpredictable challenges of a twenty-first century characterized by rapid technical and scientific advance and obsolescence. In many regions of the world, stable and abiding cultural value systems began to experience fragmentation associated with an acceleration and multiplication of extra-political flashpoints. On both national and international stages, a sense of disunity began to crystallize around issues of socioeconomic equity in the very contentious areas of race, religion, wealth, and sexuality. Consequently, interactive classrooms with the potential to promote autonomous thinking skills during sustained periods of equitable participation became increasingly attractive as places that could prepare young learners for the unpredictable transitions ahead (Central Council for Education, 1996).

In the years leading toward the twenty-first century, the confidence of the Japanese public in the efficacy of national educational policy began to diminish into disapproval and apathy. New policy courses created new pressures for educators around how the curriculum should nurture *zenjin* aptitudes and attitudes. For example, the Japanese government's MEXT responded decisively with a widely publicized commitment to nurture in students the "zest for life" (Central Council for Education, 1996; Sugita, 2012; MEXT, n.d. a). The zest for life (*ikiru chikara*) is a policy initiative taken in response to a perceived decline in young learners' "basic abilities and skills to discover, learn, consider, and judge issues independently and to act in order to solve problems in a better way" (MEXT, n.d. b, "Various Skills and Natures Suggested until Now," para. 1). It is a program through which MEXT seeks to encourage "rich humanity in order to control oneself, collaborate with others, and think of others; and the health and physical strength to live vigorously" (MEXT, n.d. b, "Various Skills and Natures Suggested until Now," para. 1). Sugita (2012), in a MEXT speech on the development of the "whole child," commented, "a *balanced* intellect, goodness, and body comes down to the concept of a 'zest for life'" (p. 5, emphasis added).

As a movement taking place outside Japan, formative assessment was not without political zest of its own. It became a common theme at educational conferences and the subject of increasingly frequent requests for government funding. The Organisation for Economic Cooperation and Development (OECD) designated formative assessment as a key research hub in 2002, reflecting and shaping a "quiet revolution" (Hutchinson & Hayward, 2005, p. 244) as formative assessments were integrated into the national policy frameworks of numerous education systems worldwide (OECD, 2005a). Subsequent international studies debated the claims that classroom teachers can, through dialogic feedback activities, "awaken a whole series of functions" required for autonomous, and therefore mature, thinking (Vygotsky, 1987, p. 212), as well as collaborative learning (Assessment Reform Group, 1999; OECD, 2005a, 2005b; Linquisti, 2014).

Introduction

We see in the OECD (2016) statistical report that Japan scores significantly above the average levels related to performance and outcome equity. However, it is perhaps the ethnographic research conducted by Shinkawa and Arimoto (2012), as they documented the very challenging aftermath of the 2011 Fukushima cataclysm, that foregrounds the themes guiding the construction of this chapter. They observed the social reproduction of "altruism even in adversity," noting that Japanese interrelationships (*kankei*) are "rooted in thousands of years of Japanese tradition and [have] withstood outside influences" (p. 67). Shinkawa and Arimoto (2012), of Tohoku University, surveyed secondary students using the Education for Sustainable Development competency questionnaire. It was found that traditional cultural values assisted in the construction of resilient attitudes among the Japanese secondary students in their sample by supporting "cooperative working" or "stress-managing" competencies (p. 67).

The OECD's report on the 2015 PISA states that "the Japanese school system ensures equity in education opportunities" (2016, p. 1). Further, it makes the connection between examination performance and outcome equity: "Japan ... achieves high levels of performance and equity in education outcomes as assessed in PISA 2015, with 10% or less of the variation in student performance attributed to differences in students' socio-economic status" (p. 6). This finding emphasizes the cultural importance attached to outcome equity. It is a fundamentally important measure of whole-school success. This is partly because the role of Japanese teachers is much more diverse than "exam prep" since Japanese teachers consider the holistic development of students as the most important goal in education (Kasanage, 2013).

In concise terms, contingent feedback interactions follow a basic rule. That is, where there are two interactants (an interactant can be any participant, adult or child) A and B, the quality of the interaction *depends* on the extent of inter-subjectivity as follows: if B senses A's intentions accurately in that specific moment, then B is able to interact in ways that sustain the interaction to the satisfaction of A. The process of contingent assistance (cf. Vygotsky, 1987) is an interactive turn-taking social strategy. Contingent interaction sustains the learning task to successful completion, emphasizing cooperation with others, rejecting control over others. Contingent interaction is the *sine qua non* required for successful outcomes in collective settings, and yet stable intersubjective states are elusive and difficult to sustain. This is a formidable challenge for teachers, some of whom may even struggle to keep their students inside the classroom. More optimistically, in assessment terms, contingent interactivity is the basis for more effective or, more specifically, *reciprocal* feedback (Clark, 2012; Clark & Dumas, 2015). "Interactive turn-taking" therefore means much more than two or more learners working together. It is a strategy, and from the constructivist ideal learners are interactive when they assist each other equally and mutually while attempting to solve a particular challenge or problem. Equality is defined here as the level of authority or control over the task; pairs exhibiting a high level of equality have the ability to take direction from each other. Mutuality means the extent of engagement between each other's contributions. As dimensions of equality and mutuality extend, we see the emergence of reciprocal interaction – a more advanced iteration of contingent turn-taking. In due course, it will be seen that the immediate and contingent feedback, the synchronous aspect of formative assessment, is the social norm inside Japanese classrooms, particularly in mathematics.

In general, theoretical similarities, even across cultures, create a firm and flexible basis for comparative analysis of classroom feedback practices. This kind of comparative analysis is, as the OECD indicates, of particular importance where it relates to learning environments that support outcome equity. The OECD notes that in Western contexts, the interactive (or constructivist) foundation of "formative assessment has been shown to be highly effective in raising the level of student attainment, increasing equity of student outcomes, and improving students' ability to learn" (2005b, p. 2). The OECD's praise for interactive styles of assessment that ensure outcome equity parallels the dialogic teaching styles found in Japanese classrooms. Inevitably, then, the tacit questions and propositions guiding the construction of this chapter revolve around constructivist and equitable learning environments. Of particular relevance here is *kankei*, the Japanese word for interrelationships described as equitable, mutual, reciprocal, intersubjective, harmonious, stable, and balanced. The international research community knows that such relationships engage learners, motivating them to express their ideas and to assist each other toward a successful outcome. Put another way, Japanese classrooms optimize or balance stability (often perceived as formality) with interactivity, supporting "good learning" by the method of synchronous collection and strategic use of whole-group feedback (Inoue, 2010). It seems reasonable to denote the quality of *kankei* found in many Japanese classrooms as simply "contingent plus."

The Legacy of Masataro Sawayanagi's "New Education Movement"

As I sit here at the Graduate School of Education (GSE) of Tohoku University (established 1907), I am mindful of this university's foundational relevance to this interdisciplinary exploration of classroom feedback practice in Japan. The GSE's work, including that of the Japanese Assessment for Learning Network (JAfLN), has been made more meaningful by the foundational work of Dr. Masataro Sawayanagi (1865–1937), who was Tohoku University's first president, inaugurated in 1911, and before that, in 1906, a former vice-minister for education. Almost inevitably, his sincere commitment to the integration of global perspectives into traditional discourses led to his appointment as president of the very progressive Kyoto University in 1913. Sawayanagi, the son of a samurai of the Matsumoto clan, is little known outside Japan. In remarkable contrast, his sustainable vision for education has prompted a laudatory admiration here. Japanese historians consider him to be "one of the truly great figures in the history of modern Japanese education" (T. Kobayashi, 1990, p. 43). At Tohoku, Sawayanagi's emphasis on resolving school-related issues through dialogue with students earned him the accolade of "master president." Today, Sawayanagi is remembered and celebrated for his socially accomplished approach to education and his commitment to the development of mature thinking among his young students.

Creative integrations and adaptations of new and, due to its external origin, contentious knowledge were ignited by the advent of the Meiji Restoration (1868–1912). Under the direction of the Meiji government, a now unified Japan emerged from national isolation, and after more than two centuries drew a deep breath before the plunge into the modern industrial age. In this "new world," the elite Tohoku and Kyoto universities debated ideological modernizations associated with Japan's reintegration with the industrial world. What followed was an era remarkable for its highly active interest in the "state of the art." The new Meiji administration dispatched numerous educational missions to nations in Europe and North America. In due course, they returned with notions of decentralization, local school boards, and teacher autonomy. The formation of the Meiji government was an event with profound impact that propelled global research so that Japan had among the best economic, trade, technological, and cultural intelligence in the world. Ezra Vogel, in his very popular account of Japanese socioeconomics, remarked that, "in post-industrial society, knowledge . . . became a great rage in Japan's leading circles. But, these leading circles were merely articulating the latest formulation of what already had become conventional Japanese wisdom, the supreme importance of the pursuit of knowledge" (1979, p. 27).

It was against this backdrop of global intelligence-gathering that, in 1917, Sawayanagi founded the New Education Movement (NEM, *Shin Kyoiku Undo*). The NEM's protagonists were united by an intimate affinity with creative, student-centered teaching methods based on *zenjin* educational values – to promote autonomous learning strategies and to provide equitable opportunities for students to approach the Japanese ideal of the whole person. The NEM thrived at this time. In close correlation with John Dewey's laboratory school in the United States (founded in 1894), Sawayanagi founded Seijyo Elementary School in 1917. (Note that Dewey visited Japan in 1919.) It was a facility devoted to research, experiment, and educational innovation. Sawaya-nagi's vision connected powerfully with many of his contemporaries, including a notable junior associate of Sawayanagi's and a figure of considerable relevance to any discussion on twenty-first-century classroom practice, Kuniyoshi Obara (1887–1977). The NEM was significant because it provided Obara with an incubator that he used to enculture his students with *zenjin* education from 1921. Obara is just one influential figure from a pantheon of radical Japanese reformers of the early twentieth century. However, it is the ideal of *zenjin* that has shaped the contours of the Japanese national curriculum and the classroom feedback practices it legitimizes.

General provisions for *zenjin* education appear in the newest versions of the Japanese National Curriculum's "Courses of Study." These were issued between 2011 and 2013 and call specifically for the education of the "total child." The courses propose that the balanced development of students is encouraged through lessons called *tokubitsu katsudo*. Usually abbreviated to *tokkatsu* (special projects), these lessons were formalized as a regular curriculum subject by former Minister of Education Michita Sakata (in office 1968–1971). Sakata was strongly influenced by Obara's ideas and publicly stated his conviction of the benefits of *zenjin* education (M. Kobayashi, 2004). Since then, general provisions for *zenjin* education have been present in the guidelines for formal education issued by MEXT. In 2012, Director Hiroshi Sugita announced the priorities of *zenjin* education: "we decided to emphasise the fostering of abilities to build personal relationships, participating in society and encouraging autonomous abilities" (p. 1). In the same speech, Sugita encouraged teachers to "instruct with the intention of … fostering the ability for each child to do his or her very best in collaborating" (p. 2).

"Special projects" entail student leadership and coordination of various nonsubject activities taking place at lunch, club events, and student councils. The *tokkatsu* lessons are offered in addition to core curricular disciplines (e.g., mathematics, science, reading, and social studies), contributing less than 4% to the overall teaching hours at both elementary and junior high school levels (University of Tokyo, 2017). *Tokkatsu* represents a uniquely Japanese practice made by the energetic conjunction of Japanese cultural philosophy and imported intellectualism. Obara's formulation of *zenjin* education provides an enduring example of the creative integration of ideas from non-Japanese contexts into Japanese policy frameworks and institutional systems. Obara's standing as an intellectual leader of the time explains his legacy. By 1918, Obara was acknowledged as one of eight leading protagonists of the NEM, each with their own unique specialty in holistic student-centered education. In possession of an advanced capacity to think analogously, he demonstrated a remarkable skill in making conceptual connections requiring high levels of cultural literacy and reasoning ability. Obara fed his intellectual gifts with a fascination for the ancient and modern theories of philosophy, religious traditions, and political ideologies. Commendably, he explored them as an honorable civil servant might, weighing all sides of a philosophical and ideological theory before deciding on its contribution to the enrichment of human perspectives. By 1919, Sawayanagi, recognizing that Obara was a passionate and knowledgeable innovator, had invited him to oversee the day-to-day implementation of the Seijyo Elementary School project.

As coordinator for the project, Obara considered Sawayanagi's original problem of autonomy and refined his personal perspectives on thinking and learning (M. Kobayashi, 2004). He informed his work through consideration of influential European thinkers. The European Enlightenment (ending in the late eighteenth century) had ushered in a new European social and political order. This period of European history offered much to attract the proponents of Japan's radical NEM. The term "enlightenment" was defined by Immanuel Kant (1724–1804) as humankind's release from its self-incurred immaturity by the acquisition and development of autonomous thinking competences. "Immaturity," said Kant in 1794, "is the inability to use one's own understanding without the guidance of another" (p. 1), a view that later became the unitary purpose of the NEM. The Enlightenment brought philosophical change powered by the challenge to the existing order and the high value attached to autonomous thinking. These ideas resonated deeply with the membership of the NEM, with profound implications for educational practice. Accordingly, Obara advocated for "free development" and confidently asserted that his methods of instruction would ensure the optimal development of the *zenjin* personality in each and every one of his students. For Obara, this entailed the optimization of six basic values, drawn from Buddhist tradition and global philosophy (e.g., Plato), and that corresponded with the cultural activities of mankind (M. Kobayashi, 2004), namely: (1) truth as the ideal of academe, (2) goodness as the ideal of morality, (3) beauty as the ideal of art, (4) holiness as the ideal of religion, (5) health as the ideal of the body, and (6) wealth as the ideal of livelihood (Ajisaka, 1960). He attached the highest importance to these universal human values, proposing that they are attainable through the crafting of individuals' unique features toward models of cultural excellence.

The task for Obara and colleagues at the Kyoto School (established 1913; Obara joined in 1915) was to deliberate on the tensions and synergies between individual development (in Western contexts, personal development is contingent on the conscious regulation of the environment for personal gain), on the one hand, and the fundamentally interconnected nature of (Japanese) culture, on the other. The conception of individual control over the environment in collective settings was described by Stanford University's Albert Bandura, with the term "personal agency." Bandura argued that "to be an agent is to influence intentionally one's functioning and life circumstances" (Bandura, 2008, p. 16). Put another way, "personal agency refers to one's capability to originate and direct actions for given purpose" (Zimmerman & Cleary, 2006, p. 45). Together they capture the key elements of personal agency as defined in the North American context as: (1) self-reference for leadership and (2) environmental influence for personal gain. Personal agency is, therefore, the personal capability to exert influence over environmental factors with the ultimate goal of attaining valued outcomes and personal goals. Continuing that argument, most individuals, irrespective of their cultural perspective, strive to gain valued outcomes. The complexity quickly begins when moving from general observations to cultural specifics. This is because the social strategies by which personal goals are attained are perceived differently by contrasting cultural values systems (see Figure 21.1). In Western contexts, personal agency is a culturally sanctioned "self-referent" social norm (Bandura 1989, p. 1175) on which American capitalism is built. In comparison, Japanese classrooms operate to eliminate asymmetrical, leadership roles in a culture that expects modesty and individual self-sacrifice in deference to group harmony.

In the Japanese classroom, personal agency is therefore covert. It is not a sanctioned cultural norm for individuals to seek gratification by overtly referencing the self. For exponents of radical constructivism, belonging, reciprocal acts of trust, and mutual respect are regarded as the values of learning in today's world. These values satisfy the innate psychological needs of the learner and sanction the kinds of classroom interactions so that students engage in the emotionally risky process of becoming *zenjin* (Willis, 2010). In Japanese classrooms, the issue of personal agency may be (for the purposes of our model) creatively integrated into existing culture as autonomy in interdependent settings and the ideals of *zenjin* education (Cave, 2016). The aim of working in support of the total child so that he or she becomes an autonomous thinker, active learner, and effective problem-solver is perhaps the greatest challenge facing educators globally. This challenge is made all the more urgent because everywhere people of all ages are faced with making complex decisions in environments characterized by flux, uncertainty, and rapid change. In 1996, the Japanese Central Council for Education predicted that Japan would face "a difficult period of rapid change, in which the way ahead would be difficult to discern" (p. 62). Whatever the way ahead may be, history has taught us that rapid changes are created by a sudden coalescence of extra-political forces that seek to contest and challenge that which they perceive as oppression. No nation may merely observe in the stillness of its own culture as the world begins to move in new and interconnected directions.

In accordance with Dr. Sawayanagi's reform agenda, Japanese administrators and school staff pay careful attention to the promotion of student autonomy and provide many opportunities for its cultivation and development (Lewis, 1995). There is consensus that working alongside school staff who enact the role of "fellow travelers" prepares learners to be confident and capable of making good decisions inside, outside, and beyond school autonomously (Bransford, Derry, Berliner, Hammerness, & Beckett, 2005; Black & William, 2009; Vogt & Rogalla, 2009; Scottish Government, 2011; Sugita, 2012). Naturally, those "good decisions" may be rendered differently according to culture and custom (see Figure 21.1). Sugita (2012), of MEXT, directs Japanese teachers to work alongside learners, urging them to "observe what children are doing," to ask "how do you suffer with them, and what do you enjoy together," and to encourage autonomy by "letting children face problems which they can manage in sincere collaboration" (p. 3).

The very deliberate and creative integration of ideas that became *zenjin* education is a strong example of the blending of traditional and new, contentious ideas into a functioning cultural framework. Obara, because of his acceptance of the Enlightenment's ideas on the duality of the mind and heart, has been described as a committed individualist. While this is certainly so, it should be recalled that his guiding purpose was to integrate powerful Western concepts into the Japanese "cultural identity" entirely. Therefore, Obara's *zenjin* education realizes the optimal development of the human personality (as embodied by the six basic values) in a well-balanced and harmonious way. For it to be otherwise would result in a certain level of community rejection (as discussed in the work of Lave and Wenger (1991), later in the chapter) and the ultimate failure of his own underlying method. Manifestly, as a nation Japan attaches a great deal of value to cultural philosophies related to balance and harmony, explored next.

Buddhism as the "Background Theory" behind High-Quality Learning Environments

While the Japanese academy collaborated in constructing frameworks made from philosophical alloys, as a nation Japan was (and still is) a reflective society, self-aware, but within the means of their cultural identity. As Fereshteh (1992) observed, the Japanese "are alert to the end to maintain their own cultural values and practices at the core of any new system adopted. They regard culture as an integral, dynamic part of their society and economy" (p. 23). Therefore, Japan as a nation is sensitive to the deconstruction of its cultural identity that threatens to turn undeniable truths, thousands of years in the making, into uncertainties with multiple interpretations. This perception, not exclusive to Japan at all, is associated with internationalized lifestyles, globalized political systems, competition of economic interests, and networking patterns that have become organized at the surface layer of society in ways that seem to no longer feel the pull and draw of traditional cultural values.

Despite populist agitation to the contrary, Japan's cultural identity and the tacit background theories that constrain social norms remain resistant to the unchecked intrusion of destabilizing global forces (Shinkawa & Arimoto, 2012). In concise terms, background theories or cultural philosophies "constrain ways in which issues are conceived and types of explanations one gives, and frame one's descriptions of what needs explaining" (Thompson, 2002, p. 197). If those cultural constraints are breached, then it is expected that corrective sociopolitical forces will interlock in ways that characterize breaches as illegitimate. Buddhist tradition, as an aspect of Japanese culture, is therefore producer, constrainer, and, when triggered, gatekeeper of classroom community norms. It is worth noting that the Thompson quotation above was taken from a publication dedicated to radical constructivism. There is a basis for a comprehensive heuristic agreement between Buddhist background theory and radical constructivism. Certainly, both exert similar influences over group learning. Theoretical similarities will be discussed later in this chapter.

The activists who participated in the NEM's membership enjoyed an intimate involvement with world philosophies. It was their passion to integrate them into the tradition of balance and harmony seen as the foundational principles for human life (Fereshteh, 1992). The foundational values and tacit beliefs that define cultural systems exist at a deeper level in the sense that they are hidden and unarticulated social assumptions, understood by all to their fullest potential. In undeniably pervasive abstraction sometimes difficult to grasp, the ancient values of Buddhism "live" inside Japanese classrooms in these tacit forms. The impact of Buddhist thought can be illustrated by two key tenets that facilitate balanced and equitable interrelationships on which interactive styles of assessment depend. One is "citta," which translates as "heart or mind." The other is the *Brahma-viharas*, the four "divine abiding" or mental states.

In the ancient Pali language of India – widely studied as the language of the earliest extant literature of Buddhism – the word *citta* describes a conceptual nexus between "mind" (cognitive functions) and "heart" (affective functions). The idiom "to learn by heart" emphasizes depth in learning, attainable only when learners are encouraged to express themselves. This may sound like an invitation to chaos. On the contrary, citta recognizes the balanced weighting of cognitive and socioemotional perspectives on learning, and why balance is important for *zenjin* development. (For general information, see Collaborative for Academic, Social, and Emotional Learning, www.casel.org/.)

It is widely understood that Japanese cultural philosophy places high implicit value on the socioemotional aspects of social life and learning. The "mind-heart nexus" is, perhaps without their intent, implied in Black and Wiliam's (2009) reference to learners' "inner mental life." As a single concept, inner mental life suggests the interior complexity of the "heart or mind nexus." It would seem safe to presume that Buddhist canon was not in Black and Wiliam's deliberations in that paper of 2009, entitled "Developing the Theory of Formative Assessment." Coincidentally, then, these differing theoretical constructs, one from twentieth-century social cognition, the other from traditions thousands of years old, underpin similarities in interactive learning environments of the twenty-first century. When educators from self-referent cultures (e.g., North America) accept that their students' emotional and motivational states are influential over feedback production, they have then adapted their teaching to meet the needs not just of the student but of the whole child. And, although obvious, it may be noted that the needs of an effective learner are not met by "protecting the child," a concern explored in early Western studies on formative assessment (see Pryor & Torrance, 1996). In Japan, expert teachers favor interactive styles that elicit learners' recondite knowledge for synchronous whole-group feedback. In doing so, they are balancing cognitive needs with emotional/motivational needs to attain valuable and successful outcomes. School-level plans, therefore, operate to legitimize and reproduce interactive assessment methods that pursue *zenjin* outcomes (Sugita, 2012; MEXT, n.d. a) and assure outcome equity (OECD, 2005a, 2016). One important outcome for Japan is the weakening of the correlation between socioeconomic status and examination results that creates the very asymmetrical achievement gaps experienced by other nations.

Zenjin assessment activities have been confirmed to promote equity among children studying in other Asian contexts. For example, in Hong Kong, Cheng, Lam, and Chan (2008) found that "the quality of group processes played a pivotal role because both high and low achievers were able to benefit when group processes were of high quality" (p. 205). *Zenjin* assessment practices depend on interactive approaches that have the potential to provide assessment data that deepen understanding of the "wholeness" of the learner. Wholeness is a traditional concept pursued through *bhavana* – the process of becoming mentally cultivated. The process of "becoming" is, by its own description, a transitional process. Bostock and Wood (2014) suggested that transitions are profound periods of change and transformation, and children in schools "should be studied and managed to ensure that [they] are able to grow and thrive during these difficult phases in their education" (p. 3). The balanced cultivation of learners' "inner mental" lives is also potentially transformative. This idea can be seen in Popham's (2008) concise discussion of formative assessments, entitled *Transformative Assessment*.

Another key Buddhist concept of relevance to any discussion on interactive feedback in the specific cultural context of Japanese classrooms is the *Brahma-viharas*. The ancient text in which they appear states the four virtues of "metta" (loving kindness), "karuna" (compassion), "mudita" (sympathetic joy), and "upekka" (equanimity). These endemic cultural meta-values, which may sound a little like romantic evocations from mythopoetry, have in reality a prevailing and pervasive influence over learning relationships. It is a teacher's responsibility to model these virtues so students may at first through observation reproduce interactive feedback strategies. Success occurs when young learners internalize the virtues and see themselves as becoming interactive and autonomous learners. First, metta addresses the quality of human relationships (e.g., caring and goodwill). Supportive relationships improve academic self-concepts and energize learners' interconnectedness with the learning environment. Such robust interrelationships improve the quality of "formative feedback." Careful whole-group probing and elicitation guides young learners in the acquisition of autonomous thinking skills. However, simply instructing students to work harder or recalculate their answers is not feedback that promotes autonomous learning because it does not strategically guide (or scaffold) learning by informing students how or why they need to do this. If positive learning identities are to form, then the insecurity inherent to guesswork should be eliminated by effective scaffolding as observed in Stigler and Hiebert's (1999) seminal papers on lesson study in Japanese classrooms. Effective scaffolding, as seen in the foundational work of Wood, Bruner, and Ross (1976), means providing assistance *only* when the student is unable to complete the next step of a task. To intervene too early would frustrate the development of learners' capacities to gain control over their autonomous learning strategies. Feedback becomes formative when it is used as information to adapt the content and timing of teachers' dialogues in ways that meet student needs (Sadler, 1989). More specifically, students are provided with instruction or thoughtful questioning that scaffolds further inquiry and deepens cognitive processing.

Second, karuna guides practices that alleviate suffering and recognize that all beings are engaged in some aspect of struggle. As such, it is unwise to judge others hastily. Such values have numerous implications for learning environments, including *zenjin* approaches to classroom assessment and rigorous approaches to academic research and inquiry. The third virtue, mudita, synonymous with the reciprocal aspects of intersubjectivity, is the capacity to enjoy the accomplishments of others and reject jealousy. Teachers model a collaborative environment that emphasizes that individual success is both a consequence of and a contribution to the whole community. The fourth and final virtue of the Brahma-viharas is upekka, or equanimity. This is to understand impermanence and insubstantiality as natural qualities of reality. It is a source of introspection and interconnection that deepens awareness of the true nature of assessment events unfolding in the classroom.

The importance of the affective component of the mind or heart nexus is implicit in Schilbach et al.'s (2013) comprehensive scientific review of brain-to-brain interaction. Schilbach and colleagues found that emotional engagement is required in order to gain intersubjective states of consciousness – a necessary condition for the recruitment of the neural reward-related (dopamine) networks to occur. The relevance of intersubjectivity to educational practice is two-fold. The first component is the extent to which the "hidden" ideas, intentions, and values of one participant are accessible to, understood, and reciprocated by others. The second stems from the increasingly relevant empirical domain of social neuroscience, which clarifies intersubjectivity as the basis for contingent interaction that may recruit the dopamine-releasing networks. As desirable as this sounds, we also know from our own personal experience of others that a stable intersubjective state is sometimes elusive and difficult to sustain. Regulation is needed to reproduce stable learning communities, a fact by no means lost on the global research community. In his MEXT speech, Sugita (2012) called specifically for the "discipline and stability" required to "understand children … construct a bond with them," and, in reference to Buddhist tract, "build a classroom community" where learners face the prospect of classroom assessment with equanimity (p. 3). In England, the year-long "SPRinG programme" was aimed at addressing the wide gap between the potential of group interaction to promote learning and its limited use in schools. The project involved working with primary school teachers to develop strategies for enhancing group work and dialogue and to implement a relational and group-skills training program (Baines, Rubie-Davis, & Blatchford, 2009). Twenty-first-century neuroscientific findings (e.g., Allen & Williams, 2011) verified Japanese cultural philosophy's prevailing and pervasive message and indicated that verbal consensus-building, as one would expect to find in formative assessment settings, creates a stable learning environment.

There is a broad intercultural consensus that for all human beings there is the possibility of transformation through mental cultivation, which results ultimately in heightened mindfulness. Kabat-Zinn (2013) expressed this concept well in English: "Mindfulness means paying attention in a particular way; on purpose, in the present moment, and non-judgementally" (p. xxvii). In the ancient Pali language, the word is "sati," which can also mean alertness, recollection, or retention – words that relate directly to the moment-to-moment processes for gathering information from the world around us. Implicit in the idea of mindfulness is impartiality and outcome equity. The inquiry then becomes one of how might practitioners conceptualize and facilitate an interactive learning environment? The capacity of classroom teachers to capitalize on spontaneous opportunities to engage in high-quality feedback practices resides in their mindfulness. The Japanese word for mindfulness is *kizuki* (Arimoto, 2017); it approximates to Kounin's term "with-it-ness" (Kounin, 1977) or, alternatively, realizing, becoming aware of, or noticing (Sakamoto, 2011). *Kizuki* is unique to Japanese culture, drawing from Buddhist teachings about skills that build an attentiveness required for synchronous feedback. Nichiren (1222–1282), a monk known for his devotion to Buddhist studies, provided some quite ancient thoughts on feedback: "a person can know another's mind by listening to his voice. This is because the physical aspect reveals the spiritual aspect. The physical and the spiritual, which are one in essence, manifest themselves as two distinct aspects" (Thien, 2004, p. 256). In the context of assessment, the term *kizuki* conveys the cultivation of teachers' whole focus in order to develop insights into the true nature of their students' learning.

Interpreting "Constructivism" Inside the Japanese Classroom

> Exploring mathematics with groups of people is inherently a cultural practice.
> (Kazemi, Elliott, Hubbard, Carroll, & Mumme, 2007, p. 797)

The purpose of this section is to describe in "optimal definition" the culturally produced classroom processes associated with the collection and use of learning evidence inside the mathematics classrooms of Japanese elementary schools. We coin the term "optimal definition" in recognition of Wiliam's insightful observation that universal definitions are not useful here because "all research findings are generalizations and as such are either too general to be useful or too specific to be universally applicable" (Wiliam & Leahy, 2007 p. 39). While this is undoubtedly true, there is a sense of irony in the admission that some limited generalizability is possible in the Japanese context, even if it is merely the sequence of transitions between lesson stages in mathematics lessons. This is because there is a stable, almost "canonical" order to these lessons. While a traditional and stable "lesson blueprint" exists, it should be remembered that teachers acquire the skills required for a whole-class dialogic style of teaching only after rigorous lesson study (Shimizu, 1999).

In mathematics lessons, teachers typically transition among four distinct lesson stages: *hatsumon* (posing a problem, often termed the "hook" question), *kikan-shido* (instruction at students' desks), *neriage* (in-depth dialogic interaction), and *matome* (summing up). Of particular interest for their potential to provide high-quality feedback are stages two (*kikan-shido*) and three (*neriage*). Stage two provides opportunities for observations of student work and some individual questioning. Stage three, *neriage*, is the "heart" of the lesson and provides opportunities for the collection and use of synchronous formative feedback (Clark, 2012) on a whole-group basis. The term *neriage* relates to the work of a craftsman and embodies the spirit of a true worker or artisan with good spirit, technique, and physical condition. When it is applied to classroom interaction, the *neriage* stage alludes to elevating, elaborating, and kneading, not clay, but the substance of student reasoning using blackboard and peer equitable assessment interaction in the whole class.

In the language of the neo-Vygotskian constructivists Goos, Galbraith, and Renshaw (2002), whole-group feedback strategies are "best understood as involving the mutual adjustment and appropriation of ideas" (p. 195) inside the "collaborative ZPD [zone of proximal development]" (cf. Vygotsky, 1978). For many educators, the often-quoted constructivist concept of the "zone of proximal development," originated by Vygotsky, elucidates classroom feedback practices most completely. The ZPD is the conceptual gap, or distance between the current level of understanding, and the next (or proximal) level of understanding. Vygotskian theory guides practitioners to reject reductionist modes of thinking. Both Buddhist philosophy and Vygotskian theory concur on the importance of contingent social interaction. However, Japanese cultural tradition constrains social norms in ways that require a more specific term than "contingent." Japanese interrelationships depend on *reciprocity*, or in the language of the constructivist, collaboration. To illustrate the inseparability of self and environment as they interact to create meaning, Vygotsky (1987) analogizes that in order to understand how water extinguishes a flame one does not attempt to reduce it to its elements. To do so means that the scientist will "discover, to his chagrin that hydrogen burns and oxygen sustains combustion. He will never succeed in explaining the characteristics of the whole by analyzing the characteristics of the elements" (p. 45). In accordance with constructivist theory, traditional Japanese values reproduce the social norms from which reciprocal learning interactions arise (see Figure 21.1).

Radical constructivists Lave and Wenger (1991) completed their anthropological study of craft apprenticeships in rural West Africa and concluded that "learning involves the whole person; it implies not only a relation to social communities – it implies becoming a full participant, a member, a kind of person" (p. 3). The constructivism of Lave supports the formative assessment literature's emphasis on sharing assessment criteria, learning goals, and collaborative learning. For example, Lave (1991) observed of the Vygotskian novice–expert relationship that "newcomers furnished with comprehensive

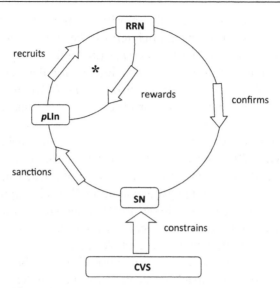

Figure 21.1 *Schematic describing the processes linking cultural value systems (CVS), social norms (SN), "positive" learning interactions (pLIn), and the dopamine reward-related networks (RRN) to be found in the human mid-brain region. Positive is denoted with a lowercase* p *because there is no objective measure of whether an interaction is positive. It is a cultural value judgment, and as such differs between cultural contexts. * Denotes bidirectional, mutually reinforcing relationship.*

goals, an initial view of the whole, improvising within the multiply structured field of mature practice with near peers and exemplars of mature practice – these are characteristic of communities of practice that re-produce themselves successfully" (p. 72). Lave and Wenger's fieldwork supports the proposition that the use of formative assessment creates active and engaged participants with an increasing potential to acquire "mastery . . . without didactic structuring and in such a fashion that knowledgeable skill is part of the construction of new identities of mastery in practice" (Lave, 1991, p. 64). This is seen in the Japanese public school system's strategy of interyear collaborations between older and younger students who learn together for their mutual benefit. In Japan, the cross-grade study partner system is an energetic national strategy, entirely consistent with the MEXT focus on the positive association between autonomous life skills and equitable collaboration skills.

Constructivist practices are ubiquitous, and therefore the observations of Lave and Wenger are also consistent with the perspectives of the early twentieth-century New Education Movement and with twenty-first-century policy perspectives (Sugita, 2012). The rationale behind Lave and Wenger's concept of social reproduction – legitimate peripheral participation (LPP) in "social communities" – intersects with aspects of Japanese social structure: hierarchical social structures that exist as the foundation for culturally sanctioned processes that, despite the vertical structure, promote collaboration and stability in pursuit of wholeness. It also shares a great deal of spirit with the practice of Japanese lesson study. Consistent with the discussion on construct-ivism, Shimahara (1998) described the uniqueness of the Japanese model of lesson study as "craft knowledge" based on "apprenticeship through which occupational practice from the past is perpetuated" (p. 451). Shimahara (1998) noted that when teachers are engaged in lesson study, they are collect-ively "committed to creating and regenerating craft knowledge of teaching" (p. 451), because Japanese teachers' activities are embedded in their lives.

LPP is, in part, a process of becoming "whole." As seen in the fieldwork of Lave and Wenger (1991) and foundational studies on contingent feedback (Vygotsky, 1987), learners share knowledge and learn best from each other through reciprocal interaction (cooperation) as opposed to didactic "top-down" instruction and assessment (control). Classrooms that nurture reciprocal learn-ing relationships establish a cultural ambience, or climate, that encapsulates students within a uniquely harmonious sociocultural context for an interactive style of assessment and feedback. This (1) negates the psychological risks associated with being verbally assessed in front of the whole room and (2) promotes a sense of self-worth among students as valuable contributors whether their answers are right or wrong. The assurance of equitable learning environ-ments is a constant across the theoretical spectrum, ranging from social cogni-tion theories (as seen in Bandura's social cognitive theory) to radical constructivism (as in Lave and Wenger's LPP) and the theoretical space in between where theories of formative assessment are conceived (Clark, 2012). The process of "becoming" through participation in community norms and the outcome of wholeness are manifest in the active social construction of legitim-ate identities as interactive learners (Lave, 1991; Wiliam, Bartholomew & Reay, 2004; Willis, 2010).

The emphasis on the social negotiation of meaning is entirely consonant with Japanese learning policy and practice. In this chapter we have seen that this is particularly true of the dialogic *neriage* stage of mathematics lessons. In the Vygotskian conception of interactive learning, students traverse the ZPD by interacting either with peers who have the knowledge to assist or with experts (e.g., teachers). The Japanese Central Council for Education (1996) emphasized that parents are also important participants. If "competences for positive living" are to be cultivated, it is important for schools, parents, and the community to work together as partners (as cited in Shinkawa & Arimoto, 2012, p. 62). In this environment, young learners may work alongside adults in synchronicity. In the twenty-first-century classroom, many teachers of every cultural extraction are encouraged to use well-practiced observational and verbal strategies to elicit feedback in a process that Schön called "reflection in action" (1987). Wenger (1998) described the social component of Schön's reflection in action as possessing "a flavour of continuous interaction, of grad-ual achievement and of give and take" (p. 53). Here, "continuous interaction . . . of give and take" parallels the sustained and reciprocal norms of social inter-action expected of Japanese students.

Teachers who have become professionally adapted to the use of dialogic feedback practices, such as those seen in *neriage* and formative feedback lesson stages are, according to the US National Research Council (2000), "adaptive experts." These are expert teachers who are flexible and able to respond contingently by modifying existing or inventing new procedures to meet learners' moment-to-moment needs. Such practitioners are more likely to innovate approaches that better equip them to capitalize on opportunities and solve problems that could otherwise appear mystifying (Hatano & Oura, 2003). Bransford et al. (2005) noted the difference between adaptive experts and "routine experts." They emphasized that for students to become effective learners, they need to be taught by teachers who have received initial and continuing training (as seen in Japanese lesson study) in interactive feedback strategies (Black & Wiliam, 1998; Vogt & Rogalla, 2009; Inoue, 2010). Routine experts have a range of core competencies that they consistently deploy across the span of their lifetimes to attain increasing efficiency. Adaptive experts, however, have core competencies such as "adaptability, creativity and innovativeness." They are "people who aren't focused only on payoffs but do the best they can to learn, adapt, improve" (Benkler, 2011, p. 85). In Benkler's vision of a process without payoffs, we see the concept of altruism, a concept residing at the deeper levels of Japanese culture. The quest for the adaptive expert, as described earlier, is consonant with the cultivation of professional skills during Japanese lesson study. US-based Japanese authority on mathematics education Noriyuki Inoue and colleagues presented a paper entitled "Deconstructing adaptive teacher expertise for inquiry-based teaching in Japanese elementary classrooms: Neriage as inter-subjective pedagogy for social mind-storming" at the 2016 European Educational Research Association conference (Inoue, Asada, Maeda, & Nakamura, 2016). In Inoue et al.'s title, there are many keywords of relevance to the discussions in this chapter; "inquiry-based," "inter-subjective," and "social mind-storming" are particularly evocative collocations. The adaptive-expert model, in its idealized form, is described by Bransford et al. (2005) as "the gold standard." No matter how benchmarks and standards are described, it seems reasonable to expect that the criteria recognizing teachers' quality as interactive assessors would be intrinsically similar for cross-cultural contexts of *neriage*, formative assessment, and adaptive expertise. How, then, do Inoue et al.'s claims of "inter-subjective pedagogy" demonstrate their sociocultural foundation in the practical reality of the Japanese mathematics lesson? We turn to that next.

An Introduction to Strategic Interactions Inside Japanese Mathematics Classrooms

The inherent systemic stability typical of Japanese classrooms makes it possible to move from the general sense of "a math lesson in Japan" to the more specific "Japanese mathematics lesson" or what Shulman (2005) terms as "signature pedagogy." Japanese lesson study tends to prescribe whole-class interaction, so students have the opportunity to engage in feedback that raises whole-class attainment rather than that of individual students. The skill of directing questions to the "collective student" was found in the practice of expert Japanese mathematics teachers, and typically absent from that of novices, who tended to treat students' questions as being from individual learners (Bromme & Steinbring, 1994). Inoue (2010) worked with fourth- and fifth-grade mathematics teachers in San Diego, California, who wanted to develop *neriage*-like skills. Participating teachers reported that interacting with the collective student was a "major problem" and could not be established as a legitimate social norm. Some teachers scaffolded their lessons heavily, distributing written prompts to help students begin thinking and articulating their ideas to the group.

The teachers in the study overcame their tacit preconceptions around cultural identity, requiring only two months to transition into more competent facilitators of whole-group student interaction, in part by interjecting their own ideas less frequently. Black and Wiliam (2006), in their research on the dialogic classroom with UK and US teachers, reported similar findings: "the task of developing an interactive style of classroom dialogue required a radical change in teaching style for many teachers ... some were well over a year into the project before such changes were achieved" (p. 14). As with all transitions, community cohesion is integral to success, as displayed in the "highly interactive and complex discussions" (Inoue, 2010, p. 13) that took place among teachers during rewarding (collaborative) meetings.

The Japanese Mathematics Lesson Deconstructed

The following discussion is applicable to any curriculum subject that can be taught through inquiry and problem-solving. It continues the trend in this chapter of emphasizing mathematics as an important discipline and a key research area. The Japanese mathematics lesson, the structure of which was introduced earlier in the chapter, again opens with the *hatsumon*. This opening question should be refined so that it engages student attention. It deals with concepts, yet it can be based on a simple math problem, such as 84 divided by 14. The task is not to calculate the answer; the point is to understand that both dividend (84) and divisor (14) can be divided by the same number without changing the result. The *hatsumon* often deals with the reconstruction of generalizable concepts of this kind to similar problems. To plan for and effectively set up lessons where learners talk about meta-strategies is seen as particularly important by Pellegrino et al. (2001). In their policy document for the National Research Council, they emphasized that assessments should assess the "efficiency and appropriateness" of students' problem-solving skills: "Assessments should focus on identifying the specific strategies children are using for problem solving, giving particular consideration to where those strategies fall on a developmental continuum of efficiency and appropriateness for a particular domain of knowledge and skill" (p. 3). In mathematics as in life, if problem-solving strategies are to be reconstructed successfully, then learners must have a strong understanding of the underlying principles of what was learned. In this way, they can recognize novel situations that relate closely to those previously encountered, and deploy *zenjin* strategies to resolve any challenges and problems.

In the second, *kikan-shido* stage, teachers gather evidence of the students' problem-solving methods through observation. It is a generally silent stage of collection used along with evidence collected from teachers' prior experience of teaching this topic to other students. Some teachers will also use questioning to elicit evidence of individual learning if they think it is useful to the "collective student" in the next group-discussion stage of the lesson. While doing so, they decide which student groups will be the first to attend the board so that the third stage, the heart of the lesson called *neriage*, may begin.

In accordance with the Japanese emphasis on consensual meaning-making, teacher and students engage in a "dynamic" and "collaborative" (Shimizu, 1999) process known as *neriage*. Inoue et al. (2016) described it as "inter-subjective pedagogy for cultural mind-storming." *Neriage* is an ancient term borrowed from the traditional pottery-craft industry. It offers a rich cultural metaphor that deconstructs classroom dialogue as the "kneading," "layering," and "polishing" of students' ideas. Inoue (2010) emphasized whole-class con-sensus building dialogue as the *sine qua non* of successful learning because it assists "students [to] build consensus on the best mathematical strategy and think deeply about problem-solving" (p. 5). In Japanese society, consensus-building is the social norm. In everyday conversation, phrases such as *so desu ne* (yes, I see your point) create a sense of reciprocal understanding resembling agreement. They are intended to facilitate further harmonious interaction. Such courteous sensitivities are called *kizukai* (or *kikubari*), meaning alertness and attention to others' needs or feelings. This requires not only accommodative positive behavior but also *enryo* (self-imposed restraint) to avoid causing *mei-waku*, an extremely common word that covers a comprehensive gamut of meanings, including trouble, burden, inconvenience, annoyance, displeasure, and discomfort.

As a microcosm of wider social life, the Japanese classroom is fully engaged with interactions that build and consolidate consensus (Takahashi, 2008; Inoue, 2010; Walshaw 2011). Walshaw (2011) remarked that "*neriage* is centred on whole-class discussions in which the teacher compares and contrasts different students' strategies and, rather than pointing to the best solution, works to build consensus amongst students" (p. 2). The reciprocal interactions of *neriage* parallel the "synchronous feedback" (Black & Wiliam, 2009) at the heart of a more effective dialogic style of teaching. In the abstract, *neriage* and formative feedback originate in the heart–mind nexus. It is therefore entirely logical to state that where the needs of the *zenjin* are not being met, it is just as damaging to *neriage* as to formative feedback, or any kind of interactive assessment founded on interrelationships. It is, after all, a logical justification for the general adoption of *zenjin* approaches to classroom instruction and assessment.

Neriage has been described as the "heart of the lesson [that] begins *after* students come up with solutions" (Takahashi, 2008). After students have done their best to formulate solutions (in the *kikan-shido* stage), students are assisted in their efforts to uncover important mathematical ideas as they analyze and compare solutions. In the *neriage* stage, students are carefully guided by the teacher as they critically analyze, compare, and contrast the shared ideas. The concept of *neriage* also uses the artisan (*waza*) as a symbol for the whole person, who is in possession of good spirit, technique, and physical condition. It is by more than rhetorical connection that the *neriage* metaphor signals to all participants that this stage of the lesson is a culturally venerated process. As such, it surpasses superficial student presentations (micro-summative assessments) by accommodating a careful, multiphase collection of learning evidence for immediate (synchronous) use or for use later, asynchronously (Black & Wiliam, 2009; Clark, 2012).

During *neriage*, students are called on to consider issues like efficiency, generalizability, and similarity to previously learned ideas (Takahashi, 2008). This is more clearly illustrated in a video funded by the US Department of Education (Lesson Study Group, n.d.). In the video, Takahashi interacts with US fourth-grade students as they calculate the area of a polygon. However, the desired learning outcome is not to find the area. The "big idea" is for students to reconstruct the same method in order to find the areas of similar yet novel shapes. In the video, students are seen working in pairs or small groups. At the end of the group-work phase, the students are invited to the marker board where they explain their method while the teacher probes their conceptual understanding and annotates a picture of the polygon with their ideas. Eventually, six different methods of solution are written on the marker board. In the latter part of the lesson, the teacher asks the students how they are different.

From *neriage*, the lesson transitions to the fourth and final stage: *matome* (summing up). Although *neriage* is seen as the heart of the lesson, the overall quality of the lesson depends on planning and monitoring during *kikan-shido* and the essential reflection during *matome*. Japanese teachers see *matome* as indispensible. Shimizu (1999) noted that *matome* "is identified as a critical difference" (p. 111) between Japanese classroom activities and those documented elsewhere. Japanese mathematics teachers, through rigorous lesson study, are practiced in making "a final and careful comment on students' work in terms of mathematical sophistication" by "theorizing key ideas and applications of the ideas to new problems" (Inoue et al., 2016, p. 2). In the aforementioned US Department of Education video, the lesson is shown to end with a clear statement from the teacher on the general applicability of the "agreed on" method: "Let's use the way that we solved this problem with other shapes." In the Japanese context, "consensus building discussions" (Inoue, 2010) reproduce and reward reciprocity and diminish the negative motivational states associated with public comparison.

The *neriage* stage's constructivist methods create a direct parallel with the methods arising from Vygotsky's ZPD or Wood's (1976) scaffolding. All refer to forms of assisted learning, and "assisted learning is the method by which instructional and motivational goals are integrated" (Sivan, 1986, p. 211). If the integration of these goals is to take place, then teachers, their students, and their peers need to sustain *intersubjectivity* (Walker, 2010). This is an interpersonal process that entails the making of subjective inferences in order to gain insights about the intentions and perspectives of others. Subjective inference is a fundamental process that determines whether interactions are contingent and support learning, or whether they are noncontingent and will not. This process of meaning-making has been described as a *neural basis* for learning relationships (Clark & Dumas, 2015). Higher-level intersubjectivity (or "cognitive empathy," a term that combines mind and heart) reveals the actions and emotional states of others and forms the basis for contingent responses that sustain learning interactions to a successful conclusion. In Japan, intersubjectivity plays a particularly powerful role in sustaining the reciprocity required for legitimate learning interactions. Lebra (1976) explains that "implicit, nonverbal, intuitive communication" is valued above an "explicit, verbal exchange of information" (p. 46). In Japan's unique cultural circumstance, intersubjectivity maintains and sustains culturally sanctioned reciprocal interrelationships. Indeed, reciprocal interactions exist at the very center of effective social and learning interactions, as the neuroscientific work of Sakaiya et al. (2013) indicates, discussed next.

Cultural Values, Neural Reward, and "Positive" Learning Interactions

Sakaiya et al. (2013), a team of research scientists at the University of Tokyo, conducted a neuroimaging study to investigate neural recruitment during live face-to-face interaction. They reported two findings with major implications for learning. First, the intensity of *emotion* associated with reciprocal styles of interaction presents in the mesolimbic dopamine reward system of the brain. Put another way, when humans engage in reciprocal interactions in pursuit of a common outcome, the mid-brain structures produce dopamine, a chemical that creates a sense of well-being and even excitement. In terms of their general findings, Sakaiya et al.'s study confirmed those of an earlier study by Redcay et al. (2010). However, to pause briefly on a quite salient cultural point, the Japanese study focused intentionally on the cultural cornerstone of "reciprocal" social interactions, going as far to specify that Japanese society may not function at all without reciprocal relationships. In contrast, Redcay et al.'s functional magnetic resonance imaging study in the North American context does not confer a similar emphasis on interrelationships. It does, however, confirm that those key neural structures recruited for everyday social interaction (right temporoparietal junction, anterior cingulate cortex, and right superior temporal sulcus) are "consistently linked" to the activation of the dopaminergic reward system. The same study emphasized "the powerful and pervasive drive" (p. 7) for humans to seek out social interactions and reiterated that contingent interactions with another person recruits the reward systems (Redcay, et al., 2010; Guionnet et al., 2012; Krill & Platek, 2012; Sakaiya et al., 2013; Schilbach et al., 2013). The neuroscientific evidence regarding contingent interaction provides empirical basis for Black and Wiliam's notional "moments of contingency" (2009, p. 10). These "moments" are described as a series of opportunities to interact in ways that further learning. Moments may be created by an accomplished teacher, and where they arise spontaneously, moments should be capitalized on immediately. This requires synchronous, yet well-considered adjustments in learning discourse. In formative environments, such moments of contingency arise continuously and can become teachable moments when teachers listen carefully, probe into students' conceptual understanding, and respond in ways that construct further understanding from learners' previous answers. In addition, contingent interactions cultivate autonomous verbal reasoning in collective settings. So, when a teacher is in a contingent iinteraction, he or she is also scaffolding learning in the constructivist tradition.

In related neuroscientific work, US scientists Salamone and Correa (2012) found that the simple expectation of a rewarding interaction based on past experience recruits dopamine production. This response makes it more likely that learners will engage enthusiastically and sustain the next interaction to a mutually agreeable conclusion. In a carefully structured group-learning ecology, the dopamine effect has a clear potential to motivate, reinforcing engagement and succeeding negative psychological states caused by teachers' negative public comparisons between students. However, Salamone and Correa (2012) emphasized that beneficial outcomes are not inevitable or equally distributed among the participants, so that there is significant variability in how children identify themselves as good or poor learners in any cultural context. The second, and equally important, finding by Sakaiya and colleagues (2013) was that intersubjectivity is so essential that without it, cooperative human relationships appear impossible. Although the emphasis on the intersubjective basis for reciprocal social interaction arises from unique cultural tradition, it is also a proposition supported by European research, for example, as noted in Schilbach et al.'s (2013) German-based review of the neural basis for social interaction (also see Clark & Dumas, 2015). Such findings suggest the inherent capacity of Japanese communities to reproduce reciprocal relationships for successful *zenjin* outcomes.

What Is a "Positive" Learning Interaction?

"Positive" learning interactions are, on the surface, definitively "good," particularly for classrooms that claim to value interactive styles of assessment. Right? Perhaps not: the idea of "positive" is entirely subjective, depending on cultural perception. Findings from empirical psychology (Kitayama, Marksus,

& Kurokawa, 2000) and social neuroscience (Sakaiya et al., 2013) indicate that cultural values place unique constraints and pose problems around the social norms from which legitimate and rewarding moment-to-moment interactions arise. Kitayama et al.'s study found that cultural values constrain social interaction, and where those constraints are breached, cultural values regard those interactions as erroneous. Neural rewards are available only when people are engaged in culturally sanctioned modes of social interaction. This relationship is elaborated on in Figure 21.1.

Just as the field of social neuroscience began to explain the neural (intrinsic) rewards experienced during social interaction, Kitayama et al. (2000) published their psychological study on cultural values, motivation, and social interaction. They drew their sample from Japanese and US college students. Kitayama et al. hypothesized as follows: "Feelings of well-being are associated with independence and interpersonal disengagement in America, and with inter-dependence and interpersonal engagement in Japan" (p. 97). Contrasting datasets were expected based on the given differences in culture and the resultant social psychology of the nations under review. These differences were framed as "culturally sanctioned views." In the United States, the view of the self as independent is associated with asymmetrical relationships and social disengagement. The social reproduction of this view entails "asserting and protecting one's own rights, acting on the basis of one's own attitudes or judgements, and separating or distinguishing the self from the context" (p. 95). In comparison, the Japanese view of the self as *inter*dependent is reflected in a socially engaging disposition, which emphasizes empathy, personal sacrifice, and a uniquely constructivist perspective on the relationship between self and significant others in the social environment (Lebra, 1976, 2004).

Participants from both countries were provided with a list of "positive" emotions of two types. The first type, "interpersonally *disengaging* positive emotions," included superiority, pride, and "top of the world"; generally speaking it is the nationalistic concept of "number one." The second type, "interpersonally *engaging* positive emotions," included closeness, friendliness, and respect. Kitayama and colleagues (2000) found that the US students in the sample derived more intrinsic pleasure from socially disengaging emotions such as feelings of superiority during an interaction. In contrast, their Japanese counterparts reported a greater sense of well-being when experiencing socially engaging positive emotions, such as those experienced during reciprocal interaction.

Reflection

This chapter has placed heavy emphasis on the importance of cultural influence over whole-group dialogic processes and on the interconnectedness that Japanese students find intrinsically rewarding. More specifically, it explored how culture constrains the social norms that sanction legitimate community participation from within. Research in this area would benefit greatly from new and interdisciplinary branches of neuroscience, such as "sociocultural neuroscience" (see Sakaiya et al., 2013) and "educational neuroscience" (see Clark & Dumas, 2016). Regrettably, many otherwise brilliant scientists look to the past and reject interdisciplinary studies that seek to blend social psychology and neuroscience together as mixing oil and water. We contest this and note that one of the fundamental pillars supporting the link between education and neuroscience is the ability of the brain to learn. This challenges the perspective that the human brain and learning should be viewed in different ways and, further, suggests a neural basis for learning.

From the global perspective, it is correct to say that Japanese cultural values constrain social norms so that "Japanese society tends to value formality in public contexts. This is true of schools in Japan. Hence, formality is more important than creativity" (Takanashi, 2004, p. 9). Yet, in Japan, formality is better understood as stability, a necessary condition for intersubjectivity. Eurocentric evocations of formative assessment's creative and spontaneous qualities are treated as items of only potential interest in non-Western contexts, not least for their self-referent bases. For example, North American researchers Macintyre, Buck, and Beckenhauer (2007) enthusiastically described the "qualities integral to formative assessments" as "resisting imposed routine, demanding reason alongside ongoing judgments" (p. 6). This proposition raises the question of how these qualities might be transformed and integrated as a legitimate community practice in non-self-referent contexts such as Japan. In the same paragraph, the authors go on to describe formative assessment as "a creative enterprise, consideration of alternatives, openness, and inventiveness" (p. 6). These dynamic qualities of imagination and creation are seen as fundamental to success across cultures, and from a Japanese perspective are essential to and constitutive of *zenjin*. As this chapter moves toward its conclusion, it is appropriate to encourage further cross-cultural and interdisciplinary studies on the fine grain of classroom dialogue, and how legitimate learning identities are constructed through reciprocal interactions in the heart and mind nexus. So it is complex, and from our earlier discussion we understand that any so-called positive frameworks for activity are transformed by the cultural context to which they are applied. Consequently, formulations of creativity and formality are problematized differently depending on where they exist.

The discussion presented in this chapter suggests that care should be taken not to read too much into or mishandle the word "formality" in the Japanese context. A compelling body of evidence (as seen in OECD reports) supports the contention that Japanese interrelationships ensure successful task outcomes, even in times of extreme crisis (Shinkawa & Arimoto, 2012). Consider the words of Catherine Lewis, a distinguished research scholar from Mills College in Oakland, California. In a personal communication, she reflected on the Fukushima disasters that shook the Tohoku region and the world in 2011, remarking:

in the U.S., the newspaper accounts of the Tohoku tragedy impressed Americans with their descriptions of the way tens of thousands of displaced people were able to organize survival in schools and other public buildings, by working together ... I was struck by how well the basic habits of mind and heart learned in elementary school serve Japanese adults: the sense of responsibility, awareness of others' needs and feelings, and commitment to everyone's welfare ... I don't know if any other country so successfully integrates academic learning, social learning, and ethical learning.
(personal communication, 2014)

This chapter has in part discussed a framework connecting the role of culture and social and classroom interaction in the cultivation and reproduction of the basic habits of mind and heart. These are based squarely on the high value attached to the concept of *kankei* (interrelationships) as the foundation of cultural identity. Put another way, Japanese cultural identity is created in the mind or heart nexus. When teachers in Western contexts cultivate postintervention awareness (*kizuki*) of their students' emotional and motivational needs, they have adapted "their own work to meet pupils' needs" (Black & Wiliam, 2010, p. 82). Perhaps with careful pre- and in-service moderation, all teachers can reproduce a community of adaptive experts by their commitment to the dialogic and collaborative essence at the heart of the formative assessment movement. *Zenjin* education requires teachers to possess and model the expert regulation of relational skills, so transcending didactic methods that disaffect large numbers of students in all cultural contexts. This is seen in Sugita's (2012) speech to novice teachers, in which he analogizes that teachers should never "use reins and whips by force," because such methods "are ineffective" (p. 6).

We argue for discursive progress in the educational research sciences. Video examples of what interactive whole-group dialogue looks like in practical settings are the essential stimuli for successful outcomes from intercultural discussion. Underpinning this effort, universities need to build robust mixed-methods research capacities in order to conduct complex and international collaborations and test the hypothesis that "Teachers, regardless of their cultural identity, resist interacting with their students inside the inherently motivating heart-mind nexus." Fundamentally, it is the pervasive influence of the (European) Enlightenment over Western contexts, and strongly emphasized in the United States, that continues to value the mind over emotion and discredits emotion as a distraction from "mature" thought. We have also seen, and not without a sense of irony, how fractious European ideals were successfully integrated into Japanese cultural identity by local reformers tacitly guided toward balanced and harmonious interrelationships. In terms of what is intellectually producible, one must remember that the products of critical scholarship and creative development are constrained and sanctioned (or not) by prevailing cultural philosophies. In this regard, this chapter has built a case to suggest that thousands of years of Japanese cultural tradition are a powerful reproducer of learning communities organized to sustain reciprocal and intrinsically rewarding learning and feedback interactions.

References

Ajisaka, T. (1960). *Education by Dr. Obara*. Tokyo: Tamagawa University Press.

Allen, M., & Williams, G. (2011). Consciousness, plasticity, and connectomics: The role of intersubjectivity in human cognition. *Frontiers in Psychology, 2*(20).

Arimoto, M. (2017). The prospect of educational assessment as a secret ingredient of effective pedagogy in the context of Japanese kizuki (with-it-ness) based on evidence-informed principles for effective teaching and learning. *Annual Bulletin, Graduate School of Education, Tohoku University, 3*, 10–35.

Assessment Reform Group. (1999). *Assessment for learning: Beyond the black box*. Cambridge School of Education, Cambridge University.

Baines, E., Rubie-Davies, C., & Blatchford, P. (2009). Improving pupil group work interaction and dialogue in primary classrooms: Results from a year-long intervention study. *Cambridge Journal of Education, 39*, 95–117.

Bandura, A. (1989). Human agency in social cognitive theory. *American Psychologist, 44*, 1175–1184.

Bandura, A. (2008). The reconstruction of "free will" from the agentic perspective of social cognition theory. In J. Baer, J. C. Kaufman, & R. F. Baumeister (Eds.), *Are we free? Psychology and free will* (pp. 86–127). Oxford: Oxford University Press.

Benkler, Y. (2011). The unselfish gene. *Harvard Business Review, 89*(7–8), 77–85.

Black, P., & Wiliam, D. (1998). *Inside the black box: Raising standards through classroom assessment*. London: School of Education, King's College.

Black, P., & Wiliam, D. (2006). Assessment for learning in the classroom. In J. Gardner (Ed.), *Assessment and Learning* (pp. 9–25). London: Sage.

Black, P., & Wiliam, D. (2009). Developing the theory of formative assessment. *Educational Assessment, Evaluation and Accountability, 21*, 5–31.

Black, P., & Wiliam, D. (2010). Inside the black box: Raising standards through classroom assessment. *Phi Kappan Delta, 92*, 81–90.

Bostock, J., & Wood, J. (2014). *Supporting student transitions 14–19: Approaches to teaching and learning*. Abingdon, UK: Routledge.

Bransford, J., Derry, S., Berliner, D., Hammerness, K., & Beckett, K. L. (2005). Theories of learning and their roles in teaching. In L. Darling-Hammond & J. Bransford (Eds.), *Preparing teachers for a changing world: What teachers should learn and be able to do* (pp. 40–87). San Francisco, CA: Jossey-Bass.

Bromme, R., & Steinbring, H. (1994). Interactive development of subject matter in the mathematics classroom. *Educational Studies in Mathematics, 27*, 217–248.

Cave, P. (2016). *Schooling selves: Autonomy, interdependence and reform in Japanese junior high education*. Chicago, IL: University of Chicago.

Central Council for Education/Ministry of Education. (1996). *Priorities and prospects for a lifelong learning society: Increasing diversification and sophistication; the future of lifelong learning; encouraging zest for living*. Tokyo: MEXT. Retrieved from www.mext.go.jp/b_menu/hakusho/html/hpae199601/hpae199601_2_042.html.

Cheng, R. W., Lam, S.-F., & Chan, J. C. (2008). When high achievers and low achievers work in the same group: The roles of group heterogeneity and processes in project based learning. *British Journal of Educational Psychology, 78*, 205–221.

Clark, I. (2011). Formative assessment: Policy, perspectives and practice. *Florida Journal of Educational Administration & Policy, 4*, 158–180.

Clark, I. (2012). Formative assessment: Assessment is for self-regulated learning. *Educational Psychology Review, 24,* 205–249.

Clark, I., & Dumas, G. (2015). Toward a neural basis for peer-interaction: What makes peer-learning tick? *Frontiers in Psychology, 6.*

Clark, I., & Dumas, G. (2016). The regulation of task performance: A trans-disciplinary review. *Frontiers in Psychology, 6,* 1862.

Fereshteh, M. H. (1992). The U.S. and Japanese education: Should they be compared? Paper presented at Lehigh University's Conference on Education and Economics in Technologically Advancing Countries, Bethlehem, PA.

Goos, M., Galbraith, P., & Renshaw, P. (2002). Socially mediated meta-cognition: Creating collaborative zones of proximal development in small group problem solving. *Educational Studies in Mathematics, 49,* 192–223.

Guionnet, S., Nadel, J., Bertasi, E., Sperduti, M., Delaveau, P., & Fossati, P. (2012). Reciprocal imitation: Toward a neural basis of social interaction. *Cerebral Cortex, 22,* 971–978.

Hatano, G., & Oura, Y. (2003). Commentary: Reconceptualizing school learning using insight from expertise research. *Educational Researcher, 32*(8), 26–29.

Hutchinson, C., & Hayward, L. (2005). The journey so far: Assessment for learning in Scotland. *Curriculum Journal, 16,* 225–248.

Inoue, N. (2010). Zen and the art of *neriage*: Facilitating consensus building in mathematics inquiry lessons through lesson study. *Journal of Mathematic Teacher Education, 14,* 5–23.

Inoue, N., Asada, A., Maeda, M., & Nakamura, S. (2016, August). Deconstructing adaptive teacher expertise for inquiry-based teaching in Japanese elementary classrooms: Neriage as inter-subjective pedagogy for social mind-storming. Paper presented at the ECER 2016 Leading Education conference, Dublin, Ireland.

Kabat-Zinn, J. (2013). *Full catastrophe living* (rev. edn.). New York: Bantam Books.

Kant, I. (1784). An answer to the question: "What is enlightenment?" Retrieved from https://web.cn.edu/kwheeler/documents/What_is_Enlightenment.pdf.

Kazemi, E., Elliott, R., Hubbard, A., Carroll, C., & Mumme, J. (2007). Doing mathematics in professional development: Theorizing teacher learning with and through socio-mathematical norms. In *Proceedings of the 29th Annual Meeting of the North American Chapter of the International Group for the Psychology of Mathematics Education.* Stateline (Lake Tahoe), NV: University of Nevada, Reno.

Kitayama, S., Markus, H., & Kurokawa, M. (2000). Culture, emotion, and well-being: Good feelings in Japan and the United States. *Cognition and Emotion, 14,* 93–124.

Kobayashi, M. (2004). Prospects. UNESCO International Bureau of Education, vol. 34, no. 2, 222–239. Retrieved from www.ibe.unesco.org/sites/default/files/obara.pdf.

Kobayashi, T. (1990). Masataro Sawayanagi (1865–1937) and the revised elementary code of 1900. *Biography, 13,* 43–56.

Kounin, J. (1977). *Discipline and group management in classrooms.* Huntington, NY: Krieger.

Krill, A. L., & Platek, S. M. (2012). Working together may be better: Activation of reward centers during a cooperative maze task. *PLoS ONE, 2,* e30613.

Kusanagi, K. (2013). The bureaucratising of lesson study: A Javanese case. *Mathematics Teacher Education and Development, 16*, 171–200.

Lave, J. (1991). Situating learning in communities of practice. In L. Resnick, J. Levine, & S. Teasley (Eds.), *Perspectives on socially shared cognition* (pp. 63–82). Washington, DC: APA.

Lave, J., & Wenger, E. (1991). *Situated learning: Legitimate peripheral participation.* New York: Cambridge University Press.

Lebra, R. S. (1976). *Japanese pattern of behavior.* Honolulu: University of Hawaii Press.

Lebra, R. S. (2004). *The Japanese self in cultural logic.* Honolulu: Hawaii University Press.

Lesson Study Group. (n.d.). Teaching through problem solving: Students do mathematics to learn mathematics. Neriage. Retrieved from http://preservice.lesson research.net/polygon-overview/neriage/.

Lewis, C. (1995). *Educating heart and minds: Reflections on Japanese pre-school and elementary education.* Cambridge: Cambridge University Press.

Linquisti, R. (2014). *Supporting formative assessment for deeper learning: A primer for policymakers.* Washington, DC: Council of Chief State School Officers.

Macintyre, L. M., Buck, G., & Beckenhauer, A. (2007). Formative assessment requires artistic vision. *International Journal of Education & the Arts, 8*(4), 1–23.

Ministry for Education (MEXT). (n.d. a). *Improvement of academic abilities: Courses of study.* Retrieved from www.mext.go.jp/en/policy/education/elsec/title02/detail 02/1373859.htm.

Ministry for Education (MEXT). (n.d. b). *Four basic policy directions.* Retrieved from www.mext.go.jp/en/policy/education/lawandplan/title01/detail01/sdetail01/ 1373808.htm.

National Research Council. (2000). *How people learn: Brain, mind, experience, and school* (expanded edn.). Washington, DC: National Academies Press.

Organisation for Economic Cooperation and Development (OECD). (2005a). *Formative Assessment: Improving learning in secondary classrooms.* Centre for Educational Research and Innovation (CERI). Paris: OECD.

Organisation for Economic Cooperation and Development (OECD). (2005b). *Formative Assessment: Improving learning in secondary classrooms.* Policy Brief, November 2005. OECD Observer. Paris: OECD. Retrieved from www.oecd.org/edu/ ceri/35661078.pdf.

Organisation for Economic Cooperation and Development (OECD). (2016). *Country note: Japan. Programme for International Student Assessment: Results from PISA 2015.* Paris, France: OECD. Retrieved from www.oecd.org/pisa/PISA-2015-Japan.pdf.

Pellegrino, J. W., Chudowsky, N., & Glaser, R. (Eds.) (2001). *Knowing what students know: The science and design of educational assessment.* Washington, DC: National Academy Press.

Popham, W. J. (2008). *Transformative assessment.* Alexandria, VA: Association for Supervision and Curriculum Development.

Pryor, J., & Torrance, H. (1996). Teacher–pupil interaction in formative assessment: Assessing the work or protecting the child? *Curriculum Journal, 7*, 205–226.

Redcay, E., Dodell-Feder, D., Pearrow, M., Mavros, P., Kleiner, M., Gabrieli, J., & Saxe, R. (2010). Live face-to-face interaction during fMRI: A new tool for social cognitive neuroscience. *Neuroimage, 50*, 1639–1647.

Sadler, D. R. (1989). Formative assessment and the design of instructional systems. *Instructional Science, 18*, 119–144.

Sakaiya, S., Shiraito,Y., Kato, J., Ide, H., Okada, K., Takano, K., & Kansaku, K. (2013). Neural correlate of human reciprocity in social interactions. *Frontiers in Neuroscience, 7*, 239.

Sakamoto, N. (2011). Professional development through "kizuki": Cognitive, emotional and collegiate awareness. *Teacher Development, 15*, 187–203.

Salamone, J., & Correa, M. (2012). The mysterious motivational functions of mesolimbic dopamine. *Neuron, 76*, 470–485.

Schilbach, L., Timmermans, B., Reddy, V., Costall, A., Bente, G., Schlict, T., et al. (2013). Toward a second-person neuroscience. *Behavioral and Brain Sciences, 36*, 393–462.

Schön, D. (1987). *Educating the reflective practitioner.* San Francisco, CA: Jossey-Bass.

Scottish Government. (2011). Curriculum for excellence: Building the curriculum 5: A framework for learning and teaching. Edinburgh: Scottish Government. Retrieved from www.educationscotland.gov.uk/Images/BtC5Framework_tcm4-653230.pdf.

Shimahara, N. K. (1998). The Japanese model of professional development: Teaching as craft. *Teaching and Teacher Education, 14*, 451–462.

Shimizu, Y. (1999). Aspects of mathematics teacher education in Japan: Focusing on teacher's roles. *Journal of Mathematics Education, 2*, 107–116.

Shinkawa, M., & Arimoto, M. (2012). Research for Japanese-like competency and assessment through challenges of eager schools for sustainability after the great earthquake and tsunami. *International Journal of Sustainable Development, 3*, 61–69.

Shulman, L. (2005). Signature pedagogies in the professions. *Daedalus, 134*, 52–59.

Sivan, E. (1986). Motivation in social constructivist theory. *Educational Psychology, 21*, 209–23–3.

Stigler, J. W., & Hiebert, J. (1999). *The teaching gap: Best ideas from the world's teachers for improving education in the classroom.* New York: Free Press.

Sugita, H. (2012). Excerpts taken from a lecture given to novice Japanese teachers in light of the full implementation of Special Activities (tokkatsu) in the New Japanese Curriculum. Retrieved from www.p.u-tokyo.ac.jp/~tsunelab/tokkatsu/cms/wp-content/uploads/2016/03/sugita.pdf.

Takahashi, A. (2008). Neriage: An essential piece of a problem-based lesson. Teaching through problem solving: A Japanese approach. Paper presented at the annual conference of the National Council of Teachers of Mathematics, Salt Lake City, UT.

Takanashi, Y. (2004). TEFL and communication styles in Japanese culture. *Language Culture and Curriculum, 17*, 1–14.

Thien, K. (2004) *Buddhist general semantics: A new approach to Buddhist religion and its philosophy.* New York: iUniverse.

Thompson, P. (2002). Didactic objects and didactic models in radical constructivism. In K. Gravemeijer, R. Lehrer, B. van Oers, & L. Verschaffel (Eds.), *Symbolizing, modeling, and tool use in mathematics education* (pp. 191–212). Dordrecht: Kluwer.

Tsuneyoshi, R. (2017). Educating the whole child: The Japanese model of educating the whole child. Graduate School of Education, University of Tokyo. Retrieved from www.p.u-tokyo.ac.jp/~tsunelab/tokkatsu/edwc/.

Vogel, E. (1979). *Japan as number one: Lessons for America*. Lincoln, NE: iUniverse. com.

Vogt, F., & Rogalla, M. (2009). Developing adaptive teaching competency through coaching. *Teaching and Teacher Education, 25*, 1051–1060.

Vygotsky, L. S.(1978). *Mind in society: The development of higher psychological processes*. Cambridge, MA: Harvard University Press.

Vygotsky, L. S. (1987). Thinking and speech. In R. W. Rieber & A. S. Carton (Eds.), *The collected works of L. S. Vygotsky*, vol. 1: *Problems of general psychology* (pp. 39–285). New York: Plenum.

Walker, R. (2010). Socio-cultural issues in motivation. In P. Peterson, E. Baker, & B. McGaw (Eds.), *International encyclopaedia of education* (pp. 712–717). Oxford: Elsevier.

Walshaw, M. (2011). Working with teachers to enable both student and teacher learning. *Journal of Mathematics Teacher Education, 14*, 1–4.

Wenger, E. (1998). *Communities of practice: Learning, meaning and identity*. Cambridge: Cambridge University Press.

Wiliam, D., Bartholomew, H., & Reay, D. (2004). Assessment, learning and identity. In P. Valero and R. Zevenbergen (Eds.), *Researching the socio-political dimensions of mathematics education: Issues of power theory and methodology* (pp. 43–61). Dordrecht: Kluwer.

Wiliam, D., & Leahy, S. (2007). A theoretical foundation for formative assessment. In H. McMillan (Ed.), *Formative assessment classroom: Theory into practice* (pp. 29–42). New York: Teachers College Press.

Willis, J. (2010). Assessment for learning as a participative pedagogy. *Assessment Matters, 2*, 65–84.

Wood, D. J., Bruner, J. S., & Ross, G. (1976). The role of tutoring in problem solving. *Journal of Child Psychiatry and Psychology, 17*, 89–100.

Young, V., & Kim, D. (2010). Using assessments for instructional improvement: A literature review. *Education Policy Analysis Archives, 18*(19), 1–40.

Zimmerman, B., & Cleary, T. (2006). Adolescents' development of personal agency. In T. Urban and F. Pajares (Eds.), *Self-efficacy beliefs of adolescents* (pp. 45–70). Greenwich, CT: Information Age Publishing.

22 Instructional Feedback in Animals

Allison B. Kaufman and Michele M. Pagel

Amelia Bedelia took out three eggs.

"I wonder why they need to be separated. They've been together all day and nothing happened."

But Amelia Bedelia separated those eggs.

"Pair the vegetables!" Amelia Bedelia laughed.

"Here, you two go together – and you two. Now be careful, or I'll be separating you, too."

(Parish, 1993, pp. 40–41)

Introduction

A chapter on feedback in animals is probably not the first thing that comes to mind when opening *The Cambridge Handbook of Instructional Feedback*. In fact, it probably isn't even the nineteenth or twentieth. But communication is hard. Particularly when a person's language (or one's personal understanding of it) isn't the same as another's. If Amelia Bedelia's employer had understood that her mistakes were feedback on how they phrased their requests, it would have been a much shorter series of books. Without language, the challenge is even greater – feedback is typically written or spoken; it is almost always linguistic. In the absence of language, actions and reactions must be interpreted as feedback – this is the challenge when working with nonhuman animals.

Despite the focus of this chapter, the challenge of communicating and providing feedback nonlinguistically is not the sole province of nonhumans. Imagine you are a teacher's aide in a preschool who has just been told the newest student is deaf and cannot speak (is mute). It is your job to help this child adjust to the classroom setting. You must teach her:

- Who the teachers are and how to move between classes, the lunchroom, and the playground at appropriate times
- How to ask for something she needs
- How to sit calmly in a circle with the other children
- To allow adults to manipulate her body – for example, to check her for injury if she falls or to help her wash her hands
- How to play with a toy that is new to her, for example, that a jack-in-the-box is funny, not scary.

You do not have a common language with your new charge. How will you know if you have gotten your message across correctly? And, in turn, how will she know if she has completed an assigned task to your satisfaction? The type of feedback you give each other cannot be the typical feedback between teacher and student.

Animal trainers work within these constraints daily. Not only must instruction be given in alternative forms, but feedback requires elaborate specificity. In this chapter, we will discuss feedback in the context of a system that allows for a "dialogue" of actions: operant conditioning.

Very generally, if two people, two animals, or a person and an animal are engaging in a dialogue via operant conditioning, A requests something of B. It could be to fetch a ball, do math homework, or eat dinner. B's compliance is a form of feedback – was A's message conveyed appropriately? (We are assuming, of course, that all Bs are well behaved and eager to please.) Dogs that fetch balls on request and children who do math homework when asked are providing a form of feedback: "Your message has been received clearly." Amelia Bedelia, as she has every intention of obeying, is providing feedback as well: "Your message must be tailored differently for me." Once the task done, A's reaction to the task is again a form of feedback, this time providing information to B with regard to the success of the task. A dog treat or an extra hour of television may indicate a good job of fetching or homework well done, while an early bedtime might indicate the opposite.

The Basics of Operant Conditioning

Operant conditioning occurs when the frequency of a behavior is either increased or decreased by the immediate consequence of that behavior (Skinner, 1938). It is one of the most successful methods of behavioral conditioning or modification available when working with animals (Pryor, 1999; Ramirez, 1999; Kuczaj & Xitco, 2002; Bailey et al., 2010) and is easily applied to humans as well (Pryor, 1999). It is the basis for the type of feedback in animals addressed in this chapter. The terminology associated with operant conditioning is simple yet very nuanced.

Positive, Negative, Reward, Punishment

Four terms form the basic system of identification of outcomes in operant conditioning. The terms "positive" and "negative" indicate directionality of the outcome, whether something is added to the situation or environment or something is taken away. This is complicated because the terms "positive" and "negative" have their own connotations with respect to good and bad. In operant conditioning, these connotations are not relevant, a fact that is often confusing to those new to the method. A positive outcome, or an addition, can be in the form of object – money or a toy, for example. However, it can also be less tangible. Hitting is a considered "positive" – it is the addition of the force created by your hand. Speech is a positive operant outcome as well – regardless of the content of the speech – because sound is added to the situation. A negative outcome includes removing a tangible object – i.e., taking away money or a favorite toy – but also includes less tangible things. Removal of a hand placing pressure on a child to force them to sit down is a negative outcome. Removal of restrictions such as early release from jail or a child being allowed to leave his room is also a negative operant outcome. These terms come from the medical field, where positive means that something is present (could be as bad as the presence of cancer), and negative means the absence of something ("the results of the tests were negative" is usually good news!).

The terms "reinforcement" and "punishment" as used in operant conditioning must also be separated from their traditional good and bad connotations. Reinforcement is defined as an action that is intended to increase the likelihood that a behavior will occur in the future (Skinner, 1938). A dog sitting next to his owner can receive positive reinforcement in the form of a treat (something given to increase the likelihood of quiet sitting in the future) or negative reinforcement in the form of the relaxation of pressure on a leash (removal of the pressure that occurred when the dog was impatiently pulling on the lead). Punishment, on the other hand, is intended to decrease the likelihood of the behavior's occurrence (Walters & Grusec, 1977). If the dog bolts away and reaches the end of the leash, there is a sudden and uncomfortable yank backward – this is positive punishment, as the addition of the yank decreases the likelihood the dog will bolt in the future due to the unpleasant consequence. If the owner picks up the bone the dog was chewing previous to running off, this negative punishment also provides the dog feedback on the consequences of his behavior.

Research has shown many times that operant conditioning – i.e., these four ideas in combination – is the one of the most productive ways to communicate feedback to nonhuman animals (e.g., Skinner, 1938; Ramirez, 1999). It is clearly understood, fast at conveying a message, and has the lowest risk of creating unwanted fears or behaviors. In addition, as will be detailed later in this chapter, it can be applied to provide feedback to both humans and animals. In fact, for an excellent and highly enjoyable "how to," see Skinner (1951, found online fairly easily), which directly categorizes operant conditioning as a form of feedback and which discusses both animal and humans, despite the title.

Primary Reinforcement

Primary reinforcement is, very basically, anything that is naturally reinforcing due to innate survival value (Premack, 1965, 1971). Generally, this amounts to food, water, and sex. Without food or water, the individual will not survive. Without reproduction, the species will not survive. It is the type of reinforcement most often associated with conditioning and, in most cases, the most powerful type of reinforcement (Skinner, 1938; Ramirez, 1999; Kuczaj & Xitco, 2002).

Secondary Reinforcement

Because animals under human care are maintained at their optimal weight, as opposed to slightly under it as might be the case in a lab, primary reinforcement may not always be as motivating (Kuczaj & Xitco, 2002). This makes nonfood reinforcement (i.e., secondary reinforcement) an important factor. In addition, the common usage of this type of reinforcement lends credibility to the idea that animals are willing participants in training (and learning) sessions (Ramirez, 1996), as animals may be satiated at different times during the day but still participate in training sessions because of the high value of secondary reinforcers (Kuczaj & Xitco, 2002). Some have even argued that in situations such as this, the secondary reinforcer is powerful enough to be considered a primary reinforcer (Bekoff & Byers, 1998; Kuczaj & Xitco, 2002). In one scenario, a killer whale learned a new husbandry behavior solely via tactile reinforcements (rubs, pats, etc.) in the same amount of time as did conspecifics being rewarded with food (unpublished manuscript cited in Kuczaj & Xitco, 2002).

Secondary reinforcement is often thought of as such because it has to be paired with primary reinforcement in order to take on a reinforcing quality (Hull, 1943) – i.e., rubbing or petting a wild animal is not naturally reinforcing in many cases, but over time may elicit the same response from the animal as a primary reinforcer would if paired properly (Williams, 1994; Ramirez, 1996; Pearce & Bouton, 2001). For example, if a trainer always presents a specific ball to a seal paired with a handful of fish, over time, through classical conditioning, the seal would show the same enthusiasm for the ball alone as it would when presented with fish. When conditioned successfully, a secondary reinforcer can be a very powerful tool in a trainer's toolbox.

Careful conditioning of the secondary reinforcer is key. As much care should be spent conditioning a secondary reinforcer as when training an animal in a new behavior. It helps to consider training the new reinforcer as making deposits in a training savings account: if you don't deposit enough positive association with primary reinforcement, you won't have enough positive history for the animal to want to work for the secondary reinforcer alone.

Secondary reinforcers may not work for all individuals. One of the most common pitfalls of using secondary reinforcers is assuming the secondary reinforcer has been completely conditioned when in fact it has not. A properly conditioned secondary reinforcer will provide marked behavioral feedback, similar to the individual's reaction when presented with primary reinforcement (Ramirez, 1996). Without these careful observations, the trainer may assume something is reinforcing to the animal when it is not. Similarly, some animals have a higher biological drive than others, so it may be difficult to mix the use of secondary reinforcement in a training session if the animal is too focused on primary reinforcement; behaviors that are normally reinforced with secondary reinforcement may be refused in favor of those typically reinforced with primary. In all cases, these are important feedback reactions to be monitored to make for better – and less frustrating – communication for both human and nonhuman.

The Bridge

The bridge is perhaps one of the most important and powerful secondary reinforcers.[1] It serves to bridge the gap between correct behavior and the reinforcement for that behavior and communicates to an animal "yes, that's it right there!" (Pryor, 1975). Thus, it is both a behavior marker and the messenger that the reward is on its way. As an event marker it must be delivered precisely, to mark the exact point at which the animal offers the behavior correctly. As such, the item used as a bridge should be capable of being delivered with a near split-second accuracy. Commonly used bridging devices include dog whistles, clickers, a tap on a metal bucket, pointing, and a specific spoken word. The bridge gains its value from its close association with primary reinforcement, and thus is one of the first and most important behaviors to train any animal (Pryor, 1975; Ramirez, 1999). The conditioning of the bridge consists of pairing the bridging stimulus with food in a basic classical conditioning paradigm. Just as Pavlov paired a bell enough times with food that the bell came to represent food (Pavlov, 1927), one might, for example, give a seal a fish every time a whistle is blown, so that the seal develops an association with the whistle as a means of receiving primary reinforcement (Ramirez, 1999; Kuczaj & Xitco, 2002). When this association is repeated enough times, the bridge becomes reinforcing in and of itself. A checkmark on a piece of paper has no inherent value to a person, but if it is paired enough times with the message "your homework is correct," seeing the checkmark becomes inherently rewarding. Or, for example, a paycheck at the end of the week makes you happy even though that paycheck is just a piece of paper and you don't get excited by every other random piece of paper you encounter. The paycheck does, however, have strong associations. For example, you can't eat the paycheck, but it symbolizes food for your family; you can't wear the paycheck, but it symbolizes the clothing you can buy with it; nor can you use the paycheck for shelter, but you can pay your rent with it.

    In general animal training practice, timing is king. The bridge should come just as the animal is performing the correct behavior and primary reinforcement

---

1 In fact, some have argued that the bridge often becomes powerful enough to be considered primary reinforcement. We follow in the tradition of Ramirez (1996), who considered the bridge a secondary reinforcer regardless of its strength due to the fact it must be initially conditioned to the animal.

as soon as possible thereafter (Ramirez, 1999; Kuczaj & Xitco, 2002). An early or late bridge runs the risk of occurring during a nonoptimal time – for example, in training a hippo to hold her mouth open for a dental exam, it is essential to bridge at the apex of the open mouth – i.e., the full potential of the behavior. If a bridge is delivered at the wrong time (for example, the hippo is bridged while she is starting to close her mouth), then the hippo is getting bridged incorrectly, and the trainer is accidentally reinforcing a behavior that is not up to the correct criteria. When this happens, the hippo finds she can receive a bridge and reward for opening her mouth to only three-quarters the fully open size for the exam, followed by half the mouth's fully open size, and thus half the potential for the behavior. The criteria for the original behavior of "open mouth" is not being met, making a thorough dental exam not possible, necessitating that the behavior be reworked to accomplish the original goal. This is why bridging to criteria is critical to the training process and one of the most important skills a trainer should learn.

However, there are some exceptions to the timing rule, particularly in highly cognitive species. Some studies in humans have shown increased strengthening of correct behaviors in response to feedback when there is a lag between the behavior and the feedback. This increased performance is thought to be due to additional time to process variations of the behavior distinctly and is not seen when the goal of the feedback is to correct behavior (Smith & Kimball, 2010).

Additional Types of Secondary Reinforcers

Tactile reinforcement, or touches, are highly reinforcing to some species and not at all to others. It is important for trainers to have an understanding of the natural behavioral tendencies of the species they work with (Ramirez, 1996), for while a dolphin may actively seek out poolside rubdowns from their trainers outside training sessions, an antelope may prefer to avoid physical contact at all cost. While in theory when utilizing the proper behavioral conditioning techniques almost anything can be accomplished, when the purpose is to condition a strong secondary reinforcer, it is best to set the animal up for success with something that is positive, or at least neutral, to start with (Ramirez, 1999; Kuczaj & Xitco, 2002).

Toys are one of the most varied and versatile categories of secondary reinforcers. Many types of toys, although artificial, can appeal to the natural tendencies of the animal, thus making them good candidates to be used as secondary reinforcers (Ramirez, 1996). Examples include a police dog being rewarded with a game of tug with its handler, a dolphin being presented with a toy made of car wash strips (replicating kelp strands that dolphins play with in the wild) after a successful husbandry exam, or a parrot being given a popsicle stick to shred after a voluntary nail trim. Toys in this category can become extremely strong conditioned reinforcers (Bekoff & Byers, 1998; Kuczaj et al., 2002; Paulos, Trone, & Kuczaj, 2010).

However, toys that are less innate and intuitive to an animal's natural tendencies also have the potential to become strong secondary reinforcers if they are consistently paired with food and conditioned correctly. For example, in the second author's (MP) personal experience, while a seal in the wild would not naturally seek out a small plastic ball, MP was able to so strongly condition a small yellow ball as a secondary reinforcer for a female harbor seal that the ball could serve as the only form of reinforcement during training sessions in which the seal was not motivated by food. This became particularly vital when MP was able to maintain a voluntary ultrasound behavior with the seal during the later stages of pregnancy when motivation was sporadic and the animal was not consistently participating in structured training sessions.

When dealing with animals, verbal reinforcement is perhaps one of the most commonly used, and misused, forms of secondary reinforcement. The use of specific words such as "Good" and "Yes" are frequently utilized in dog training, sometimes serving as a bridge, but often also serving as the conditioned reinforcer/secondary reinforcement (Pryor, 1999). Most animals quickly learn that verbal praise has an intrinsic value to them. Generally, when reinforcement is verbal, tone matters more than actual words. For example, if "Good" is the trainer's word of choice, then the word must be delivered in a consistent tone and manner by all trainers working that animal. If one trainer delivers "Good" in a low-energy, monotone way, and the other trainer delivers "Good" in an excited, high-pitched way, both trainers are not using the same conditioned reinforcer and over time the animal's response to it will deteriorate. Verbal reinforcement therefore needs to be used carefully, be relied on as a secondary reinforcer only if the animal shows a distinct positive reaction when presented with it, and only if all trainers can use it with accuracy and consistency (Ramirez, 1999).

Operant Conditioning at Home and School

Conditioning Pets and Other Animals

As an understanding of the ability of operant conditioning to foster communication between human and animal grew, it became increasingly common outside traditional training situations. Post–World War II, operant conditioning became common not only for training dogs for military, law enforcement, and hunting, but also as a way to teach our pets at home – and can now be found being put to use to train every type of animal from horses to snakes to goldfish (Pryor, 1999; Emer, Mora, Harvey, & Grace, 2015; Chiandetti, Avella, Fongaro, & Cerri, 2016; R2 Fish School, n.d.). Preferred methods of behavioral conditioning over the years have seemed to follow the trends of the day, dependent on what method dominated the popular culture of the time. Best-selling books, television shows, corporate marketing campaigns, and blogs have all been responsible for fueling the popularity of different training techniques.

From the choke chain and negative reinforcement popularity in the 1950s to the clicker and positive reinforcement taking over in the 1980s, behavioral conditioning has always been an evolving science (Hiby, Rooney, & Bradshaw, 2004). In the next section, we discuss two of the most prominent trends, one with a reinforcement-based methodology and one with a punishment-based one.

Perhaps the most influential proponent of positive reinforcement training and a key figure in teaching nontrainers how to use the principles in everyday life, Karen Pryor began her career as a dolphin trainer in 1963 (Pryor, 1975). The newly constructed Sea Life Park, on the island of Oahu, Hawaii, would soon become the birthplace of positive reinforcement training in the marine mammal field (Pryor, 2014). Pryor developed training techniques that revolutionized the animal training field, creating a line of communication between trainer and animal that opened a new world of feedback between the two. Her training methods are widely adapted to suit all species of animals and have become the standard behavioral conditioning technique for animals in zoos and aquariums (Pryor, 1999). Karen Pryor's methods were popularized with her development of clicker training, in which she used a pocket-sized clicking device as a bridging stimulus, allowing the trainer to effectively mark and reinforce the desired behavior quickly, thus increasing training accuracy and efficiency. Not only is it readily accepted by animals, but clicker training also lends itself to being easily taught to the layman/novice trainer. Pryor has authored several books, including what is considered by most professional trainers as the gold standard, *Don't Shoot the Dog* (1999), which breaks down the nuances of behavioral conditioning into examples that are easy to understand. In addition, she is the founder of both Karen Pryor Clicker Training and the Karen Pryor Academy, which teach and provide certification for modern force-free trainers.

Clicker training has become one of the most widely used methods of training by both laypeople and behaviorists, if not *the* most widely used, and has been adapted to all variety of species (Pryor, 1999). The technique has been used with great success in both educational and athletic situations, as will be discussed in later sections.

Worth a mention is also the controversial Cesar Millan, a self-taught dog trainer who gained almost immediate fame with the launch of his television show *Dog Whisperer with Cesar Millan* in 2004. Millan's philosophy revolves around the theory that dog owners need to establish themselves, in his words, as a "calm, assertive" pack leader and that dogs possess three primary needs: exercise, discipline, and affection (Millan, n.d.). While this line of thinking is not completely off-base, it relies heavily on old science, research on the pack behavior of wolves, and has been the subject of recent debate (see, e.g., van Kerkhove, 2004). The most controversial aspect of the Millan method is "touch," in which the trainer makes physical contact with the dog to "focus" or "distract." Often the touch is depicted as a quick, firm tap or poke that catches the dog by surprise.

In operant conditioning terms, touch is directionally positive (i.e., adding to the situation). It can be reinforcing (increasing the likelihood of the previous actions) or punishing (decreasing the likelihood of the previous actions). Tactile reinforcements as discussed above are specifically used in a positive manner. Tactile punishments (i.e., "positive punishment") are meant to be aversive feedback; the intent is to decrease whatever incorrect behavior had been occurring.

In many ways, this issue has already been addressed extensively in educational feedback. Corporal punishment has long been shown to be less effective than positive methods for correcting behavior, and positive punishments create fear and adversity when used as behavioral feedback in both humans and animals (Dubanoski, Inaba, & Gerkewicz, 1983; Greydanus et al., 2003; Hiby et al., 2004). In addition, they merely point out that an incorrect behavior has occurred; they fail to model the correct behavior (i.e., "don't run" versus "walk").

Although he does still enjoy some support, the majority of the scientific community and accredited training professionals or facilities have rejected positive punishment as a method of feedback (Ramirez, 1999; Davis & Harris, 2006). However, Millan's media presence leaves the impression that these training methods are somehow sanctioned, approved, and safe for use because they are broadcast on national television, when in fact – as has been demonstrated in the classroom – positive punishment can easily make the short transition to abuse in the hands of an overzealous teacher or trainer (Dubanoski et al., 1983; Greydanus et al., 2003).

Conditioning People

Like humans, animals monitor both the existence of the feedback and the quality of it. A variety of species has demonstrated awareness of the quality of reinforcement, a preference for types of reinforcement, and even a willingness to wait for a preferred item (Bentosela, Jakovcevic, Elgier, Mustaca, & Papini, 2009; Stevens, Rosati, Heilbronner, & Muhlhoff, 2011). This might be considered akin to the quality of feedback in humans (e.g., the common recommendation to pick out something specific to compliment in a child's drawing). When the quality or quantity of reinforcement declines, performance suffers; likewise, performance increases with an increase in quality or quantity of reinforcement (Pubols, 1960). In a related principle, variation in the timing and quantity of reinforcement tends to increase interest and create behaviors that are less vulnerable to extinction (Kuczaj & Xitco, 2002).

Feedback via operant conditioning is common in people, although it is not often identified as such – compliments, rewards, limitations, restrictions, and the removal thereof are all ways of communicating that a particular behavior is desirable. However, while the advantages of these techniques are well established in the scientific literature (Skinner, 1951; McAllister, Stachowiak, Baer, & Conderman, 1969; Altman & Linton, 1971; van de Vijver, Ridderinkhof, & de Wit, 2015), and perhaps not unknown among parents and school districts, implementation has been slow due to the hold of more traditional discipline-based feedback techniques (Maag, 2001; Sugai & Horner, 2002; Sigler & Aamidor, 2005). In some situations, an actual bridge has become very useful for teaching, making for a more formal use of operant conditioning.

TAGteach (TAGteach International, n.d.) and other similar movements use a clicker (or other bridge) as a teaching tool. This idea has been particularly helpful to coaches in particular sports – for example, gymnastics – who find they can "mark" an athlete at the exact moment his or her body is in the correct position. This allows the athlete to feel the position at the moment it is occurring, instead of having to recall it later. The bridge has also allowed those working with young children and special needs populations to break down difficult tasks such as shoelace tying. Feedback can be provided at several points along the way during the tying process, both encouraging the child and noting that he or she has mastered the smaller steps within the larger skill.

Conclusion

From the very first dog that lay at our ancestors' feet beside an ancient campfire, man's relationship with animals, as hunting partners, protectors, and beasts of burden, has continued to evolve over the millennia. Humans have long since recognized the benefit of the domestication of various species. Animals were trained to help humans fight our wars, hunt our food, and establish our civilizations – they became key to our existence. This link further cemented the desire to know more about the methods of training animals. The scientific study of animal behavior – and the understanding of feedback – aided by the rise of the theory of operant conditioning has allowed animal care to move out of the laboratory setting and to find success in partnerships that range from therapy horses to naval dolphins to zoo animal stewardship. In this way, operant conditioning has opened up the lines of communication and tapped into the potential of the human–animal partnership.

References

Altman, K. I., & Linton, T. E. (1971). Operant conditioning in the classroom setting: A review of the research. *Journal of Educational Research*, *64*, 277–286.

Bailey, R., Bihm, E. M., Gillaspy, J. A., Abbott, H. J., Lammers, W. J., & Lammers, W. (2010). More misbehavior of organisms: A Psi Chi lecture by Marian and Robert Bailey. *Psychological Record*, *60*, 505–522.

Bekoff, M., & Byers, J. A. (1998). *Animal play*. New York: Cambridge University Press.

Bentosela, M., Jakovcevic, A., Elgier, A. M., Mustaca, A. E., & Papini, M. R. (2009). Incentive contrast in domestic dogs (*Canis familiaris*). *Journal of Comparative Psychology*, *123*, 125–130.

Chiandetti, C., Avella, S., Fongaro, E., & Cerri, F. (2016). Can clicker training facilitate conditioning in dogs? *Applied Animal Behaviour Science*, *184*, 109–116.

Davis, C., & Harris, G. (2006). Redefining our relationships with the animals we train: Leadership and posture. *Soundings, 31*(4), 6–8.

Dubanoski, R. A., Inaba, M., & Gerkewicz, K. (1983). Corporal punishment in schools: Myths, problems and alternatives. *Child Abuse & Neglect, 7*(3), 271–278.

Emer, S., Mora, C., Harvey, M., & Grace, M. (2015). Predators in training: Operant conditioning of novel behavior in wild Burmese pythons (*Python molurus bivitattus*). *Animal Cognition, 18*, 269–278.

Greydanus, D. E., Pratt, H. D., Richard Spates, C., Blake-Dreher, A. E., Greydanus-Gearhart, M. A., & Patel, D. R. (2003). Corporal punishment in schools. *Journal of Adolescent Health, 32*, 385–393.

Hiby, E., Rooney, N., & Bradshaw, J. (2004). Dog training methods: Their use, effectiveness and interaction with behaviour and welfare. *Animal Welfare, 13*, 63–69.

Hull, C. L. (1943). *Principles of behavior.* New York: Appleton-Century.

Kuczaj, S. A., Lacinak, T., Fad, O., Trone, M., Solangi, M., & Ramos, J. A. (2002). Keeping environmental enrichment enriching. *International Journal of Comparative Psychology, 15*, 127–137.

Kuczaj, S. A., & Xitco, M. J. (2002). It takes more than fish: The psychology of marine mammal training. *International Journal of Comparative Psychology, 15*, 186–200.

Maag, J. W. (2001). Rewarded by punishment: Reflections on the disuse of positive reinforcement in schools. *Exceptional Children, 67*, 173–186.

McAllister, L. W., Stachowiak, J. G., Baer, D. M., & Conderman, L. (1969). The application of operant conditioning techniques in a secondary school classroom. *Journal of Applied Behavior Analysis, 2*, 277–285.

Millan, C. (n.d.). Cesar's way: Achieving balance and harmony. Retrieved from www.cesarsway.com/.

Parish, P. (1993). *Thank you Amelia Bedelia.* New York: Harper Collins.

Paulos, R. D., Trone, M., & Kuczaj, S. A. (2010). Play in wild and captive cetaceans. *International Journal of Comparative Psychology, 23*, 701–722.

Pavlov, I. (1927). *Conditioned reflexes* (G. V. Anrep, trans.). London: Oxford University Press.

Pearce, J. M., & Bouton, M. E. (2001). Theories of associative learning in animals. *Annual Review of Psychology, 52*, 111–139.

Premack, D. (1965). Reinforcement theory. In D. Levine (Ed.), *Nebraska Symposium on Motivation.* Lincoln: University of Nebraska Press.

Premack, D. (1971). Catching up with common sense or two sides of a generalization: Reinforcement and punishment. In R. Glaser (Ed.), *The nature of reinforcement* (pp. 121–150). New York: Academic Press.

Pryor, K. W. (1975). *Lads before the wind: Diary of a dolphin trainer.* New York: Harper and Row.

Pryor, K. W. (1999). *Don't shoot the dog: The new art of teaching and training.* New York: Bantam Books.

Pryor, K. W. (2014). Historical perspectives: A dolphin journey. *Aquatic Mammals, 40*, 104–114.

Pubols, B. H. (1960). Incentive magnitude, learning, and performance in animals. *Psychological Bulletin, 57*, 89–115.

R2 Fish School. (n.d.). The complete kit to teach your fish amazing tricks. Retrieved from www.r2fishschool.com/.

Ramirez, K. (1996). Secondary reinforcers as an indespensible tool: The effectiveness of non-food reinforcers. *Marine Mammals: Public Display and Research, 2*(1), 42–31.

Ramirez, K. (1999). *Animal training.* Chicago, IL: John G. Shedd Aquarium.

Sigler, E. A., & Aamidor, S. (2005). From positive reinforcement to positive behaviors: An everyday guide for the practitioner. *Early Childhood Education Journal, 32,* 249–253.

Skinner, B. F. (1938). *The behavior of organisms: An experimental analysis.* New York: Appleton-Century.

Skinner, B. F. (1951). How to teach animals. *Scientific American, 185*(6), 26–29.

Smith, T. A., & Kimball, D. R. (2010). Learning from feedback: Spacing and the delay-retention effect. *Journal of Experimental Psychology: Learning, Memory, and Cognition, 36,* 80–95.

Stevens, J. R., Rosati, A. G., Heilbronner, S. R., & Muhlhoff, N. (2011). Waiting for grapes: Expectancy and delayed gratification in bonobos. *International Journal of Comparative Psychology, 24,* 99–111.

Sugai, G., & Horner, R. (2002). The evolution of discipline practices: School-wide positive behavior supports. *Child & Family Behavior Therapy, 24,* 23–50.

TAGteach International. (n.d.). Retrieved from www.tagteach.com/.

van de Vijver, I., Ridderinkhof, K. R., & de Wit, S. (2015). Age-related changes in deterministic learning from positive versus negative performance feedback. *Aging, Neuropsychology, and Cognition, 22,* 595–619.

van Kerkhove, W. (2004). A fresh look at the wolf-pack theory of companion-animal dog social behavior. *Journal of Applied Animal Welfare Science, 7,* 279–285.

Walters, G. C., & Grusec, J. F. (1977). *Punishment.* San Francisco, CA: W. H. Freeman.

Williams, B. A. (1994). Conditioned reinforcement: Experimental and theoretical issues. *The Behavior Analyst, 17,* 261–285.

PART IV

Student Responses to Feedback

23 The Emotional Dynamics of Feedback from the Student's Point of View

Rick Stiggins

Without question, the feedback we provide to students represents one of the most powerful teaching and learning tools we have at our disposal. Done well, it helps students zero in on the keys to the improvement of their performance. When we reflect on matters of effective feedback in the classroom, most often our attention is drawn to its formulation and delivery. In other words, we think about how to make it effective from the teacher's (or information sender's) point of view – we center on making sure we have the right content, proper timing, and effective delivery of feedback. If it is formulated and given well, we tend to assume that it will serve its intended purpose. To be sure, these are very important considerations. The criteria or characteristics by which we judge the quality of feedback from the teacher's side of the information-sharing equation have been clearly articulated and are addressed in other chapters of this book.

However, in my opinion, in order to develop a comprehensive picture of the foundations of effective feedback, we also must explore feedback effectiveness from the student's (information recipient's) perspective. In doing so, we need to pay particular attention to the student's frame of mind when they interact with the feedback, and their mental state often depends on their relationship with their teacher at the time information is shared. This chapter explores the emotional dynamics of feedback from these points of view. My basic premise is that feedback cannot serve its intended purpose unless and until the recipient understands the meaning of information provided, is confident (or open) enough to accept it, and is prepared to act on it productively.

Understand the Feedback Environment

To set the stage for this discussion of the student's perspective, let's step back and consider feedback in the larger context of the classroom assessment environment (Chappuis, Commodore, & Stiggins, 2017). Assessment is the process of gathering information to inform instructional decisions. This process works effectively to promote student academic well-being only when the feedback provider begins with a clear vision of why, what, and how they are assessing. What is the *purpose* for the assessment? Who is the decision maker? What decision is this particular assessment to inform? And, therefore, what information must the assessment provide? In addition, the assessor must begin with clear vision of the *learning target* to be assessed. This underpins the development or selection of *quality assessment* exercises and scoring schemes reflective of that target. In other words, the purpose, target, and quality of the assessment all must contribute to the gathering of dependable evidence of student achievement. The quality and impact of feedback turns, in part, on the quality of the evidence underpinning the information being shared. With dependable evidence in hand, the assessor can *communicate the assessment results* to the intended user in a confident, timely, and understandable manner.

Regarding assessment purpose, we assess for either of two reasons depending on the context: to support student learning or to certify it, that is, for formative or summative reasons. Feedback is important in both of these contexts, but its role is different in each. When our purpose is to support learning, the recipient is the learner and feedback must describe attributes of student work back to them in a form and using terms and examples they understand and that reveal to the student how they can perform at a higher level the next time. However, in a summative context, the communication task is to judge and report how each student performed in relation to preestablished achievement expectations. Here we communicate about the sufficiency of student learning at a particular point in time both to the student and to others invested in promoting student well-being.

By way of orientation, for the remainder of this chapter, I am going to focus primarily on the formative assessment context while connecting also to summative applications as we go. I have chosen this emphasis because it is in the support learning context that the student–teacher relationship contributes the most to the effectiveness of feedback. But that partnership can be important in summative contexts too. I will illustrate this with classroom examples.

Further with respect to orientation, I will be bringing the student into the feedback process as a full partner with their teacher when appropriate on the formative side. Common wisdom has had us defining formative assessment as a process that gives teachers more frequent information on student achievement so they can design instruction in ways that help students grow. This is a good *partial* definition. But the revolutionary insight of the past decade is that students are active assessors of their own achievement too, and they make decisions based on their interpretation of their own performance. When they receive a test score, grade, or more descriptive information, they evaluate their results and ask themselves these kinds of instructionally relevant questions:

- Can I learn this or am I just too dense or far behind?
- Is learning this worth the amount of energy I will need to expend to master it?
- Is trying to learn this worth the risk that I might fail – again – in public?

Based on their own judgment about the evidence of their learning success or lack of it as reflected in the feedback they receive, they decide what to do about that performance. They can decide to press ahead and strive for learning success, or they can just give up in hopelessness. The heartbreak is that if they decide to give up in hopelessness, the learning stops before their teacher ever entered the game with their judgments and decisions about how to help. In other words, if students come down on the wrong side of the above questions, the results can be catastrophic.

Let me illustrate what can happen in the mind of a student by sharing a personal story of my struggles to learn to read in third grade – a story I have told often in workshops and at conferences. Note as you read that the feedback that led to my demise as a learner was summative in nature – the report card grading system.

Struggling to Learn to Read

My story begins in third grade in a small town in western New York State. Miss G. was my teacher. Visualize twenty-five of us seated in straight rows in alphabetical order. There was Eddie A. at the head of the first row over by the windows. Next came Jim B., then Judy C. My name is Stiggins, so I was near the end of the last row – way over by the bulletin boards. Only Dave W. sat behind me, and Terry S. was just in front of me.

When the time came for instruction in reading, Miss G. would instruct us to take out our reading books and open to a particular page, the story we were to read that day. She would turn to Eddie A. and nod – he knew his job was to rise from his desk, stand with proper posture, and read the first paragraph of the story aloud for others to hear. When he finished, Jim B. would follow, and so we would go down the row.

Now, for reasons that we understand today but didn't back then, I have great difficulty with oral reading fluency. My eyes, brain, and mouth are not "wired" to work effectively together – a reality I have accommodated as an adult. But back then it was a very big problem. I was constantly at risk of embarrassing myself in a very public manner. So I needed a risk management strategy – a way to minimize the embarrassment. This is the one I used: I would count the number of students in class that day, count down the paragraphs to find mine, and practice reading it silently to myself. I found that, if I could be a few minutes with my passage, I could almost memorize it and then stand and recite it, thus not embarrassing myself when it was my turn.

However, about halfway through the story, my strategy would begin to reveal its shortcomings when Miss G. asked a comprehension question and spontaneously called on me to answer it. I couldn't answer it – I didn't even know what the question was because I wasn't listening, I was practicing. But Miss G. didn't know this. So she filed away her first piece of data for "data-based decision making": Rick isn't getting this … hopefully a kind of formative cue.

In any event, we proceed down the rows and Terry S. (right in front of me) is reading his paragraph. As he does, fear rages within me because I'm next – sweaty palms, heart-pounding stark terror. Seriously!

Terry finishes. Rick, you're on. As I am about to rise from my desk, Miss G. says, "Terry you did that so beautifully and your paragraph was so short. Would you read another one for us?" So he reads my passage far better than I ever could have and I am compelled to try to read an unpracticed piece, making a fool of myself once again.

My worst nightmare was when Miss G. turned to what I used to call "reading roulette" – where she would call on us at random to read. I knew was going to get slammed – it was just a matter of time – and I was powerless to prevent it.

Anyway, now Miss G. has her second piece of data and she decides to send notes home to my parents informing them that "Rick can't read." Now I'm a good enough reader to read these notes, and I see a serious problem brewing. At the end of the first grading period, on my report card, next to "Reading," there appears a great big F – clearly a summative intervention.

Why is that F there? Two reasons: First, it informs both me and my family that my achievement is at a low level, and if the target is oral reading proficiency, it conveys an accurate message. Second, the F is supposed to be a motivator – to get me going so I would not continue to fail in the future. It was supposed to be a kick in the pants (my Dad took that part literally).

So Mom, Dad, and Miss G. launch a frontal attack on Rick, the nonreader. "You have to try harder," they admonished. Nevertheless, the second report card: "Reading: F." A trend or trajectory of failure begins to seem inevitable to me.

As the story continues to unfold, put Miss G., Mom, and Dad aside for a moment and focus on me. The next crucial decision was mine. At some point in the progression of those failures, I said to myself, "Rick you're a nonreader. It will always be so. So get over it." And I stopped trying. I gave up in hopelessness. Do you think that was what Mom, Dad and Miss G. wanted me to do? Of course not. They wanted just the opposite. But this is what they got.

I held that academic self-concept of Rick as a nonreader all the way through high school. And, of course, reading proficiency underpinned academic success in all aspects of my course work. "Not a good student" doesn't begin to describe my life in junior high and high school. Now understand that I didn't have a bad life back then – I was a pretty good athlete, girl watcher, and partier. But none of it included Rick the learner, because I was sure I was incapable of mastering school stuff. I had no confidence at all as a learner. In the rank order of our senior class, I ranked low and for good reason.

The classroom assessment and summative grading process had done its work – had had its effect. Its impact was deep and long lasting. As my teammates took college entrance exams, I didn't bother. What was the point? As they headed to university, I headed somewhere else. But, as it turned out, the inferences I had drawn about myself as a learner were wrong. Later, I will complete the story with details about how the assessment and evaluation process actually formed the foundation of my turn-around experience. But first, let's delve more deeply into my state of mind at the end of high school.

The Emotional Dynamics of Being Evaluated

My struggles with reading proficiency with all of its spinoff implications for my achievement in school subjects played out in ways that aligned very comfortably with the mission of our schools at that time. That mission was to produce a dependable rank order of students based on achievement at the end of high school; that is, the system was supposed to produce winners and losers. Some of us were supposed to give up in hopelessness so we could occupy the low ranks. The more spread the summative grading system produced among students with respect to their achievement (as reflected in cumulative GPAs), the more dependable would be the rank order. My place in the pecking order was very clear to me and I acted accordingly, as I was supposed to.

But the societal problem that has emerged over the past two decades is that we have come to realize the shortcomings of this institutional mission. It no longer meets our educational or workplace needs. Because of the rapid evolution of technology and increase in our cultural diversity, we now understand that any student who leaves school without certain essential lifelong learning skills will not be able to survive socially or economically, let alone contribute. We have come to understand that those who drop out or finish low in the rank order typically fail to develop the lifelong learner proficiencies that we now see as essential.

So, our community and educational leaders have expanded the mission of our schools to include this additional lifelong learner priority. Educators are instructed to "leave no student behind," to make sure "every student succeeds." Schools have been told to narrow chronically wide achievement gaps, promote universal high school graduation, and make sure every student is ready for college or workplace training. I submit that this is a new assignment that has profound implications for the role of assessment and feedback in our schools.

If our educators are to fulfill this mission of promoting much higher levels of academic success for all, *we can no longer have any students giving up in hopelessness*. Hopelessness arises when the feedback students receive leads them to the conclusion that learning success is beyond reach for them – it's too late, I'm too far behind, why try? Obviously, this is a crucial emotional dynamic from the student's point of view. It focuses on their sense of being in control of their own academic success. Albert Bandura (1994) refers to this sense as self-efficacy. In the paragraphs that follow, he marks both ends of a continuum of this personal construct:

> A strong sense of efficacy enhances human accomplishment and personal well-being in many ways. People with high assurance in their capabilities approach difficult tasks as challenges to be mastered rather than as threats to be avoided. Such an efficacious outlook fosters intrinsic interest and deep engrossment in activities. They set themselves challenging goals and maintain strong commitment to them. They heighten and sustain their efforts in the face of failure. They quickly recover their sense of efficacy after failures or setbacks. *They attribute failure to insufficient effort or deficient knowledge and skills which*

are acquirable. They approach threatening situations with assurance that they can exercise control over them. Such an efficacious outlook produces personal accomplishments, reduces stress and lowers vulnerability ...

In contrast, people who doubt their capabilities shy away from difficult tasks which they view as personal threats. They have low aspirations and weak commitment to the goals they choose to pursue. When faced with difficult tasks, they dwell on their personal deficiencies, on the obstacles they will encounter, and all kinds of adverse outcomes rather than concentrate on how to perform successfully. They slacken their efforts and give up quickly in the face of difficulties. They are slow to recover their sense of efficacy following failure or setbacks. *Because they view insufficient performance as deficient aptitude it does not require much failure for them to lose faith in their capabilities.* (p. 71, emphasis added)

In practical terms, the anchor points at the ends of the continuum are found in the two sentences in italics. Each refers to the attributions of the reasons for success or failure. One has the learner in possession of the inner reserves needed to power past the occasional negative feedback to the promise of success with greater effort. This is a sense of being in control of one's own outcomes. At the other end, however, the learner sees inadequate academic ability as the cause of failure. In this case, this leads to the inference that failure is inevitable and so negative feedback spells defeat. The question is, how can we use the assessment/feedback process to promote the kind of universal academic success implied in "every student succeeds" – at least with respect to the mastery of lifelong learner proficiencies?

I found part of the answer in the work of Rosabeth Moss Kanter in her book *Confidence: How Winning Streaks and Losing Begin and End.* Professor Kanter speaks of confidence as ebbing and flowing, not as events or episodes but rather as tendencies, patterns, or trajectories. In essence, expectations of success or failure can become self-fulfilling prophesies. Winning can become contagious. "Success makes it easier to view events in a positive light, to generate optimism ... easier to aim high ... easier to find the energy to work hard because it looks as if hard work will pay off" (p. 29). In effect, success becomes the cause of even more success. This must become our universal emotional aspiration for our students if schools are to fulfill their expanded mission of universal lifelong learner proficiency. On the other hand, Kantor points out, "losing streaks begin in response to a sense of failure, and failure makes people feel out of control. It is just one more step to a pervasive sense of powerlessness, and powerlessness corrodes confidence" (p. 97). This is the deep trap into which I fell in my struggles to learn to read. When it comes to the development of lifelong learner proficiencies, hopelessness is no longer an acceptable emotional dynamic within learners.

We help students build and maintain a strong sense of academic self-efficacy when we help them understand that their role in their classroom assessment environment is (1) to strive to understand what success looks like from the beginning of the learning and (2) to analyze each formative assessment for evidence of or keys to their own improvement over time. The teacher's support role is to be sure students gain access to the evidence they need from each formative assessment to determine how they can do better the next time. This is precisely why our national assessment spotlight has been steadily shifting from merely summative to far more frequent formative applications.

Once again, as above, to understand the practicalities of how to get students on winning streaks and keep them there, we need to see the matter of feedback in the context of the larger picture of classroom assessment couched in terms of productive teaching and learning.

In my opinion, this has been most clearly and appropriately accomplished by Jan Chappuis (2015) in her teacher guidebook, *Seven Strategies of Assessment for Leaning*. She is influenced in her thinking by Royce Sadler (1998), who advised us to make sure students are made aware from the very beginning of instruction of answers to three key instructional questions: Where am I going? Where am I now in relation to the target? And how can I close the gap between the two? Or, what am I trying to learn? What have I already learned? And how can I get there most effectively? Chappuis builds her practical assessment for learning strategies around these as follows:

Where am I going?

1. Provide students with a clear vision of the learning target in terms they can understand from the very beginning of instruction.
2. Provide examples of strong and weak work, again, from the outset so the pathway to success becomes clear to them too.

Where am I now?

3. Offer continuous access to descriptive feedback during learning so students can see how to improve step-by-step, get on winning streaks, and gain confidence with each new success.
4. Teach student the skills of self-assessment so they can see increments in their own capabilities, attribute them to their own hard work, and partner with their teacher in deciding what comes next in their learning.

How can I close the gap?

5. Use evidence of student needs to plan focused lessons designed to help students understand how to move forward.
6. Follow focused instruction with practice and feedback, again, so students can focus their revisions and see growth coming about for them due to themselves.
7. Provide students with opportunities to track their own progress, describe it with examples of progressively better work, and share their successes with others.

These elements in Chappuis's progression all contribute to a formative assessment/feedback loop intended to promote each student's sense of control over their own academic well-being. Here's how: Students become clear about the learning target from the beginning of instruction through their teacher's transformation of expectations into student-friendly language accompanied by relevant examples of student work ranging from poor to mid-range to excellent work. With this understanding, they develop the conceptual sense and vocabulary they will need later to comprehend the meaning of whatever descriptive feedback they receive on the journey to success. With this background, as the ongoing descriptive feedback flows in, they will see precisely how to revise their work in ways that promote ever-better performance. As they track their own success and see their gap narrowing with focused instruction, and as evidence of that success begins to accumulate, the positive effect of their own assertive actions will become apparent over time and a strong sense of academic self-efficacy will grow with them.

Hidden in plain sight within this scenario is a profoundly important transformation in the emotional dynamics of feedback from the student's point of view. Not only can students build the inner reserves needed to remain resilient to occasional negative feedback, but they actually come to understand that it helps them attain even stronger growth. In other words, their frame of mind remains continuously open to ways feedback can set them up for success. This is an essential lifelong learner dynamic. Further, given the kind of understanding developed in students by starting the progression with an understanding of the target, as students attain higher levels of mastery of it they can begin to generate their own descriptive feedback and partner with their teacher in planning what comes next in their learning. If the kind of learning experience promised and delivered with Chappuis's seven strategies of assessment for learning does not represent the foundation for becoming a lifelong learner, I don't know what does.

Let's consider why this progression and the feedback that results work to maintain student confidence and promote gains in student achievement. Incidentally, those gains range from half to three-quarters of a standard deviation increase in achievement with the greatest gains accruing for struggling learners (Black & Wiliam, 1998). They arise because assessment for learning strategies provide the learner with insights about their own learning success that trigger productive emotional reactions within the student.

For example, initial insight into the target and the path they will follow to attain it can trigger a confidence within the learner that they will have a way to know they are getting closer, that the gap is narrowing. If left to guess at the meaning of success, the learner is left with uncertainty about how to act productively in their own best interest. This can be a learning-stopper by triggering a sense of vulnerability.

Further, having continuous access to descriptive feedback while they are learning can add to a student's sense of confidence that their actions are leading to better-quality work. The result will be an ever-stronger sense of academic self-efficacy. In the absence of such information, as they struggle to learn, they have no way to judge the efficacy of their actions. Again, vulnerability. This sense of being at risk becomes even more dangerous if students fall into a tumble over time of what they come to accept as inevitable failure. When the occasional failure turns into a losing streak, mere vulnerability transforms into hopelessness. And so it becomes clear that the role of feedback during learning must be either (1) to provide evidence of the gap narrowing for the student or (2) to permit students to infer what actions on their part will narrow that gap. In Kanter's parlance, we must strive to get all students on winning streaks and keep them there. This is the kind of learning environment that Bandura, as quoted above, would contend will move students to the efficacious end of his continuum.

In their comprehensive synthesis of research on effective communication in the classroom, Hattie and Temperley (2007) provide details on the kinds of feedback that are most likely to give rise to strong gains in student achievement. "Feedback is effective," they point out, "when it consists of information about progress and/or about how to proceed" (p. 89). In other words, it focuses student attention on the learning target in such a manner as to describe their strengths and areas in need of improvement in terms they can understand, so it becomes clear to them how to do better the next time. It arrives for the student while they are in the process of learning and growing so they have time and opportunity to apply it to the improvement of their work. And it arrives in manageable amounts so as not to overwhelm the student with so much input that they become confused and unable to respond.

The Foundations of Feedback Success

At the outset and throughout this chapter, I have repeatedly emphasized how important it is to build toward truly effective feedback by developing a totally feedback-friendly classroom assessment environment. I repeat this admonition one more time below for emphasis. And then I will illustrate it with the assessment/feedback experience that turned my learning life around, giving rise to the kind of success we dream of for all of our students.

Success begins for the teacher/assessor/feedback-giver with a clear purpose of every assessment. Is it intended to support learning or judge its sufficiency in relation to expectations? Will feedback show the way to higher levels of performance or depict achievement at a point in time in relation to preset expectations? Ultimately, the resulting feedback will vary in its content and delivery depending on the purpose.

Second, the teacher must begin the assessment process with a clear vision of the learning target to be assessed and the progression students will follow from start to learning success. Obviously, instruction and the assessment exercises and scoring will figure here. But more importantly, presentation of the target to learners from the beginning of the learning provides them with the conceptual understanding and vocabulary they need to make meaning of the feedback they will receive along the way.

Third, the assessment must be of high quality, delivering dependable evidence of the current level of student achievement. This forms the backbone of the feedback to be delivered and acted on by the learner. We do great harm by providing students with feedback that is based on assessments that misrepresent their achievement.

Next is the communication of assessment results to the intended user. When the recipient is the student and the intent is to support their ongoing learning, it needs to be descriptive feedback that they understand and have been prepared to act on. But in summative contexts, feedback is effective only when the information shared shows the student and others how their performance compared with preset and public achievement expectations.

Finally, when the purpose of the assessment and feedback is to support student learning, maximum support can be provided when students have been involved in a self-assessment process from the outset as they are learning, having accomplished the following:

- Come to understand the learning target and the pathway to it
- Learned to interpret their own assessment results as they related to their ultimate achievement destination
- Received or generated and acted on feedback providing insights about how to improve
- Had the opportunity to regularly reflect on and interact with others about their growth and development.

As it turned out, my turn-around experience after years of believing that I would never be a good reader or learner included each of these active ingredients.

Learning Success as a Motivator for Students

After high school and a brief technical school experience, I enlisted in the Air Force. The Vietnam War was raging; we had a draft at that time by lottery; I had drawn a low number and essentially had no choice. After basic training, I was ordered to aircraft mechanic's school. This was a fifteen-week school divided into five two-week segments. Segment one centered on mastery of knowledge of airplane systems – engines, electronics, hydraulics, avionics, airframe, etc. After ten eight-hour days of instruction, we had to pass a hundred-item final exam to go on to segment two.

But it was here that I remember something happening that I had never experienced before in school: on day one, the instructors gave us a copy of the final exam that had been taken by the previous class. They said it would not be our final, but it would cover the same range and kinds of material. So we should use it to our advantage in our studies. Each day at the end of instruction as our last activity, we would find the items on that test related to the learning of that day, figure out the right answer and why the incorrect answers were wrong. This kind of feedback for learning helped us understand expectations, zero in on and grow toward excellence with great precision, and understand the assessment process. It built our confidence.

In the end, we took that final exam and I remember scoring near 100%. Two things about that: First, I had never scored that high on any exam in any context. I was stunned. A small glow of confidence I had never experienced before was lighted within me. I had been scared but maybe I was going to be okay.

Second, most of the other airmen scored very high also. This was new too. In high school if this happened, the teachers would have been chastised for being too easy – for giving too many As. But remember, the Air Force is not seeking a dependable rank order of mechanics by the end of school. The institutional mission was different. They need for every one of us to be a really good mechanic. Pilot's lives hang in the balance. The mission of these master technicians was to promote universal competence.

With our solid foundation of knowledge in hand, we went on to school segment two. Here we were to learn how to use that knowledge to diagnose problems with airplane systems: why is this engine not working? Where is the electrical short in this apparatus? etc. They had developed sets of apparatus for the various systems in which they would create a variety of problems – purposely make things go wrong – and our task was to learn how to solve the problem. On day one of this segment, they demonstrated with instructors thinking out loud as they solved problems they set up and posed for each other. After two weeks of instruction actually using the various simulated systems, we were confronted with ten such problems we had not seen before, and, to move on, we had to diagnose almost all of them correctly. I got them all. Two segments, two big successes: I was on a little winning streak! And I was just a little bit more confident. Maybe I had been wrong all along about my own "smarts."

No need to string this out. This kind of learning and success went on for the rest of the program – clear learning targets, continuous descriptive feedback and self-assessment as we learned, rigorous accountability, and very high rates of student success. I finishing with a very high level of performance and was publicly recognized for it. I was on a very real winning streak now and felt a kind of control over my own well-being that I had never felt before. And it was all because the technical instructors in this school understood how to weave the assessment into the learning in ways that promoted (and did not merely measure) success.

Thanks to those airmen, I had confidence enough to risking taking some college courses while in the military and received very high grades – again, very different from my previous academic experiences. As a result, on returning to civilian life, I had enough confidence to enroll in college full time and proceeded through seven straight years to a PhD from Michigan State.

I don't share this part of the story to be boastful. I share it to make the point that the emotional dynamics of an assessment/feedback environment can be managed in simple ways that set up learners for unprecedented levels of success – levels they may have thought unattainable. Given a new institutional mission for our schools that is very much like that of this Air Force training staff – that is, universal mastery of essential learning targets – we can and should learn much from their clear thinking about how to use feedback during learning to promote student success.

References

Bandura, A. (1994). Self-efficacy. In V. S. Ramachaudran (Ed.), *Encyclopedia of human behavior*, vol. 4, 71–81. New York: Academic Press.

Black, P., & Wiliam, D. (1998). Assessment and classroom learning. *Educational Assessment: Principles, Policy and Practice, 5*, 7–74.

Black, P., & Wiliam, D. (2010). Inside the black box: Raising standards through classroom assessment. *Phi Delta Kappan, 80*, 139–148.

Chappuis, J. (2015). *Seven strategies of assessment for learning* (2nd edn.). Hoboken, NJ: Pearson Education.

Chappuis, S., Commodore, C., & Stiggins, R. (2017). *Balanced assessment systems: Leadership, quality and the role of classroom assessment.* Thousand Oaks, CA: Corwin.

Hattie, J., & Timperley, H. (2007). The power of feedback. *Review of Educational Research, 77*, 81–112.

Kanter, R. M. (2004). *Confidence: How winning streaks and losing streaks begin and end.* New York: Crown Business.

Sadler, R. (1998). Formative assessment: Revisiting the territory. *Assessment in Education, 5*, 77–84.

24 Facilitating Students' Active Engagement with Feedback

Anders Jonsson and Ernesto Panadero

There is an increasing consensus that the quality of students' engagement with, and use of, the feedback they receive is a critical element of feedback effectiveness. Winstone, Nash, Parker, and Rowntree (2016) use the term "proactive recipience" to emphasize the active contribution and responsibility of the learners who are the recipients and who have to engage with the feedback they receive. On the other hand, there is ample evidence suggesting that students' engagement with their feedback is usually not very productive. For instance, Brown and Glover (2006) wrote that their interviews with students showed that the students did not act on feedback to improve their work, although they did value receiving it. The same message is reiterated in other studies, where many students reported not reading their feedback or using it rarely, if at all (MacDonald, 1991; MacLellan, 2001; Sinclair & Cleland, 2007). Therefore, there is a pressing need for more research on how to understand and improve students' engagement with their feedback (Jonsson, 2013; Winstone et al., 2016).

The aim of this chapter is to bring together research on students' use of feedback in order to provide a picture of what kind of research has been conducted and what we currently know about how to facilitate students' engagement with their feedback. The main sources for the chapter are two recent reviews by Jonsson (2013) and Winstone et al. (2016). These two reviews complement each other by having slightly different foci and analyzing and presenting their findings differently.

The chapter is structured as follows: First, we present a general overview of existing research into students' use of feedback based on the two reviews. This overview outlines how the respective searches for studies were performed and describes characteristics of the outcomes. Second, we summarize a taxonomy of "recipience processes" used by Winstone et al. (2016) to categorize interventions aiming for improved student engagement with feedback. Third, we present an overview of factors that may moderate students' engagement with the feedback they receive. Finally, conclusions based on the previous sections are drawn regarding recommendations for practice on how students' engagement with feedback may be facilitated.

An Overview of Research on Students' Use of Feedback

In 2013, Jonsson (2013) published a literature review aiming to identify the difficulties students face when using feedback. This review focused on research in higher education and on feedback provided by educators (i.e., not peers, computers, etc.). Furthermore, a time limit for the search was set to 1990. Data were collected by starting from a number of recent publications (2009–2010). The reference lists in these articles were then used to find new articles, continuing iteratively throughout the review process, a method referred to as "snowballing."

In total, 103 studies were included in the review. These studies varied across academic subjects (e.g., humanities, technology, business), and the feedback studied consisted almost exclusively of written comments on students' written work (mostly essays). Research designs encompassed mostly questionnaires and interviews, sometimes in combination. A number of studies complemented students' perceptions with analyses of examination results or teacher feedback. Only very few studies were found that went into detail about students' strategies for handling feedback. In fact, only two studies investigated mechanisms behind students' use of feedback in vivo by employing think-aloud protocols to record students' verbal reports during revisions of essays (Dessner, 1991; Dohrer, 1991). Consequently, all but two studies investigated students' use of feedback through "indirect" measures, such as studying changes made in revised drafts or by asking students about how they used their feedback retrospectively. Therefore, according to the 2013 review findings, the evidence available on students' actual use of feedback was quite scarce.

The main contribution made by this review was a thematic analysis of factors influencing students' use of feedback. A small number of factors were identified that were recognized as important in several studies. These factors are presented as five themes, including commonly reported obstacles for using feedback, as well as possible ways to promote a more productive use of the feedback. One of the major barriers for using feedback formatively is that students do not find the feedback useful, for instance, because they are not given the opportunity to revise their assignments. Another problem identified in the review is the lack of congruence between students' preferences for feedback and the kinds of feedback that actually seem to aid them in using it productively. The optimal feedback for formative use may not necessarily be specific, detailed, positive, and individualized, as is often assumed. Instead, less specific and less individualized feedback that forces students to actively engage with the information may actually be more productive for student learning. Yet another barrier for using feedback formatively is the authority expressed through the feedback, including grades or marks, since some students do not question such authoritative feedback. This means that these students may choose to avoid difficult and cumbersome revisions, which could potentially improve the quality of their performance. Instead, they may focus on revisions that are perceived as easier and safer, such as form and mechanics, in order to optimize their chances to obtain high grades or marks without too much effort.

While the aforementioned obstacles depend largely on the teacher, there are also factors identified in the review that depend on the students. These factors include the lack of strategies for using the feedback students receive and the lack of understanding of the academic terminology. Obviously, if students do not know what to do with the feedback or do not understand it, then asking them for revisions will not help. To overcome these barriers, substantial changes to the instructional process (e.g., the opportunity to engage in dialogue with the teacher using model answers or exemplars along with the feedback) are in order (Jonsson, 2013).

In 2016, Winstone and her colleagues published a literature review focusing on factors that may affect learners' engagement with feedback, while also aiming to describe different feedback interventions along with the processes they have targeted. It is notable that even though the search performed by Winstone et al. (2016) was both broader (i.e., no time limit, not only higher education, not only educator feedback, and not only empirical research) and used a more thorough methodology (i.e., searching databases with keywords, resulting in 4,862 initial hits), the outcome did not differ considerably from the review by Jonsson (2013). In total, 195 studies were included, all published between 1985 and 2014, and more than 80% contained some form of empirical data. Among the 159 empirical studies, only eleven included students from primary and secondary schools. In studies that included students from higher education, participants from different disciplines were represented, such as social sciences, STEM, health and social care, and arts and humanities. Most of the empirical studies focused on feedback as provided by an educator (81%), although some focused on different sources of feedback or on multiple sources, such as peer and self-feedback. The most common method was surveys (55%), but many studies also used focus groups (23%) and/or individual interviews (21%). A number of studies used quantitative research methods, including a few with quasi-experimental and experimental designs.

The main contributions made by this review are the systematic presentation of potential moderators of proactive recipience, organized around an interpersonal communication model, and the proposal of a framework for categorizing interventions designed to influence students' use of feedback. This latter framework includes both the components that the interventions target and researchers' rationales for the development of such interventions. The taxonomy is a particularly important contribution because it organizes existing research and serves as a guide for future research. It may also guide practitioners when identifying problems to be addressed and when planning possible solutions (Winstone et al., 2016). Both of these contributions will be presented in more detail in the upcoming sections, starting with the framework for categorizing feedback interventions.

A Taxonomy of Recipience Processes

As presented above, one of the aims of the review by Winstone et al. (2016) was to identify pedagogical interventions for supporting students' engagement with feedback. The authors systematized the "recipience processes" (i.e., the processes that the recipient could activate) that these interventions targeted and presented a taxonomy of such processes. Their analyses included 105 studies that detailed the outcomes of interventions designed to support students' use of feedback. Studies were categorized in two ways: (1) by the components of the interventions, including the outcomes, and (2) by the rationale for the interventions.

Starting with the components of the interventions, this classification resulted in fourteen main categories (Table 24.1) that were often used in combination with each other. These individual components were grouped in four clusters with conceptual similarities.

In their analysis, Winstone et al. (2016) also categorized the rationale for the interventions resulting in four recipience processes:

1. *Self-appraisal* means making judgments about oneself, such as students' own traits or behavior. This process supports proactive recipience by empowering students to assess their own strengths and weaknesses, thereby reducing their reliance on external sources of judgment.
2. *Assessment literacy* means understanding the grading process and using it to assess one's own performance. This process supports proactive recipience by allowing the students (1) to understand the relation between assessment, learning, and what is expected; (2) to evaluate their own and others'

Table 24.1 *Intervention components and clusters identified by Winstone et al. (2016)*

Cluster	Intervention Component
Internalizing and applying standards	Peer assessment
	Self-assessment
	Engaging with grading criteria
	Dialogue and discussion
Sustainable monitoring	Action planning
	Portfolio
Collective provision of training	Feedback workshop
	Feedback resources
	Exemplar assignments
Manner of feedback delivery	Formative assessment/resubmission
	Feedback without a grade
	Tailored feedback
	Presentation of feedback
	Technology

performance against certain criteria; (3) to understand terminology and concepts used in feedback; and (4) to be familiar with ways of assessing and giving feedback. (Price, Rust, O'Donovan, Handley, & Bryant, 2012, pp. 10–11)

3. *Goal-setting* refers to students' ability to articulate desired outcomes, which in turn requires them to adopt some kind of strategy to reach these outcomes. *Self-regulation* means planning, monitoring, and evaluating progress and strategies, thereby subsuming the process of goal-setting. These processes support proactive recipience by empowering students to translate their goals into plans of action and to review and adjust their performance and strategies in order to reach these goals.

4. *Engagement and motivation* is about being open to receiving feedback. Such engagement requires a commitment to change and development, paying attention to the feedback, and being prepared to use it. This process supports proactive recipience by facilitating the motivation to read and understand feedback.

In order to avoid excessive details, only the clusters are presented below and not the individual components. Instead, examples of findings are mentioned briefly, along with one study summarized in more detail. For a more detailed presentation of individual components, see Winstone et al. (2016).

Internalizing and Applying Standards

In this cluster of studies, several intervention components included activities such as self- and peer assessment, where students were expected to become familiar with assessment standards. These interventions were often designed to target self-appraisal and assessment literacy but were also designed for the purposes of enhancing engagement and motivation. Findings from studies showed, for instance, that self-assessment was perceived to improve students' capacity to question their own work or develop their understanding of educators' tacit knowledge and the criteria used for assessment. Other findings showed that students appreciated interventions directed toward engagement with assessment criteria and that students were particularly open to guidance received during one-on-one feedback dialogues (Winstone et al., 2016).

As an example, Al-Barakat and Al-Hassan (2009) investigated how preservice teachers perceived the use of peer assessment during their workplace-based education (or "practicum"). Semi-structured interviews showed that students believed that peer assessment had several benefits, such as supporting the development of "instructional competencies" and making sound assessments of their own classroom performance.

Sustainable Monitoring

In this cluster of studies, students were engaged in documenting and tracking how their performance and feedback changed over time and reflected on these changes. Several recipience processes were targeted through action planning and portfolios, but the most common was goal-setting and self-regulation. Findings from studies show, for instance, that students' engagement with feedback was facilitated by encouraging or requiring them to produce different kinds of action plans. Another finding was that keeping a portfolio of assessed work was perceived positively by students and facilitated engagement in reflection (Winstone et al., 2016).

As an example, Altahawi, Sisk, Poloskey, Hicks, and Dannefer (2012) investigated how medical students perceived a competence-based assessment portfolio system. This particular system was built around competence standards and continuous formative feedback, with no grades. These findings, based on individual narratives, showed that respondents independently suggested that the portfolio system had enhanced their training in ways that prior systems (which included grades) had not, particularly concerning self-reflective skills.

Collective Provision of Training

In this cluster of studies, some intervention components involved collectively supporting groups of students. Resources, such as workshops or exemplar assignments, were designed to extend students' concepts of feedback and to aid them in understanding and using their feedback and/or to be prepared for their own emotional responses to feedback. These interventions were mainly implemented for assessment literacy purposes. Findings from studies show that students who used a feedback guide perceived that this made them engage more with their feedback than they normally would. Another finding was that students engaged with and appreciated the opportunity to access exemplars of completed assignments (Winstone et al., 2016).

As an example, Cartney (2010) used peer assessment as a vehicle to engage social work students with assessment criteria. As part of this intervention, a workshop was held to explain the processes of giving each other feedback. The findings, based on focus-group interviews, showed that there was a general agreement among students that the feedback had supported them in improving their work. Moreover, several students claimed that they had started to seek feedback from peers in courses that did not include a formal peer assessment element.

Manner of Feedback Delivery

In this cluster of studies, a number of intervention components focused on how feedback was delivered, whether formative or summative, or in terms of content, presentation, or style. This cluster included the largest category of intervention components, which was technology. These interventions were mainly implemented for engagement and motivation purposes. Findings from studies demonstrated that students perceived that not receiving any grades made them take more notice of their feedback. Other findings revealed that students believed that they were more likely to use their feedback if they had specifically requested it. Students were also receptive to feedback that was delivered through digital learning environments (Winstone et al., 2016).

As an example, Wingate (2010) investigated the impact of formative feedback on the development of academic writing for first-year undergraduate students. The findings, based on text analysis and interviews, showed that students who had made use of their feedback improved in the areas criticized. However, for several students the same problems persisted because they had paid little attention to their feedback and had not acted on it.

Summary and Conclusions for Future Research

The reviewed research demonstrated a number of positive effects of feedback interventions on students' engagement with feedback. However, most of this research was based on self-reported data only. More research using other kinds of data (e.g., comparing first and second drafts) and other kinds of research designs (e.g., experimental conditions) is needed in order to substantiate claims made from self-reported data.

Winstone et al. (2016) showed that far more interventions targeted students' motivation to use their feedback, as compared with goal-setting and self-regulation. The primary focus for several of these studies was on students' satisfaction with feedback, rather than their actual use of it. Since goal-setting and self-regulation could be considered key goals of education (Wiggins, 1998), there is a need for more interventions aiming for improved student engagement with feedback as a means of fostering students' self-regulation.

By far, the most common intervention component was technology used for feedback delivery, whereas components pertaining to the cluster "collective provision of training" were relatively rare in the interventions. Further, the components in the cluster "sustainable monitoring" were also rarely used. Still, both of these clusters of intervention components could be important tools for students' autonomy and self-regulation. More research is needed where interventions aimed at improving student engagement with feedback provide (1) tools and strategies for students to track their progress, such as action planning and portfolios, and (2) training and resources, such as workshops and exemplars – especially in combination with means to foster students' self-regulation.

The research reviewed in Winstone et al. (2016) reported a number of difficulties with the interventions. For example, the described interventions were often time-consuming to set up and/or to implement. Furthermore, several interventions were difficult for students to understand, and students engaged with them less than expected. Researchers could focus on designing interventions that are scalable and possible to implement and use within the scope of regular instruction.

Last, because most individual intervention components were explored in only a few studies, relatively little is known about the transferability of effects across contexts, as well as long-term effects. Here the taxonomy by Winstone et al. (2016)

could support future research by providing a stronger theoretical organization and coherence for studies to come.

Factors Moderating Students' Engagement with Feedback

In this section, moderators that have been seen to influence how students engage with their feedback will be discussed. Winstone et al. (2016) note that despite several examples of how to create "actionable feedback," there is still limited information for educators on how to change learners' behavior from passive to more active receivers and seekers of feedback. To bridge this gap, Winstone et al. (2016) presented an overview of factors that might positively influence students' proactive recipience.

Although meta-analysis might be considered the optimal methodology for comparing different moderating variables, both Jonsson (2013) and Winstone et al. (2016) used a narrative review approach. This was justified by the large number of empirical studies and potential moderators that both reviews included, making full coverage of all potential moderators unfeasible. However, while Jonsson (2013) conducted a thematic analysis of the studies reviewed, in Winstone et al. (2016) the findings were presented according to a model of interpersonal communication. In the current chapter, the latter model will be used to organize our discussion, which means that factors are grouped into the following categories: receiver variables, sender variables, variables that pertain to the message, and those that relate to the learning context (Figure 24.1). The reader should keep in mind that these categories are purely organizational entities. Furthermore, within these categories, findings from both reviews are presented, as well as findings from other relevant sources. In particular, Lipnevich, Berg, and Smith (2016) have proposed a model that has some overlap with

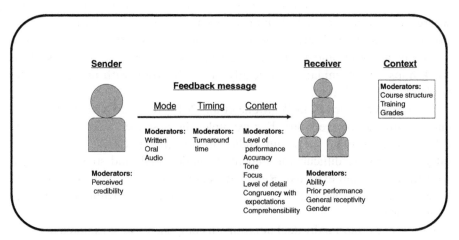

Figure 24.1 *An overview of factors moderating students' engagement with feedback.*

the communication model used by Winstone et al. (2016), but focusing more on the mechanisms guiding student receptivity to feedback. The "feedback-student interaction model" by Lipnevich et al. (2016) will be used to elaborate further on the categories below where appropriate.

The Receiver

Individual differences among students may influence how feedback is used. We know this already from studies on the effectiveness of formative feedback, where low-achieving students may benefit from feedback with different characteristics than high-achieving students (e.g., Shute, 2008). Lipnevich et al. (2016) therefore raise the question: While acknowledging that some part of the feedback process is likely to be context dependent, are some students generally more receptive to feedback as compared with others? And if this is the case, how modifiable is this characteristic? These authors suggest three factors that may affect how students engage with feedback: ability, prior performance, and general receptivity.

A number of moderators associated with ability and prior performance have been investigated empirically, and findings suggest that students with positive academic self-concept, high self-efficacy, good self-regulation skills, and high achievement are more likely to engage with their feedback. There are exceptions, however, to this general picture, and some suggestions on how to improve students' engagement with feedback are based on theoretical considerations only and have not been empirically tested (e.g., Handley, Price, & Millar, 2011). It is therefore difficult to draw any firm conclusions about how students' individual characteristics may serve as moderators of proactive recipience.

Regarding general receptivity, this factor has been shown to be a strong predictor of emotional reactions to feedback (Smith, Berg, Kendall-Smith, & Lipnevich, 2013). It has also been suggested that students need to have a clear understanding of the purposes of feedback and carry responsibility for realizing the potential benefits of the feedback. Without having a good grip on these feedback fundamentals and, hence, willingness to engage, students are presumably less likely to use feedback productively. Studies in this category are usually based on interviews with teachers, asking about their perceptions of students' use of feedback (e.g., Bailey & Garner, 2010; Carless, Salter, Yang, & Lam, 2011).

In addition to the factors suggested by Lipnevich et al. (2016), there are indications of gender differences, where females are more likely to engage with their feedback as compared with males (e.g., Baadte & Schnotz, 2014).

The Sender

Just as there are individual differences among students that may influence how feedback is used, there are individual differences among teachers (and other feedback providers). This is a separate category in the model by Winstone et al. (2016) but part of the context in the Lipnevich et al. (2016) model. One factor raised by both, however, is trust, which has been operationalized in terms of perceived credibility of the teacher. For example, Bing-You, Paterson, and Levine (1997) presented several aspects of the sender, which according to the medical students interviewed would cause them to disbelieve or discount their feedback, even if delivered adequately. These aspects are students' perceptions of sender characteristics (e.g., trust and respect, level of knowledge), students' observation of sender behavior (e.g., attention, uneasiness), the content of the feedback (e.g., focus on insignificant areas, feedback inconsistent with perceived performance), and the method of delivering feedback (e.g., judgmental, in a group setting).

Another situation where the sender of feedback is of great importance is in peer assessment. A recent review by Panadero (2016) analyzed a range of social and interpersonal effects of peer assessment. One of the key factors for student involvement in peer assessment is not only the trust in the other as an assessor (i.e., receiving feedback and/or a grade from a peer) but also the trust in oneself as an assessor. These aspects are discussed by Panadero, Jonsson, and Alqassab in Chapter 18 in this volume.

The Message

Characteristics of the feedback message are a variegated collection of factors, a number of which have been investigated in relation to student learning (e.g., Hattie & Timperley, 2007). First, a distinction can be made regarding how the message is delivered, when it is delivered, and the content of the feedback.

In regard to how the message is delivered, most people may associate feedback with written comments. However, feedback messages can be delivered in a variety of ways. Even if we limit ourselves to written feedback, this can be delivered as a coherent narrative, as annotations in the margin, as drawings, symbols, color markings in rubrics, etc. Similarly, oral feedback can be delivered face to face, via Skype, or as audio recordings. Modern smartphones allow for easy video recording and editing, making it possible to create multimedia feedback, for instance, by filming a student during physical education and highlighting incorrect movements with colors, arrows, or lines. Only a few of these ways to deliver feedback have been systematically investigated, and neither Winstone et al. (2016) nor Lipnevich et al. (2016) include this category of moderating factors. However, in the review by Jonsson (2013) it is reported that students claim to appreciate a combination of oral (preferably one-on-one) and written feedback, but that the time constraints of most teachers make individual dialogue with each student problematic. The use of audio feedback, on the other hand, has been shown to alleviate these difficulties as it provides a way to increase the amount of feedback communicated to the students as compared with written feedback, without being more time consuming (Kirschner, Vanden Brink, & Meester, 1991; Pearce & Ackley, 1995; Huang, 2000).

Regarding the timing of feedback delivery, Winstone et al. (2016) claim that students typically engage less with their feedback if they have to wait longer. Lipnevich et al. (2016), on the other hand, note that findings about preferable turnaround times for feedback are inconclusive, because this feature interacts with other factors, such as task difficulty. In her review on formative feedback, Shute (2008) suggested using immediate feedback for difficult tasks, while using delayed feedback for relatively simple tasks. However, this broad categorization of feedback as either immediate or delayed may sometimes be misleading. A good example is when students receive automatized computer feedback, which is delayed by thirty seconds (see, e.g., Schroth, 1992), as compared with students handing in assignments for teacher feedback who may have to wait for days, or even weeks, to receive their feedback. It is also difficult to envision how to provide immediate feedback for complex (and presumably difficult) tasks, such as an argumentative essays, without compromising the quality of the feedback.

Regarding the content of the feedback, the message can vary along several dimensions, such as whether it is concise or extensive, specific or vague, detailed or sketchy, positive or critical, individualized or general, focused on content or structure, personal or neutral, giving advice or asking questions, etc. Most of these characteristics have not been systematically investigated and it is therefore not known which factors may contribute the most to students' engagement with feedback. The following section will describe the subdivisions by Lipnevich et al. (2016), which include aspects such as level of performance, timeliness (discussed above), accuracy, tone, focus, level of detail, congruency with expectations, and comprehensibility.

Lipnevich et al. (2016) suggest that the extent to which feedback provides information about students' performance in relation to existing learning objectives, and whether this information is positive or negative, needs to be considered. Similarly, Winstone et al. (2016) propose that high-quality feedback (i.e., feedback clarifying what good performance involves and providing opportunities to close the gap between current and desired levels of performance) should be more important as compared with quantity. However, no references are made to empirical research in order to back up this assertion. Instead, reference is made to a study where students were *not* more likely to use feedback that they perceived to be of higher quality (Bounds et al., 2013). Consequently, the influence of high-quality feedback, as defined above, needs further attention by future research.

Regarding positive versus negative feedback messages, Winstone et al. (2016) discuss studies showing that students engaged more with positive feedback and found it more useful, but that senior students were less dependent on the valence of the feedback as compared with junior students. Jonsson (2013), on the other hand, suggests that there might exist a conflict between what students prefer and what is likely to contribute to productive learning and that the positive versus negative framing of the message can be regarded as yet another instance of this conflict. For instance, whereas many students prefer positive comments, such comments have been shown to lead to less change (Ferris, 1997). Researchers also recognize that students need critical comments in order to improve, even if these comments may be perceived as negative (Drew, 2001; Higgins, Hartley, & Skelton, 2002; Whitington, Glover, & Harley, 2004; Holmes & Papageorgiou,

2009). In sum, simplistic approaches to the valence of feedback might not capture the complex interactions involved, and more holistic approaches may therefore be needed.

Another aspect of content is accuracy. Lipnevich et al. (2016) suggest that students' engagement with feedback may be affected by whether the students perceive that the teacher has made an accurate assessment of their work. Examples include instances when teachers give comments that are not relevant, erroneous, or do not match the quality of students' work.

An aspect of the message that has proven to be important for moderating students' use of feedback is its tone. Winstone et al. (2016) give examples of ineffective approaches, such as unmotivational, unconstructive, and insensitive comments. Jonsson (2013) specifically highlights an authoritarian tone as less productive for students' use of feedback. To be perceived as less authoritative, teachers need to avoid an insensitive tone, giving mainly evaluative comments, and using imperatives. With regard to students' emotional reactions, Lipnevich et al. (2016) suggest that tone might be the single most critical aspect of feedback.

Yet another aspect is the focus of feedback, where Winstone et al. (2016) make a distinction between task-level and process-level feedback (Hattie & Timperley, 2007). They propose that process-level feedback should have greater utility as compared with task-level feedback.

However, as shown by Walker (2009), students may find task-specific feedback more useful when revising work that is going to be handed in again, but prefer process-level feedback for future assignments. This means that process-level feedback is not necessarily more useful per se. Instead, what is perceived as most useful depends on what the feedback should be used for. If the students are engaged with one particular assignment, which is to be revised, they want more task-specific feedback so that they can make improvements for the final version. If the particular task is not to be handed in again, but students are required to apply their skills on new assignments instead, they are likely to find process-level feedback more useful (Jonsson, 2013).

The sixth aspect of content put forth by Lipnevich et al. (2016) is the detail and extent of the feedback that students receive. Both Jonsson (2013) and Winstone et al. (2016) note that student surveys indicate that the amount of feedback is important for student satisfaction with feedback. However, even though many students seem to prefer a lot of feedback, the length of the comments does not necessarily influence whether students use the feedback. Less important but copious comments may also overshadow more important aspects of feedback (Vardi, 2009). Still, longer comments may have a positive impact on revisions – if they are used (Ferris, 1997; Treglia, 2009). According to Jonsson (2013), this is another instance of the conflict between what students prefer and what is likely to contribute to productive learning. While there is substantive evidence that students appreciate specific, detailed, and individualized comments on their own work and that they make both more revisions and more accurate revisions if told exactly what to do, revisions based on such highly specific and directive feedback do not necessarily improve the quality of students' texts.

The seventh aspect of content is comprehensibility. As evident from research in this area, many students have problems understanding the meaning of the terms that teachers use or the criteria that teachers make reference to, ultimately hindering their engagement with feedback. Both Jonsson (2013) and Winstone et al. (2016) suggest that academic terminology is one major barrier in this regard. For instance, Winstone et al. (2016) claim that educators use the language contained within formal grading policies and grade descriptors as a basis of their feedback, and this language is generally inaccessible to students. Therefore, students need to become familiar with the specific terminology in order to better understand feedback. Strategies for achieving this are discussed later in the section "Facilitating Proactive Recipience: Recommendations for Practice."

The final aspect of content is congruency with expectations, which means that this aspect involves an interaction between the student (i.e., his or her expectations) and feedback. As proposed by Lipnevich et al. (2016), there may be a match or a mismatch between what the student receives and what he or she expected at any level of performance. Mismatches, in particular, may heavily influence whether or how the feedback is acted on. A special case of congruency with expectations involves the interaction with another aspect of feedback, namely, whether the qualitative feedback is accompanied by a judgment expressed on a scale, such as scores, marks, or grades. There is research indicating that grades often trigger disappointment, which may reduce students' future engagement, and that such emotional responses depend on students' expectations (Kahu, Stephens, Leach, & Zepke, 2015). This influence of students' grade expectations has also been shown to affect students' processing of feedback (Pitt & Norton, 2016). Students' reactions to grades will be further explored in the next section, as an aspect of the context.

The Context

Lipnevich et al. (2016) make reference to the work of Yang and Carless (2013) when addressing the contextual factors that might influence students' engagement with feedback. These authors suggest a dynamic interplay between the content of feedback, the social and interpersonal negotiation of feedback, and the organization and management of feedback (i.e., a structural dimension). From their analysis, three different levels of barriers for dialogic feedback are outlined (i.e., student-, teacher-, and institution-related barriers).

One of the major institutional-related constraints for dialogic feedback is the modularized structure in higher education (Carless et al., 2011; Yang & Carless, 2013), which is an aspect also noted by both Jonsson (2013) and Winstone et al. (2016). Yang and Carless (2013) suggest that "Integrated multi-stage assignments generally facilitate timely comments and student uptake of feedback. An assignment divided into two or more phases permits iterative feedback cycles which facilitate engagement with feedback and the prospects of improvement from one task to the other" (p. 291).

However, as exemplified by Taras (2006), who collected data from six undergraduate programs across three faculties comprising 166 courses and 426 different assessments, only five of these 166 modules allowed for an iterative feedback cycle. Further, students seem to be given feedback at the very end of (or even after) the course, which means that there are no opportunities for them to use their feedback in that specific context. As opposed to situations where the opportunity for revision is mandatory, feedback in these situations is often perceived as irrelevant by the students (Jonsson, 2013; Winstone et al., 2016).

Another feature of the context described by both Jonsson (2013) and Winstone et al. (2016) is related to students' insufficient training in the use feedback. This is revealed in surveys asking students whether they feel that they have received adequate guidance on how to understand and use feedback (e.g., Bevan, Badge, Cann, Wilmott, & Scott, 2008) and in interviews with students and through think-aloud-protocols (e.g., Porte, 1996; Furnborough & Truman, 2009).

A third aspect of the context relates to whether the feedback is accompanied by a judgment expressed on a scale, such as scores, marks, or grades. According to Winstone et al. (2016), students often focus heavily on the grades at the expense of their engagement with the qualitative feedback. In a number of studies, students also claim to appreciate grades, especially when they are accompanied with an explanation (e.g., Walker, 2009; Ferguson, 2011). Still, grades are problematic for several reasons. For instance, grades make many students do their best to comply with the teacher's comments, even if this means compromising their own intentions (e.g., Hyland, 1998; Zhao, 2010). Moreover, when the effort of compliance is perceived as too large, many students make changes they think will pay off in terms of grades (Dohrer, 1991; Porte, 1996; McDowell, 2008). This strategy typically changes students' focus away from larger, text-based revisions, toward smaller (and safer) surface revisions (e.g., Ashwell, 2000; Williams, 2004).

Other problematic effects of grades have to do with the fact that receiving a low grade can have detrimental effects on students' self-perception and that students receiving high grades do not read their feedback when they are satisfied with the grade awarded (e.g., Brown, 2007; Vardi, 2009). For example, Lipnevich and Smith (2009a) investigated the effects of providing grades in combination with different feedback conditions for psychology students. They found that detailed descriptive feedback was most effective when delivered without a grade. Furthermore, in follow-up focus group interviews (Lipnevich & Smith, 2009b), students consistently agreed that detailed feedback was the most effective condition. In fact, grades were seen as potential hindrances to improvement. Students who received low marks on their first draft were often discouraged, whereas students who received high marks had little motivation to modify their work. In the latter case, some of these students were afraid that changes might result in lower grades.

Taken together, current research suggests that grades may constitute one of the major barriers to productive use of feedback. Grades have been shown to interact negatively with students' engagement with feedback in several ways, such as (1) students compromising their own ideas in order to comply with teachers' comments, (2) students focusing on surface changes in order to "play it safe," (3) grades affecting self-perception of students with low self-esteem, and (4) grades triggering negative emotions, especially when receiving a lower mark than expected.

Summary and Conclusions for Future Research

There are a very large number of factors potentially affecting students' engagement with feedback. In this section, the models provided by Lipnevich et al. (2016) and Winstone et al. (2016) have been used to organize the findings into a more coherent structure. These models can also be used to guide future research in order to support a more systematic exploration of these factors.

To date, most factors have been investigated by only a few studies. Winstone et al. (2016) therefore conclude that any of their categories (i.e., receiver, sender, message, or context) may substantially moderate students' proactive recipience, but for the individual moderators evidence is not so strong in terms of quantity and/or strength. This would imply that basically all research in this area is welcome. However, it is not possible to investigate all conceivable factors in all imaginable situations and contexts, and – as suggested by Carless et al. (2011) and as evident from the discussion about grades above – there are also significant interactions between the categories in the model used by Winstone et al. (2016). Moreover, not all factors are possible to affect within the frames of regular instruction. This means that it is not feasible, and maybe not meaningful, to keep addressing each of these factors in isolation from each other. Instead, it could be wise to focus research on factors that (1) potentially have a more comprehensive effect, (2) can be combined into "batteries" that address barriers at more than one level according to the model by Yang and Carless (2013), and (3) are possible to implement and/or affect within the frames of regular instruction. Examples of such factors will be provided in the next section outlining possible ways to facilitate students' engagement with feedback.

Facilitating Proactive Recipience: Recommendations for Practice

As evident from the above review of students' engagement with feedback, current research is scattered across a landscape of many different possible moderators, where each individual moderator is investigated in only one or a few studies. In the review by Winstone et al. (2016), this is also how the findings are presented, making it difficult to formulate any tentative recommendations for how to facilitate students' productive use of feedback.

The review by Jonsson (2013), on the other hand, is based on a thematic analysis of the studies, which means that the findings are presented as themes transcending several studies. It is still not possible to evaluate the relative strength of these themes, but recommendations can at least be made based on findings from more than a few studies. In the following section, we present overarching themes that have been grouped into three important conditions for productive use of feedback: (1) feedback is perceived as useful by the students; (2) students know what to do with the feedback they receive; and (3) feedback is delivered without a grade.

Condition 1: Feedback Needs to Be Perceived as Useful by the Students

The most commonly expressed reason for not engaging with feedback is that the students do not find it useful. The reasons for not finding feedback useful may differ, however, and at least three major aspects of usability as perceived by the students can be identified.

The first aspect is whether students are required to, or have the opportunity to, use their feedback within the course or module. As mentioned above, students are often given feedback at the very end of (or even after) the course, which means that there is no opportunity for them to use their feedback within that particular course. Furthermore, feedback may also be highly task specific and bear no relationship to studies in future modules. The students tend to perceive such feedback as irrelevant to them and do not necessarily see the point of engaging with their feedback. This situation is in contrast with studies where students have been expected to use their feedback, either by making revisions of a task or by using the feedback on similar tasks in the near future, where most of feedback comments are in fact attended to by the students (e.g., Paulus, 1999; Zhao, 2010; Zimbardi et al., 2016). A fundamental requirement for facilitating productive use of feedback would therefore be to include the opportunity for students to use their feedback within the current course or module.

The second aspect of usability is whether feedback contains information that can be acted on. Students generally perceive feedback negatively if it does not provide enough information to be helpful (Drew, 2001; Higgins et al., 2002; Ferguson, 2011). Theoretically, high-quality feedback should scaffold improved performance and self-regulation, but as noted above, no clear connection has yet been established between the quality of the feedback (at least as perceived by the students) and students' engagement with feedback.

The third aspect of usability is whether feedback is understandable by the students. As noted above, many students have problems understanding teachers' use of academic terminology or technical jargon, preventing them from engaging constructively with feedback. On the one hand, it could be recommended that teachers avoid the language contained within formal grading policies and grade descriptors as the basis of their feedback, but, on the other hand, the subject-specific discourse is part of what students need to learn and therefore cannot be avoided. However, research does suggest a number of ways for students to become familiar with the discourse and thus to better understand their feedback. For instance, providing model answers or exemplars along with the feedback, or by engaging the students in work with explicit assessment criteria, are examples of resources that can support students' understanding of the academic discourse (e.g., Case, 2007; Huxham, 2007). Another way for students to become familiar with the discourse is to engage in dialogue with the teacher, but time often does not allow for teachers to have dialogues with each individual student. However, some of the dialogue with teachers may be replaced or complemented by using audio feedback. As noted above, students are more likely to open audio files (as opposed to collecting written feedback) and to actually use the feedback (Ice, Curtis, Phillips, & Wells, 2007; Lunt & Curran, 2010). Furthermore, the amount of feedback communicated to the students with audio feedback has been reported to be significantly greater than the amount communicated with written feedback, without necessarily being more time-consuming (Kirschner et al., 1991; Pearce & Ackley, 1995; Huang, 2000).

Condition 2: Students Need Strategies for Using Their Feedback

A major obstacle for students using their feedback productively is the lack of strategies. Students may potentially apply a number of different approaches for using feedback, such as writing down points to remember for future assignments or make reflective analyses of teacher comments (Martens & Dochy, 1997; Hyland, 2001; Orsmond, Merry, & Reiling, 2005; Orsmond & Merry, 2011). However, this active use of feedback does not seem to be the primary choice for most students (e.g., Furnborough & Truman, 2009). Instead, a number of students use feedback passively, for instance, by making a "mental note" of the feedback. They may also use it indirectly, as an indicator of progress or in order to motivate themselves (Holmes & Papageorgiou, 2009; Williams & Kane, 2009; Pokorny & Pickford, 2010), or not at all by simply erasing problematic issues raised by the teacher (Hyland, 1998).

Although the lack of strategies is a major obstacle for proactive recipience, it seems to be amendable. For instance, according to Hattie and Timperley (2007), feedback can be provided at the self-regulation level, addressing the way students monitor, direct, and regulate their actions toward the learning goal. Such feedback may lead to further engagement with the task at hand and enhanced self-efficacy. Furthermore, Burke and Pieterick (2010) suggest that workshops based around past student assignments, including feedback, can help students prepare for future feedback. Students can work in pairs or small groups and the activity can be progressive, starting from more simple (corrective) feedback and advancing toward more complex aspects of academic writing (in higher education). They also suggest a number of strategies for students to get more out of their feedback. Examples are students reflecting on how they have responded to feedback, breaking feedback down into positives and negatives, and/or preparing for tutorials.

Condition 3: Feedback Should Be Delivered without a Grade

Several researchers propose that students' engagement with feedback depends on the match between their expected and actual grades, such as students receiving high grades not reading their feedback when they are satisfied with the grade awarded. Receiving a low grade, on the other hand, tends to evoke feelings of disappointment and can have detrimental effects on self-perception of students with low self-esteem or self-efficacy. There are also a number of studies showing that grades make students less willing to challenge the teacher, which means that they do their best to comply with the teacher's comments, even if this may compromise their own intentions with the task. Moreover, when the effort is perceived as potentially too large, many students strategically focus on making changes that they think will pay off in terms of grades, typically changing students' focus away from larger revisions and toward smaller (and safer) surface revisions (Jonsson, 2013).

Summary and Implications

Three fundamental conditions for constructive engagement with feedback have been identified. First, students need to perceive feedback as useful. There are at least three different aspects of usefulness: (1) whether students are required to or have the opportunity to use feedback, (2) whether feedback contains information that can be acted on, and (3) whether feedback is understandable by the students. Second, students need strategies for actively using the feedback they received. Third, grades have been shown to interact negatively with students' engagement with feedback in several ways, affecting both learning/study strategies and students' self-perception.

Taken together, in order to support students' proactive recipience of feedback, teachers could (1) design courses where students can make use of their feedback, either by revising drafts or by using their feedback on similar assignments; (2) provide feedback that can be acted on, by giving either task-level feedback on drafts that are expected to be revised or process-level feedback on "recurring" assignments; and (3) support students' understanding of feedback by providing resources such as model answers, exemplars, or engagement with assessment criteria and/or by engaging in dialogue with the student. Since one-to-one dialogue is time consuming, this can preferably be complemented with audio feedback. Another possibility is to engage students in dialogue with their peers about feedback. Teachers could also provide explicit guidance on how to use feedback, for instance, by giving feedback at self-regulation level and/or by arranging workshops focusing on strategies for using feedback. Finally, teachers could provide students with detailed feedback without an accompanying grade.

Conclusions

This chapter started by noting that the quality of students' engagement with and use of the feedback they receive is critical for taking advantage of the formative potential of feedback. Unfortunately, much of the research in this area indicates that students' engagement with feedback is usually not very productive. However, as we showed in this chapter, it is not an easy task to identify who is to blame for this situation. Students differ in their capacity and willingness to use feedback. Teachers and other feedback providers (e.g., peers) differ in their capacity to deliver high-quality feedback and in how trustworthy they appear to the students. The content, timeliness, and mode of delivery in feedback messages can be varied almost limitlessly, as can the context surrounding the feedback process. Furthermore, and adding to the complexity, the reasons for wanting students to engage with their feedback may also differ. Reasons identified by Winstone et al. (2016) include empowering students to assess their own strengths and weaknesses, thereby reducing their reliance on external sources of judgment ("self-appraisal"); understanding the grading process and using this to assess own performance ("assessment literacy"); translating goals into plans of action and reviewing and adjusting performance and strategies in order to reach these goals ("goal-setting and self-regulation"); and facilitating the motivation to read and understand the feedback ("engagement and motivation").

In the midst of this complexity, however, there is a nucleus that can be used as a point of departure for facilitating students' engagement with feedback. As suggested above, this includes providing feedback that is useful for the students, helping them to develop constructive strategies for using feedback, and avoiding grades on individual assignments. Furthermore, a theme transcending the rationale for the interventions reviewed is empowering the students to self-assess and self-regulate. This "sustainable feedback practice" (Carless et al., 2011) is a more long-term goal with feedback, as compared with improving student performance on specific tasks, courses, or educational programs. An important next step for research on students' engagement with feedback may therefore be to distinguish between strategies that support short-term and long-term (i.e., sustainable) use of feedback, so that we do not implement practices that make the students rely more on external sources of feedback in order to increase test results or other short-term achievement. Instead, we may need to, as suggested by Carless et al. (2011), push students to involve themselves in developing self-regulatory practices consistent with sustainable feedback. This, in turn, highlights the need for interventions supporting students' understanding of the purposes of feedback and the benefits of self-regulation, as well as practices scaffolding self-regulation strategies, such as peer feedback and self-assessment (Panadero, Jonsson, & Strijbos, 2016).

References

Al-Barakat, A., & Al-Hassan, O. (2009). Peer assessment as a learning tool for enhancing student teachers' preparation. *Asia-Pacific Journal of Teacher Education, 37*, 399–413.

Altahawi, F., Sisk, B., Poloskey, S., Hicks, C., & Dannefer, E. F. (2012). Student perspectives on assessment: Experience in a competency-based portfolio system. *Medical Teacher, 34*, 221–225.

Ashwell, T. (2000). Patterns of teacher response to student writing in a multi-draft composition classroom: Is content feedback followed by form feedback the best method? *Journal of Second Language Writing, 9*, 227–257.

Baadte, C., & Schnotz, W. (2014). Feedback effects on performance, motivation and mood: Are they moderated by the learner's self-concept? *Scandinavian Journal of Educational Research, 58*, 570–591.

Bailey, R., & Garner, M. (2010). Is the feedback in higher education assessment worth the paper it is written on? Teachers' reflections on their practices. *Teaching in Higher Education, 15*, 187–198.

Bevan, R., Badge, J., Cann, A., Wilmott, C., & Scott, J. (2008). Seeing eye-to-eye? Staff and student views on feedback. *Bioscience Education Electronic Journal, 12*.

Bing-You, R. G., Paterson, J., & Levine, M. A. (1997). Feedback falling on deaf ears: Residents' receptivity to feedback tempered by sender credibility. *Medical Teacher, 19*, 40–44.

Bounds, R., Bush, C., Aghera, A., Rodriguez, N., Stansfield, R. B., & Santeen, S. A. (2013). Emergency medicine residents' self-assessments play a critical role when receiving feedback. *Academic Emergency Medicine, 20*, 1055–1061.

Brown, E., & Glover, C. (2006). Evaluating written feedback. In C. Bryan & K. Clegg (Eds.), *Innovative assessment in higher education* (pp. 81–91). London: Routledge.

Brown, J. (2007). Feedback: The student perspective. *Research in Post-Compulsory Education, 12*, 33–51.

Burke, D., & Pieterick, J. (2010). *Giving students effective written feedback*. Berkshire, UK: Open University Press.

Carless, D., Salter, D., Yang, M., & Lam, J. (2011). Developing sustainable feedback practices. *Studies in Higher Education, 36*, 395–407.

Cartney, P. (2010). Exploring the use of peer assessment as a vehicle for closing the gap between feedback given and feedback used. *Assessment & Evaluation in Higher Education, 35*, 551–564.

Case, S. (2007). Reconfiguring and realigning the assessment feedback processes for an undergraduate criminology degree. *Assessment & Evaluation in Higher Education, 32*, 285–299.

Dessner, L. E. (1991). English as a second language college writers' revision responses to teacher-written comments. Doctoral dissertation, University of Pennsylvania.

Dohrer, G. (1991). Do teachers' comments on students' papers help? *College Teaching, 39*(2), 48–51.

Drew, S. (2001). Student perceptions of what helps them learn and develop in higher education. *Teaching in Higher Education, 6*, 309–331.

Ferguson, P. (2011). Student perceptions of quality feedback in teacher education. *Assessment & Evaluation in Higher Education, 36*, 51–62.

Ferris, D. (1997). The influence of teacher commentary on student revision. *TESOL Quarterly, 31*, 315–339.

Furnborough, C., & Truman, M. (2009). Adult beginner distance language learner perceptions and use of assignment feedback. *Distance Education, 30*, 399–418.

Handley, K., Price, M., & Millar, J. (2011). Beyond "doing time": Investigating the concept of student engagement with feedback. *Oxford Review of Education, 37*, 543–560.

Hattie, J., & Timperley, H. (2007). The power of feedback. *Review of Educational Research, 77*, 81–112.

Higgins, R., Hartley, P., & Skelton, A. (2002). The conscientious consumer: Reconsidering the role of assessment feedback in student learning. *Studies in Higher Education, 27*, 53–64.

Holmes, K., & Papageorgiou, G. (2009). Good, bad and insufficient: Students' expectations, perceptions and uses of feedback. *Journal of Hospitality Leisure Sport & Tourism Education, 8*, 85–96.

Huang, S. (2000). A quantitative analysis of audiotaped and written feedback produced for students' writing and students' perceptions of the two feedback methods. *Tunghai Journal, 41*, 199–232.

Huxham, M. (2007). Fast and effective feedback: Are model answers the answer? *Assessment & Evaluation in Higher Education, 32*, 601–611.

Hyland, F. (1998). The impact of teacher written feedback on individual writers. *Journal of Second Language Writing, 7*, 255–286.

Hyland, F. (2001). Providing effective support: Investigating feedback to distance language learners. *Open Learning, 16*, 233–247.

Ice, P., Curtis, R., Phillips, P., & Wells, J. (2007). Using asynchronous audio feedback to enhance teaching presence and students sense of community. *Journal of Asynchronous Learning Networks, 11*(2), 3–25.

Jonsson, A. (2013). Facilitating productive use of feedback in higher education. *Active Learning in Higher Education, 14*, 63–76.

Kahu, E., Stephens, C., Leach, L., & Zepke, N. (2015). Linking academic emotions and student engagement: Mature-aged distance students' transition to university. *Journal of Further and Higher Education, 39*, 481–497.

Kirschner, P. A., Van den Brink, H., & Meester, M. (1991). Audiotape feedback for essays in distance education. *Innovative Higher Education, 15*, 185–195.

Lipnevich, A. A., & Smith, J. K. (2009a). The effects of differential feedback on student examination performance. *Journal of Experimental Psychology: Applied, 15*, 319–333.

Lipnevich, A. A., Berg, D. A. G., & Smith, J. K. (2016). Toward a model of student response to feedback. In G. T. L. Brown & L. R. Harris (Eds.), *Human factors and social conditions of assessment* (pp. 169–185). New York: Routledge.

Lipnevich, A. A., & Smith, J. K. (2009b). "I really need feedback to learn": Students' perspectives on the effectiveness of the differential feedback messages. *Educational Assessment, Evaluation and Accountability, 21*, 347–367.

Lunt, T., & Curran, J. (2010). "Are you listening please?" The advantages of electronic audio feedback compared to written feedback. *Assessment & Evaluation in Higher Education, 35,* 759–769.

MacDonald, R. B. (1991). Developmental students' processing of teacher feedback in composition instruction. *Review of Research in Developmental Education, 8*(5), 1–5.

MacLellan, E. (2001). Assessment for learning: The differing perceptions of tutors and students. *Assessment & Evaluation in Higher Education, 26,* 307–318.

Martens, R., & Dochy, F. (1997). Assessment and feedback as student support devices. *Studies in Educational Evaluation, 23,* 257–273.

McDowell, L. (2008). Students' experiences of feedback on academic assignments in higher education: Implications for practice. In A. Havnes & L. McDowell (Eds.), *Balancing dilemmas in assessment and learning in contemporary education* (pp. 237–249). New York: Routledge.

Orsmond, P., & Merry, S. (2011). Feedback alignment: Effective and ineffective links between tutors' and students' understanding of coursework feedback. *Assessment & Evaluation in Higher Education, 36,* 125–136.

Orsmond, P., Merry, S., & Reiling, K. (2005). Biology students' utilization of tutors' formative feedback: A qualitative interview study. *Assessment & Evaluation in Higher Education, 30,* 369–386.

Panadero, E. (2016). Is it safe? Social, interpersonal, and human effects of peer assessment: A review and future directions. In G. T. L. Brown & L. R. Harris (Eds.), *Human factors and social conditions of assessment* (pp. 247–266). New York: Routledge.

Panadero, E., Jonsson, A., & Strijbos, J. W. (2016). Scaffolding self-regulated learning through self-assessment and peer assessment: Guidelines for classroom implementation. In D. Laveault & L. Allal (Eds.), *Assessment for learning: Meeting the challenge of implementation* (pp. 311–326). Boston: Springer.

Paulus, T. (1999). The effect of peer and teacher feedback on student writing. *Journal of Second Language Writing, 8,* 265–289.

Pearce, C. G., & Ackley, R. J. (1995). Audiotaped feedback in business writing: An exploratory study. *Business Communication Quarterly, 58*(4), 31–34.

Pitt, E., & Norton, L. (2016). "Now that's the feedback I want!" Students' reactions to feedback on graded work and what they do with it. *Assessment & Evaluation in Higher Education, 42,* 499–516.

Pokorny, H., & Pickford, P. (2010). Complexity, cues and relationships: Student perceptions of feedback. *Active Learning in Higher Education, 11,* 21–30.

Porte, G. (1996). When writing fails: How academic context and past learning experiences shape revision. *System, 24,* 107–116.

Price, M., Rust, C., O'Donovan, B., Handley, K., & Bryant, R. (2012). *Assessment literacy: The foundation for improving student learning.* Oxford: Oxford Centre for Staff and Learning Development.

Schroth, M. L. (1992). The effects of delay of feedback on a delayed concept formation transfer task. *Contemporary Educational Psychology, 17*(4), 78–82.

Shute, V. J. (2008). Focus on formative feedback. *Review of Educational Research, 78,* 153–189.

Sinclair, H. K., & Cleland, J. A. (2007). Undergraduate medical students: Who seeks formative feedback? *Medical Education, 41,* 580–582.

Smith, J. K., Berg, D., Kendall-Smith, M., & Lipnevich, A. A. (2013). Response to feedback: How we perceive what we receive. Paper presented at the annual meeting of the New Zealand Association for Research in Education, Dunedin, New Zealand.

Taras, M. (2006). Do unto others or not: Equity in feedback for undergraduates. *Assessment & Evaluation in Higher Education, 31*, 365–377.

Treglia, M. O. (2009). Teacher-written commentary in college writing composition: How does it impact student revisions? *Composition Studies, 37*, 67–86.

Vardi, I. (2009). The relationship between feedback and change in tertiary student writing in the disciplines. *International Journal of Teaching and Learning in Higher Education, 20*, 350–361.

Walker, M. (2009). An investigation into written comments on assignments: Do students find them usable? *Assessment & Evaluation in Higher Education, 34*, 67–78.

Whitington, V., Glover, A., & Harley, F. (2004). Preservice early childhood students' perceptions of written feedback on their essays. *Early Child Development and Care, 174*, 321–337.

Wiggins, G. (1998). *Educative assessment.* San Francisco, CA: Jossey-Bass.

Williams, J. (2004). Tutoring and revision: Second language writers in the writing center. *Journal of Second Language Writing, 13*, 173–201.

Williams, J., & Kane, D. (2009). Assessment and feedback: Institutional experiences of student feedback, 1996 to 2007. *Higher Education Quarterly, 63*, 264–286.

Wingate, U. (2010). The impact of formative feedback on the development of academic writing. *Assessment & Evaluation in Higher Education, 35*, 519–533.

Winstone, N. E., Nash, R. A., Parker, M., & Rowntree, J. (2016). Supporting learners' agentic engagement with feedback: A systematic review and a taxonomy of recipience processes. *Educational Psychologist, 52*, 17–37.

Yang, M., & Carless, D. (2013). The feedback triangle and the enhancement of dialogic feedback processes. *Teaching in Higher Education, 18*, 285–297.

Zhao, H. (2010). Investigating learners' use and understanding of peer and teacher feedback on writing: A comparative study in a Chinese English writing classroom. *Assessing Writing, 15*, 3–17.

Zimbardi, K., Colthorpe, K., Dekker, A., Engstrom, C., Bugarcic, A., Worthy, P., Victor, R., Chunduri, P., Lluka, L., & Long, P. (2016). Are they using my feedback? The extent of students' feedback use has a large impact on subsequent academic performance. *Assessment & Evaluation in Higher Education, 42*, 625–644.

25 Performance Feedback and Emotions

Thomas Goetz, Anastasiya A. Lipnevich, Maike Krannich, and Katarzyna Gogol

I was really hurt. I was devastated. Although I knew that I haven't done well the feedback was quite negative only the first sentence said it was a nice attempt, but then a long row of negative things.

(Katya, interview, in Shields, 2015, p. 620)

Students' emotions greatly influence the way in which they are able to receive and process feedback.

(Värlander, 2008, p. 146)

Summary

This chapter discusses the relations between performance feedback and emotions in educational settings. First, we define the complex constructs of "feedback" and "emotions." Second, we outline existing theoretical approaches and empirical findings of the relations between feedback and emotions and consider potential moderators and mediators of those relations. Third, we summarize the theoretical approaches and existing findings on the relations between performance feedback and emotions in a comprehensive model. Finally, we offer suggestions for future directions.

Introduction

Feedback and emotions are omnipresent in education. Both constructs are of very high relevance with respect to future learning, behavior, and career choice (e.g., Krannich, Goetz, Lipnevich, & Roos, 2017). Above and beyond the effects of both constructs on various performance outcomes, emotions represent a cluster of crucial outcome variables in their own right. For example, Fredrickson (2001) states that "positive emotions are worth cultivating, not just as end states in themselves but also as means to achieving psychological growth and improved well-being over time" (p. 218; for positive emotions in the context of "positive psychology," see also Seligman & Csikszentmihalyi, 2000).

Intuitively, one might assume that feedback and emotions are reciprocally linked, either directly and/or via potential moderating and mediating mechanisms. Feedback (e.g., positive feedback on achievement) can directly (e.g., enjoying the good grade) or indirectly (e.g., by fostering high control cognitions) elicit strong emotions (e.g., enjoyment, pride), which, in turn, might have an impact on subsequent learning behavior (e.g., high amount of self-regulated learning) and consequently learning outcomes. Positive learning outcomes can, in turn, influence subsequent reactions to feedback. However, only a few theoretical assumptions and empirical results currently exist that describe the direct and indirect interplay between feedback and emotions. Reviews on feedback (e.g., Hattie & Timperley, 2007) typically do not mention emotions, and the emotion literature rarely explicitly mentions feedback as an antecedent or consequence of emotions. An exception to this is Pekrun's (2006) control-value theory that describes antecedents and effects of academic emotions. In this model feedback is explicitly mentioned as an antecedent of emotions, with emotions subsequently affecting achievement outcomes and consequently further receptivity of feedback. A further exception is research on test anxiety, which dates back to the 1950s (Sarason & Mandler, 1952; Zeidner, 2007). In this literature, the relations between anxiety and achievement outcomes as one facet of feedback are outlined (see meta-analyses of Hembree, 1988; Seipp, 1991; Ma, 1999).

In this chapter we focus on the relations between instructional feedback and student performance and emotions. It is an aim of this chapter to synthesize existing theoretical approaches and empirical data and to develop a heuristic model summarizing the interplay between performance feedback and emotions by taking potential moderators and mediators of those relations into account. Further, and based on this model, we outline avenues for future research in this field.

Definition of Feedback and Emotions

Our lives are an ongoing, bidirectional interaction between ourselves and the environment. We continuously impact our environment and, in turn, are impacted by it. Thus, similar to the title of Karl Popper's (1999) essay, "All Life Is Problem Solving," life is an ongoing feedback process that is filled to the brim with "natural" feedback processes as well as consciously initiated actions on the environment that humans undertake to achieve their goals (Kluger & DeNisi, 1996). Numerous definitions of feedback have been outlined in this volume (see Chapters 1–4). Due to our focus on performance feedback, in this chapter, we employ a definition by Hattie and Timperly (2007): "Feedback is information provided by an agent (e.g., teacher, peer, book, parent, self, experience) regarding aspects of one's performance or understanding" (p. 102). Thus, feedback is engendered by performance and/or understanding. It is important to note that this definition includes self-evaluations related to achievement, such as judging the quality of one's oral answer to a question posed by the teacher. However, beyond the importance of performance feedback given by others, the self is always relevant in the feedback process as feedback gets consistently interpreted and classified with respect to specific frames of references, like internal or social comparisons or self-defined criteria (e.g., individual goals, criteria, and thresholds for "good" or "bad" performance; cf. Marsh, 1986, 1990; Goetz, Frenzel, Hall, & Pekrun, 2008).

Similarly, numerous definitions of emotions have been proposed in the literature (see Kleinginna & Kleinginna, 1981; Lewis & Haviland-Jones, 2000). Prominent definitions entail a componential perspective (e.g., Scherer, 1984; Damasio, 2004), in which emotions are viewed as multicomponent, coordinated processes of psychological subsystems that include affective, cognitive, motivational, expressive, and peripheral physiological processes. Anxiety, for example, is an emotion comprising uneasy, nervous feelings; worries about possible negative events and outcomes; motivation to avoid the situation; physiological activation; and a specific facial expression. Enjoyment, on the other hand, comprises happy feelings, positive perceptions and thoughts, motivation to stay in the situation, physiological activation, and happy expression.

In the context of performance feedback, achievement emotions play a pivotal role. They can be defined as emotions pertaining to achievement activities or achievement outcomes (Pekrun, 2006). In addition to this object focus (activity vs. outcome), they can be grouped with respect to their valence (positive vs. negative or, simply put, pleasant vs. unpleasant). Taking both object focus and valence into account renders a 2×2 classification (Pekrun et al., 2006) grouping these emotions as follows: (1) activity/positive (e.g., enjoyment), (2) activity/negative (e.g., boredom, anger), (3) outcome/positive (e.g., hope, pride), and (4) outcome/negative (e.g., anxiety, hopelessness, shame). As feedback can refer to both activities and outcomes, all four groups of emotions might be relevant in the context of the relations between feedback and emotions. Teachers provide feedback on both the process and product of activity such that the emotions elicited would inevitably vary across Pekrun's (2006) dimensions of valence and object focus.

Related to the assumingly high relevance of outcome emotions in the field of feedback-emotion relations, Johnson and Connelly (2014) argue that it is important to differentiate emotions that are induced by the feedback message itself (e.g., good achievement results, i.e., outcome emotions like pride and shame) and emotions that are involved in the feedback exchange (e.g., enjoyment of the feedback provider). It can be assumed that emotions of the feedback provider and emotions of the feedback receiver depend on the feedback message itself (i.e., positive or negative in nature) and its interpretation (e.g., based on individual goals and criteria). Further, it can be assumed that emotions of the feedback provider and the emotions of the receiver of the feedback dynamically interact (i.e., emotional transmission processes; e.g., Frenzel, Goetz, Lüdtke, Pekrun, & Sutton, 2009). Beyond the direct emotional contagion (Hatfield, Cacioppo, & Rapson, 1994) that is the transmission of emotions among interaction partners by mimicking emotional expression and immediately adopting each other's emotions, rather complex processes of emotional transmission may be taking place in the context of education (and beyond). For example, results of a study by Taxer and Frenzel (2012; see also van Doorn, van Kleef, &

van der Pligt, 2014) indicate that the emotions of the feedback receiver following a negative achievement outcome can strongly differ based on the emotions demonstrated by the feedback provider: anger expressed by the teacher might result in students' feelings of hope, as students may interpret anger as an indicator of teacher's high belief of students' ability to achieve better results (i.e., anger of the feedback provider increasing the self-concept of the feedback receiver resulting in hope). This scenario may work in a highly supportive environment and will depend on strong positive student–teacher relationship. In contrast, teacher's pity might result in hopelessness of the feedback receiver, as it may be construed by a student as the teacher's belief in the student's lack of ability (e.g., due to low intelligence) to achieve better results. However, beyond such initial empirical results we lack knowledge on the complex interplay between the emotions of the feedback providers (be they teachers or peers) and the receiver of the feedback. Thus, we focus in this chapter on emotions as induced by the feedback message itself.

Direct Relations between Performance Feedback and Emotions

The Role of Feedback and Emotion Valence (Positive vs. Negative)

Based on the existing literature on performance feedback and emotions, Goetz and Hall (2013) suggest that the valence (positive vs. negative; pleasant vs. unpleasant) of both feedback and emotions plays a crucial role with respect to the relations between the constructs. Generally, positive feedback is related to positive emotions and negative feedback is related to negative emotions. The majority of studies investigating the relations between performance feedback and emotions do not allow for conclusions on causal relations, but there is initial evidence demonstrating such links; we present these findings below. These studies were done in different (academic) disciplines and across age groups (e.g., Nicaise et al., 2007, for school students in the context of physical education; Lipnevich & Smith, 2009a, 2009b, in tertiary education; for an overview, see Goetz and Hall, 2013). The existing empirical findings show that positive feedback is typically related to positive emotions, negative feedback is related to negative emotions – and vice versa.

However, things are not always straightforward, as it is not always clear whether feedback is "positive" or "negative" in nature. Inherently, a numerical score or a letter grade do not carry any valence, positive or negative. However, depending on the context, task, and student, grade becomes one of the most emotionally charged pieces of feedback that a student may receive in an instructional context. For one student 80/100 is a very desirable outcome that will elicit a slew of positive emotions, whereas for another student 80/100 is a detrimental outcome resulting in intense negative emotions. Student characteristics, prior performance, and teacher expectations may affect differential receptivity of identical grades (see later sections for discussion of mediators and moderators).

Lipnevich and Smith (2009a) report the results of a large experimental study that examined differential effects of individualized comments, grades, praise, and source of information on student performance and emotions. The researchers revealed that a mere presence of grade had a significant effect on students' reported negative affect. Students who received a grade had higher negative affect (and lower reported levels of self-efficacy) than their counterparts for whom their grade was unknown. Lipnevich and Smith (2009a) manipulated the source of feedback and examined the effects of various types of feedback across students of different ability levels. The findings demonstrated that the grade from the instructor had a negative effect on performance and significantly enhanced negative affect. This was not the case for students who received virtually identical feedback with an understanding that it came from the computer. It is reasonable to presume that the computer-based grade was viewed as being less judgmental or personally directed than the instructor-based grade. Subsequent focus group discussions (Lipnevich & Smith, 2009b) supported this speculation, with many focus group participants mentioning that seeing their grade made them think that they could not possibly improve their work to earn a passing score. The grade caused them "to panic," "to feel ashamed," or "to get angry" at themselves and the professor. Any of these emotions could hinder students' improvement on the task at hand, and obviously, they did. Interestingly, there were no differences in emotions as a result of praise. Inherently positive in valence, a statement of encouragement or praise presented in the study did not influence positive emotions. Praise did affect motivation, but in an unusual fashion, where students presented with a laudatory statement reported lower levels of motivation than those who were not (Lipnevich and Smith, 2009a, 2009b). Overall, the most common types of feedback offered in an instructional setting result in changes in student emotions, which, in turn, may affect student performance on a task.

To gain a deeper understanding of the complex links among feedback and emotions, we further examined the data collected in the Lipnevich (2007) dissertation (as reported in Lipnevich & Smith, 2009a, 2009b) for the purposes of this chapter. We investigated relations between feedback and discrete emotions that students experienced immediately following the presentation of feedback. Interestingly, but not surprisingly, we found that receiving a grade, as opposed to written comments, increased student ratings on distressed, upset, scared, hostile, ashamed, nervous, and afraid – all negative emotions. Additionally, we also saw a decrease in pride when grades were given compared with written comments. Further, in order to explore the relation between feedback condition, emotions elicited, and differences in student essay scores, we tested a mediation path model. We hypothesized that emotion played a mediational role in the relation between feedback type and differences in essay score. Both direct and indirect paths were included in the model in order to test negative affect as a mediator in the relation between grade condition and revised essay score.

Additionally, exploratory path analyses were conducted with various discrete emotions that were highly correlated with feedback condition and differences in student scores. We found that the discrete negative emotions of upset and ashamed were significant mediators in the relation between feedback condition and differences in essay scores. Additionally – and interestingly – we also found the emotion of pride negatively predicted change in essay scores. Decreases in pride, as a result of grade opposed to comment, led to smaller improvements in essay scores. Predicted relations changed when we considered the positive emotion of pride. The direct effect of feedback condition on difference in essay scores from draft to the final performance on an essay remained the same, demonstrating that grades predicted less change in essay scores. However, the condition of grade elicited a decrease in the experience of pride. This negatively predicted differences in essay score, suggesting that students improved their scores less when they experienced a decrease in a positive emotion. This study provides evidence of the close links between feedback and emotions, and warrants further exploration. Further, unlike Kluger, Lewinsohn, and Aiello's (1994) quasi-experimental study that showed positive effects of achievement outcomes (grades) on pleasantness, the results of Lipnevich and Smith (2009a, 2009b) showed no differences in positive affect for students of all ability levels or depending on scores presented to them (i.e., 50/100 or 100/100 did not result in changes in positive affect).

Above and beyond the fact that it is often not quite clear whether feedback is "positive" or "negative" in nature, it is important to emphasize that numerous studies have revealed that positive and negative affect are not merely the opposite ends of a single continuum and should be regarded as separable phenomena (e.g., Diener & Emmons, 1985; Watson, Clark, & Tellegen, 1988; Cacioppo & Berntson, 1994). Hence, we should not always expect an emotional response well aligned and proportional in valence and intensity to the valence and intensity of a feedback message.

Concerning the strength of relations, the average correlation between achievement outcomes and emotions across single positive and negative emotions (e.g., enjoyment, pride, anxiety, anger, boredom) is |.25| (Goetz & Hall, 2013; for meta-analyses especially in the field of test anxiety, see Hembree, 1988; Seipp, 1991; Ma, 1999). Although this correlation is not very high (medium in terms of effect size; Cohen, 1988), it is important to note that even weak effects may have a strong cumulative impact due to the omnipresence of feedback situations and emotions in academic settings.

Causality in the Feedback/Emotion Relations

When it comes to causal relations between feedback and emotions, the admittedly minimal existing empirical evidence indicates that performance feedback and emotions are linked by reciprocal causality. A recent longitudinal study by Pekrun et al. (2017) (n = 3,425 school students from grades five to nine) revealed positive reciprocal relations between achievement outcomes (end-of-year grades and test scores) and positive emotions (enjoyment, pride) as well as negative reciprocal relations between achievement outcomes and negative emotions (anger, anxiety, shame, hopelessness, boredom). By employing two longitudinal studies, Pekrun et al. (2010, 2014) demonstrated that negative achievement enhanced boredom, which in turn had negative effects on subsequent achievement. This study showed further support for the assumption of reciprocal causality between feedback and emotions.

The Role of the Achievement Level of the Reference Group

With respect to the effects of performance feedback on emotions, empirical evidence suggests that is important to take into account the achievement level of the reference group (e.g., average grade level of the school class) in addition to the individual performance (e.g., math grade). By referring to the big-fish-little-pond effect (BFLPE; Marsh, 1987), Goetz et al. (2004) used a longitudinal study design ($n = 1,762$ school students, mathematics domain) and found that high individual achievement (investigated via a math achievement test) led to an increase in enjoyment and a decrease in anxiety, whereas high average class achievement (mean class score on the math achievement test) resulted in the opposite effects. In other words, the achievement level of the reference group (classmates) had negative effects on individual emotional experiences. Although not directly referring to performance feedback, findings by Zeidner and Schleyer (1999; $n = 1,020$ gifted elementary school students, across-domain approach) also indicate that the achievement level of the reference group has an impact on individual emotions. They found that gifted students in mixed ability regular classes (i.e., big fish) reported lower test anxiety than their counterparts (i.e., little fish) in special classes for the gifted. By analyzing a subsample of the study by Zeidner and Schleyer (1999), namely, the gifted students attending special gifted classes ($n = 769$), Goetz, Preckel, Zeidner, and Schleyer (2008) found that individual grades were negatively related to test anxiety, while the average achievement of the class was positively related to test anxiety. In sum, these studies indicate that both individual performance feedback and the perceived performance level of the reference group have an impact on emotions.

The Role of Performance Feedback across Domains

Interestingly, studies suggest that feedback presented in one domain may influence emotions in a different domain. For example, referring to the internal/external frame of reference model (Marsh, 1986, 1990), Goetz, Frenzel, Hall, and Pekrun (2008) found that in a study of 1,380 high school students, mathematics performance (grades), assessed in the previous academic year, positively predicted enjoyment in mathematics classes and negatively predicted enjoyment in language classes. Language class performance (grades) positively predicted enjoyment in language classes and negatively predicted enjoyment in mathematics classes. Thus, emotional experiences in a specific academic domain seem to be impacted not only by the performance feedback within the domain but also by performance feedback in other domains.

Moderators and Mediators of the Relations between Feedback and Emotions

Latham and Locke (1991) argue that the effects of feedback are difficult to predict without taking other variables into account: "Actually, feedback is only information, that is, data, and as such has no necessary consequences at all" (p. 224). In fact, performance feedback is often just a number (e.g., grades; Sticca et al., 2017) and the role of additional variables must be considered when judging the effects of feedback on emotions. Vice versa, the effects of emotions on achievement outcomes and corresponding performance feedback seem also rarely to be predictable without taking further variables into account.

Thus, knowledge of moderators and mediators of the relations between performance feedback and emotions seems to be important with respect to understand the "net relations" (i.e., |.25|; see above) between both constructs. Further, such knowledge is crucial with respect to practical implications. For example, modifying the levels of a specific moderator in students (e.g., enhancing meta-cognitions on feedback) might decrease negative effects of negative performance feedback on emotions. As for mediators (e.g., appraisals of control), they might be considered when giving performance feedback (e.g., fostering control cognitions even the feedback is negative in nature), for example, with respect to decreasing negative effects of negative performance feedback on emotions. Moderators and mediators can be assumed to play a pivotal role with respect to their effects of performance feedback on emotions and vice versa.

In the next sections we outline the variables that are mentioned in the literature as moderators and mediators of the relations between performance feedback and emotions by taking the causal relations into account (reciprocal relations: feedback ↔ emotions; unidirectional relations: feedback → emotion, emotion → feedback). Figure 25.1 depicts moderating and mediating variables discussed in the current chapter.

Feedback ↔ Emotions: Moderators

Level of Generalization. The research literature suggests that the level of generalization may moderate the strength of relations between feedback and emotions (Goetz & Hall, 2013). More specifically, relations are stronger when both performance feedback and emotions refer to a specific academic domain (e.g., feedback on mathematics and math emotions) as compared with both constructs referring to a more generalized area (e.g., GPA and school-related emotions; for possible explanations, see Brunswik, 1952; Goetz et al., 2006).

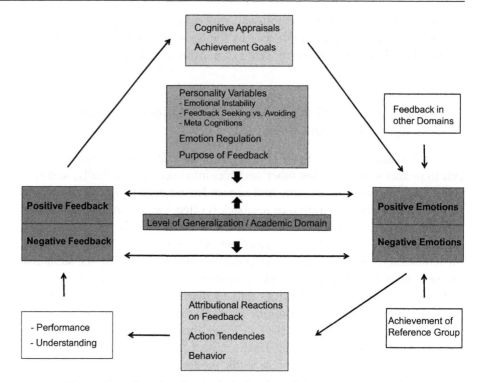

Figure 25.1 *Relations between feedback and emotions: reciprocal causality, moderators, and mediators.*

In other words, a "fit" of the levels of generalization can be assumed to result in stronger relations (cf. Gogol, Brunner, Preckel, Goetz, & Martin, 2016).

Academic Domain. The strength of relations between performance feedback and emotions may also depend on the nature of the academic domain (e.g., language arts, mathematics). For example, in their meta-analysis of research in formative assessment, Kingston and Nash (2011) found that formative assessment practices, including feedback, were more effective in language arts than in mathematics or science. In contrast, Goetz et al. (2007) found relations to be stronger in mathematics and the science domains as compared with the verbal domains. Possible explanations for those findings are outlined in Goetz et al. (2010). For example, when compared with the language domains, mathematics and science have been found to be less subjective and have clearer criteria for assessment, resulting in greater alignment between performance feedback and emotions in these domains. This is reflected in higher reliabilities and validities of grades and emotion scales in math and science domains as compared with the language domains (cf. Sticca et al., 2017). The inconsistent findings show that the role of the academic domain in feedback–emotions relations is certainly a fruitful area of research for future investigations, and we hope new studies will shed light on feedback–emotions contingencies across domains.

Feedback → Emotion: Moderators

Personality Variables. In the literature, three personality variables are mentioned with respect to moderating the effects of feedback on emotions. Niemann et al. (2014) refer to emotional instability and suggest that emotionally unstable persons (i.e., with high levels of neuroticism; McCrae & Costa, 2008) would react to negative feedback with more anger than emotionally stable persons. This assumption was confirmed in their experimental study ($N = 84$ adults), in which participants received negative feedback (low score on a scale ranging from 1 (very bad) to 10 (outstanding)) on a working task for a marketing company. Neuroticism moderated the effect of negative feedback on anger with highly neurotic persons experiencing higher levels of anger. Further, Fong et al. (2016) refer to feedback-seeking versus feedback-avoiding and found ($N = 270$ undergraduate students) that feedback-seekers (i.e., with high values on the item "I look forward to receiving feedback"; see Cassidy, Ziv, Metha, & Feeney, 2003) as compared with feedback-avoiders experienced higher pleasant emotions and lower unpleasant emotions with respect to constructive and negative feedback. In other words, feedback-seeking versus feedback-avoiding moderated the effect of feedback on emotions. Finally, in the context of medical education, Sargeant et al. (2008) ($N = 28$ physicians) employed a qualitative interview study approach and found that meta-cognitions (i.e., a facet of self-regulation) could reduce negative emotions following negative feedback (see also Chapter 13 in this volume). More specifically, they argue that reflection on emotional reactions following negative feedback can reduce negative emotional experiences. In other words, meta-cognition can be assumed to moderate the effects of negative feedback on negative emotions. In sum, (1) emotional instability, (2) feedback-seeking versus feedback-avoiding characteristics, and (3) meta-cognitions have been found to be significant moderators of the relation between feedback and emotions.

Emotion Regulation. Raftery and Bizer (2009) proposed that emotion regulation (Gross, 1998; Gross & John, 2003) would have an impact on how people responded to negative feedback. In their quasi-experimental investigation ($N = 144$ undergraduates) they showed that reappraisers (i.e., people thinking about a situation to change its emotional impact) who received negative feedback (poor performance) completed a further test more quickly and performed better as compared with people who received moderate feedback (performance slightly above average). The authors found no such effects for suppressors (i.e., people inhibiting emotion-expressive behavior). Thus, individual differences in reappraisal and suppression seem to be meaningful with respect to the impact of negative feedback on subsequent cognitive performance. Thus, the specific way of regulating emotions that individuals employ after negative feedback has been received seems to moderate the effects of feedback on performance. As emotions are at the focus of emotion regulation, it can be assumed that emotion regulation moderates the impact of feedback on emotions.

Purpose of Feedback. Rowe, Fitness, and Wood (2014) conducted an interview study and investigated university students' emotions related to anticipating and receiving feedback (21 students and 15 teachers). The researchers concluded that the purpose of feedback moderated its effects on students' emotions. For both positive and negative feedback, the effects on emotions differed according to the purpose of the feedback (i.e., whether it focused on evaluation or was used to support student learning). In other words, whether feedback was used for formative or summative purposes moderated the link between feedback and emotions (see Chapter 4 in this volume for a detailed discussion of summative versus formative purposes of feedback). The authors argue that evaluative feedback may be associated with "achievement emotions" (according to Pekrun et al., 2002; e.g., pride, enjoyment, anxiety), and the more formative type of feedback may be linked to both achievement and "social" emotions (e.g., gratitude, love). Sargeant et al. (2008) ($N = 28$ physicians) found that the effects of negative feedback on emotions strongly differed according to whether the focus of the feedback was the task or the self. Negative emotional reactions were found to be weaker when the task was in focus. This finding is consistent with the literature on formative feedback. As Hattie and Timperley (2007) suggest, task, process, and self-regulation feedback may be more effective in promoting improvement compared with the person-level feedback, which is self-focused and, thus, more emotionally charged. Depletion of cognitive resources that results from students' focus on the self and not the task may impede the constructive use of feedback, and their performance is likely to decrease or stay the same (Baumeister et al., 1990).

Feedback → Emotion: Mediators

Cognitive Appraisals. According to Pekrun's (2006) control-value theory of achievement emotions, feedback on success and failure (outlined in the theory as an aspect of the social environment) should have an impact on the feedback receiver's emotions via his or her appraisals of control (e.g., expectations, attributions) and values (e.g., intrinsic and extrinsic). In other words, performance feedback should have effects on feedback receivers' control and value cognitions that in turn should have an impact on emotions. The effects of feedback on control and value depend on the type of feedback. It is possible to give feedback in a way that it has specific effects on appraisals of control and value (e.g., giving negative performance feedback by outlining that this might have deep consequences for a future career might reduce levels of control and increase the judgment of the value of the achievement outcome). High levels of control are assumed to align with positive emotions, whereas low levels of control typically coincide with negative emotions. Value is assumed to increase both positive and negative emotions, with the exception of boredom, which should decrease with increasing value. However, it is important to note that there are different types of value (e.g., intrinsic value, utility, costs, attainment; Gaspard et al., 2015), which might be differentiated with respect to their mediating role.

The few existing studies on the relations between feedback, appraisals, and emotions are in line with the aforementioned assumptions. In a study of 577 high school students, Goetz (2004) found that positive performance feedback (grades) increased both students' control cognitions (self-concept) and value cognitions (achievement value). Control, in turn, reduced anxiety and increased enjoyment. In contrast, value increased both anxiety and enjoyment. Further, encouraging feedback on negative performance (e.g., "When I receive a bad grade my math teacher is cheering me up") increased achievement value, which increased both anxiety and enjoyment. These results indicate that even "positive" ways of giving feedback can result in negative emotions via increasing extrinsic value cognitions. Pekrun, Goetz, Daniels, Stupnisky, and Perry (2010; $N = 287$ university students) focused on boredom and found that grades increased both students' control and value cognitions, with both types of appraisals reducing student experiences of boredom.

Beyond studies referring to Pekrun's (2006) control-value theory there are very few findings indicating that cognitive appraisals mediate the relations between performance feedback and emotions. However, most of those studies do not explicitly mention and test this mediation assumption (e.g., Turner and Schallert, 2001).

Achievement Goals. Pekrun, Cuscak, Murayama, Elliot, and Thomas (2014) developed a theoretical model on the effects of anticipated feedback on academic emotions, in which they assumed that achievement goals would mediate the effects of feedback on emotions. Anticipated feedback in this study was defined as the expectation of students about the kinds of performance feedback they expected to receive. Self-referential feedback (referring to individual competence developments related to past performance) and normative feedback (referring to competence relative to other students' performance) were differentiated. This approach groups academic emotions with respect to their valence dimension (positive vs. negative; i.e., pleasant vs. unpleasant) and with respect to activity versus outcome focus (see above, definition of emotions). Goals in this study were conceptualized according to the trichotomous goal model (i.e., mastery goals, performance-approach goals, performance-avoidance goals; Elliot & McGregor, 2001). Thus, achievement goals were assumed to mediate the effects of feedback on emotions. To summarize, according to this model, self-referential feedback should promote the adoption of mastery goals, while anticipating feedback should promote the adoption of both performance-approach and performance-avoidance goals. Further, mastery goal orientation should have an effect on activity emotions (e.g., enhancing enjoyment, reducing anger); performance approach goals should have effects on positive-outcome emotions related to success (e.g., enhancing hope and pride); and performance avoidance goals should affect negative-outcome emotions related to failure (e.g., enhancing anxiety, hopelessness, shame, and relief). In Pekrun et al.'s (2014) experimental study ($N = 153$ high school students), participants were informed that they would receive self-referential feedback, normative feedback, or no feedback at all in a test-taking situation. The hypotheses were mainly confirmed and the study found that achievement goals mediate the effect between feedback and emotions. The main implication of this study is that self-referential feedback is clearly preferable to normative feedback with respect to its impact on achievement goals and students' academic emotions.

Emotion → Feedback: Mediators

Attitudinal Reactions on Feedback. Niemann et al. (2014) assumed that emotions involved in a feedback process have an impact on attitudinal reactions to the feedback. Such attitudes can be expected to have an impact on performance and, consequently, on further performance feedback. The researchers found ($N = 47$ undergraduates) that negative feedback increased anger in students, which in turn had effects on the attributional reactions: anger reduced the liking of the feedback provider (e.g., response to the item "I think that my subordinate is a pleasant person"); it lowered the perceived ability of the feedback provider (e.g., "I think that my subordinate is able to give useful comments"); and it also reduced feedback acceptance (e.g., "My subordinate rightfully criticized me"). In line with those findings, Sargeant et al. (2008) found that negative feelings following feedback reduced the acceptance of the feedback. Beyond the state of current research findings, it could further be assumed that the attributional reactions to feedback have an impact on subsequent performance and consequently on the acceptance of the performance feedback. Thus, attributional reactions can be presumed to mediate the effect of emotions on performance feedback.

Action Tendencies. Belschak, Jacobs, and Den Hartog (2008) suggested that emotions involved in a feedback process influenced individuals' specific actions. In their scenario study ($N = 101$ working adults) they found that positive emotions (enjoyment, relief, pride, contentment, enthusiasm) involved in the feedback process resulted in increased positive extra-role behaviors (organizational citizenship behavior), whereas negative emotions (anger, anxiety, frustration, disappointment, guilt, shame) increased negative extra-role behaviors (counterproductive behavior, turnover intention). Therefore, action tendencies appear to impact subsequent performance and, consequently, performance feedback; they can be assumed to mediate the effect of emotions on performance feedback.

Behavior. By referring to dual process models (e.g., Chaiken & Trope, 1999), Baumeister, Vohls, DeWall, and Zhang (2007) argue that emotions represent a feedback system that influences behavior. Emotions can be assumed to stimulate cognitive processing following a specific outcome. From this perspective, feedback on achievement activates an "emotional feedback system," which in turn has an impact on subsequent behavior. Thus, emotions involved in a feedback process mediate the effects of (external) feedback on performance. In line with this mediation assumption, Fishbach, Eyal, and Finkelstein (2010) argue that "the affective response is not a side effect or an epiphenomenon of the feedback, but rather the underlying mechanism by which feedback influences behavior" (p. 523). Also in line with this mediation assumption, Pekrun (2006) argued that emotions have an impact on performance via activation of cognitive resources, motivation to learn, and individuals' use of specific learning strategies and self-regulated learning processes (see also Goetz & Hall, 2013). However, to date, there has been little empirical evidence on the causal mechanisms leading to the effects of emotions on academic outcomes (for cross-sectional findings, see Goetz, 2004; Pekrun et al., 2004, 2011).

Summarizing the Current State of Our Knowledge on the Relations between Feedback and Emotions

Figure 25.1 summarizes the current state of our knowledge on the relations between feedback and emotions in a heuristic model. As outlined earlier, the existing cumulative empirical evidence on the outlined relations, moderators, and mediators strongly differs across constructs and is for some aspects quite clear (e.g., valence (positive vs. negative) as a moderator of the reciprocal relations), while for other aspects it is rather scarce (e.g., feedback-seeking vs. feedback-avoiding as a moderator of the impact of feedback on emotions). The majority of the existing empirical evidence on the relations between feedback and emotions is based on studies in which feedback was assessed via achievement outcomes (test scores, course grades, GPA).

Avenues for Future Research on the Relations between Feedback and Emotions

Taking Different Types of Feedback into Account. As outlined above, most studies on the relations between performance feedback and emotions refer to achievement outcomes as provided by test scores, course grades, and GPA. Thus, we lack knowledge on the relations between other types of performance feedback (e.g., oral feedback, computer-based feedback, immediate process feedback) and emotions. Future studies might take other taxonomies and purposes of feedback into account (e.g., formative vs. summative feedback, correction, reinforcement, forensic diagnosis, benchmarking, longitudinal development; Price, Handley, Miller, & O'Donovan, 2010; progress feedback vs. gap feedback; Voerman, Korthagen, Meijer, Simons, 2014; Chapter 3 in this volume). Of note is that we (the authors of this chapter and our collaborators) are currently embarking on a study that will investigate student emotional responses to feedback provided on a written task. We will examine these effects longitudinally.

Taking the Emotions of the Feedback Provider into Account. As outlined above, Johnson and Connelly (2014) argued that emotions that were induced by the feedback message itself (e.g., good achievement results, i.e. outcome emotions) as well as emotions that were communicated in the feedback exchange (e.g., enjoyment of the feedback provider) should be taken into account. Research is lacking on the latter aspect, and to our knowledge, there are no studies that focused on both aspects simultaneously. As for the emotions involved in the feedback exchange, emotional transmission processes should be investigated (Frenzel et al., 2009). Studies may examine how emotions of the feedback provider and the feedback receiver interact in an oral or written feedback process.

Taking Intraindividual Relations into Account. Although most of the theoretical approaches on the relations between performance feedback and emotions (e.g., control-value theory; Pekrun, 2006) refer to intraindividual mechanisms (cf. Molenaar, 2004; Voelkle, Brose, Schmiedek, & Lindenberger, 2014), nearly all existing studies focus on interindividual relations from which it is hardly ever possible to extrapolate to intraindividual relations (Schmitz & Skinner, 1993; Goetz et al., 2016). Future studies might investigate intraindividual relations by assessing feedback, emotions, and moderating as well as mediating variables repeatedly within persons over time. Longitudinal questionnaire studies or experience-sampling methods can be effectively used for these purposes (Csikszentmihalyi & Larson, 1987; Hektner, Schmidt, & Csikszentmihalyi, 2007). Intraindividual analyses of longitudinal data and intraindividual time-series analyses (cf. Schmitz & Skinner, 1993) might be helpful to shed light into the intraindividual relations between performance feedback and emotions. As argued by Voelkle et al. (2014), findings on the intraindividual level are a prerequisite to support theoretical assumptions on intraindividual functioning and to develop intervention programs for individuals.

Theory Development. Above and beyond the model presented in this chapter, it is important to develop empirically sound theories describing the interplay between performance feedback and emotions. Such theories might be based on the results of studies on intraindividual relations between both variables. They would be helpful for further research in this field and for bringing different theoretical approaches together (e.g., those from feedback and emotion research and from educational and work psychology).

Developing Intervention Studies. There is a clear lack of intervention studies with respect to providing feedback with the purposes of eliciting differential emotions and also with respect to emotions being beneficial concerning achievement outcomes and subsequent performance feedback. Such studies might take existing findings on the moderators and mediators of the relations between feedback and emotions into account and should be based on results of studies on intraindividual relations between performance feedback and emotions. In conclusion, we offer the following quotes that came from a focus group discussion, in which students described their reactions to feedback messages (Lipnevich, 2007): "I saw my grade and froze. I can't really improve that much from 55 [referring to the score]. I am going to fail it. I felt quite mad" or "I was upset because I thought I did a lot better. I stared at it for, like, fifteen minutes before I could start making some changes. I kept thinking that I failed the exam." Similarly, "I felt super happy and proud that I scored so highly.

I submitted my essay and left. I didn't need to improve my score beyond 92. I was satisfied." Interestingly, these quotes from students include the discussion of mediators and moderators of the link between feedback, emotions, and performance, thus presenting additional evidence that these relations do in fact exist, are meaningful, and should be further explored.

References

Barbalet, J. (2002). Introduction: Why emotions are crucial. In J. Barbalet (Ed.), *Emotions in sociology*. Oxford: Blackwell.

Baumeister, R. F., Hutton, D. G., & Cairns, K. J. (1990). Negative effects of praise on skilled performance. *Basic and Applied Social Psychology, 11*(2), 131–148.

Baumeister, R. F., Vohs, K. D., DeWall, C. N., & Zhang, L. (2007). How emotion shapes behavior: Feedback, anticipation, and reflection, rather than direct causation. *Personality and Social Psychology Review, 11*, 167–203.

Becker, E. S., Keller, M. M., Goetz, T., Frenzel, A. C., & Taxer, J. L. (2015). Antecedents of teachers' emotions in the classroom: An intraindividual approach. *Frontiers in Psychology, 6*, 635.

Belschak, F. D., Jacobs, G., & Den Hartog, D. N. (2008). Feedback, emotions, and action tendencies: Emotional consequences of feedback from one's supervisor. *Zeitschrift für Arbeits- und Organisationspsychologie, 52*(3), 147–152.

Brunswik, E. (1952). *The conceptual framework of psychology*. Chicago, IL: University of Chicago Press.

Cacioppo, J. T., & Berntson, G. G. (1994). Relationship between attitudes and evaluative space: A critical review, with emphasis on the separability of positive and negative substrates. *Psychological Bulletin, 115*, 401–423.

Cassidy, J., Ziv, Y., Mehta, T. G., & Feeney, B. C. (2003). Feedback seeking in children and adolescents: Associations with self-perceptions, attachment representations, and depression. *Child Development, 74*, 612–628.

Chaiken, S., & Trope, Y. (Eds.) (1999). *Dual-process theories in social psychology*. New York: Guilford.

Cohen, J. (1988). *Statistical power analysis for the behavioral sciences*. Hillsdale, NJ: Lawrence Erlbaum Associates.

Covington, M. V., & Beery, R. (1976). *Self-worth and school learning*. New York: Holt, Rinehart & Winston.

Csikszentmihalyi, M., & Larson, R. (1987). Validity and reliability of the experience-sampling method. *Journal of Nervous and Mental Diseases, 9*, 526–536.

Damasio, A. R. (2004). Emotions and feelings: A neurobiological perspective. In A. S. R. Manstead, N. Frijda, & A. Fischer (Eds.), *Feelings and emotions* (pp. 49–57). Cambridge: Cambridge University Press.

Diener, E., & Emmons, R. A. (1984). The independence of positive and negative affect. *Journal of Personality and Social Psychology, 47*(5), 1105–1117.

Elliot, A. J., & McGregor, H. A. (2001). A 2 x 2 achievement goal framework. *Journal of Personality and Social Psychology, 80*, 501–519.

Falchikov, N., & Boud, D. (2007). Assessment and emotion: The impact of being assessed. In D. Boud & N. Falchikov (Eds.), *Rethinking assessment in higher education: Learning for the longer term* (pp. 144–156). London: Routledge.

Fishbach, A., Eyal, T., & Finkelstein, S. R. (2010). How positive and negative feedback motivate goal pursuit. *Social and Personality Psychology Compass*, *4*, 517–530.

Fong, C. J., Warner, J. R., Williams, K. M., Schallert, D. L., Chen, L. H., Williamson, Z. H., & Lin, S. (2016). Deconstructing constructive criticism: The nature of academic emotions associated with constructive, positive, and negative feedback. *Learning and Individual Differences*, *49*, 393–399.

Fredrickson, B. L. (2001). The role of positive emotions in positive psychology. *American Psychologist*, *56*(3), 218–226.

Frenzel, A. C., Goetz, T., Lüdtke, O., Pekrun, R., & Sutton, R. E. (2009). Emotional transmission in the classroom: Exploring the relationship between teacher and student enjoyment. *Journal of Educational Psychology*, *101*(3), 705–716.

Frenzel, A. C., Pekrun, R., Goetz, T., Daniels, L. M., Durksen, T. L., Becker-Kurz, B., & Klassen, R. (2016). Measuring teachers' enjoyment, anger, and anxiety: The Teacher Emotions Scales (TES). *Contemporary Educational Psychology*, *46*, 148–163.

Gaspard, H., Dicke, A.-L., Flunger, B., Schreier, B., Häfner, I., Trautwein, U., & Nagengast, B. (2015). More value through greater differentiation: Gender differences in value beliefs about math. *Journal of Educational Psychology*, *107*, 663–677.

Goetz, T. (2004). *Emotionales Erleben und selbstreguliertes Lernen bei Schülern im Fach Mathematik [Students' emotional experiences and self-regulated learning in mathematics]*. München: Utz.

Goetz, T., Cronjaeger, H., Frenzel, A. C., Lüdtke, O., & Hall, N. C. (2010). Academic self-concept and emotion relations: Domain specificity and age effects. *Contemporary Educational Psychology*, *35*, 44–58.

Goetz, T., Frenzel, C. A., Hall, N. C., & Pekrun, R. (2008). Antecedents of academic emotions: Testing the internal/external frame of reference model for academic enjoyment. *Contemporary Educational Psychology*, *33*, 9–33.

Goetz, T., Frenzel, C. A., Pekrun, R., Hall, N. C., & Lüdtke, O. (2007). Between- and within-domain relations of students' academic emotions. *Journal of Educational Psychology*, *99*(4), 715–733.

Goetz, T., Haag, L., Lipnevich, A. A., Keller, M. M., Frenzel, A. C., & Collier, A. P. M. (2014). Between-domain relations of students' academic emotions and their judgments of school domain similarity. *Frontiers in Psychology*, *5*, 1153.

Goetz, T., & Hall, N. C. (2013). Emotion and achievement in the classroom. In J. Hattie & E. M. Anderman (Eds.), *International guide to student achievement* (pp. 192–195). New York: Routledge.

Goetz, T., Hall, N. C., Frenzel, A. C., & Pekrun, R. (2006). A hierarchical conceptualization of enjoyment in students. *Learning and Instruction*, *16*, 323–338.

Goetz, T., Preckel, F., Zeidner, M., & Schleyer, E. (2008). Big fish in big ponds: A multilevel analysis of test anxiety and achievement in special gifted classes. *Anxiety, Stress and Coping*, *21*(2), 185–198.

Goetz, T., Sticca, F., Pekrun, R., Murayama, K., & Elliot, A. J. (2016). Intraindividual relations between achievement goals and discrete achievement emotions: An experience sampling approach. *Learning and Instruction*, *41*, 115–125.

Gogol, K., Brunner, M., Preckel, F., Goetz, T., & Martin, R. (2016). Developmental dynamics of general and school-subject-specific components of academic self-concept, academic interest, and academic anxiety. *Frontiers in Psychology*, *7*, 356.

Gross, J. J. (1998). The emerging field of emotion regulation: An integrative review. *Review of General Psychology, 2,* 271–299.

Gross, J. J., & John, O. P. (2003). Individual differences in two emotion regulation processes: Implications for affect, relationships, and well-being. *Journal of Personality and Social Psychology, 85,* 348–362.

Hargreaves, E. (2013). Inquiring into children's experiences of teacher feedback: Reconceptualising assessment for learning. *Oxford Review of Education, 39,* 229–246.

Hatfield, E., Cacioppo, J. R., & Rapson, R. L. (1994). Emotional contagion. *Current Directions in Psychological Science, 2,* 96–99.

Hattie, J., & Timperley, H. (2007). The power of feedback. *Review of Educational Research, 77,* 81–112.

Hektner, J. M., Schmidt, J. A., & Csikszentmihalyi, M. (2007). *Experience sampling method: Measuring the quality of everyday life.* Thousand Oaks, CA: Sage.

Hembree, R. (1988). Correlates, causes, effects, and treatment of test anxiety. *Review of Educational Research, 58,* 47–77.

Idson, L. C., & Higgins, E. T. (2000). How current feedback and chronic effectiveness influence motivation: Everything to gain versus everything to lose. *European Journal of Social Psychology, 30,* 583–592.

Ilgen, D. R., & Davis, C. A. (2000). Bearing bad news: Reactions to negative performance feedback. *Applied Psychology: An International Review, 49,* 550–565.

Johnson, G., & Connelly, S. (2014). Negative emotions in informal feedback: The benefits of disappointment and drawbacks of anger. *Human Relations, 67*(10), 1265–1290.

Kingston, N. & Nash, B. (2011). Formative assessment: A meta-analysis and a call for research. *Educational Measurement: Issues and Practice, 30*(4), 28–37.

Kleinginna, P. R., & Kleinginna, A. M. (1981). A categorized list of emotion definitions, with suggestions for a consensual definition. *Motivation and Emotion, 5,* 345–379.

Kluger, A. N., & DeNisi, A. (1996). The effects of feedback interventions on performance: A historical review, a metaanalysis, and a preliminary feedback intervention theory. *Psychological Bulletin, 119,* 254–284.

Kluger, A. N., Lewinsohn, S., & Aiello, J. R. (1994). The influence of feedback on mood: Linear effects on pleasantness and curvilinear effects on arousal. *Organizational Behavior and Human Decision Processes, 60,* 276–299.

Krannich, M., Goetz, T., Lipnevich, A. A., & Roos, A.-L. (2017, April). It's boring I won't do that: State and trait boredom predicting students' career aspirations. Paper presented at the annual meeting of the American Educational Research Association, San Antonio, TX.

Latham, G. P., & Locke, E. A. (1991). Self-regulation through goal setting. *Organizational Behavior and Human Decision Processes, 50,* 212–247.

Lewis, M., & Haviland-Jones, J. M. (Eds.). (2000). *Handbook of emotions.* New York: Guilford.

Lipnevich, A. A. (2007). Response to assessment feedback: The effects of grades, praise, and source of information. Rutgers the State University of New Jersey–New Brunswick.

Lipnevich, A. A., & Smith, J. K. (2009a). "I really need feedback to learn": Students' perspectives on the effectiveness of the differential feedback messages. *Educational Assessment, Evaluation and Accountability, 21,* 347–367.

Lipnevich, A. A., & Smith, J. K. (2009b). Russian and American perspectives on self-regulated learning. *International Journal of Creativity and Problem Solving, 19*, 83–100.

Ma, X. (1999). A meta-analysis of the relationship between anxiety toward mathematics and achievement in mathematics. *Journal for Research in Mathematics Education, 30*(5), 520–540.

Marsh, H. W. (1986). Verbal and math self-concepts: An internal/external frame of reference model. *American Educational Research Journal, 23*, 129–149.

Marsh, H. W. (1987). The big-fish-little-pond effect on academic self-concept. *Journal of Educational Psychology, 79*(3), 280–295.

Marsh, H. W. (1990). Influences of internal and external frames of reference on the formation of math and English self-concepts. *Journal of Educational Psychology, 82*, 107–116.

McCrae, R. R., & Costa, P. T. J. (2008). Empirical and theoretical status of the five-factor model of personality traits. In G. J. Boyle, G. Matthews, & D. H. Saklofske (Eds.), *The Sage handbook of personality theory and assessment* (pp. 273–294). Thousand Oaks, CA: Sage.

Molenaar, P. C. M. (2004). A manifesto on psychology as idiographic science: Bringing the person back into scientific psychology, this time forever. *Measurement, 2*, 201–218.

Nicaise, V., Bois, J. E., Fairclough, S. J., Amorose, A. J., & Cogérino, G. (2007). Girls' and boys' perceptions of physical education teachers' feedback: Effects on performance and psychological responses. *Journal of Sports Sciences, 25*(8), 915–926.

Niemann, J., Wisse, B., Rus, D., Van Yperen, N. W., & Sassenberg, K. (2014). Anger and attitudinal reactions to negative feedback: The effects of emotional instability and power. *Motivation and Emotion, 38*(5), 687–699.

Núñez-Peña, M. I., Bono, R., & Suárez-Pellicioni, M. (2015). Feedback on students' performance: A possible way of reducing the negative effect of math anxiety in higher education. *International Journal of Educational Research, 70*, 80–87.

Parkinson, B., & Manstead, A. S. R. (1992). Appraisal as a cause of emotion. In M. S. Clark (Ed.), *Emotions: Review of personality and social psychology* (pp. 122–149). Newbury Park, CA: Sage.

Pekrun, R. (2006). The control-value theory of achievement emotions: Assumptions, corollaries, and implications for educational research and practice. *Educational Psychology Review, 18*, 315–341.

Pekrun, R., Cusack, A., Murayama, K., Elliot, A. J., & Thomas, K. (2014). The power of anticipated feedback: Effects on students' achievement goals and achievement emotions. *Learning and Instruction, 29*, 115–124.

Pekrun, R., Elliot, A. J., & Maier, M. A. (2006). Achievement goals and discrete achievement emotions: A theoretical model and prospective test. *Journal of Educational Psychology, 98*, 583–597.

Pekrun, R., Elliot, A. J., & Maier, M. A. (2009). Achievement goals and achievement emotions: Testing a model of their joint relations with academic performance. *Journal of Educational Psychology, 101*, 115–135.

Pekrun, R., Goetz, T., Daniels, L. M., Stupnisky, R. H., & Perry, R. P. (2010). Boredom in achievement settings: Exploring control-value antecedents and performance outcomes of a neglected emotion. *Journal of Educational Psychology, 102*(3), 531–549.

Pekrun, R., Goetz, T., Frenzel, A. C., Barchfeld, P., & Perry, R. P. (2011). Measuring emotions in students' learning and performance: The Achievement Emotions Questionnaire (AEQ). *Contemporary Educational Psychology*, *36*(1), 36–48.

Pekrun, R., Goetz, T., Perry, R. P., Kramer, K., Hochstadt, M., & Molfenter, S. (2004). Beyond test anxiety: Development and validation of the Test Emotions Questionnaire (TEQ). *Anxiety, Stress, and Coping*, *17*(3), 287–316.

Pekrun, R., Goetz, T., Titz, W., & Perry, R. P. (2002). Academic emotions in students' self-regulated learning and achievement: A program of qualitative and quantitative research. *Educational Psychologist*, *37*(2), 91–105.

Pekrun, R., Hall, N. C., Goetz, T., & Perry, R. P. (2014). Boredom and academic achievement: Testing a model of reciprocal causation. *Journal of Educational Psychology*, *106*(3), 696–710.

Pekrun, R., Lichtenfeld, S., Marsh, H. W., Murayama, K., & Goetz, T. (2017). Achievement emotions and academic performance: Longitudinal models of reciprocal effects. *Child Development*, *88*, 1653–1670.

Popper, K. (1999). *All life is problem solving*. New York: Abingdon.

Price, M., Handley, K., Millar, J., & O'Donovan, B. (2010). Feedback: All that effort, but what is the effect? *Assessment & Evaluation in Higher Education*, *35*(3), 277–289.

Raftery, J. N., & Bizer, G. Y. (2009). Negative feedback and performance: The moderating effect of emotion regulation. *Personality and Individual Differences*, *47*(5), 481–486.

Rowe, A. D., Fitness, J., & Wood, L. N. (2014). The role and functionality of emotions in feedback at university: A qualitative study. *Australian Educational Researcher*, *41*(3), 283–309.

Sarason, S. B., & Mandler, G. (1952). Some correlates of test anxiety. *Journal of Abnormal and Social Psychology*, *47*(4), 810–817.

Sargeant, J., Mann, K., Sinclair, D., Van Der Vleuten, C., & Metsemakers, J. (2008). Understanding the influence of emotions and reflection upon multi-source feedback acceptance and use. *Advances in Health Sciences Education*, *13*, 275–288.

Scherer, K. R. (1984). On the nature and function of emotion: A component process approach. In K. R. Scherer & P. Ekman (Eds.), *Approaches to emotion* (pp. 293–317). Hillsdale, NJ: Erlbaum.

Scherer, K. R. (2000). Emotions as episodes of subsystems synchronization driven by nonlinear appraisal processes. In M. D. Lewis & I. Granic (Eds.), *Emotion, development, and self-organization* (pp. 70–99). Cambridge: Cambridge University Press.

Schmitz, B., & Skinner, E. A. (1993). Perceived control, effort, and academic performance: Interindividual, intraindividual, and multivariate time series analyses. *Journal of Personality and Social Psychology*, *64*, 1010–1028.

Seipp, B. (1991). Anxiety and academic performance: A meta-analysis of findings. *Anxiety Research*, *4*, 27–41.

Seligman, M. E. P., & Csikszentmihalyi, M. (2000). Positive psychology: An introduction. *American Psychologist*, *55*(1), 5–14.

Shields, S. (2015). "My work is bleeding": Exploring students' emotional responses to first-year assignment feedback. *Teaching in Higher Education*, *20*(6), 614–624.

Shrauger, J. S., & Rosenberg, S. E. (1970). Self-esteem and the effects of success and failure feedback on performance. *Journal of Personality*, *38*, 404–417.

Sticca, F., Goetz, T., Nett, U. E., Hubbard, K., & Haag, L. (2017). Short- and long-term effects of over-reporting of grades on academic self-concept and achievement. *Journal of Educational Psychology, 109*, 842–854.

Stough, L. M., & Emmer, E. T. (1998). Teachers' emotions and test feedback. *Qualitative Studies in Education, 11*(2), 541–600.

Taxer, J. L., & Frenzel, A. C. (2012, July). The influence of teachers' emotions on students' self-concepts, attributions, expectations, persistence and emotions. Paper presented at the Junior Researchers of EARLI Conference, Regensburg, Germany.

Turner, J. E., & Schallert, D. L. (2001). Expectancy–value relationships of shame reactions and shame resiliency. *Journal of Educational Psychology, 93*, 320–329.

van Doorn, E. A., van Kleef, G. A., & van der Pligt, J. (2014). How instructors' emotional expressions shape students' learning performance: The roles of anger, happiness, and regulatory focus. *Journal of Experimental Psychology: General, 143*(3), 980–984.

Van Kleef, G. A. (2008). Emotion in conflict and negotiation: Introducing the emotions as social information (EASI) model. In N. M. Ashkanasy & C. L. Cooper (Eds.), *Research companion to emotion in organizations* (pp. 392–404). London: Edward Elgar.

Van Kleef, G. A. (2009). How emotions regulate social life: The emotions as social information (EASI) model. *Current Directions in Psychological Science, 18*(3), 184–188.

Värlander, S. (2008). The role of students' emotions in formal feedback situations. *Teaching in Higher Education, 13*(2), 145–156.

Voelkle, M. C., Brose, A., Schmiedek, F., & Lindenberger, U. (2014). Towards a unified framework for the study of between-person and within-person structures: Building a bridge between two research paradigms. *Multivariate Behavioral Research, 49*, 193–213.

Voerman, L., Korthagen, F. A., Meijer, P. C., & Simons, R. J. (2014). Feedback revisited: Adding perspectives based on positive psychology. Implications for theory and classroom practice. *Teaching and Teacher Education, 43*, 91–98.

Waterhouse, I. K., & Child, I. L. (1953). Frustration and the quality of performance. *Journal of Personality, 21*, 298–311.

Watson, D., Clark, L. A., & Tellegen, A. (1988). Development and validation of brief measures of positive and negative affect: The PANAS Scales. *Journal of Personality and Social Psychology, 54*, 1063–1070.

Young, P. (2000). "I might as well give up": Self-esteem and mature students' feelings about feedback on assignments. *Journal of Further & Higher Education, 24*(3), 409–418.

Zeidner, M. (1998). *Test anxiety: The state of the art.* New York: Plenum Press.

Zeidner, M. (2007). Test anxiety in educational contexts: Concepts, findings, and future directions. In P. A. Schutz & R. Pekrun (Eds.), *Emotion in education* (pp. 165–184). London: Academic Press.

Zeidner, M., & Schleyer, E. J. (1999). The big-fish-little-pond effect for academic self concept, test anxiety, and school grades in gifted children. *Contemporary Educational Psychology, 24*, 305–329.

26 The Relationship between Creativity and Feedback

Molly Holinger and James C. Kaufman

Creativity is usually treated as a dependent variable (Forgeard & Kaufman, 2016). In other words, most studies emphasize how the physical environment, individual differences, or interactions with other people or other factors can help improve creativity. This focus is not surprising; the most exciting aspect of creativity may be inspiration. The questions of how we get our ideas or what might break writer's block or how we might try to listen to our inner muse are captivating. Yet the process of revision – as slow and frustrating as it can be – is what allows people to grow as creators (Kaufman & Beghetto, 2013b). Feedback – so essential to the process of revision – is a comparatively understudied topic. Yet revisions are just as important as inspiration. Feedback is essential to the successful refinement of ideas and thus to creativity itself.

Feedback (and the related construct of evaluation) may be less studied in creativity research but is prevalent in most aspects of life around the world. Two million US high schoolers will get their SAT scores as well as grades for up to 300 assignments or assessments each year (Stone & Heen, 2014). Between 50% and 90% of employees will be subject to performance reviews (Green, 2013). Every year, more than 800 million business hours are spent on the annual review process (Stone & Heen, 2014).

Abundance, however, does not equal effectiveness. According to their meta-analysis of feedback interventions, Kluger and DeNisi (1996) concluded that feedback interventions can have greatly different results, from helping to hurting to no effect. To illustrate the mercurial nature of feedback, a study of organizational leaders (Amabile, Schatzel, Moneta, & Kramer, 2004) found that the monitoring behavior (of which feedback was a subcomponent) was the *only* leader behavior that significantly related both positively and negatively to perceived leader support. Employees reacted positively to monitoring that led to a sense of safety and support and negatively to monitoring that included nonactionable negative feedback. Feedback has unquestionably powerful effects, but to varying degrees and directions based on personality traits, task type, and contextual factors.

Winnie and Butler (1994) defined feedback as "information with which a learner can confirm, add to, overwrite, tune, or restructure information in memory, whether that information is domain knowledge, meta-cognitive knowledge, beliefs about self and tasks, or cognitive tactics and strategies" (p. 5740). Used in the most casual sense, feedback can include any evaluative information that leads to learning. Some occurs naturally and is detected (e.g., a disapproving facial expression); some results from an action and is observed (e.g., the death of a plant from overwatering); and some is deliberately given or demanded (e.g., a teacher's comments on a student's work). Feedback can include suggestions for improvement, but often does not.

Feedback that is personal (such as "You need to get better at something" or "You are good at this") has less impact, regardless of its positive or negative valence. One reason is that no learning takes place. Teachers tend to give underperforming students more praise, a less effective form of feedback because it provides little direction for improvement (Hattie & Timperley, 2007). Praise can even damage performance (Kluger & DeNisi, 1996), especially creative performance (Hennessey, 2010). Task-related feedback is more effective, particularly when a correct solution is given. Well-constructed feedback bridges the gap between misunderstanding and understanding by providing direct, clear, and relevant information about a particular task. Therefore, in cases where the receiver has no point of reference (such as no prior knowledge or skills that can be used to improve), instruction is more appropriate than feedback.

Beyond these broad considerations, there are several ways that feedback can be used to nurture, maintain, or stimulate creativity. We have grouped these theories and studies under three approaches: motivational, cognitive, and personality/individual differences.

Three Approaches to Considering Creativity and Feedback

An initial look at the feedback literature might make the manager, teacher, or artist wary of feedback as a means of enhancing creative performance. Feedback has been shown to benefit rote tasks more than complex tasks and may even undermine performance on complex tasks, at least when performance was assessed over a short time frame (Kluger & DeNisi, 1996). Furthermore, revealing the correct response has been shown to make feedback more effective, but often in creativity there is no "correct response."

On one hand, feedback has been shown to enhance creative performance (Yuan & Zhou, 2008; de Stobbeleir, Ashford, & Buyens, 2011). On the other hand, person-focused feedback (as opposed to process-focused) can even run the risk of a creator wanting to give up entirely (Beghetto, 2014). Indeed, the creativity–feedback relationship is quite inconsistent (much as the general performance–feedback relationship). We will now explore the different considerations regarding feedback and creativity that can determine whether feedback helps, hurts, or does not affect creativity.

The Motivational Approach

Intrinsic motivation is performing an activity out of a genuine desire or passion for the task. Someone with intrinsic motivation experiences enjoyment and a need for growth or learning. In contrast, extrinsic motivation is when someone is engaged in an activity for an external reward, such as payment, credit, or praise (Deci & Ryan, 1985, 2008). Intrinsic motivation is generally considered to be more closely linked with creativity (Amabile, 1996), although there has been some debate (Eisenberger & Shanock, 2003). We will highlight key points of this larger discussion that are the most relevant to the question of feedback.

Several components of intrinsic motivation suggest some best practices for giving feedback. For example, competence is a key component of intrinsic motivation (Amabile et al., 2004). Feeling competent enables someone to feel a level of mastery about a particular field (Hennessey, in press). Someone who aims for mastering a task wants to learn and is less concerned about the specific final outcome (Miele, Finn, & Molden, 2011). Some have proposed that competence and intrinsic motivation have a reciprocal relationship. For example, students who care about school performance showed higher intrinsic motivation for reading, which then led to increased reading performance, which further led to increased intrinsic reading motivation (Schaffner, Phillipp, & Sciefele, 2016).

Given that creativity involves solving complex, ambiguous problems that are inherently challenging, paying attention to the creator's perceived competence is important. Constructive, informational feedback has been demonstrated to be particularly effective (Ligon, Graham, Edwards, Osburn, & Hunter, 2012). Intrinsic motivation leads to greater immersion and experimentation in one's work (Ruscio, Whitney, & Amabile, 1998); the more that an environment can help support this connection, the better (Puccio & Cabra, 2010). Creativity thrives in a supportive, noncontrolling environment in which individuals adopt a growth mindset and are willing to make mistakes in the pursuit of mastery (Oldham & Cummings, 1996; Dweck, 2006). Rather than pursuing a perceived outcome desired by their superior, individuals focus on exploration and skill development. Informational feedback provides necessary learning without damaging personal competence, given that it is often perceived as providing relevant and instructive information to accomplish a task rather than an indication of inadequacy. Generally, feedback that builds on someone's previous attempts to accomplish a task has been shown to be effective (Hattie & Timperley, 2007).

To the extent that informational practices can positively influence intrinsic motivation, overly controlling practices can negate it (Deci & Ryan, 1985). For example, close monitoring is a behavior in which supervisors micromanage, constantly watching their employees to make sure that their work is completed in an approved and expected fashion (Zhou & George, 2001). Zhou (2003) found that close monitoring by supervisors lessened creative performance, even when surrounded by creative co-workers, though there was less of a negative impact for less-creative people. Similarly, individuals who anticipated constructive, informational evaluation were significantly more creative than those who expected judgmental evaluation (Shalley & Perry-Smith, 2001). Anticipated evaluation also impacts how someone approaches a task. Regulatory focus theory (Higgins, 1998) proposes two types of foci: promotion and prevention. People with a promotion focus seek to succeed and improve even at the risk of making mistakes; in taking what is called an "eager" approach, they are more likely to rely on intuition and aim for personal goals. In contrast, people with a prevention focus try to avoid errors and emphasize security. In taking what is called a "vigilant" approach, they are likely to be deliberate and cautious and consider what other people (such as supervisors) would prefer (Cesario & Higgins, 2008; Cornwell & Higgins, 2016). Wang, Wang, Liu, and Dong (2017) studied the relationship between creativity and feedback under the guise of regulatory focus. They found two interesting results. First, they found that people who were led to expect a controlling evaluation of their creative work were more likely to take a vigilant approach. Those people who were led to expect an informational evaluation were more likely to take an eager approach Second, the match between focus and expected evaluation is important. People with a promotion focus were more creative when they anticipated an informational evaluation; in contrast, however, people with a prevention focus were more creative when they anticipated a controlling evaluation.

Evaluation is not the same thing as feedback; the focus is often more on appraisal or judgment than improvement. However, the two concepts are related. Merely the threat of evaluation can undermine creative performance (Amabile, 1979) and decrease feelings of competence (King & Gurland, 2007). There are several individual difference variables that can moderate the impact of evaluation. For example, gender differences play a role. J. Baer (1997) asked eighth-graders to write poems and stories. One group expected to be evaluated and the other group did not. The boys wrote equally creative work regardless of condition. By contrast, the girls were significantly less creative when anticipating evaluation. In an expansion of the study, J. Baer (1998) tested whether the anticipation of informational feedback as opposed to broad evaluation would cause less of a decline in girls' creativity. As with anticipating evaluation, there was some decreased creativity, but it was greatly reduced to the point of not being significant. J. Baer (1998) also replicated his earlier findings and found that younger boys showed increased creativity if they expected evaluation. Similar discrepancies found in competitive situations (Conti, Collins, & Picariello, 2001) and group creativity (M. Baer, Vadera, Leenders, & Oldham, 2014) are notable, given that there are generally no gender differences in creative ability (J. Baer & Kaufman, 2008).

Gender is, of course, one of several variables that moderate evaluation. For example, high levels of initial intrinsic motivation mediate the impact of extrinsic motivators, including evaluation (Amabile, 1996). J. Baer (1998) further suggested that low levels of initial motivation can lead to evaluation being more damaging. In addition, a study of computer programmers found that experts were negatively affected by the threat of evaluation, whereas novices were actually positively affected (Conti & Amabile, 1995). This pattern suggests that skill level may be another mediating variable, a topic we will return to when discussing the individual-differences approach to feedback.

There are several instances where people want to receive feedback and will be less creative without it. For example, a person working alone who is trying to be creative will perform better if he or she is expecting feedback (Shalley, 1995). Consistent with Wang et al.'s (2017) study discussed earlier, someone with a high need for structure thrives on feedback, such that even receiving controlling feedback is preferable to receiving none (Slijkhuis, Rietzschel, & Van Yperen, 2013). Similarly, such people will not be harmed by close monitoring (Rietzschel, Slijkhuis, & Yperen, 2014).

The Cognitive Approach

Another approach to considering how feedback and creativity are related is to take a cognitive perspective. The creative process entails alternating stages of divergent thinking and convergent thinking. Divergent thinking involves free-wheeling thought aimed at generating a large number of ideas (Guilford, 1950; Mumford, 2003). Novelty tends to arrive later in the idea production process after someone has exhausted initial, less original ideas (Milgram & Rabkin, 1980). Convergent thinking utilizes focused thought in which one sorts or refines ideas. The creative process usually requires both types of thinking. For example, brainstorming is a tool used to promote divergent thinking. It recommends that people defer judgment during the initial phase of idea production (Osborn, 1953). Criticism is then reintroduced during the idea-selection (or convergent thinking) phase. One study found that the expectation of evaluation during idea production has been shown to inhibit divergent thinking but improve the idea appropriateness during convergent thinking (Yuan & Zhou, 2008). The most creative ideas came when people expected evaluation during the convergent thinking phase but not in the divergent thinking phase. Why would this pattern emerge? Divergent thinking is a heuristic activity, demanding complex cognitive tasks such as making remote associations between discrepant concepts (Mednick, 1962). External evaluation causes a person to be distracted, thereby increasing cognitive load and depleting the mental resources available. In addition, the authors noted that the external evaluation itself does not decrease divergent thinking; rather, it is the expectation of this evaluation (Yuan & Zhou, 2008). Convergent thinking is more algorithmic in nature but nevertheless demands effort. It requires focused attention and draws on domain knowledge and established processes to make decisions. As a result, expectation of evaluation can improve performance. There is some evidence that feedback benefits creative performance even in jobs that are largely routine based (Hackman & Oldham, 1975), supporting the idea that algorithmic tasks benefit from evaluation.

The type of creative thinking used can often depend (and vary wildly) on the domain (Kaufman & Baer, 2002). It is worth noting that the latter half of the ideation phase, in which ideas are refined or discarded, tends to reduce novelty in certain domains more than others. Creative products are typically defined as being both novel and task appropriate (Hennessey & Amabile, 2010;

Kaufman, 2016). There is variation across domains; Cropley and Cropley (2010; see also Cropley & Kaufman, 2012) highlight the contrast between functional and aesthetic creativity. Aesthetic creativity tends to have a broader conception of what constitutes task appropriateness. For example, a poem may have to follow a specific format (such as a sonnet), but the core task requirement is to be insightful, beautiful, or entertaining. The underlying purpose is aesthetic. In contrast, however, a bridge's primary task requirement is to be sturdy and safe. A bridge will be judged as more creative if is aesthetically pleasing – but if it collapses, then it is not creative at all. Aesthetic creativity demands a high degree of novelty and less appropriateness as compared with functional creativity, which demands a high degree of appropriateness as opposed to novelty. Therefore, the relevance of evaluation varies according to the desired degree of novelty in a task or domain.

The discrepancies of the effects of external evaluation may be rooted in the cognitive aspects of creativity. It is understandable that studies that treat creative process as a single unit and studies that separately analyze the different stages may find inconsistent conclusions on how creativity relates to feedback and evaluation. Consider that Scott, Leritz, and Mumford's (2004) meta-analysis on the effectiveness of creativity training found that cognitive approaches were most effective in improving overall creative performance. Other approaches, which included confluence (cognitive supplemented with something else), motivational, or personality factors, were less useful. This pattern may also apply to the best way to understand how feedback or evaluation can strengthen creativity.

The Personality/Individual-Differences Approach

Are certain types of people more likely to respond positively or negatively to feedback on creative work? A recurring theme across most studies is that regardless of feedback, openness to experience is typically the personality factor most linked to creativity (Feist, 1998; Jauk, Benedek, & Neubauer, 2014). Studies that seek the equation for the highest creative performance will often include this factor. For example, George and Zhou (2001) found that people high on openness who were engaged in open-ended tasks and received positive feedback were the most creative. Similarly, Oldham and Cummings (1996) found a larger patent output and higher manager-rated creativity in employees (1) who were working on heuristic tasks; (2) who were monitored in a supportive, informational style; and (3) who rated themselves highly on the Creative Personality Scale (Gough, 1979), which incorporates self-beliefs of both creativity and openness.

Others have studied how personality mediates the creativity–feedback relationship. For example, people who are low on both emotional stability and extraversion are notably less creative if they believe they will be evaluated. People who are high on extraversion and openness are less likely to be impacted at all by the threat of evaluation (Chamorro-Premuzic & Reichenbacher, 2008; see also Cheek & Stahl, 1986).

Personality is not the only individual difference variable related to creativity and feedback. Consider the difference between people who are passive feedback-receivers and those who are active feedback-seekers. Just the act of seeking feedback can be empowering and enable the creator to self-regulate (Crommelinck & Anseel, 2013). Instead of receiving feedback according to someone else's timetable, it allows the creator to request more frequent feedback at the time that it is most desired. In the workplace, managers rarely have the opportunity to closely monitor employee creativity across all stages of the creative process, particularly when the process is broken down in smaller substages (Zhou, 2003). Even when this chance does present itself, as previously mentioned, employees who are closely monitored may see their boss as controlling and be adversely affected by the feedback (Amabile et al., 2004).

If employees are allowed to have more say in when they receive feedback, it can help uncover positive attributes. Feedback-seeking behavior has been linked to enhanced job performance and learning (Crommerlick & Anseel, 2013). Further, studies have shown that feedback-seeking helps people adapt to new work environments by offering a clear understanding of organizational norms and standards.

According to the model proposed by Ashford and Cummings (1983), individuals seek out feedback through either inquiry or monitoring or some combination of the two. Inquiry is when individuals explicitly request feedback from others, whereas monitoring entails observing one's circumstances and how other people act and thereby forming indirect conclusions regarding one's personal performance. Individuals prone to monitoring (as opposed to inquiry) risk misreading subtle cues in their environment (Crommelinck & Anseel, 2013). The trade-off is that directly asking for feedback comes with "image costs" – in other words, seeking feedback can make an employee seem less knowledgeable or confident of his or her abilities (de Stobbeleir et al., 2011). It is interesting to note that the same concern for maintaining one's image can also lead someone to suppress creative ideas given the potential for ridicule or criticism (Sternberg & Lubart, 1995).

This concept extends from the individual to the organization. A creativity-supporting climate can reduce employee reluctance to expressing creativity (Zhou & George, 2001). Might it have similar implications for feedback seeking? De Stobbeleir et al. (2011) compared supervisor ratings of employee creativity with the employees' self-reports of feedback-seeking behavior. They found that the frequency of inquiry-based feedback-seeking was significantly associated with creative performance, but there was no association between creativity and monitoring-based feedback-seeking. In addition, employees were more likely to seek out feedback when they felt their creativity was supported. A culture that encourages feedback-seeking aims to establish a bottom-up approach to enhancing organizational creativity. This approach allows individual behaviors (such as feedback-seeking) to help drive organizational-level change. In the "top-down" approach, organizations attempt to establish the climate based on policies and rules.

The Goldilocks Principle, Creative Mortification, and Creative Mollification

One recent approach to studying creativity development is the Four C Model of Creativity, which expands the traditional little-c/Big-C dichotomy of everyday and eminent creativity by adding mini-c (Beghetto & Kaufman, 2007, 2009, 2013, 2014) and Pro-c (Kaufman & Beghetto, 2009, 2013a, 2013b). Mini-c is personal creativity, or the meaningful micro-moments of insight that happen to all of us, whereas Pro-c is expert-level creativity. One of the concepts discussed in the model was the Goldilocks Principle. This idea is that there is an optimal level of feedback that can be given to a developing creator that strikes the ideal mix of encouragement and directions for improvement.

It is a difficult balance beam to walk and there are many ways to fail. Sometimes, as Beghetto (2010) proposes, ideas can simply be killed softly by being ignored, dismissed, or postponed. Not giving any feedback is not the solution. There is another extreme of giving harsh, critical feedback that holds someone to an unreasonable standard. Such sharp criticism can make the receiver feel intense shame. This feeling, which Beghetto (2014) dubs creative mortification, can kill someone's desire to ever create.

The opposite extreme, although less discussed, can be equally devastating. Some creators go through much of their lives being overpraised. Their creative work is met with general compliments or bland exhortations. Perhaps the critic does not want to risk hurting feelings, or else they are afraid of confrontation. In any event, these people develop their creativity without receiving authentic and constructive feedback that helps them grow. As a result, these people can develop an inaccurate sense of their own creative abilities (Kaufman, Evans, & Baer, 2010; Kaufman, Beghetto, & Watson, 2016). Although often given with the best intentions, such "creative mollification" is just as detrimental as the pointed belittlement of creative mortification. At some point, these people will encounter an accurate assessment of their abilities; the resulting impact may leave them just as voiceless as those who encounter creative mortification.

Conclusion

As with many areas in creativity, the right level of feedback requires a delicate balance. On one hand, feedback can potentially lead to immediate underperformance by damaging intrinsic motivation or inhibiting divergent thinking, as well as more lasting underperformance in the case of creative mortification. Yet neglecting feedback closes the door to improvement. As someone strives to move past mini-c or even little-c, inspiration alone no longer suffices.

Let us review feedback practices according to their impact on creativity. Two broad feedback practices tend to help and enhance creativity. The first is feedback that *preserves the creator's sense of competence.* Competence is associated with intrinsic motivation, which, in turn, is often associated with creativity. The second is when the creator *engages in feedback-seeking behavior*. Directly asking for feedback (or "inquiry-based" feedback) is associated with increased creative performance (de Stobbeleir et al., 2011); in addition, it occurs more frequently in creativity-supporting environments.

There are also practices that can decrease creativity. Most notably is when someone *gives general praise*, which does not offer areas of improvement for the creator to seek out, and when people give *person-focused feedback*, which is not only less effective but can be directly harmful.

Finally, there are feedback practices whose ultimate success is dependent on the interaction between the creator, the mentor/supervisor, and the context. One such mixed practice is *giving controlling feedback*. Although informational feedback is generally considered to be more helpful, it is also true that individuals with a prevention focus or a high need for structure may benefit from controlling feedback. Another practice is when the environment *creates an expectation of evaluation*. The expectation of evaluation is often a negative thing. A deleterious impact on creativity is especially true for individuals who are more emotionally unstable or introverted compared with people who are more emotionally stable and extroverted. However, there are times when the relationship between creativity and expected evaluation can be quite nuanced, with variables such as gender and age playing a role. For example, adolescent boys showed increased creativity with expectation of evaluation. In addition, expected evaluation hinders divergent thinking and facilitates convergent thinking. Although divergent thinking is more traditionally associated with creativity, convergent thinking is certainly also related. This specific pattern may show some benefit for novices, although it is also likely to deter the creativity of experts.

What is the take-home message on creativity and feedback? A basic best practices formula does emerge. A creative personality paired with open-ended or heuristic tasks and with supportive, informational feedback leads to increased creativity. However, most types of feedback do not fall as simply into "good" or "bad" categories. The human element – what drives us, how we think, and who we are – is often a wild card in choosing the ideal type of feedback to give. If you know your students, workers, or mentees well, then you should be able to use the information in this chapter to select the best type of feedback strategies to use. Unfortunately, it is more complicated and nuanced than "one size fits all" (like much of creativity research).

References

Amabile, T. M. (1979). Effects of external evaluation on artistic creativity. *Journal of Personality and Social Psychology, 37*, 221–233.

Amabile, T. M. (1996). *Creativity in context: Update to "The Social Psychology of Creativity."* Boulder, CO: Westview Press.

Amabile, T. M., Schatzel, E. A., Moneta, G. B., & Kramer, S. J. (2004). Leader behaviors and the work environment for creativity: Perceived leader support. *Leadership Quarterly, 15*, 5–32.

Ashford, S. J., & Cummings, L. L. (1983). Feedback as an individual resource: Personal strategies of creating information. *Organizational Behavior and Human Performance, 32*, 370–398.

Baer, J. (1997). Gender differences in the effects of anticipated evaluation on creativity. *Creativity Research Journal, 10*, 25–31.

Baer, J. (1998). Gender differences in the effects of extrinsic motivation on creativity. *Journal of Creative Behavior, 32*, 18–37.

Baer, J., & Kaufman, J. C. (2008). Gender differences in creativity. *Journal of Creative Behavior, 42*, 75–106.

Baer, M., Vadera, A. K., Leenders, R. J., & Oldham, G. R. (2014). Intergroup competition as a double-edged sword: How sex composition regulates the effects of competition on group creativity. *Organization Science, 25*, 892–908.

Beghetto, R. A. (2010). Intellectual hide-and-seek: Prospective teachers' prior experiences with creativity suppression. *International Journal of Creativity & Problem Solving, 20*, 29–36.

Beghetto, R. A. (2014). Creative mortification: An initial exploration. *Psychology of Aesthetics, Creativity, and the Arts, 8*, 266–276.

Beghetto, R. A., & Kaufman, J. C. (2007). Toward a broader conception of creativity: A case for "mini-c" creativity. *Psychology of Aesthetics, Creativity, and the Arts, 1*, 13–79.

Beghetto, R. A., & Kaufman, J. C. (2009). Intellectual estuaries: Connecting learning and creativity in programs of advanced academics. *Journal of Advanced Academics, 20*, 296–324.

Beghetto, R. A., & Kaufman, J. C. (2013). Fundamentals of creativity. *Educational Leadership, 70*, 10–15.

Beghetto, R. A., & Kaufman, J. C. (2014). Classroom contexts for creativity. *High Ability Studies, 25*, 53–69.

Cesario, J., & Higgins, E. T. (2008). Making message recipients "feel right": How nonverbal cues can increase persuasion. *Psychological Science, 19*, 415–420.

Chamorro-Premuzic, T., & Reichenbacher, L. (2008). Effects of personality and threat of evaluation on divergent and convergent thinking. *Journal of Research in Personality, 42*, 1095–1101.

Cheek, J. M., & Stahl, S. (1986). Shyness and verbal creativity. *Journal of Research in Personality, 20*, 51–61.

Conti, R., & Amabile, T. M. (1995, April). *Problem solving among computer science students: The effects of skill, evaluation expectation, and personality on solution quality*. Paper presented at the annual meeting of the Eastern Psychological Association, Boston.

Conti, R., Collins, M., & Picariello, M. (2001). The impact of competition on intrinsic motivation and creativity: Considering gender, gender segregation, and gender role orientation. *Personality and Individual Differences, 30*, 1273–1289.

Cornwell, J. M., & Higgins, E. T. (2016). Eager feelings and vigilant reasons: Regulatory focus differences in judging moral wrongs. *Journal of Experimental Psychology: General, 145*, 338–355.

Crommelinck, M., & Anseel, F. (2013). Understanding and encouraging feedback-seeking behavior: A literature review. *Medical Education, 47*, 232–241.

Cropley, D. H., & Cropley, A. J. (2010). Functional creativity: Products and the generation of effective novelty. In J. C. Kaufman & R. J. Sternberg (Eds.), *Cambridge handbook of creativity* (pp. 301–320). New York: Cambridge University Press.

Cropley, D. H., & Kaufman, J. C. (2012). Measuring functional creativity: Empirical validation of the Creative Solution Diagnosis Scale (CSDS). *Journal of Creative Behavior, 46*, 119–137.

Deci, E. L., & Ryan, R. M. (1985). *Intrinsic motivation and self-determination in human behavior*. New York: Plenum.

Deci, E. L., & Ryan, R. M. (2008). Self-determination theory: A macrotheory of human motivation, development, and health. *Canadian Psychology, 49*, 182–185.

de Stobbeleir, K. E., Ashford, S. J., & Buyens, D. (2011). Self-regulation of creativity at work: The role of feedback-seeking behavior in creative performance. *Academy of Management Journal, 54*, 811–831.

Dweck, C. S. (2006). *Mindset: The new psychology of success*. New York: Random House.

Eisenberger, R., & Shanock, L. (2003). Rewards, intrinsic motivation, and creativity: A case study of conceptual and methodological isolation. *Creativity Research Journal, 15*, 121–130.

Feist, G. J. (1998). A meta-analysis of personality in scientific and artistic creativity. *Personality and Social Psychology Review, 2*, 290–309.

Forgeard, M. J. C., & Kaufman, J. C. (2016). Who cares about imagination, creativity, and innovation, and why? A review. *Psychology of Aesthetics, Creativity, and the Arts, 10*, 250–269.

George, J. M., & Zhou, J. (2001). When openness to experience and conscientiousness are related to creative behavior: An interactional approach. *Journal of Applied Psychology, 86*, 513–524.

Gough, H. G. (1979). A creative personality scale for the adjective check list. *Journal of Personality and Social Psychology, 37*, 1398–1405.

Green, C. (2013, May). Improving performance review policies for managers and employees. *Westchester Magazine*. Retrieved from www.westchestermagazine.com/914-INC/Q2-2013/Improving-Performance-Review-Policies-for-Managers-and-Employees/.

Guilford, J. P. (1950). Creativity. *American Psychologist, 5*, 444–454.

Hackman, J. R., & Oldham, G. R. (1975). Development of the job diagnostic survey. *Journal of Applied Psychology, 60*, 159–170.

Hattie, J., & Timperley, H. (2007). The power of feedback. *Review of Educational Research, 77*, 81–112.

Hennessey, B. A. (2010). Intrinsic motivation and creativity in the classroom: Have we come full circle? In R. A. Beghetto & J. C. Kaufman (Eds.), *Nurturing creativity in the classroom* (pp. 329–361). New York: Cambridge University Press.

Hennessey, B. A. (in press). Motivation and creativity. In J. C. Kaufman & R. J. Sternberg (Eds.), *Cambridge handbook of creativity* (2nd edn.). New York: Cambridge University Press.

Hennessey, B. A., & Amabile, T. M. (2010). Creativity. *Annual Review of Psychology, 61*, 569–598.

Higgins, E. T. (1998). Promotion and prevention: Regulatory focus as a motivational principle. *Advances in Experimental Social Psychology, 30*, 1–46.

Jauk, E., Benedek, M., & Neubauer, A. C. (2014). The road to creative achievement: A latent variable model of ability and personality predictors. *European Journal of Personality, 28*, 95–105.

Kaufman, J. C. (2016). *Creativity 101* (2nd Ed.). New York: Springer.

Kaufman, J. C., & Baer, J. (2002). Could Steven Spielberg manage the Yankees? Creative thinking in different domains. *Korean Journal of Thinking & Problem Solving, 12*, 5–15.

Kaufman, J. C., & Beghetto, R. A. (2009). Beyond big and little: The Four C Model of creativity. *Review of General Psychology, 13*, 1–12.

Kaufman, J. C., & Beghetto, R. A. (2013a). Do people recognize the Four Cs? Examining layperson conceptions of creativity. *Psychology of Aesthetics, Creativity, and the Arts, 7*, 229–236.

Kaufman, J. C., & Beghetto, R. A. (2013b). In praise of Clark Kent: Creative metacognition and the importance of teaching kids when (not) to be creative. *Roeper Review, 35*, 155–165.

Kaufman, J. C., Beghetto, R A., & Watson, C. (2016). Creative metacognition and self-ratings of creative performance: A 4-C perspective. *Learning and Individual Differences, 51*, 394–399.

Kaufman, J. C., Evans, M. L., & Baer, J. (2010). The American Idol effect: Are students good judges of their creativity across domains? *Empirical Studies of the Arts, 28*, 3–17.

King, L. A., & Gurland, S. T. (2007). Creativity and experience of a creative task: Person and environment effects. *Journal of Research in Personality, 41*, 1252–1259.

Kluger, A. N., & DeNisi, A. (1996). The effects of feedback interventions on performance: A historical review, a meta-analysis, and a preliminary feedback intervention theory. *Psychological Bulletin, 119*, 254–284.

Ligon, G. S., Graham, K. A., Edwards, A., Osburn, H. K., & Hunter, S. T. (2012). Performance management: Appraising performance, providing feedback. In M. D. Mumford (Ed.), *The organizational handbook of creativity* (pp. 633–666). Amsterdam: Elsevier.

Mednick, S. A. (1962). The associative basis of the creative process. *Psychological Review, 69*, 220–232.

Miele, D. B., Finn, B., & Molden, D. C. (2011). Does easily learned mean easily remembered? It depends on your beliefs about intelligence. *Psychological Science, 22*, 320–324.

Milgram, R. M., & Rabkin, L. (1980). Developmental test of Mednick's associative hierarchies of original thinking. *Developmental Psychology, 16*, 220–232.

Mumford, M. D. (2003). Where have we been, where are we going? Taking stock in creativity research. *Creativity Research Journal, 15*, 107–120.

Oldham, G. R., & Cummings, A. (1996). Employee creativity: Personal and contextual factors at work. *Academy of Management Journal, 39*, 607–634.

Osborn, A. F. (1953). *Applied imagination: Principles and procedures of creative problem-solving*. New York: Scribner's Sons.

Puccio, G. J., & Cabra, J. F. (2010). Organizational creativity: A systems approach. In J. C. Kaufman & R. J. Sternberg (Eds.), *The Cambridge handbook of creativity* (pp. 145–173). New York: Cambridge University Press.

Rietzschel, E. F., Slijkhuis, M., & Van Yperen, N. W. (2014). Close monitoring as a contextual stimulator: How need for structure affects the relation between close monitoring and work outcomes. *European Journal of Work and Organizational Psychology*, *23*, 394–404.

Ruscio, J., Whitney, D. M., & Amabile, T. M. (1998). Looking inside the fishbowl of creativity: Verbal and behavioral predictors of creative performance. *Creativity Research Journal*, *11*, 243–263.

Schaffner, E., Philipp, M., & Schiefele, U. (2016). Reciprocal effects between intrinsic reading motivation and reading competence? A cross-lagged panel model for academic track and nonacademic track students. *Journal of Research in Reading*, *39*, 19–36.

Scott, G., Leritz, L., & Mumford, M. D. (2004). The effectiveness of creativity training: A quantitative review. *Creativity Research Journal*, *16*, 361–388.

Shalley, C. (1995). Effects of coaction, expected evaluation, and goal setting on creativity and productivity. *Academy of Management Journal*, *38*, 483–503.

Shalley, C. E., & Perry-Smith, J. E. (2001). Effects of social-psychological factors on creative performance: The role of informational and controlling expected evaluation and modeling experience. *Organizational Behavior and Human Decision Processes*, *84*, 1–22.

Slijkhuis, J. M., Rietzschel, E. F., & Van Yperen, N. W. (2013). How evaluation and need for structure affect motivation and creativity. *European Journal of Work and Organizational Psychology*, *22*, 15–25.

Sternberg, R. J., & Lubart, T. I. (1995). *Defying the crowd.* New York: Free Press.

Stone, D., & Heen, S. (2014). *Thanks for the feedback: The science and art of receiving feedback well.* New York: Penguin Books.

Wang, J., Wang, L., Liu, R., & Dong, H. (2017). How expected evaluation influences creativity: Regulatory focus as moderator. *Motivation and Emotion*, *41*, 147–157.

Winnie, P. H., & Butler, D. L. (1994). Student cognition in learning from teaching. In T. Husen & T. Postlewaite (Eds.), *International encyclopedia of education* (2nd edn., pp. 5738–5745). Oxford: Pergamon.

Yuan, F., & Zhou, J. (2008). Differential effects of expected external evaluation on different parts of the creative idea production process and on final product creativity. *Creativity Research Journal*, *20*, 391–403.

Zhou, J. (2003). When the presence of creative coworkers is related to creativity: Role of supervisor close monitoring, developmental feedback, and creative personality. *Journal of Applied Psychology*, *88*, 413–422.

Zhou, J., & George, J. M. (2001). When job dissatisfaction leads to creativity: Encouraging the expression of voice. *Academy of Management Journal*, *44*, 682–696.

PART V

Concluding Remarks

27 Instructional Feedback

Analysis, Synthesis, and Extrapolation

Jeffrey K. Smith and Anastasiya A. Lipnevich

Introduction

Instructional feedback is the process through which individuals receive information concerning their learning or production efforts that should enable them to improve their work. Feedback might come from a teacher, a peer, or from the learner simply observing the results of his or her efforts. It might include information on where the learner currently is, where the learner is headed, or advice on what the next steps in learning might be. It is closely related to and often includes, or is included in, formative assessment. We decided to focus this volume on instructional feedback as opposed to formative assessment for several reasons. One is that there already are a number of good edited works on formative assessment, but fewer on instructional feedback. Another was that we felt that instructional feedback was really "the heart of the matter." The provision of information to the student about his or her progress is the *sine qua non* of helping students in their learning.

We look at the research on instructional feedback from a decades-old perspective from the seminal work of Scriven (1967), Bloom (1968), Ramaprasad (1983), and Black and Wiliam (1998), and they, in turn, examine great scholars from other fields, most notably physics, as described by Wiliam (Chapter 1 in this volume). We are further enlightened by a series of thoughtful reviews of the research in instructional feedback and the closely related area of formative assessment (see, e.g., Crooks, 1988; Kluger & DeNisi, 1996; Hattie & Timperley, 2007; Shute, 2008). The reader can see these classic works cited time and again in the preceding chapters.

Our approach to inviting authors was to cast our nets widely and to entice scholars to contribute by offering as much free rein in their writing as possible. We wanted people to be able to say things that were on their minds that they had not expressed before. We also wanted to be expansive in our coverage of the topic. We wanted to look at feedback in various subject areas and age levels as well as general consideration of the topic. We wanted to garner research on variables that impact on feedback and that feedback impacts on. We wanted to get perspectives outside traditional Western approaches. As a consequence, we not only have contributions that provide a rigorous review and analysis of certain areas, we also have heartfelt calls for certain directions and approaches to be taken in the field. It has been a long and sometimes difficult journey, but we are thrilled to have been able to present this compendium to the reader, and we offer our profound thanks to the scholars who have selflessly contributed to this work.

What Is Instructional Feedback?

Almost every chapter in this volume begins with some discussion about what instructional feedback is. Many chapters make reference to Ramaprasad (1983), and this is a good starting point. Frequently, the notion that instructional feedback provides information about where a student is, where the student is going, and how to bridge the gap between the two is proffered. But we wonder if this three-pronged approach is actually the correct one. What if the students are only given information on where they are and how to improve? What if there is no information on what the ultimate goal is? What if there is no ultimate goal other than "improvement"? If we are working with a fourth-grade student on general problem-solving in mathematics or on comprehension skills in reading, it is reasonable to argue that we have a sense of the appropriate trajectory, but not the ultimate destination. Hence, the gap between current status and the desired status is something of a fiction. To push this argument a bit further, what if there is only information about current status? If a student is only informed about how well he or she is currently performing, is that feedback? Stobart (Chapter 2), citing Eraut (2007), argues for the following definition of feedback:

> Any communication that gives some access to other people's opinions, feelings, thoughts or judgements about one's own performance.   (p. 6)

We think this alternative has much to offer. But we would push this definition a step further in terms of opening up the definition of feedback. We do not think the communication has to come from another person. It does not technically have to be a communication. It might come from something inorganic. Imagine an archer. She lets fly with an arrow and sees that she has overshot her target. She ponders what she did (maybe she even has video-recorded the shot during a training session). She makes adjustments in her technique and tries again. No one has assessed her actions or spoken to her. The flight of the arrow is the feedback. It does not involve people or opinions, feelings, thoughts, or judgments. It simply is information concerning a performance. It knows nothing of the archer's status at the sport, nor her most recent efforts at improvement, nor of the archer she aspires to be. And yet it is hard to argue that it is not feedback. Furthermore, it is unbiased, immediate, and highly pertinent to improvement. Consider Hattie and Timperley's (2007) approach:

> Feedback is information provided by an agent (e.g., teacher, peer, book, parent, self, experience) regarding aspects of one's performance or understanding.   (p. 102)

At the risk of focusing too much on small distinctions, we would like to see the definition include some notion that the information influences the learner with regard to the performance. Hence, we offer:

> *Any information about a performance that a learner can use to improve that performance or grow in the general domain of the performance.*

This definition allows for feedback to come from any source and includes learning in the general domain of the performance in addition to that specific performance. A person receiving feedback on a piece of writing may be able to use that feedback to improve that particular piece of writing and to improve writing skills in general. This definition is similar to the one that Wiliam (Chapter 1) cites from Kulhavy (1977): "any of the numerous procedures that are used to tell a learner if an instructional response is right or wrong" (p. 211). But we do not want to limit feedback to information about right and wrong, as many things that we work on in life are more complex than right or wrong. Something could be "right" and still have the potential to be "better." This may seem a quibble, but it is important to consider the small issues when thinking of definitions.

And to the end of small issues, Wiliam (Chapter 1) points out that there is an important distinction to be made between the notions of *performance* and *learning*. If a learner receives feedback about a performance (let us say, an essay) that leads to improvement in a subsequent version of that performance (a second draft of the essay), but makes the same mistake in the following, related performance (the next essay written), where are we in terms of the effectiveness of the feedback? And on the other hand, if feedback does not affect current performance (for example, if there is no second draft to be done), but the learner does not make the same mistake in the future, is the feedback effective? We think all would agree that the answer here would be *yes*, and thus, we need to include learning along with improvement in performance in a definition of feedback.

Unpacking Instructional Feedback: How Is It Related to Formative Assessment?

We tend to think of instructional feedback as a response to some sort of performance or effort by a student. We think about formative assessment and assessment for learning in much the same way. Is there utility in thinking about instructional feedback as something distinct from formative assessment? As Guskey (Chapter 19) points out, Bloom took the revolutionary distinction of formative and summative evaluation developed by Scriven and applied it to diagnostic classroom assessment processes in his development of mastery learning theory (Bloom, 1968; Bloom, Hastings, & Madaus, 1971). In his writings and teaching, Bloom would explain that formative assessment allowed teachers to provide the feedback and correctives necessary to improve learning. He clearly distinguished between formative assessment, which was a process through which information was gained on learners, and feedback, which was then provided to learners by teachers in order to improve learning. Brookhart (Chapter 3) presents an excellent review of formative and summative assessment, and how each can contribute to student learning.

Wiliam (Chapter 1) focuses on this question and develops an answer that we fundamentally agree with. Feedback is a component of formative assessment, whether that feedback is directed toward a particular learner's progress or toward the efforts of a teacher working with a class in general. In this fashion, formative assessment encompasses feedback, as feedback is an integral part of the formative assessment process. But formative assessment also involves setting tasks, relating those tasks to the curriculum or learning objectives, etc., whereas feedback does not necessarily involve such components (it might just be observing the flight of an arrow). Thus, at the same time, and somewhat paradoxically, it is possible to think of formative assessment as one approach to feedback among many others. Thus, each term encompasses the other, depending on one's perspective.

How Does Instructional Feedback Vary by Subject Matter and Age?

One of our goals in this volume was to allow subject-matter specialists and specialists in teaching students of different ages the opportunity to talk about the uniqueness of their various specialities. What is clear here is that feedback in music instruction (Parkes, Chapter 10) is incredibly different from feedback in writing instruction (Graham, Chapter 7) or in math instruction (Small & Lin, Chapter 8; Ruiz-Primo & Kroog, Chapter 9). Although there are similarities, tertiary education (van der Meer & Dawson, Chapter 12) presents problems wholly unrelated to those encountered in primary education (Tan & Wong, Chapter 6). And feedback in medical schools (Sargeant & Watling, Chapter 13) and the workplace (Athota & Malik, Chapter 14) are entirely different again. Perhaps the chapter that brings the differences most clearly into focus in this volume is the one on feedback in animal learning (Kaufman & Pagel, Chapter 22). So what is it that we see that holds these various areas together, and what is it about them that is distinct?

Starting with distinctions, several dimensions can be seen. One has to do with the impacts that curricular differences have on feedback. Mathematics feedback is more likely to focus on specific issues that are currently being taught than feedback in reading or writing where growth is somewhat more amorphous. This is not to say that mathematics does not also focus on the broader issues of quantitative reasoning and problem-solving, but looking at feedback, particularly at the primary level, one sees feedback being provided on very specific problems. If one is working with students on the characteristics of triangles, then feedback will focus on just that. In writing, using metaphoric language focuses not on a small number of metaphors but on the broader processes of thinking metaphorically and their impact on the reader.

A second difference that can be seen has to do with the age and level of development of the learner. As learners become more sophisticated, they can process feedback more broadly defined and can handle feedback that is presented in a straightforward and direct fashion (for the most part). They can also process more feedback being presented at once. Younger learners can be overwhelmed by too much information being presented at one time. Furthermore, the nature of the relationship between the provider of feedback and the student differs. For a second-grade student, the teacher is often pretty close to being a surrogate parent, whereas a teaching assistant marking a college introductory biology class assignment may be totally anonymous to the receiver of the feedback.

Looking more closely at the differences in feedback across levels of schooling, there are specific characteristics of feedback that are unique to the secondary school setting. Among these are the pressure for students to do well on standardized achievement measures, the demands of providing grades that are critical to students' chances of getting into a desired college, and the student to teacher ratio (Boyer, 1983). The typical secondary school teacher has an average class size of 26.8 students; with four to five classes that a typical teacher has each year, that means well over 100 students to attend to. To spend five minutes per student on devising individualized feedback on a single assignment would take a teacher six hours of working without a break (see, e.g., Price, Smith, & Berg, 2017)! Another issue of importance at the secondary level are the substantial differences in what is being taught in various subject areas. What students are learning in an English class differs dramatically from what they are learning in a German or a physics class, or in instrumental music. With regard to feedback, one size clearly does not fit all. In sum, the three key factors to take into consideration when looking at the issue of feedback at the secondary level are the number of students, striking differences in subject areas, and the need to provide fair grades that will inevitably affect students' future academic paths.

At the primary level, the numbers are much smaller, and the subject areas, while distinct, are less differentiated than at the secondary level. Developing reading and mathematical skills take precedence over other areas of the curriculum. Grades, while somewhat important, pale in comparison to their importance at the secondary level. In comparing to tertiary instruction, the differences are equally dramatic. College faculty may deal with very large numbers of students, but in such courses there is typically little or no instructional feedback provided and assessment is often done with multiple-choice tests. For those classes that are much smaller this situation changes, but again, presentation of instructional feedback remains somewhat limited. And there are no standardized tests to worry about.

Moving to similarities, feedback needs to come from a trusted source in all settings. If we do not have faith in the accuracy of the feedback, we are unlikely to attend to it. If students do not make active use of the feedback provided, it has little or no value in instruction (Jonsson & Panadero, Chapter 24). We also see that the use of self- and peer assessment can be effective and efficient tools at all levels of instruction, although some scaffolding will be necessary with younger students (Andrade, Chapter 17; Panadero, Jonsson, & Alqassab, Chapter 18). In one of the most revealing and intriguing chapters in the volume, the use of clickers as a bridge (a type of secondary reinforcement) in animal training made a lightbulb light up for us (Kaufman & Pagel, Chapter 22). Learners need to know as precisely as possible what they are doing right and where they can improve. This is universal. When working with animals, you cannot have a conversation with them. They cannot ask questions and get a refined assessment of their performance. The clicker is the opportunity to signal to the animal, "Yes, just NOW!" The click can be delivered as a secondary reinforcement more quickly and more accurately than a primary reinforcer (say, food). In music, the instructor will frequently stop a learner at the exact point in which an error was made (Parkes, Chapter 10). A teacher working with a student on an essay can write a note right next to a problematic section of the essay (or a particularly good one). The accuracy of the feedback to the performance does not require a clicker. But accuracy is key in all feedback.

Also common across subject areas and ages is that a general positive emotional experience with the feedback greatly enhances its effectiveness in most settings (Goetz, Lipnevich, Krannich, & Gogol, Chapter 25). Feedback is one of the strongest sources and antecedents of emotions in a classroom, and appreciating its power to elicit various affective responses is a key to using it for student improvement. Although it may be the case that "a kick in the rear" will be motivational in some settings, the research does not support it as a general approach. That is, certain negative emotions in moderate doses may stimulate the learner to work harder (Goetz et al., Chapter 25); elevated negative emotions will serve as deterrents to performance.

What Do We Say and How Do They Hear It?

Stiggins (Chapter 23) presents the reader with a moving personal story from one of the leading figures in the history of formative assessment and teaching, and one that we feel will resonate strongly with many readers. At the end of the day, we are reminded of the admonition of one of our colleagues (Joseph Zelnick of Rutgers University) to a group of student teachers about to engage in teacher/parent conferences: "You've got to remember that these are the very best children that these people have. They aren't keeping the talented ones safe at home." And so we become very much vested in the notion of what we say to students and how they hear and respond to what we say. We have three excellent chapters on noncognitive issues and feedback (Murano, Martin, Burrus, & Roberts, Chapter 11; Jonsson & Panadero, Chapter 24; Goetz et al., Chapter 25) and another solely dedicated to looking at the kind of language we use in providing feedback to students (Murray, Gasson, & Smith, Chapter 4).

It is not hard to think of times when all of us have eagerly anticipated feedback, or dreaded it, or were on the fence depending on what the feedback contained. We know that some individuals tend to typically seek out feedback while others typically avoid it, but we also know that response to feedback is often dependent on the situation. In our earlier work (Lipnevich, Berg, and Smith, 2016) we proposed a model of feedback receptivity, and we feel it can be a useful tool to consider the complexity of feedback. Feedback is always received in context, and it may be a setting and subject area where the student is comfortable or uncomfortable, and where the outcomes are very important to the student or less so. Hence, the consequences of such feedback will be variable. Feedback can be viewed as supportive and thus may elicit positive emotions, or it may be perceived as potentially negatively consequential for the student and, thus, be anxiety-producing. It may be delivered in a classroom environment that is friendly and collaborative or in a competitive space and serve as a source of social comparison. Furthermore, feedback may vary on a number of factors. It may be detailed or sparse, aligned with the student's level and expectations or not. It may be painfully honest but delivered in a strongly supportive fashion or be unpleasantly judgmental. Students receiving it may have vast background knowledge in the domain or be complete novices. They may be positively or negatively disposed toward feedback in general.

When a student receives feedback, affective and cognitive responses follow. The student may experience dismay, joy, a feeling of pride or embarrassment, worry about how parents or peers will react, have a sense of having disappointed the teacher or themselves in their performance, or of having made the teacher proud. In reading through the feedback, the student might be confused by the comments or fully appreciative of them. From this amalgam of affect and cognition, students will act adaptively or maladaptively. They will work on the assignment, taking the suggestions made by the teacher into account, or perhaps discount what has been said in order to protect their sense of self-worth. And finally, how the student reacts to and acts on the feedback will affect who the student is, what the student knows and can do in this area, and how the student will respond in the next cycle of feedback. The feedback may trigger responses that generalize across settings and subject areas or may remain specific to situations highly similar to this one, and generate responses in other domains.

In related thinking on these issues, Panadero et al. (Chapter 18) look at current research on peer assessment and find that issues of trust are essential for such feedback to be effective. Goetz et al. (Chapter 25) examine the emotional reactions that students have to feedback. They remind us that feedback has affective consequences as well as cognitive ones and that those noncognitive consequences have impact on the receipt of subsequent feedback. Hence, it is always essential to attend to the emotional as well as the academic aspects of the message that is delivered to learners. Murano et al. (Chapter 11) turn the tables on this issue by looking at how important noncognitive factors in schooling can be affected by feedback. We want students to achieve in the domains of math, reading, and science, for certain, but we also have a host of noncognitive objectives in schooling, and these authors show us how the research in cognitive areas generalizes to the noncognitive. Finally, the chapter by Murray et al. (Chapter 4) presents an approach to categorizing written feedback and shows that the nature of feedback that is provided is highly dependent on who is providing the feedback.

How Do We Study Instructional Feedback?

The conduct of research on instructional feedback involves a number of challenges for the researcher, as pointed out by Brown and Harris (Chapter 5). To begin, instruction occurs in widely different subject areas and at many different levels. One of our goals in this volume was to solicit work from scholars researching different levels and in different areas, and the comparisons and contrasts we see are stark. Instructional feedback for elementary school mathematics differs dramatically from what is presented to university-level students developing their writing skills. As discussed above, there are commonalities for certain, but there are also differences that simply have to be acknowledged in the design of any research study. Such problems are not unique to studying feedback, however; they are endemic to the study of education. They limit our ability to generalize from one study to another, but they are challenges, not barriers.

A much tougher nut to crack in the conduct of research on instructional feedback has to do with the very nature of feedback. Instructional feedback does not exist in a vacuum; a host of contextual effects need to be taken into consideration. Instructional feedback, in a classroom setting, occurs typically between a student and the student's teacher. The student knows the teacher and vice versa. Every feedback message that is sent and received is peculiar to the history of the relationship between the student and the teacher. The assignment handed in by the student (or even the work being done in class as the teacher traverses the classroom) is part of a chain of interactions between teacher and student. It may be exceptionally good (or poor) work for this student; it may represent a breakthrough in understanding (or a regression back to a previous state); it may demonstrate exceptional effort or a sloppy job. And the response to this work given by the teacher may be viewed as harsh by the student or highly encouraging; it might be eagerly consumed or totally ignored. The teacher may have given the work short shrift because of a heavy workload or a crying baby in the middle of marking. These are all factors that enter into the equation of instructional feedback.

We enter into that equation from a research perspective without a strong handle on what has happened or is happening. And we are faced with the dilemma of either trying to observe without interfering in the process or trying to implement an intervention or experimental condition to see how that influences any of a set of possible outcomes (cognitive, affective, or behavioral). If we take an observational approach, we are likely to get results that are long on ecological validity, but may suffer from susceptibility to a host of alternative explanations of the phenomenon we observe. If we intervene experimentally, we are more likely to be able to attribute outcomes to experimental manipulation, but do not know if the findings will replicate in real-life settings. So, what are we to do?

A facile answer would be: both. And although that answer is certainly true as far as it goes, it does not really answer the question in a satisfactory way. What we really need is "Both at the same time." We would argue that we need to be able to work in real classroom settings and engage in experimental manipulations that allow for less ambiguous attributions of cause without creating such an artificial setting that we are doubtful of the generalizability of those results. A good example of the kind of work we are talking about can be seen in a study by Price, Smith, and Berg (2017). Working within a real classroom setting, this team of academic and school-based researchers randomly assigned students in writing classes to different kinds of instructional feedback on their work, in this instance comparing individualized personal feedback on an essay to annotated exemplars of high-quality essays on the same or similar topics. They found that the effects of the two approaches were roughly similar in terms of the quality of the revisions that students produced on their draft essays (after having received personalized feedback or annotated exemplars). They also found that students preferred the personalized feedback, but liked the annotated exemplars as well. Finally, they found that the annotated exemplar approach was far more time-efficient for the teacher. This study was limited by sample size, the specificity of the school in which it was conducted, and the use of teacher as researcher. At the same time, it provides a highly enlightening look at what happened in two real classrooms when a randomized experiment was conducted looking at the effects of two radically different approaches to feedback. We believe this represents exactly the kind of research that the field needs.

Indeed, we have conducted similar work at the university level (Lipnevich & Smith, 2009). Our study involved a much larger sample and more elaborate design; these were afforded to us by the nature of working in a large, introductory psychology class at a major state university. We found that detailed feedback, without the use of praise or a tentative grade, produced the best results in terms of students revising their work. In a second study (Lipnevich, McCallen, Miles Pace, & Smith, 2014), we compared the effects of rubrics and exemplars as instructional feedback in an experimental setting. We found that students prefer exemplars but are more productive when using rubrics. Each of the three studies had the advantages of randomization in situ, a powerful tool for drawing conclusions that can be attributed to manipulations in real-life settings. Each also had the limitation of the setting and subject matter in which they were conducted, awaiting replication and extension.

Another problem and, again, a very difficult one, has to do with the difference between production and learning in instructional feedback research. It is one thing to note that a piece of student work has improved as the result of receiving feedback on that work, and another to see if the student has experienced cognitive growth in the area where the feedback was given. Without question, we need more studies that focus on the latter.

What Kinds of Students Do We Want to Raise?

Three of the chapters (Tan & Wong, Chapter 6; Kanjee, Chapter 20; Arimoto & Clark, Chapter 21) present perspectives from outside a traditional Western perspective. They bring home to us powerful reminders that not only is education not the same around the world, but societies are not the same around the world. Arimoto and Clark, in particular, argue for a very different model of what kinds of students societies strive to raise, and how instructional feedback interacts with those different goals. At a very fundamental level, they question the notion that we want our children to strive to succeed, to be excellent, to be creative and innovative, to stand out from the crowd. The very act of saying, "this is where you should be headed" presumes that it is the teacher (or the curriculum) who should make that decision, and not the learner. Kaufman and Pagel (Chapter 22) present a dramatic counterpoint to the Arimoto and Clark perspective. In animal training, the notion of what the animal wants to do or learn is simply not something we consider. On the other hand, since the ability of animals to communicate to humans is limited, then feedback has to take on a very different dimension. Here an unabashed use of behavioral techniques is called for. In thinking about feedback and its effects, we usually do not step back and ask broader contextual questions at a societal level. Perhaps we should.

Whither Feedback in a Brave New World?

Guskey (Chapter 19) explains that Bloom wanted to replicate the instructional setting of one student with a highly skilled tutor in his development of mastery learning theory. Formative assessment played a critical role in Bloom's thinking. And mastery learning has seen its successes (and failures). But the goal of mastery learning (one student, one skilled tutor) remains a challenge for us in developing instructional feedback approaches. Price, Smith, and Berg (2017) found that providing individualized feedback took much more time on the part of the teacher as using annotated exemplars. But one might ask if the use of an annotated exemplar, or a rubric (see, e.g., Andrade & Du, 2005; Lipnevich, McCallen, Pace, & Smith, 2014), can even rightfully be considered feedback. We think clearly that these are forms of feedback, but others may disagree as no information about the student's performance is directly provided; it must be inferred by the student by comparing the student work to the exemplar or rubric specification.

The question of how we can provide effective feedback in an efficient fashion is, in our opinion, a major challenge for the field. We have turned to peer assessment (Panadero et al., Chapter 18), self-assessment (Andrade, Chapter 17), and technology (Munshi & Deneen, Chapter 15; Homer, Ober, & Plass, Chapter 16) in our efforts to assist the classroom teacher in providing quality feedback to students. As our technology becomes more sophisticated, the ability to provide feedback via technological means becomes more widely available. As is always the case with technology and education, this is a bit of a double-edged sword. Educators do not really have a sterling record when it comes to the effective use of technology. However, we are ever hopeful and encourage the reader to give careful consideration to the Homer and Ober's and Munshi and Deneen's efforts in this regard.

Where to from Here?

There are a number of things that we know about instructional feedback due to the excellent work of people who have provided these chapters and the scholars whose work they have relied on. In this final section, we look at the issues that we feel the field needs to address in the immediate and longer-term future.

To begin, we feel the field needs to look carefully not at feedback as a generic notion but much more specifically at the types and nature of feedback that is provided. We see progress along those lines in the research of Hattie and Timperley (2007) and Shute (2008), but we also see the need for much more refinement along these lines. The work of Murray et al. (Chapter 4) advances this refinement, but more work can be done. If we can more precisely define the nature of the feedback that is provided, we can more precisely understand its effects.

A second area in need of more work has to do with the efficiency of feedback. In a workshop one of us gave recently, we spent a fair amount of time explaining a particular approach and why it would be effective. At the conclusion of the presentation, one of the teachers in the audience raised his hand and said, "You do realize that I have 100 students?" We simply must push ourselves to look for ways to help teachers in providing effective feedback that does not require hours and hours of work on their part. That is why we are hopeful about the use of peer feedback, rubrics, exemplars, computer-assisted feedback, instructional games and the feedback provided therein, and self-feedback. Self-feedback, in particular, seems important to us and may in fact represent the ultimate form of feedback. It not only helps the student with the immediate content being worked on but develops the ability to self-assess at the same time. Having students work from exemplars and rubrics, with the guidance of a teacher, appears to generate good results efficiently.

Next, we believe that the field will benefit tremendously by looking at the noncognitive aspects of feedback, both the influences of noncognitive variables on feedback and the influences of feedback on noncognitive variables. Concerns such as motivation, the development of self-efficacy, resilience, and others come into play in the complex matrix of the delivery and receipt of feedback.

Finally, we need to take a very broad view of feedback as part of instruction, and ask ourselves what kind of students we strive to see. We often simply take for granted that our primary goal should be to see students excel, reach their maximum potential, and be the best. But in doing so, do we ignore concerns about the development of a just and equitable society? This takes the question into one of educational philosophy more than educational research, but we should always keep our eyes on the long view as well as the wonder and awe of the immediacy of day-to-day classroom life.

We hope this summary helps to unfold the complexities of how students respond to feedback and highlights potential areas for future research. Tremendous progress has been made in the domain of instructional feedback; we look forward to the continuation of this progress and hope that the reader will join in those efforts.

References

Andrade, H., & Du, Y. (2005). Student perspectives on rubric-referenced assessment. *Practical Assessment, Research & Evaluation, 10*(3), 1–11.

Black, P., & Wiliam, D. (1998). Assessment and classroom learning. *Assessment in Education: Principles, Policy and Practice, 5*(1), 7–74.

Bloom, B. S. (1968). Learning for mastery. *Evaluation Comment (UCLA-CSIEP), 1*(2), 1–12.

Bloom, B. S., Hastings, J. T., & Madaus, G. (1971). *Handbook on formative and summative evaluation of student learning.* New York: McGraw-Hill.

Boyer, E. L. (1983). *High school: A report on secondary education in America.* New York: Harper & Row.

Crooks, T. J. (1988). The impact of classroom evaluation practices on students. *Review of Educational Research, 58*(4), 438–481.

Eraut, M (2007). Feedback and formative assessment in the workplace, 3rd seminar, Assessment of Significant Learning Outcomes Project. Retrieved from www.researchgate.net/publication/237739544_ASSESSMENT_OF_GNIFICANT_LEARNING_OUTCOMES_3RD_SEMINAR_Feedback_andFormative_Assessment_in_the_Workplace1.

Hattie, J., & Timperley, H. (2007). The power of feedback. *Review of Educational Research, 77*(1), 81–112.

Kluger, A. N., & DeNisi, A. (1996). The effects of feedback interventions on performance: A historical review, a meta-analysis, and a preliminary feedback intervention theory. *Psychological Bulletin, 119*(2), 254–284.

Kulhavy, R. W. (1977). Feedback in written instruction. *Review of Educational Research, 47*, 211–232.

Lipnevich, A. A., Berg, D. A. G., & Smith, J. K. (2016). Toward a model of student response to feedback. In G. T. L. Brown & L. R. Harris (Eds.), *Handbook of human social conditions in assessment* (pp. 169–185). Abingdon: Routledge.

Lipnevich, A. A., McCallen, L. N., Miles Pace, K., & Smith, J. K. (2014). Mind the gap! Students' use of exemplars and detailed rubrics as formative assessment. *Instructional Science, 42*(4), 539–559.

Lipnevich, A. A., & Smith, J. K. (2009). Effects of differential feedback on students' examination performance. *Journal of Experimental Psychology: Applied, 15*(4), 319–333.

Natriello, G. (1987). The impact of evaluation processes on students. *Educational Psychologist, 22*(2), 155–175.

Price, D., Smith, J. K., & Berg, D. A. G. (2017). Personalised feedback and annotated exemplars in the writing classroom: An experimental study in situ. *Assessment Matters, 11*, 122–144.

Ramaprasad, A. (1983). On the definition of feedback. *Behavioral Science, 28*(1), 4–13.

Sadler, D. R. (1989). Formative assessment and the design of instructional systems. *Instructional Science, 18*, 119–144.

Scriven, M. (1967). The methodology of evaluation. In R. W. Tyler, R. M. Gagne, & M. Scriven (Eds.), *Perspectives of curriculum evaluation* (pp. 39–83). Chicago, IL: Rand McNally.

Shute, V. J. (2008). Focus on formative feedback. *Review of Educational Research, 78*(1), 153–189.

Index